Khorat Plateau
Pages 272–285

Mekong River Valley
Pages 286–307

Nong Khai

Loei

Udon Thani

Mukdahan

Khon Kaen

NORTHEAST THAILAND

Ubon Ratchathani

Khorat

Western Seaboard
Pages 328–345

Eastern Seaboard
Pages 316–327

Chanthaburi

Ko Chang

Gulf of Thailand

Bangkok
Pages 74–159

0 kilometers 100
0 miles 100

attani

Yala Narathiwat

EYEWITNESS TRAVEL

THAILAND

EYEWITNESS TRAVEL

THAILAND

DK

Penguin Random House

Project Editor Rosalyn Thiro
Art Editors Ian Midson, David Rowley
Editors Jonathan Cox, Marcus Hardy, Tim Hollis,
Lesley McCave, Sean O'Connor
US Editors Mary Sutherland, Michael Wise
Designers Susan Blackburn, Des Hemsley, Tim Mann,
Malcolm Parchment, Adrian Waite
Map Coordinators Emily Green, David Pugh
Researcher Warangkana Nibhatsukit

Contributors
Philip Cornwel-Smith, Andrew Forbes, Tim Forsyth, Rachel Harrison, David Henley,
John Hoskin, Gavin Pattison, Jonathan Rigg, Sarah Rooney, Ken Scott

Photographers
Philip Blenkinsop, Stuart Isett, Kim Sayer, Michael Spencer

Illustrators
Stephen Conlin, Gary Cross, Richard Draper,
Roger Hutchins, Chris Orr & Assocs, John Woodcock

Printed and bound in China
First American edition, 1997
16 17 18 19 10 9 8 7 6 5 4 3 2 1

Published in the United States by: DK Publishing,
345 Hudson Street, New York, New York 10014

**Reprinted with revisions 1999, 2000, 2001, 2002,
2004, 2006, 2008, 2010, 2012, 2014, 2016**

Copyright © 1997, 2016 Dorling Kindersley Limited, London
A Penguin Random House company

A catalog record for this book is available from the Library of Congress.

ISSN 1542-1554

ISBN 978-1-4654-4130-0

Transliteration of Thai words in this book mostly follows the
General System recommended by the Thai Royal Institute, but visitors
will encounter many variant spellings in Thailand.

Throughout this book, floors are referred to in accordance
with European usage, i.e. the "first floor" is one floor up.

MIX
Paper from
responsible sources
FSC™ C018179
www.fsc.org

**The information in this
DK Eyewitness Travel Guide is checked regularly/annually.**
Every effort has been made to ensure that this book is as up-to-date as possible
at the time of going to press. Some details, however, such as telephone numbers,
opening hours, prices, gallery hanging arrangements and travel information are
liable to change. The publishers cannot accept responsibility for any consequences
arising from the use of this book, nor for any material on third party websites, and
cannot guarantee that any website address in this book will be a suitable source of
travel information. We value the views and suggestions of our readers very highly.
Please write to: Publisher, DK Eyewitness Travel Guides, Dorling Kindersley,
80 Strand, London, WC2R 0RL, UK, or email: travelguides@dk.com.

Front cover main image: A view of the *chedi* at Wat Chana Songkhram, Sukhothai

◀ Replica of the Sanphet Prasat Palace, Ayutthaya's lost monument, in Ancient City, Bangkok

Contents

How to Use This Guide **6**

Lakshman and Sita, characters
from the Ramakien

Introducing
Thailand

Bangkok

Wat Pan Tao in Chiang Mai

Hat Maenam, a beach on Ko Samui in the Gulf of Thailand

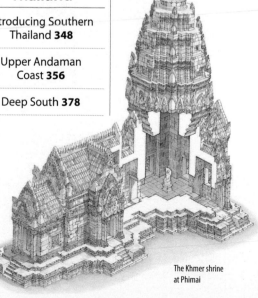
The Khmer shrine
at Phimai

HOW TO USE THIS GUIDE

This guide helps you get the most from your vacation in Thailand. It provides detailed practical information and expert recommendations. *Introducing Thailand* maps the country and sets it in its historical and cultural context. The five regional chapters, plus *Bangkok*, describe important sights, using maps, pictures, and illustrations. Features cover topics from architecture and crafts to wildlife and sports. Hotel and restaurant recommendations are found in *Travelers' Needs*. The *Survival Guide* has information on everything from transportation to personal safety.

Bangkok

The center of Bangkok has been divided into five sightseeing areas. Each has its own chapter, which opens with a list of the sights described. The *Farther Afield* section covers the best sights outside the center. All sights are numbered and plotted on an area map. The information for each sight follows the map's numerical order, making sights easy to locate within the chapter.

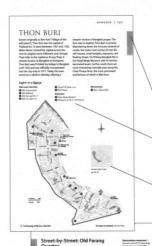

1 Area Map

For easy reference, the sights are numbered and located on a map. Sights in the city center are also marked on the Street Finder on pages 148–59.

All pages relating to Bangkok have the same colored thumb tabs.

Sights at a Glance lists the chapter's sights by category: *Wats* and Palaces; Museums and Monuments; Parks and Districts; Markets and Notable Roads.

A locator map shows where you are in relation to other areas of the city center.

2 Street-by-Street Map

This gives a bird's-eye view of the key areas in each chapter.

Stars indicate the sights that no visitor should miss.

A suggested route for a walk is shown in red.

3 Detailed Information

The sights in Bangkok are described individually. Addresses, telephone numbers, opening hours, and other practical information are also provided. The key to the symbols used is on the back flap of the book.

Thailand Area by Area

Apart from Bangkok, Thailand has been divided into 10 regions, each of which has a separate chapter. The most interesting towns and places to visit have been numbered on a Regional Map.

1 Introduction
The landscape and character of each region is outlined here, showing how the area has developed and what it has to offer the visitor today.

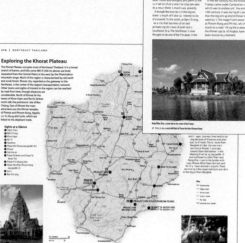

KHORAT PLATEAU

Each area of Thailand can be identified quickly by its color coding, shown on the inside front cover.

2 Regional Map
This shows the main road network and gives an illustrated overview of the whole region. All entries are numbered, and there are also useful tips on getting around the region by car, train, and other forms of transportation.

Exploring the Khorat Plateau

3 Detailed Information
All the important towns and other places to visit are described individually. They are listed in order, following the numbering on the Regional Map. Within each entry, there is detailed information on important buildings and other sights.

For all the top sights,
a Visitors' Checklist provides the practical information you need to plan your visit.

Story boxes explore related topics.

Prasat Hin Phimai

4 Thailand's Top Sights
These are given one or more full pages. Three-dimensional illustrations reveal the layouts and interiors of historic monuments. Interesting town and city centers are given street by street maps, featuring individual sights.

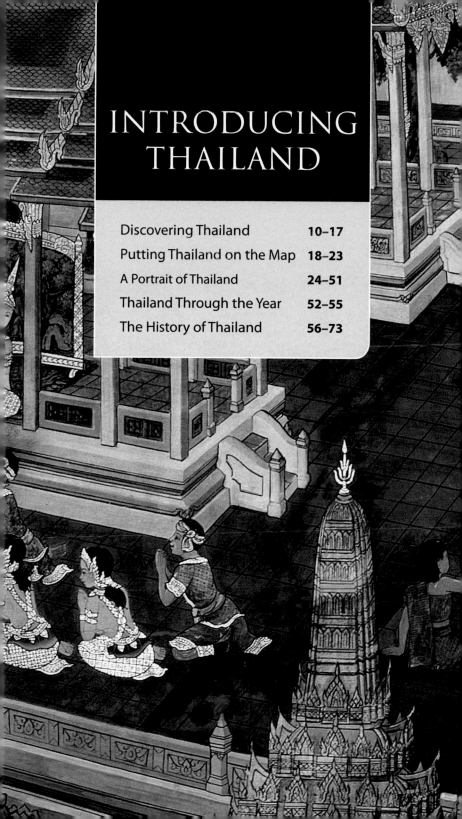

INTRODUCING THAILAND

DISCOVERING THAILAND

The following tours have been designed to cover the best areas for experiencing the many pleasures of Thailand while keeping long-distance travel to a minimum. The two-day tours introduce Thailand's main cities, Bangkok and Chiang Mai. Next, a one-week tour north from Chiang Mai introduces the rural and culturally diverse highlands. The country's rich historical past is uncovered in a one-week tour of the capitals of four kingdoms that have flourished here, from the Sukhothai kingdom in the north, founded in the 13th century, to the current Chakri dynasty, which has ruled from Bangkok since 1782. A one-week itinerary in the northeast covers areas of both cultural interest and great natural beauty. Of course, no trip to Thailand is complete without sampling the country's superb beaches and islands. The final two itineraries cover a week on the shores of the Eastern Seaboard (a short trip from Bangkok) and a week on the spectacular beaches of Southern Thailand. Follow and combine your favorite tours, or simply seek inspiration.

A Week in the Far North of Thailand

- Raft the **Mae Taeng River** and trek through the jungle astride an elephant.
- Enjoy a nature walk or visit sacred caves in **Chiang Dao**.
- Sample fragrant Chinese tea, grown in the mountain-top village of **Mae Salong**.
- Admire spectacular views from the temple of **Wat Phra That Doi Tung**.

- Shop in the busy market of **Mae Sai**, where Thailand and Myanmar (Burma) meet.
- Discover the history of the Golden Triangle at the fascinating **House of Opium** museum.
- Gaze across the Mekong River from the historical town of **Chiang Saen**.
- Take in the elaborate woodcarvings of **Wat Phra Kaeo** in Chiang Rai.

Ancient Capitals of Thailand

- Explore the magnificent royal sites of **Bangkok**.
- Wander through the former splendor of **Ayutthaya**, the capital of Siam before Bangkok.
- Cycle through the majestic temples of **Sukhothai**, the first capital of Siam.
- Enjoy the little-visited splendor of the ancient city of **Si Satchanalai**.
- Delve into the history of the northern capital **Chiang Mai**, and visit the city's many *wats*.

Thailand's Southern Beaches

- See the bright lights of **Patong** after dark, and enjoy a tranquil seafood dinner on the waterfront.
- Cruise on a long-tail boat among the limestone stacks and sea caves of **Phangnga Bay**.
- Watch the sun set at the **Big Buddha statue** on Bangrak beach.
- Wander through the historic streets of **Phuket Town**.
- Ride an elephant and explore **Ko Samui's** interior jungles, mountains and caves.

0 kilometers 100

0 miles 100

Wat Phra Kaeo in Bangkok, home to the famous Emerald Buddha

◀ Mural paintings at the Grand Palace, Bangkok

Key

— A Week in the Far North of Thailand

— Ancient Capitals of Thailand

— Thailand's Southern Beaches

— A Week on the Eastern Seaboard

— A Week in Thailand's Northeast

Mae Sai
Doi Tung Sop Ruak
Mae Salong Chiang Saen
Chiang Rai
Doi Chiang Dao Mekong
Mae Taeng Wiang Pa Pao
Chiang Mai Nan
Lampang Nan
Si Satchanalai Chiang Khan Than Thip Falls Mekong
Sukhothai Phu Rua National Park Loei Nong Khai Nakhon Phanom
Phu Kradung National Park Mukdahan
THAILAND Chi
Prasat Hin Phimai
Khorat Prasat Hin Khao Phnom Rung
Chao
Ayutthaya
Bangkok
Pattaya Chanthaburi
Ko Samet Laem Ngop
Ko Chang Ko Wai
Gulf of Thailand
Ang Thong Marine National Park Ko Samui
Phangnga Bay
Phuket Town Ko Phi Phi
tong
Andaman Sea

A Week on the Eastern Seaboard

- Find a slice of paradise on **Ko Wai**, one of numerous pristine islets south of Ko Chang.
- Walk the entire east coast of tiny **Ko Samet**, discovering each bay's unique character.
- Taste fresh spring rolls in the Vietnamese Quarter of **Chanthaburi**.
- Dive into dense jungle to reach Ko Chang's **Khlong Phlu waterfall**.
- Snorkel over shipwrecks in **Ao Sa Lak Phet**.

The imposing temple ruins of Wat Phra Si Sanphet, Ayutthaya

A Week in Thailand's Northeast

- Enjoy incredible sweeping vistas from the summit of **Phu Kradung National Park**.
- Sample superb wine from the vineyards of the **Phu Rua National Park**.
- Watch the world go by in the chic riverside cafés of **Chiang Khan**.

- Visit breathtaking temples in **Nong Khai**.
- Tuck in to spicy local delicacies in **Khorat**, a city famous for its food.
- Explore two superb Khmer sites: the ruins at **Prasat Hin Phimai**, and the once-Hindu temple complex of **Prasat Hin Khao Phnom Rung**.

2 Days in Bangkok

Thailand's vibrant capital dazzles visitors with its array of contrasts – serene temples, gardens, and royal palaces amid ultra-modern skyscrapers and bustling city crowds.

- **Arriving** Bangkok's Suvarnabhumi International Airport lies 18 miles (29 km) east of the city. A high-speed rail link reaches various parts of the city, and there are plenty of taxis. Don Muang Airport, north of Bangkok, handles budget carriers.
- **Moving on** Flights to Chiang Mai leave from both airports, buses from the Northern Bus Terminal (Morchit) and trains from the downtown Hua Lampong Railway Station.

Day 1

Morning Bangkok is huge, but its best sights are found within a fairly small area along the Chao Phraya River. **Wat Phra Kaeo** *(pp84–7)* holds one of Thailand's most esteemed cultural artifacts, a small jade Buddha image. Ornate pavilions and gilded *chedi* (pagodas) fill the compound, which is surrounded by a walkway decorated with scenes from the Ramakien *(pp44–5)*.

Residence of the first six kings of the current Chakri dynasty, the **Grand Palace** *(pp84–5 and pp88–9)* is a mixture of traditional Thai and European Neo-Classical architecture. Most impressive is the Dusit Throne Hall, which contains the original teak throne of the dynasty's founder.

Afternoon As a counterpoint to the intense atmosphere of Wat Phra Kaeo, explore sprawling **Wat Pho** *(pp96–7)*. The magnificent central *bot* (chapel) contains a bronze Buddha image salvaged from the former capital, Ayutthaya, and the immense Reclining Buddha exudes serenity. After absorbing the atmosphere here, try a therapeutic massage in the temple's traditional medical school.

An aerial view of the bright lights of Bangkok at dusk

Day 2

Morning Jim Thompson House *(pp124–5)* is the former home of an American entrepreneur who revitalized the Thai silk industry after World War II. The six traditional teak houses within the shady compound contain superb collections of Asian art, including sculpture from the 7th century, antique Thai ceramics, Burmese wood carvings and Ming porcelain.

Afternoon Near Jim Thompson House are a wide choice of modern shopping malls, from the elegant **Siam Paragon** *(p143)* to the bazaar-like atmosphere at **Mahboonkrong** *(p143)*, which sells gadgets and clothing at bargain prices. More shopping on nearby Ploenchit Road can be followed by a visit to the **Erawan Shrine** *(p122)*, where traditional Thai dancers perform in honor of the Hindu god Indra, held holy by Buddhist Thais.

> **To extend your trip...**
> Enjoy some fresh air and greenery at the elegant **Dusit Park** *(pp106–7)* or the popular and central **Lumphini Park** *(p121)*.

2 Days in Chiang Mai

In the 14th century, Chiang Mai was the capital of an independent kingdom. Today it is known for its beguiling blend of ancient and modern, thriving culture and art scenes, charming and hospitable people, and its proximity to mountainous hill-tribe areas.

- **Arriving** Chiang Mai International Airport has flights to and from other Asian cities as well as domestic services. The airport is a few miles from the city center.
- **Moving on** Buses and minivans cover the northern region. Express buses and a train run to Bangkok. Car and motorcycle hires are readily available.

Day 1

Morning Start at the splendid **Wat Phra Sing** *(p230)* near the center of the old city, and then walk down tree-lined Ratchadamnoen Road to historic **Wat Chedi Luang** *(p230)*. A few blocks to the northeast, relax in the peaceful shady compound of **Wat Chiang Man** *(p230)*, the city's oldest *wat*.

Afternoon From Chiang Mai Zoo, at the foot of the mountain, board a minibus for the winding 7-mile (12-km) climb up **Doi Suthep** *(pp226–7)*. The temple of **Wat Doi Suthep**, originally constructed in the

Wat Phra Sing, the largest temple in Chiang Mai

14th century, attracts a steady stream of worshipers and visitors who admire the gilded central *chedi* (pagoda) and the panoramic views. In the evening, go shopping in the **Night Bazaar** (p230).

Day 2
Morning Explore **Warorot Market** (p230), where fresh food, spices, and local clothing (upstairs) are on offer. From the Chinese shrine west of the market, walk south along the small road, where hill tribes sell hand-woven cloth to local merchants.

Afternoon Take a cruise on the **Ping River** (p231); the boats leave from Wat Chaimongkol. Afterwards, watch the sun set over dinner or a drink in the Wat Gate neighborhood on the east side of the river along Charoenrat Road.

The iconic golden *chedi* of Wat Doi Suthep in Chiang Mai

A Week in the Far North of Thailand

- **Airports** Arrive and depart from Chiang Mai International Airport.
- **Transport** This itinerary is ideal for self-driving, which offers the most flexibility, although a good network of buses and (faster) minivans cover all the stops on this tour.

Day 1: Mae Taeng
Drive an hour north of Chiang Mai to the verdant **Mae Taeng Valley** (p225). The scenery is stunning, and there are fantastic opportunities to go river rafting, or trekking to hill-tribe villages. Stay the night in Mae Taeng.

Day 2: Chiang Dao
Head further north the next morning, and you'll soon spot the looming massif of **Doi Chiang Dao** (p224). Take a lantern-lit tour around the sacred cave and temple at the base of the mountain, or opt for a walking or cycling tour in the rugged countryside. There are a number of pleasant guesthouses nearby.

Day 3: Mae Salong
The mountain-top village of **Mae Salong** (p246) has a unique history; it was once a base for Chinese nationalist troops fleeing Mao's Communists. Now the economy thrives on growing fragrant Chinese tea, which tastes especially good on misty mornings.

Day 4: Doi Tung to Mae Sai
Winding through superb mountainous scenery, you'll soon reach **Doi Tung** (p247). The temple at its summit, **Wat Phra That Doi Tung** (p247), affords incredible views of the surrounding mountains and valley below. Don't miss **Doi Tung Royal Villa** (p247), a former royal palace. Head down to the border town of **Mae Sai** (p250), the gateway to Myanmar (Burma). What Mae Sai lacks in traditional beauty, the market makes up for in vivacity, as Thais bargain over the latest products from China.

Day 5: Golden Triangle to Chiang Saen
Just east of Mae Sai, visit the excellent **House of Opium museum** (p252), which tells the story of this infamous commodity. Stop at the village of **Sop Ruak** (p252), where you'll see the riverine meeting point of Thailand, Myanmar, and Laos – the center of the area known as the Golden Triangle because of its links to the opium trade. Stay in the pleasant town of

Chiang Saen (pp252–3), and take an evening stroll to the wide Mekong River, where you can watch porters unload the boats.

Day 6: Chiang Rai
The provincial capital of **Chiang Rai** (pp254–5) is growing, but the city center still exudes small-town charm – notice the old teak shop-houses along Tanalai Rd, and admire the wood carvings in **Wat Phra Kaeo** (p254), once the home of the Emerald Buddha that is now housed in the Bangkok temple of the same name.

Day 7: Chiang Rai to Chiang Mai
The return 3-hour drive to Chiang Mai is a pleasant and scenic tour, passing through hills and then a long valley of rice cultivation. Stop at the town of **Wiang Pa Pao** (p256) and, for a scenic return to Chiang Mai, turn right and continue to the small market town of **Phrao** (p224). Stock up on traditional textiles and locally grown fruit, then meander through a quiet hill-bounded valley to your destination.

> **To extend your trip...**
> From Chiang Rai, head to the rarely visited mountainous province of **Nan** (pp258–9), once an independent statelet. While there, admire the murals and elegant architecture of **Wat Phumin** (pp260–61).

Ancient Capitals of Thailand

- **Airports** Bangkok Airways offers daily flights from Suvarnabhumi International Airport to Sukhothai. To continue to Chiang Mai by air requires first going to Phitsanulok, 40 miles (60 km) east of Sukhothai.

- **Transport** Self-driving is recommended. Trains, buses, and minivans all reach nearby Ayutthaya from Bangkok. From Ayutthaya, trains travel to Phitsanulok, and buses reach Sukhothai town directly. Continuing north to Chiang Mai, there are buses from Sukhothai and trains from Phitsanulok.

Day 1: Bangkok
See day 1 of the Bangkok city itinerary. If time permits, visit the **National Museum** (pp92–3); it holds some of the best artifacts from the sites you'll be visiting.

Day 2: Ayutthaya
In the morning, drive or take a bus to **Ayutthaya** (pp180–85), which was the cosmopolitan capital of Siam from the 14th century until it was razed by Burmese invaders in 1767. The Historical Park includes over a dozen temples; most have now been restored, although those left in ruins still manage to evoke the former splendor of this once great city. Sites are spread out, so take a driven tour or rent a bicycle to get the most out of your visit. For an informative orientation, start at the **Ayutthaya Historical Study Center** (p182). Admire the elegant corncob-shaped *prang* (a Khmer-style *chedi*, or pagoda) at **Wat Phra Ram** (p181) and wander the sprawling grounds of **Wat Phra Si Sanphet** (pp182–3).

Day 3: Ayutthaya
Start the day at **Wat Phra Mahathat** (p180), the largest temple complex in Ayutthaya, then get a *tuk-tuk* (motorized trishaw) to **Wat Yai Chai Mongkhon** (p185), which lies just off the island and is home

A Buddha image reflected in lotus ponds at Sukhothai Historical Park

to a magnificent reclining Buddha. See a unique strand of Thai Buddhism that embraces Chinese folk religion (with firecrackers and fortune telling) at the nearby **Wat Phanan Choeng** (p185). In the evening, take a boat ride around the island, viewing the beautifully lit temples of old Ayutthaya.

Day 4: Sukhothai
Leave in the morning for Sukhothai (meaning "dawn of happiness"), the site of a 13th-century kingdom considered by Thais to be the source of their language and culture. A UNESCO World Heritage Site, **Sukhothai Historical Park** (pp198–9) lies in the center of a lush green valley. The park is huge so it's best to rent a bicycle at the entrance to travel between sites. Start with **Wat Mahathat** (pp200–1) in the center of the walled royal city, and admire its elegant *chedi* and magnificent Buddha. Choose from a variety of cafés and guesthouses nearby after the park closes at 6pm.

Day 5: Sukhothai
Spend the day exploring the temples surrounding the Royal City. Just outside the east gate, compare the bell-shaped *chedi* at **Wat Chang Lom** (p199), with the elegant Sukhothai style at nearby **Wat Chedi Sung** (p199). To the north, admire the immense Buddha image of **Wat Si Chum** (p199). **Wat Saphan Hin** (p201) lies to the west atop a small hill, which affords fine views over the valley.

Day 6: Si Satchanalai
Take a morning trip to Si Satchanalai from Sukhothai or, if you're driving, stop on the way to Chiang Mai. **Si Satchanalai-Chalieng Historical Park** (pp202–3) is located on the banks of the Yom River, which adds to the peaceful atmosphere here. The largest temple, **Wat Chang Lom** (p204), sports a Sri Lankan-style, bell-shaped *chedi*. A lone *chedi* is all that remains of **Wat Suwan Khiri** (p203), but the views from the hilltop it perches on, of the rivers and rice fields beyond, are spectacular.

Day 7: Chiang Mai
See day 1 of the Chiang Mai city itinerary.

To extend your trip…

Stop in at **Lampang** (p240–41) on the way to Chiang Mai and explore the town in a horse-drawn carriage.

Wat Chang Lom in Si Satchanalai-Chalieng Historical Park

For practical information on traveling around Thailand, see pp472–81

A Week in Thailand's Northeast

- **Airports** Fly into Loei from Bangkok, or start this tour from Khorat, and fly back to Bangkok from Loei, or to Chiang Mai from nearby Udon Thani.

- **Transport** This itinerary is ideal for self-driving, but buses and minivans cover the northern part of the trip and there are both trains and buses from Nong Khai to Khorat and on to Bangkok. Driving time between Nong Khai and Khorat is about 4 hours.

Prasat Hin Phimai, a beautifully restored Khmer temple complex close to Khorat

Day 1: Loei

Fly to the quiet town of Loei, and head for **Phu Kradung National Park** *(pp290–91)*, a superb mountainous environment with a year-round cool climate that encourages unique flora and fauna. It's a 3-mile (5-km) walk to the summit, where the park offers accommodation. The sunrise vistas from here are magnificent. If the walk doesn't suit you, opt instead for the nearby **Phu Rua National Park** *(p292)*, where the cool breezes have made the area Thailand's flower and wine-growing center.

Day 2: Chiang Khan

North of Loei, on the Mekong River, visit the charming town of **Chiang Khan** *(p294)*, with its old teakwood shop-houses and riverside esplanade. Chiang Khan has become a favorite weekend trip for young Bangkokians and is full of trendy boutiques, coffee shops, and great places to stay.

Days 3: Chiang Khan to Nong Khai

Savor the splendid views of the river, waterfalls, and small villages untouched by time on the road that winds along the Mekong between Chiang Khan and **Nong Khai** *(pp296–7)*. Stop on the way for a lunch of fresh river fish, and cool off at the **Than Thip Falls** *(p295)* near Sangkhom.

Day 4: Nong Khai

The busy town of **Nong Khai** is situated on the Mekong River where the Friendship Bridge connects to the Lao capital of Vientiane. Its close trading position with Laos ensures that there are many bargains to be had in the bustling **Indochina Market** *(p296)*. Perhaps the most amazing sight in Nong Khai is the inimitable **Wat Khaek** *(p297)*. Here, an eccentric yogi assembled a fantastic collection of bizarre statuary drawn from Buddhist and Hindu traditions and his own imagination. Spend the evening in one of the restaurants or bars along the Rimkhong (the riverside road).

Day 5: Khorat

From Nong Khai, travel south to **Khorat** *(pp278–9)* and visit the **Thao Suranari Monument** *(p279)*, dedicated to a local heroine who defeated Lao invaders with feminine guile. Have dinner in the lively **Night Market** *(p279)*; Khorat is famous for its spicy regional dishes and barbecued chicken.

Day 6: Prasat Hin Phimai

Take a day trip from Khorat to the nearby **Prasat Hin Phimai** *(pp280–81)*, a thousand-year-old Khmer site that has been beautifully restored. Both Buddhist and Hindu iconography abound here. The intricate carvings of Hindu deities in pink sandstone are awe-inspiring, and the Buddha statue at the temple's epicenter is superlative.

Day 7: Prasat Hin Khao Phnom Rung

Take a second trip from Khorat to **Prasat Hin Khao Phnom Rung** *(pp284–5)*. Once a Hindu temple, this is considered one of the best examples of Khmer architecture in Thailand. To understand the symbolism of the buildings in the complex, stop in at the visitor information center at the front gate. Hindus believe that as you walk over the three *naga* bridges approaching the central sanctuary, you are leaving the temporal world and entering the home of the god Shiva. Drive to Khorat Airport in the afternoon, or continue your journey.

> **To extend your trip...**
> After Nong Khai, follow the Mekong south through the picturesque riverside towns of **Nakhon Phanom** *(p300)* and **Mukdahan** *(p302)*, and rejoin the road to Khorat further south.

Steps to the temple compound at Prasat Hin Khao Phnom Rung

A Week on the Eastern Seaboard

- **Airports** There are flights between Bangkok and Trat, a town close to the ferries to Ko Chang.
- **Transport** Regular bus services reach the area from Bangkok's Eastern Bus Terminal and directly from Suvarnabhumi International Airport. A passenger ferry runs to Ko Samet from the village of Ban Pae. Both car and passenger ferries go from Laem Ngop port near Trat to Ko Chang.

Day 1: Pattaya

Pattaya *(p321)* is about 2 hours by bus or car from Bangkok. Walk along Pattaya's **Beach Road** admiring the colorful fishing boats in this wide bay. In the evening, have a look at South Pattaya's **Walking Street**, a brightly lit throng of go-go bars, discos, and open-air beer bars. North Pattaya is slightly more restrained, although the most famous transvestite cabaret shows are here. Even mellower is the adjacent bay of **Naklua** *(p321)*, where excellent seafood goes for a fraction of the price nearby.

Day 2: Ko Samet

A few hours from Pattaya, by road, ferry, and a short minibus ride, are the powdery white sands of **Ko Samet** *(pp322–3)*. Spend the day basking on one of the island's fantastic beaches. Opt for **Hat Sai Kaeo** *(p322)* if you fancy a lively beach with lots of restaurants and bars. **Ao Phai** *(p322)* bay is smaller, quieter, and more picturesque.

Day 3: Ko Samet

Put on some solid footwear and strike out towards the southern tip of the island at the deserted **Ao Toei,** stopping to rest in the leafy shade of each headland. Each bay has its own distinct character. Fresh coconuts provide excellent refreshment en route, or stop into a luxury resort for high tea.

Day 4: Chanthaburi

Back on the mainland, travel to the charming town of **Chanthaburi** *(pp324–5)*. Take a stroll along the river, visit the **gem market** *(p325)*, and try the fresh (uncooked) spring rolls in the town's **Vietnamese Quarter** *(p324)*.

Day 5: Ko Chang

Much bigger than Ko Samet, **Ko Chang** *(pp326–7)* offers a wide variety of experiences such as fishing, diving and snorkeling. Take the short ferry ride from Laem Ngop on the mainland and catch a minibus to **Hat Sai Khao** beach *(p326)* for beach barbecues, live music, and fire-juggling shows. Alternatively, travel to **Hat Khlong Phrao** *(p326)* for the

The refreshing Khlong Phlu Waterfall on Ko Chang

best seafood on the island. The short walk to the **Khlong Phlu Waterfall** *(p327)* offers a good look at the dense jungle of the island.

Day 6: Day trip to Ko Wai

From Bang Bao village on the southern tip of the island, catch a boat to **Ko Wai** *(p327)*, a pristine islet. Snorkel or swim in the crystal-clear waters and take in the stunning views of the surrounding islands in the Ko Chang archipelago. Stay in Ko Wai or return to Ko Chang in the evening.

Day 7: Ko Chang

Back in Ko Chang, spend the morning on one of the isolated beaches on the southern coast. **Ao Sa Lak Phet** *(p326)* is near a traditional fishing village, and from here you can go snorkeling over eerie sunken ships from World War II. From the mainland, it's an hour's flight or about a 5-hour drive to Bangkok.

> **To extend your trip…**
> Visit **Ko Mak** *(p327)* and **Ko Kut** *(p327)*, two islets off the southern tip of Ko Chang.

A view of the bay at Pattaya

For practical information on traveling around Thailand, see pp472–81

Thailand's Southern Beaches

- **Airports** Fly into Ko Samui International Airport from Bangkok and from Samui to Phuket International Airport. From Phuket you can fly back to Bangkok or on to other destinations, including Europe.
- **Transport** Both car ferry and passenger ferries reach Ko Samui from the mainland, and Phuket is connected to the mainland by bridge, so self-drive is another option for this tour. Buses also connect Samui and Phuket.

Day 1: Ko Samui

Choose one the two best beaches on Ko Samui's east coast: **Hat Chaweng** (p342) is longer and has more entertainment options; **Hat Lamai** (p342) is better for families. Both are great for swimming and water sports, from windsurfing to parasailing. At sunset, visit the **Big Buddha statue** near Hat Bangrak (p341), on the island's quieter north coast. Dine at one of the excellent restaurants in the nearby fisherman's village at **Hat Bophut** (p341).

The limestone islet Ko Tapu, which lies just off the coast of Phangnga Bay

The pristine waters of the Angthong National Marine Park

Day 2: Ko Samui

Head inland to the **Namuang waterfall** (p342). Walk to the falls, and cool off in the clear pool at their base. Afterwards, take a Thai cooking class or play a round of golf on one of Samui's many world-class courses.

Day 3: Angthong National Marine Park

Catch a boat from Ko Samui to this beautiful and undeveloped group of some 40 islands (pp344–5). Explore via kayak, go snorkeling, or hike to caves on the wild interior of one of the islands. Return to Ko Samui in the afternoon and fly or drive to Phuket.

Day 4: Phuket

Spend a morning in charming **Phuket Town** (pp364–5) visiting two Chinese temples, **Bang Niew** (p364) and **Chui Tui** (p365) established by the Chinese immigrants who flocked to the tin mines here in the 19th century. Both celebrate the Taoist tradition and the often raucous ambience is unlike the serenity that prevails in Buddhist temples. The **Chinese Mansions** (p364), once home to tin barons, are a fascinating mixture of Asian and Western architecture. After lunch, head for the secluded beaches of **Hat Nai Yang** or **Hat Nai Thon** (p366) at the northern end of the west coast of the island.

Day 5: Phangnga Bay

A day trip to **Phangnga Bay** (pp368–71), reveals the spectacular limestone stacks and hidden sea caves that create a home for the marine and avian life for which it is famous. For the best views, hire a long-tail boat or join a sea kayaking tour for some cave paddling.

Day 6: Patong Beach

No trip to Phuket is complete without a visit to **Patong Beach** (p366). Every seaside diversion is offered here, from jet skis to late-night discos. **Hat Kata and Hat Karon** (p366) to the south, while developed, are more relaxing.

Day 7: Ko Phi Phi

Take a morning boat from Phuket for a day trip to this spectacular island (pp376–7). Cool off in one of the hip cafés in **Ban Ton Sai** (p376) village, then step across the isthmus where you'll find a lovely bay bounded by coconut palms and limestone crags. A steep but quick walk leads to a magnificent viewpoint. Alternatively, walk along the level trail to **Hat Yao** (p376) and go snorkeling on the reef, where iridescent fish dart among the vivid coral. Return to Phuket for the sunset.

> **To extend your trip...**
> The **Ko Surin** and **Ko Similan** archipelagos (p361), north of Phuket, are home to spectacular and world-famous diving sites, such as Burma Banks. The waters are crystal clear.

Putting Thailand on the Map

Thailand is located at the heart of Southeast Asia, between the Indian Ocean and the South China Sea. The country covers 198,000 sq miles (513,000 sq km) and has a population of 68 million, the majority of whom are concentrated in the fertile Central Plains and in the capital, Bangkok. The verdant North is mainly mountainous, and towering ranges run along the long western border with Myanmar (Burma). In contrast, the Northeast is a flat, poor, arid region. Much of the eastern border with Laos is defined by the Mekong River. Further south are the hills of northern Cambodia. Thailand's Southern peninsula offers many of the best beaches and islands.

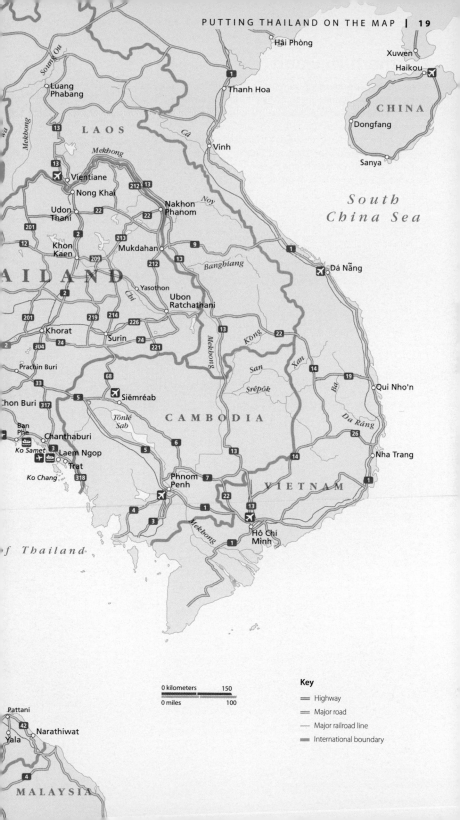

Northern Thailand

An extensive road network covers most of the North, Northeast, and Central Plains of Thailand. Air-conditioned buses run between many of the major towns, and local buses are plentiful. Only in isolated border areas are road links unreliable. The railroad system connects Bangkok to the Central Plains and Chiang Mai. Bangkok, Chiang Mai, and Chiang Rai have international airports, and many major towns are served by domestic flights.

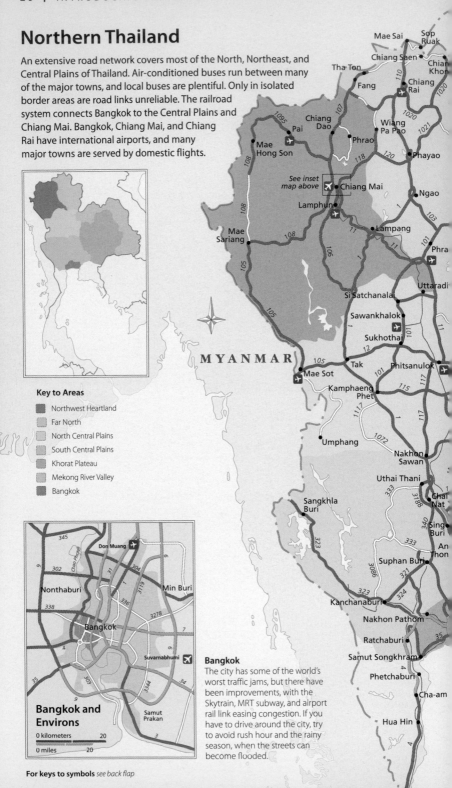

Key to Areas

- Northwest Heartland
- Far North
- North Central Plains
- South Central Plains
- Khorat Plateau
- Mekong River Valley
- Bangkok

MYANMAR

Bangkok and Environs

0 kilometers   20
0 miles   20

Bangkok

The city has some of the world's worst traffic jams, but there have been improvements, with the Skytrain, MRT subway, and airport rail link easing congestion. If you have to drive around the city, try to avoid rush hour and the rainy season, when the streets can become flooded.

For keys to symbols *see back flap*

Chiang Mai
Chiang Mai has good road and rail links with Bangkok and the rest of Thailand. The "Super Highway" connects to the airport and main routes into the city. City roads can be very congested at rush hour.

Chiang Mai and Environs

Doi Saket

San Sai

DOI SUTHEP

Chiang Mai

San Kamphaeng

Saraphi

0 kilometers 10
0 miles 5

LAOS

Nong Bua

Nan

Chiang Khan

Vientiane

Nong Khai

Loei

Udon Thani

Ban Chiang

Nakhon Phanom

Renu Nakhon

That Phanom

Sakhon Nakhon

Phetchabun

Khon Kaen

Kalasin

Mukdahan

Maha Sarakham

Roi Et

Selaphum

Khemmarat

Chaiyaphum

Bua Yai

Yasothon

Suwannaphum

Khong Chiam

Ubon Ratchathani

Phimai

Buri Ram

Khorat (Nakhon Ratchasima)

Surin

Sirindhorn Dam

Phra Phutthabat

Saraburi

Ayutthaya

Bang Pa-in

Prachin Buri

CAMBODIA

See inset map, left

Bangkok

Chachoengsao

Aranyaprathet

Chon Buri

Ko sichang

Si Racha

Pattaya

Rayong

Ban Phe

Chanthaburi

attahip

Ko Samet

Laem Ngop

Trat

Ko Chang

0 kilometers 100
0 miles 50

Key

Highway
Major road
Minor road
Railroad line
International border

Southern Thailand

Thailand's long coastline, fine beaches, and idyllic offshore islands are a major attraction for visitors to the Gulf of Thailand and the South. Good-quality roads stretch from the Cambodian border in the east to the Malaysian border in the south and along the western Andaman Sea coast. Air-conditioned buses operate regularly between the main towns. There is one north-south railroad line from Bangkok that passes through, or has connections with, most of the towns on the Gulf of Thailand. The Eastern Seaboard has good road connections with Bangkok, but the railroad line terminates at Sattahip. Ferry services from ports to the main islands are frequent, and it is possible to buy tickets in Bangkok that combine train, bus, and ferry trips. Many towns have regional airports; Ko Samui, Phuket, Hat Yai, and Krabi are also served by international flights.

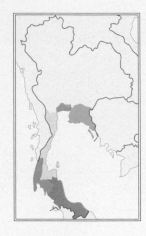

Key to Areas

 Eastern Seaboard

Bangkok

Western Seaboard

Upper Andaman Coast

Deep South

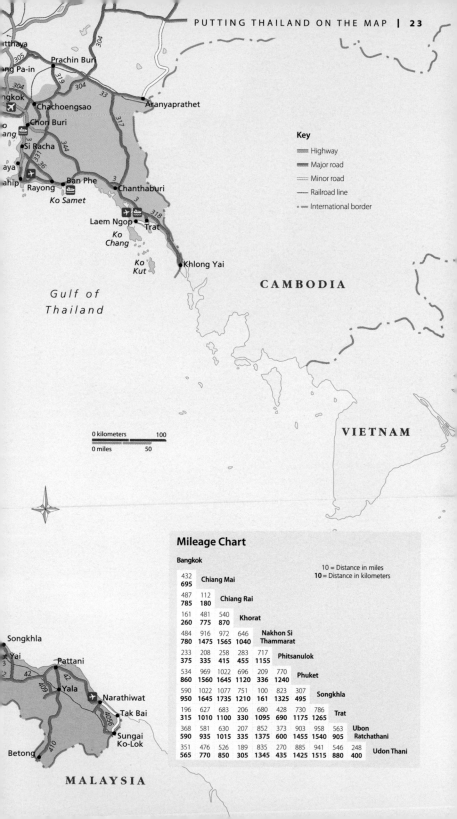

Key

Highway
Major road
Minor road
Railroad line
International border

Gulf of Thailand

CAMBODIA

VIETNAM

MALAYSIA

Mileage Chart

Bangkok										
432										
695	**Chiang Mai**					10 = Distance in miles				
487	112					**10** = Distance in kilometers				
785	**180**	**Chiang Rai**								
161	481	540								
260	**775**	**870**	**Khorat**							
484	916	972	646		Nakhon Si					
780	**1475**	**1565**	**1040**	**Thammarat**						
233	208	258	283	717						
375	**335**	**415**	**455**	**1155**	**Phitsanulok**					
534	969	1022	696	209	770					
860	**1560**	**1645**	**1120**	**336**	**1240**	**Phuket**				
590	1022	1077	751	100	823	307				
950	**1645**	**1735**	**1210**	**161**	**1325**	**495**	**Songkhla**			
196	627	683	206	680	428	730	786			
315	**1010**	**1100**	**330**	**1095**	**690**	**1175**	**1265**	**Trat**		
368	581	630	207	852	373	903	958	563	Ubon	
590	**935**	**1015**	**335**	**1375**	**600**	**1455**	**1540**	**905**	**Ratchathani**	
351	476	526	189	835	270	885	941	546	248	
565	**770**	**850**	**305**	**1345**	**435**	**1425**	**1515**	**880**	**400**	**Udon Thani**

A PORTRAIT OF THAILAND

Set within a lush, tropical landscape, Thailand is a theater of cultural and sensual contrasts for the visitor. The long, rich heritage and abundant natural resources of this proud Buddhist nation jostle for space within the dynamism of a country undergoing economic boom and bust. In turns zestful and tranquil, resplendent and subtle, Thailand is always compelling.

Thailand is located in a fertile monsoon belt midway between India and China, the two civilizations that have molded Southeast Asia. But the Thais have long delighted in their distinctive culture. For instance, though the Tai (rather than Thai) ethnic group probably originated in Southern China sometime in the first millennium AD, their tonal language is quite unlike any form of Chinese. Moreover, the elegant Thai script, though derived from that of ancient Southern India, is distinct.

Today, Thailand is a member of the Association of Southeast Asian Nations (ASEAN), though Thais still take pride in a long tradition of independence. Unlike all its immediate neighbors, Myanmar (Burma), Laos, Cambodia, and Malaysia, the country never fell to a European colonial power. More fundamentally, though, the Thai sense of identity is allied with Theravada Buddhism and the monarchy. Both have been dignified institutions since the Sukhothai period (13th–14th century), an era when the first real Thai kingdom flourished. Indeed, the colors of the modern Thai flag (thong trai rong) symbolize the nation (red), the three forces of Buddhism (white), and the monarchy (blue).

Today, the great majority of Thailand's 63 million inhabitants regard themselves as Thai. Hill tribes are the most obvious ethnic minority groups, but it is the Chinese who form the largest (and most integrated) group.

Colorful *korlae* fishing boats in the clear waters of Southern Thailand

◀ Buddhist monks at the ruins of Wat Phra Si Sanphet, Ayutthaya

Bangkok is a sprawling modern metropolis with a continually evolving skyline

Northeast, and South. Each region also has its own topographical identity. The North is an area of forested mountains, where hill-tribe minorities coexist with mainstream society. In the South, the narrow Kra Peninsula presents a 2,500-km (1,500-mile) coastline with a hilly interior of rainforests and rubber plantations. Malay-Muslim culture is a major influence here.

Between these two extremes are the Central Plains, the cradle of Thai civilization and a fertile, rice-growing region. Near the mouth of the Chao Phraya River, the capital, Bangkok, sprawls ever farther each year. Its palatial splendor can still be discerned, but the city is among the world's most congested and polluted, despite great efforts to clean the air and local rivers. Different again is Northeast Thailand (also widely known as Isan), the poorest part of the country occupying the Khorat Plateau, its eastern border with Laos defined by the Mekong River. In this semiarid region traditional farming communities, many of them Thai-Lao, eke out a subsistence living.

The various peoples live relatively peaceably nowadays, though in 1939, in a wave of nationalism encouraged by Prime Minister Phibun Songkram, the country's name was changed from Siam to Prathet Thai (Thailand), or "land of the Thai people."

The country is divided into four main regions, and there are many subtle differences between the peoples and dialects of the Central Plains, North,

Economic Development

Rice and other agricultural crops were long the mainstays of the Thai economy, and farming is still highly respected.

Green terraced rice field in Doi Inthanon National Park in the Northwest Heartland

Noodle vendor at Damnoen Saduak Floating Market, a colorful and popular sight near Bangkok

Transport infrastructure remains a weak point, resulting in Bangkok's notorious traffic chaos. Commerce and communications are concentrated in Bangkok, while the rest of the country remains largely rural.

Raw materials top the country's list of imports, and the leading exports include garments, electrical goods, mechanical equipment, seafood products, rice, rubber, gems, and jewelry.

The environment has taken many blows in the last 50 years, and forest cover has declined from 70 percent of the land to less than 20 percent. Many animal species have lost their habitats and been hunted almost to extinction. However, conservation awareness is increasing, and measures are being taken to preserve what remains of the nation's rich natural bounty.

From the mid-1980s, however, a concerted export drive triggered an unprecedented economic boom. For several years, Thailand enjoyed double-digit growth and was known as one of Asia's "tiger" economies. Economic growth came to an abrupt halt, however, in a chain of events that began in May 1997 with financial speculation against the Thai *baht*. Flotation of the *baht* in July pushed the economies of various Asian countries, including Thailand, Indonesia, and South Korea, into crisis. While Thai politicians blamed everyone from bankers to city-dwellers, the people of Thailand immediately suffered, with large-scale redundancies, pay cuts, and repossessions.

Muslim Thai in Southern Thailand

Society and Politics

In spite of the pressures of change, Thai society is relatively stable. There is no caste system, but the social hierarchy, topped by the monarchy, is

Thailand has since recovered fully, and Bangkok's skyline is seeing much construction work. Tourism is still the single largest foreign exchange earner. The Tourism Authority of Thailand (TAT) revived the "Amazing Thailand Year," which was a great success in 1998. In 2006 Thailand recorded 13.8 million visitors, and though this figure dropped in 2008, 2013 saw a significant rise again. Bangkok and the beach resorts attract most of the visitors, followed by Chiang Mai and the North. Thailand's deluxe hotels and luxurious spa resorts are some of the finest in the world.

Elephant in Bangkok, surprisingly not a rare sight

quite rigid. Social standing is dictated mainly by wealth and family connections. Women have less standing than men, despite playing a major role in the economy, mainly as laborers and white-collar workers. However, in 2011, Thailand elected its first female prime minister, Yingluck Shinawatra, sister of deposed PM Thaksin Shinawatra. Three years later, she was charged with dereliction of duty and forced out of office. Elders are always accorded respect within families and in society.

Seated Buddha image, one of thousands in Thailand

Hierarchy permeates daily life in many ways. The traditional greeting, the *wai*, in which the hands are brought together near the chin, is always initiated by the inferior, and the height of the *wai* reflects the social gap between the parties. If the gap is extreme, inferiors may approach their superiors on their knees. Other rules of etiquette, such as never raising the voice, transcend class. Despite such rules for themselves, Thais are renowned for their tolerance of other cultures and friendliness to visitors. Offense is taken only if there is any perceived disrespect to the King or Buddhism.

Garland of jasmine, a ubiquitous sight

There is no criticism of the King in Thailand's press. Constitutional since 1932, the monarchy is revered almost as much as when kings were *chakravatin,* or "king of kings." Kingship and religion are inextricably linked in Thailand. The present monarch, King Bhumibol Adulyadej (Rama IX), served as a monk in his youth and presides over some major religious ceremonies.

He is the longest-reigning living monarch in the world, having ascended to the throne in 1946, and has won widespread respect for his devotion to Thai welfare and environmental projects.

The monkhood (*sangha*), some 250,000 strong, plays a crucial social role. Most teenage boys become novice monks for a while, which is seen as fortuitous for their families, especially their mothers, as well as a rite of passage. Some enter the monkhood properly later in life and may choose its austere precepts for life. Monks conduct numerous Buddhist rites, ranging from festivals to everyday blessings and other social events. In rural areas, they traditionally play an important role as teachers, a profession that in Thailand is perhaps held higher in regard than anywhere else in the world.

In contrast, politicians are held in far less respect, and the Thai press openly criticizes the running of the country. The economic boom and bust of the 1980s and 1990s exerted considerable pressure on Thai society. The extended family remains important, but it has

Lisu hill-tribe women and children in their colorful traditional clothing

Monks chanting in Pali, the language of Theravada Buddhism

countless Buddha images and murals, and decorative arts, such as woodcarving, stucco, gilt, lacquer, colored glass mosaic, and mother of pearl inlay, are all used to striking effect.

The literary tradition of Thailand is confined mostly to classic tales, the most important of which is the Ramakien, an ancient moral epic with its origins in the Indian Ramayana. Such sagas provided the narrative content for the once-thriving performing arts, best preserved today in highly stylized classical dance-drama called *khon* and *lakhon*. Thailand's most notable literary figure is the 19th-century poet Sunthorn Phu.

become an idealized concept espoused by conservative groups. As soon as they are old enough, many young people move away from their towns and villages to find work in the city, sending money back to their parents each month.

Thai Culture and Arts

Thailand's classical arts have developed almost exclusively (and anonymously) in the service of Theravada Buddhism. Accordingly, the best showcase is the *wat*, where traditional architecture, typified by sweeping, multitiered roofs,

Lakhon dancers at a Buddhist shrine

Thai cinema continues to go from strength to strength. In 2002, *Sut Sanaeha* ("Blissfully Yours"), the story of a romance between a Thai woman and an illegal Burmese immigrant, was selected for special consideration at the Cannes Film Festival, and the 2008 film *Ploy* was premiered there during Director's Fortnight. The Bangkok International Film Festival was launched in 2002.

On the sports front, Thailand's unique style of kick-boxing draws big crowds, while other traditional pastimes range from *takraw*, a game not unlike volleyball, but using the feet, to kite-flying. Numerous colorful festivals, many linked to both Buddhism and the changing seasons, are celebrated with exuberance. Whatever the activity, Thais believe that life should be *sanuk* – "fun." *Sanuk* can be found in all things, from eating – something for which Thais have a passion – to simply going for a stroll with friends.

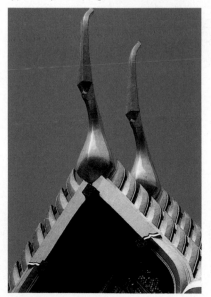

Cho fas, or roof finials, at the Grand Palace, Bangkok

Monsoon Country

The rice cycle, upon which the Thais have long believed their health, wealth, and happiness depends, is governed by the advance and retreat of the monsoon rains. As most people in the kingdom define themselves as *chao na*, rice farmers, the monsoon could be said to govern the cycle of life. This analogy is seen clearly in many Thai beliefs and practices. The rice goddess must be honored before cultivation if the crop is to be bountiful. The rice grain contains a spirit *(kwan)* and is planted in the rainy season to become "pregnant." The Thai word for irrigation *(chon prathan)* translates as gift of water."

The Central Plains of Thailand enjoy good conditions for wet rice cultivation. The flat paddies become flooded in the rainy season.

Bundles of rice seedlings ready for transplanting

Transplanting takes place in the rainy season, when the heavy clay soil is saturated.

A "calling for rains" Buddha image – a standing posture with both arms pointing to the earth – is found in some Northern *wats*. The rice crop depends on rain.

Songkran, or Thai New Year, in April, is a water festival marking the imminent end of the cool, dry season. People celebrate by pouring or throwing water over each other.

Monsoon Seasons

"Monsoon" comes from the Arabic mawsim (season). It refers to South Asia's seasonal winds (not heavy rain). In Thailand, the southwest monsoon is the rainy season; the northeast monsoon is dry, called the cool season; and between these periods is the hot season.

The southwest monsoon comes from the Indian Ocean with rain-laden clouds, from about June to October. Most days there are downpours, though Thailand's east coast is fairly dry.

Flooding in Bangkok at the end of the rainy season

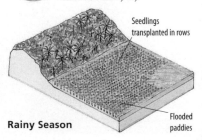

Seedlings transplanted in rows

Rainy Season

Flooded paddies

Machinery has replaced animals on many farms, reflecting the increasing mechanization of the Thai farming industry. However, plowing and cultivating the land is still hard work.

The main harvest for lowland wet rice cultivation takes place in the middle of the cool season. Entire families and villages labor in the fields at this busy time, cutting off the golden stalks with sickles.

Water channel between fields

Seedlings need to be semisubmerged

Threshing is usually undertaken in the rice fields by the same laborers who have harvested the crop. The stalks are beaten to separate the grain from the chaff. The grain is then dried in the sun.

Transplanting

Since most varieties of rice can only propagate in flood conditions, rice seedlings may initially be nurtured in nursery fields, where irrigation can be carefully managed and monitored. Later these seedlings will be transplanted into flooded paddies.

The northeast monsoon from central Asia usually blows from November to March, bringing relatively cool, dry conditions to Thailand, though rains often affect the east coast.

Between the two monsoons the land heats up, creating an area of low pressure above it. Eventually the high pressure over the Indian Ocean moves inland, and the monsoon cycle begins again.

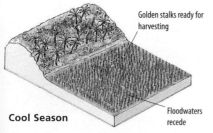

Golden stalks ready for harvesting

Cool Season

Floodwaters recede

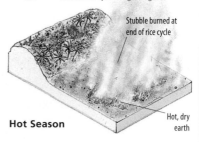

Stubble burned at end of rice cycle

Hot Season

Hot, dry earth

The Landscape and Wildlife of Thailand

Thailand stretches from south of the tropic of Cancer to about 620 miles (1,000 km) north of the equator; its tropical climate is affected by two monsoons *(see pp30–31)*. Varied topography and a gentle climate have led to a rich diversity of flora and fauna. Limestone hills in the North are clad in dense tropical forest. Open forest is more usual in the Northeast and Central Plains while the South and Gulf have superb coastlines and pockets of rainforest. Many habitats are threatened by industry and tourism; deforestation is rife, and some animal species face extinction *(see p223)*. As a result, many national parks have been established. The first, Khao Yai *(see pp188–9)*, opened in 1962.

Coconut palms on the island of Ko Samui in the Gulf of Thailand

Montane Tropical Forest

This type of forest is made up mostly of broadleaf evergreens and some deciduous trees such as laurel, oak, and chestnut. Mosses, ferns, and epiphytic orchids, growing on other plants, are common.

Atlas moths are the world's largest species. The female is larger than the male.

Serow, a type of antelope, are becoming increasingly rare in the hills of Northern Thailand.

Palm civets are nocturnal. They are found in tropical forests, but may also live near humans and eat cultivated fruit.

Open Forest

The most common trees in the open forest, also called savanna forest, are dipterocarps, a family of trees native to Southeast Asia. The ground around them is often carpeted by coarse scrub.

Sambar, Thailand's largest deer, can be seen on the Central Plains and in the Northeast.

Capped gibbons are found mainly on the southern edge of Northeast Thailand. They are extremely agile.

Wild boars have been heavily hunted in the past. They feed mainly on grass.

Thai Flowers

The diversity of Thailand's flowers reflects its range of natural habitats. Most famous of all are its orchids; there are some 1,300 different varieties. Unfortunately, illegal collection has led to their growing rarity in the wild. Other flowers are used as spices and for medicinal purposes.

The mallow flower, a relative of the hibiscus, is common throughout Southeast Asia.

Lotus lilies' seed pods and stems are edible. Other lilies are grown for ornament only.

Mountain pitcher plants are insectivorous. Their prey falls into the "pitcher" where the plant's juices slowly dissolve it.

Orchids *(see p224)* come mainly from Northern Thailand; they are prized for their beauty.

Wetlands

Freshwater swamp forests have been decimated by farming, though some survive in the South. River basins and man-made lakes and ponds can be found all over Thailand.

Dusky leaf-monkeys are found in the Thai-Malay peninsula. Three other species of leaf-monkey also live in Thailand.

Coastal Forest

The seeds of trees such as pines and Indian almond are transported on sea currents; thus ribbons of coastal forest are found all over Southeast Asia. Thailand's coastal forests are now threatened by farming and tourism.

Green turtles are the only herbivorous sea turtles; they feed on sea grass and algae and are nocturnal.

Lizards are common in island forests. Most eat insects, though some species eat mice and small birds.

Painted storks migrate to Thailand's swamps to breed. During this time the pigment in their faces turns pink.

Purple swamp hens are common. Long-toed feet allow them to walk on floating vegetation.

Crested wood partridges are found in the South, in areas of coastal, lowland forest.

Thai Buddhism

At least 90 percent of Thais practice Theravada Buddhism. This was first brought to the region from India around the 3rd century BC and is based on the ancient Pali canon of the Buddha's teachings (Tripitaka). However, Thai practice incorporates many Hindu, Tantric, and Mahayana Buddhist influences. The worship of Buddha images, for instance, is a Mahayana Buddhist practice. Animist beliefs in spirits and the magical and in astrology are also widespread. Thais believe that Buddhism is one of three forces that give their kingdom its strength, the other two being the monarchy and nationhood. Religious rituals color daily life, especially in the form of merit-making *(see p133)*.

King Bhumibol, like many kings before him, spent time as a monk. For Thais, this act reinforces the notion that Buddhism and the monarchy are unified powers.

Siddhartha sets out to attain Enlightenment.

Most Thai males are ordained as monks at adolescence – a major rite of passage. They usually spend at least a few months as monks, earning merit for themselves and their families. Few Thai women become nuns.

Applying gold leaf to Buddha images is a popular act of merit-making. Books of gold leaf can be readily purchased at temples, and the thin leaves are applied in profusion on Buddha images, *wat* decoration, and murals.

Story of the Buddha

The Buddha was born Prince Siddhartha Gautama in India in the 6th century BC. He gave up his riches to seek Enlightenment, and later taught the way to nirvana. Statues of the Buddha (see p177) and murals depicting his previous 10 lives (jatakas) abound in Thailand.

The family is held in high regard in Thailand. A senior monk will be asked by the family for his blessing at child-naming ceremonies, weddings, to bless a new house or car, or simply after a donation to the *wat* has been made. Children are taught the simple moral codes of Buddhism from an early age.

Walking meditation is practiced by most monks. Here, the most senior monk leads the line walking around the temple clockwise. Meditation on the nature of existence is a major way in which Buddhists progress toward Enlightenment – Buddha literally means "One who is Enlightened."

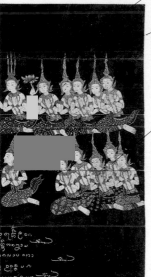

Vishnu, with four arms, is one of the three principal Hindu gods.

Thai folding book painting, c.1900

Heavenly beings *(devas)* bear the Prince through the air.

A ring of jasmine symbolizes the beauty of the Buddha's teachings and, as it perishes, the impermanence of all life. Vendors offer wreaths of jasmine to be hung in cars and shrines.

Cremation ceremonies are sober but not morbid; they are a rite of passage from this life to the next. The scale of the pyre reflects the status of the deceased. Chulalongkorn's funeral *(see pp70–71)* was one of the grandest.

Incantations in the ancient Pali script

Ritualistic tattooing is an ancient Hindu-Buddhist custom. Such tattoos are believed to act as powerful talismans against bad forces.

The Basic Tenets of Buddhism

Buddhist cosmology encompasses many states of being and heavenly realms. Buddhists believe in perpetual reincarnation, whereby each life is influenced by the actions and deeds of the previous one. This underlying philosophy of cause and effect, known as *karma*, is symbolized by the "wheel of law." Enlightenment *(nirvana)* is the only state that will end the cycle of rebirth. To reach this, Buddhists try to develop morality, meditation, and then wisdom (the "three pillars"). Following certain codes of behavior in each life, including the basic principles of tolerance and nonviolence, assists in this aim.

The "wheel of law" on the Thai flag of Buddhism

The *Wat* Complex

A *wat* is a collection of buildings within an enclosure serving two purposes: Buddhist monastery, temple, and community center. There are about 30,000 *wats* in Thailand. Their construction is often funded by wealthy patrons – contributing to a *wat* is a good way to make merit *(see p133)*. Each period of Thai history has seen modifications to *wat* architecture, and the exact layout and style of buildings vary considerably. However, the basic layout of most *wats* follows set principles, as do the functions of different buildings.

A *mondop* is a square-based structure topped with either a spire, as pictured here with the *mondop* at Wat Phra Kaeo *(see pp84–7)*, or a cruciform roof. The edifice contains an object of worship or sacred texts.

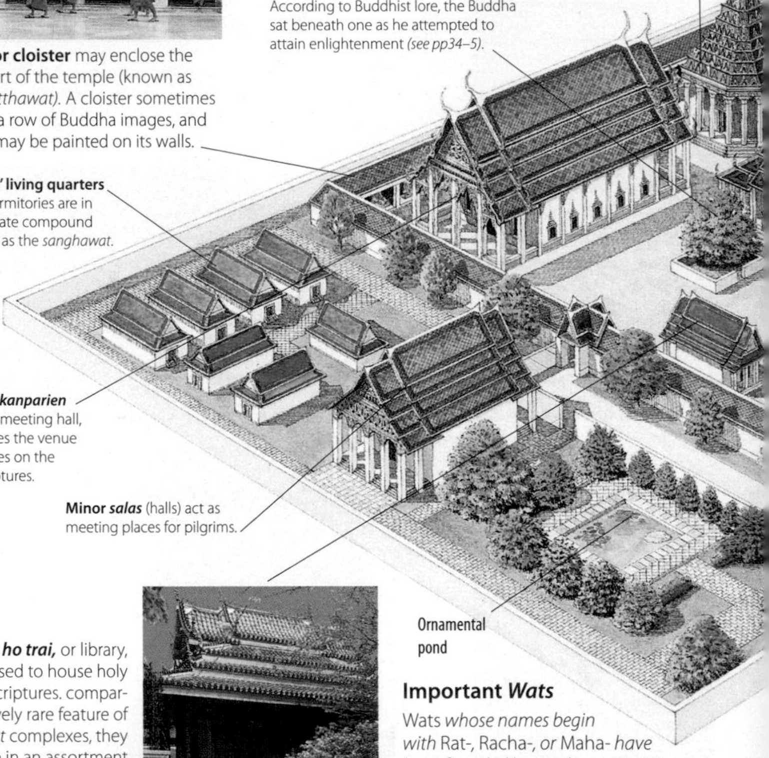

A wall or cloister may enclose the main part of the temple (known as the *phutthawat*). A cloister sometimes houses a row of Buddha images, and murals may be painted on its walls.

A Bodhi tree is found in many *wats*. According to Buddhist lore, the Buddha sat beneath one as he attempted to attain enlightenment *(see pp34–5)*.

Monks' living quarters and dormitories are in a separate compound known as the *sanghawat*.

The *sala kanparien* is a small meeting hall, sometimes the venue for lectures on the holy scriptures.

Minor *salas* (halls) act as meeting places for pilgrims.

Ornamental pond

The *ho trai*, or library, is used to house holy scriptures. comparatively rare feature of *wat* complexes, they come in an assortment of shapes and sizes; this one at Wat Paknam in Bangkok is typical of a *ho trai* in a city *wat*. A *ho trai* in the countryside may have a high base, or be surrounded by water to minimize damage from insects.

Important *Wats*

Wats *whose names begin with* Rat-, Racha-, *or* Maha- *have been founded by royalty, or contain highly revered objects (with names often prefaced by* Phra*). There are about 180 important* wats *in Thailand, and this imagined* wat *is typical. The* bot *and* wihan *are grand affairs, and there are a number of minor* salas, *as well as extensive monks' quarters. Lesser* wats *have fewer buildings and sometimes no* wihan.

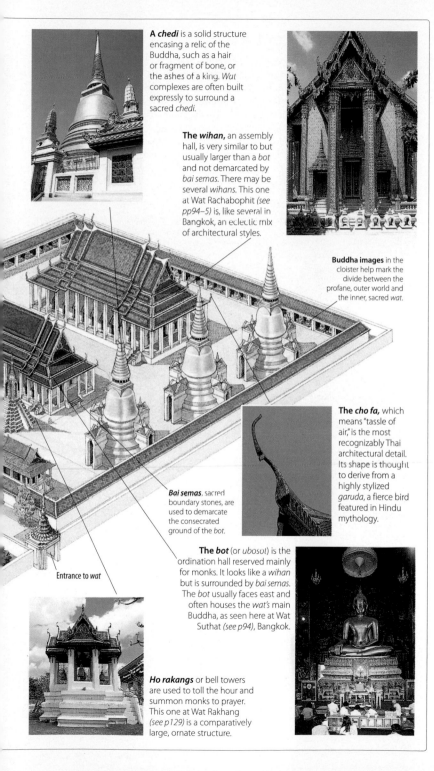

A **chedi** is a solid structure encasing a relic of the Buddha, such as a hair or fragment of bone, or the ashes of a king. *Wat* complexes are often built expressly to surround a sacred *chedi*.

The **wihan,** an assembly hall, is very similar to but usually larger than a *bot* and not demarcated by *bai semas*. There may be several wihans. This one at Wat Rachabophit *(see pp94–5)* is, like several in Bangkok, an eclectic mix of architectural styles.

Buddha images in the cloister help mark the divide between the profane, outer world and the inner, sacred *wat*.

The **cho fa,** which means "tassle of air," is the most recognizably Thai architectural detail. Its shape is thought to derive from a highly stylized *garuda*, a fierce bird featured in Hindu mythology.

Bai semas, sacred boundary stones, are used to demarcate the consecrated ground of the *bot*.

Entrance to *wat*

The **bot** (or *ubosot*) is the ordination hall reserved mainly for monks. It looks like a *wihan* but is surrounded by *bai semas*. The *bot* usually faces east and often houses the *wat's* main Buddha, as seen here at Wat Suthat *(see p94)*, Bangkok.

Ho rakangs or bell towers are used to toll the hour and summon monks to prayer. This one at Wat Rakhang *(see p129)* is a comparatively large, ornate structure.

Religious Architecture

Thailand's religious sites span more than 11 centuries. The
materials used to build them invariably determine how much of
each site can be seen today. Hindu-Buddhist Khmer temples were
built of stone and, where restored, are fairly complete. Generally,
all that is left of the *wihans* and *bots (see pp36–7)* of the Buddhist
temples at Sukhothai and Ayutthaya are foundations and stone
pillars, though some stone structures such as *chedis* and *mondops*
are still standing. There are many fine examples of later Lanna and
Rattanakosin Buddhist temples.

Gilded pediment of *wihan*, Wat
Saket *(see p91)*

Khmer (9th to 13th Centuries)

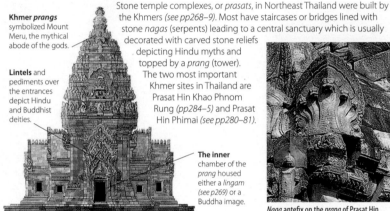

Khmer *prangs*
symbolized Mount
Meru, the mythical
abode of the gods.

Lintels and
pediments over
the entrances
depict Hindu
and Buddhist
deities.

Stone temple complexes, or *prasats*, in Northeast Thailand were built by
the Khmers *(see pp268–9)*. Most have staircases or bridges lined with
stone *nagas* (serpents) leading to a central sanctuary which is usually
decorated with carved stone reliefs
depicting Hindu myths and
topped by a *prang* (tower).
The two most important
Khmer sites in Thailand are
Prasat Hin Khao Phnom
Rung *(pp284–5)* and Prasat
Hin Phimai *(see pp280–81)*.

The inner
chamber of the
prang housed
either a *lingam*
(see p269) or a
Buddha image.

Central sanctuary of Prasat Hin Khao Phnom Rung

Naga antefix on the *prang* of Prasat Hin
Khao Phnom Rung

Sukhothai (Mid-13th to 15th Centuries)

The cities of Sukhothai *(see pp198–9)* and Si Satchanalai *(see pp202–4)*
witnessed the most radical architectural leap in Thai history. Amid
sacred Khmer ruins, King Si Intharathit *(see p62)* and his successors
built *wihans* and *bots* to house Buddha images. *Chedis*, modeled
on Sri Lankan bell-shaped reliquary towers *(see p202)*, were added.
Vast new temple complexes, such as Wat Mahathat *(see pp200–1)*,
sometimes incor-
porated a unique
development, the
lotus-bud *chedi*.

Central lotus-
bud *chedi*

Small *chedis*
surround the
main one.

Niches
(foreground)
once housed
stucco
Buddhas.

Some *chedis*
(background)
show Khmer
influence.

A frieze of
walking monks is
carved around
the base.

Mondop housing a Buddha image at
Wat Si Chum *(see p199)*

Six (illustrated) of the nine *chedis* at the heart of Wat Mahathat

Ayutthaya (Mid-14th to Late 18th Centuries)

The architects of Ayutthaya *(see pp180–85)* looked to the past, subtly modifying such features as Khmer *prangs* and Sri Lankan-style *chedis*. Temple buildings were ornate structures, with elaborate *hang hong* and door and window pediments. Few *bots* or *wihans* survived the Burmese sack of 1767 *(see pp64–5)*; one exception is Wat Na Phra Men *(see p184)*.

Carved Buddhas sit in the niches of the *prang*.

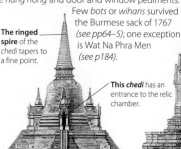

The ringed spire of the *chedi* tapers to a fine point.

This *chedi* has an entrance to the relic chamber.

Surviving Ayutthayan *wihan* of Wat Na Phra Men

Sri Lankan-style *chedi* of Wat Phra Si Sanphet *(see pp182–3)*

Bullet-shaped *prang* of Wat Ratchaburana *(see p180)*

Lanna (mid-13th to 19th Centuries)

Religious buildings during the Lanna period in the North *(see pp66–7)* were inspired first by Dvaravati architecture *(see pp60–61)*, then later by Sukhothai, Indian, and Sri Lankan styles. Lanna's golden age was in the 14th–15th centuries. Unfortunately, few buildings remain from this period. Later 18th-19th-century *wats*, seen in such towns as Chiang Mai *(see pp228–31)*, often feature intricate woodcarving, gilded *hang hong*, and murals.

Square-based *chedi* of Wat Chiang Man, Chiang Mai

Intricately carved and gilded gables

Low, sweeping roofline

Hang hong, Wat Phan Tao, Chiang Mai

Lanna *wihan* of Wat Phra Sing, Chiang Mai

Rattanakosin (late 18th Century to Present)

After the devastation of Ayutthaya, the Thais attempted to recreate their lost past. The first *bots* and *wihans* built in the new capital, Bangkok, were similar to Ayutthayan structures; the most notable examples can be seen at Wat Phra Kaeo *(see pp86–7)*. Later temple buildings were grander and more elaborate. In the 19th century, buildings such as Wat Benchamabophit *(see pp110–11)* and Wat Rachabophit *(see pp94–5)* were built incorporating Western elements. The Rattanakosin style is also known as the Bangkok style.

Gilded *hang hong* and detailing set off the green, red, and orange of the roof tiles.

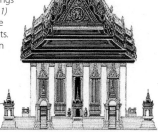

Western-style stained-glass window, Wat Benchamabophit

Eight *bai semas* (boundary stones) encircle the *bot*.

Early Rattanakosin *bot*, Wat Suthat *(p94)*

Traditional Thai Houses

Traditional Thai houses are well adapted to the tropical climate. Many are raised on stilts to protect from flooding. A steeply slanting roof helps to channel rainwater off the house, and natural materials such as hardwoods, bamboo, and dried leaves help keep the building cool. The design also reflects spiritual beliefs. The innermost room is believed to be the abode of the spirits of family ancestors, and this is usually used as the sleeping quarters. Traditional Thai houses are most often seen in rural areas, though grand versions may be found in cities.

Plantation house, Northern Thailand

Northern Houses

Northern Thailand can be relatively cool. As a result, the windows of Northern houses are smaller than those in the rest of the country. The kitchen and living areas are often joined together, which makes good use of the available heat. Outer walls are commonly built to slope outward, toward the roof, for strength. In more rural areas of Northern Thailand some houses have thatched roofs.

Traditional Northern houses, constructed from teak

Decorative *kalae*, a traditional feature of Northern houses

Plain *kalae*

Slanted walls

Front veranda

Typically the whole structure of a Northern house is raised on pillars. An open balcony running along the front of the house is common, as are plain or decorative *kalae*.

Central Plains Houses

In the hot Central Plains, a large, centrally situated veranda is the dominant feature of many traditional houses and acts for much of the year as an outside living area. Some houses in the Central Plains have covered verandas running along the sides of the main structure. Sometimes, a communal veranda will have several houses clustered around it. Houses found in the Central Plains tend to have wood-paneled walls.

Wood-paneled gable

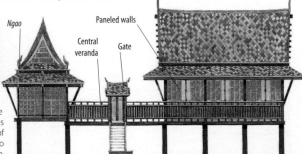

Ngao

Paneled walls

Central veranda

Gate

The gables often have decorative features called *ngaos*, the origins of which can be traced to Khmer architecture.

Houses on Water

River houses can be found in the Central Plains. The *khlongs* of early Bangkok *(see p129)* had many floating shop-houses. Such houses are very practical in areas prone to seasonal flooding. Houses can either be anchored to posts above the water line, or built on bamboo rafts so that during flood conditions they are able to float on the rising waters.

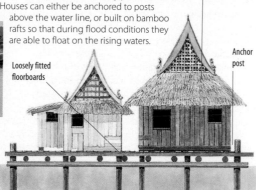

Thatched roof

Anchor post

Loosely fitted floorboards

Floating houses, Sangkhla Buri *(see p172)*

Houses close to the river's edge are often anchored on posts. Floorboards are loosely fitted so that they move with the water beneath them.

Royal Houses

Royal houses and mansions are typically a mixture of Thai temple and house styles and Western architecture. The main structural material of such buildings is usually teak, which gives them their distinctive rich, red color. Windows and doors usually have ornate frames and pediments, which are themselves sometimes decorated in gilt bronze.

Window pediment, Prince of Lampang's Palace *(see p141)*

Cho fa

Teakwood roof tiles

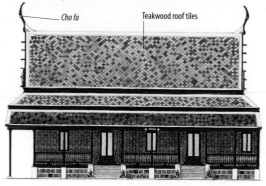

The Red House at the National Museum *(see pp92–3)* is a typical royal house. As its name reflects, it is built entirely of teak and, like a temple, has *cho fas*.

Spirit Houses

Spirit houses can be found on the grounds of many Thai homes. They are small structures, usually elevated on a pole, and house the spiritual guardian of the property. Resembling both dollhouses and bird-tables, they come in a wide collection of styles: sometimes simple replicas of the houses to which they belong, at other times elaborate models of religious buildings. Spirit houses are erected to placate the spirits of the land, traditionally before the construction of the main building begins. They are then adorned daily with incense, flowers, and food to further mollify the spirits. Spirit worship predates Theravada Buddhism *(see pp34–5)*, but the flexibility of Thai religion means that worship of the Buddha and spirits is a normal part of daily life.

Decorated spirit house

The Art of Thai Food

Thai food is justifiably renowned for its quality and
diversity – and for being as much a feast for the eyes as
for the stomach. The simplest of dishes is often served with
a carved carrot flower or a scallion tassel; a full-blown Royal
Thai meal in a high-class restaurant may be accompanied
by spectacular virtuoso fruit and vegetable carvings.
The cooking and presentation techniques of Thai cuisine
are so respected that Bangkok's celebrated cooking schools
attract pupils from all over the world. For the majority of
Thais, eating is an informal, social activity. Whether it is an
important family occasion, such as a wedding, an impromptu
outdoor garden party, or a colorful festival, food will play a
central role. Many restaurants serving Northern *khantoke*
dinners may be aimed at tourists, but the principle of
communal sharing of food is genuinely Thai.

The pre-rice planting festival
in Northern Thailand, like many
Thai festivals, involves the preparation and consumption of a
wide variety of food.

White radish petals around a
papaya heart

Royal Thai cuisine
is based on the
dishes that at
one time were
served only at the
Thai court. It is
characterized
by complex
cooking methods
and elaborate
decoration.
Royal Thai cooking
also often uses
ingredients that are
(or were) expensive,
such as ice for
chilled dishes.

Cucumber carved
into leaves

Papaya has a firm
texture and is a
popular fruit to carve.

Radish

Fruit and Vegetable Carving

Few visitors to Thailand fail to be impressed by the exquisitely
carved fruit and vegetables that accompany many dishes in
restaurants. Scallions are transformed
into tassels and chrysanthemums;
carrots and chilies become flowers;
and tomatoes are magically turned
into roses. The practice was once
the preserve of the women of the
royal court. Today, most Thai chefs
know the basic carving skills, but
few have the dexterity and
application needed to master the
more advanced techniques. Skilled
practitioners, capable of producing
astonishingly elaborate creations,
are highly esteemed.

Khantoke is a traditional way of eating
in Northern Thailand. Guests sit on
raised platforms around a circular
table and share a selection of typical
Northern dishes served with sticky rice.

Demonstrating the art of
vegetable carving

Cooking schools provide trainee chefs and interested amateurs with a grounding in Thai cooking techniques, although most chefs learn their trade over a period of years in a restaurant kitchen. The most famous schools are in Bangkok (see p451).

Miang kham, a snack dish of ginger, coconut, lemons, red onions, dried shrimps, peanuts, and a syrup sauce, is presented here with a typical Thai attention to detail. The idea that food should look as good as it tastes applies to simple as well as elaborate dishes.

Thai pumpkin

Carrot

Pumpkin

Beets, expensive in Thailand, are sometimes replaced by dyed carrots.

Rice is endowed with spiritual significance in Thailand (see pp30–31) as well as being the central pillar of the country's cuisine. Here, Brahmins present offerings of rice in a Bangkok temple.

Luk chub are utterly exquisite sweetmeats made to resemble tiny vegetables. Because few people possess the skills to make them, they are quite expensive, but well worth trying nonetheless.

Cucumber petals

A communal meal is the subject of this 19th-century temple mural. Although the Thais are inveterate snackers, sitting down for a full meal is still an important social event. Weddings and funerals are never without food and drink for all guests to enjoy. Eating out of doors, in a pavilion or a garden, is a popular way of dining in Thailand and is known as *suan ahan*. On Sundays many *wats* host a large communal meal.

The Ramakien

The Ramakien, the Thai version of the Indian Ramayana, is an allegory of the triumph of good over evil. The hero, Rama, is a paragon of virtue – the ideal king. The villain, the demon king Tosakan, is a tragic character of great dignity. This epic tale is thought to have become established after the Thais occupied Angkor in the 15th century. It has been an inspiration for painting and classical drama. All the Chakri kings have taken Rama as one of their names, and the old capital of Ayutthaya *(see pp180–85)* was named after Ayodhya, a fictional kingdom in the story.

Hun krabok (rod puppets), in a scene from the Ramakien

Monkey armies accompany Rama to Longka.

Buildings and chariots are painted in Thai style even though the story is set in India and Sri Lanka.

Rama is a skilled archer, as this bas-relief marble panel at Wat Pho *(see pp96–7)* shows. Rama wins Sita's hand by stringing a bow that no other suitor is even able to lift.

The Story

Rama, the heir to the throne of Ayodhya, is sent into exile for 14 years, through the intrigues of his stepmother. His wife, Sita, and brother Lakshman go with him deep into the forest. Tosakan, the demon king of Longka (Sri Lanka), abducts Sita and carries her off to his island kingdom in the hope of marrying her. The brothers pursue him. Hanuman, the white monkey god, volunteers his services. Together they win the alliance of two monkey kings, Sukrip and Chompupan, each with a powerful army. They march south to the coast opposite Longka. The monkey armies build a road of stone through the sea and lay siege to Longka. Many victorious battles are waged against Tosakan's demon armies. Finally, when all his champions have been defeated, Tosakan fights Rama and is killed. Rama then crowns his ally, Piphek (Tosakan's banished brother), as King of Longka and returns with Sita to resume his reign in Ayodhya.

Mural at Wat Phra Kaeo: Hanuman using his tail as a bridge

Many demons were overcome by Rama during his forest exile. Some recognized his divine nature. As they died, his blessings released them from the punishment of being reincarnated as demons in the next life.

Nang yai **shadow plays** *(see p389)*, based on the Ramakien, were first documented in the 15th century. Today this art form is rarely performed in Thailand but can still be seen in Cambodia.

In this view, the sea is narrowed to allow both countries in the tale to be seen.

Rama in the chariot rides high above his followers, as befits a king.

The Main Characters

Hundreds of characters are featured in the many episodes of the epic Ramakien. However, the central thread of the drama is carried by the five most important figures, who are described below.

Rama, often depicted with a deep green face, is an incarnation of the god Vishnu. Rama's purpose is to defeat the demon race whose power threatens the gods.

Sita, the daughter of Tosakan's consort and incarnation of the goddess Lakshmi, remains loyal to Rama while held captive by the evil Tosakan.

Lakshman, Rama's loyal younger brother, is often shown in gold. He accompanies Rama into exile in the forest.

Ramakien Murals at Wat Phra Kaeo

The Ramakien is beautifully depicted through a series of 178 colorful murals, dating from the late 18th century, at Wat Phra Kaeo (see pp84–7). In this scene Hanuman displays his supernatural powers to assist Rama in rescuing Sita by building a stone causeway across the sea.

Hanuman, the white monkey, son of the wind god, is totally devoted to Rama, but still finds time to seduce beautiful women.

Hanuman finds Sita imprisoned by the wicked king of Longka, Tosakan. He gives her Rama's ring and tells her she will soon be rescued.

Tosakan (meaning "ten necks"), the demon king of Longka, has multiple heads and arms. In the Indian version of the Ramayana he is called Ravanna.

Thai Theater and Music

The two principal forms of classical Thai drama are *khon* and *lakhon*. *Khon* was first performed in the royal court in the 15th century, with story lines taken from the Ramakien *(see pp44–5)*. The more graceful *lakhon*, which also features elements from the *jataka* tales *(see p34)*, was originally performed inside the palace, but moved outside at a later date. Both *khon* and *lakhon* involve slow, highly stylized, angular dance movements set to the music of a *piphat* ensemble.

Students learn gestures by imitating their teacher. Training begins at an early age (when limbs are still supple) and includes a sequence of moves known as the Alphabet of Dancing *(mae bot)*.

White mask of Hanuman *(see p45)*

Ganesh, the elephant god

Khon masks, decorated with gold and jewelry, are treated as sacred objects with supernatural powers.

Graceful gestures typify classical Thai drama. Here, weapons are raised to attack the enemy.

Lavish costumes, made of heavy brocade and adorned with jewelry, are modeled on traditional court garments.

Khon and **lakhon performances** are often staged at outdoor shrines. Dancers are hired to perform to the resident god by supplicants whose wishes have been granted.

A Khon Performance

In khon drama, demons and monkeys wear masks, while human heroes and celestial beings sport crowns. As the story is told mainly through gestures, khon can be enjoyed by non-Thais. Visitors today are most likely to see performances at restaurants catering to tourists.

Instruments of Classical Thai Music

Ranat (xylophones)

Thailand's classical music originated in the Sukhothai era. The basic melody is set by the composer, but, as no notation is used, each musician varies the tune and adopts the character of the instrument, like actors in a play. A tuned percussion ensemble, or *piphat*, accompanies theater performances and boxing matches *(see p48)*. A *mahori* ensemble includes stringed instruments.

A *mahori* ensemble shown in a mural

The keys of a flat xylophone produce a different tone from those of a curved one.

Likay, by far the most popular type of dance-drama, is a satirical form of *khon* and *lakhon*. The actors wear gaudy costumes and the plot derives from ancient tales laced with improvised jokes and puns.

Khon and **lakhon** troupes, employed by the royal palace until the early 20th century, are now based at Bangkok's Fine Arts Department.

Finger extensions emphasizing the graceful curves of a dancer's hands, are seen in *lakhon* performances and in "nail dances" of the North.

This mural at Wat Benchamabophit, Bangkok, depicts a scene from a *khon* performance. In it, Erawan, the elephant mount of Indra, descends from heaven.

Natural-looking makeup enhances the features of characters who do not wear masks. This replaces a heavy white paint that was traditionally worn.

Hun krabok puppets, rodded marionettes, are operated by hidden threads pulled from under the costume. *Hun krabok* performances are very rare today.

Khong wong lek (small gong circle)

Chake ("crocodile")

The hollowed hardwood body is inlaid with ivory.

Small gongs are struck by the player to give the tune's basic melody.

The strings of a *chake* are plucked. It accompanies fiddles and flutes in a string ensemble.

A *piphat mon* ensemble, including a vertical gong circle, plays at funerals.

Thai Boxing

Thai boxing *(muay thai)*, Thailand's unique national sport, is gaining popularity worldwide. It was first documented in 1411, but probably evolved from an earlier form of armed combat, *krabi-krabong*. *Muay thai* is highly ritualistic – many techniques are inspired by battle stories from the Ramakien *(see pp44–5)*. The country's first famous boxer was Nai Khanom Dtom, who in 1774 defeated 10 Burmese fighters. Due to a high injury rate, the sport was banned in the 1920s. In 1937 it was revived with rules for protecting fighters.

In the stadium, the audience becomes excited, shouting encouragement to the boxers. Thais bet furiously, often staking large sums on their favorite fighter. Bouts between famous boxers can be sold out well in advance.

This manuscript, which dates from the early 20th century, depicts a fight between two Thai boxers.

Training gear varies in style from camp to camp.

Phone Kingphet was the first world champion Thai boxer. He trained in the cool climate of Phu Kradung National Park *(see pp290–91)* in preparation for his numerous bouts abroad.

Feet are kept bare in training sessions, though ankle covers may be worn for protection during a match.

A ringside *piphat* band is an essential element of a Thai boxing match. During the opening ceremony, the music is soft in tone; when the fighting begins it switches to a more upbeat "fight melody." As the action becomes more frenzied, the music increases in tempo, adding tension to the match.

Types of Moves

Points are awarded for each blow to the opponent. The groin is not a valid target, and biting and head-butting are not allowed. A match may end with a spectacular knockout.

The jumping downward strike elbow is a physically demanding move. It gives the boxer an excellent vantage point over his opponent.

Amulets *(see p83)*, worn around one or both biceps during the match, are believed to offer protection to the boxer while fighting. They consist of a piece of cord that usually contains a Buddha image or an herb that is thought to be lucky.

Where to See Thai Boxing

Matches are held at Ratchadamnoen Stadium (p445) every Mon, Wed, Thu & Sun. Lumphini Stadium (p445) has matches on Tue, Fri & Sat. For other towns, check sites. Several TV channels now televise Thai Boxing.

Fists are bound with cloth for protection during training. Before 1937, glass-impregnated hemp was often used, to injure the opponent.

The *wai kru*, a ritual bow, is the first part of the *ram muay*, a gesture of respect to the trainer *(kru)* and the spirit of boxing. In honor of their training camp, boxers often take its name as their surname.

Before the match, the boxer performs a slow, solemn dance *(ram muay)*. The exact movements differ according to the boxer's camp, but usually involve sweeping arm motions, which are said to draw the power of earth, air, fire, and water into the body.

Thai Boxing Versus Western Boxing

Thai boxing, or "kick boxing," exerts parts of the body not used in Western boxing, such as the feet and elbows. Thai boxing matches are also faster paced, and are thus limited to five rounds of three minutes, each separated by a short break. Professional boxers, who may start the rigorous training as young as six, often retire by 25. Several Thai boxers have won Western boxing titles.

Knee hooks can be devastating. To perform a "rising knee," aimed at either the head or body, the boxer pushes down his rival's head, bringing his knee up to hit it.

Kicks are common in Thai boxing. A high kick to the neck, as shown here, may knock out a rival. A push kick, in which one boxer pushes the sole of his foot into the face of the other, is regarded as a great insult to the opponent.

Elbows deliver fierce blows to the face, and, like knee strikes, are often decisive in matches. An elbow strike is more powerful than a punch, the weakest blow.

Festivals in Thailand

Thai festivals are rarely solemn occasions, and few countries celebrate them with so much fun and color. Annual rites and festivities, marking religious devotion or the passage of seasons, have long been an integral part of Thai life. A 13th-century inscription reads: "Whoever wants to make merry, does so; whoever wants to laugh, does so." This still applies today, with dozens of festivities taking place each month. The main festivals, such as Songkran, are celebrated nationwide, with the most exuberant activities taking place in Bangkok and other major cities. Each region has its own unique festivals, too. Many festival dates change each year, as they follow the lunar calendar.

Decorated oxen, paraded for Bangkok's Royal Plowing Ceremony

Bangkok

Songkran, the Thai New Year, is celebrated nationally from April 12–14 (see p52). In Bangkok, festivities take place at Sanam Luang, where a revered Buddha image is bathed as part of the merit-making rituals. Over the years, the festival has become a boisterous affair involving water-throwing, when few people escape getting soaked.

Visakha Bucha (see pp52–3), in May, marks the birth, Enlightenment, and death of the Buddha, all said to have occurred on the same day of the year. It is celebrated with candlelight processions around important temples.

The Royal Plowing Ceremony is held at Sanam Luang at the start of the rice-planting season in May (see p52). The display features oxen plowing and Brahmin priests sowing rice seeds. The oxen predict the coming year's harvest by selecting one of several types of food offered to them.

The Golden Mount Fair (see p54) is in November. With its carnival, performers, and candlelight processions, this is Thailand's best temple fair.

December's Trooping of the Colors in the Royal Plaza is the best of many nationwide celebrations marking King Bhumibol's birthday (see p55).

Central Plains

Every March, pilgrims flock to the Temple of the Holy Footprint near Saraburi for the elaborate Phra Phutthabat Fair (see p52), which has theater and folk music performances.

Full-moon night in November is the occasion for Loy Krathong. It is celebrated throughout the country, but magically amid the ruins of Old Sukhothai (see p199), where it is said to have originated. The festival is held in honor of Mae Kongkha, the goddess of waterways, and takes place by rivers, lakes, and ponds. Small, lotus-shaped vessels carrying offerings for Mae Kongkha are floated to take away the sins of the past year and to bring good luck for the future.

Khwae River Bridge Week (late November/early December), held at Kanchanaburi, marks the building of the infamous bridge with historical displays and a dramatic sound and light show.

Northern Thailand

Bo Sang, which is famous for its hand-painted umbrellas, holds an Umbrella Fair every January. Umbrella painting competitions, umbrella exhibitions, parades, and a "Miss Bo Sang" beauty contest are part of the festival.

Northern Thailand shows off its beautiful blooms to full effect during Chiang Mai's Festival of Flowers in February, when parades of lavish floral floats fill the town with color. Events include floral exhibitions, handicraft sales, and a beauty pageant.

Mae Hong Son comes alive during its Poi Sang Long Festival, held in late March or early April. The highlight of this Buddhist festival is a mass ordination ceremony for

Painting umbrellas for the Umbrella Festival in Bo Sang

Young Buddhist novices at the Poi Sang Long Festival in Mae Hong Son

Shan boys. Wearing sumptuous costumes, the novices parade through the town before exchanging their finery for simple monks' robes in a symbolic gesture of renouncing worldly goods.

Northeast Thailand

Northeast Thailand is renowned for its unique festivals. In May, the town of Yasothon hosts the Bun Bang Fai (Rocket Festival), perhaps the most thrilling of Thailand's regional celebrations. This two-day event, accompanied by much high-spirited revelry, is staged to ensure plentiful rains during the coming rice-planting season. On the first day there is a parade of carnival floats, as well as carnivals, music, and folk dancing. The next day, huge, home-made rockets are set off.

Dan Sai in Loei Province is known for the Phi Ta Khon Festival (see p293), held in

Mud-covered revelers at Dan Sai, Northeast Thailand

June or July. Celebrations begin with a parade. Locals dressed as ghosts follow a Buddha image through the streets of town to make Buddhist merit and call for rain.

Ubon Ratchathani has a Candle Festival in July, its own version of the nationally celebrated "beginning of the rains retreat," or Khao Phansa (see p53). As part of the celebrations, huge, intricately carved beeswax candles are exhibited on floats in the town before being presented to temples, where they burn throughout the rainy season.

The national holiday of "end of the rains retreat," or Ok Phansa, is celebrated in particular style at Nakhon Phanom in October with the Illuminated Boat Procession. Intricately fashioned model boats carrying single candles are set adrift on the Mekong River at nightfall.

Gulf of Thailand

Modern-style merrymaking is found at Pattaya, which hosts the week-long Pattaya Festival in April. Floral float parades, beauty contests, and fireworks displays feature amid a non stop carnival atmosphere. One of Thailand's most colorful water festivals is the Receiving of the Lotus Festival, which is celebrated in late October at Bang Phli, just south of Bangkok. Here, Ok Phansa is marked by a

ceremony in which a locally revered Buddha image is showered with thousands of lotus buds while it is paraded by barge along Khlong Samrong, the local canal. Lively crowds, thronging the canal banks, throw flowers until only the image's head remains visible above the mounting floral offerings. Other events include boat races, boxing matches fought on poles placed across the canal, and likay theater shows.

Displays of self-mortification, part of the Vegetarian Festival, Phuket

Southern Thailand

Traditional Southern culture gets an airing at the week-long Narathiwat Fair (last week of September). This features races between brightly painted traditional korlae fishing boats (see p394), as well as dove-cooing contests and performances of Southern music and dance.

For sheer spectacle, it is hard to beat Phuket's Vegetarian Festival (late September/early October, see p364). This nine-day festival, marking the start of Taoist Lent, is celebrated by people of Chinese ancestry. During the festival followers eat only vegetarian food and take part in acts of self-mortification, such as piercing the body with skewers, with no apparent harm.

THAILAND THROUGH THE YEAR

The Thai year revolves around the monsoon seasons – which dictate the year's farming activities – and the religious calendar. Most religious festivals are Buddhist, and often observed on significant days of the lunar cycle, such as full moon. Festivals may also mark a seasonal change, such as the end of the rains, or a related agricultural event, such as the beginning of the planting season. The three seasons – wet, cool, and hot – are produced by the Southwest and Northeast monsoons *(see pp30–31)*. At the start of the wet season farmers plant rice seedlings. The rice-growing period is the traditional time for boys to enter the monkhood for a few weeks. In the cool season the drier weather ripens the crop, which is gathered before the hot season. Village life then slows down. During most weeks a festival is held somewhere in the country, especially in the cool season.

Hot Season

High temperatures combined with high humidity make this an uncomfortable time, April being especially hot. With the fields empty and rivers running low, the landscape appears faded and spent in the bright sunshine. Considering the heat, it is not surprising that Thailand's traditional New Year, Songkran, is celebrated with water.

March

ASEAN Barred Ground Dove Fair *(first week)*, Yala. Dove-singing contest that attracts bird lovers from as far away as Cambodia, Malaysia, Singapore, and Indonesia.
Phra Phutthabat Fair *(first or second week)*, Saraburi. Celebration of the annual pilgrimage to the Temple of the Holy Footprint *(see p176)*.
Phra That Chaw Hae Fair *(third week)*. A colorful procession of townspeople, all dressed in

Water throwing during Songkran celebrations in Chiang Mai

traditional Lanna attire, carry robes to cover the *chedi*.
Poi Sang Long Festival *(late Mar/early Apr)*, Mae Hong Son. Mass ordination of 15- and 16-year-old-boys, who dress up as princes in memory of the Buddha's origins.

April

Chakri Day *(Apr 6)*. Commemorates Rama I founding the Chakri dynasty. The Royal Pantheon – which displays statues of former kings – in Wat Phra Kaeo's grounds, Bangkok, is open to the public on this day only.
Songkran *(Apr 12–14)*. Traditional Thai New Year. Celebrated nationwide, but Chiang Mai has the reputation for the most fun *(see p240)*.
Pattaya Festival *(mid-Apr)*. Features a week of food and floral floats, beauty contests, and a huge firework display.

Phnom Rung Fair *(Apr full moon)*. Daytime procession and a nighttime sound and light show at Prasat Hin Khao Phnom Rung *(see pp284–5)*.

May

Coronation Day *(May 5)*. Ceremony to mark the crowning of King Bhumibol.
Royal Plowing Ceremony *(early May)*, Bangkok. Observes the official start of the rice-planting season with an elaborate royal rite at Bangkok's Sanam Luang.
Bun Bang Fai (Rocket) Festival *(second week)*, Northeast Thailand. Home-made rockets are fired to ensure plentiful rains amid a carnival atmosphere. Celebrated exuberantly at Yasothon *(see p278)*.
Visakha Bucha *(May full moon)*. Most important date on the Buddhist calendar.

Temple of the Holy Footprint during the Phra Phutthabat Fair

Average Daily Hours of Sunshine

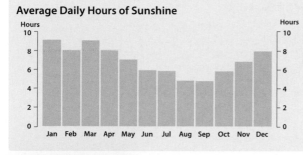

Sunshine Chart
Even during the rainy season, most days have some sunshine. The tropical sun can be fierce, and precautions against sunburn and sunstroke should be taken. Sunscreen, a sun hat and sunglasses are highly recommended. Drink plenty of water to reduce the risk of dehydration.

Visakha Bucha celebrations at Wat Benchamabophit, Bangkok

Celebrates the birth, Enlightenment, and death of the Buddha. Sermons and candle-lit processions at temples.

Rainy Season

The rural scene comes alive with the advent of the annual rains, which soften the soil ready for plowing. Once the rice has been planted, there is a lull in farming activity. This coincides with the annual three-month Buddhist Rains Retreat, the period when young men traditionally enter the monkhood for a brief period. This is something that young Thai men should do at least once in their lives. The rainy season is a good time to observe the ordination ceremonies held throughout Thailand, which blend high-spirited festivities with deep religious feelings.

June
Phi Ta Khon Festival (Jun/Jul), Loei. An event unique to the Dan Sai district of Loei province, comprising masked players reenacting the legend of Prince Vessandon, the Buddha's penultimate incarnation (see p293).

July
Asanha Bucha (Jul full moon). Second of the year's three major Buddhist festivals. Commemorates the anniversary of the Lord Buddha's first sermon to his first five disciples.
Khao Phansa (Jul full moon). Marks the start of the three-month Buddhist Rains Retreat (which is also referred to as Buddhist Lent), when monks remain in their temples to devote themselves to study and meditation. Young men are ordained for short periods.

Young man in ordination robes

Candle Festival (Jul full moon),
Ubon Ratchathani. Unique festival held in the Northeast to mark the beginning of Khao Phansa. Features parades of carved candles (made by villagers from all over the province) displayed on floats and later presented to temples throughout the city. Some candles are several meters tall (see p307).

August
Her Majesty the Queen's Birthday (Aug 12).
Buildings and streets are lavishly decorated in honor of Queen Sirikit's birthday. The most elaborate decorations can be seen in Bangkok, especially along Ratchadamnoen Avenue and around the Grand Palace, where the streets and government offices are exuberantly adorned with colored lights.

Parade of candles at the Ubon Ratchathani Candle Festival

Average Monthly Rainfall (Bangkok)

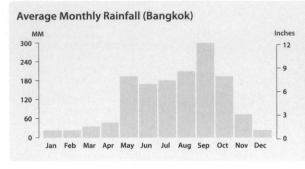

Rainfall Chart
Thailand's rainfall is not evenly distributed. The southern peninsula has the highest, some 95 inches (2,400 mm) annually; the north and central regions receive 51 inches (1,300 mm). In many places, torrential rain falls almost daily during the rainy season, from June to October.

September
Food and Fruits Fair *(first week)*, Nakhon Pathom. Held at Thailand's largest Buddhist temple, Phra Pathom Chedi. Cooking, folk theater, and floral floats.
Phichit Boat Races *(Sep)*, Nan. This annual regatta takes place on the Nan river as part of the Nan Provincial Fair and features traditional low-slung boats.
Narathiwat Fair *(last week)*. A good opportunity to experience Southern culture.

Mangoes on display at Nakhon Pathom

October
Vegetarian Festival *(early Oct)*. Trang and Phuket provinces *(see p364)*. Self-mortification rituals following abstinence from meat.
Chulalongkorn Day *(Oct 23)*, Bangkok. Commemorates the death of Rama V (King Chulalongkorn). Floral tributes are placed by the King's equestrian statue by the Royal Plaza in Bangkok.
Receiving of the Lotus Festival *(late Oct)*, Bang Phli *(see p51)*. The end of the rains celebrated by pouring lotus buds over a locally revered Budda image.
Ok Phansa *(Oct full moon)*. Nationwide celebration of the Lord Buddha's reappearance on Earth after a season spent preaching in heaven. Marks the end of the Buddhist Rains Retreat.
Krathin *(begins Oct full moon)*. One-month period during which monks are presented with new robes.
Nan Boat Races *(late Oct)*. Festive regatta *(see p259)*.
Illuminated Boat Procession *(Oct full moon)*, Nakhon Phanom. Boats with candles and offerings set afloat down the Mekong River. Entertainments provided in the town *(see p300)*.

Cool Season

After the rains, the skies clear and the air cools to a comfortable warmth. The countryside looks its best, lush and green from the rains, with full rivers and waterfalls. In general this is the best time to visit Thailand, especially during the coolest months of December and January. Numerous festivals, to celebrate of the end of the rains, afford a period of relaxation before rural activity climaxes with the rice harvest in December and January.

November
Golden Mount Fair *(first week)*, Bangkok. Thailand's largest temple fair, held at the foot of the Golden Mount.
Elephant Roundup *(third week)*, Surin. Annual spectacle honoring the many and varied roles played by the elephant in Thailand's development *(see p282)*. More than 150 elephants take part in displays of forestry skills and a mock battle.
Khwae River Bridge Week *(late Nov/early Dec)*, Kanchanaburi. Commemorates the construction of the bridge by POWs and slave labor.
Loy Krathong *(Nov full moon)*. One of Thailand's best-loved national festivals. Pays homage to the goddess of rivers and waterways, Mae Khongkha. In the evening, people gather at rivers, lakes, and ponds to float *krathongs*. Sukhothai is the best place to watch this festival *(see p199)*.

Colorful spectacle of the boat races at Nan in Northern Thailand

Average Monthly Temperature (Bangkok)

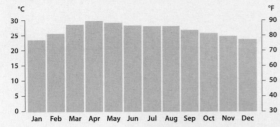

Temperature Chart
For visitors from temperate climes, Thailand is hot and humid throughout the year, especially in the South. It is uncomfortably so during April and May, pleasantly so in November and December. Though it is less humid in Northern Thailand, it can be chilly at night during the coolest months.

December
Trooping of the Colors *(Dec 3)*, Royal Plaza, Bangkok. A very impressive ceremony that offers a vivid picture of regal pageantry. It is presided over by the king and queen and features members of the elite Royal Guards, arrayed in bright dress uniform. The guardsmen swear allegiance to the King and march past members of the royal family.
His Majesty the King's Birthday *(Dec 5)*. Government and private buildings throughout Thailand are elaborately decorated, and the area around the Grand Palace is illuminated. In the evening, crowds gather around Sanam Luang for celebrations. On the King's and the Queen's birthdays, no alcohol is served in bars or sold in stores. This occasion shows the deep respect Thais have for their King.

Soldiers in dress uniform for the Trooping of the Colors in Bangkok

January
Chinese New Year *(Jan/Feb)*. Not an official holiday, but this three-day festival is widely observed by the large number of Thais of Chinese origin.
Umbrella Fair *(mid-Jan)*, Bo Sang, Chiang Mai province. Celebrates traditional paper and wood umbrella making *(see p232)*.
Don Chedi Memorial Fair *(late Jan)*, Suphan Buri province. Marks the victory of King Naresuan of Ayutthaya over the Burmese. The highlight of the events is an elephant-back duel.

February
Festival of Flowers *(first week)*, Chiang Mai. Beautiful blooms of the north displayed on floral float parades.
Kite Flying Season *(Feb–Apr)*, Sanam Luang, Bangkok. Colorful displays and kite flying contests.
Makha Bucha *(Feb full moon)*. Third of the year's major Buddhist festivals. Merit-making and candlelit processions at temples.

Celebrations for the King's Birthday

Public Holidays

Western New Year's Day (Jan 1)

Makha Bucha (Feb or Mar full moon)

Chakri Day (Apr 6)

Thai New Year – Songkran (Apr 12–14)

Labour Day (May 1)

Coronation Day (May 5)

Royal Plowing Ceremony (early May)

Visakha Bucha Day (May full moon)

Asanha Bucha and Khao Phansa (Jul full moon)

Queen's Birthday (Aug 12)

Chulalongkorn Day (Oct 23)

King's Birthday (Dec 5)

Constitution Day (Dec 10)

Western New Year's Eve (Dec 31)

THE HISTORY OF THAILAND

The history of Thailand is that of an area rather than of a single nation, and over the centuries numerous peoples have made their home in this region. The most recent were the Tai of Southern China, who migrated south in the first millennium AD, and from whom most Thais are descended.

Prehistoric Thailand was once regarded as a cultural backwater. In the Northeast of the country, however, archaeologists uncovered the earliest evidence of agriculture and metallurgy in Southeast Asia. Also among the finds were ceramic pots, some dating as far back as 3000 BC, that display a high level of artistic skill.

The earliest known powers in the region were the Dvaravati Kingdom (6th–11th centuries AD), the Sumatran-based Srivijaya Empire (7th–13th centuries), and the Khmer Empire (9th–13th centuries) based at Angkor (see pp268–9), all of which were heavily influenced by Indian culture and religion.

The Lanna Kingdom in the North and the Sukhothai Kingdom, which imported Theravada Buddhism to Thailand, in the Central Plains grew in power from around the 12th century. Of all its kings, Ramkamhaeng (1279–98) stands out: part heroic myth, part historical figure.

Sukhothai was conquered by the Kingdom of Ayutthaya – also Tai – in the 14th century. At its height ruling most of what is now Thailand, the city of Ayutthaya saw the arrival of the first Europeans. The city was destroyed by the Burmese in 1767. A new city, Krung Thep (Bangkok), was built farther south, on the Chao Phraya River, and the Chakri dynasty founded. In the 19th century Kings Mongkut and Chulalongkorn modernized Thailand, and the country resisted colonization by France and Britain.

The 1932 revolution ended absolute monarchy, and in 1939 Phibun Songkram, formerly a soldier in the Thai army, changed the country's name from Siam to Thailand. There have been a number of military coups since then, and a cycle of economic boom and bust in the 1980s and 1990s. In 2014, the military deposed Prime Minister Shinawatra and established an interim government.

Dutch map of the city of Ayutthaya, probably drawn in the 17th century

◀ Chakri painted screen, dating from the late 18th century

Prehistoric Thailand

Hunter-gatherers were already established in the area of modern-day Thailand by around 40,000 BC. They lived in semi-permanent settlements and made tools from wood and stone. Ancient seed husks found in caves in Northern Thailand have led to speculation that agriculture began to develop around 9000 BC. Rice was being cultivated around 3000 BC. Subsequently, in the area of Ban Chiang, elaborate pottery and bronze work began to be produced. This Bronze Age culture is believed by some historians to be the earliest in the world.

Prehistoric Sites

The flared rim and slightly more complex geometric pattern on this black and white, cord-incised pot were new stylistic features.

Ban Kao Tripod
This three-legged, terracotta pot was made by Neolithic artisans around 2100 BC. It was found at Ban Kao *(see p174)* in the Central Plains.

Bronze Axe Head
The earliest bronze artifacts found at Ban Chiang, such as this axe head, are thought to date from about 2100 BC.

Molded shoulders

A black and white pattern was created by incising the clay with cord.

Clay feet

2100 BC

c.1600 BC

Clay Molds
Clay molds confirm that bronze objects were cast at Ban Chiang and not imported from elsewhere.

Ban Chiang Pottery

Pots found at Ban Chiang (see p276) date from 2100 BC to AD 200. Until their discovery in 1966, this area of Southeast Asia was thought to have produced little of cultural merit in prehistoric times. These, and other finds, show that the indigenous peoples were capable of producing sophisticated, beautiful works of art.

40,000 BC Hunter-gatherers in area of modern-day Thailand		*Bronze spearhead* 	**2100–1500 BC** Bronze artifacts and elaborate cord-marked pottery created at Ban Chiang	**1000 BC** Cave and cliff paintings at Pha Taem *(pp302–3)*	
	6000 BC First pottery created by inhabitants of Spirit Cave	**3000 BC** Domestication of animals (pigs, dogs, chickens, and cattle)			
50,000 BC	**5000 BC**	**4000 BC**	**3000 BC**	**2000 BC**	100
	3500 BC Rice chaff left in Banyan Valley Cave – beginning of rice cultivation		**2000 BC** Clay and bronze pots created at Ban Kao	**1000 BC** Bronze animals cast at Don Tha Phet	
	9000–7000 BC Seed and plant husks left in caves in Northern Thailand may indicate the beginnings of agriculture				

Iron Age Rooster
A find of bronze and iron artifacts at Don Tha Phet, near Kanchanaburi (see p174), includes this iron rooster from about 1000 BC.

Cave Painting
These paintings at Pha Taem date from around 1000 BC. The artists were probably descended from the early inhabitants of Ban Chiang.

Paint rather than cord is used to create a complex geometric pattern.

300 BC–AD 1

Rust-colored geometric designs were painted on a beige ground.

300 BC–AD 200

Where to See Prehistoric Thailand
At Ban Chiang (see p276) visitors can see burial sites and artifacts housed in the Ban Chiang National Museum. More Ban Chiang artifacts can be seen in the Bangkok National Museum (pp92–3). At Ban Kao (p174) there are burial sites and a museum, and cave paintings can be seen at Pha Taem (pp302–3) and Phu Phrabat Historical Park (p299).

Burial sites at Ban Chiang were filled with pots that were placed around the dead.

Narrow stand

Bronze Bracelets
As well as practical objects, the craftsmen of Ban Chiang were skilled at making elaborate jewelry. These bracelets probably date from the height of Ban Chiang's Bronze Age, around 300–200 BC.

500 BC Bronzeware created at Ban Na Di

1st–6th centuries AD Indianized Kingdom of Funan exerts strong cultural influence on the area around the Central Plains

AD 1	100	200	300	AD 400

1st century AD Indian merchants begin to arrive in the Thai peninsula (see pp350–51)

Ban Chiang pot (300 BC–AD 200)

3rd–5th centuries Kingdom of Dan Sun in South flourishes and trades with Indian merchants

Limestone sculpture of Vishnu (4th century AD)

The First States

From the first few centuries BC Hindu and Buddhist missionaries from India and Sri Lanka came to Southeast Asia. Over the next millennium distinctly Indianized kingdoms emerged. The Dvaravati Kingdom (6th–11th centuries) flourished in what is now the heart of Thailand; the Srivijaya Empire of Sumatra (7th–13th centuries) was strong in the peninsula *(see pp350–51)*; while the Khmer Empire (9th–13th centuries) expanded from Cambodia *(see pp268–9)*. The Tai, from southern China, migrated to the area from the 11th century onward.

Khmer Empire in AD 960

☐ Extent of Khmer Empire

Flying Buddha (8th–9th centuries) This Dvaravati sculpture shows the Buddha on the back of Panaspati, a strange beast that comprises Nandin the bull, Shiva's mount, and a garuda (a mythical bird).

Vishnu, asleep on the back of the *naga*, dreams of a new universe.

Stone Relief Dvaravati craftsmen were renowned for their stonework. They excelled at bas-reliefs such as this one, at Wat Suthat *(see p94)*, which depicts Buddhist and Hindu figures.

Dvaravati Deities Dvaravati bas-reliefs, found in a cave near Saraburi, central Thailand, depict Brahma, Vishnu, the Buddha, and flying figures.

The naga (serpent) bearing Vishnu represents the Milky Sea of Eternity.

Early 6th century Mon people establish Dvaravati culture. They have already inherited Buddhism from Indian missionaries

7th century Srivijaya civilization expands from Sumatra

8th century Tai people inhabit the upland valleys of Laos, northern Vietnam, and southern China

Dvaravati coin

500	600	700	800

Dvaravati stucco head

AD 661 Haripunchai said to be founded at Lamphun, Northern Thailand *(see p233)*, by Buddhist holymen

7th century Chamadevi of Lop Buri becomes Queen of the Dvaravati Kingdom

9th century Khmer Empire founded at Angkor

Devaraja

This Khmer bas-relief, one of many found at Angkor Wat *(see pp268–9)*, shows the god-king, or *devaraja*, King Suryavarman II (1113–50).

Where to See the First States

Dvaravati, Srivijayan, and Khmer artifacts can be seen at the Bangkok National Museum *(see pp92–3)* as well as at other regional national museums. Two Dvaravati-style *chedis* can be seen at Wat Chama Thewi in Lamphun *(p233)*. Phra Boromathat Chaiya *(p337)* is the best-surviving example of a Srivijayan temple. Khmer sites in Thailand include Prasat Hin Phimai *(pp280–81)* and Prasat Hin Khao Phnom Rung *(pp284–5)*.

Terra-cotta Lion (8th-century) Dvaravati figures, such as this lion from Phetchaburi *(see pp332–3)*, were influenced by earlier Gupta art from India.

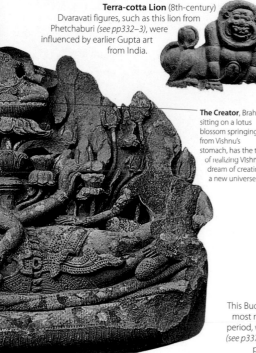

The Creator, Brahma, sitting on a lotus blossom springing from Vishnu's stomach, has the task of realizing Vishnu's dream of creating a new universe.

Prasat Hin Phimai was built mostly during the reign of Suryavarman I in the 11th century.

Srivijayan Buddha

This Buddha image, one of the most notable of the Srivijaya period, was found in Chaiya *(see p337)*, an ancient city in peninsular Thailand.

Khmer Lintel

The Khmers built temples throughout their vast empire, many of which are in present-day Northeast Thailand. Intricate stone carvings are a striking feature of the monuments – the characters depicted (see p45) are mainly Hindu, though some are Mahayana Buddhist. This lintel, from Prasat Hin Khao Phnom Rung (see pp284–5), depicts a Hindu creation myth.

11th–13th centuries Lop Buri incorporated into Khmer Empire as a significant provincial capital	**1001–1002** Reign of Udayadityavarman, who invades Haripunchai (Lamphun) following an assault on Lop Buri		**1229–43** Reign of Indravarman II
		1115–55 Lop Buri tries to assert its independence from Khmer control	
900	**1000**	**1100**	**1200**
10th–12th centuries Srivijaya becomes involved in ruinous wars with Chola state in India	**11th–12th centuries** Population of Tai people increases in areas of present-day Thailand, then under Khmer control	**1113–50** Reign of Suryavarman II

Lop Buri Buddha | **1181–1220** Reign of Jayavarman VII, the most powerful and innovative of the Khmer kings |

The Kingdom of Sukhothai

Sukhothai was the first notable kingdom of the Tai people, centered around the city of Sukhothai (see pp198–201) in the Central Plains. The Khmers referred to the Tai as Siam, a name that came to be used for this and subsequent Tai kingdoms. Theravada Buddhism achieved new expression during the Sukhothai period, in innovative architecture and images of the Buddha finely cast in bronze. Sukhothai was made powerful by its most illustrious ruler, Ramkamhaeng, but by 1320 was only a local power again.

Sukhothai in 1300

☐ Sukhothai Kingdom

Potteries and other industries were located north of the city.

Minor *wats* on low hills

Wat Chang Lom, the symbolic power center

Ramkamhaeng (c.1279–98)
This modern relief depicts Ramkamhaeng, Sukhothai's most illustrious ruler. He extended the kingdom and negotiated treaties with neighboring states.

Inscription No. 1 (1292)
Ramkamhaeng is credited with inventing the Thai alphabet and using it to record the history of Sukhothai on this stone.

Rice fields and houses

Roof Decoration
Ceramics were used to adorn buildings. This one is from the 14th century.

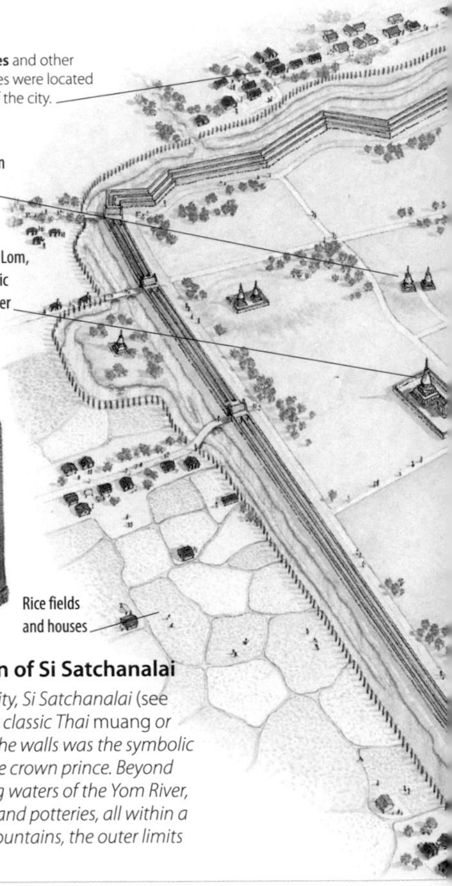

Reconstruction of Si Satchanalai

Sukhothai's twin city, Si Satchanalai (see pp202–3) was the classic Thai muang or city-state. Within the walls was the symbolic power center of the crown prince. Beyond were the life-giving waters of the Yom River, rice fields, homes, and potteries, all within a ring of forested mountains, the outer limits of the muang.

King Ramkamhaeng

c.1240s Si Intharathit is first known king of Sukhothai

c.1279 Ramkamhaeng is made king; during his reign Sukhothai becomes a large kingdom

1287 Ramkamhaeng forges alliance with states of Lanna (see pp66–7) and Phayao

1240

1260

1280

1283 According to legend, Ramkamhaeng modifies Sri Lankan script to create Thai alphabet

c.1270–79 Reign of Ban Muang; Sukhothai remains merely a local power

1294 Ramkamhaeng campaigns in the south, near Phetchaburi

Slate Engraving
This 14th-century engraving shows the Buddha being reincarnated as a horse. It is one of a series discovered at Wat Si Chum (see p199) at Sukhothai.

Where to See the Sukhothai Kingdom

The main sites are Sukhothai itself (see pp198–201), Si Satchanalai (pp202–4), and Kamphaeng Phet (pp196–7). Artifacts are housed in the Bangkok National Museum (pp92–3), the Ramkamhaeng National Museum (pp198–9), the Sawankha Woranayok National Museum (p204), and the Kamphaeng Phet National Museum (see p196).

Minor *wat*

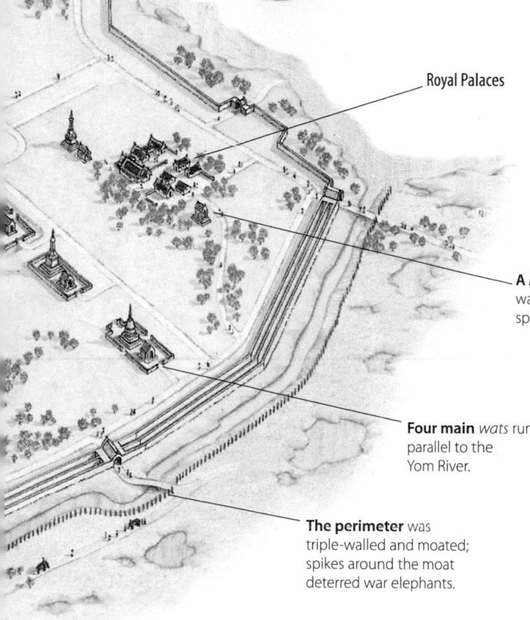

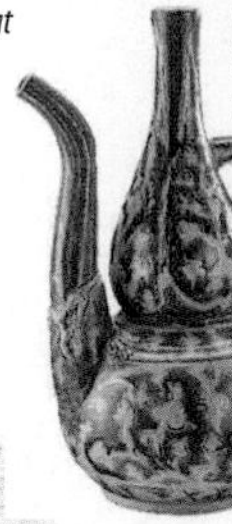

Sangkhalok Pottery
Sawankhalok was the old name for Si Satchanalai, where many kilns (see pp164–5) were sited. From this derives the name Sangkhalok, given to 13th–15th-century pottery from the Sukhothai Kingdom.

Rapids

Wat Sa Si (see p199) is just one of dozens of *wats* at Sukhothai Historical Park.

Royal Palaces

A *lak muang* (city pillar) was built to appease the spirits of the land.

Four main *wats* run parallel to the Yom River.

Walking Buddha
New, sophisticated techniques for casting bronze produced this classic 14th-century Walking Buddha image.

The perimeter was triple-walled and moated; spikes around the moat deterred war elephants.

1298 Ramkamhaeng dies

End of 13th century Sukhothai first called Siam by Chinese

14th to 15th century *Sangkhalok bowl*

1346–7 Reign of Ngua Nam Thom

1300

1320

1340

1298–1346 Reign of Lo Thai, who succeeds Ramkamhaeng. Empire begins to unravel

14th to 15th century Sukhothai stoneware

1321 Tak, formerly part of Sukhothai, falls under Lanna control; Sukhothai is now a small kingdom, one of many competing states

1347–68 Reign of Maha Thammaracha I

The Kingdom of Ayutthaya

Ayutthaya supplanted Sukhothai as the most powerful kingdom in Siam in the mid-14th century and by 1438 had incorporated it into its empire. By the mid-16th century Ayutthaya controlled the entire Central Plains area and at its height held sway over much of what is now Thailand. The Ayutthaya period saw military, legal, and administrative reforms and a flowering of the arts, as well as diplomatic and trade links with the West *(see pp166–7)*. Its end came after years of conflict with Burma, when in 1767 the capital was sacked.

Ayutthaya in 1540

☐ Kingdom of Ayutthaya

Ayutthayan Frescoes
Few frescoes have survived. These, from the 15th century, are from Wat Ratchaburana in Ayutthaya *(see pp180–85)*.

Gold Elephant
The Ayutthayans were masters at working gold. This elephant, studded with gems and crafted to look as though it is paying homage, was discovered in Wat Ratchaburana.

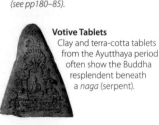

Votive Tablets
Clay and terra-cotta tablets from the Ayutthaya period often show the Buddha resplendent beneath a *naga* (serpent).

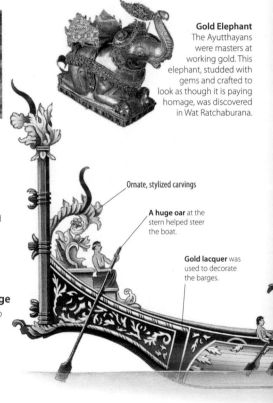

Ornate, stylized carvings

A huge oar at the stern helped steer the boat.

Gold lacquer was used to decorate the barges.

Reconstruction of a Royal Barge
When foreigners (farangs) first came to Ayutthaya, they often met the sight of grand royal barges. This illustration is based on French engravings in some of the first accounts of the opulent city of Ayutthaya to reach the West.

1351 Ayutthaya is established and Ramathibodi I becomes king

1409–24 Reign of Intharacha

1448–88 Reign of Borommatrailokanat, who introduces far reaching administrative and legal reforms

| 1350 | 1400 | 1450 | 1500 |

1388-95 Ramesuan captures Chiang Mai in Lanna *(pp66–7)*

1424-48 Borommaracha II conquers Angkor

1491–1529 Reign of Ramathibodi II

1507-15 Ayutthaya at war with Lanna

Ayutthayan coin

Gilded Lacquer Cabinet
The craftsmen of Ayutthaya were adept at working wood. The doors of this cabinet are inlaid with gold; the pattern is of trees. Other such cabinets depict scenes from the *jataka* or Westerners.

Where to See Ayutthaya

The city of Ayutthaya in the South Central Plains has some of the most spectacular ruins in Thailand *(see pp180–85)*. Ayutthayan artifacts are housed in the Chao Sam Phraya National Museum *(p182)* and in the Bangkok National Museum *(pp92–3)*.

Wat Chai Watthanaram, built by King Prasat Thong in 1630.

Door Panel from Ayutthaya
This 17th to 18th century wood panel once formed part of the door of a temple. It was discovered in Wat Huntra in Ayutthaya.

Carving of the king

Royal insignia

The oarsmen would chant barge songs to keep paddling in time.

Deva Figure
Carved "angels," such as this 18th-century figure, were used in religious ceremonies.

Ayutthayan soldier

1585–7 Naresuan defeats Burmese twice

1555 Naresuan is born

1593 Naresuan defeats Burmese at Battle of Nong Sarai *(pp66–7)*

1660 Narai tries to take Chiang Mai and Lampang in Lanna from Burmese rule, but is repelled by a Burmese army

1685 First French mission in Ayutthaya

1766 Burmese forces, after taking Chiang Mai, besiege Ayutthaya

| 1550 | 1600 | 1650 | 1700 | 1750 |

1564 Burmese invade the kingdom of Ayutthaya

1608 Siam sends its first diplomatic mission to Europe

1569–90 Ayutthaya under Burmese rule

1662 Narai invades Burma

1688 Narai's death leads to "revolution" in Ayutthaya

King Narai

1767 Ayutthaya sacked, capital moves to Thon Buri

Lanna and Burmese Kingdoms

The northern kingdom of Lanna was established at the same time as Sukhothai and endured for 600 years. Its first ruler, Mengrai, extended Lanna rule into Burma (now Myanmar), and the reigns of Ku Na and Tilok saw a golden age. Wars with Burma and Ayutthaya in the 16th and 17th centuries, however, led to decline. Ayutthaya had driven the Burmese out of Lanna once before, but in 1615 the Burmese took back the Lanna capital, Chiang Mai, for almost a century. In the late 1700s, newly allied Siamese and Lanna forces drove the Burmese out. Lanna remained autonomous into the 19th century.

Lanna in 1540

☐ Lanna Kingdom

Golden Door
Decorated with gold leaf, this temple door is at Wat Phra That Lampang Luang (*see pp238–9*), one of the oldest Lanna structures in Thailand.

Naresuan, on his elephant, engages the Burmese crown prince.

Ayutthayan soldiers, in traditional helmets, rally round Naresuan.

Lanna Elephant
This bronze elephant, from the 16th century, was used as a pedestal upon which Buddhist merit offerings were presented.

Bronze Buddha
Buddha images such as this one from the 14th–15th century are regarded as the pinnacle of classical Lanna art. After the Burmese took the north, this style of Lanna art declined.

Battle of Nong Sarai (1593)

The Burmese attempted to control all of Siam, and in 1564, invaded Ayutthaya. This 19th-century painting shows the Battle of Nong Sarai, when Naresuan (1590–1605) defeated the Burmese crown prince and Ayutthaya gained independence. In 1598 Ayutthaya drove Burma from the north, but in the 17th century the Burmese retook it.

1259–1317 Reign of Mengrai; northern principalities unified

1289 Mengrai extends Lanna control into Burma

1292 Chiang Mai founded

1355–85 Reign of Ku Na leads to period of stability

1441–82 Reign of Tilok

1442–3 Ayutthaya sends an army against Lanna

1250	1300	1350	1400	1450	1500

1281 Mengrai conquers Haripunchai (*p233*)

1262 Chiang Rai (*pp254–5*) founded

1369 Ku Na invites a Sukhothai monk, a follower of Sri Lankan Buddhism (*p202*), to establish a monastery in Chiang Mai

King Mengrai

1456–7 Lanna and Ayutthaya are engaged in a protracted war for control of the upper Central Plains

Model *Wihan*
Models of *wihans* are common throughout Thailand. This Lanna one, from the 18th–19th century, cast in bronze, has a high base, an exaggerated version of the bases found on many Lanna temple buidings.

Where to See Lanna and Burmese Thailand

Lanna artifacts can be seen in national museums at Chiang Mai, Lamphun *(see p233)*, and Bangkok. Chiang Mai *(pp228–31)*, Chiang Khong *(p253)*, Lamphun, and Lampang *(p240)* all have buildings that date from the Lanna period. Mae Hong Son *(pp220–21)* and Phrae *(pp262–3)* have buildings showing Burmese influence.

The *ho trai* (scripture library) of Wat Phra Sing, Chiang Mai, is one of the most notable late Lanna structures in Thailand.

Burmese Dancer
This temple mural of a Burmese dancing girl is from Chiang Mai *(see pp228–31)*. A number of *wats* in the North bear similar indications of Burmese occupation.

Burmese soldiers wear simple bandanas around their heads.

Lanna Coin
During the 18th and 19th centuries, bronze rings were used as coinage in the Lanna Kingdom.

Lanna Wood Carvings
The pediment of the 19th-century *wihan* at Wat Pan Tao *(see p229)* is typical of the elaborate work produced by Lanna wood carvers.

19th-century Lanna box

1558 Burmese take Chiang Mai for the first time

1590 Ayutthaya establishes independence from Burma at Battle of Nong Sarai

1660 Narai of Ayutthaya attempts to wrest control of North from Burmese but is repulsed

1550	1600	1650	1700	1750	1800

1615 Burma regains control over Lanna

1598 Naresuan of Ayutthaya expels Burma from the North, though this is short-lived

15th to 17th century Lanna Buddha

1727 General Thip proclaims himself king of Lampang after defeating Burmese

1776 Taksin of Thon Buri and Kawila of Lampang reconquer Chiang Mai

The Early Chakri Dynasty

After the sack of Ayutthaya, Taksin, an army general, established a new capital at Thon Buri, on the west bank of the Chao Phraya opposite what would later become Bangkok. He became king in 1768, and in 10 years Siam was a regional power again. However, he became increasingly despotic and, in 1782, was ousted by the military commander Chao Phraya Chakri, who was later pronounced King Rama I. Chakri's descendant, King Mongkut (Rama IV), modernized Siam, opening it up to foreign trade and influence.

Siam in 1809

☐ Siamese territories

Chakri Kings
The reigns of Ramas I, II, and III signaled an era of stable monarchical rule. Rama II was a literary man, while Rama III was a great merchant.

Khlongs are an important means of transportation

Chakri Throne
The Busabok Mala Maha Piman Throne was built in the reign of Rama I for important occasions. It is in the Grand Palace *(see pp84–9)*.

The Grand Palace
(see pp84–9) was founded in the late 18th century; by the mid-19th century it is already vast.

Sir John Bowring
The Bowring Treaty (1855) allowed the British free trade. Later, Siam forged similar treaties with other colonial powers, thus avoiding annexation.

1768 Taksin begins to re-establish Siamese Empire

Ramakien mural

1800 Burmese finally expelled from Siam

1797 Rama I "writes" Ramakien *(see pp44–5)*

1813 Siam withdraws from Cambodia leaving Vietnam as dominant power

| 1770 | 1780 | 1790 | 1800 | 1810 |

1782 Rama I overthrows an increasingly despotic Taksin; relocates capital

1783 Wat Phra Kaeo begun

1785 Massive Burmese invasion repulsed

1805 Rama I appoints a committee of judges to reform Siamese law

1808–24 Reign of Rama II

Thai Etiquette (1855)
In mid-19th century Siam, prostrating oneself before a superior was common. It was officially abolished by Rama V *(see pp70–71)*.

(see pp70–71)

Where to See Early Chakri Thailand

Almost all the best examples of architecture from the early Chakri – or Rattanakosin *(see p39)* – period can be seen in Bangkok. The earliest Chakri building is the *bot* of Wat Phra Kaeo *(p84)*. Other examples include the *bot* of Wat Suthat *(p94)*, the *wihan* of Wat Suthat, Wat Pho *(pp96–7)*, and Phra Nakhon Khiri in Phetchaburi *(p334)*.

Wat Suthat, built in the early 19th century by Rama I, is the site of Bangkok's tallest *wihan*.

Mongkut (1851–68)
Before coming to the throne, Mongkut, pictured here with his favorite wife, traveled widely, meeting many Westerners.

Thon Buri, on the western bank of the Chao Phraya, is still just a small town.

Early Bangkok (Krung Thep)

The Siamese capital was moved from Thon Buri to the east of the river in 1782 as a defense against the Burmese. Its official 43-syllable name matches the majesterial plans that Rama I had for his new city: the first two words, "Krung Thep," mean "city of angels." This mural from 1864 shows the temples and river houses of early Bangkok.

King Mongkut Mural
In this mural King Mongkut is in his palace observing an eclipse through a telescope, his subjects below him.

1824–51 Reign of Rama III

Chakri coin

1840s Siam dominant in Cambodia

1855 Signing of the Bowring Treaty

1820	1830	1840	1850	1860

1826 Limited trade agreement, Burney Treaty, signed

1830s Siam goes to war in Cambodia, to defend Buddhism against the Vietnamese

1827 Vientiane is sacked by Siamese army

Rama IV (1851)

1868 Mongkut, Rama IV, dies. 15-year-old King Chulalongkorn accedes to the throne, his powers constrained by the appointment of a regent

Reign of King Chulalongkorn

Perhaps the greatest king of the Chakri dynasty, Chulalongkorn (1868–1910) carried on the modernization of Siam that his father, Mongkut, had started. Financial reforms were made, the government restructured, and slavery abolished. Reform angered older ministers, the "conservatives" *(hua boran)*, and led to the Front Palace Crisis of 1875. This was also a time when Britain and France were consolidating their positions in Southeast Asia. Chulalongkorn's policies and diplomacy kept the colonial powers at bay, though parts of Burma, Laos, Cambodia, and the Malay states were ceded to them.

Siam in 1909

◻ Siamese territories

▨ Ceded territories

Rama V
Chulalongkorn (Rama V) came to the throne, under the guidance of a regent, at the age of 15. He had received an excellent Thai and Western education and was well qualified for the task of reforming Siam.

Soldiers attending the cremation wore colonial uniforms.

Drummers wore traditional Thai headdresses.

Life on the Khlongs
At the end of the 19th century, and into the 20th, Bangkok was known as the "Venice of the East" *(see p129).*

Classical Dancers at Court
Many Siamese traditions, among them classical dance, remained unchanged. Scenes such as this were often recorded with the aid of new technology – photography.

1874 Chulalongkorn (Rama V) introduces a series of reforms that anger the "conservatives" or *hua boran*

1887 Prince Devawongse attends the celebrations, in London, of Queen Victoria's 50th year; the prince studies European government with a view to reform in Siam

1870

1875

1880

1885

1874 Thai High Commissioner sent to govern Lanna

1875 Front Palace Crisis – the "conservatives" demonstrate their anger. Chulalongkorn has to tone down some of his reforms

1885 Enlightened Prince Devawongse made Foreign Minister

Tile detail, Wat Rachabophit

1888 New administrative system, centralizing power, is introduced

Franco-Siamese Crisis

In an attempt to consolidate her hold over Indochina, in 1893 France asserted sovereignty over Siamese-controlled Laos. This cartoon shows a French "wolf" hungrily assessing a Siamese "lamb."

Chulalongkorn's body was cremated in this funeral tower.

Cremation of Chulalongkorn

Chulalongkorn's cremation, held in Bangkok in 1910, was a grand state affair. As a great reformer, he was idealized by his subjects, and even today the people of Thailand commemorate his death on Chulalongkorn Day (see p54).

Where to See Late Chakri Thailand

During the latter part of the 19th century there was little change in the basic style of religious buildings. Chulalongkorn, however, left his mark on some buildings in Bangkok. Wat Benchamabophit *(see pp110–11)* employs an eclectic mixture of Chinese, Italian, and Khmer styles, while Wat Rachabophit *(pp94–5)* displays traditional Thai and Western motifs.

At Wat Rachabopit, Rama V had the interior decorated in Italianate-Thai style.

Modern Developments

Chulalongkorn promoted many new ideas; cars appeared in Bangkok at the beginning of the 20th century.

1893 French take control of Laos; leads to Franco-Siamese Crisis

French gunboat

1910 Chulalongkorn dies. His son Vajiravudh (Rama VI) comes to throne

1907 Cambodia ceded to the French

| 1890 | 1895 | 1900 | 1905 | 1910 |

1892 New ministries are created to govern Siam

1893 Paknam Incident – French gunboats sail up the Chao Phraya River

1905 After years of gradual reform, slavery is finally abolished

1909 Siamese sovereignty over the Malayan states of Kelantan, Perlis, Terengganu, and Kedah ceded to the British

Modern Thailand

In 1932 Siam became a constitutional monarchy. Under Prime Minister Phibun Songkram, the 1930s saw rising nationalism: the country was renamed Prathet Thai (Thailand) and sided with Japan in World War II. However, during the Vietnam War, fear of Communism led Thailand to help the US. A number of military coups have since hindered democratization; in 2006 the ousting of Prime Minister Thaksin Shinawatra caused political division. Shinawatra's sister, Yingluck, was elected Prime Minister in 2011 but political stability remains elusive.

ASEAN in 2008

☐ Association of SE Asian Nations

King Vajiravudh
Chulalongkorn's son Vajiravudh (1910–25) clashed with his father's senior advisors. To build a following of his own he created the elite corps, the Wild Tigers, in 1911.

Democracy Monument
A meeting place during prodemocracy rallies, the monument was built in 1939 to mark the revolution of 1932. To this day it serves as the nexus of demonstrations.

Commercial buildings by the Waterfront

Wat Phra Kaeo

Modern Bangkok
With an official population of around 9.5 million (though unofficially it could be closer to 15 million), Bangkok is one of the most frenetic, congested, and polluted cities in the world. It is also a colorful city where old traditions are still important. The 1982 Bangkok Bicentennial and the celebrations of Bhumibol's 50th year as King in 1996 (shown here), featured splendid royal barges.

	1920	1930	1940	1950	1960

1911 Wild Tigers, an elite paramilitary corps, formed

1935 Prajadhipok abdicates, Ananda Mahidol becomes king

1938 Phibun Songkram becomes Prime Minister

1959 Sarit Thanarat becomes Prime Minister in coup

1932 Revolution; Siam made a constitutional monarchy

1939 Phibun renames Siam

1946 Phibun resigns; Pridi Phanomyong forms government

1917 Siam sends a small force of men to fight on the side of the Allies in WWI

1925 Prajadhipok becomes king

1940 Thais invade Laos and Cambodia after fall of France to Germany

1946 Mahidol killed; Bhumibol made king

1967 Thailand becomes founder member of the Association of Southeast Asian Nations (ASEAN)

1934–8 Increasing power struggle between Phibun Songkram and Pridi Phanomyong

1941 Phibun capitulates to Japan; Pridi Phanomyong organizes underground resistance

Phibun Songkram

Traffic Congestion
Modern Bangkok has a reputation for severe traffic jams, but the Skytrain, airport rail link, and underground have eased traffic congestion.

Where to See Modern Thailand

Apart from palaces and *wats*, most 20th-century architecture in Thailand, particularly in Bangkok, tends to be very dull and functional. However, some of the many edifices built in the 1980s and 1990s are worth a look if only for their sheer outrageousness *(see p123)*. Modern resort hotels sometimes incorporate traditional touches.

King Bhumibol
Against a backdrop of unstable politics, the revered King Bhumibol (Rama IX) has represented virtue and stability. Through his authority, the military coup and bloody demonstrations of 1992 were ended.

The Robot Building, in downtown Bangkok, was designed by Sumet Jumsai in the mid-1980s.

Ayutthaya-style barge

Stylish riverside apartments

Tourism
Despite the 2004 tsunami and the closure of Bangkok's main airport in late 2008 by anti-government protestors, Thailand remains popular with tourists.

1973–6 Turbulent democratic government; student demonstrations

1988 Fully democratic elections

2004 December 26, west coast of Southern Thailand hit by a tsunami – some 5,300 deaths

1997 Thai economy collapses

2008 Thailand returns to civilian rule

2011 Yingluck Shinawatra elected Prime Minister

| 1970 | 1980 | 1990 | 2000 | 2010 | 2020 |

1976 Massacre of students at Thammasat University brings huge support for the CPT *(see p292)*

1980s CPT a spent force; Thailand enters a period of rapid economic growth

1992 Massacre of pro-democracy demonstrators in Bangkok followed by democratic elections

King Bhumibol

2006 Bloodless military coup deposes Prime Minister Thaksin Shinawatra

2014 Government is ousted; military assumes control of political positions

BANGKOK

Introducing Bangkok

Thailand's capital, straddling the great Chao Phraya River, 12 miles (20 km) upstream from the Gulf of Thailand, is an exuberant, exhilarating metropolis of eight and a half million people. Founded by Rama I in 1782, this relatively young city is known to Thais as Krung Thep ("city of angels"), a shortened form of a full name in excess of 150 letters. Bangkok may be a lesson in the dangers of uncontrolled urban expansion, but it is also one of the world's most exciting cities. It is highly regarded for its trendy nightclubs and cosmopolitan dining scene, and its markets, shops, magnificent *wats*, museums, palaces, and parks offer something for everyone.

The National Museum *(see pp92–3)* contains a wealth of treasures, such as this 7th–8th-century head of the Buddha.

The Grand Palace and Wat Phra Kaeo complex *(see pp84–9)* is Bangkok's premier tourist attraction. The sacred Emerald Buddha, or Phra Kaeo, is housed in one of many splendid buildings.

Wat Pho *(see pp96–7)* is one of the oldest temples in the capital, dating originally from the 16th century. It is also a famous center for traditional medicine and contains the much respected Institute of Massage.

Wat Arun *(see pp130–31)*, otherwise known as the Temple of Dawn, is one of Bangkok's best known landmarks. Its Khmer-influenced *prangs* are encrusted with thousands of pieces of broken porcelain.

◀ Mosaic-encrusted wall of Phra Mondop, Grand Palace, Bangkok

Dusit Park *(see pp106–7)*, with its leafy walkways, fascinating museums, Vimanmek Palace, and neighboring zoo, has enough attractions to provide a full day's sightseeing.

0 meters   1000
0 yards   1000

DUSIT
(see pp104–13)

PHITSANULOK

LAN LUANG

PETCHABURI

PAMA V

RAMA I

HINATOWN
(see pp98–103)

RAMA IV

DOWNTOWN
(see pp114–25)

RAMA IV

Jim Thompson House
(see pp124–5), a beautifully decorated series of teak buildings, was once home to the famed American silk merchant.

Chinatown *(see pp98–103)*
is one of Bangkok's most hectic, colorful, and intoxicating districts. Narrow streets overflow with markets and shops, such as this religious goods emporium.

The Old Farang Quarter *(see pp116–17)*
was the commercial hub for foreigners in the 19th century. Some colonial buildings, such as the Portuguese Embassy, survive.

Greater Bangkok Area

0 kilometers   20
0 miles   15

Pathum
Thani

Nakhon
Pathom

Nonthaburi   Min Buri

BANGKOK

Ratchaburi

Samut
Prakan

Samut
Sakhon

Samut
Songkhram   *Gulf of Thailand*

For keys to symbols *see back flap*

A River View of Bangkok

The two great rivers of the North, the Ping and the Nan, join at Nakhon Sawan in the Central Plains to form the Chao Phraya ("river of kings"), Thailand's most important waterway. This vital transportation link drains some of the country's most fertile rice-growing land. The stretch shown here is actually a canal, built in the 16th century as a shortcut at a point where the Chao Phraya took a huge meander along what is now Khlong Bangkok Noi and Khlong Bangkok Yai. Along this busy "royal mile" you can catch glimpses of the Grand Palace, temples, and colonial buildings, and experience a flavor of old Bangkok's colorful riverfront.

A typical Chao Phraya barge, transporting goods along the river

To Phrapin-klao Bridge

The Buddhaisawan Chapel in the National Museum *(see pp92–3)* is home to the Phra Buddha Sing, one of the most venerated Buddha images in Thailand after the Emerald Buddha. Elsewhere in the museum is a fabulous collection of arts and crafts from every period of Thai history. Exhibits include Buddha images, weapons, and pottery.

Riverboats on the Chao Phraya

The Chao Phraya is a major transportation artery, for both goods and people. Hefty rice barges, tiny boats laden with fruit and vegetables, and a variety of ferry services continually ply the river. No visitor to Bangkok should miss seeing the city from the water, and jumping on the Chao Phraya Express is one of the easiest and cheapest ways to do so. The stops are indicated on the Street Finder (maps 1–2, 5–6). There are also cross-river ferries from almost every river pier, as well as countless long-tail boats that operate as buses or can be specially chartered to explore the city's *khlongs*.

| 0 meters | 200 |
| 0 yards | 200 |

Wat Rakhang *(see p129)* is a little visited but rewarding temple containing fine murals painted in the 1920s.

Long-tail boat on the Chao Phraya

Wat Phra Kaeo *(see pp84–7)* contains one of Thailand's most sacred Buddha images, the Emerald Buddha. The temple and palace complex is a superb collection of buildings with lavish decorative details.

Sanam Luang, ("field of kings"), the venue for national ceremonies, is one of Bangkok's few open spaces.

Locator Map
See Street Finder map 1

Wat Pho *(see pp96–7)*, the city's oldest temple, dates from the 17th century. It is famed for its school of massage, as well as for fine details such as this painting of a Chinese soldier.

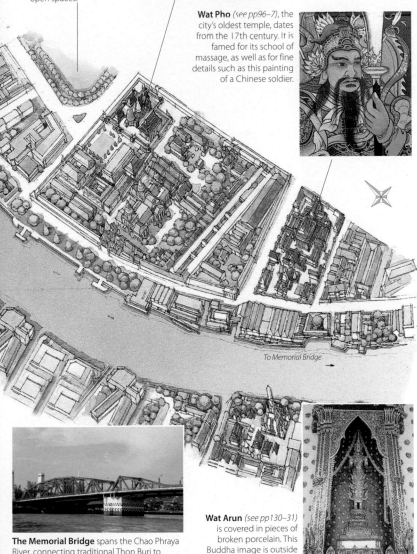

To Memorial Bridge

The Memorial Bridge spans the Chao Phraya River, connecting traditional Thon Buri to the modern Downtown area.

Wat Arun *(see pp130–31)* is covered in pieces of broken porcelain. This Buddha image is outside the main *bot*.

OLD CITY

As the spiritual and historical heart of Bangkok, the Old City is dense with temples and shrines. Known as Rattanakosin, this was the center of the new capital Rama I founded in 1782 *(see pp68–9)*. Remnants of a defensive wall can be seen between the Golden Mount and Wat Rachanadda. Some of Thailand's finest Rattanakosin period architecture is within the Old City. The foremost example is the Grand Palace, within which is Wat Phra Kaeo, home of the country's most venerated image, the Emerald Buddha. South of here is Wat Pho, one of the city's oldest temples, while to the north lies Sanam Luang ("field of kings"), the site of royal ceremonies. Alongside Sanam Luang, the National Museum contains Southeast Asia's most impressive artifacts. Two Buddhist universities in temples nearby: Wat Mahathat and Wat Bowonniwet. The latter is famed for its murals combining Western and traditional Thai styles.

Sights at a Glance

Wats

① Grand Palace and Wat Phra Kaeo pp84–9
② Wat Mahathat
⑤ Wat Bowonniwet
⑦ Wat Rachanadda
⑧ Wat Saket and the Golden Mount
⑪ Wat Suthat and the Giant Swing
⑫ Wat Rachabophit
⑬ Wat Rachapradit
⑭ Wat Pho pp96–7

Museums and Galleries

③ National Museum pp92–3
④ National Gallery
⑮ Museum of Siam

Notable Roads and Districts

⑨ Monk's Bowl Village
⑩ Bamrung Muang Road

Monuments

⑥ Democracy Monument

0 meters 500
0 yards 500

See also Street Finder pp148–59

◀ Reclining Buddha, Wat Pho

For keys to symbols *see back flap*

Street-by-Street: Around Sanam Luang

สนามหลวง

Sanam Luang ("field of kings" or "royal ground") is one of the few sizable open spaces in Bangkok. It is the traditional site for royal cremations, the annual kite flying festival, and the Royal Plowing Ceremony (see p52). Spiritually speaking, this area is one of the luckiest in the city, with the Grand Palace, the Lak Muang (City Pillar) shrine, and the Amulet Market bordering Sanam Luang. Neighboring streets overflow with salesmen hawking lotions, potions, and amulets for luck, love, or protection from evil spirits. Astrologers gather to chart your stars or read your palm. Notable sights include Wat Mahathat, Thailand's most revered center of Buddhist studies, and the National Museum, which charts Thailand's fascinating history.

Locator Map
See Street Finder map 1

Phra Chan Pier

❷ Wat Mahathat
Meditation classes are held at the Buddhist university within this temple's compound. Dating from the 18th century, the *wat* is more notable for its bustling atmosphere than its buildings

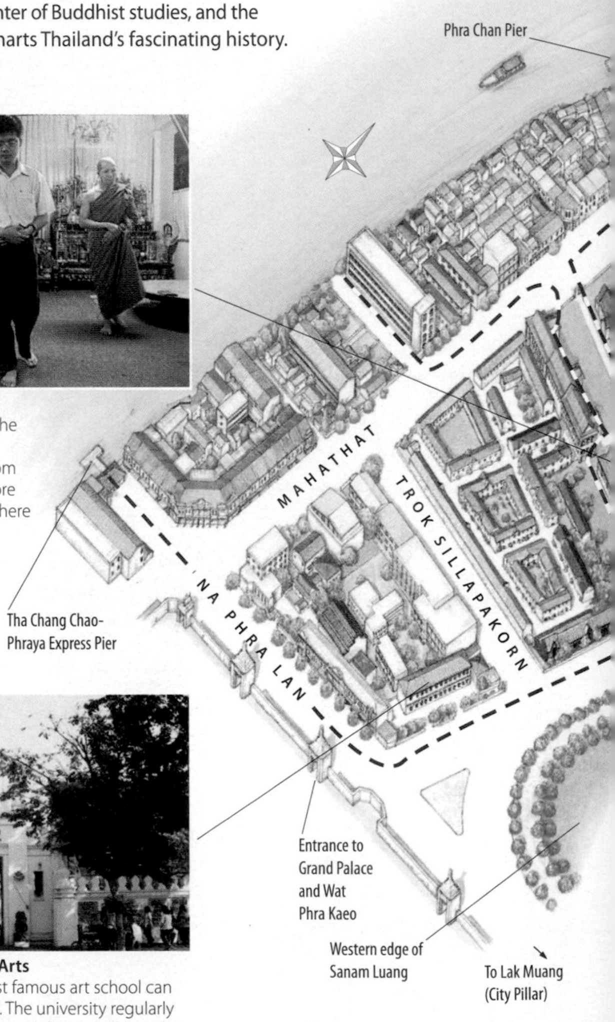

Tha Chang Chao-
Phraya Express Pier

MAHATHAT

TROK SILLAPAKORN

NA PHRA LAN

Entrance to
Grand Palace
and Wat
Phra Kaeo

Western edge of
Sanam Luang

To Lak Muang
(City Pillar)

Silpakorn University of Fine Arts
The entrance to Thailand's most famous art school can be found on Na Phra Lan Road. The university regularly puts on excellent art shows in its exhibition hall. See the signs outside the entrance for details and opening times.

Key

— Suggested route

Amulets

The Thais are a highly superstitious people – those who do not wear some form of protective or lucky amulet are firmly in a minority. Amulets come in myriad forms and are sold in specialty markets, often near spiritually auspicious sites. Although many are religious in nature – such as tiny Buddha images and copies of sacred statues – others are designed for more practical purposes, such as model phalluses to ensure sexual potency. Amulets are such a big business that there are even magazines dedicated to them.

A selection of charms sold at stalls around Sanam Luang

Thammasat University, notable for its law and political science faculties, was the scene of student riots in the 1970s *(see p73)*.

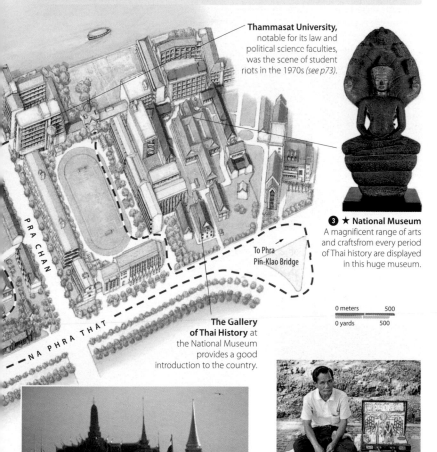

❸ ★ National Museum
A magnificent range of arts and craftsfrom every period of Thai history are displayed in this huge museum.

To Phra Pin-Klao Bridge

PRA CHAN

NA PHRA THAT

The Gallery of Thai History at the National Museum provides a good introduction to the country.

| 0 meters | 500 |
| 0 yards | 500 |

Fortune Teller at Sanam Luang
Many Thais set great store by the predictions of fortune tellers and often visit those who gather on Sanam Luang near Wat Phra Kaeo.

★ Kite Flying at Sanam Luang
King Chulalongkorn (1868–1910) was an avid kite flyer and permitted Sanam Luang to be used for the sport. Fiercely contested kite fights can often be witnessed here between February and April.

❶ Grand Palace and Wat Phra Kaeo

พระบรมมหาราชวังและวัดพระแก้ว

Construction of this remarkable site began in 1782, to mark the founding of the new capital and provide a resting place for the sacred Emerald Buddha (Phra Kaeo) and a residence for the king. Surrounded by walls stretching for 2,080 yards (1,900 m), the complex was once a self-sufficient city within a city. The royal family now lives in Dusit, but Wat Phra Kaeo is still Thailand's holiest temple – visitors must cover their knees and heels before entering.

Wat Phra Kaeo's skyline, as seen from Sanam Luang

★ *Bot* of the Emerald Buddha
Devotees make offerings to the Emerald Buddha at the entrance to the *bot*, the most important building in the *wat*.

★ Ramakien Gallery
Extending clockwise all the way around the cloisters are 178 panels depicting the complete story of the Ramakien.

1750	1800	1850	1900	1950
	1783 Work begins on Wat Phra Kaeo, Dusit Throne Hall, and Phra Maha Monthien	**1855** New buildings epitomize fusion of Eastern and Western styles		**1925** Rama VII chooses to live in the less formal Chitrlada Palace at Dusit. Grand Palace reserved for special occasions
1782 Official founding of new capital	**1809** Rama II introduces Chinese details	**1840s** Women's quarter laid out as a city within a city	**1880** Chulalongkorn, the last king to make major additions, involves 26 half-brothers in renovation of Wat Phra Kaeo	**1932** Chakri Dynasty's 150th year celebrated at palace **1982** Renovation of the complex

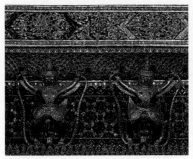

Decorative Gilt Figures
Encircling the exterior of the *bot* are 112 *garudas* (mythical beasts that are half-man, half-bird). They are shown holding *nagas* (serpents) and are typical of the *wat's* dazzling decorative details.

VISITORS' CHECKLIST

Practical Information
Na Phra Lan Rd. **Map** 1 C5. **Tel** 0-2623-5500. **Open** 8:30am–3:30pm daily. **Closed** ceremonies. includes Vimanmek Mansion *(see pp108–9)* and Ananta Samakhom Throne Room *(see p109)*. in *bot*. **palaces.thai.net**

Transport
1, 3, 25, 33, 39, 53.
Chang, Tien.

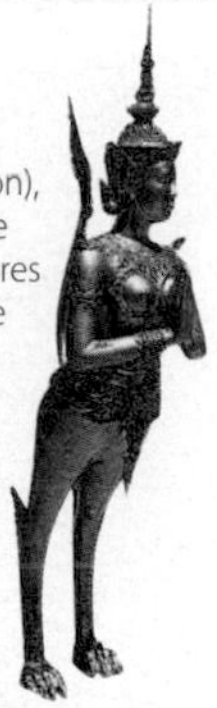

Apsonsi
A mythical creature (half-woman, half-lion), Apsonsi is one of the beautiful gilded figures on the upper terrace of Wat Phra Kaeo.

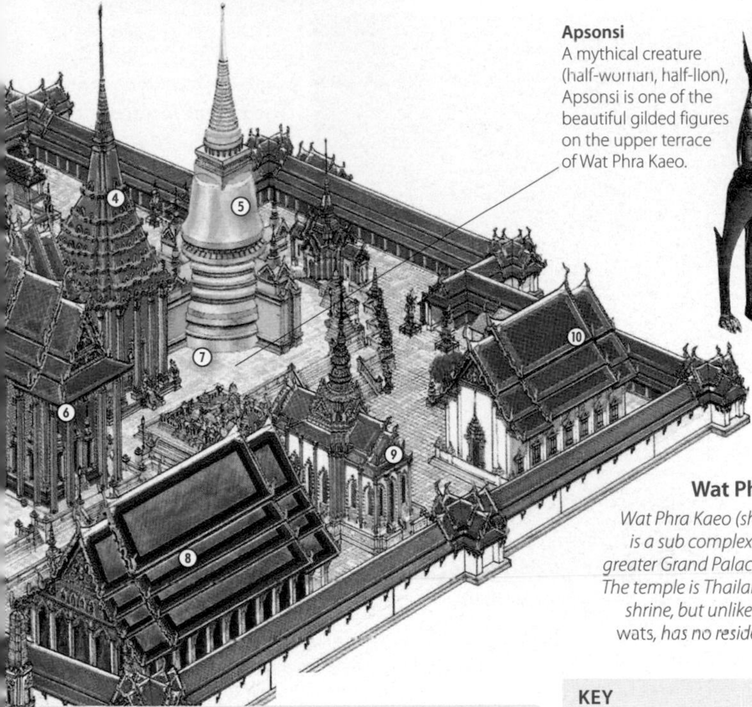

Wat Phra Kaeo

Wat Phra Kaeo (shown here) is a sub complex within the greater Grand Palace complex. The temple is Thailand's holiest shrine, but unlike other Thai wats, has no resident monks.

KEY

① **Eight *prangs*** border the east side of the *wat*.

② **Chapel of the Gandharara Buddha**

③ **Emerald Buddha**

④ **Phra Mondop (library)**

⑤ **The Phra Si Rattana Chedi** contains a piece of the Buddha's breastbone.

⑥ **The Royal Pantheon**

⑦ **Upper Terrace**

⑧ **The Ho Phra Monthien Tham** is the auxiliary library.

⑨ **Wihan Yot**

⑩ **Ho Phra Nak (royal mausoleum)**

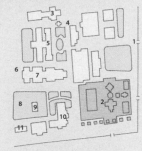

Grand Palace and Wat Phra Kaeo

1 Entrance
2 Wat Phra Kaeo complex
3 Dusit Throne Hall
4 Aphonphimok Pavilion
5 Chakri Throne Hall
6 Inner Palace
7 Phra Maha Monthien Buildings
8 Siwalai Gardens
9 Rama IV Chapel
10 Boromphiman Mansion
11 Audience Chamber

Key
Wat Phra Kaeo complex
Lawns
Buildings

Exploring Wat Phra Kaeo

When Rama I established the new capital of Bangkok in 1782 his ambition was to construct a royal temple along the lines of the grand chapels of previous capital cities. Symbolizing the simultaneous founding of the Chakri dynasty, this temple was to surpass its larger Sukhothai and Ayutthaya predecessors in the splendor of its design and decoration. The result of his vision was Wat Phra Kaeo, or Temple of the Emerald Buddha (officially known as Wat Phra Si Rattana Sasadaram), so called because the *bot* houses the Emerald Buddha image, brought here from Wat Arun *(see pp130–31)* in 1785.

The Emerald Buddha crowning the ornate gilded altar inside the *bot*

The Bot and Peripheral Buildings

The most sacred building within the palace complex, the *bot* of Wat Phra Kaeo was erected to house what is still the most revered image of the Buddha in Thailand: the Emerald Buddha.

The exterior doors and windows of the *bot* are inlaid with delicate mother-of-pearl designs. Along the marble base supporting the structure runs a series of gilt bronze *garudas* (half bird, half human). The staircase of the main entrance is guarded by Cambodian-style stone lions, or *singhas*. Inside, the surprisingly small image of the Emerald Buddha sits in a glass case high above a golden

altar. Carved from a single piece of jade (not emerald), it is 26 in (66 cm) tall and has a lap span of 19 in (48 cm). The Buddha has been attributed to the late Lanna School of the 15th century. It is dressed in one of three costumes: a crown and jewelry for the summer season; a golden shawl in winter; and a gilded monastic robe and headdress in the rainy season. The reigning monarch or a prince appointed by him presides over each changing of the Buddha's attire in a deeply symbolic ceremony. Inside the *bot* are murals from the reign of Rama III (1824–51). They depict the classic subjects of Thai mural painting, namely the Traiphum (Buddhist cosmology),

the Buddha's victory over Mara (the god of death), and scenes from the previous lives of the Buddha – the *jatakas*. Around the temple are 12 open-sided *salas* (small pavilions) built as contemplative shelters.

Southeast of the *bot* is the 19th-century **Chapel of the Gandharara Buddha**. The bronze image of the Buddha calling the rains housed here is used in the Royal Plowing Ceremony in May *(see p50)*. The bell in the nearby belfry is rung only on special occasions such as New Year's Day.

The Upper Terrace

Of the four structures on this elevated terrace, the **Phra Si Rattana Chedi**, at the western end, is the most striking. It was built by King Mongkut (Rama IV) to enshrine a piece of the Buddha's breastbone. The golden tiles decorating the exterior were later added by King Chulalongkorn (Rama V).

The adjacent **Phra Mondop**, used as a library, was built by Rama I as a hall to house Buddhist scriptures. Although the Library is closed to the public, the exterior is splendid in itself. The Javanese Buddha images on the four outer corners are copies of early 9th-century originals, which are now in the museum near the entrance to the palace complex. Outside the building are memorials to all the kings of the present Chakri dynasty, and bronze elephant statues

The ornate entrance to the Phra Mondop (used as a library) at Wat Phra Kaew

Mural depicting a scene from the Ramakien in the Ramakien Gallery

representing the royal white elephants *(see p110)* from the first five reigns of the dynasty *(see pp68–9)*.

To the north of the *mondop* is a model of Angkor Wat in northwest Cambodia *(see pp268–9)*. The model was commissioned by Rama IV to show his people the scale and gracious splendor of 12th-century Khmer architecture – Cambodia during his reign being under Thai rule.

The **Royal Pantheon** houses life-size statues of the Chakri kings. Rama IV had intended the hall to hold the Emerald Buddha, but decided that it was too small. The pantheon is open to the public only on Chakri Day *(see p52)*.

The Northern Terrace

Ho Phra Nak was originally constructed by Rama I in the late 18th century to enshrine the Nak (literally, alloy of gold, silver, and copper) Buddha image that had been rescued from Ayutthaya. Rama III, however, demolished the original hall, preferring to build the present brick and mortar structure to house the ashes of minor members of the

royal family. The Nak Buddha was moved into the neighboring **Wihan Yot**, which is shaped like a Greek cross and decorated with Chinese porcelain.

Also on the Northern Terrace is the **Ho Phra Monthien Tham**, or Auxiliary Library, built by the brother of Rama I. The door panels, inlaid with mother-of-pearl, were salvaged from Ayutthaya's Wat Borom Buddharam. Inside, Buddhist scriptures are stored in fine cabinets.

Ramakien figure outside *chedi*

The Prangs, Yakshas, and Ramakien Gallery

Surrounding the temple complex is the cloisterlike Ramakien Gallery, decorated with lavishly painted and meticulously restored murals. This is Thailand's most extensive depiction of the ancient legend of the Ramakien *(see pp44–5)*. The 178 panels were originally painted in the late 18th century, but damage from humidity means that frequent renovation is necessary. The murals are divided by marble pillars inscribed with verses relating the story, which begins opposite Wihan Yot and proceeds in a clockwise direction.

Guarding each gateway to the gallery is a pair of *yakshas* (demons). Placed here during the reign of Rama II, they are said to protect the Emerald Buddha from evil spirits. Each one represents a different character from the Ramakien myth: the green one, for example, symbolizes Tosakan, or the demon king.

The eight different-colored *prangs* on the edge of the temple complex are intricately decorated with Chinese porcelain. They represent the eight elements of the Buddhist religion, including the Buddha, the Dharma (law), the *sangha* (monkhood), and the *bhiksunis* (female Buddhists).

The Legend of the Emerald Buddha

In 1434 lightning struck the *chedi* of Wat Phra Kaeo in Chiang Rai in Northern Thailand *(see pp254–5)*, revealing a simple stucco image. The abbot of the temple kept it in his residence until the flaking plaster exposed a jadeite image beneath. Upon learning of the discovery, the king of Chiang Mai sent an army of elephants to bring the image to him. The elephant bearing the Emerald Buddha, however, refused to take the road to Chiang Mai, and, treating this as an auspicious sign, the entourage re-routed to Lampang. The image was moved several more times over the next century, then was taken to Haw Pha Kaew in Laos *(see pp298–9)* in 1552. It was not until General Chakri (later Rama I) captured Vientiane in 1778 that the Emerald Buddha was returned to Thailand. It was kept in Wat Arun *(see pp130–31)* for 15 years, before a grand river procession brought it to its current resting place on March 5, 1785.

The small Emerald Buddha inside the *bot*

Exploring the Grand Palace

Built at the same time as Wat Phra Kaeo, the Grand Palace was the king's official residence from 1782 to 1946, although King Chulalongkorn (Rama V) was the last monarch to live here. Today, the royal family resides at Chitrlada Palace (see p110). Throughout the palace's history, many structures have been altered. Within the complex there are a few functioning government buildings, such as the Ministry of Finance, but most others are unused. Important ceremonies are still held in the Dusit Throne Hall and the Amarin Winichai Hall.

Dusit Throne Hall

This cross-shaped throne hall was originally built in 1784 as a reproduction of one of Ayutthaya's grandest buildings, Sanphet Maha Prasat (see pp182–3). Five years later the hall was struck by lightning and rebuilt on a smaller scale. Crowned with a sumptuously decorated tiered spire, it is one of the finest examples of early Rattanakosin architecture (see p39). Inside is a masterpiece of Thai art: the original Rama I teak throne, inlaid with mother-of-pearl. In the south wing is a window in the form of a throne. The hall is used for the annual Coronation Day celebrations (see p52).

Aphonphimok Pavilion

King Mongkut (Rama IV) built this small wooden structure as a royal changing room for when he was giving audiences at the Dusit Throne Hall. The king would be carried on a palanquin to the pavilion's shoulder-high first step. Inside the building he would change into the appropriate apparel for the occasion. The pavilion's simple structure, complemented by its elaborate decoration, makes it a building of perfect proportions: indeed, it is considered a glory of Thai architecture. It inspired Rama V so much so that he had a replica built at Bang Pa-in (see p185).

Elephant statue by Chakri Throne Hall

Chakri Throne Hall

Also known as the Grand Palace Throne Hall, Chakri Maha Prasat was built in Neo-Classical style by the British architect John Chinitz. Rama V commissioned the building in 1882 to mark the centenary of the Chakri dynasty, a fact reflected in the theme of the sumptuous decoration. The structure was originally intended to have a domed roof, but the royal court decided that a Thai-style roof would be more appropriate, in keeping with the area.

Housed on the top floor of the Central Hall are the ashes of royal monarchs, and the first floor – the only floor open to the public – acts as the main audience hall where the King receives ambassadors and entertains foreign monarchs; artifacts from the King's armory are on display here.

Behind the Niello Throne in the Chakri Throne Room is the emblem of the Chakri dynasty: a discus and trident. The paintings in the room depict diplomatic missions, including Queen Victoria welcoming Rama IV's ambassador in London. The East Wing is used as a reception room for royal guests. The long hall connecting the Central Hall with this wing is lined with portraits of the Chakri dynasty. In the West Wing is the queen's personal reception room. Portraits of the principal queens of Rama IV, Rama V, and Rama VII decorate the hall between the Central Hall and this wing.

Phra Maha Monthien Buildings

This cluster of connected buildings, located to the east of the Chakri Throne Hall, is the "Grand Residence" of the palace complex.

The focal point of the 18th-century **Amarin Winichai Hall**, the northernmost building of the group, is Rama I's boat-shaped Busabok Mala Throne. When an audience was present, two curtains hid the throne as the king ascended, and, with an elaborate fanfare, the curtains were drawn back to reveal the king wearing a loose, golden gown and seeming to float on the prowlike part of the throne. In the 19th century two British ambassadors were received in such manner here; John Crawfurd by Rama II and Sir

Exterior of the Dusit Throne Hall, with its elegant multitiered spire

For hotels and restaurants see pp402–11 and pp418–33

Lavish decor of the connecting hall of the Chakri Throne Hall's West Wing

John Bowring by Rama IV. The hall is now used for some state ceremonies.

Connected to the hall by a gateway through which only the king, queen, and royal children may walk is the **Phaisan Thaksin Hall**. This was used by Rama I as a private hall when dining with family, friends, and members of the royal court. In 1809 a Borom Rachaphisek Ceremony was performed in this hall to mark the coronation of the new king, Rama II. On the high altar is the Phra Siam Thewathirat, a highly venerated guardian figure, placed here by Rama IV.

The third building is the **Chakraphat Phiman Hall**. It served as a residence for the first three Chakri kings. It is still the custom for a newly crowned king to spend a night here as part of his coronation.

Inner Palace

Behind a gateway to the left of the Chakri Throne Hall is the entrance to the Inner Palace, which is closed to the public. Until the time of Rama VII, the palace was inhabited solely by women of the royal family: principal wives, minor wives, and daughters. Apart from sons, who had to leave the palace on reaching puberty, the king was the only male allowed to live within its walls. The palace functioned as a small city, with

its own government and laws, complete with prison cells. Under the strict guidance of a formidable "Directress of the Inside," a small army of uniformed officers policed the area.

Rama III renovated the overcrowded and precarious wooden structures and, in the late 19th century, Rama V built small, fantastical Victorian style palaces here for his favorite consorts. Because his successor, Rama VI, had only one wife, the complex was left virtually empty, and it eventually fell into disrepair.

One of the palace buildings that continues to function is the finishing school for the daughters of high-society Thai families. The girls are taught flower weaving, royal cuisine, and social etiquette.

Siwalai Gardens

These beautiful gardens, which are sadly now closed to the public, lie east of the Inner Palace and contain the **Phra Buddha Ratana Sathan**, a personal chapel built by Rama IV. The pavilion is covered in gray marble and decorated with white and blue glass mosaics. The marble *bai sema* (boundary stones) are inlaid with the insignia of Rama V, who placed the stones here, Rama II, who had the gardens laid out, and Rama IV.

The Neo-Classical **Boromphiman Mansion** in the gardens was built by Rama V as a residence for the Crown Prince (later King Rama VI). The building served as a temporary residence for several kings: Rama VII, Rama VIII, and Rama IX (King Bhumibol). Today it is used as a guest house for visiting dignitaries.

Audience Chamber

Visible from outside the palace walls, this chamber – Phra Thinang Sutthaisawan Prasat – is located between Thewaphithak and Sakchaisit gates. It was built by Rama I as a place to grant an audience during royal ceremonies and to watch the training of his elephants. Rama III strengthened the wooden structure with brick, and decorative features were added later. These include the crowning spire and ornamental cast-iron motifs.

Mosaic-decorated Phra Buddha Ratana Sathan in the Siwalai Gardens

Entrance to the Buddhist University at Wat Mahathat

❷ Wat Mahathat

วัดมหาธาตุ

3 Maharaj Rd. **Map** 1 C4. **Tel** 0-2221-5999. AC: 203, 506. Chang Maharaj. **Open** daily.

This is a large, busy temple complex, interesting more for its atmosphere than for its architecture. Dating from the 1700s, the *wihan* and *bot* were both rebuilt between 1844 and 1851. The *mondop*, which gives the temple its name – "temple of the great relic" – has a cruciform roof, a feature rarely found in Bangkok.

The *wat* is the national center for the Mahanikai monastic sect, and it holds one of Bangkok's two Buddhist universities (meditation classes are offered here at 7am, 1pm, and 6pm in Section Five, near the monks' quarters). There is also a traditional herbal medicine market, and, on weekends, numerous stalls selling a wide range of goods.

❸ National Museum

พิพิธภัณฑสถานแห่งชาติ

See pp92–3.

❹ National Gallery

หอศิลป์แห่งชาติ

4 Chao Fa Rd. **Map** 2 D4. **Tel** 0-2281-2224. AC: 506. Phra Athit. **Open** 9am–4pm Wed–Sun. **Closed** public hols.

Thailand's main art gallery, housed in the old mint building, was established in 1977. It concentrates on modern Thai and international art. Initially the gallery suffered from lack of funds, but in 1989 further wings were added. The high-ceilinged, spacious halls now attract exhibitions from all over Asia. Temporary shows of prominent Asian artists are often better than many of the permanent exhibits. Modern art can also be found at the Bangkok Art and Culture Center *(see p122)*. Check the *Bangkok Post* for other exhibitions in the city.

Modern sculpture at the National Gallery

❺ Wat Bowonniwet

วัดบวรนิเวศน์

248 Phra Sumen Rd. **Map** 2 D4. **Tel** 0-2281-5052. 12, 15, 56; AC: 511 (Express). **Open** 8am–5pm daily.

Hidden in quiet, tree-filled grounds, this mid-19th-century temple was constructed by Rama III. The style bears his trademark Chinese influence. A central gilded *chedi* is flanked by two symmetrical chapels, the most interesting of which is next to Phra Sumen Road. The interior murals are attributed to monk-painter Khrua In Khong, who is famous for the introduction of Western perspective into Thai temple murals. As court painter to King Mongkut (Rama IV) he was exposed to Western ideas and adapted these to a Thai setting. The result was a series of murals that on first glance look wholly Western, but that portray the same Buddhist allegories found in traditional Thai murals. For instance, a physician healing a blind man can be interpreted as the illuminating power of Buddhism. The images are all the more remarkable for the fact that Khrua In Khong never traveled to the West. The main Buddha image, Phra Buddha Chinasara, is one of the best examples from the Sukhothai period.

King Mongkut served as abbot here during his 27 years in the monkhood and founded the strict Tammayut sect of Buddhism, for which the temple is now the headquarters. Since Mongkut, many Thai kings have served their monkhoods at the *wat*, including the current monarch, King Bhumibol (Rama IX). The temple also houses Thailand's second Buddhist university. Across the road from the temple is a Buddhist bookstore that sells English-language publications.

Mid-19th-century, Western-style mural at Wat Bowonniwet

❻ Democracy Monument

อนุสาวรีย์ประชาธิปไตย

Ratchadamnoen Klang. **Map** 2 E4.
🚌 AC: 503, 509, 511. **Open** daily.

A focal point during pro-democracy demonstrations, this monument (built 1939) commemorates the revolution of 1932 (see p72). Each feature symbolizes the date of the establishment of Thailand's constitutional monarchy, on June 24, 1932.

The four wing towers are each 79 ft (24 m) high. The 75 cannons indicate the year 2475 of the Buddhist Era (1932), and the pedestal, containing a copy of the constitution, is 10 ft (3 m) high, referring to the third month of the Thai calendar (June).

The structure was designed by Silpa Bhirasi, an Italian sculptor who took a Thai name and citizenship.

Central edifice of Democracy Monument (1939)

❼ Wat Rachanadda

วัดราชนัดดา

Maha Chai Rd. **Map** 2 E5.
🚌 2, 44, 59; AC: 79, 503, 511.
Open 9am–4pm daily.

The most interesting feature at Wat Rachanadda (also often spelled Ratchanaddaram) is the metal monastery. Originally conceived as a *chedi* to complement the temple, it evolved into an elaborate

One of hundreds of meditation cells at Wat Rachanadda

meditation chamber modeled on a 3rd-century BC Sri Lankan temple (the original is now ruined). Passages dissect each level, running north to south and east to west. The meditation cells are at each intersection.

In the temple's courtyard is Bangkok's best amulet market. Tourists may face disapproval if they attempt to take talismans home as souvenirs. Across the road, behind the old city walls, is the Doves' Village, where singing doves are sold for competitions.

❽ Wat Saket and the Golden Mount

วัดสระเกศและภูเขาทอง

Chakkaphatdi Phong Rd. **Map** 2 F5.
🚌 8, 15, 37, 47, 49; AC: 38, 543.
Open 7:30am–5:30pm daily. 🎫
🎫 Golden Mount Fair (Nov).

Built by Rama I in the late 18th century, Wat Saket is one of the oldest temples in Bangkok. Visitors come to climb the artificial hill topped with a golden tower within the grounds. Rama III built the first Golden Mount, but the soft soil led to its collapse. King Chulalongkorn (Rama V) provided the necessary technology to create the 250-ft (76-m) high representation of the mythical Mount Meru seen today. It is believed to house relics of the Buddha presented to Rama V by the Viceroy of India. A circular staircase lined

with strange monuments and tombs leads to the top, where there is a small sanctuary. The wonderful panoramic view from the gallery takes in the Grand Palace, Wat Pho, and Wat Arun. The octagonal building opposite, Mahakan Fort, is one of 14 original watchtowers of the city walls.

Until the 1960s the Golden Mount was one of the highest points in Bangkok. Today, it still forms a prominent landmark, although it is dwarfed by skyscrapers (see p123).

During the 19th century the grounds of Wat Saket served a macabre function as a crematorium. The bodies of the poor were sometimes left for vultures and dogs. By contrast, a fair with dancing and a candle procession is now held on the grounds in November.

The Golden Mount, a distinctive Bangkok landmark

❸ National Museum

พิพิธภัณฑสถานแห่งชาติ

The National Museum has one of the largest and most comprehensive collections in Southeast Asia and provides an excellent introduction to the arts, crafts, and history of Thailand. Two of the museum buildings, the 18th-century Wang Na Palace and Buddhaisawan Chapel, are works of art in themselves. The chapel contains the venerated Phra Buddha Sihing image, and an eclectic selection of artifacts from ancient weaponry to shadow puppets. The two wings of the museum are devoted mainly to art and sculpture. Other attractions include galleries of history and prehistory and the Royal Funeral Chariots Gallery. The labeling of the collection is not always helpful, so taking one of the frequent, free guided tours is highly recommended.

Doors of Throne Hall
These beautifully decorated black and gold lacquered doors to the Wang Na Palace date from the 19th century and show a strong Chinese influence.

Phra Buddha Sihing
The history of this image, one of Thailand's holiest after the Emerald Buddha, is shrouded in legend. It probably dates from the 13th century and was brought here from Chiang Mai by Rama I in 1787.

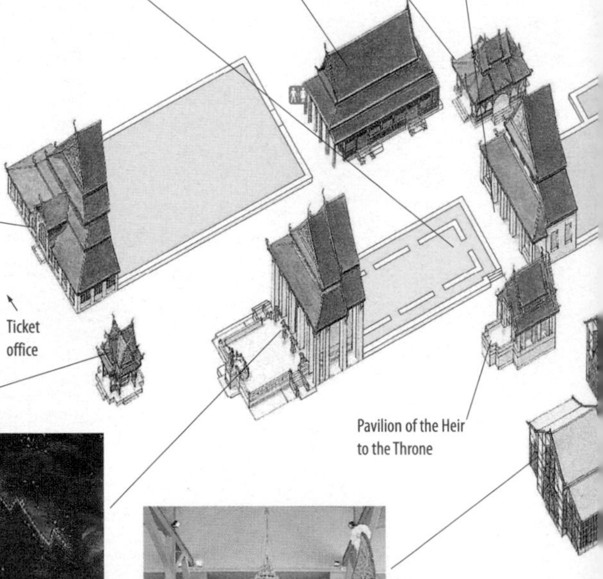

King Rama IV Pavilion

Red Pavilion

The Gallery of Thai History houses the 13th-century Ramkamhaeng Stone. This is thought to be inscribed with the earliest extant example of the Thai script.

Ticket office

King Vajiravudh Pavilion

Pavilion of the Heir to the Throne

★ Buddhaisawan Chapel
Built in 1787, this beautiful building is decorated with some of the best Rattanakosin period murals in Thailand.

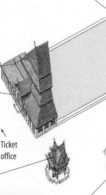

★ Royal Funeral Chariots Gallery
Several lavishly decorated, gilded teak chariots used in royal funeral processions can be seen in this gallery, including Racharot Noi, built in 1795.

For hotels and restaurants see pp402–11 and pp418–33

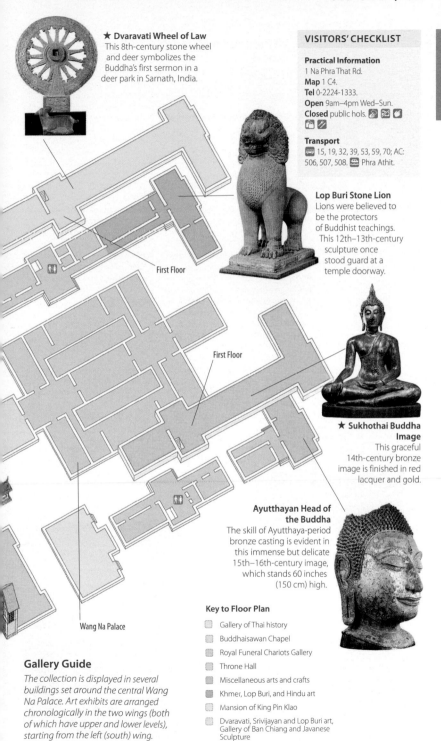

★ Dvaravati Wheel of Law
This 8th-century stone wheel and deer symbolizes the Buddha's first sermon in a deer park in Sarnath, India.

VISITORS' CHECKLIST

Practical Information
1 Na Phra That Rd.
Map 1 C4.
Tel 0-2224-1333.
Open 9am–4pm Wed–Sun.
Closed public hols.

Transport
15, 19, 32, 39, 53, 59, 70; AC: 506, 507, 508. Phra Athit.

First Floor

Lop Buri Stone Lion
Lions were believed to be the protectors of Buddhist teachings. This 12th–13th-century sculpture once stood guard at a temple doorway.

First Floor

★ Sukhothai Buddha Image
This graceful 14th-century bronze image is finished in red lacquer and gold.

Ayutthayan Head of the Buddha
The skill of Ayutthaya-period bronze casting is evident in this immense but delicate 15th–16th-century image, which stands 60 inches (150 cm) high.

Wang Na Palace

Key to Floor Plan

- Gallery of Thai history
- Buddhaisawan Chapel
- Royal Funeral Chariots Gallery
- Throne Hall
- Miscellaneous arts and crafts
- Khmer, Lop Buri, and Hindu art
- Mansion of King Pin Klao
- Dvaravati, Srivijayan and Lop Buri art, Gallery of Ban Chiang and Javanese Sculpture
- Lanna, Sukhothai, Ayutthayan, and Rattanakosin art

Gallery Guide

The collection is displayed in several buildings set around the central Wang Na Palace. Art exhibits are arranged chronologically in the two wings (both of which have upper and lower levels), starting from the left (south) wing. The ticket office, near the entrance on Na Phra That Road, sells guidebooks.

Monk's bowl being heated to blacken and finish the surface

❾ Monk's Bowl Village (Ban Bat)

บ้านบาตร

Bamrung Muang Rd, Soi Ban Bat. **Map** 2 F5. 🚌 AC: 508.

Monks' bowls were first used 2,500 years ago and are still widely used today in Buddhist countries for early morning alms-gathering *(see p133)*. Such bowls have been made at Monk's Bowl Village in Bangkok since the late 18th century. The village once stretched as far as Wat Saket *(see p91)*, but modern developments have reduced the village to just three homes and a cluster of small workshops. This area may be hard to find amid the maze of *sois*, but the bowls are sold at Wat Suthat.

The process of bowl making is time consuming and requires eight pieces of metal, representing the eight spokes of the wheel of Dharma. The first strip is beaten into a circular form to make the rim. Three pieces are then beaten to create a cross-shaped skeleton. Four triangular pieces complete the sides. After being welded in a kiln, the bowl is shaped, filed smooth, and fired again to give an enamel-like surface. About 20 bowls are produced daily in the village.

At the center of the maze of alleyways next to the small village hall is an unusual and intriguing shrine, constructed from old Chinese cylinder bellows, that is dedicated to the "Holy Teacher and Ancestor."

❿ Bamrung Muang Road

ถนนบำรุงเมือง

Map 2 F5. 🚌 AC: 508.

Bamrung Muang, like Charoen Krung *(see pp118–19)*, was an elephant trail until the 20th century, when it became one of Thailand's first paved roads. The stretch between Maha Chai Road and the Giant Swing provides an enlightening peek into the thriving business behind the Buddhist practice of merit-making. Along here the road is lined with shops selling religious paraphernalia: monks' robes, votive candles, and Buddha images of all shapes and sizes, many rather incongruously packaged in cellophane. Monks shop here for temple essentials; other people buy offerings and shrines for the home. Although the religious objects look enticing to tourists, they are not intended as souvenirs: images of the Buddha cannot be taken out of the country without an export license *(see p459)*.

⓫ Wat Suthat and the Giant Swing

วัดสุทัศน์และเสาชิงช้า

Bamrung Muang Rd. **Map** 2 E5. 🚌 10, 12, 19, 35, 42, 56, 96. **Open** 8:30am– 4pm daily *(wihan* Sat & Sun only).

There are several superlatives for Wat Suthat, a temple that was begun by Rama I in 1807 and completed by Rama III. Its *wihan* is the largest in Bangkok. The art and architecture beautifully exemplify Rattanakosin style *(see p39)*. Its central Buddha, at 26 ft (8 m) high, is one of the largest surviving Sukhothai bronzes. This image was moved from Wat Mahathat in Sukhothai *(see pp62–3)* to Bangkok by Rama I.

The murals in the immense *wihan* are some of the most celebrated in Thailand. Amazingly intricate, they depict the Traiphum (Buddhist cosmology) and were restored in the 1980s. The teak doors to the *wihan* are carved in five delicate layers and stand 18 ft (5.5 m) high. (One made by Rama II is now in the National Museum.) The cloister around the outside of the *wihan* is lined with 156 golden Buddha images.

The square in front of Wat Suthat used to feature the Giant Swing, the remains of a swing used for a Brahmin ceremony. After standing for 224 years, this was moved in 2007 to Devasathan Brahmin temple and replaced by a new swing made from six 100-year-old teak trees.

⓬ Wat Rachabophit

วัดราชบพิตร

Fuang Nakhon Rd. **Map** 2 D5. **Tel** 0-2222-3930. 🚌 2, 60; AC: 501, 502, 512. 🚢 Tien. **Open** 8am–5pm daily.

The circular form of Wat Rachabophit is a successful architectural blend of East and West. Construction of the temple began under King Chulalongkorn (Rama V) in 1869 and continued for over 20 years. The whole complex is splendidly decorated with porcelain tiles, which were

View through the immense portal of the *wihan* at Wat Suthat

made in China. The focal point is the central, Sri Lankan-style, gilded *chedi,* whose full height from the terrace is 140 ft (43 m).

Inside the *wat* are four Buddha images, each facing one of the cardinal points. Leading off from the circular gallery are the *bot* to the north, the *wihan* to the south, and two lesser *wihans* to the east and west: an unusual layout for a Thai *wat.*

East-West flourishes permeate the complex. The 10 door panels and 28 window panels of the *bot* are decorated with mother-of-pearl inlay that illustrates the insignia of five royal orders. The moldings over the door depict King Chulalongkorn's seal. The carved, painted guards on the doors are distinctively *farang* (European), and the interior is decorated in an incongruous Italian Renaissance style.

Accessible through the temple grounds (parallel to Khlong Lot) is a fascinating royal cemetery rarely explored by visitors. The monuments to members of King Chulalongkorn's family are an eccentric mix of Khmer, Thai, and European styles.

Rows of tiny carved figures on eaves of the *bot* at Wat Rachapradit

⑬ Wat Rachapradit
วัดราชประดิษฐ์

Saran Rom Rd. **Map** 2 D5.
Tel 0-2223-8215. AC: 501, 502, 512. Tien.
Open 8am–6pm daily.

Located in the northeast corner of the former Saranrom Palace gardens (now the Ministry of Foreign Affairs), this charming, peaceful temple is rarely visited by tourists. It was built in the mid-19th century by King Mongkut (Rama IV) and his East-meets-West taste in architecture is apparent in the choice of building materials. The main *wihan,* for instance, is covered in forbidding gray marble. The interior murals were painted in the late 19th century and depict the festivals of the Thai lunar calendar. Among other scenes are some extravagant preparations for the Giant Swing ceremony, people celebrating the annual Loy Krathong water festival, and an image of King Mongkut observing an eclipse of the moon *(see p69).* Striking carvings adorn the doors, eaves, and gables of the temple. Other notable edifices in the grounds of the *wat* include graceful pavilions, Khmer-style *prangs,* and a gray marble *chedi.* Near to Wat Rachapradit,

Farang, Wat Rachabophit

next to Khlong Lot, is a small gilded boar, a shrine to Queen Saowapha Phongsi (King Chulalongkorn's consort), who was born in the year of the pig.

⑭ Wat Pho
วัดโพธิ์

See pp96–7.

⑮ Museum of Siam
พิพิธภัณฑ์สยาม

Sanam Chai Rd. **Map** 5 C1. **Tel** 0-2225-2777. 12, 47; AC: 3, 82. Thien.
Open 10am–6pm Tue–Sun & public holidays. **Closed** Songkran Holiday, New Year's Eve, New Year's Day.
🖥 📷 **W museumsiam.org**

The Museum of Siam is housed in the former Ministry of Commerce – a handsome Italianate building that was designed by Mario Tamagno. The project was finished in 1922 and was converted into its present incarnation in 2007. A Milanese architect, Tamagno was also the designer of many other important Bangkok landmarks, including the Ananta Samakhom Throne Hall *(see p111).*

The Museum of Siam is spread over three floors and features excellent permanent interactive exhibits that explore what it means to be Thai through ancient and contemporary history. Buddhism, village life, and politics and communication are some of the themes that are examined.

The Swing in Action

Sao Ching Cha, the "Giant Swing" at Wat Suthat, was built in 1784 by Rama I. During ceremonies – Brahmin in origin – teams of four would swing in 180-degree arcs up to 82 ft (25 m) high. One participant would try to bite off a sack of gold hung from tall poles. The event, linked to the god Shiva swinging in the heavens, caused many deaths and was abolished in 1935.

Young Brahmins performing on Sao Ching Cha

⑭ Wat Pho

วัดโพธิ์

Officially known as Wat Phra Chetuphon, Wat Pho is not only Bangkok's oldest and largest temple but also Thailand's foremost center for public education. Unlike the Grand Palace *(see pp84–9)*, it has a lively and lived-in dilapidated grandeur. In the 1780s Rama I rebuilt the original 16th-century temple on this site and enlarged the complex. In 1832 Rama III built the Chapel of the Reclining Buddha, housing the stunning image, and turned the temple into a place of learning. Today Wat Pho is a traditional medicine center, of which the famous Institute of Massage is a part. Nearby on Chetuphon Road is the temple monastery, home to some 300 monks.

Wihan
The western *wihan* is one of four around the main *bot*.

★ **Medicine Pavilion**
Embedded in the inner walls of this pavilion are stone plaques showing massage points. The pavilion is now a souvenir shop.

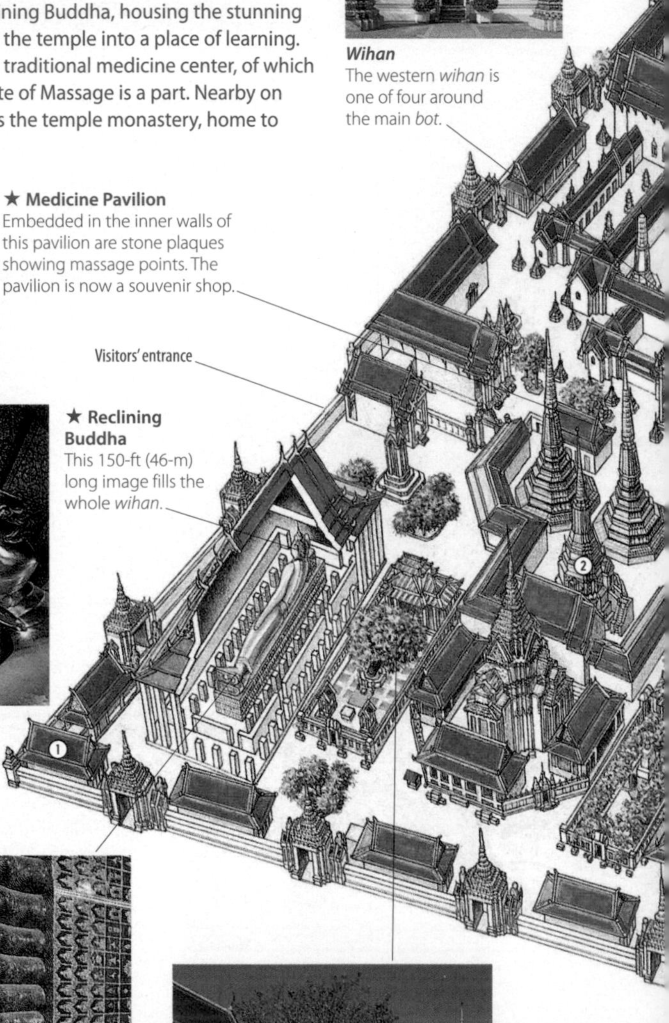

Visitors' entrance

★ **Reclining Buddha**
This 150-ft (46-m) long image fills the whole *wihan*.

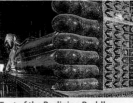

Feet of the Reclining Buddha
The striking, intricate mother-of-pearl images on the soles of the feet of the gilded plaster and brick Reclining Buddha represent the 108 *lakshanas*, which are the auspicious signs of the true Buddha.

Bodhi Tree
It is said that this grew from a cutting of the tree under which the Buddha meditated in India.

Ceramic Decoration
This porcelain design is on the Phra Si Sanphet Chedi.

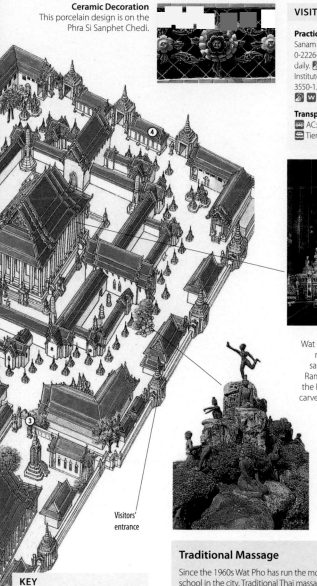

VISITORS' CHECKLIST

Practical Information
Sanam Chai Rd. **Map** 5 C1. **Tel**
0-2226-0335. **Open** 9am–5pm
daily. 🏛 📷 🅦 watpho.com
Institute of Massage: **Tel** 0-2622-
3550-1. **Open** 8:30am–6pm daily.
📷 🅦 watpomassage.com

Transport
🚌 AC: 25, 32, 44, 60, 508.
🚤 Tien, Chang, Rachinee.

Main *Bot*
Wat Pho's *bot* houses a bronze meditating Buddha image salvaged from Ayutthaya by Rama I's brother. Scenes from the Ramakien (see pp44–5) are carved into the outer base and inner doors.

Miniature Mountains
This tiny stone mountain by the southern *wihan* is one of several within the complex. The statues of naked hermits are posed in the different positions of healing massage.

Visitors'
entrance

KEY

① **Small buildings** at this end of the *wat* are reserved for children.

② **The Phra Si Sanphet Chedi** encases the remains of a sacred Buddha image.

③ ***Farang*** guards stand at the compound's inner gates. These huge stone statues with big noses, beards, and top hats are caricatures of Westerners.

④ **Institute of Massage**

Traditional Massage

Since the 1960s Wat Pho has run the most respected massage school in the city. Traditional Thai massage (nuat paen boran) supposedly dates from the time of the Buddha and is related to Chinese acupuncture and Indian yoga. The highly trained masseurs at the *wat* specialize in pulling and stretching the limbs and torso to relieve various ailments ranging from general tension to viruses. Visitors can experience a massage or learn the art through a 10- or 15-day course in Thai or English.

Braving a traditional Thai massage
at Wat Pho

CHINATOWN

Bangkok's Chinese residents originally lived in the area where the Old City is today. When Rama I decided to move his capital across the river in 1782, the entire community was relocated. Since then the district around Yaowarat and Sampeng roads has been the focus of Chinese life in the city, although now it is also home to a small Indian community. Once the financial center of Bangkok, Chinatown remains a thriving, bustling, noisy area. Between the two great traffic-choked thoroughfares of Yaowarat Road and Charoen Krung Road lies a maze of narrow alleyways packed with market stalls. The most accessible are the wholesale fabric market of Sampeng Lane and the diverse offerings of the vendors along Soi Isara Nuphap. Other major markets in Chinatown include Pak Khlong, Nakorn Kasem, and Phahurat. Near to Hua Lamphong Station is Wat Traimit with its splendid interior and huge gold Buddha image.

The area is peppered with Chinese shrines, many of which combine elements of Confucianism, Taoism, Mahayana Buddhism, and animism. Old Chinese noodle shops patronized by mahjong-playing, undershirt-clad men make interesting snack spots.

Sights at a Glance

Wats

❹ Wat Traimit

Markets

❶ Pak Khlong Market
❷ Phahurat Market
❸ Nakorn Kasem

Historic Buildings

❺ Hua Lamphong Station

0 meters   500
0 yards   500

See also Street Finder pp148–59

◀ Ornate temple decoration, Chinatown

For keys to symbols *see back flap*

Street-by-Street: Central Chinatown

เยาวราช

This area is Chinatown at its most atmospheric, with its vibrant colors, pungent smells, overwhelming cacophony, and frenetic bustle. A cross-section of the district can be experienced by walking up Soi Isara Nuphap from Ratchawong pier. After Songwat Road, with its old wooden buildings, the street is lined with wholesale spice shops. Past the fabric market of Sampeng Lane, the sidewalk is crowded with fresh and preserved foods. Once over Yaowarat Road, with its countless gold shops and Chinese herbal medicine stores, snack stalls predominate before giving way, after crossing traffic-choked Charoen Krung Road, to sellers of Chinese religious paraphernalia.

Kao Market
Fresh produce, such as mushrooms, is sold at Kao ("old") Market, which has been here since the late 18th century.

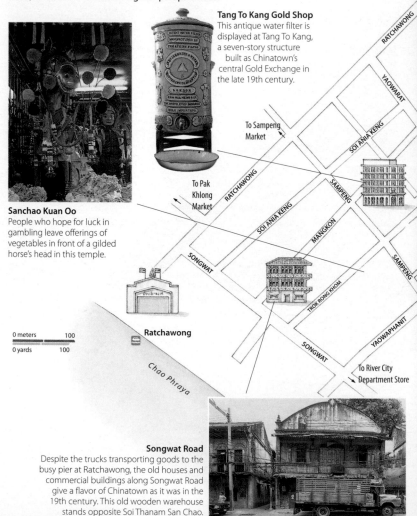

Tang To Kang Gold Shop
This antique water filter is displayed at Tang To Kang, a seven-story structure built as Chinatown's central Gold Exchange in the late 19th century.

To Sampeng Market

To Pak Khlong Market

Sanchao Kuan Oo
People who hope for luck in gambling leave offerings of vegetables in front of a gilded horse's head in this temple.

RATCHAWONG

YAOWARAT

SOI ANIA KENG

RATCHAWONG

SOI ANIA KENG

SAMPENG

MANGKON

SAMPENG

SONGWAT

TROK RONG KHOM

YAOWAPHANIT

YAOWAPHANIT

0 meters 100
0 yards 100

Ratchawong

SONGWAT

To River City Department Store

Chao Phraya

Songwat Road
Despite the trucks transporting goods to the busy pier at Ratchawong, the old houses and commercial buildings along Songwat Road give a flavor of Chinatown as it was in the 19th century. This old wooden warehouse stands opposite Soi Thanam San Chao.

For hotels and restaurants see pp402–11 and pp418–33

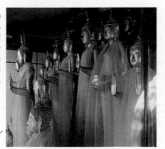

★ Leng Noi Yee
This Buddhist shrine combines elements of Confucianism and Taoism, attracting a wide range of devotees. The main chamber contains several gilded Buddha images.

DUSIT
OLD CITY
CHINATOWN
THON BURI
DOWNTOWN

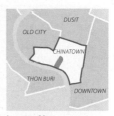

Locator Map
See Street Finder map 6

CHAROEN KRUNG
SOI CHAROEN KRUNG 10
PHLAB PHLA CHAI
SOI ISARA NUPHAP
PLEANG NAM
CHAROEN KRUNG
YAOWARAT
To Hua Lamphong Station
To Wat Traimit

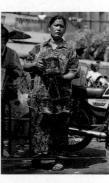

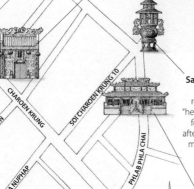

Sanchao Dtai Hong Kong
At this popular temple relatives of the dead burn "hell's banknotes" to provide for their loved ones in the afterlife *(see p103)*. Devotees make merit by buying and freeing caged birds.

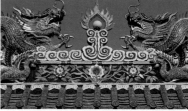

Li Thi Miew
This atmospheric temple within a courtyard is topped by fierce dragons. Inside, incense smoke swirls around statues of Taoist deities.

This picturesque sausage shop is said to date from the 19th century.

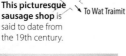

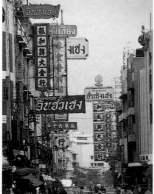

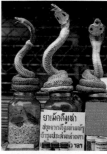

Mai Market
Mai ("new") Market can't boast the pedigree of Kao Market, but it is still a good source of everyday and unusual items like snake parts for Chinese medicine.

★ Yaowarat Road
One of Chinatown's main traffic arteries, this bustling road is packed with gold shops, herbal sellers, cafés, and restaurants.

For keys to symbols *see back flap*

Vendor selling a wide range of chilies, Pak Khlong Market

❶ Pak Khlong Market

ตลาดปากคลอง

Maharaj Rd. **Map** 5 C1. 🚌 AC: 501, 512. 🚤 Rachinee, Pak Khlong. **Open** daily.

Open 24 hours a day, Pak Khlong Market provides the city with fresh flowers and vegetables. Known for offering the best array of flowers in Thailand, it is a one-stop florist's dream. Deliveries arrive from 1am and by dawn the display has roses, orchids, lotus, jasmine, and Dutch tulips. The widest variety of blooms can be seen at 9am. Visitors can buy bouquets or floral basket arrangements.

❷ Phahurat Market

ตลาดพาหุรัด

Phahurat Rd. **Map** 6 D1. 🚌 6, 37, 82, 88; AC: 3, 82.

This predominantly Indian market offers all the tastes, sights, and smells of Bombay. The main bazaar, which spills out around Phahurat and Chak Phet roads, specializes in fabrics. Downstairs, cloth merchants sell anything from tablecloths to wedding saris. The dimly lit upstairs section is devoted to traditional Indian accessories such as sandals and ornate jewelry. In the surrounding streets are many delicious "hole-in-the-wall" Indian restaurants

and samosa stalls. Off Chakphet Road is Siri Guru Singh Sabha, a traditional Sikh temple.

❸ Nakorn Kasem

นครเกษม

Charoen Krung Rd. **Map** 6 E1. 🚌 AC: 501, 507.

Popularly known as Thieves' Market because stolen goods were allegedly once sold here, Nakorn Kasem has discarded its illicit past and now has a miscellaneous collection of shops selling metal wares, musical instruments, and a wide range of ornaments.

Nearby is Saphan Han Market, a covered market along both sides of Khlong Ong Ang. Its specialty is electrical goods. The area is filled with smells wafting from nearby noodle stalls.

❹ Wat Traimit

วัดไตรมิตร

Tri Mit Rd. **Map** 6 F2. 🚌 1, 4, 11, 25, 53, 73; AC: 501, 507. **Open** 9am–5pm daily.

Also called the Temple of the Golden Buddha, Wat Traimit houses the world's largest solid gold Buddha. The gleaming 13-ft (4-m) high 13th-century Sukho-thai image is made of 18-carat gold and weighs five tons.

The Buddha was discovered by accident in 1955. While

extending the port of Bangkok, workers for the East Asiatic Company unearthed what appeared to be a plain stucco Buddha. The image was kept at Wat Traimit under a makeshift shelter for 20 years, until a crane dropped it while moving it to a more permanent shelter. The plaster cracked, revealing the gold Buddha beneath.

The statue had likely been encased in stucco to hide it from Burmese ransackers – a common practice during the Ayutthaya period *(see pp64–5)*.

Local Chinese residents come here to worship the Golden Buddha and to make merit by rubbing gold leaf on the temple's smaller Buddha images.

Wat Traimit, which houses the revered Golden Buddha image

❺ Hua Lampong Station

สถานีหัวลำโพง

Rama IV Rd. **Map** 7 A2. **Tel** 1690. Ⓜ Hua Lampong. 🚌 4, 21, 25, 29, 34, 40, 48, 109; AC: 501, 507, 529. 🌐 railway.co.th

King Chulalongkorn (Rama V), a great champion of modern-ization, was the instigator of rail travel in Thailand. The first railroad line, begun in 1891, was a private line from Paknam to Hua Lampong. Today, the historic station is Bangkok's main rail junction. From here, trains leave for the North, Northeast, the Central Plains, and the South. The city's other station, Bangkok Noi, serves only the South.

The Chinese in Thailand

The first Chinese immigrants arrived in Thailand as merchants in the 12th century. During the late 18th and early 19th centuries, following years of war in Thailand (*see pp68–9*), Chinese immigration was encouraged in order to help rebuild the economy. The subsequent integration of the Chinese into Thai society was so successful that by the mid-19th century half of Bangkok's population was of pure or mixed Chinese blood. There have been periods of anti-Chinese feeling and immigration restrictions, but the Chinese still dominate Thailand's commercial sector. Chinese traditions and beliefs remain strong in their communities.

Leng Noi Yee Temple in Bangkok is an important Mahayana Buddhist shrine that also incorporates elements of Taoism and Confucianism. The temple, with its glazed ceramic gables topped by Chinese dragons, is the focal point of the annual Vegetarian Festival (*see p51*).

"Hell's banknotes" are a form of *kong tek* – paper replicas of real objects, burned to provide for the dead during their next life.

Intricate Chinese designs feature on many utensils, such as these pan covers.

Fresh vegetables are essential to many Chinese dishes.

Chinese Shop-Houses

Shop-houses are a common feature of Chinatown. The family lives on the first floor while the ground floor is devoted to the family business, whether it is a small workshop or a store selling, for example, food or household goods.

Chinese opera, performed by traveling troupes, features a dramatic mixture of martial arts, acrobatics, singing, and dance.

Dim sum, literally "touch the heart," can be sampled in many of the area's Chinese restaurants. The bite-size snacks include shrimp toast and pork dumplings.

Sign painting is not just a decorative art form. These good luck messages, written in gold, are said to ward off evil and sickness. They are displayed in great numbers during the Chinese New Year.

DUSIT

Dusit is the center of Thai officialdom and an oasis of relative calm in a chaotic city. Tree-lined avenues, *khlongs*, old buildings, and the low skyline have all been preserved here. King Chulalongkorn laid out the district along European lines, with grand vistas, broad boulevards, and a geometric road grid surrounding his palaces. A century later it is still the royal quarter. Ratchadamnoen Avenue ("royal way") leads up to Vimanmek Mansion and the royal museums in Dusit

Park. Nearby is the royal "marble" temple of Wat Benchamabophit and Chitrlada Palace, the king and queen's residence. Political power is also concentrated in Dusit. The National Assembly, Government House, several ministries, and the Prime Minister's house are located here. By contrast, horse racing at the Royal Turf Club, *muay thai* boxing at Ratchadamnoen Stadium, and animal encounters at the landscaped Dusit Zoo provide popular public entertainment.

Sights at a Glance

Wats and Churches
2 Dusit's Christian Churches
4 Wat Indrawihan
10 Wat Benchamabophit

Museums
5 Vimanmek Mansion
6 SUPPORT Museum

Notable Roads
9 Phitsanulok Road
11 Ratchadamnoen Avenue

Landmark Buildings
8 Chitrlada Palace

Markets
3 Thewet Flower Market

Parks and Zoos
1 *Dusit Park pp106–7*
7 Dusit Zoo

See also Street Finder
pp148–59

◀ Vimanmek Mansion, Dusit

For keys to symbols *see back flap*

❶ Dusit Park

แผนผังสวนดุสิต

This magnificent park is the major attraction of the Dusit area. King Chulalongkorn (ruled 1868–1910), the first Thai sovereign to visit Europe, was determined to Westernize Bangkok, and the manicured gardens, genteel architecture, and teak mansions in Dusit Park all bear testimony to his efforts. Highlights include Vimanmek Mansion – the world's largest golden teak building – and the graceful Abhisek Dusit Throne Hall, which houses the SUPPORT Museum of traditional arts and crafts. A visit to the park and the neighboring zoo *(see p109)* can easily occupy a whole day.

Locator Map
See Street Finder maps 2, 3

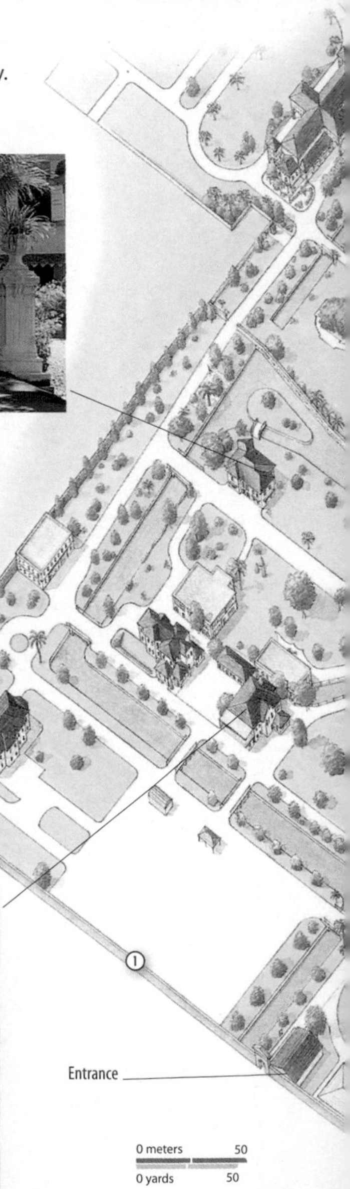

King Bhumibol's Photographic Museums
Most of the photographs in these museums were taken by King Bhumibol, an avid photographer. The royal family features in many.

Royal Paraphernalia Museum
Photographs and paintings of regal figures from the Chakri dynasty, such as this portrait of Maha Uparaja Bovornvijaya Jarn, the deputy king to King Rama V, can be seen in this museum.

Antique Textile Exhibition Hall
This small collection includes a range of fabrics favored by the court of King Rama V, such as satin. There are also displays of the different types of Thai silk from all over Thailand.

KEY

① Perimeter wall
② Canal
③ Bridge

Entrance

0 meters   50
0 yards   50

★ **Abhisek Dusit Throne Hall**
This hall *(see p109)* is a fancifully ornamented white edifice. The major attraction inside is the SUPPORT Museum, with its collection of traditional, crafted artifacts, such as works using the exquisitely colored wings of jewel beetles.

VISITORS' CHECKLIST

Practical Information
Map 2 F1. 📞 0-2628-6300-9, ext 0#. Vimanmek Mansion: **Open** 9:30am–3:15pm daily (tickets sold till 3pm). 📷 compulsory. SUPPORT Museum: **Open** 9:30am–3:15pm daily. All other buildings: **Open** 9am–4pm daily. **Closed** for royal ceremonies. 🎫 Royal Mansion ticket (valid 30 days) inc adm to Dusit Park and all buildings. 📷 in buildings. 🌐 **palaces.thai.net**

Transport
🚌 56, 70; AC: 70, 510, 515.

Lakeside Pavilion
An elegant pavilion behind Vimanmek Palace affords a pleasant view across the lake to some particularly fine traditional Thai teak houses. The farther bank is, however, closed to visitors.

★ **Vimanmek Mansion**
More like a Victorian mansion than a Thai palace, this three-storied, golden teak structure *(see pp108–9)* was built using wooden pegs instead of nails. The palace is full of intriguing artifacts.

Old Clock Museum
This museum houses the collection of clocks acquired by Kings Rama V and Rama IX on their trips to Europe. It includes timepieces of European, American, and Japanese origin.

❷ Dusit's Christian Churches

โบสถ์ดุสิตคริสเตียน

Map 2 E1. 🚌 3, 9, 30, 53; AC: 506; MB: 8, 10.

By the bank of the Chao Phraya River, just south of Ratchawithi Road, is a small group of Christian churches.

The first of these, **St. Francis Xavier Church**, is near Krung Thon Bridge. Built in the early 1850s, it is notable for the statue of the saint atop its triple-arched portico frontage. Among its congregation are members of the local Vietnamese Catholic community, who settled here in 1934.

Just south is the smaller **Church of the Immaculate Conception**. It was originally constructed in 1674, during King Narai's reign (see pp64–5), by Father Louis Laneau for the early Portuguese community. It was then rebuilt in 1847 by French missionaries, and within its grounds is a smaller church known as Wat Noi. Some Cambodian refugees settled here in the late 17th century and still live in the parish. They take part in religious festivals here, hence the church's nickname, the Cambodian Church.

Wat Noi houses the **Wat Mae Phrae Museum** (no set opening times), which contains a statue of the Virgin Mary. The statue is venerated in an annual ceremony held each October.

Porticoed entrance of St. Francis Xavier Church

Modern mural of a reclining Buddha, Wat Indrawihan

❸ Thewet Flower Market

ตลาดดอกไม้เทเวศน์

Krung Kasem Rd. **Map** 2 E2. 🚌 AC: 506. National Library: Samsen Rd. **Open** 9:30am–7:30pm daily.

One of Bangkok's premier plant and garden markets flanks both sides of Khlong Phadung Krung Kasem, west of Samsen Road. It stocks a huge range of goods, including ornamental garden pots, orchids, trees, and pond bases. Although Thewet Flower Market is not as vast as Chatuchak Market (see p139), its prices are generally lower. It is a pleasant place to browse, even if you buy nothing.

Ornamental garden pots at Thewet Flower Market

Around the corner is the **National Library**, which contains a large collection of books in Thai and English. A number of Thai paintings hang in the lobby. The exterior incorporates several traditional Thai architectural touches (see pp38–9), as do many government offices in the area.

❹ Wat Indrawihan

วัดอินทรวิหาร

Wisut Kasat Rd. **Map** 2 E3. 🚌 3, 53; AC: 506. **Open** daily.

You cannot miss the reason for Wat Indrawihan's fame: an impressive 105-ft (32-m) standing Buddha. The statue was commissioned in the mid-19th century by King Mongkut (Rama IV) to enshrine a relic of the Buddha from Sri Lanka. (Relics such as fragments of bone and hair are housed in countless Buddhist monuments worldwide.)

While admittedly not the most beautiful of Buddha images because of its rather flattened features, it stands out attractively against the sky. Its enormous toes make a bizarre altar for the many offerings presented, including garlands of flowers.

Inside the bot of Wat In (a popular abbreviation for the temple) are hundreds of Bencharong (five-color) funerary urns. Traditional-style, modern murals can also be seen inside the bot. In another, smaller building, "lucky" water is sold in plastic bags.

❺ Vimanmek Mansion

พระที่นั่งวิมานเมฆ

Ratchawithi Rd. **Map** 2 F1. **Tel** 0-2628-6300-9 (ext 0#). 🚌 56, 70; AC: 70, 510, 515. **Open** 9:30am–3:15pm daily. **Closed** 1–6 Jan. 🎟 (free for Grand Palace ticket holders). 📷 inside. 🎥 compulsory. 🌐 palaces.thai.net

Constructed entirely without nails, the world's largest golden teak building was reassembled on this site in 1901, after being moved from its original location on Ko Sichang (see pp320–21).

It soon became a favored retreat of King Chulalongkorn (Rama V) and his family and concubines while they were waiting for nearby Chitrlada Palace *(see p110)* to be completed. Apart from the king, the mansion was for women only. After closing in 1935 and falling into disrepair, this "celestial residence" was magnificently restored in 1982 at the request of Queen Sirikit for Bangkok's bicentennial celebrations *(see pp72–3)*.

The guided tour takes in 30 of the 81 rooms via circuitous corridors. Highlights include the audience chambers, the music room, sweeping staircases, and the king's apartments, which are contained within an octagonal tower. The palace was the first building in Thailand to have electricity and an indoor bathroom; an early light bulb and a showerhead are two of the items on display.

Treasures from the Rattanakosin era include porcelain, furniture, betel-nut sets, the first Thai alphabet typewriter, hunting trophies, and royal photographs. King Chulalongkorn was known for his taste in Western-style design, and the palace, with its verandas and high ceilings, is reminiscent of a Victorian mansion.

Although the tour allows little time inside, visitors can walk around outside or sit in a lakeside porch, where Thai dancing *(see pp46–7)* and disquieting monkey acrobatics are staged twice daily.

Domed ceiling of the Ananta Samakhom Throne Hall

❻ SUPPORT Museum

พิพิธภัณฑ์ศิลปาชีพ

Ratchawithi Rd. **Map** 2 F1.
Tel 0-2628-6300. 🚌 AC: 510, 515.
Open 9:30am–3:15pm daily. 📷

Housed in the Abhisek Dusit Throne Hall beside Vimanmek Palace (and included on the same ticket), the SUPPORT Museum is a showcase for traditional crafts that have been saved from decline by Queen Sirikit, founder of the Promotion of Supplementary Occupations and Related Techniques (SUPPORT). One such craft is *yan lipao* weaving, which originated in Nakhon Si Thammarat *(see pp382–3)*. The fine reed used in *yan lipao* lends itself to intricate patterns, its sheen giving the end product a luster.

Crafts on display include nielloware, rattan, bamboo, celadon, lacquerware, and an art form that uses the iridescent green-blue wings of jewel beetles. Some of the designs were created by members of the royal family. One of the training centers for SUPPORT is at the Bang Sai Folk Arts and Crafts Center near Bang Pa-in *(see p185)*. South Abhisek Dusit is another throne hall, **Ananta Samakorn**. Dating from 1912,

this ornate, Italianate building once housed the parliament. Today it is used for royal receptions and private functions. Its spectacular interior is open to the public only on Children's Day, the second Saturday in January.

❼ Dusit Zoo

สวนสัตว์ดุสิต (เขาดิน)

Rama V & Ratchawithi rds. **Map** 3 A2.
Tel 0-2281-2000. 🚌 AC: 510, 515.
Open 8am–6pm daily. 📷
🌐 zoothailand.org

Forming a green wedge between Dusit Park and Chitrlada Palace are the lush gardens of Dusit Zoo. One of Asia's better zoos, it has reasonable space for birds and large mammals such as tigers, bears, elephants, and hippos, although some of the other enclosures are much more confining. There is a Reptile House and a recreation of an African Savanna. The grounds were originally the private botanical gardens of Rama V, and some varieties of tropical flora are still cultivated here. The lawns, lakes, and wooded glades are ideal for relaxing strolls and watching Thai families enjoying a day out.

Vimanmek Mansion, the summer residence of Rama V

Black bear in Dusit Zoo

❽ Chitrlada Palace

พระตำหนักจิตรลดา

Ratchawithi & Rama V rds. **Map** 3 B2.
🚌 18, 28; AC: 510. **Closed** to public.

The permanent residence of the king and queen is an early 20th-century palace set in extensive grounds (closed to the public), east of Dusit Zoo. Although the palace is hidden from view, the buildings used by King Bhumibol (Rama IX) for agricultural and industrial experiments are visible. In 1993 he became the first monarch in the world to earn a patent – for a waste water aerator.

The grounds also contain the Chitrlada School, for children of the royal family.

The perimeter of the palace is illuminated from the King's Birthday (Dec 5) to New Year.

A portrait of King Bhumibol

❾ Phitsanulok Road

ถนนพิษณุโลก

Map 2 E2. 🚌 16, 23, 201, 505.

A number of important state institutions are located along this major avenue, which cuts through the heart of Dusit. Traveling northwest past the Mission Hospital at the Sawankhalok Road end, the first of interest is **Ban Phitsanulok**. This mansion has been the official residence of the prime minister since it was restored in 1982. It was originally built in 1925 by Rama VI for Major General Phraya Aniruttheva. Designed by the same Italian architects who built the Ananta Samakorn Throne Hall *(see p109)*, it is a riot of Venetian Gothic, with floral-shaped mullioned windows, spindly crenellations, and a sweeping curved wing. It is not open to the public, and guests rarely stay overnight, because the mansion is supposedly haunted. On the opposite side of the road is the grassy oval of the **Royal Turf Club**, one of Bangkok's two major horse-racing tracks *(see p121)*. Races alternate between the two tracks, and are held here from 12:30pm to 6:30pm every other Sunday. The stands fill with bettors from all levels of Thai society. Experiencing the banter and furious betting can often be as much fun as watching the race itself. The most prominent annual event that takes place here is the King's Cup, also known as the Derby Cup, on

Filling in the results at the end of a race at the Royal Turf Club

the first or second weekend of January.

Government House, to the west, just past the Nakhon Pathom Road turning, is a fanciful, cream-colored Neo-Venetian style building. It is now used to house the prime minister's office, and it is closed to the public.

❿ Wat Benchama-bophit

วัดเบญจมบพิตร

69 Rama V Rd. **Map** 3 A3.
Tel 0-2281-2501. 🚌 3, 16, 23, 505.
Open 8:30am–5:30pm daily.

European influence on Thai architecture *(see pp38–9)* is exemplified by Wat Benchamabophit, the last major temple to be built in central Bangkok. In 1899 King Chulalongkorn (Rama V) commissioned his brother Prince

Royal White Elephants

The importance of the white elephant *(chang samkhan)* in Thailand derives from a 2,500-year-old tale. Queen Maya, once barren, became pregnant with the future Buddha after dreaming of a white elephant entering her womb. Ever since the 13th century, when King Ramkamhaeng gave the

Old manuscript depicting a white elephant

animal great prestige, the reigning monarch's importance has been judged in part according to the number of white elephants he owns. Indeed, the white elephant's status as a national icon was symbolized by its presence on the Siamese flag until 1917. The origin of the phrase "white elephant," meaning a large, useless investment, lies in the Thai tradition according to which all white elephants must belong to the king. They cannot be used for work and, therefore, have to be cared for at huge expense. Though referred to as white, the elephants are not fully albino. But tradition states that seven parts of their body – the eyes, palate, nails, tail hair, skin, hairs, and testicles – must be close to white.

Singhas guarding the entrance to Wat Benchamabophit

Naris and the Italian architect Hercules Manfredi to design a new *bot* and cloister for the original Ayutthaya-period temple which stood on the site. The nickname for the new *wat* ("Marble Temple") is derived from the gray Carrara marble used to clad the walls.

Laid out in cruciform with cascading roof levels, the *bot* is elegantly proportioned. It contains another successful fusion of traditions: intricate Victorian-style stained-glass windows depicting scenes from Thai mythology. In the room of the ashes of Rama V is the most revered copy of Phitsanulok's Phra Phuttha Chinarat *(see pp164–5)*, with a pointed halo. In the cloister are 53 different Buddha images, originals and copies of images from around Thailand and other Buddhist countries, assembled by Rama V.

Within the *wat* is one of the three sets of doors inlaid with mother-of-pearl that were salvaged from Wat Borom Buddharam in Ayutthaya. The building

in which Rama V lived as a monk features murals depicting events that occurred during his reign.

Wat Benchamabophit is a popular location for witnessing monastic rituals, from Buddhist holiday processions to the daily alms round *(see p133)*, in which merit-makers donate food to the monks lined up outside the *wat* along Nakhon Pathom Road. This is a reversal of the usual practice where the monks go out in search of alms.

⓫ Ratchadamnoen Avenue

ถนนราชดำเนิน

Map 2 D4. 🚌 15, 33, 39, 70, 159, 201; AC: 511, 503, 157, 170, 183.

Planned by King Mongkut (Rama IV) in the style of a European boulevard, this thoroughfare has three parts.

The first section, Ratchadamnoen Nai ("inner"), starts at Lak Muang and skirts **Sanam Luang** *(see pp82–3)*, before veering east at the Royal Hotel as Ratchadamnoen Klang("middle"). From here it passes the **Democracy Monument** *(see p91)* and 1930s mansions – a vista featured in the movie *Good Morning, Vietnam*.

Just across Khlong Banglamphu, Ratchadamnoen Nok ("outer") turns north into the Dusit area. This stretch, shaded by trees, is flanked by ministries, the main TAT headquarters, and **Ratchadamnoen Boxing Stadium** *(see p49)*. Just before the ornate double bridge over Khlong Phadung Krung Kasem is the Thai-influenced modern building of the United Nations Economic and Social Commission for Asia and the Pacific (ESCAP).

The avenue ends at the domed **Ananta Samakhom Throne Hall** *(see p109)*, which looms up beyond the Chulalongkorn Equestrian Statue in the parade ground, the site of December's Trooping of the Colors ceremony *(see p55)*.

Ratchadamnoen Avenue is decorated and illuminated in December as part of King Bhumibol's birthday festivities.

Annual Trooping of the Colors ceremony, Ratchadamnoen Avenue

European-inspired Wat Benchamabophit ▶

DOWNTOWN

The center of Bangkok's vast and continually expanding downtown is the area spanning Silom and Ploenchit roads. The business district originated in the 19th century in the Old Farang quarter of Charoen Krung Road, where charming colonial buildings have been conserved around the Oriental Hotel. The concrete canyon of Silom is the preserve of business people by day, but after dark its northern end is the heart of city nightlife. Farther north, showcase stores line Ploenchit and Rama I roads, while the stalls of Silom Road and Siam Square provide cheaper shopping. Amid the tower blocks, Lumphini Park provides green relief, and a few traditional Thai buildings remain, such as Jim Thompson House and Suan Pakkad Palace.

Sights at a Glance

Wats, Shrines, and Churches

2 Assumption Cathedral
5 Maha Uma Devi Temple
12 Erawan Shrine
13 Wat Pathum Wanaram

Museums and Libraries

6 Neilson-Hays Library
15 Bangkok Art and Culture Center
16 Jim Thompson House pp124–5
18 Suan Pakkad Palace

Notable Roads and Districts

3 Charoen Krung (New) Road
4 Silom Road
7 Patpong
14 Siam Square
17 Pratunam

Parks and Sports Grounds

9 Lumphini Park
11 Royal Bangkok Sports Club

Historic Buildings

1 Mandarin Oriental Hotel
10 Chulalongkorn University

Zoos

8 Snake Farm

See also Street Finder
pp148–59

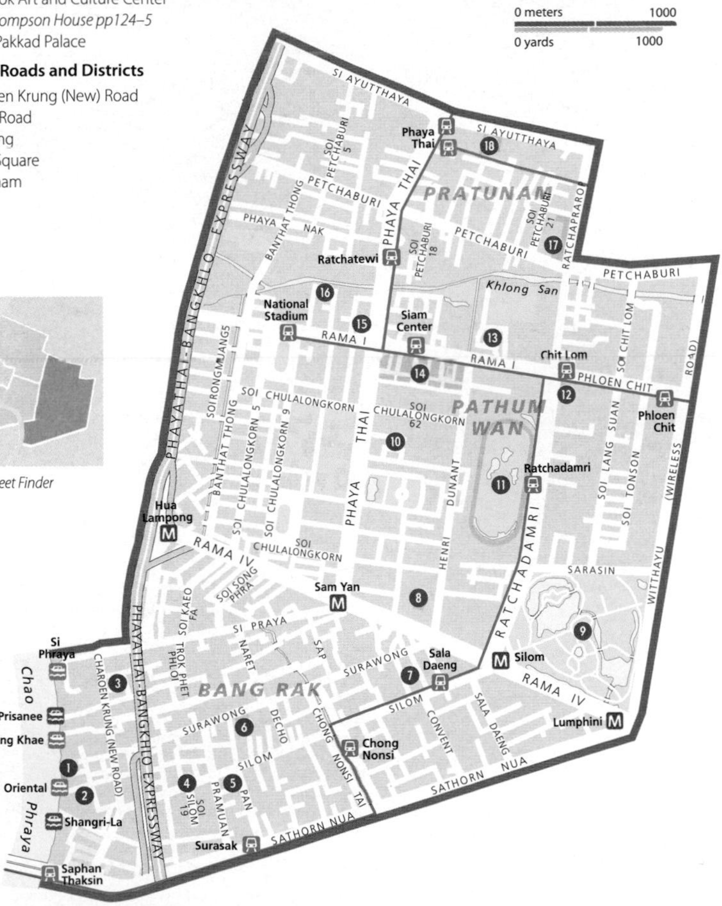

0 meters   1000
0 yards   1000

Bangkok's downtown area at night

For keys to symbols see back flap

Street-by-Street: Old Farang Quarter

ย่านที่อยู่ของฝรั่งสมัยก่อน(ย่านเจริญกรุง)

This area was Bangkok's original port and foreign commercial district in the 19th century. In 1820 Portugal was granted land in Bangkok, which resulted in the construction of the Portuguese Embassy. Embassies of other countries, such as France, soon followed. These outside influences created an amalgam of Western and Eastern architectural styles. Charoen Krung (New) Road, the first road in Thailand to be paved, cuts through the Old Farang Quarter and is home to gem traders, tailors, and antique dealers. The elegant Assumption Cathedral faces Bangkok's only European-style square. The Quarter's back streets are surprisingly quiet and contain some attractive wooden houses.

Harmonique restaurant is one of a row of Chinese shop houses built around 1900.

To Portuguese Embassy and GPO

SOI 34

SOI 36

House of Gems
is a tiny shop/museum selling rocks and fossils. Geological oddities – such as dinosaur droppings and tektites (glassy meteorites) – can be seen here.

The Old Customs House was built in the 1880s. Its exterior is now crumbling.

The French Embassy features pitched roofs and carved verandas.

The Haroon Mosque
is a quaint stucco building with a Muslim graveyard. The mosque, which faces Mecca, is off a street lined with wooden houses.

❶ ★ Mandarin Oriental Hotel
The world-renowned Mandarin Oriental Hotel was established in 1876 by two Danish sea captains. In 1958 a new structure (the Tower Wing) was added, and in 1976 the 10-story River Wing opened.

The China House, one of Bangkok's most expensive restaurants, is in a building dating from the reign of King Vajiravudh (*see p71*). The structure next door, the Commercial Co. of Siam, was erected in the same era.

Locator Map
See Street Finder map 6

❷ ★ **Assumption Cathedral**
This elegantly decorated cathedral was built in 1910. The cathedral's Rococo interior features a high, vaulted ceiling and a striking marble altar from France.

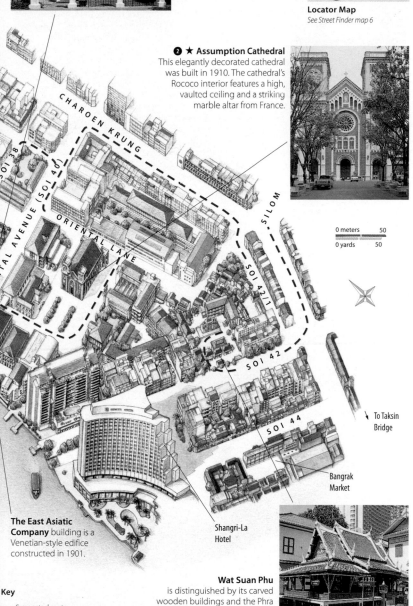

0 meters 50

0 yards 50

To Taksin Bridge

Bangrak Market

Shangri-La Hotel

The East Asiatic Company building is a Venetian-style edifice constructed in 1901.

Wat Suan Phu is distinguished by its carved wooden buildings and the Phra Bodhisattva Kuan-Im, a Chinese shrine over a carp pond.

Key

— Suggested route

Neo-Classical façade of the Authors' Wing of the Mandarin Oriental Hotel

❶ Mandarin Oriental Hotel

โรงแรมโอเรียนเต็ล

Oriental Ave, off Charoen Krung Rd.
Map 6 F4. **Tel** 0-2659-9000. 🚌 35, 75.
🚤 Oriental. **W** **mandarinoriental.com/bangkok**

Repeatedly voted the world's best hotel for its service and attention to detail, the Mandarin Oriental was Thailand's first large hotel. It was established in 1876 and completely rebuilt in 1887. More wings have since been added. The hotel owes much of its charm to the Armenian Sarkies brothers, creators of the luxurious Raffles Hotel in Singapore, and boasts lavish decor and a spectacular setting on the banks of the Chao Phraya River.

The original, white-shuttered wing contains the renowned Authors' Suites. Somerset Maugham was one such author who stayed here in the 1920s. Recovering from a bout of malaria, he wrote of the "dust and heat and noise and whiteness and more dust" of Bangkok, though his perception of the city was to change once he was able to explore the *wats* and *khlongs*.

Classic, English-style high tea is served in the Authors' Lounge of the hotel, a riot of potted plants and wicker chairs. A teak barge shuttles back and forth to the Sala Rim Naam on the

opposite bank, one of the hotel's eight highly acclaimed restaurants. Performances of traditional dance are staged here as guests dine. The hotel runs a respected school of Thai cookery.

❷ Assumption Cathedral

วัดอัสสัมชัญ

Oriental Lane, off Charoen Krung Rd.
Map 6 F4. 🚌 35, 75. **Open** daily.

This Romanesque-style brick edifice was built in 1910 on the site of an earlier cathedral. Its rose window is flanked by twin squat towers. The richly ornamented, Rococo interior is dominated by a lofty, barrel-arched blue ceiling patterned with gold starbursts.

The cathedral faces a tree-shaded piazza, the site of several other Western-style buildings. These include the modern Assumption College, the Neo-Classical Catholic Mission, and the Renaissance-style Catholic Center.

❸ Charoen Krung (New) Road

ถนนเจริญกรุง

Map 6 F2. 🚤 1; AC: 504.

Skirting the Chao Phraya River – from Wat Pho through Chinatown and on to Yannawa – Charoen Krung, or New Road (as it is often also called) is one of Bangkok's oldest thoroughfares.

Linking the Customs House and many trading companies, the road was once the center of Bangkok's European community. At their insistence it became Thailand's first paved highway. Still home to the gem and antique trades, today the road is choked with traffic pollution and noise, but side streets, lined with trees and old wooden buildings, can be blissfully serene. Along the road is the imposing **General Post Office**, whose light-brown stone façade is adorned with reliefs of *garudas* (mythical beasts, half bird, half human). In front is a statue of King

The airy and luxurious lobby of the Mandarin Oriental Hotel

Chulalongkorn. The coin and stamp stalls (open Sundays) outside the post office and the **Bangrak Market** (open daily), selling clothing and fruit, give the area vibrancy.

❹ Silom Road

ถนนสีลม

Map 7 A4. AC: 177, 504, 514, 532, 544. Ⓜ Silom. Ⓡ Saladaeng (skytrain).

The commercial heart of Bangkok, Silom Road is becoming a polluted canyon of skyscrapers, shopping malls, and elevated railway lines, though the area used to consist of orchards flanking a canal. One feature that remains unchanged is the many thousands of barn swallows that nest here from October to March.

Towards the river end of the road, and also on parallel Surawong Road, are several gem and silk shops. Near Patpong (*see p120*) is the Dusit Thani Hotel that overlooks Lumphini Park and the bustle of the local nightlife. Close by is Convent Road, taking its name from the **Carmelite Convent**, and also home to the Gothic-style **Anglican Christ Church**, built in 1904.

❺ Maha Uma Devi Temple

วัดศรีมหาอุมาเทวี

Corner of Silom and Pan rds. **Map** 7 B4. AC: 76, 502, 504. **Open** 7am–6pm daily. Deepavali (Nov).

Tamils founded this colorful Hindu temple during the 1860s. They were part of an influx of Indians who decided to move to Bangkok when India was handed over to the British Crown in 1858.

The main temple building is topped by a gold-plated copper dome above a 20-ft (6-m) high façade depicting various Hindu

Multicolored deities on the roof of Maha Uma Devi Temple

Street vendor pushing his cart

gods. Always buzzing with activity, and often with live Indian music, the temple is also the focus for Deepavali (Festival of Lights) celebrations in November. An oil-lamp ritual is held most days at noon, and on Fridays at 11:30am there is a *prasada* (vegetarian ceremony), in which blessed food is distributed to devotees. Although some Thais might call the temple Wat Khaek ("Indians' temple"), a common cultural heritage means that many local Thais and Chinese also regularly worship here. The Hindu deities Shiva and Ganesh feature in Thai Buddhism, and Hindus regard the Buddha as one of the incarnations of Vishnu.

❻ Neilson-Hays Library

ห้องสมุดเนลสันเฮยส์

195 Surawong Rd. **Map** 7 B4. **Tel** 0-2233-1731. 16, 93. **Open** 9:30am–5pm Tue–Sun. Ⓦ neilsonhayslibrary.com

Housed within an elegant building beside the British Club is the Neilson-Hays Library. Its 20,000 volumes form one of Southeast Asia's finest English-language collections.

The library was built in 1921 in honor of Jennie Neilson-Hays, who was the mainstay of the Bangkok Library Association between 1895 and 1920. The internal domed rotunda is used as a modern art gallery.

Western Writers in Bangkok

Western impressions of Thailand were for a long time heavily influenced by just one author – Anna Leonowens. An English teacher at the court of King Mongkut (Rama IV), Leonowens wrote the book that inspired the musical *The King and I*. However, the portrayal of the king as a comic figure stirred up anger in the country, and the book is now regarded as an unreliable historical source. Less controversially, Joseph Conrad wrote about his journey up the Chao Phraya in *The Shadow Line*, and Somerset Maugham described his impressions of Thailand in *The Gentleman in the Parlour*. These are just two of the Western authors commemorated by suites at the Oriental Hotel. Others include Noël Coward, Gore Vidal, Graham Greene, and Barbara Cartland. The Oriental has also ventured into other literary projects: it is the site for the annual prize-giving ceremony of the SEAWrite Award, established in 1969 to promote contact between writers in Southeast Asian countries.

Joseph Conrad in 1904

Looking for bargains at a night market in Patpong

❼ Patpong

พัฒน์พงษ์

Silom Rd, Patpong 1 and 2. **Map** 7 C3.
🚌 AC: 76, 177, 504, 514. Ⓜ Silom.
🚊 Sala Daeng (skytrain).

The private streets of Patpong 1 and 2, named after the one-time owner, Chinese millionaire Khun Patpongpanit, comprise what is probably the world's most notorious red-light district. In the 1960s the area was the home of Bangkok's entertainment scene – the go-go bars sprang up to satisfy airline crews and US GIs on leave during the Vietnam War. Since the 1970s, the sex shows have been sustained mainly through tourist patronage. A less visible gay scene exists in adjacent Soi Silom 4, while Soi Taniya's hostess bars are frequented mainly by Japanese clients.

The tourist police department monitors Patpong, and the area is surprisingly safe. A night market, with stalls selling souvenirs and original and fake fashions, gives the area a thin veneer of respectability. A bookstore in the center of Patpong is one of Southeast Asia's major outlets for books on feminism and exploitation. Many visitors come to Patpong out of curiosity rather than to indulge in the flesh trade.

❽ Snake Farm

สวนงู

Rama IV Rd. **Map** 7 C3.
Tel 0-2252- 0161. 🚌 AC: 50, 507.
Ⓜ Silom. 🚊 Sala Daeng (skytrain).
Open 8:30am–4:30pm Mon–Fri,
8:30am–noon Sat, Sun & public hols
(shows at 10:30am, 2pm). 🚻 📷

The Queen Saowapha Snake Farm is run by the Thai Red Cross. It makes snakebite serums and informs the public about local snakes. Unlike the tourist-oriented farms, the emphasis is on education. Demonstrations of venom milking take place twice daily (once daily on weekends), preceded by an explanatory slide show. Handlers open a snake's mouth and pierce the cellophane lid of a glass jar with its fangs. The milky venom then squirts harmlessly into the jar.

Cobra before milking, Snake Farm

Sex Workers and Their Clients in Thailand

Historically, prostitution in Thailand was reinforced by the institution of polygamy. Both are now illegal, but the use of prostitutes by Thai men is still widespread. Every town has at least one massage parlor. The glitzy brothels of Patpong and such towns as Pattaya and Hat Yai may form the foreign perception of the Thai sex industry, but they are a relatively recent development, dating from the presence of US servicemen in Thailand during the Vietnam War. Some estimates put the number of sex workers as high as two million, but a more realistic figure is 250,000, one fifth of whom are male. The majority of prostitutes work for Thai clients, but a few service the many tourists who come for so-called "sex holidays." Increasingly, concern about exploitation, pedophilia, AIDS, and sex tourism is being voiced around the world, and countries such as Sweden now prosecute their nationals caught paying for sex with children abroad.

Many prostitutes come from the poorest regions of Thailand or neighboring countries such as Myanmar. The income, and a somewhat fatalistic attitude, can outweigh any social disapproval they may face. But some do not become involved in the industry willingly, and cases of beatings and imprisonment are not uncommon. Health problems, stigma, lack of skills, and death from AIDS (see p467) spell grim prospects for all sex workers.

Despite a government campaign and the work of programs by charities such as Empower, research from 2010 estimates the number of prostitutes infected at 10 percent for the whole country, and up to 50 percent for provinces adjacent to the Myanmar border.

Gaudy nightclub sign in central Bangkok

Perfecting the art of tai chi chuan early one morning in Lumphini Park

9 Lumphini Park
สวนลุมพินี

Map 8 D3. 🚌 14; AC: 50, 507.
Ⓜ Silom, Lumphini. 🚊 Sala Daeng
(skytrain). **Open** 5:30am–9pm daily.

Named after the Buddha's
birthplace in Nepal, Bangkok's
main greenbelt sprawls around
two boating lakes. Dominating
the Silom Road corner of the
park is a statue of Rama VI.

The best time to visit is early
morning, when it is used by
Thais for jogging and Chinese
for practicing t'ai chi ch'uan. The
superstitious can be seen
consuming fresh snake blood
and bile to keep ill health at
bay, purchased from stalls along
the park's northern edge. The
park is a relaxing place to stroll
and observe elderly Chinese
playing chess, and impromptu
games of *takraw* (a type of
volleyball in which the hands
may not be used).

10 Chulalongkorn University
มหาวิทยาลัยจุฬาลงกรณ์

Phya Thai Rd. **Map** 7 C2. 🚌 16, 40, 47,
50; AC: 501; MB: 1. **Tel** 0-2215-0871.
Imaging Tech Museum: **Tel** 0-2218-
5583. **Open** 10:30am–3:30pm Mon–
Fri. 🖼 Art Gallery: **Tel** 0-2218-2965.
Open daily. **Closed** public hols.
Museum of Natural History:
Open 10am–3:30pm daily.

Dedicated to the modern-
minded king who founded it,
this is Thailand's oldest, richest,

and most prestigious
university. Chulalongkorn's
central gardens, between the
busy Phya Thai and Henri
Dunant roads, are the site of
several attractive buildings and
a pond that is often used
during the festival of Loy
Krathong (see p54).

The **Imaging Technology
Museum**, south of the
lake, features hands-on
photographic displays,
including a room where you
can develop and print your own
film, and exhibitions of high-
quality photography from
Thailand and other countries.
Nearby are an auditorium,
used mainly for classical
concerts, a contemporary **Art
Gallery**, which stages various
temporary exhibitions, and a
Museum of Natural History.

11 Royal Bangkok Sports Club
ราชกรีฑาสโมสร

Henry Dunant Rd. **Map** 8 D2.
🚌 16, 21; AC: 141. **Tel** 0-2255-4158.
Open 9am–6pm alternate Sun for
races only. 🖼 Ⓦ rbsc.org

Considered to be Thailand's
most exclusive social institution,
the RBSC has a waiting list to
prove it. It offers a wide range
of sports to its members –
including rugby, soccer, and
field hockey – who form some
of the top Thai teams in these
sports. Nonmembers may enter
to watch horse races at the
club, one of Thailand's two
principal race courses; the
other is the Royal Turf Club on
Phitsanulok Road (see p110).

Gambling is virtually a
national institution in Thailand,
and the RBSC gives Bangkokians
the perfect opportunity to
indulge in one of their favorite
pastimes. On race days,
thousands of bettors from all
social classes flock to the track.
As the start of the race draws
near, betting becomes furious,
and huge electronic screens
track the odds on each horse
and the total money wagered.
Visitors are welcome to join in,
and should watch the screens
for clues as to which horse to
bet on; you may have to ask for
help to fill out one of the Thai-
language betting slips.

Horses on the home stretch, Royal Bangkok Sports Club

The vast interior of the Siam Center, one of Thailand's first shopping malls

⑫ Erawan Shrine

พระพรหมเอราวัณ

Ratchadamri Rd. **Map** 8 D1.
🚍 AC: 501, 504, 505. 🚈 Rachadamri, Chit Lom, or Siam Center (skytrain).

Drivers take their hands off the steering wheel to *wai* (a gesture of respect) as they pass the Erawan Shrine, such is the widespread faith in the luck that this landmark brings. The construction of the original Erawan Hotel in the 1950s, on the site now occupied by the Grand Hyatt Erawan Hotel, was plagued by a series of mishaps. In order to counteract the bad spirits believed to be causing the problems, this shrine dedicated to Indra and his elephant mount, Erawan, was erected in front of the hotel. Ever since, the somewhat gaudy monument has been decked

Dancers in traditional Thai costume performing at the Erawan Shrine

with garlands, carved wooden elephants, and other offerings in the hope of, or thanks for, good fortune. By the shrine are women in traditional costume. Anyone wishing to express gratitude for good fortune can pay the dancers a fee, and they will do a thankyou dance around it.

Near the shrine, and along Ploenchit and Sukhumvit roads, are several of Bangkok's most upscale shopping complexes *(see pp142–3)*, including Sogo, Siam Center, World Trade Center, Gay Sorn Plaza, Amarin Plaza, Le Meridien, and the swankiest of them all, the Siam Paragon.

⑬ Wat Pathum Wanaram

วัดปทุมวนาราม

Rama I Rd. **Map** 8 D1. 🚍 AC: 25, 501, 508. 🚈 Siam Center (skytrain).
Open 9am–4pm daily.

The main reason for visiting the Pathum Wanaram temple is to see Phra Meru Mas, a reconstruction of the crematorium of the late Princess Mother. Following her cremation at Sanam Luang *(see pp82–3)* in March 1996, her remains were transferred to these grounds in an elaborate procession. The crematorium is a rare example of ancient craftmanship, featuring ornate stencils and lacquered sculptures. It represents Mount Meru, the heavenly abode of the gods.

⑭ Siam Square

สยามสแควร์

Rama I Rd. **Map** 7 C1. 🚍 AC: 25, 501, 508. 🚈 Siam (skytrain).

Street shopping is fast disappearing in Bangkok as shopping malls proliferate. The principal exception to this phenomenon is the network of *sois* (alleys) collectively known as Siam Square, between Chulalongkorn University *(see p121)* and the Siam Center.

The square is packed with independent shops and stalls selling, in particular, music, books, accessories, and clothing – much of it by enterprising young Thai designers.

Rama I Road, on one side of the square, is the showcase for Thailand's movie industry. Three grand theaters – the Scala, the Lido, and the Siam – are located here. On the western edge of the square, on Phaya Thai Road, is the **Mahboonkrong Center** (MBK), which houses a department store and various shops and stalls. Beyond it is the **National Stadium**, Thailand's main arena for major soccer and other sports events. However, the future of the entire district looks uncertain: it is feared that the land may be redeveloped when its lease expires.

⑮ Bangkok Art and Culture Center

หอกลจรณมฮรรหแหจครจเกพฝฑวมตร

939 Rama I Rd. **Map** 7 C1. **Tel** 0-2214-6630. 🚍 AC: 15, 16, 501, 508, 529.
🚈 National Stadium (skytrain).
Open 10am–9pm Tue–Sun. 📷 for special exhibitions and performances.
🔲 ♿ 🏛 🆆 bacc.or.th

The Bangkok Art and Culture Center offers visitors an enjoyable insight into Thai culture and society. This striking 11-story building is home to galleries, performance spaces, and a library. The center displays over 300 contemporary works of art by Thai and international artists and hosts regular exhibitions alongside an exciting events program.

Bargain-price clothing for sale at Pratunam Market

⑯ Jim Thompson House

บ้านจิมทอมป์สัน

See pp124–5.

⑰ Pratunam

ประตูน้ำ

Map 4 E5. ⊞ 12; AC: 504.

Pratunam district is worth a brief visit. The lively and colorful **Pratunam Market** is a vast maze of stalls, stores, and workshops, trading mostly in clothing and fashion accessories. Just west of the market is the Modernist **Baiyoke Tower**, which reigned briefly as the tallest building in Bangkok from 1987 until 1995. Despite evidence of settling in

the surrounding ground, permission was granted for construction of the adjacent **Baiyoke Tower II**, which was completed in 1997.

⑱ Suan Pakkad Palace

วังสวนผักกาด

352 Si Ayutthaya Rd. **Map** 4 D4. **Tel** 0-2245-4934. ⊞ AC: 201, 513. 🚇 Phaya Thai (skytrain). **Open** 9am–4pm daily. 🅿 📷 🅦 **suanpakkad.com**

This palace, a group of five traditional teak houses, was originally the home of Prince and Princess Chumbhot. The houses were assembled in the 1950s within a lush garden landscaped out of a cabbage patch – *suan pakkad* in Thai – that gives the palace its name. Each building has been converted into a museum, and together they house an impressive private collection of art and artifacts that once belonged to the royal couple.

The eclectic assortment ranges from Khmer sculpture, betel-nut sets, and pieces of antique lacquered furniture, to Thai musical instruments and exquisite shells and crystals. More important, perhaps, is the first-class collection of whorl-patterned red and white Bronze

Age pottery, excavated from tombs at Ban Chiang *(see p276)* in Northeast Thailand. The highlight for most visitors, though, is the Lacquer Pavilion, which was built from two exquisite temple buildings retrieved by Prince Chumbhot from Ayutthaya province.

Immaculately crafted, charmingly detailed black and gold lacquered murals inside each edifice depict scenes from the Buddha's life and the Ramakien *(see pp44–5)*. They also portray ordinary Thai life from just before the fall of Ayutthaya in 1767 *(see pp64–5)*. These murals are some of the only ones to survive from the Ayutthaya period. Scenes include foreign traders exchanging goods, graphic battle scenes, and gruesome depictions of hell.

Elegant façade of the Lacquer Pavilion at Suan Pakkad Palace

Bangkok's Modern Architecture

An apparently endless mass of dull concrete towers, monotonous rows of shop-houses, and gaudy mock-classical edifices give Bangkok the overall impression of a sprawling urban jungle rather than the Oriental splendor visitors might expect.

Nonetheless, there are some modern buildings within the city that were designed by visionary architects. Postmodern architecture of an international standard is particularly noticeable along Sathorn Tai and Silom roads. Other interesting buildings include the Thai Airways headquarters and the triple-towered "Elephant Building."

One of Bangkok's most progressive design companies is Plan Architecture, responsible for striking buildings such as the Baiyoke Towers I and II, the bullet-shaped Vanit Building II on Soi Chidlom, and the narrow Thai Wah II Tower on Sathorn Tai Road. Thailand's most famous, and perhaps most witty, modern landmark is probably the Bank of Asia's head office on Sathorn Tai Road, nicknamed the "Robot Building" *(see p73)*.

Two sophisticated examples of Thai Modernism, both hotels, were designed by Westerners. The roof of the Siam Inter-Continental was designed to resemble a traditional "Mongkut" crown, and the gardens of the Sukhothai evoke the serene waterscape of the old capital of the same name *(see pp198–201)*.

One of the Baiyoke Towers, in downtown Bangkok

In the 21st century, Bangkok's skyline continues to change, with additions such as the Siam Paragon, Central World, and many flashy apartment buildings and chic hotels.

⑯ Jim Thompson House

บ้านจิมทอมป์สัน

One of the best-preserved traditional Thai houses in Bangkok and finest museums in the country is the former home of Jim Thompson. The entrepreneurial American revived the art of Thai silk weaving *(see pp270–71)* following its demise during World War II. His house stands in a flower-filled garden across from the ancient silk weavers' quarter of Ban Khrua. In 1959 Thompson dismantled six teak houses in Ban Khrua and Ayutthaya province and reassembled them here in an unconventional layout. Thompson was an avid collector of antiquities and artworks from all over Southeast Asia. His distinguished array, which spans 14 centuries, is attractively displayed, and left much as it was when he mysteriously disappeared in 1967. Unlike many other domestic museums, this feels like a lived-in home.

Master Bedroom
Fine 19th-century paintings of the *jataka* tales line the walls of this room.

First floor

Ground floor

Guest bedrooms

★ *Jataka* Paintings
This panel, in the entrance hall, is one of eight early 19th-century paintings in the house showing scenes from the Vessantara *jataka (see p34)*. These depict Prince Vessantara as an incarnation of the Buddha.

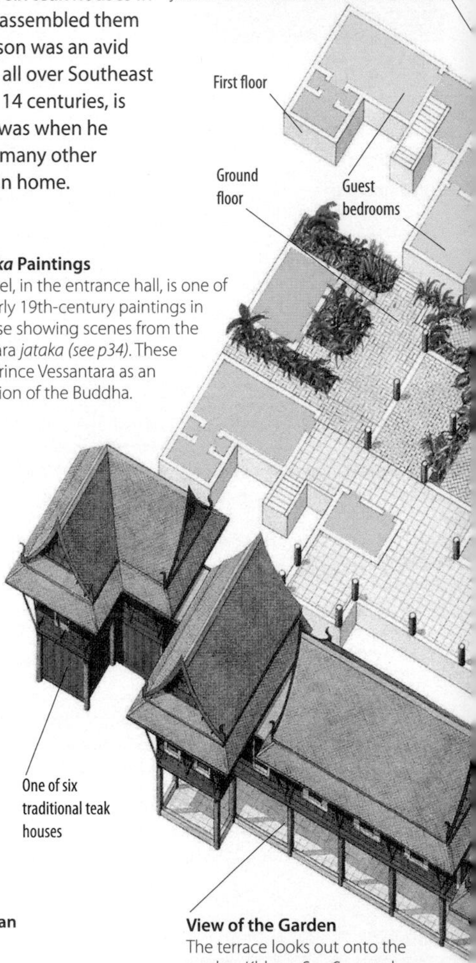

★ Burmese Carvings
This wooden figure of an animist Nat spirit is among Thompson's extensive collection of Burmese images. When Buddhism developed in Burma, it incorporated the preexisting worship of Nat spirits.

One of six traditional teak houses

Key to Floor Plan

- ☐ Bedrooms
- ▨ Study
- ☐ Entrance hall
- ☐ Drawing room
- ☐ Dining room
- ☐ Secure room
- ☐ Bencharong room
- ☐ Silk Pavilion
- ☐ Other exhibition space

View of the Garden
The terrace looks out onto the garden, Khlong San Sap, and across to Ban Khrua.

Drawing Room
Situated on the right is a 14th-century U Thong sandstone head of the Buddha, while the 18th-century carved wooden figures in the alcoves are of Burmese spirits.

VISITORS' CHECKLIST

Practical Information
Map 3 C5. **Tel** 0-2216-7368.
6 Soi Kasemsan 2, Rama I Rd.
Open 9am–5pm daily. 🔲 🔲
🔲 compulsory. 🔲 🔲
W jimthompsonhouse.com

Transport
🚌 15, 48, 204; AC: 508. 🚉
National Stadium (skytrain).

The *khlong* (canal) was once used by silk weavers, who dried threads of silk on poles along the banks.

Porcelain Chamberpot
This cat, made of Chinese porcelain, is in one of the guest bedrooms.

Dining Room
Beautiful blue and white Ming porcelain adorns the walls of this room.

★ Dvaravati Torso of the Buddha
This torso, made of limestone, is in the garden. Dating from the early Dvaravati period (7th century), it is said to be one of the oldest surviving Buddha images in Southeast Asia.

Spirit house with offerings

Entrance

The teak houses, the oldest dating from 1800, were erected with some walls reversed so that exterior carvings now face the interior.

Who was Jim Thompson?

An architect by profession, Thailand's most famous American came here in 1945 as the Bangkok head of the Office of Strategic Services (OSS), a forerunner of the CIA. In 1948 he founded the Thai Silk Company Ltd., turning the ailing industry into a thriving business once again. Thompson became a social celebrity in Bangkok and finally achieved mythical status following his disappearance on Easter Sunday 1967 while walking in the Cameron Highlands in Malaysia. Explanations for his vanishing include falling from a path or having a heart attack to more sinister suggestions of CIA involvement.

Jim Thompson inspecting Thai silk in 1964

THON BURI

Known originally as Ban Kok ("village of the wild plum"), Thon Buri was the capital of Thailand for 15 years between 1767 and 1782. When Rama I moved his capital across the river its original name followed, and, though Thais refer to the capital as Krung Thep, it remains known as Bangkok to foreigners. Thon Buri wasn't linked by bridge to Bangkok until 1932 and was officially incorporated into the city only in 1971. Today this area preserves a distinct identity, offering a sleepier version of Bangkok proper. The best way to explore Thon Buri is by boat. Meandering down the intricate network of canals, the visitor sees scenes of river life – stilt houses, small temples, mansions, and floating shops. On Khlong Bangkok Noi is the Royal Barge Museum with its lavishly decorated boats. Farther south there are some interesting riverside *wats* along the Chao Phraya River, the most prominent and famous of which is Wat Arun.

Sights at a Glance

Wats and Churches
1. Wat Suwannaram
4. Wat Rakhang
5. *Wat Arun pp130–31*
6. Wat Kanlayanimit
7. Church of Santa Cruz
8. Wat Prayun

Museums
2. Royal Barge Museum
3. Museums at the Siriraj Hospital

Monuments
9. Taksin Monument

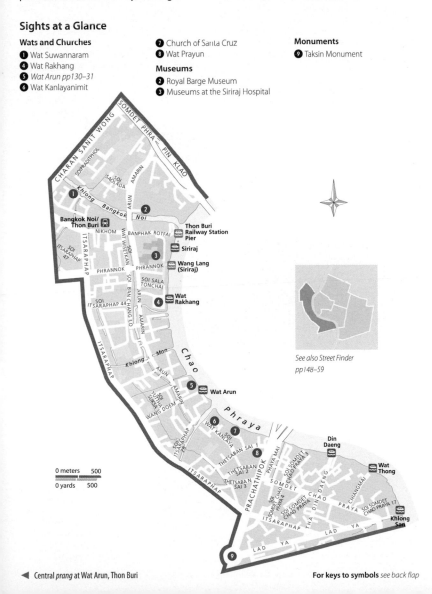

See also Street Finder pp148–59

0 meters 500
0 yards 500

◀ Central *prang* at Wat Arun, Thon Buri

For keys to symbols *see back flap*

Buddha in classic *bhumisparsa mudra* posture, Wat Suwannaram

❶ Wat Suwannaram

วัดสุวรรณาราม

Charan Sanit Wong Rd, Khlong Bangkok Noi. **Map** 1 A3. 🚤 hire a long-tail from any pier. **Open** daily.

Wat Suwannaram was constructed by Rama I on the foundations of a temple dating from the Ayutthaya era. It was renovated by Rama III and finally completed in 1831. The temple complex provides a graceful example of early Rattanakosin architecture (*see p39*), in which a few traces of the Ayutthaya style still linger. The well-restored murals of the main *wihan,* some of the best of the early 19th century, are attributed to two renowned painters of the third reign, Luang Vichit Chetsada and Krua Khonpae.

Western perspective had not permeated Thai mural painting at the time: scenes are depicted as aerial views with figures shown at the same size whether they are in the foreground or background. On the side panels are depictions of the last 10 tales of the *jataka* (the Buddha's previous lives). On the south wall are the Buddhist cosmological kingdoms, and the entrance wall is dominated by a lively scene of the Buddha's victory over Mara. Notice the hairstyles of the third reign (1824–51): the heads of both sexes are shaven to leave a small patch of hair at the top. Also, look for a Christian cross on a hermit's hut, evidence that missionaries were active in Thailand at the time.

❷ Royal Barge Museum

พิพิธภัณฑ์เรือพระที่นั่ง

Khlong Bangkok Noi. **Map** 1 B3. **Tel** 0-2424-0004. 🚌 7, 9,19. 🚤 hire a long-tail from Chang pier. **Open** 9am–5pm daily. 🚫 📷

Housed within a huge warehouse-like structure is a collection of Thailand's most ostentatious boats, the royal barges. Paintings of fabulous Ayutthayan barges (*see pp64–5*) engaged in battles and stately processions, together with archive photographs of royal barge ceremonies in Bangkok over the last 150 years, have provided some of the most splendid visions of Thailand presented to the world via postcards and tourist brochures. Nowadays, though, the vessels are rarely seen cruising the Chao Phraya River, since they have been housed at the museum since 1967. The barges are reproductions of some built 200 years ago by Rama I, who had copied Ayutthayan originals.

Hongsa, on prow of the king's barge

In 1981 most of the royal barges underwent an expensive face-lift. They came out in all their gilded glory during the 1982 Bangkok Bicentennial celebrations (*see p72*), for the King's 60th birthday in 1987, and for the Golden Jubilee of his reign on November 7, 1996. For such auspicious occasions more than 50 barges sail in a lengthy procession down the Chao Phraya. Most of the 2,000 oarsmen – dressed in traditional uniforms – are sea cadets, a fitting crew for boats that were once the naval fleet.

The vessel in the center of the museum, *Supphanahongsa* ("golden swan"), is the most important royal barge. Made from a single piece of teak, it is over 165 ft (50 m) long and weighs 15 tons. In action it requires a highly trained crew of 64. The mythical, swanlike bird Hongsa rears up from its prow. Anantanagaraj, a barge bearing a multiheaded *naga* and a

Superbly detailed 19th-century mural at Wat Suwannaram

Ferocious figurehead on a gun barge built in the reign of Rama I

Buddha image, is reserved for conveying monks' robes. Narai Song Suban Rama IX is the first barge to be built during the present king's reign. It is 145 ft (44 m) long and can carry 50 people.

❸ Museums at the Siriraj Hospital

พิพิธภัณฑ์โรงพยาบาลศิริราช

Arun Amarin Rd. **Map** 1 B4. **Tel** 0-2419-2618. 81, 91. Phrannok and Wang Lang. **Open** 10am–5pm Mon, Wed–Sun. **Closed** public hols. **W** si.mahidol.ac.th/museums

Six medical museums are located at this hospital, of which the **Museum of Forensic Medicine** is the best known. It houses gruesome objects,

such as the preserved figure of Si-oui, a man who suffocated and ate seven children. Thai parents often threaten naughty children with his ghost. In the **Congdon Museum of Anatomy** are still-born Siamese twins. Such twins are so named because the famous Chan and In, who toured the world in the mid-19th century, were from Siam, as Thailand was then known.

❹ Wat Rakhang

วัดระฆัง

Soi Wat Rakhang. **Map** 1 B5. 57, 83. Chang pier to Wat Rakhang. **Open** daily.

Wat Rakhang was the last major temple to be constructed by Rama I in the early 19th century. The fine murals in the main

wihan, which were painted between 1922 and 1923 by a monk Phra Wanawatwichit, include recognizable scenes of Bangkok. Though the capital has changed much since then, the Grand Palace, which stands just across the river from Wat Rakhang, is easy to identify. In the murals, the palace is shown in the middle of an imaginary attack. There is also an elaborate depiction of a royal barge procession.

The raised wooden library *(ho trai)* of Wat Rakhang, in the west of the compound, was used as a residence by Rama I before he became king. The building's eave supports, delicately carved bookcases, and gold and black doors are period masterpieces. Inside the library are murals depicting scenes from the Ramakien and a portrait of Rama I.

Wooden façade of the raised library at Wat Rakhang

Living on Water: the Era of the Thai Khlongs

Ayutthaya and Bangkok, both on the flood plain of the Chao Phraya River, were cities that grew along countless little canals and streams known as *khlongs*. Bangkok was once a floating city. In the 1840s all but about 10 percent of its population of 400,000 lived on the *khlongs*. Houses built on rafts could be moored wherever there was space *(see p41)*.

Stilt houses lining the banks of the *khlongs* provided a somewhat more stable habitat. Although roads now cover most of Bangkok's eastern waterways, many still exist in Thon Buri, where life still largely revolves around the *khlongs*. Children splashing in the water are a common sight, and early each morning waterborne vendors cruise up and down, selling everything from Chinese pastries and coffee to fruit, vegetables, and cooking utensils. The favored *khlong* vessel today is the long-tailed powerboat – one was memorably commandeered by Roger Moore as James Bond in the movie *The Man with the Golden Gun*. Visitors can easily charter their own from Chang pier to explore the Thon Buri *khlongs*.

Bangkok in the 1890s, before the age of roads and land-based dwellings

❺ Wat Arun

วัดอรุณ

Wat Arun, named after Aruna, the Indian god of dawn, is a striking Bangkok landmark. It owes its name to the legend that, in October 1767, King Taksin arrived here at sunrise from the sacked capital, Ayutthaya. He soon enlarged the tiny temple that stood on the site into a Royal Chapel to house the Emerald Buddha *(see pp86–7)*. Rama II and Rama III were responsible for the size of the current temple: the main *prang* is 260 ft (79 m) high and the circumference of its base is 768 ft (234 m). In the 19th century King Mongkut (Rama IV) added the ornamentation created with broken pieces of porcelain. The monument's style, deriving mainly from Khmer architecture *(see pp268–9)*, is unique in Thailand.

Multicolored Tiers
Rows of demons, decorated with pieces of porcelain, line the exterior of a minor *prang*.

★ River View of Temple
This popular image of Wat Arun, as seen from the Chao Phraya, appears on the 10-*baht* coin and in the Tourism Authority of Thailand (TAT) logo.

Central Monument of Wat Arun

The monument's design symbolizes Hindu-Buddhist cosmology. The central prang (tower) is the mythical Mount Meru, and its ornamental tiers are worlds within worlds. The layout of four minor prangs around a central one is a symbolic mandala shape.

One of the eight entrances

Chinese Guards
These figures, at the entrances to the terrace, complement the Chinese-style porcelain decorating the *prangs*.

KEY

① **Minor *prangs*** at each corner of the wat

② **Top terrace**

③ **Indra's weapon**, the *vajra* or thunderbolt, at the crest

④ **Mondops** at the cardinal points

Gallery of the *Bot*
Elsewhere in the temple complex are the usual buildings found in a *wat*. This image of the Buddha in the main *bot* sits above the ashes of devotees.

Symbolic Levels

The Devaphum (top) is the peak of Mount Meru, rising above four subsidiary peaks. It denotes six heavens within seven realms of happiness.

The Tavatimsa Heaven (central section), where all desires are fulfilled, is guarded at the four cardinal points by the Hindu god Indra.

The Traiphum (base) represents 31 realms of existence across the three worlds (Desire, Form, and Formless) of the Buddhist universe.

VISITORS' CHECKLIST

Practical Information
Arun Amarin Rd. **Map** 5 B1.
Open 7am–5pm daily.

Transport
19, 57, 83. Tien to Wat Arun.

Stairs on the Central *Prang*
The steep steps represent the difficulties of reaching higher levels of existence. Visitors can climb halfway up when restoration work allows.

Small Cove
On the second level of the central *prang* are many small coves, inside which are *kinnari*, mythological creatures, half-bird, half-human.

Decoration of the Four Minor *Prangs*
Inside the niches of each minor *prang* are statues of Nayu, the god of wind, on horseback.

★ Ceramic Details
Much of the colorful porcelain decorating the *prangs* was donated by local people. The flowers above and below the "demon bears" are said to evoke the vegetation of Mount Meru, home of the gods.

❻ Wat Kanlayanimit
วัดกัลยาณมิตร

Soi Wat Kanlaya. **Map** 5 B2. 🚌 2, 8;
AC: 2 to Pak Klong Talad, then cross
the river by ferry at the pier.
Open 8:30am–4:30pm daily.

This dilapidated temple complex
is one of the five temples built
in Bangkok by Rama III (ruled
1824–51). Rama liked Chinese
design, as can be seen from the
statuary dotted around the
courtyard (brought to Thailand
as ballast on empty rice barges
returning from China) and the
Chinese-style polygonal *chedi*.

The complex's immense
wihan contains a large sitting
Buddha image. In the temple
grounds is the biggest bronze
bell in Thailand.

Near the *wat*, on the other
side of Khlong Bangkok Yai, is
Wichai Prasit Fortress, built to
guard the river approach to
Thon Buri when Ayutthaya was
the dominant city in Thailand
(*see pp64–5*).

Thailand's biggest bronze bell, in the bell
tower of Wat Kalayanimit

❼ Church of Santa Cruz
วัดซางตาครู้ส

Soi Kudi Chin. **Map** 5 C2. 🚌 2, 8 to Pak
Klong Talad then cross the river by
ferry at the pier, or express boat to
Saphan Phut pier. **Open** 6am and 7pm
Sun (for Mass). 🚫 inside the church.

This pastel yellow church is one
of the most prominent reminders
of the community of Portuguese

Newly released turtles feeding on fruit in the pond at Wat Prayun

merchants and missionaries
who lived here in the mid-19th
century. The church was built in
the late 18th century, when Thon
Buri was the capital of Thailand
(*see pp68–9*). It was rebuilt by
Bishop Pallegoix in 1834, and
again in 1913. The church is
known in Thai as Wat Kuti Chin
("Chinese monastic residence"),
from the Chinese influences in
its architecture.

Although only a few houses of
Portuguese origin remain in the
muddle of alleyways
surrounding the temple, the
Portuguese legacy can still be
seen in the private Catholic
shrines that are tucked away
among Thai shop-houses.

❽ Wat Prayun
วัดประยูร

Pratchathipok Rd. **Map** 5 C2. 🚌 6, 43,
or express boat to Saphan Phut pier.
Open 7am–4:30pm daily.

The unusual artificial hill at the
entrance to this temple was
created on a whim of Rama III.
While reading by candlelight,
the king observed the
interesting wax formation of
the melting candle.
He then asked one of
his courtiers, Prayun
Bunnag, to create a
hill in the same
shape. The hill is
dotted with bizarre
shrines, miniature
chedis, *prangs*,
grottoes, and tiny
temples, but is perhaps most
memorable for its ornamental
pond, filled with hundreds of

turtles. Devotees buy the turtles
nearby and then release them
into the pond. This act of setting
free confined creatures (more
commonly releasing caged
birds) is a way of gaining merit
for future lives.

The temple *bot* is punctuated
with doors and window shutters
decorated with mother-of-pearl.
The large *chedi* has a circular
cloister that is surmounted by
smaller *chedis*.

❾ Taksin Monument
อนุสาวรีย์พระเจ้าตากสิน

Pratchathipok Rd. **Map** 5 C4.
🚌 21, 40, 43, 82.

Located on the busy Wong-
wian Yai traffic circle, this
20th-century equestrian
statue commemorates King
Taksin (ruled 1767–82), who
moved the capital to Thon
Buri after the destruction of
Ayutthaya by the Burmese
in 1767.

In 1950 the commission to
design the monument was
given to Professor Silpa Bhirasri,
the Italian "father" of Thai
modern art who
took a Thai name
and citizenship. The
striking statue took
three years to
complete and was
finally unveiled in
1954. Each year, on
December 28 – the
anniversary of King
Taksin's coronation – many Thais
come to pay homage at the
statue.

Detail of King Taksin
Monument

Popular Buddhist Rituals

The act of merit-making is an essential part of religious life in Thailand *(see pp34–5)*. Practiced both by monks and lay people, it reflects an awareness that good deeds lead to good outcomes, such as happiness, either in this life or the next (as a more fortunate rebirth). To accumulate merit is a way of taking responsibility for one's own *karma* (destiny). Becoming a monk, even for a short period, or sponsoring the ordination of a monk, is the highest form of making merit, and a devout Buddhist monk adheres to strict rules in his daily life. In some rituals – such as the alms round – the lives of monks and lay people interact. Other everyday habits of ordinary people focus on the local temple: the shared act of decorating a Buddhist shrine strengthens community ties. Devout lay people, meanwhile, may meditate and worship at a private shrine in their own home.

The daily alms round *(bintabat)* takes place shortly after dawn, when monks leave their temples to search for their daily meal. Giving food to monks is a popular way for lay people to earn merit and practice generosity (the act of *dana*). Monks are permitted to eat only food that has been offered to them, and they must consume it before noon.

Meditation purifies the mind and clears it of distractions. It is practiced regularly by all monks and some lay people.

Shaving the head is a ritual for monks on the day of the full moon. This mural shows a novice being shaved for ordination.

Gold leaf put on the Buddha image honors his teachings.

Pavilion at Wat Phra Kaeo

Offerings for the Buddha are usually symbolic. Lotus buds represent the purity of the Buddha's thoughts.

Incense sticks, in groups of three, symbolize the Buddha, the *dharma* (teachings), and the *sangha* (monkhood). Candles stand for the light of understanding.

Visits to the *Wat*

Many lay people in Thailand go to their local wat at least once a week. Typically they make offerings to an image of the Buddha, listen to the monks chanting and to a dharma talk, and receive blessings. Food is prepared to offer to the monks and as a communal meal. The local community often funds building or restoration projects.

FARTHER AFIELD

Many interesting sights lie outside central Bangkok. Extending eastward is Sukhumvit Road, with a plethora of shops, restaurants, small galleries, and museums. Shopaholics will also not want to miss the superb Chatuchak Market or the spectacle of Damnoen Saduak Floating Market, west of the city. To the south and east are a clutch of theme and amusement parks, including the Erawan Museum and the Ancient City, a tranquil park with replicas of Thai monuments. At the Crocodile Farm

reptile wrestling is the major attraction, and Safari World offers further wildlife encounters. Culture lovers will enjoy the art and antiques in the Prasart Museum. Pleasant day trips include the green suburb of Nonthaburi and, to the west, the relaxed provincial towns of Ratchaburi and Nakhon Pathom. The latter is the site of the world's tallest Buddhist monument, Phra Pathom Chedi. Another popular excursion is west to the Thai culture shows at the Sampran Riverside.

Sights at a Glance

Towns
1. Ratchaburi
4. Nakhon Pathom
5. Nonthaburi

Museums and Cultural Theme Parks
3. Sampran Riverside
10. Prasart Museum
11. Ancient City
13. Erawan Museum

Notable Roads
7. Sukhumvit Road

Swimming Pools
9. Siam Park

Markets
2. Damnoen Saduak Floating Market
6. Chatuchak Market

Zoos
8. Safari World
12. Crocodile Farm

Key

- Main sightseeing area
- Built-up area
- Highway
- Major road
- Minor road

0 kilometers 25
0 miles 25

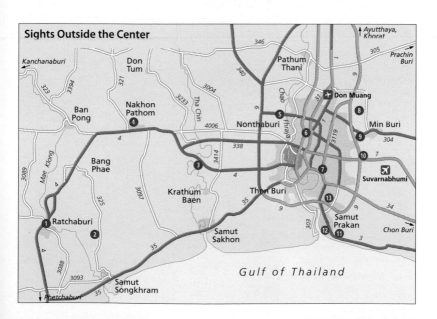

Sights Outside the Center

Ayutthaya, Khorat
346
Prachin Buri
305
Kanchanaburi
Don Tum
Pathum Thani
Don Muang
323 3394
321
340
Ban Pong
Nakhon Pathom 4
3233 3004
Chao Phraya
9
31
8 Min Buri
Tha Chin
4006 Nonthaburi
5
3119 304
9
Mae Klong
Bang Phae
338
6
3414
10 7
4
Krathum Baen
Thon Buri
Suvarnabhumi
3089
325 3097
4
35
13
303 34
1 Ratchaburi
Samut Prakan
Chon Buri
2
Samut Sakhon
12 11
3
35
9
3088
3093
35
Samut Songkhram
Phetchaburi
35

Gulf of Thailand

◀ Erawan Museum's "Stairway to Heaven," Samut Prakan

Palm-shaded Wat Mahathat, the main sight at Ratchaburi

❶ Ratchaburi

ราชบุรี

Ratchaburi province. 🗺 195,977. 🚉
🚌 ℹ️ TAT, Phetchaburi (0-3247-1005).

Originally an estuarial port at the mouth of the Klong River, Ratchaburi is now 19 miles (30 km) from the ocean. During the Ayutthaya period (*see pp64–5*) the town was sacked twice, in 1765 and 1767, by invading Burmese armies en route to besiege the capital city of Ayutthaya.

Nowadays, Ratchaburi makes a pleasant place to stop on the way to Kanchanaburi and the Western Seaboard. Some visitors stay overnight if visiting Damnoen Saduak Floating Market the next morning.

The town has few sights, but Wat Mahathat is worth a visit. Its *prang*, allegedly modeled on the main *prang* at Angkor Wat (*see pp268–9*), dates from the 15th century, although the temple complex may have been founded as early as the 8th or 9th century. Inside the *prang* are traces of murals from the 15th century, and partially restored stucco work.

Artifacts in the **Ratchaburi National Museum** include archaeological finds such as fine Khmer sculptures and stucco decorations excavated from Muang Khu Bua, a Dvaravati site south of Ratchaburi.

🏛 **Ratchaburi National Museum**
Woradej Rd. **Tel** 0-3232-1513.
Open 9am–4pm Wed–Sat.
Closed public hols. ♿
🌐 nationalmuseums.f_inearts.go.th

Environs
The caves of Khao Ngu, 4 miles (6 km) northwest of Ratchaburi on Highway 3087, contain some early Dvaravati art. The splendid reliefs of Buddha images found in Tham Rusi and Tham Fa Tho are probably of greatest interest. Aggressive macaques gather in the area around the caves.

❷ Damnoen Saduak Floating Market

ตลาดน้ำดำเนินสะดวก

1 mile (2 km) W of Damnoen Saduak, Ratchaburi province. 🚉 🚌
🚤 or join tour from Bangkok.
Open 4–11am daily. ℹ️ TAT, Phetchaburi (0-3247-1005).

Like the numerous floating markets in Bangkok, the Damnoen Saduak market is also organized almost exclusively for tourists.

Located near Damnoen Saduak – 62 miles (100 km) southwest of Bangkok – the market is a labyrinth of narrow *khlongs* (canals). The small wooden boats are paddled mainly by female traders, some of whom are dressed in traditional blue farmers' shirts – *mo hom* – and conical straw hats. The fresh produce, including fruit, vegetables, and spices, comes straight from the farm. For the benefit of the tourists, some boats sell souvenir straw hats and refreshments.

The floating market actually consists of three markets. The largest, **Ton Khem**, is on Khlong Damnoen Saduak. On the parallel *khlong* is **Hia Kui**, where structures anchored to the banks function as warehouses selling souvenirs to large tour groups. To the south, on a smaller *khlong*, is **Khun Phitak**, which is the least crowded market.

The best way of getting around the three markets is by boat: trips can be taken along the *khlongs* or to see nearby coconut plantations. The best time to arrive is between 7am and 9am, when the Floating Market is in full swing.

Trading Thai-style at the bustling Damnoen Saduak Floating Market

Thai Fruits and Vegetables

Thailand's climate and soil conditions are conducive to the cultivation of a huge variety of fruits and vegetables throughout the year. Well-known tropical fruits, including papaya, watermelon, mango, and pineapple, are unmistakable, but the orchards and farms of Thailand also offer a wealth of produce that may be less familiar to many visitors. Among the not-to-be-missed treats are the mangosteen, the grapefruitlike pomelo, the much-prized durian, and the sweet-fleshed, hairy rambutan. Thai fruits are sold sliced as snacks by street vendors everywhere, and the full range of fresh produce can be seen at most markets.

Longans have a transparent, succulent flesh around a smooth pit.

Mangoes can be eaten unripe and sour (green) or ripe and sweet (yellow).

Mangosteens are a favorite with Thais. Their tasty flesh has a melt-in-the-mouth texture.

Durians are the king of Thai fruit. The pungent smell and flavor are an acquired taste.

Guavas, crisp and sour fruits, are best enjoyed with a sweet chili dip or as a refreshing juice.

Jackfruits, similar in appearance to durians, only larger, have a sticky flesh with a tangy flavor.

Gourds

Pea eggplant

Baby tomatoes

Eggplant

Thai vegetables include several types of makhua (the tomato and eggplant family). Gourds and eggplant are frequently used in curries.

Scallions

Cilantro

Chilies

Thai cuisine makes liberal use of chilies, galingal, tamarind, and lemon grass to flavor dishes, balancing spiciness with coconut milk and sugar. Cilantro and scallions are popular garnishes.

The peaceful, immaculately maintained Sampran Riverside

❸ Sampran Riverside

สามพราน ริเวอร์ไซต์

Off Hwy 4, 20 miles (32 km) W of Bangkok. **Tel** 0-3432-2544.
🚌 M: 15; AC: to Nakom Pathom or Suphan Buri, or tour from Bangkok.
Open 8am–6pm daily (shows 1:30pm & 2:45pm). 🎫
🌐 sampranriverside.com

This well-manicured garden, west of Bangkok, was formerly known as the Rose Garden Riverside. Here visitors can walk or cycle through the lush greenery, take a boat ride on the river, swim and even play tennis. A tour of the Organic Farm offers visitors a chance to learn about traditional Thai farming methods and buy some of the produce. However, the chief attraction for visitors is the daily show of culture. Packed into the one-hour show are traditional Thai dancing *(see pp46–7)*, ancient sword fighting, a Thai wedding, the ordination of a monk *(see p34)* and Thai boxing *(see pp48–9)*. The model Thai village within the grounds is a showcase for fruit-carving, basket weaving, and other crafts.

Environs

Farther west, on the way to Nakhon Pathom, the **Thai Human Imagery Museum** has fiberglass statues of historical Thai figures, including the Chakri kings *(see pp68–9)* and some renowned monks.

🏛 **Thai Human Imagery Museum**
Pinklao-Nakhonchaisri Hwy, km 31.
Tel 0-3433-2607. **Open** daily. 🎫

❹ Nakhon Pathom

นครปฐม

Nakhon Pathom province. 🗺 167,500. 🚍 🚌 ℹ TAT, Bangkok (0-2250-5500), TAT, Kanchanaburi (0-3451-1200). 🛒 daily. 🎏 Food and Fruit Fair (Sep 1–7); Phra Pathom Chedi Fair (Nov).

Some 42 miles (67 km) to the west of Bangkok, Nakhon Pathom was a major center of the Dvaravati Kingdom, which thrived from the 6th to the 11th centuries AD *(see pp60–61)*.

The highlight of the town is the **Phra Pathom Chedi**, on Phetkasem Highway. This huge monument, housing a large standing Buddha image, is one of the most important places of pilgrimage in Thailand. The original *stupa* (a non-Thai *chedi*) on this site is thought to have been built sometime between the 2nd century BC and the 5th century AD. It commemorated the first Buddhist missionaries in Thailand, allegedly sent here from India in the 3rd century BC. The building fell into decay in the 11th century and was not restored until the early 19th century, when King Mongkut had the old shrine encased in a *chedi*. The spire was completed by King Chulalongkorn. The *chedi* dominates the town and, at 395 ft (120 m) in height, is the tallest Buddhist *stupa* in the world.

Southeast of the *chedi* is the **Phra Pathom Chedi National Museum**, which has a fascinating collection of locally excavated pieces from the Dvaravati period, including the stone Wheels of the Law 23 els from Chedi Chula Prathon, a 7th to 8th century monument east of town.

West of the *chedi* is the early 20th-century **Sanam Chandra Palace**. Parts of the palace are open to the public, and the peaceful grounds are a good place from which to view the palace's unusual mix of architectural styles.

🏛 **Phra Pathom Chedi National Museum**
Khwa Phra Rd. **Tel** 0-3427-0300.
Open Wed–Sun.
Closed public hols. 🎫

🏛 **Sanam Chandra Palace**
Off Phetkasem Hwy. **Tel** 0-3427-0222.
Open Tue–Sun. 🎫

Nakhon Pathom's *chedi*, the world's tallest Buddhist monument

Nonthaburi pier, as seen from the Chao Phraya River

➎ Nonthaburi

นนทบุรี

Nonthaburi province. 🖼 46,500. 🚌 🚇 ℹ TAT, Bangkok (1672); TAT, Ayutthaya (0-3524-6076). 🚢 daily. 🥭 Fruit Fair (Apr–Jun).

Approximately 6 miles (10 km) north of Bangkok, Nonthaburi offers a relaxing slice of provincial life. The town is best reached by riverboat from one of Bangkok's express piers. The journey takes 50 minutes and offers several interesting sights, the first of which is the Royal Boat House near Wat Sam Phraya pier, where some of the royal barges are kept. Others are housed at the Royal Barge Museum in Thon Buri (see pp128–9). Past the Krung Thon Bridge is a small community of rice barges on the east bank, and shortly before Nonthaburi pier is **Wat Khian**, a temple that is half-submerged in the river.

Nonthaburi has a pleasant, provincial atmosphere that contrasts with the chaos and pollution of the capital just down the river. The town is particularly well known for the quality of its durian fruit (see p137) – reflected in the unusual decoration of the lampposts on the promenade. You may find the famously smelly fruit for sale in Nonthaburi's colorful, lively market by the side of the river. A round-trip boat ride

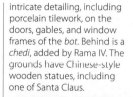
Door of *bot*, Wat Chalerm Phrakiet

from Nonthaburi along Khlong Om will take you on a slow-paced journey through durian plantations and past riverside houses. The tiny river island of **Ko Kret**, accessible only by boat, is home to a community of craftsmen, who are famous for their distinctive style of pottery.

Another worthwhile excursion from Nonthaburi is the river journey to **Wat Chalerm Phrakiet**, on the west bank of the Chao Phraya. The *wat* occupies the site of a 17th-century fortress, built by Rama III in the 19th century for his mother. A particularly striking feature is the intricate detailing, including porcelain tilework, on the doors, gables, and window frames of the *bot*. Behind is a *chedi*, added by Rama IV. The grounds have Chinese-style wooden statues, including one of Santa Claus.

➏ Chatuchak Market

ตลาดจตุจักร

Chatuchak district. 🚌 AC: 38, 502, 503, 509, 510, 512, 517, 518, 521, 523. Ⓜ Kampangphet. 🚇 Mo Chit (skytrain). ℹ TAT, Bangkok (1672). **Open** 7am–6pm Sat & Sun. 🌐 chatuchak.org

Thailand's biggest market is staged each weekend in a northern suburb of Bangkok, between the Northern Bus Terminal and Bangsu Railroad Station. It moved here in 1982 because it had outgrown its original site on Sanam Luang (see pp82–3). This chaotic mass of more than 15,000 stalls occupies the space of over five football fields. It is always full of throngs of eager shoppers, many of whom spend a whole day browsing among the merchandise displays.

The huge variety of goods for sale ranges from seafood to antiques, and from Siamese fighting fish to secondhand jeans. The plant section offers a good introduction to Thai flora, while the food stalls display every conceivable ingredient of Thai food, fresh from the farm or the sea. The antique and hill-tribe sections sell a good selection of artifacts and textiles, both fake and genuine, from all over Thailand and neighboring countries.

The market has been referred to as the "wildlife supermarket of the world," due to the sale of some endangered species here, such as leaf monkeys. Despite efforts to stop this, it is still continuing.

Traditional Thai wooden figures for sale at Chatuchak Market

❼ Sukhumvit Road

ถนนสุขุมวิท

Phra Khanong district. 🚇 🚌 AC: 38, 501, 508, 511, 513.

This road begins at the eastern end of Bangkok's downtown and continues all the way to the Cambodian border in Trat province *(see p327)*. In Bangkok it is the main thoroughfare of an expanding business quarter popular with foreigners.

Though it is a long way from Bangkok's best-known sights, the area has numerous good quality, moderately priced hotels and restaurants, and a few attractions of its own.

Foremost of these is the **Siam Society**, which was founded in the early 1900s (by a group of Thais and foreign residents under the patronage of Rama VI) to research, rediscover, and preserve Thai culture. Within the grounds are two traditional teakwood Northern Thai houses that comprise the country's only genuine ethnological museum. The Kamthieng House, a farm dwelling, was transported piece by piece in the 1960s to Bangkok from the bank of the Ping River, near Chiang Mai. The Sangaroon House is a later addition donated by the architect Sangaroon Ratagasikorn who – inspired by the utilitarian

Bangkok's Mass Transit System along busy Sukhumvit Road

beauty of rural utensils – amassed a sizable collection. It is a good example of Central Plains style *(see p40)*. Also on the grounds is a reference library on Thai culture, open to visitors. The *Journal of the Siam Society* is one of Asia's most respected publications on art history, culture, and society.

Located next to the Eastern Bus Terminal, the **Bangkok Planetarium**, with its hands-on exhibitions, may be of some interest to those people who have time to spare while waiting for a bus.

Sculpture at the Queen's Park

The **Queen's Park** (or Benjasiri Park) is between sois 22 and 24, while the larger **King Rama IX Park** is farther out toward Samut Prakan. With its botanical gardens and area for water sports, this park is one of Bangkok's most pleasant oases. The park also has an exhibition on the king's life.

🏛 **Siam Society**
131 Soi Asoke, Sukhumvit Rd, Soi 21.
Tel 0-2661-6470. **Open** Tue–Sat.
🌐 siam-society.org

🏛 **Bangkok Planetarium**
928 Sukhumvit Rd. **Tel** 0-2392-1773.
Open Tue–Sun. **Closed** public hols.
📷 🌐 sciplanet.org

🌳 **Queen's Park**
By Soi 22, Sukhumvit Rd. **Open** daily.

🌳 **King Rama IX Park**
Soi Udomsuk, Sukhumvit Rd, Soi 103.
Tel 0-2328-1385. **Open** daily. 📷 🚻

A mockup of a traditional sleeping area in the Kamthieng House

❽ Safari World

ซาฟารีเวิลด์

99 Panyaintra Road, Minburi district.
Tel 0-2914-4100. 🚌 60, 71 & AC: 501 to Fashion Island Center, then *songthaew*. **Open** 9am–5pm daily.
📷 🌐 safariworld.com

This car-safari park offers eight different natural habitats over a 3-mile (5-km) drive. Animals on view include tigers, elephants, giraffes, lions, zebras, and rare species such as white pandas. A marine park features dolphin shows. There are also elephant and orangutan shows, and a bird park.

❾ Siam Park

สวนสยาม

203 Suan Siam Road, Khan Na Yao district. **Tel** 0-2919-7200. 🚌 AC: 519.
Open 10am–6pm Mon–Fri, 9am–7pm Sat, Sun & public hols.
📷 🌐 siamparkcity.com

Siam Park is a great place to cool off from the heat of the Thai sun. Its attractions include huge waterslides, a gentle whirlpool, and an artificial lake. Water permeates Thai culture in many ways, not least at Songkran (New Year), when everyone gets soaked on the streets *(see p52 and p240)*.

The facilities are well maintained, and there are restaurants and lifeguards. There is also an amusement park with rickety fairground rides and a small zoo. As Bangkok families descend upon the park in numbers at the weekend, it's best to visit during the week.

⑩ Prasart Museum

พิพิธภัณฑ์ปราสาท

9 Soi Krungthepkretha 4a, Bang Kapi district. **Tel** 0-2379-3601. M: 10. **Open** Tue–Sun. compulsory (book in advance).

The privately owned Prasart Museum is known to relatively few tourists and Bangkokians, but the journey out to this elegant museum, set in landscaped tropical gardens, will be worthwhile for anyone who loves Thai art. The collector, Prasart Vongsakul, started to acquire Thai antiques in 1965 when he was only 12 years old.

Ornate interior of Lanna Pavilion at the Prasart Museum

⑪ Ancient City

เมืองโบราณ

Sukhumvit Rd, Bangpu, Samut Prakan province. **Tel** 0-2709-1644. AC: 511 to the end of the line, then take the 36 mini-bus. **Open** 8am–5pm daily. W ancientcitygroup.com

Muang Boran, or "Ancient City," is an outdoor cultural theme park financed and created in the early 1970s by the art-loving philanthropic owner of Thailand's largest Mercedes-Benz dealership.

The park makes a surprisingly worthwhile visit. The peaceful grounds, shaped roughly like Thailand itself, display numerous replicas of important monuments in Thailand as well as actual buildings and sculptures that have been restored to their former grandeur. Replicas are one third real size.

All the Thai art periods are represented, including a few mythical and literary ones such as at the Garden of Phra Aphaimani, inspired by a 19th-century verse play *(see p322)*. Some of the buildings – for example the Sanphet Prasat Palace, which once stood near Wat Phra Si Sanphet in Ayutthaya *(see pp182–3)* – are reconstructions of monuments destroyed centuries ago in battle and so provide the only testaments to past glories.

⑫ Crocodile Farm

ฟาร์มจระเข้

Old Sukhumvit Highway, Samut Prakan province. **Tel** 0-2387-0020. AC: 511 to Samut Prakan, then *songthaew*, or join tour from Bangkok. **Open** 8am–6pm daily.

The largest of Thailand's (and, supposedly, the world's) crocodile farms, this breeding park/zoo is home to some 30,000 reptiles. Fresh- and saltwater species, from South American caimans to crocodiles from the Nile, can be seen here.

In the breeding section you can see crocodiles hatching and in various stages of growth. You can also see them transformed into handbags and key rings in the souvenir shop. Wrestling shows are held regularly, and feeding time happens at 4:30–5:30pm. A visit to the crocodile farm is popularly combined with a day trip to the Ancient City.

Wrestling, the most spectacular show at the Crocodile Farm

⑬ Erawan Museum

พิพิธภัณฑ์ช้างเอราวัณ

99/9 Moo 1, Bangmuangmai Samut Prakan province. **Tel** 0-2371-3135. 25, 142, 365; AC: 102, 507, 511, 536. **Open** 8am–5pm daily. W erawan-museum.com

A monumental three-headed bronze elephant stands astride the Erawan Museum, making it visible for miles around. Inside is a large collection of ancient religious objects, including a number of priceless Buddha statues.

The exterior of the building's lower story is decorated with tiny pink enamel tiles in the style of Thai Benjaron ceramics. An elaborate double staircase, which takes you up inside the body of the elephant, dominates the upper levels. There is also an elevator that travels up one of the hind legs. Outside, the tranquil gardens contain ponds and fountains in a variety of styles.

Reconstruction of the Prince of Lampang's Palace, Ancient City

SHOPPING IN BANGKOK

Bangkok is a veritable shoppers' paradise, with its profusion of retail outlets, high quality of goods, and surprisingly low prices. Staff in department stores are super-attentive – some might say overly so – and whether it's designer clothes, traditional crafts, or electronic equipment you're after, there are some great deals to be had. Don't miss the fun of bargaining in the open-air markets, where vendors will often drop their prices by 30 percent or more. Beware of the energy-sapping heat and humidity of mid-afternoon, and limit your buying spree to one or two locations per day.

Crowds thronging Mahboonkrong shopping mall

Practical Information

Opening hours are usually early morning to mid-afternoon in fresh markets, 10am–10pm in shopping malls, and 24 hours in convenience stores. Credit cards are accepted in shopping malls and modern boutiques, but market vendors expect cash payment. VAT refunds are available, but the shop where the item is bought must fill out a form for customs, which can be time-consuming, so it is only worth it for significant savings. Bargaining is expected at street stalls and markets, but prices are fixed in department stores and boutiques. For more information, see page 434.

Shopping Districts

Boutiques and markets are scattered all over the city, but an especially high concentration of shopping outlets can be found around Siam Square and Silom, Ploenchit, and Sukhumvit roads.

Shopping Malls

CentralWorld leads the way in the race to be Bangkok's best and biggest mall; indeed, this is Southeast Asia's largest shopping complex. Another favourite shopping destination is **Siam Paragon**, where you can buy anything from a sports car to a bowl of noodles. **Mahboonkrong** (or MBK) feels more like a street market spread over eight floors. Other centrally located malls are **Siam Center** and **Siam Discovery**, **Emporium**, **Silom Complex**, **Amarin Plaza**, **Gaysorn Plaza**, and **Erawan**.

Markets

No self-respecting shopaholic can claim to know Bangkok without having experienced the city's vast **Chatuchak Market**

A stall at Chatuchak Market, the country's biggest open-air market

(see p139), said to be the world's largest open-air market. Pick up a map and be selective, since you'll never get round it all in a day.

Bangkok's night markets in the Khao San, Patpong, and Sukhumvit Sois 3–15 regions, which consist of simple stalls set up each evening on the sidewalk, make it possible to combine souvenir shopping with dining and clubbing in case you're pushed for time.

Jim Thompson, one of the most reputable outlets for silk products

Silk and Cotton

Thai silk is renowned for its high quality, unique designs, and reasonable price. Be aware that in the night markets, some items that claim to be silk are, in fact, made of synthetic fabric. To be sure you're getting the real thing, it pays to visit a reputable shop, such as **Jim Thompson**, which has outlets in many top hotels. If you know what you're looking for, head for **Phahurat Market**, where prices are cheaper.

Thai cotton is also a good deal. The eye-catching designs on items like bedspreads and cushion covers make it a distinctive souvenir.

Clothes

With prices only a fraction of what they are in the West, it makes sense to stock up on clothes, either off the peg in shopping malls or tailor-made to order. Tailors abound in all tourist areas, but workmanship varies, so visit a reputable tailor such as **Raja's Fashions** or **Marzotto**, and allow several days for preparation and fittings.

Antiques

Examples of ancient crafts are available in many shops, but few of these are genuine antiques, for which a permit from the Fine Arts Department is required for export. A couple of reliable outlets are the **River City Complex**, which has four floors of antique furniture, carvings, and old maps, and **OP Place**, with rare collectibles like sculptures and prints.

Thai Crafts

From silverware to celadon, from lacquerware to woodcarvings, from basketware to hand-woven textiles, the variety of Thai crafts is rich indeed. Good places to see a wide range of crafts include **Chatuchak Market** *(see p139)*, **Narai Phand**, **Silom Village**, and **Nandakwang**.

Hand-painted umbrellas can be found in many craft centers

Gems and Jewelry

As with antiques, extreme caution should be exercised when buying gems or jewelry, since potential customers are often exposed to sophisticated scams. Serious shoppers should browse the glittering displays of jewelry at **Peninsula Plaza** or the gem boutiques at reliable hotels.

Electronic Goods

Computer equipment, video games, cameras, and mobile phones are on sale in shopping malls throughout the city, but one place that specializes in such goods is **Pantip Plaza**. Customers should be aware that some items on sale, such as software, are pirated and offer no money-back guarantee.

Books

Book addicts should explore the massive selection at **Asia Books** and **Kinokuniya Books**. Other bookstore chains with outlets in central Bangkok are **B2S** and **Bookazine**.

DIRECTORY

Shopping Malls

Amarin Plaza
Ploenchit Rd. **Map** 8 D1.
Tel 0-2650-4704.
W amarinplaza.com

CentralWorld
Ratchadamri Rd.
Map 8 D1.
Tel 0-2793-7400.
W centralworld.co.th

Emporium
Sukhumvit Soi 24–26.
Tel 0-2269-1000.
W emporiumthailand.com

Erawan
Ploenchit Rd. **Map** 8 D1.
Tel 0-2250-7777.
W erawanbangkok.com

Gaysorn Plaza
Ploenchit Rd. **Map** 8 D1.
Tel 0-2656-1149.
W gaysornplaza.com

Mahboonkrong (MBK)
Phayathai Rd. **Map** 7 C1.
Tel 0-2217-9111.
W mbk-center.co.th

Siam Center/Siam Discovery
Rama I Rd. **Map** 7 C1.
Tel 0-2658-1000.
W siamcenter.co.th

Siam Paragon
Rama I Rd. **Map** 7 C1.
Tel 0-2610-8000.
W siamparagon.co.th

Silom Complex
Silom Rd. **Map** 8 D4.
Tel 0-2632-1199.
W silomcomplex.net

Silk and Cotton

Jim Thompson
9 Surawong Rd.
Map 7 C3.
Tel 0-2632-8100.

Phahurat Market
Phahurat. **Map** 6 D1.

Clothes

Marzotto
3 Soi Shangri-La Hotel,
Charoen Krung Rd.
Map 6 F5.
Tel 0-2233-2880.

Raja's Fashions
Sukhumvit Rd, between
Soi 6 & Soi 8.
Tel 0-2253-8379.

Antiques

OP Place
Charoen Krung Rd,
Soi 38 (near Mandarin
Oriental Hotel).
Map 6 F4.

River City Complex
23 Trok Rongnamkaeng
Yotha Rd. **Map** 6 F3.
Tel 0-2237-0077.
W rivercity.co.th

Thai Crafts

Nandakwang
Sukhumvit Soi 23.
Tel 0-2664-0017.
W nandakwang.com

Narai Phand
973 Ploenchit Rd.
Map 8 D1.
Tel 0-2656-0398.

Silom Village
Silom Rd. **Map** 7 A4.
Tel 0-2234-4448.
W silomvillage.co.th

Gems and Jewelry

Peninsula Plaza
Ratchadamri Rd.
Map 8 D1.
Tel 0-2253-9791.

Electronic Goods

Pantip Plaza
Petchburi Rd. **Map** 4 D5.
Tel 0-2250-1555.
W pantipplaza.com

Books

Asia Books
Siam Discovery Mall.
Tel 0-2715-9000.
W asiabooks.com

B2S
CentralWorld,
Ratchadamri Rd.
Map 8 D1.

Bookazine
Silom Complex, Silom Rd.
Map 8 D4.

Kinokuniya Books
Siam Paragon
(also in Emporium and
CentralWorld). **Map** 7 C1.

Bangkok's Markets

Markets are a fundamental part of Bangkok life. Both specialty and general markets provide great browsing, whether you are interested in flowers or fabrics, sarongs or stamps. Do not try to take in too many markets in one outing – focus on one area and explore that in depth. Nancy Chandler's *Map of Bangkok*, readily available locally, can be a great help in planning a market sortie.

Banglamphu Market is a typical neighborhood market with general stalls displaying food, shoes, clothes, and assorted bric-a-brac.

Khao San Road Market may take up only one tiny road, but it has become a legend among backpackers as a source of almost anything imaginable. In addition to rucksacks, hiking boots, and other travelers' equipment, it is good for secondhand books, jewelry, clothes, bags, and pirated DVDs.

Pak Khlong Market *(see p102)* is the most lively and atmospheric wholesale fresh produce market in the capital. Open 24 hours a day, it is best viewed – and cheapest – between 10pm and 5am, when exotic blooms line the pavements along with fruit and vegetables.

0 meters 500
0 yards 500

Key to Market Locations in Bangkok

① Thewet Flower Market
② Banglamphu Market
③ Khao San Road Market
④ Bo Be Market
⑤ Nakorn Kasem (Thieves' Market)
⑥ Stamp Market
⑦ Phahurat Market
⑧ Pak Khlong Market
⑨ Sampeng Lane Market
⑩ Kao Market
⑪ Pratunam Market
⑫ Patpong/Silom Market
⑬ Bangrak Market

Phahurat Market *(see p102)* is the commercial hub of Bangkok's Indian community. Fabric sellers and tailors predominate, and the air is filled with the aroma of Indian food and spices.

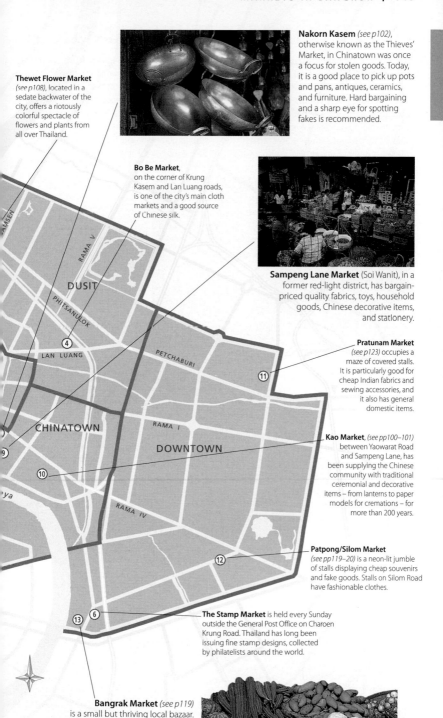

Nakorn Kasem *(see p102)*, otherwise known as the Thieves' Market, in Chinatown was once a focus for stolen goods. Today, it is a good place to pick up pots and pans, antiques, ceramics, and furniture. Hard bargaining and a sharp eye for spotting fakes is recommended.

Thewet Flower Market *(see p108)*, located in a sedate backwater of the city, offers a riotously colorful spectacle of flowers and plants from all over Thailand.

Bo Be Market, on the corner of Krung Kasem and Lan Luang roads, is one of the city's main cloth markets and a good source of Chinese silk.

Sampeng Lane Market (Soi Wanit), in a former red-light district, has bargain-priced quality fabrics, toys, household goods, Chinese decorative items, and stationery.

Pratunam Market *(see p123)* occupies a maze of covered stalls. It is particularly good for cheap Indian fabrics and sewing accessories, and it also has general domestic items.

Kao Market, *(see pp100–101)* between Yaowarat Road and Sampeng Lane, has been supplying the Chinese community with traditional ceremonial and decorative items – from lanterns to paper models for cremations – for more than 200 years.

Patpong/Silom Market *(see pp119–20)* is a neon-lit jumble of stalls displaying cheap souvenirs and fake goods. Stalls on Silom Road have fashionable clothes.

The Stamp Market is held every Sunday outside the General Post Office on Charoen Krung Road. Thailand has long been issuing fine stamp designs, collected by philatelists around the world.

Bangrak Market *(see p119)* is a small but thriving local bazaar. Many of the top hotels buy their fruit, vegetables, meat, and seafood from here. The market also has fabric and clothes stands.

ENTERTAINMENT IN BANGKOK

Bangkok provides a bewildering range of entertainment, from classical puppet theater to nightclubs. One of the most popular choices for short-stay visitors is a cultural show accompanied by a Thai meal, but there are plenty of alternatives, such as transvestite cabaret shows or an unusual cocktail at one of the city's bars with a view.

Many restaurants and bars feature live music, ranging from traditional Thai ballads to rock classics, while the city's discos provide a melting pot in which locals and foreigners discover mutual tastes. If you are going to any event that starts at a particular time, be sure to plan your journey well in advance to beat Bangkok's notorious traffic.

Thai women in traditional dress dancing at Siam Niramit

General Information

For information about upcoming events, consult the English-language newspapers **Bangkok Post** and **The Nation**, or pick up one of the free magazines, like **BK**, that are distributed at tourist locations. Tickets for events are usually easy to come by: ask at your hotel desk or at any travel agent, or book online at www. thaiticketmaster.com. For more information, see p442.

Cultural Shows and Theater

If you're in the mood for a cultural extravaganza, then book for the nightly show at **Siam Niramit**, which features spectacular sets and more than 500 elaborately dressed performers. Classical dance shows with buffet or à la carte dinners can be enjoyed at **Sala Rim Nam** and **Silom Village**, while the city's top cabaret location is **Calypso Cabaret** in Asiatique, an entertainment venue south of the city center. For performances of *khon*, or classical

masked drama, head for the **Sala Chalermkrung Theatre** or the **National Theatre**.

In addition to famous Thai puppetry, the **Aksra Theatre**'s performances include scenes from the classic *Ramakien* masked dance drama, as well as other traditional Thai dance.

Muay Thai

Those who prefer visceral rather than intellectual entertainment should head to the local Thai boxing ring to view this traditional martial art. Thai boxing, or *muay thai*, is the national sport, and bouts always draw a large crowd. Spectators like to bet on the

outcome of the matches, and cheer excitedly for their chosen fighter.

At **Ratchadamnoen Stadium** and **Lumphini Stadium**, you can watch the boxers prepare for their bouts with slow, mindful movements to the accompaniment of wailing instruments.

Cinemas

It may seem strange to travel all the way to Thailand and end up going to the cinema, but with their air-conditioned interiors, comfortable seats, and cheap prices, they can make the perfect antidote to a tiring shopping spree. Most cinemas these days are located in shopping malls, such as the **Paragon Cineplex** in Siam Paragon and the **Major Cineplex** in CentralWorld Plaza, though a few independent cinemas still exist, such as the **Scala** and **Lido** in Siam Square, which occasionally show arthouse or independent films. The Thai national anthem is played before every showing, and everybody is expected to stand, including foreign visitors. The website www. movieseer. com has details of what films are showing.

The colorful foyer of the Major Cineplex in CentralWorld

The crowded bar and dancefloor at the popular Q Bar, Bangkok

Bars and Nightclubs

Bangkok has an astonishing range of bars, from the hole-in-the-wall **Adhere the 13th**, with an in-house band playing funky music, to the super-chic **Sky Bar**, where the city's high-flyers sip cocktails and gaze down on their domain from the 63rd floor. Competition for custom is fierce, and many bars feature live bands in an effort to draw in the crowds – for example, **Saxophone** offers a heady mix of jazz, blues, and reggae, while **Hard Rock Café** has bands playing covers of rock classics. Visitors itching to shake their stuff at a disco are also catered for at venues like **Sugar Club**, **Q Bar**, **Ku De Ta**, and at the gay nightclub **DJ Station**. Sophisticated travelers looking for an elegant environment should make their way to **Diplomat Bar**, **Moon Bar**, or **Syn Bar**.

Bangkok has long been known for its tolerance of a wide variety of sexual tastes, and Silom Sois 2 and 4 are lined with gay bars, such as **Telephone Pub**. The three main areas of hostess and go-go bars are the infamous **Patpong 1 and 2** (off Silom Road), **Nana Plaza** (Sukhumvit Soi 4), and **Soi Cowboy** (Sukhumvit Soi 21–23). Many are curious to drop into one of these bars, but it's best to avoid the upstairs bars on Patpong, where scams often leave foreign visitors with an empty wallet.

The neon lights of Soi Cowboy, one of Bangkok's red-light districts

DIRECTORY

Cultural Shows and Theater

Aksra Theatre
Rangnam Rd.
Map 4 E4.
Tel 1-2677-8888.

Calypso Cabaret
Asiatique, 2194 Charoenkrung.
Tel 0-2688-1415.
w calypso cabaret.com

National Theatre
Rachinee Rd. **Map** 1 C4.
Tel 0-2224-1342.

Sala Chalermkrung Theatre
Charoen Krung Rd.
Map 6 D1.
Tel 0-2222-0434.

Sala Rim Nam
Oriental Hotel,
48 Oriental Avenue.
Map 6 F4.
Tel 0-2659-9000.

Siam Niramit
Ratchada Theatre, 19 Tiam Ruammit Rd.
Tel 0-2649-9222.
w siamniramit.com

Silom Village

Silom Rd.
Map 7 A4.
Tel 0-2234-4448.
w silomvillage.co.th

Muay Thai

Lumphini Stadium
6 Ramintra Rd.
Tel 0-2284-3141.
w muaythailumpinee.net

Ratchadamnoen Stadium
Ratchadamnoen Nok Rd.
Map 2 F4.
Tel 0-2281-4205.
w rajadamnern.com

Cinemas

Lido
Siam Square. **Map** 7 C1.
Tel 0-2252-6498.

Major Cineplex
1121/39 Sukhumvit.
Tel 0-2381-4855.

Paragon Cineplex
Siam Paragon, Rama I Rd.
Map 7 C1.
Tel 0-2129-4635.

Scala

Siam Square.
Map 7 C1.
Tel 0-2251-2861.

Bars and Nightclubs

Adhere the 13th
13 Samsen Rd. **Map** 2 D3.
Tel 08-9769-4613.

Diplomat Bar
Conrad Hotel, Wireless Rd.
Map 8 E2.
Tel 0-2690-9999.

DJ Station
Silom Soi 2.
Map 7 C4.
Tel 0-2266-4029.
w djstation.com

Hard Rock Café
Siam Square.
Map 7 C1.
Tel 0-2251-0797.
w hardrockcafe.co.th

Ku De Ta
98 North Sathorn Rd.
Map 7 C4.
Tel 0-2108-2000.

Moon Bar
Banyan Tree Hotel,
South Sathorn Rd.
Map 8 D4.
Tel 0-2679-1200.

Q Bar

Sukhumvit Soi 11.
Tel 0-2252-3274.

Saxophone
3/8 Victory Monument.
Map 4 E3.
Tel 0-2246-5472.

Sky Bar
63rd Floor, State Tower,
Silom Rd.
Map 7 A5.
Tel 0-2624-9999.
w lebua.com

Sugar Club
37 Sukhumvit 11.
Tel 08-2308-2346.

Syn Bar
Swissotel Nai Lert Park,
Wireless Rd.
Map 8 E1.
Tel 0-2253-0123.

Telephone Pub
Silom Soi 4.
Map 7 C4.
Tel 0-2234-3279.
w telephonepub.com

BANGKOK STREET FINDER

Finding your way around Bangkok can be a challenge. The lack of standard transliterations for Thai words means that the street names listed here will not always match those seen on street signs. Additionally, some streets are known by more than one name – for example, Charoen Krung Road is New Road and Wireless Road is Witthayu Road. Most major roads *(thanons)* have numerous numbered (and sometimes named) *sois* and *troks* (minor roads and lanes) leading from them. Odd-numbered *sois* usually lead off one side of a road, even numbers off the other. Be warned that there can be considerable distances between *sois* – for instance, *sois* 6 and 36 off Petchaburi Road are more than 2 miles (3 km) apart. Major sights, markets, and ferry piers are also listed in this gazetteer.

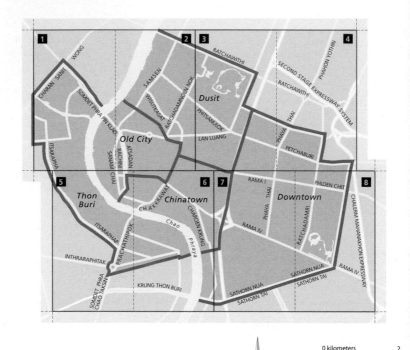

Key

Major sight	Riverboat pier	Church
Place of interest	Chao Phraya Express pier	Mosque
Other building	Tourist information	Railroad line
Subway station	Hospital with emergency room	Skytrain route
Railroad station	Police station	Airport rail
Skytrain station	Wat	Expressway
Airport rail link	Hindu temple	Street market

0 kilometers 2
0 miles 1

Scale of Map Pages

0 meters 400
0 yards 400

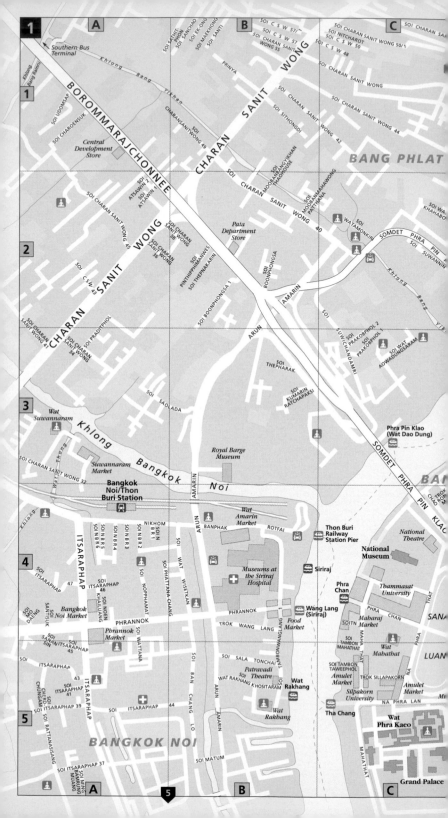

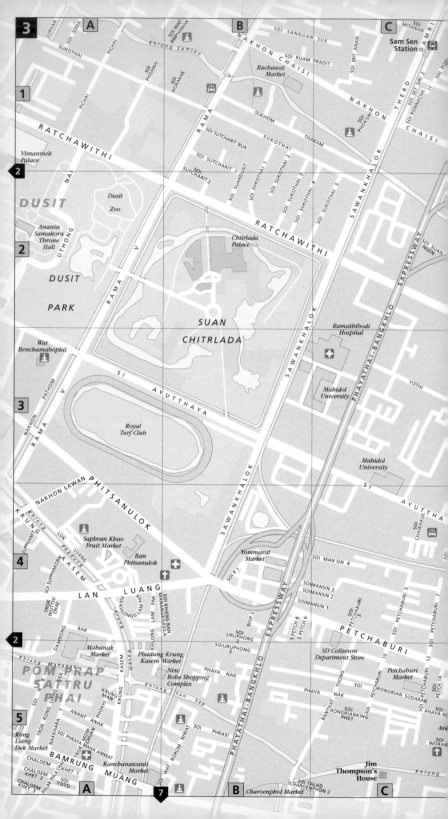

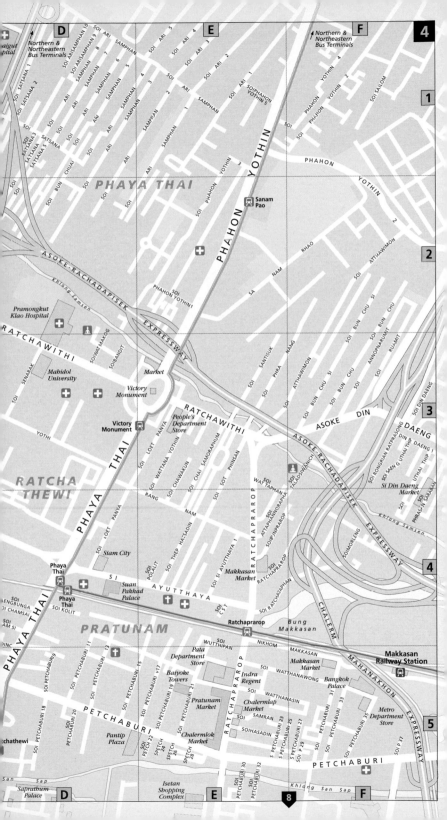

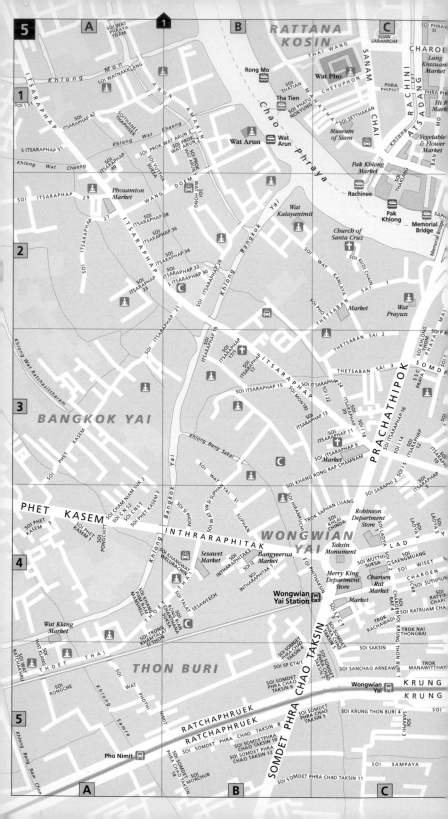

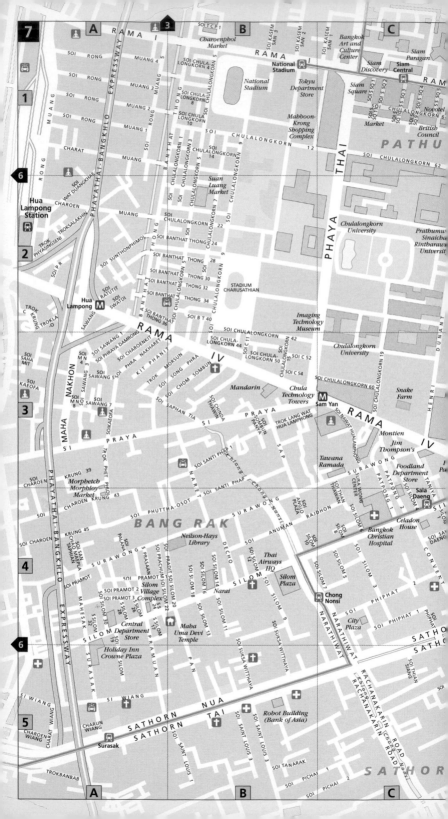

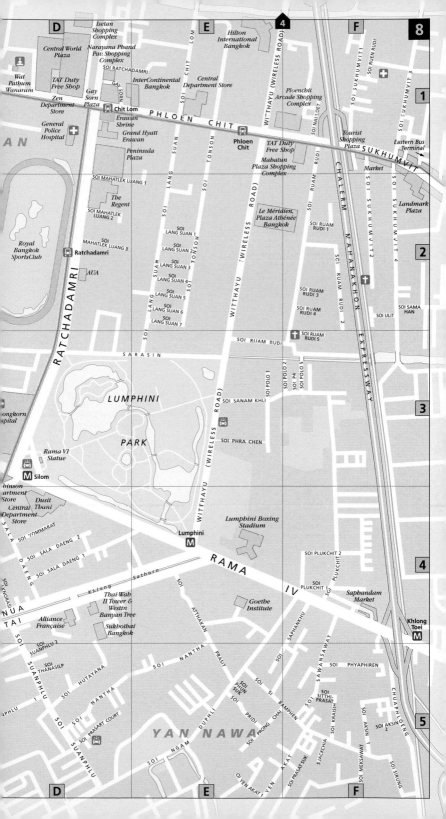

THE CENTRAL PLAINS

Introducing the Central Plains

The fertile plains stretching northward from Bangkok are
the nation's rice basket and the historic heartland of the
Tai people. Here lie the impressive ruined cities of the old
Sukhothai *(see pp62–3)* and Ayutthaya kingdoms *(see pp64–5)*.
Today this is the country's most wealthy and densely
populated region, with fast-expanding towns surrounded
by fields of sugar cane and rice. In the forested hills that
border the Central Plains are national parks with
spectacular waterfalls and a wide range of wildlife,
providing a pleasant scenic contrast.

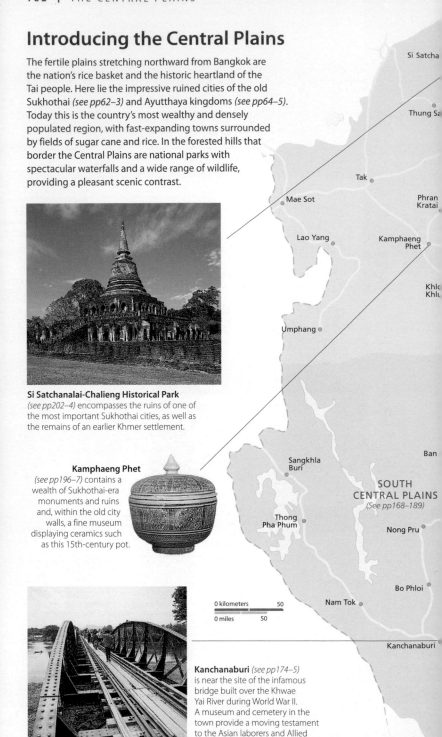

Si Satchanalai-Chalieng Historical Park
(see pp202–4) encompasses the ruins of one of
the most important Sukhothai cities, as well as
the remains of an earlier Khmer settlement.

Kamphaeng Phet
(see pp196–7) contains a
wealth of Sukhothai-era
monuments and ruins
and, within the old city
walls, a fine museum
displaying ceramics such
as this 15th-century pot.

Kanchanaburi *(see pp174–5)*
is near the site of the infamous
bridge built over the Khwae
Yai River during World War II.
A museum and cemetery in the
town provide a moving testament
to the Asian laborers and Allied
troops who died.

Si Satcha

Thung Sa

Tak

Mae Sot

Phran
Kratai

Lao Yang

Kamphaeng
Phet

Khlo
Khlu

Umphang

Sangkhla
Buri

Ban

SOUTH
CENTRAL PLAINS
(See pp168–189)

Thong
Pha Phum

Nong Pru

Bo Phloi

Nam Tok

Kanchanaburi

0 kilometers 50

0 miles 50

◀ Seated Buddha image at Wat Mahathat, Sukhothai Historical Park

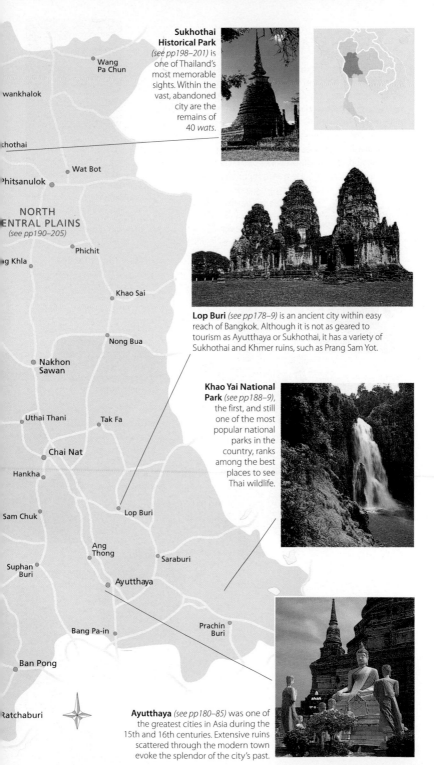

Sukhothai Historical Park *(see pp198–201)* is one of Thailand's most memorable sights. Within the vast, abandoned city are the remains of 40 *wats*.

Wang Pa Chun

wankhalok

khothai

Wat Bot

Phitsanulok

NORTH CENTRAL PLAINS *(see pp190–205)*

Phichit

g Khla

Khao Sai

Nong Bua

Nakhon Sawan

Uthai Thani

Tak Fa

Chai Nat

Hankha

Sam Chuk

Lop Buri

Ang Thong

Saraburi

Suphan Buri

Ayutthaya

Bang Pa-in

Prachin Buri

Ban Pong

Ratchaburi

Lop Buri *(see pp178–9)* is an ancient city within easy reach of Bangkok. Although it is not as geared to tourism as Ayutthaya or Sukhothai, it has a variety of Sukhothai and Khmer ruins, such as Prang Sam Yot.

Khao Yai National Park *(see pp188–9)*, the first, and still one of the most popular national parks in the country, ranks among the best places to see Thai wildlife.

Ayutthaya *(see pp180–85)* was one of the greatest cities in Asia during the 15th and 16th centuries. Extensive ruins scattered through the modern town evoke the splendor of the city's past.

Sukhothai Art

The prolific artisans of the Sukhothai School (late 13th–15th centuries) adapted stylistic elements from Sri Lanka, Burma, and other neighboring countries to produce some of Thailand's finest works of art. Numerous Buddha images of immense beauty and fluidity were cast in bronze. The "Walking" Buddha – a posture that is otherwise rare in Buddhist art – is perhaps the best-known artistic achievement of the period. The Sangkhalok *(see p204)* ceramics industry also flourished, and its fine wares, including pale blue-green celadons, were exported all over Asia until the middle of the 16th century.

The Walking Buddha posture possibly represents the Buddha's descent from Tavatimsa Heaven after he had visited his mother.

Bronze replaced stone as the preferred material for Buddha images during the Sukhothai period. It allowed a far more delicate detailing of the Buddha's hair and facial features.

Phitsanulok Buddha

Located in Wat Phra Si Rattana Mahathat in Phitsanulok, this 14th-century Buddha image, known properly as Phra Phuttha Chinarat, is one of the most revered in all of Thailand, second only to the Emerald Buddha in Bangkok. Cast in bronze and later gilded, the serene figure is a supreme example of late Sukhothai art.

This bronze Vishnu, a Hindu god, is in the classic Sukhothai style. Brahmin priests, who presided over some court ceremonies, probably ordered figures like this to be made.

Wedge-shaped joints

The flame like "halo" around Phra Phuttha Chinarat, ending in *naga* heads, is unique.

Fingers all of the same length

Sukhothai *bai semas* (boundary stones, *see p37*) were fashioned from slate into leaf shapes. This one, at Wat Sorasak in Sukhothai, is inscribed with details of a land grant.

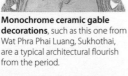

Monochrome ceramic gable decorations, such as this one from Wat Phra Phai Luang, Sukhothai, are a typical architectural flourish from the period.

Ceramic finials, found on many roofs, were sometimes fashioned as dragons. Such decorations show a fusion of Khmer and Chinese styles.

Sangkhalok ware, such as this delightful, brown monochrome elephant, are often well preserved. Fine pieces like this were produced from the mid-14th century onward, when exports boomed.

King Vajiravudh (1910–25) was highly active in the early archaeological work at Sukhothai: he was a totally untrained but enthusiastic excavator.

Fish-and-flower motifs, painted beneath the glaze, were popular for bowls and plates. Such items were exported as far afield as Japan.

Tightly curled hair drawn into flamelike finial

Arched nose and eyebrows

Gently smiling mouth

Diaphanous robes

Figurines sometimes feature a bulge by the mouth, which may depict the chewing of fermented tea. Female figures are common, often carrying babies.

Pouring vessels, known as *kendis*, were sometimes zoomorphic, like this earthenware piece in the shape of a duck.

The Ban Ko Noi Kilns

The remains of 200 brick kilns were excavated at Ban Noi (see p203) near Si Satchanalai in 1980–87. Some contain the pots that were being fired when the kilns were abandoned. There are also a number of kiln sites at Sukhothai.

Entrance

Chimney

Foreigners in Ayutthaya

Throughout the 16th and 17th centuries Ayutthaya was one of the most important trading centers in Asia, attracting not only merchants but also missionaries, adventurers, and mercenaries from around the world. Portuguese visitors arriving in the 16th century found a riverine city of canals and magnificent flotillas of barges. They brought firearms to trade and military advisers to help Ayutthaya against the Burmese. The Dutch and English followed in the 17th century and established trading warehouses. The Japanese came to buy animal hides, while French Jesuits and Persians competed for religious converts. Some foreigners, including Constantine Phaulkon, sought political influence.

St. Joseph's Church *(see p184)* stands south of Ayutthaya's main island. Originally built during the reign of King Narai (1656–88) by French missionaries, it has been restored many times since.

Lacquerware was a specialty of Ayutthaya. Like other aspects of life in the city, the decorative arts reflected the influence of foreigners or *farangs*. These doors depict *farang* traders.

Map of Ayutthaya

The involvement of Europeans in Siamese affairs led to the publication of several maps of Ayutthaya. This French map, probably an 18th-century copy of one drawn in the 17th century, shows the location of the French, Portuguese, and Siamese quarters. The European spelling of Ayutthaya at that time was Iudia.

Royal Palace

Siamese quarter

Chao Phraya River

The first French to arrive in Ayutthaya, in 1662, were Jesuit missionaries. In 1681 the French asked permission for a full diplomatic mission to visit the city. It arrived in 1685, headed by the envoy from Louis XIV, Chevalier de Chaumont. A Siamese envoy later returned with him to France. This painting shows him being received at court by the Sun King, Louis XIV.

French Jesuit missionaries came to Ayutthaya to convert King Narai to Catholicism. They failed in this but encouraged him to cultivate an interest in astronomy. This illustration shows him watching a lunar eclipse in 1685. Following the Jesuits' tutelage he watched a partial solar eclipse in 1688. Narai favored the Jesuits and gave them land to build churches and schools.

Chilies were first imported from South America by the Portuguese, who established a trading treaty with the Siamese in 1516. They quickly grew in popularity, and today chilies are an essential ingredient in numerous Thai dishes.

Siamese quarter   Chinese quarter

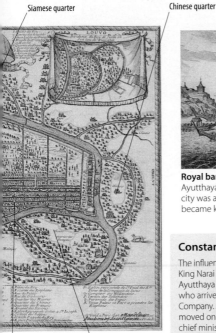

French quarter   Portuguese quarter

Royal barges and other boats crowded the waterways of Ayutthaya. Often the first sight that greeted visitors to the city was a convoy of royal barges. As a result, Ayutthaya became known as the "Venice of the East."

Constantine Phaulkon

The influence of foreigners in Ayutthaya was greatest under King Narai (1656–88). Most notorious of those who came to Ayutthaya was the Greek adventurer Constantine Phaulkon, who arrived in 1678 in the employ of the English East India Company. Attracting the attention of Narai, he quickly moved on to become the king's personal confidant and chief minister. He later advised Narai against Dutch and English interests in Ayutthaya. The French, meanwhile, were allowed to station 600 soldiers in the kingdom. Amid much political wrangling in court, Narai was viewed as cultivating strong ties with Louis XIV, whose ambition was to convert him and Siam to Catholicism, and some people feared a French takeover. When Narai died in 1688 all ties with Westerners were cut, and Phaulkon was executed.

Constantine Phaulkon, prostrate before the Siamese king, Narai

The VOC (Dutch East India Company) first visited Ayutthaya in 1604. A trading warehouse was set up in 1634, but by the 1670s trade had declined. The warehouse in Ayutthaya was later destroyed by the Burmese.

SOUTH CENTRAL PLAINS

For centuries, the broad flood plain of the Chao Phraya, which bisects the South Central Plains north to south, has been Thailand's rice basket as well as its most densely populated region. The river remains a vital link between the country's cultural heartland and its present-day capital, Bangkok. The old capital of Ayutthaya, upstream from Bangkok, is the region's most popular sight.

Ayutthaya was one of the greatest mercantile centers in Asia during the 14th–18th centuries. Its fabulous temples and palaces, built around the confluence of the Chao Phraya, Lop Buri, and Pasak Rivers, were regarded with wonder by foreigners. In 1767 it was sacked by the Burmese, and the capital was forced to move downstream to Bangkok. The remains of monuments from the earlier period stand among more modern buidings and each day attract hundreds of visitors on round-trips from Bangkok.

Kanchanaburi, to the west of Bangkok, is another popular day trip from the capital. During World War II the Japanese built a railroad from here to the Three Pagodas Pass near Burma, along an old Burmese invasion route. Little of the railroad was ever used, but at Kanchanaburi visitors can see poignant reminders of this grueling episode, when thousands of Asian laborers and Allied POWs died.

Despite these and other noteworthy sights, the region still has relatively few tourist facilities. Towns such as Lop Buri – an old Khmer outpost with several Khmer *prangs* – and the pilgrimage site of Phra Phutthabat are unknown to the majority of tourists.

There is some accommodation in the Khwae Noi River Valley, along the route to the Three Pagodas Pass. This region is surrounded by a vast expanse of forest and grassland, including two wildlife sanctuaries and the Erawan, Sai Yok, and Chaloem Rattanakosin national parks. At the eastern edge of the South Central Plains, Khao Yai, the oldest national park, is the best place in Thailand to see wild elephants and many other animals.

The bridge over the Khwae Yai River at Kanchanaburi, a poignant reminder of World War II

◄ Walkway at Wat Chai Watthanaram, Ayutthaya

Exploring the South Central Plains

The Chao Phraya River basin is fertile terrain, perfect for rice production. It is no coincidence that the kingdoms of Lop Buri and, later, Ayutthaya, the capital of which is the main sight of the region, were founded here. East of the wide plain, Khao Yai is the country's oldest and most accessible national park. Kanchanaburi, in the west, is the site of the notorious Death Railroad of World War II. From there, a road winds up to the Three Pagodas Pass on the Burmese border, passing near numerous national parks and wildlife sanctuaries.

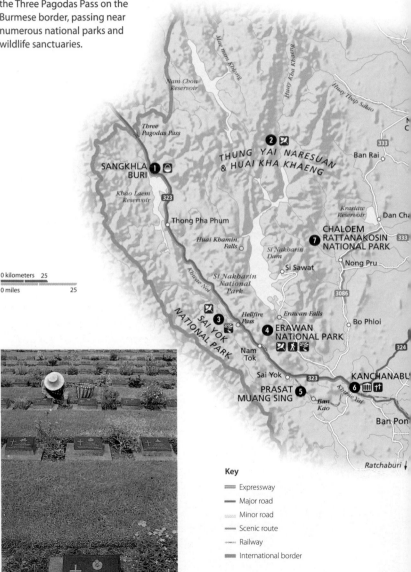

Nam Chon Reservoir

Mae nam Khwae

Huay Kha Khaeng

Huay Tbap Sduo

Three Pagodas Pass

2 THUNG YAI NARESUAN & HUAI KHA KHAENG

Ban Rai

333

SANGKHLA BURI 1

Khao Laem Reservoir

323

Thong Pha Phum

Huai Khamin Falls

Krasiaw Reservoir

Dan Cha

CHALOEM RATTANAKOSIN NATIONAL PARK 7

333

Si Nakharin Dam

Nong Pru

Si Sawat

0 kilometers 25
0 miles 25

Khwae Noi

Si Nakharin National Park

3086

SAI YOK NATIONAL PARK 3

Hellfire Pass

Erawan Falls

ERAWAN NATIONAL PARK 4

Bo Phloi

Nam Tok

324

Sai Yok

323

KANCHANABU 6

PRASAT MUANG SING 5

Ban Kao

Khwae Yai

Ban Pon

Ratchaburi

Memorial stones at POW cemetery, Kanchanaburi

Key

— Expressway
— Major road
···· Minor road
— Scenic route
···· Railway
— International border

For hotels and restaurants see pp402–11 and pp418–33

Getting Around

Many hotels in Bangkok arrange day tours of
Ayutthaya and Kanchanaburi. Boat tours up the
Chao Phraya River, from Bangkok to Ayutthaya via
Bang Pa-in, are also popular. Roads from Bangkok fan
out across the region, providing fast and easy access
by bus or car, though leaving Bangkok itself is time
consuming. Kanchanaburi,
Ayutthaya, and Lop
Buri can be all
reached by rail.

Buddhas at Wat Yai Chai Mongkhon, Ayutthaya

Chanthara Phisan Hall, on grounds of King Narai's Palace, Lop Buri

Sights at a Glance

1. Sangkhla Buri
2. Thung Yai Naresuan and Huai Kha Khaeng
3. Sai Yok National Park
4. Erawan National Park
5. Prasat Muang Sing
6. Kanchanaburi
7. Chaloem Rattanakosin National Park
8. Suphan Buri
9. Ang Thong
10. Lop Buri pp178–9
11. Phra Phutthabat
12. Ayutthaya pp180–85
13. Bang Pa-in
14. Khao Yai National Park pp188–9

For keys to symbols see back flap

On the way to market, Three Pagodas Pass

❶ Sangkhla Buri

สังขละบุรี

Kanchanaburi province. 36,000. from Kanchanaburi. TAT, Kanchanaburi (0-3451-1200). daily.

In the center of Sangkhla Buri is a market where, among other things, you can buy Burmese curries and samosas, as well as books written in the Mon language.

However, the main attraction of this isolated trading town, which is populated by Mon and Karen tribespeople (see p210) as well as Thais, is its serene lakeside location. The lake, which visitors can explore by rowing boat, is actually a large reservoir, formed by the damming of the Khwae Noi River farther downstream. Sometimes, late in the dry season, drowned remains of old villages and forests can be seen sticking up out of the calm surface of the lake's waters.

The north shore of the lake is overlooked by the unusual *chedi* of **Wat Wangwiwekaram**. In the covered gallery beside it a daily market sells goods, including *lungis* (sarongs) and simple woodcarvings from Myanmar (Burma), Indonesia, and elsewhere. Visitors can reach the *wat* on foot by crossing a wooden bridge that spans the wide, shallow inlet of the lake. A large settlement, consisting predominantly of Mon tribespeople, has grown up in close proximity to the *wat*. An interesting daily market is held here in the early morning.

Environs

At the **Three Pagodas Pass**, 14 miles (23 km) northwest of Sangkhla Buri, right on the Myanmar border, are situated three small, physically unimpressive, whitewashed *chedis*. For centuries this pass, which is less than 985 ft (300 m) above sea level, was used as an invasion route. During World War II, the Burma-Siam Railroad (see pp174–5) passed through here, and the route the track took can still be seen beside the Myanmar border. Nowadays, the pass is a quiet trading (and smuggling) route between the Indian Ocean to the west and mainland Southeast Asia. Visitors to this region are usually permitted to cross the border on a one-day visa (see p459) to the Myanmar town of Pyathonzu. However, the relations between Thailand and Myanmar are often uneasy, at times verging on the hostile, and this situation is prone to change at any time.

❷ Thung Yai Naresuan and Huai Kha Khaeng

เขตรักษาพันธุ์สัตว์ป่าห้วยขาแข้ง

Kanchanaburi, Tak and Uthai Thani provinces. Kanchanaburi (0-3451-1200); Forestry Dept (0-2562-0760). from Kanchanaburi. huaikhakhaeng.net

These two huge, adjacent wildlife sanctuaries, covering 2,400 sq miles (6,220 sq km) and surrounded by a further 2,320 sq miles (6,000 sq km) of protected forest, form one of the most important conservation areas in Southeast Asia. They are listed jointly as a UNESCO World Heritage Site and are home to some of Thailand's largest remaining wild elephant herds, as well as several endangered carnivores, such as tigers, clouded leopards, and Malaysian sun bears. The enormous gaur, a species of wild cattle, and the country's last wild buffalo herds also live within the sanctuary. Rare species of gibbon can also be seen.

Herd of wild buffalo, native to Thung Yai Naresuan and Huai Kha Khaeng wildlife sanctuaries

Tourist accommodations in the tranquil Sai Yok National Park

At Huai Kha Khaeng there is a nature trail, but neither wildlife sanctuary is geared up for large numbers of visitors – permission for large parties to enter the parks can be obtained from Bangkok Forestry Department.

❸ Sai Yok National Park

อุทยานแห่งชาติไทรโยค

Kanchanaburi province. Park HQ off Hwy 323, 62 miles (100 km) NW of Kanchanaburi. **Tel** 0-3468-6024. 🛈 TAT, Kanachanaburi (0-3451-1200); Forestry Dept (0-2562-0760 or 🖰 dnp.go.th for bungalow bookings). 🚐 🚌 from Kanchanaburi. 🚲

Sai Yok was the site of a large Japanese army barracks and POW labor camp during World War II. The 190-sq mile (500-sq km) national park was established in 1980 and today is renowned for its tranquil river scenery and the impressive Sai Yok Yai waterfall, which tumbles into the Khwae Noi River near to the park headquarters.

Accommodation is available in park bungalows or on pleasant houseboats, and boats can be chartered – at some expense – to some nearby caves. The caves are home to the 1-inch (3-cm) long Kitti's hog-nosed bat, considered by some to be the world's smallest mammal, and which was discovered in 1973 by Thai naturalist Kitti Thonglongya.

Environs
The Burma-Thailand Railroad Memorial Trail, south of Sai Yok, pays tribute to prisoners who died during the excavation of the Konyu railroad cut. Near to the cut, which was given the name "Hellfire Pass" by the many prisoners of war who labored through the night by torchlight, was the "Pack of Cards Bridge." This rickety 985-ft (300-m) long, 82-ft (25-m) high structure was built at perilous speed with green timber and, as a result, heavy loss of life – the structure collapsed three times during its construction.

Plaque in memory of POWs, Hellfire Pass

The trail, set up with funding from the Australian government, winds up to Konyu cutting through a bamboo grove. The railroad track has long since been removed.

❹ Erawan National Park

อุทยานแห่งชาติเอราวัณ

Kanchanaburi province. Park HQ off Hwy 3199, 40 miles (65 km) NW of Kanchanaburi. **Tel** 0-3457-4222. 🛈 TAT, Kanchanaburi (0-3451-1200); Forestry Dept (0-2562-0760 or 🖰 dnp.go.th for bungalow bookings). 🚐 🚌 from Kanchanaburi. 🚲

In the lush forest of the Erawan National Park, the nearest park to Kanchanaburi and measuring 210 sq miles (550 sq km), are the beautiful **Erawan falls**, which drop through a series of cascades and shady rock pools. While park rangers still find occasional tiger prints, visitors are more likely to see pig-tailed and rhesus macaques, and some 80 bird species. The Visitors' Center offers a slide show about the park, and there is a pleasant, 1-mile (2-km) hiking trail which climbs up beside the falls. This is one of Thailand's most popular national parks, and at weekends and holidays it gets very crowded. The large limestone cavern of Tham Wang Badan, situated on the west side of the park, contains many colorful stalactites and stalagmites.

Environs
The Huai Khamin falls, which are in nearby **Si Nakharin National Park**, do not receive as many visitors as the Erawan falls but, are nonetheless quite impressive. Visitors can make boat trips onto the Si Nakharin reservoir, either from the Kradan pier or from Si Sawat, a small market town situated on the eastern shore of the reservoir.

🔲 **Si Nakharin National Park**
67 miles (108 km) N of Kanchanaburi. **Tel** 0-3451-6667-8. **Open** daily. 🚲

The Erawan falls, named after the Hindu god Indra's elephant mount

Central sanctuary of Prasat Muang Sing near Kanchanaburi

❺ Prasat Muang Sing

ปราสาทเมืองสิงห์

Off Hwy 323, 27 miles (43 km) W of Kanchanaburi, Kanchanaburi province. 🛈 TAT, Kanchanaburi (0-3451-1200). 🚌 from Kanchanaburi to Tha Kilen, then *songthaew*. **Open** daily. 🗭

The ruins of Muang Sing beside the Khwae Noi River date from around the 13th century and mark the westernmost point of expansion of the Khmer Empire *(see pp268–9)*. Earthen ramparts surround an inner wall of laterite that forms a rough rectangle about 245 acres (1 sq km). Near the center of this are the ruins of the Buddhist sanctuary, Prasat Muang Sing. Like most Khmer temples it faces east, in alignment with the city of Angkor.

Although the Muang Sing temple complex looks Khmer, some art historians believe it was actually built by local artisans in imitation of the occupying Khmers – the sanctuary, for example, lacks the stylistic details that are normally associated with Khmer sites. It was probably built after the reign of Jayavarman VII (1181–1220) as the Khmer Empire began to decline and its power in this region was fading. A museum at the site displays artifacts excavated here.

Environs

Southeast of Muang Sing is Ban Kao, a prehistoric settlement discovered in the 1940s by Dutch archaeologist van Heekeren, a prisoner on the Burma-Siam Railroad. The **Ban Kao Museum** houses stone tools and ornaments.

🏛 **Ban Kao Museum**
22 miles (35 km) W of Kanchanaburi. **Open** 8am–4:30pm Wed–Sat. 🗭

❻ Kanchanaburi

กาญจนบุรี

Kanchanaburi province. 🖾 108,000. 🚉 🚌 🛈 TAT, Saeng Chuto Rd, Kanchanaburi (0-3451-1200). **Open** 8:30am–4:30pm. 🛒 daily. 🎏 Khwae River Bridge Week (Nov/Dec).

Though surrounded by limestone hills and expanses of sugar cane, Kanchanaburi is best known for the infamous Burma-Siam Railroad. Constructed in 1942–3, it crosses over the Khwae Yai River just to the north of Kanchanaburi town center. At the small station beside the bridge are a number of steam locomotives dating from the period. A memorial to those who died during the war was erected by the Japanese administration in 1944. Today, 47 miles (77 km) of the railroad remain, and the trip along it from Kanchanaburi to Nam Tok is one of the most interesting in Thailand. The **Thailand-Burma**

Sign, Kanchanaburi station

Railroad Center charts the history of this railroad. The building of the railroad cost the lives of more than 100,000 Asian laborers and 12,000 Allied prisoners of war. The **Kanchanaburi War Cemetery**, contains the graves of almost 7,000 mostly British and Australian prisoners and is one of two war cemeteries in the town. It is immaculately maintained by the Commonwealth War Graves Commission.

The smaller of the two cemeteries, **Chong Kai Cemetery**, contains 1,740 graves and lies on the north bank of the Khwae Noi River, a short ferry ride from the center of town. Nearby is **Wat Tham Khao Pun**, overlooking the river and the Burma-Siam Railroad, which at this point heads south toward Ban Kao and Prasat Muang Sing. In the grounds of the *wat* complex a network of narrow passages leads through a cave system filled with Buddha images.

In the **JEATH War Museum**, housed in Wat Chai Chumphon, visitors can see three replicas of the bamboo huts used to house prisoners of war in the camps that sprang up along the Burma-Siam Railroad during the war. The huts display paintings, sketches, and photographs of life in the camps and along the railroad line. JEATH is an acronym for Japan, England, Australia and America, Thailand, and Holland, some of the countries whose nationals worked on the railroad. Many survivors

Steel bridge over the Khwae Yai River, Kanchanaburi

and victims' relatives visit Kanchanaburi each year.

Accommodations here include riverside raft houses.

† Kanchanaburi War Cemetery
Saeng Chuto Rd. **Open** daily.

† Chong Kai Cemetery
Ban Kao Rd. **Open** daily.

▥ JEATH War Museum
Wisuttharangsi Rd. **Tel** 0-3451-1263.
Open 8am–6pm daily. 🖺

▥ Thailand-Burma Railroad Center
73 Jaokunneu Rd. **Tel** 0-3451-2721.
Open 9am–5pm daily. 🖺
w tbrconline.com

Farmers cultivating crops in the hills around Kanchanaburi

❼ Chaloem Rattanakosin National Park

อุทยานแห่งชาติเฉลิมรัตนโกสินทร

Kanchanaburi province. Park HQ off Hwy 3086, 60 miles (97 km) NE of Kanchanaburi. **ℹ** TAT (0-3451-1200); Forestry Dept (0-2562-0760, 0-3454-7020 or **w** dnp.go.th for bungalow bookings). 🚌 from Kanchanaburi to Nong Preu, then *songthaew*. **Open** daily. 🖺

This beautiful and isolated national park is one of Thailand's smallest, at just 23 sq miles (59 sq km). The main trail runs beside a stream which passes through a cavern, Tham Than Lot Noi, to emerge in a thickly forested, steep-sided ravine. The path continues for 8,200 ft (2,500 m), climbing steeply beside the Trai Trung falls to Tham Than Lot Yai, a limestone sinkhole, and a small Buddhist shrine. On weekday mornings you may find that you are the only visitor in this delightful spot.

The Bridge Over the Khwae Yai River and the Burma-Siam Railroad

The first railroad bridge over the Khwae Yai River, near Kanchanaburi, was built of wood, using Allied and Asian slave labor. In 1943 it was abandoned for an iron bridge, which was repeatedly bombed and damaged by the US Army Air Force from late 1944 on. In 1945, after only a short period in service, the bridge was put out of commission. After the war this infamous river crossing was immortalized in David Lean's movie, *The Bridge on the River Kwai* (1957).

The bridge was part of an immense project, the 255-mile (414-km) Burma-Siam Railroad, conceived by the Japanese after the Allies blockaded sea routes in 1942. It ran from Nong Pladuk, 30 miles (50 km) southeast of Kanchanaburi, to Thanbyuzayat near the coast in Burma. Built under appaling conditions, it operated for only two years. Around 60,000 Allied prisoners of war and 300,000 Asian laborers were forced to work 18-hour shifts on its construction, with many losing their lives to cholera, malaria, malnutrition, and most tragically to maltreatment. It is said that one man died for each tie laid. One reason for the brutal regime was that the Japanese followed a samurai code. They despised the disgrace of surrender and treated

Painting by prisoner of war in the JEATH War Museum, Kanchanaburi

the Allied prisoners of war as if they had forfeited all human rights. The present-day bridge at Kanchanaburi was rebuilt, as part of Japanese war reparations, with two girders from the Japan Bridge Company of Osaka. It has now become a place of pilgrimage for veterans. Kanchanaburi has two cemeteries and a museum, the latter, in particular, presenting a moving evocation of this harrowing episode of World War II history.

Prisoners of war on the wooden bridge over the Khwae Yai River (c.1942–3)

The beautifully tended Chong Kai Cemetery, Kanchanaburi

The Chinese shrine of San Chao Pho, Suphan Buri

❽ Suphan Buri

สุพรรณบุรี

Suphan Buri province. 🚹 111,000.
🚌 🚍 🚺 TAT, Suphan Buri (0-3553-
6030); TAT, Ayutthaya (0-3524-6077).
🎎 Don Chedi Fair (Jan 25).

Suphan Buri came to
prominence with the rise of
Ayutthaya in the 14th century.
The attractive art and architecture of the town are known
to few tourists.

Near the center of town is the
beautiful *prang* of Wat Phra Si
Rattana Mahathat, restored in
the Ayutthaya period and again
in the 20th century. At Wat Pa
Lelai, on the edge of Suphan
Buri, is a Buddha image from the
Dvaravati period *(see pp60–61)*.
To the east is San Chao Pho Lak
Muang, a Chinese shrine. Wat
Phra Rup, on the other side of
the Suphan Buri River, houses a
reclining Buddha image and a
carved wooden Footprint of the
Buddha. The *bot* of nearby Wat
Pratu San contains striking
19th-century murals of the
Buddha's life.

Environs
The large white monument of
Don Chedi, 20 miles (31 km)
from Suphan Buri, marks the
site of the Battle of Nong Sarai,
between the Burmese and Thai
forces led by King Naresuan
(see p66). The **U Thong National
Museum** houses 6th- to
11th-century Dvaravati artifacts
and Khmer art.

🏛 **U Thong National Museum**
4 miles (7 km) SW of Suphan Buri.
Open Wed–Sun. 🎟

❾ Ang Thong

อ่างทอง

Ang Thong province. 🚹 41,600.
🚍 🚺 TAT, Ayutthaya (0-3524-6077).
🚌 daily.

This small town is a useful base
from which travelers who are
interested in Thai images of the
Buddha can visit three little
known but rewarding sites
nearby. To the south of Ang
Thong, **Wat Pa Mok** houses
a reclining Buddha image
from the 15th century.
Wat Khun In Pramun is
to the northwest. In its
grounds is a huge
reclining Buddha image,
about 165 ft (50 m)
long, dating from the
Ayutthaya period.

At **Wat Chaiyo Wora
Wihan**, to the north of
Ang Thong, a *wihan* houses a
third enormous, seated image
of the Buddha from the Rattanakosin period, called the Phra
Maha Phuttha Phim.

Wat Pa Mok, which houses a 15th-century
Buddha, near Ang Thong

❿ Lop Buri

ลพบุรี

See pp178–9.

⓫ Phra Phutthabat

พระพุทธบาท

Saraburi province. 🚺 TAT, Ayutthaya
(0-3524-6077); TAT, Saraburi (0-3642-
2768). 🚌 from Saraburi, then *samlor*.
Open 7am–6pm daily.
🎎 Phra Phutthabat Fair (Mar).

In the early 17th century, King
Song Tham of Ayutthaya sent a
group of monks to Sri Lanka to
pay homage to a Footprint of the
Buddha. (According to legend,
these Footprints show where the
Lord Buddha walked upon the
Earth.) The monks were surprised
to be told by the Sri Lankans that,
according to scriptures, there was
a Footprint in Thailand. Song
Tham, on hearing this, ordered
a search for the Footprint.
It was found by a hunter
pursuing a wounded deer –
the animal vanished into
the undergrowth only to
re-emerge healed. On
closer inspection, the
hunter found a water-filled
pool shaped like a
footprint. He drank from it
and was miraculously
cured of a skin disease.
The king, on learning of
this, had a temple built
on the site, which subsequently
became one of the most sacred
places of worship in Thailand.

Today, the 5-ft (1.5-m) long
Footprint, Phra Phutthabat, lies in
an ornate *mondop*, restored in
the late 18th century after the
earlier buildings were destroyed
by the Burmese in 1765. A
museum here displays offerings
by pilgrims, who flock to the sight
each year. Phra Phutthabat is also
the name of the small town here.

Bell, Phra
Phutthabat

Environs
At **Phra Phutthachai** ("Buddha's
shadow"), about 25 miles
(40 km) southeast of Phra
Phutthabat, a faint Buddha
image, probably painted by a
hermit, adorns a cliff face.
Pilgrims often visit this site on
their way to Phra Phutthabat.

Gestures of the Buddha

Buddha images throughout Thailand for the most part follow strict rules laid down in the 3rd century AD. There are four basic postures: standing, sitting, walking, and reclining; the first three are associated with daily activities of the Buddha, the last with the Buddha's final moments on Earth as he achieved *nirvana*. These postures can be combined with hand and feet positions to create a variety of attitudes *(mudras)*, that represent key Buddhist themes. King Rama III (1824–51) drew up a list of 40 attitudes to be used by sculptors, but many of these are rare. Most images in Thailand represent a dozen or so attitudes, the seated image in *bhumisparsa mudra* occurring most frequently.

Touching the Earth

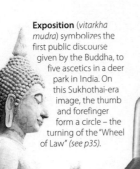

Exposition (*vitarkha mudra*) symbolizes the first public discourse given by the Buddha, to five ascetics in a deer park in India. On this Sukhothai-era image, the thumb and forefinger form a circle – the turning of the "Wheel of Law" *(see p35).*

Bhumisparsa is the most common mudra. It symbolizes an important episode in the Buddha's life when he sat in meditation under a Bodhi tree in Bodh Gaya, India, refusing to move until he attained Enlightenment. While his enemy, Mara, offered temptations such as nubile maidens and feasts, the Buddha touched the ground to attract the attention of the Earth goddess, so that she could see his resistance. Just after this he achieved Enlightenment.

Right hand pointing to the Earth

Left hand resting in lap

Legs in lotus position

Meditation (*dhyana mudra*) is signified with a sitting posture, shown by this modern Buddha image from Southern Thailand. Both hands are positioned palms up, the right over the left, as still practiced by meditating Buddhists.

Reassurance (*abhaya mudra*) symbolizes the Buddha's offer of protection to his followers. The raised right hand is also representative of an episode in which the Buddha settled a heated dispute over water.

Restraining the waters is a variation of *abhaya mudra*. The two hands of this Ayutthayan Buddha image are held palms forward, fingers pointing upward. It refers to an episode when the Buddha calmed the floodwaters of the Nairanjana, a tributary of the Ganges in northern India.

Reclining Buddhas, such as this one at Ayutthaya, usually represent the point of *parinirvana* or ultimate *nirvana*.

⑩ Street-by-Street: Lop Buri

ลพบุรี

One of Thailand's oldest cities, Lop Buri was known as Lavo in the Dvaravati period *(see pp60–61)* and subsequently became an important outpost of the Khmer Empire *(see pp268–9)*. The Khmer *prang* on the grounds of Wat Phra Si Rattana Mahathat, and those of Prang Sam Yot, date from this time. With the decline of the Khmer Empire and the rise of the Sukhothai Kingdom *(see pp62–3)*, Lop Buri struggled to retain its independence, until, in the 14th century, it was linked by marriage to the emerging state of Ayutthaya *(see pp66–7)*. It reached its political peak in the 17th century, when the Ayutthayan King Narai (1656–88) preferred to stay at Lop Buri rather than his official palace at Ayutthaya. Today, the thriving modern town of Lop Buri lies to the east of the old city.

Wat Sao Thong Thong
The *wihan* at this *wat* was modified by King Narai so the buildng could be used as a Christian chapel – he replaced Thai windows with Western-style Gothic designs.

The market sells vegetables and other foodstuffs.

★ **King Narai's Palace**
Abandoned after Narai's death, parts of the palace, including the Chanthara Phisan Hall, were later restored by King Mongkut *(see p69)*.

★ **Somdej Phra Narai National Museum**
This museum is housed in the partially restored, colonial-style Phiman Mongkut Hall of King Narai's Palace. It has a superb collection of Lop Buri Buddha images, and collections of Dvaravati, Khmer, and Ayutthayan art.

Key

— Suggested route

| 0 meters | 75 |
| 0 yards | 75 |

Phaulkon Residence
This house was built by King Narai for his favored minister, the Greek Constantine Phaulkon. Phaulkon encouraged Narai to forge close ties with the French, often excluding other foreigners, though his motive was perhaps to aid Louis XIV's attempt to convert Narai to Christianity. When this came to light it alarmed the Ayutthayan court and Phaulkon was executed (see p167).

VISITORS' CHECKLIST

Practical Information
Tel 0-3641-1458. Lop Buri province. 165,000. TAT, Naraimaharat Rd, Amphoe Mueang (0-3677-0096-7). daily. King Narai Festival (Feb). Somdej Phra Narai National Museum: **Open** 9am–4pm Wed–Sun. **Closed** public hols. King Narai's Palace: **Open** daily. Wat Phra Si Rattana Mahathat: **Open** daily. Phaulkon Residence: **Open** daily.

Transport
Na Phra Kan Rd. Phra Narai Maharat Rd

Prang Khaek
This Hindu shrine has three brick towers. It is believed by some to date as far back as the 8th century.

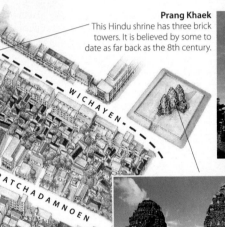

★ Prang Sam Yot
The Lop Buri style was a variation by local artisans, of already established Khmer art and architecture; this shrine is archetypal. The three *prangs* were originally consecrated as a Hindu shrine; Buddha images were added later to two of them.

To train station

★ Wat Phra Si Rattana Mahathat
This *wat* complex encloses ruins from two distinct eras. At its center is a 12th-century, Khmer *prang*, decorated with finely detailed stucco work. The site also includes Ayutthayan *chedis* and a *wihan* added by King Narai.

⑫ Ayutthaya

พระนครศรีอยุธยา

The city of Ayutthaya was founded around 1350 by Ramathibodi I (1351–69), who came here to escape an outbreak of smallpox at Lop Buri. By the early 15th century Ayutthaya had become a major power. Sukhothai *(see pp62–3)* fell to Ayutthaya in 1438. Western traders arrived in the early 16th century *(see pp166–7)*, and wrote vivid accounts of Ayutthaya's splendor. In the early 18th century, after years of war, decline set in, and in 1767 the Burmese sacked the city. Today, the ruins stand among the modern buildings of the provincial town.

Stucco and brick *singhas* around the main *chedi* of Wat Thammikarat

🏛 Wat Phra Mahathat

วัดมหาธาตุ

Corner of Cheekun Rd and Naresuan Rd. **Open** daily. 🖼

Wat Phra Mahathat is one of the largest and most important *wat* complexes in Ayutthaya. It was almost certainly founded in the late 14th century by King Borommaracha I (1370–88). Other buildings were subsequently added by his successor, Ramesuan (1388–95).

European-style Pisai Sayalak Tower, behind the Chan Kasem Palace

🏛 Wat Ratchaburana

วัดราชบูรณะ

Cheekun Rd. **Open** daily. 🖼

Across the road from Wat Mahathat is Wat Ratchaburana, its *prang* now restored. It was built in the early 15th century by King Borommaracha II (1424–48) on the cremation site of his two brothers, who died in a power struggle. Both had wanted to succeed their father, Intharacha I (1409–24), to the throne. Robbers looted

the crypt in 1957 and escaped with a huge cache of gold artifacts, only a few of which were recovered. A narrow staircase descends to the crypt where visitors can see the remains of Ayutthayan frescoes *(see p64)*.

🏛 Chan Kasem Palace

วังจันทรเกษม

Uthong Rd, opposite the night market. **Open** Wed–Sun. 🖼

In the northeast corner of the main island stands the Chan Kasem Palace or Wang Na. It was built in 1577 by the illustrious Naresuan, the son of King Maha Thammaracha (1569–90), before he became king. When Naresuan came to the throne in 1590, the palace became his permanent residence. The buildings seen today, however, date from the reign of King Mongkut (1851–68), as the palace was razed by the Burmese in 1767. It houses a large collection of Buddha images and historical artifacts. Behind the Chan Kasem Palace is the **Pisai Sayalak Tower**, once used as an astronomical observatory by King Mongkut.

🏛 Wat Thammikarat

วัดธรรมิกราช

Uthong Rd. **Open** daily. 🖼

At this picturesque site are the dilapidated remains of a large, early Ayutthayan, octagonal *chedi* surrounded by stucco and brick lions, or *singhas*. Beside the *chedi* is the ruin of a *wihan*, slowly succumbing to weeds and trees. A beautiful U Thong Buddha head recovered from here is now in the Chao Sam Phraya National Museum *(see p182)*.

🏛 Wang Luang

วังหลวง

Uthong Rd. **Open** daily. 🖼

To the west of Wat Thammikarat is Wang Luang, the northern extension of the royal palace built by King Borommatrailokanat (1448–88) in the mid-15th century. Successive monarchs added a number of pavilions and halls. Wang Luang was razed by the Burmese in 1767. The best preserved of the former royal palace buildings is the **Trimuk Pavilion**. It was built during the reign

19th-century Trimuk Pavilion, on the grounds of Wang Luang

of King Chulalongkorn (1868–1910) on the site of earlier foundations.

🏛 Wat Phra Si Sanphet
See pp182–3.

🏛 Wihan Phra Mongkhon Bophit
วิหารพระมงคลบพิตร
Si Sanphet Rd. **Open** daily. 🖼

This *wat* contains one of Thailand's largest bronze Buddha images. Now gilded, it probably dates from the late 15th century, though it has undergone numerous restorations. In 1767 Burmese invaders destroyed much of the *wihan* and damaged the image's head and right hand. The image was left open to the sky until the 1950s, when the *wihan* was rebuilt.

🏛 Wat Phra Ram
วัดพระราม
Si Sanphet Rd. **Open** daily. 🖼

A chronicle relates that Wat Phra Ram was built in 1369 on the cremation site of King Ramathibodi (1351–69) by his son, Ramesuan. The elegant *prang* visible today, however, is the result of later renovation by King Borommatrailokanat (1448–88). The *prang* is decorated with *garudas*, *nagas*, and walking Buddha images. Surrounding the *prang* are *wihans* and a *bot*. The *wat* casts beautiful and photogenic reflections in the nearby lily ponds.

15th-century, corncob-shaped *prang* at Wat Phra Ram

VISITORS' CHECKLIST

Practical Information
🗺 60,900. ℹ TAT, 108/22 Mu 4, Tambon Phratuchai Amphoe, Ayutthaya. (0-3524-6076). 🚩 daily.

Transport
🚌 Off Bang Ain Rd.
🚍 Naresuan Rd. 🚌.

🏛 Wat Lokaya Sutharam
วัดโลกยสุธาราม
W of main island. **Open** daily. 🖼

This *wat* is the site of a 140-ft (42-m) long, whitewashed reclining Buddha image. Large Buddha images such as this do not always depict the Buddha's death, but sometimes, as in this instance, an occasion when the Buddha grew 100 times in size to confront the demon Rahu. The image now lies in the open air, the original *wihan*, having been destroyed by the Burmese; 24 octagonal pillars are all that remain of this *wihan*. The *wat* also houses the ruins of a *bot* and *chedis*.

Ayutthaya Town Center

① Wat Lokaya Sutharam
② Wang Luang
③ Wat Thammikarat
④ Wat Phra Si Sanphet
⑤ Wihan Phra Mongkhon Bophit
⑥ Wat Phra Ram
⑦ Chao Sam Phraya National Museum
⑧ Ayutthaya Historical Study Center
⑨ Wat Phra Mahathat
⑩ Wat Ratchaburana
⑪ Wat Suwan Dararam
⑫ Chan Kasem Palace
⑬ Wat Na Phra Men
⑭ Wat Chai Watthanaram
⑮ St. Joseph's Church
⑯ Wat Phutthaisawan
⑰ Wat Phanan Choeng
⑱ Wat Yai Chai Mongkhon

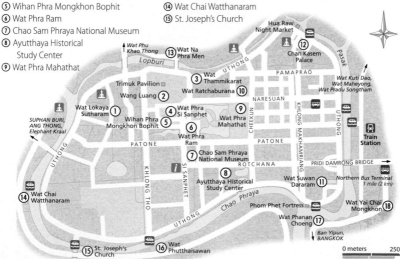

Chao Sam Phraya National Museum

พิพิธภัณฑ์เจ้าสามพระยา

Intersection of Rotchana Rd and Si Sanphet Rd. **Open** Wed–Sun.

Among the exhibits here is a small collection of gold artifacts, including a jewel-encrusted sword, gold slippers, and jewelry. Discovered in the crypt of Wat Ratchaburana's central *prang* when it was

Deity on wooden door-panel

looted in 1957, they are among the few items from the *wat* to have survived the sack of Ayutthaya by the Burmese (*see pp64–5*). Other artifacts include bronze Buddha images and wooden door panels from *wats* around Ayutthaya.

Ayutthaya Historical Study Center

ศูนย์ศึกษาประวัติศาสตร์อยุธยา

Rotchana Rd. **Open** daily.

This study center houses interesting audiovisual displays depicting Ayutthaya's history and trading relations. There is also a reconstructed model of Wat Phra Si Sanphet. Another part of the study center stands in what was the Japanese quarter at the time when Ayutthaya was at the height of its power.

Wat Suwan Dararam

วัดสุวรรณดาราราม

Near Pomphet. **Open** daily.

This temple was completely destroyed by the Burmese but later rebuilt by Rama I (1782–1809). The *ubosot* is usually locked, but it is worth requesting the key to see the murals commissioned by Rama VII (1925–35), depicting scenes from the time of King Naresuan. Among them is a mural of the Battle of Nong Sarai, which was fought against the Burmese in 1593 (*see p66*).

Nearby to Wat Suwan Dararam is a section of the old city defenses, Phom Phet, which were a strategically important lookout post over the Chao Phraya River.

Wat Phra Si Sanphet

วัดพระศรีสรรเพชญ์

Founded by King Borommatrailokanat during the 15th century as a state temple, Wat Phra Si Sanphet was later added to by his son, Ramathibodi II, who built two *chedis* to house the relics of his father and brother. The third *chedi* was built by Borommaracha IV to house the remains of Ramathibodi II. The site was extended by subsequent rulers until the Burmese sack of 1767 (*see pp64–5*). Partially renovated in the 20th century, many of its treasures are now kept in museums.

The Prasat Phra Narai was cruciform in shape. All that remains of it today are the foundations.

The ashes of Ramathibodi II (1491–1529) are enshrined in this *chedi*, built in the mid-16th century by Borommaracha IV.

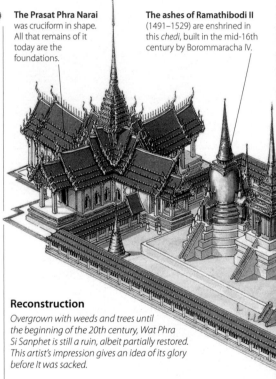

Reconstruction

Overgrown with weeds and trees until the beginning of the 20th century, Wat Phra Si Sanphet is still a ruin, albeit partially restored. This artist's impression gives an idea of its glory before it was sacked.

Drawing of *Chedis*
Lying empty after it was sacked by the Burmese, Ayutthaya became the focus of scholarly interest. Henri Mouhot, who drew this image, was one of many late 19th-century visitors. Wat Phra Si Sanphet has been under the protection of the Thai Fine Arts Department since 1927.

Three Chedis
Apart from the ashes of kings, caskets of precious Buddha images and royal regalia were buried in the chedis' central chambers.

Wooden Door
This door was probably once situated in the entrance to Wihan Phra Si Sanphet and dates from the reign of Ramathibodi II. A collection of such doors is displayed in the Chao Sam Phraya Museum.

The ashes of Borommaracha III (1463–88), the brother of Ramathibodi II, are buried in this chedi.

Entrance to Chedi
The entrance chamber to the chedi is a scaled-down version of a Khmer mandapa (entrance chamber to a Khmer sanctuary). Ayutthayan builders modified many older architectural features, such as Khmer prangs and Sri Lankan bell-shaped chedis.

The ashes of Boromma-trailokanat (1448–88) are buried in this chedi, the only one to survive the Burmese sack. The other two had to be restored.

Stairway leading to entrance of hollow chedi

A Footprint of the Lord Buddha was housed in this elegant, spired mondop.

Wihan Phra Si Sanphet
The main wihan – the entrance to the wat – once housed the principal Buddha image of Phra Si Sanphet.

Exploring Ayutthaya: The Outer Sites

The central island of Ayutthaya stands at the confluence of the Chao Phraya, Lop Buri, and Pasak rivers. The town's most imposing sites are to be found on the central island. However, a short *samlor* ride by bridge over any of the rivers, which more or less encircle it, will bring you to many more sites of interest. Wat Na Phra Men is one of Ayutthaya's most beautiful *wats*, and St. Joseph's Church offers a glimpse of Ayutthaya's connections with Western trading powers (*see pp166–7*) during the city's heyday. The main part of modern Ayutthaya sprawls to the east of the island, over the Pasak River and beyond.

A roundup of wild elephants at the elephant kraal (1890)

🏛 Wat Na Phra Men
วัดหน้าพระเมรุ

Opp Royal Palace, nr Muang Canal. **Tel** 0-3525-2163. **Open** daily. 🎫

Across a bridge to the north of the main island is Wat Na Phra Men, one of the most beautiful of Ayutthaya's monasteries, and one of the few to survive the Burmese sacking of the city in 1767 (*see pp64–5*). Thought to date from the reign of Intharacha II (1488–91), it was restored during the reign of King Borommakot (1733–58), and again in the mid-19th century. In the *wihan* is a Dvaravati seated Buddha image, Phra Kanthararat, that was moved here from Nakhon Pathom in the mid-16th century. The murals covering the *wihan* walls have now almost completely disappeared. Its doors are from the early 19th century. In the adjacent *bot* is a gilded Buddha image, probably from the reign of King Prasat Thong (1629–56).

🏛 Elephant Kraal
พระที่นั่งเพนียด

NW on Hwy 309. **Open** daily. 🎫

Farther to the north is the elephant kraal. It is thought that the original structure, built by King Yot Fa (1547–8), stood within the confines of the old city wall. The present kraal, built later, was in use well into the 19th century – wild elephants would be driven here for training as pack animals or war mounts for senior officers. In the middle of the stockade is a shrine where the elephant guardian is thought to live.

🏛 Wat Phu Khao Thong
วัดภูเขาทอง

1 mile (2 km) NW on Hwy 309. **Open** daily. 🎫

To the west, the original *chedi* of Phu Khao Thong was constructed by King Bayinnaung of Burma to celebrate his capture of Ayutthaya in 1569. Additions were made in 1744–5 by the Thai King Borommakot.

🏛 Wat Chai Watthanaram
วัดไชยวัฒนาราม

W bank of Chao Phraya River, SW of main island. **Open** daily. 🎫

This *wat* was built by King Prasat Thong in 1630. The central *prang* is surrounded by eight smaller ones, decorated with stucco reliefs depicting images such as the Buddha preaching to his mother in the Tavatimsa Heaven. All the *prangs* have been restored.

⛪ St. Joseph's Church
โบสถ์เซนต์ยอแซฟ

SW of main island on the Chao Phraya River. **Open** daily.

St. Joseph's, overlooking the Chao Phraya River, has been the site of Catholic worship for over 300 years. The original 17th-century structure was destroyed by the Burmese in 1767. The present church was built during the 19th century.

🏛 Wat Phutthaisawan
วัดพุทไธศวรรย์

S of main island. **Open** daily. 🎫

East from St. Joseph's is Wat Phutthaisawan, also located on the riverbank. It has a restored 14th-century *prang* surrounded by a cloister filled with Buddha images.

🏛 Wat Kuti Dao
วัดกุฎีดาว

E of railway station. **Open** daily. 🎫

This *wat* originally dated from the early Ayutthaya period, but the ruins here today are of an 18th-century renovation by King Phumintharacha. The *chedi* is flanked by a *wihan* and a *bot* with distinctive arched windows and doors.

Bell-shaped *chedi*, part of the ruined Wat Kuti Dao

For hotels and restaurants see pp402–11 and pp418–33

Reclining Buddha in a ruined *wihan* at Wat Yai Chai Mongkhon

🔼 Wat Yai Chai Mongkhon
วัดใหญ่ชัยมงคล

E of main island. **Open** daily. 🔼
The *chedi* here, one of the largest in Ayutthaya, was built by King Naresuan (1590–1605) to celebrate his victory over the Burmese at Nong Sarai in 1593 *(see pp66–7)*. Flanking steps up to the *chedi* are two *mondops* housing seated Buddha images. On the northeast side of the *wat* is a ruined *wihan* containing a reclining Buddha.

🔼 Wat Pradu Songtham
วัดประดู่ทรงธรรม

N of railroad station, E of main island.
Open daily.
Inside the *wihan* of Wat Pradu Songtham are the remains of murals dating from the early Rattanakosin period *(see p39)*. These recount the life of the Buddha and also show images of daily life, including one of a performance of the Ramakien at a fair. Outside is a bell tower topped by a small *chedi* from the late Ayutthaya period.

🔼 Wat Maheyong
วัดมเหยงค์

E of main island. **Open** daily.
The partially reconstructed ruins of Wat Maheyong date from the reign of King Borommaracha II (1424–48). The principal, bell-shaped *chedi* shows a clear stylistic link with earlier Sukhothai *chedis*, while all around the rectangular base are the remnants of stucco elephants. Other *chedis* at this site also show Sukhothai influence.

🔼 Wat Phanan Choeng
วัดพนัญเชิง

S of main island. **Open** daily.
This *wat* has been renovated over the years and houses the large, 14th-century, seated image of Phra Chao Phanan Choeng. The *wihan* was built in the mid-19th century.

🏛 Ban Yipun
บ้านญี่ปุ่น

S of main island. **Open** daily. 🔼
Once the site of a 17th-century Japanese settlement, today a museum here displays exhibits that explain Ayutthaya's foreign relations at the time.

---

⑬ Bang Pa-in
บางปะอิน

Phra Nakhon Si Ayutthaya province.
🚗 59,000. 🚌 🚆 🚤 ℹ️ TAT,
Ayutthaya (0-3524-6076). 🛍 daily.
🌐 palaces.thai.net

Visitors to Bang Pa-in stop off, for the most part, just to visit **Bang Pa-in Palace**, whose exuberant 19th-century buildings stand in stark contrast to nearby Ayutthaya. It is thought that a royal palace was first built at Bang Pa-in by King Prasat Thong (1629–56), to mark the birth of his son and successor, King Narai. With the defeat of Ayutthaya by the Burmese in 1767 the site fell into ruin; the present buildings date from the reigns of Mongkut (1851–68) and Chulalongkorn (1868–1910).

The beautiful pavilion, Phra Thinang Aisawan Thipha-at ("divine seat of personal freedom"), at the center of an ornamental lake, was built for Chulalongkorn in 1876, together with the Phra Thinang Warophat Phiman ("excellent and shining abode"), to the left. Behind are the terra-cotta- and white-striped lookout tower, Ho Withun Thasana, built by Chulalongkorn in 1881, and the Chinese-style mansion, Phra Thinang Wehat Chamrun, built as a gift for him by an association of Chinese merchants in 1889. Visitors can cross a canal by cable car to Wat Niwet Tham Prawat, which was built by Chulalongkorn in 1877–8.

🏛 Bang Pa-in Palace
พระราชวังบางปะอิน

Bang Pa-in district. **Tel** 0-3526-1548.
Open 8am–5pm daily. 🔼 ✏️

The Phra Thinang Aisawan Thipha-at pavilion, Bang Pa-in Palace

A statue of Buddha at Wat Phra Mahathat in Ayutthaya Historical Park ▶

⓮ Khao Yai National Park
อุทยานแห่งชาติเขาใหญ่

Established in 1962, Khao Yai was then Thailand's sole national park. Today there are well over 100, but this one remains popular. Set over 770 sq miles (2,000 sq km), the park has a wide variety of habitats, including submontane evergreen forests and grasslands. There are also several mountains of around 3,300 ft (1,000 m), including Khao Khieo. The abundant wildlife includes many endangered mammals such as elephants, gibbons, tigers and Malaysian sun bears, as well as more than 300 bird species. Visitors are advised to hire a guide for trips to more remote parts. The surrounding area offers luxurious resorts, golf courses, and even vineyards.

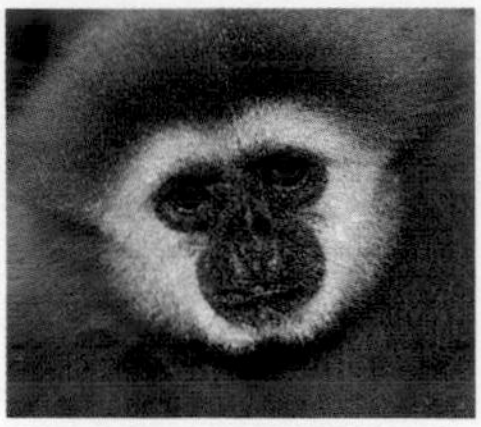

White-Handed Gibbon
These tailless apes use their long arms to move swiftly and agilely through the trees.

Saraburi

Elepha
salt lic

Watchtower•
Watchtower•

Ra
sta

▲ Kha
Khi
4,2
(1,2

Bangkok

Nakhon Nayok • ①

Endangered Species
Khao Yai is home to about 20 of the 500 or so tigers left in Thailand. These noble animals can be found surprisingly close to the park's headquarters; visitors should treat them with respect.

Siamese Fireback Pheasant
Thailand's national bird, this pheasant spends its days on the ground where it feeds on small insects, seeds, and fruit. It roosts in the trees at night.

0 kilometers   10

0 miles   10

Haeo Suwat Waterfall
Located along the upper reaches of the Lam Takhong River, this waterfall is one of many dotted around Khao Yai. From March to May each year many varieties of orchids can be seen flowering around the waterfall. Elephants have been known to drown while crossing near waterfalls when the rains are very heavy.

Submontane Evergreen Forest

This type of forest often contains deciduous trees such as chestnuts. It grows at Khao Yai's highest altitudes, 3,300 ft (1,000 m) to 4,450 ft (1,351 m) above sea level.

Khorat

Pak Chong

Khao Kamphaeng
3,196 ft (974 m)

②

Khao Wong 479 ft (146 m)

Prachin buri

Key

▬▬ Expressway
▬▬ Major road
▭▭ Minor road
■ ▪ Park border

KEY

① **Deciduous forest** grows in the park's low-lying areas.

② **Semievergreen rainforest** can be seen above 1,950 ft (600 m).

VISITORS' CHECKLIST

Practical Information
Khorat, Nakhon Nayok, Saraburi
& Prachin Buri provinces. Park HQ
off Hwy 1, NE of Bangkok.
🛈 TAT, Khorat (0-4421-3666);
Park HQ (08-6092-6529); Forestry
Dept (0-2562-0760 or for
bungalows). **Closed** in bad
weather. 🚻 📷 ♿
🆆 dnp.go.th

Transport
🚌 Pak Chong, then bus
or *songthaew*.

Sambar Stag
Sambar are the largest species of deer in Thailand and are primarily forest dwellers. Though hunted by tigers and leopards, humans are its main predator. It is now common only in well-protected conservation areas.

Earthball Fungus
This parasitic fungus is found in humid evergreen forests all over Southeast Asia. Unlike many parasites, its presence actually encourages the growth of its host.

Lam Takhong River
Rainfall in Khao Yai National Park is usually in excess of 120 inches (3,000 mm) per year. Streams swollen by the rains flow off forested slopes forming rivers, among them the Lam Takhong River. Wildlife living around this river includes kingfishers, cormorants, elephants, and macaques.

For keys to symbols *see back flap*

NORTH CENTRAL PLAINS

The farther north a visitor travels through the Central Plains, the more sparsely populated the countryside becomes – the landscape here is typified by gentle, rolling hills and rice farms. There are few interesting modern cities in this region. Its major attractions are ancient city ruins, relics of an illustrious past when competing princedoms and city-states fought each other for land and power.

Visitors to Thailand traveling north from Bangkok tend not to stop off in the North Central Plains, but instead press on to the major destination of Thailand's second city, Chiang Mai. However, some of the most fascinating ruins in Southeast Asia are found here.

In the 13th century, during the reign of King Ramkamhaeng *(see pp62–3)*, one city, Sukhothai, came to dominate the region to such an extent that its influence was felt far beyond Thailand's present borders. But its power was short-lived, and by the mid-14th century the region was once more a collection of fiefdoms. The ruins the kingdom left behind at Sukhothai, and at its satellite cities of Kamphaeng Phet and Si Satchanalai, still inspire wonder. They have been extensively restored and turned into well-managed historical parks. Other places of interest in the region include the prosperous trading center Phitsanulok, which is at the heart of a transportation network connecting the region to Bangkok and the north. This, and other towns, support a local rice-farming economy.

The hillier areas, in the west and northeast of the region, are the setting for a number of national parks and wildlife sanctuaries. These provide a much needed refuge for endangered plant and animal species *(see pp32–3)* whose habitats are threatened by the impact of illegal logging and the widespread loss of land to agriculture.

Around Mae Sot the influence of Myanmar (Burma) is felt; the town is characterized by Myanmar architecture, and a common sight is Karen and Shan tribespeople and Myanmar who cross the border at this point to trade.

Farmer raking unhusked rice, a typical rural scene in the North Central Plains

◀ Reclining Buddha and sitting Buddha at Wat Phra Kaeo, Kamphaeng Phet

Exploring the North Central Plains

This part of the country acts as a bridge between the crowded heartland of modern Thailand to the immediate south and the rolling hills of the North. The region has no big cities, and most tourists do no more than overnight in small, provincial towns near the magnificent ruins of ancient Sukhothai, the first Thai capital. Predominantly, this is rice-farming country, flanked to the east, north, and west by hills. National parks in some of the hilly areas help protect endangered flora and fauna. Magnificent forest scenery and spectacular waterfalls can be found along the western border with Myanmar (Burma), around Mae Sot and remote Umphang. Here, a hint of Myanmar spills across the border in the shape of Karen and Shan tribespeople and Myanmar architecture, goods, and food.

Buddha under *naga* at Wat Chumphon Khiri, Mae Sot

Wat Traphang Thong, a monastery surrounded by a lotus-filled pond at Sukhothai Historical Park

Key

━━ Major road

▭▭▭ Minor road

━━ Scenic route

━▭━ Railway

▬▬ International border

△ Summit

For hotels and restaurants see pp402–11 and pp418–33

Prang of Wat Phra Si Rattana Mahathat, a 14th-century temple at Phitsanulok

Getting Around

Sukhothai Historical Park is on the itineraries of many tour companies. However, most visitors use public transportation for sights in the region. Phitsanulok, an important transit hub, is the only major town in the region served by the regular train service connecting Bangkok to the North. It also has a small airport, as do Mae Sot and Sukhothai. Highway 1 passes through Kamphaeng Phet and Tak. Local buses run to all towns, and a network of main roads connects nearly all the sights. Only Umphang remains isolated, at the end of a spectacular, winding road from Mae Sot.

Sights at a Glance

① Mae Sot
② Tak
③ Umphang
④ Khlong Lan National Park
⑤ Kamphaeng Phet
⑥ Sukhothai Historical Park pp198–201
⑦ Si Satchanalai-Chalieng Historical Park pp202–4
⑧ Phitsanulok
⑨ Thung Salaeng Luang National Park

For keys to symbols *see back flap*

Wat Chumphon Khiri, Mae Sot, Tak province

❶ Mae Sot

แม่สอด

Tak province. 🗺 70,000. ✈ 🚌
ℹ TAT, Tak (0-5551-4341). 🛍 daily.

In the mid-19th century Myanmar and Shan merchants, crossing the Moei River from Myanmar (Burma) in the west, helped to establish Mae Sot as a prosperous market town. Trade in Myanmar hardwoods and gemstones, both legal and smuggled, has brought considerable wealth to this small town. Today Mae Sot retains the feel of a frontier town and makes a relaxing stopover for travelers. Gem traders, usually ethnic Chinese, can often be seen huddled on Mae Sot's pavements, negotiating with buyers from Bangkok and other parts of Thailand. Because of its location and trading history, Mae Sot has a distinct Myanmar flavor, evident in architecture and market goods.

Trilingual shop signs can be seen on the streets, Myanmar-language publications are sold in shops, and Myanmar people wearing traditional sarongs (lungis) can be seen walking along the streets.

During the morning food market – one of Thailand's most picturesque and colorful – Karen and Myanmar traders haggle with Thais and Indians.

North of the market is **Wat Chumphon Khiri**, which has a magnificent Myanmar chedi decorated with golden mosaic tiles. On the southeast side of town is the Muslim quarter; at its center is the small **Nurul Islam Mosque**.

Dotted around the town are a number of other temples that have both Karen and Shan characteristics.

Environs
Some 2 miles (3 km) west of Mae Sot is **Wat Thai Watthanaram**. In the rear courtyard is a huge, Myanmar-style, reclining Buddha image built in 1993 and a gallery of 28 seated Buddha images. A further 1,100 yards (1,000 m) beyond Wat Thai Watthanaram, a bridge over the Moei River links Mae Sot to the Myanmar border town of Myawadi. Clustered around the foot of the bridge is a market selling an odd mix of Thai, Myanmar, Indonesian, and Chinese goods.

Southeast of Mae Sot are the **Pha Charoen falls**, a very popular spot for picnicking and swimming.

Monks in the grounds of Wat Bot Mani Sibunruang, Tak

❷ Tak

ตาก

Tak province. 🗺 78,000. ✈ 🚌
ℹ TAT, Taksin Rd, Tak (0-5551-4341).
🛍 daily.

During much of the 13th century, Tak was a western outpost of the Sukhothai Kingdom. After the death of

Reclining, Myanmar-style Buddha in the courtyard of Wat Thai Watthanaram, near Mae Sot

One of many waterfalls in the Umphang Wildlife Sanctuary

King Ramkamhaeng and the subsequent collapse of the Sukhothai Empire (see pp62–3), the town came under the influence of the Lanna Kingdom (see pp66–7) to the north. Today Tak sprawls along the left bank of the Ping River, and much of the Lanna influence can still be seen in the teak houses hidden away in quiet lanes at the southern end of town. The houses here date from the late 19th and early 20th centuries.

Wat Bot Mani Sibunruang also shows Northern influences with its finely decorated, Lanna-style *bot* and a small *sala* containing a much revered Buddha image called Luang Phu Phutthamon.

Nearby is a statue of King Taksin, a former governor of Tak, who, after the sacking of Ayutthaya by Myanmar in 1767, established a new capital at Thon Buri, now part of Bangkok (see pp68–9).

Environs
The 40-sq mile (105-sq km) **Lan Sang National Park** has tracks leading to several beautiful waterfalls. These are best visited during or soon after the rainy season (see pp30–31); at other times of year there is little water. To the north of Lan Sang National Park is the **Taksin Maharat National Park**, the highlight of which is a steeply descending trail to the huge *ton krabak yai*, or big krabak

tree, which is some 165 ft (50 m) tall, and has a girth of 50 ft (16 m). The park offers bird-watching opportunities, and boasts such species as the tiger shrike and forest wagtail. Also in the park are the nine-tiered Mae Ya Pa falls.

⊠ Lan Sang National Park
12 miles (20 km) W of Tak, off Hwy 105. **Tel** 0-5557-6080.

⊠ Taksin Maharat National Park
9 miles (15 km) W of Tak, off Hwy 105. **Tel** 0-5551-1429. Forestry Dept (0-2562-0760).

❸ Umphang
อุ้มผาง

Tak province. 23,000. Mae Sot, then *songthaew*. TAT, Tak (0-5551-4341). daily.

Part of Umphang's charm lies in the journey, as the road from Mae Sot is one of Thailand's most scenic. The village – its population consisting largely of Karen tribespeople – is surrounded by the lush forests of **Umphang Wildlife Sanctuary**, rich in bird life and small mammals. Umphang has become popular for rafting, hiking, and elephant treks, but its isolation has kept most of the tourist hordes away. Here too are many cascades and rapids (including one of the country's highest waterfalls, **Thi Lo Su**), caves, and Karen settlements. Several agencies in Umphang or Mae Sot can arrange treks. Visitors should avoid school vacations, when this region is crowded and accommodations scarce.

⊠ Umphang Wildlife Sanctuary
93 miles (150 km) S of Mae Sot on Hwy 1090. Forestry Dept (0-2562-0760).

Thailand-Myanmar (Burma) Border Refugees

There are nine official refugee camps on Thailand's western border, including three main camps around Mae Sot–Mae La, Noe Po, and Umpium. Together, these camps are home to about 100,000 Myanmar refugees. The Karen tribespeople, who have long occupied an area straddling Myanmar and Thailand, are Myanmar's largest ethnic minority. The British were supposed to grant the Karen an autonomous homeland within Myanmar after World War II, but this did not happen. Following pro democracy demonstrations in Myanmar in 1988, and the subsequent crackdown, opposition MPs and ethnic minorities fled east to refugee villages. It is in such villages that the Karen organize their struggle for an independent state. The Thai government does not openly condemn Myanmar, and the Thai army does not usually intervene on behalf of the Karen.

Boy soldiers in the rebel army of the Karen tribespeople

For further information see http://theborderconsortium.org.

Waterfall in Khlong Lan National Park, Kamphaeng Phet province

❹ Khlong Lan National Park

อุทยานแห่งชาติคลองลาน

Kamphaeng Phet province. Park HQ 4 miles (6 km) off Hwy 1117, S of Kamphaeng Phet. **Tel** 0-5576-6002. TAT, Tak (0-5551-4341); Forestry Dept (0-2562-0760 inc bungalow bookings). from Kamphaeng Phet to Klonglan, then *songthaew*. **dnp.go.th**

This 116-sq mile (300-sq km) national park was formed in 1982. Formerly, the area was controlled by Communist insurgents, and inhabited by a number of hill tribes. Initially, the tribes lived within the park but were later relocated because they were regarded as a threat to the wildlife, which includes gaur, tiger, and the Asiatic black bear.

The highlight of the park is the Khlong Lan waterfall, which is easily accessible from the park headquarters. It falls 310 ft (95 m) into a pool ideal for a refreshing swim. At the foot of the road leading up to the waterfall is a small market selling Hmong handicrafts – a government rehabilitation scheme for the hill tribes relocated from the park.

The adjacent **Mae Wong National Park** is good for hiking and bird-watching. A tiger conservation project run by the WWF (www.wwf.or.th) is also located here. Until the late 1980s it was populated by Hmong, who have also been relocated. The number of birds and mammals is steadily increasing. An old road running through the center of the park, now overgrown, makes a good hiking trail. Simple bungalow accommodation is also available.

Mae Wong National Park
Park HQ SW of Kamphaeng Phet, off Hwy 1117. Forestry Dept (0-2562-0760, inc bungalow bookings). **dnp.go.th**

❺ Kamphaeng Phet

กำแพงเพชร

Kamphaeng Phet province. 164,000. TAT, Tak (0-5551-4341). daily. Nop Phra-Len Plang (Feb), Kluay Khai Muang Kamphaeng (Sep).

There has been a settlement at this site on the banks of the Ping River since the 11th century, when a northern prince, fleeing an attack by Myanmar in the area of present-day Fang *(see p246)*, brought his followers here. The community initially survived as an outpost of the Khmer Empire *(see pp60–61)* and, during the 13th century, as part of the Sukhothai Kingdom.

On the east bank lie the impressive remains of the **Old City**, dating from the early 15th century, and which once formed part of a satellite city to the mighty Sukhothai *(see pp198–201)*. Located within its walls is the **Kamphaeng Phet National Museum**. In this collection are several fine 16th-century bronzes of Hindu deities, including a standing image of Shiva and torsos of Vishnu and Lakshmi. There are also stucco and terra-cotta fragments from Kamphaeng Phet's many ruins.

The Old City walls also enclose two important ruins from the late Sukhothai period. Close to the National Museum, **Wat Phra Kaeo** is the Old City's largest site, containing the ruins of several *wihans*, a *bot* at the eastern end, a *chedi* from the late Sukhothai period, and the laterite cores of a

Renovated stone elephant at Wat Phra Kaeo, Kamphaeng Phet

Kamphaeng Phet National Museum and surrounding gardens

number of Buddha images. At the western end of the site are three more partly restored Buddha images. Neighboring **Wat Phra That** has a fine late Sukhothai, octagonal-based *chedi*. One admission charge covers all ruins in the Old City.

The modern town of Kamphaeng Phet, for the most part, sprawls to the south of the Old City. It mostly comprises commercial buildings, though it also has a riverside park and a few traditional wooden houses, as well as some tourist-oriented facilities.

A *samlor* ride northwest of the Old City are the **Aranyik Ruins**, the area of many forest *wats* once used by a meditational order called the Forest Dwelling Sect. Built during the 14th to 16th centuries, the sheer number of ruins at Aranyik attest to the popularity of the sect, which achieved prominence in Thailand during the Sukhothai era. With the assistance of UNESCO, parts of the site have now been restored and landscaped.

The *wihan* at Wat Phra Non, near the entrance, once contained a large reclining Buddha, but this is so badly damaged as to be almost indiscernible. Nevertheless, a number of laterite columns from the *wihan* are still standing. On each side of the *mondop* at Wat Phra Si Iriyabot are images of the Buddha in different postures, though all are damaged. The standing Buddha on the west side has been partially restored.

In the ruined *bot* of Wat Sing (found in the northern part of the Aranyik site) is the laterite core of a Buddha image.

Most impressive of the Aranyik *wats* is **Wat Chang Rop**, consisting mostly of the remains of a very large, square-based *chedi*, flanked by the forequarters of some elephants in laterite. On a few of these, the original stucco decoration has been restored. However, little of the Sri Lankan-style bell-shaped *chedi* is still standing. Among two dozen or so other sites dotted around Aranyik, many of them scarcely visible in thick undergrowth, Wat Awat Yai is one of the few now cleared of vegetation.

In the modern part of town, other monuments, such as the Sukhothai brick *chedi* of **Wat Kalothai**, can be seen tucked away in quiet lanes. Many such sites have now fallen into disrepair, but their sheer quantity is an indication of the importance of Kamphaeng Phet during the Sukhothai and Ayutthaya periods.

West of the city, the large, white, Myanmar-style *chedi* of **Wat Phra Boromathat** was built in the late 19th century on the site of three 13th–14th-century *chedis*, the earliest of which was constructed by King Si Intharathit of Sukhothai (c.1240–70) to house some relics of the Lord Buddha. Also to the west are the laterite walls of **Thung Setthi Fort**, which once protected this side of the city.

🏛 **Kamphaeng Phet National Museum**
Old City, behind Wat Phra Kaeo. **Tel** 0-5571-1570. **Open** 8:30am–4pm Wed–Sun. **Closed** public hols. 🎟
🌐 **finearts.go.th**

🏯 **Aranyik Ruins**
NW of Old City. **Open** daily. 🎟

🏯 **Thung Setthi Fort**
Off Hwy 1, W of town. **Open** daily.

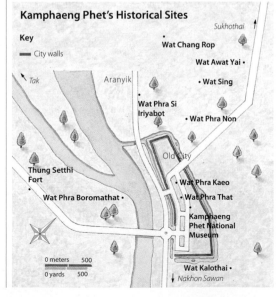

Kamphaeng Phet's Historical Sites

Sukhothai

Key
— City walls

↖ *Tak*

Aranyik

Wat Chang Rop

Wat Awat Yai •

• Wat Sing

Wat Phra Si Iriyabot

• Wat Phra Non

Old City

Thung Setthi Fort

Wat Phra Boromathat •

• Wat Phra Kaeo

• Wat Phra That

Kamphaeng Phet National Museum

0 meters 500
0 yards 500

Wat Kalothai •
↓ *Nakhon Sawan*

❻ Sukhothai Historical Park

อุทยานประวัติศาสตร์สุโขทัย

The UNESCO World Heritage site of Old Sukhothai lies to the west of the modern town. It is a potent reminder of the ancient Sukhothai Kingdom, which arose in the early 13th century from what had been a distant outpost of the Khmer Empire. Under the leadership of the Tai warrior King Ramkamhaeng, the city came to dominate the Central Plains (*see pp62–3*). The abandoned city that can be seen today is the best preserved and most popular sight in Central Thailand. Ongoing restoration has revealed the amazing symmetry of its layout and offers the visitor a remarkable insight into a time when Thai art and culture reached its apex.

Exploring Sukhothai Historical Park

The site of Old Sukhothai has around 40 temple complexes spread over an area of about 28 sq miles (70 sq km). At its center is the walled Royal City, protected by moats and ramparts. Many of the most important ruins are within this inner compound. The layout of Old Sukhothai, as with many major Thai cities (*muangs*), follows fixed principles: a large, central *wat* complex surrounded concentrically by walls, river,

rice fields, and, beyond, forested mountains. Another example of this, on a smaller scale, is Si Satchanalai (*see pp62–3*).

One way to see the ruins of the Royal City is by bicycle: shops beside the old east gate rent them by the day for a small fee. A quick test ride is advised as some are in poor condition, and an early start is recommended to avoid the midday heat.

The Royal City

Entering from the east, the first *wat* within the city walls is Wat Traphang Thong, which is situated on an islet in a small lotus-filled lake. The Sri Lankan-style *chedi* dates from the mid-14th century, and a small *mondop* beside it enshrines a stone Footprint of the Buddha, still worshiped by resident monks.

The **Ramkamhaeng National Museum** houses photographs, taken around 1900–20, of Sukhothai's ruins prior to renovation and a large collection of artifacts. At the heart of the moated city is **Wat Mahathat**

Khmer-style, laterite *prangs*, part of Wat Si Sawai

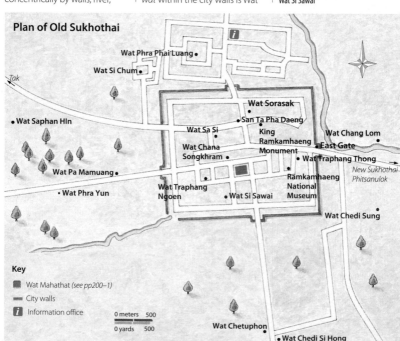

Plan of Old Sukhothai

Tak

- Wat Phra Phai Luang
- Wat Si Chum
- Wat Saphan Hin
- Wat Pa Mamuang
- Wat Phra Yun
- Wat Sorasak
- San Ta Pha Daeng
- Wat Sa Si
- Wat Chana Songkhram
- King Ramkamhaeng Monument
- Wat Chang Lom
- East Gate
- Wat Traphang Thong
- Ramkamhaeng National Museum
- Wat Traphang Ngoen
- Wat Si Sawai
- Wat Chedi Sung

New Sukhothai Phitsanulok

- Wat Chetuphon
- Wat Chedi Si Hong

Key

- ■ Wat Mahathat (*see pp200–1*)
- — City walls
- ℹ Information office

0 meters 500
0 yards 500

Façade of the Ramkamhaeng National Museum

(see pp200–1), the most important *wat* complex in Sukhothai.

Nearby, Wat Takuan has a restored, Sri Lankan bell-shaped *chedi*. Several Buddha images found in the vault of the *chedi* are thought to date from the early Sukhothai period, though they remain something of a mystery.

To the southwest, at Wat Si Sawai, are three 12th–14th-century Khmer-style *prangs*, thought to predate the Tai takeover of the city.

The *bot* of Wat Traphang Ngoen, mentioned in Ramkamhaeng's famous Inscription No. 1 (see p62), lies in an artificial rectangular lake.

Copper Buddha images and Chinese pottery were recovered from Wat Sa Si, also at the center of an artificial lake. These are now in the Ramkamhaeng National Museum.

Nearby, Wat Chana Songkhram has a restored, squat Sri Lankan-style *chedi*. A smaller *chedi* here dates from the Ayutthaya period.

To the north of Wat Mahathat is the modern **King Ramkamhaeng Monument**. Beyond lies San Ta Pha Daeng, a 12th-century Khmer shrine that once housed sandstone Hindu icons, now in the Ramkamhaeng National Museum.

Wat Sorasak, a small, brick, bell-shaped *chedi*, dates from the early 15th century. The square base is supported by 24 stucco elephants.

East of the Royal City

Wat Chang Lom, a bell-shaped *chedi* similar to one at Si Satchanalai (see p204), has 36 brick and stucco elephants around its base. It represents mythical Mount Meru, supported by elephants. Beyond is Wat Chedi Sung, a beautiful *chedi* with a high, square base typical of the late Sukhothai era.

North of the Royal City

Wat Phra Phai Luang, a Khmer-style complex, is thought to be part of the original mid-13th century settlement, built when this region was part of the Khmer Empire. Only one of the three laterite *prangs*, decorated with stucco fragments, is extant. Nearby, the *mondop* of

Wat Si Chum has an immense seated Buddha peering through an opening.

Reconstructed stucco elephant heads at Wat Sorasak

Loy Krathong at Sukhothai

Loy Krathong (see p54) occurs at the November full moon to mark the end of the rainy season and the main rice harvest. The festival has its origins in the Hindu tradition of thanking the water god for the rains. *Krathongs*, bowls fashioned out of banana leaves holding lighted candles, are floated on water after dark. Though celebrated all over Thailand, the most exuberant festivities take place at Old Sukhothai. Nowadays, the festival includes folk dancing and sound-and-light shows.

Loy Krathong festivities at the Sukhothai Historical Park

Wat Mahathat

วัดมหาธาตุ

Wat Mahathat was the spiritual center of the Sukhothai Kingdom. The central *chedi* was founded by Si Intharathit (c.1240–70), first king of Sukhothai, and rebuilt in the 1340s by Lue Thai (1298–1346) to house relics of the Buddha. Buildings were added to the complex by successive kings: by the time it was abandoned in the 16th century it had some 200 *chedis* as well as numerous *wihans* and *mondops*.

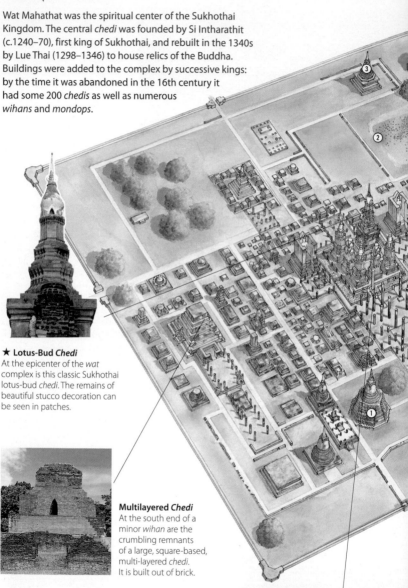

★ Lotus-Bud *Chedi*
At the epicenter of the *wat* complex is this classic Sukhothai lotus-bud *chedi*. The remains of beautiful stucco decoration can be seen in patches.

Multilayered *Chedi*
At the south end of a minor *wihan* are the crumbling remnants of a large, square-based, multi-layered *chedi*. It is built out of brick.

KEY

① Octagonal *chedi*

② Ornamental pond

③ Bell-shaped *chedi*

④ Perimeter wall

★ Frieze of Walking Monks
A stucco frieze runs around the square base of the central group of *chedis*. It depicts monks processing around the shrine – a ritual called *pradaksina*.

Remains of *Bot*
To the north of the central *chedi* are the remains of a *bot*, with a large, seated Buddha. Like all major Buddha images in Thailand, it faces east.

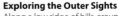

0 meters 25
0 yards 25

★ Phra Attharot Buddha Images
Flanking the central chedis are two Buddhas, both known as Phra Attharot – a literal reference to their size – housed in *mondops*.

Remains of Wihan
Aligned on an east-west axis with the central group of *chedis* is the main *wihan*. The only remains today are columns that once supported a roof and a seated Buddha image.

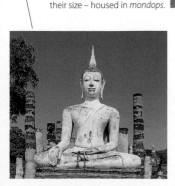

Exploring the Outer Sights
Along a low ridge of hills, around 2 miles (3.5 km) west of the ramparted royal city is another string of ruins that form part of the Sukhothai Historical Park. Most important of these is **Wat Saphan Hin**, where a 41-ft (12.5-m) high Buddha image, Phra Attharot, similar to the Buddha images of the same name at Wat Mahathat, stands on a low summit. There is another large image, similar to Phra Attharot, at Wat Phra Yun, though the head and hands are missing.

Closer to the west city wall is Wat Pa Mamuang, of archeological importance for the inscriptions discovered here relating to King Lo Thai.

To the south are the ruins of Wat Chetuphon, where a *mondop* contains the remains of four Buddha images (see p177); two are in good condition, but of the other two, one is missing below the waist and the other has virtually disappeared. At Wat Chedi Si Hong, the base of the laterite brick *chedi* is lined with elephants and divinities.

Beyond the southern edge of the Historical Park loom the hills of **Ramkamhaeng National Park**. Covering 133 sq miles (342 sq km), this is home to serow, gaur, and wild pig.

Ramkamhaeng National Park
S of Sukhothai off Hwy 101.
Tel 0-5591-0000. *i* Forestry Dept (0-2562-0760 inc bungalow bookings).
W dnp.go.th

Farmer cultivating rice in the fields surrounding Sukhothai

❼ Si Satchanalai-Chalieng Historical Park

อุทยานประวัติศาสตร์ศรีสัชนาลัย-ชะเลียง

During the 13th century, the Sukhothai Kingdom consolidated its power in the Central Plains by building a number of satellite cities. The most important of these was Si Satchanalai. Today, its ruins lie on the right bank of the Yom River, 4 miles (7 km) south of modern Si Satchanalai. One of the best examples of a Thai *muang (see pp62–3)*, it was laid out along fixed cosmological lines – temple complexes lay at its heart, surrounded by city walls, rivers, and forest. It is considered by many historians to be the apogee of Thai city planning. The nearby ruins of Chalieng are thought to be an earlier Khmer settlement, an outpost of that empire dating from the time of Jayavarman VII (1181–1220). At the height of the Sukhothai Kingdom, Si Satchanalai was twinned with the city of Sukhothai. A royal road, the Phra Ruang, linked the two.

Laterite columns and central chedi at Wat Nang Phaya

The central, lotus-bud *chedi* of Wat Chedi Chet Thaeo

Exploring the Park

The ruins of Si Satchanalai are not as grandiose as those of Sukhothai but are in some ways more interesting. They have not been as extensively restored, and fewer tourists visit the site. The ruins evoke a once powerful city that, although not a seat of government of the Sukhothai Kingdom, was the city of the deputy king and an important commercial center in the 14th and 15th centuries. Its most important trade was in ceramics *(see pp164–5)*, for which it was renowned all over Southeast Asia and China.

Today, the ruins at Si Satchanalai cover an area of roughly 18 sq miles (45 sq km) and are surrounded by a moat 40 ft (12 m) wide. A good way to tour the site is by bicycle; there is a bicycle rental store located halfway between Si Satchanalai and Chalieng. Visitors can also ride around

the ruined city on the back of an elephant. An information center located in front of the Ram Narong Gate houses a small exhibition of artifacts found at the site and photographs of Si Satchanalai's many monuments.

The Main *Wats*

At the heart of the moated city a huge Sri Lankan-style, bell-shaped *chedi* forms the centerpiece of **Wat Chang Lom** *(see p204)*. To the south is **Wat Chedi Chet Thaeo**, around whose central lotus-bud *chedi* are many smaller ones in different styles, some containing stucco Buddha images. One of these *chedis* is a smaller version of the famous lotus-bud *chedi* at Wat Mahathat at Sukhothai *(see pp200–1)*.

At **Wat Nang Phaya**, the *wihan* is decorated with fine stucco reliefs from the Ayutthaya period, especially on the exterior. There is also a Sri Lankan-style, 15th–16th-century *chedi*. The *wihan's* grille-like windows here are also characteristic of Ayutthaya, and less complete examples of this

Sri Lankan Influence

During the Sukhothai period, Theravada Buddhism, which had developed independently in Sri Lanka, arrived in Thailand. With it came Sri Lankan, bell-shaped *chedis*, reliquary towers symbolizing the ringing out of the teachings of the Buddha. The three-tiered base symbolizes hell, earth, and heaven; rings on the spire represent the 33 levels of heaven. A second layer of symbolism designates the base as the Buddha's folded robes, the *stupa* as his alms bowl and the spire as his staff. The entire *chedi* also symbolizes Mount Meru.

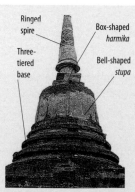

Ringed spire

Three-tiered base

Box-shaped *harmika*

Bell-shaped *stupa*

Sri Lankan-style *chedi* of Wat Suwan Khiri, overlooking Si Satchanalai

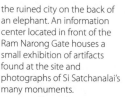

style can be seen elsewhere around the park. Nearby stands Wat Lak Muang, a small, Khmer-style shrine built as the city foundation shrine.

Minor *Wats*

On a low, wooded hill north of Wat Chang Lom stands Wat Khao Phnom Phloeng, once the site of ritual cremations. Also among the ruins are a seated Buddha, a *chedi*, and a number of columns that once supported a *wihan* roof.

On a hill top, farther west, all that remains of Wat Suwan Khiri is a single *chedi*, though there are great views from here of the rest of the city.

Beyond the City Walls

Farther west, on a mountain outside the city walls, is a row of ruined monasteries reached by a shady path. At the top of the path is the large, ruined *chedi* of Wat Khao Yai Bon.

There are many other minor ruins scattered inside and outside the moated site, and while some have been restored, others comprise little more than the base of a *wihan* or *chedi*. The *mondop* of Wat Hua Khon, for example, once contained seven stuccoed standing Buddha images; today only three are still plainly identifiable. North of the old Tao Mo Gate is Wat Kuti Rai. There are two rectangular *mondops* here, both built entirely from laterite.

Their pediments retain holes for beams, suggesting that they were once linked to other buildings. Inside one *mondop* is a seated Buddha image.

To the north are the kiln sites of Ban Pa Yuang and Ban Noi, where some of the finest Sangkhalok ceramics were produced. A sign of the times is that villagers nearby sell modern replicas to supplement their farming incomes.

Chalieng

Situated 1,090 yards (1,000 m) to the southeast is the settlement of Chalieng, predating the city of Si Satchanalai and in all likelihood built by the Khmers *(see pp268–9)* as a staging post for travelers. Some of the ruins that can be seen today date from later.

The laterite shrine of **Wat Chao Chan** was built in the Bayon style as a Mahayana Buddhist structure. The *wihan* and *mondop*, now ruins, were added later and reflect a move toward Theravada Buddhism.

Surrounded on three sides by a tight bend of the Yom River, the most important of the Chalieng sites is **Wat Phra Si Rattana Mahathat**, the buildings of which reflect a range of architectural styles from Sukhothai to Ayutthayan. The original Sukhothai lotus-bud *chedi* was built over with

VISITORS' CHECKLIST

Practical Information
41 miles (67 km) N of New Sukhothai, Sukhothai province.
🛈 Information Center (0-2250-5500) or TAT, Phitsanulok (0-5525-2743). **Open** 8:30am–4:30pm daily. 🅿️ 📷

Transport
🚌 from New Sukhothai to Si Satchanalai, then samlor.

Ancient kiln site, north of the walled city at Ban Pa Yuang

a huge Khmer-influenced, Ayutthayan *prang*, one of the finest structures of its type in Thailand. Nearby, a seated Buddha, sheltered under the head of a *naga*, sits inside a half *chedi*. Also close by are remains of stucco reliefs of walking Buddhas, said to be some of the very finest examples of Sukhothai sculpture.

Si Satchanalai-Chalieng Historical Park

↖ *Si Satchanalai*

Key

━ City walls

0 meters ——— 500
0 yards ——— 500

- Ban Noi
- Ban Pa Yuang
- Wat Kuti Rai
- Wat Hua Khon
- Tao Mo Gate
- Wat Suwan Khiri
- Wat Khao Phnom Phloeng
- 101
- Wat Khao Yai Bon
- Wat Chang Lom
- Wat Chedi Chet Thaeo
- Wat Nang Phaya
- Wat Lak Muang
- Yom
- Wat Phra Si Rattana Mahathat
- 🛈 Ram Narong Gate (entrance to walled city)
- Wat Chao Chan
- *Chalieng*
- *Sukhothai Sawankhalok*

Wat Chang Lom
วัดช้างล้อม

Built in the reign of Ramkamhaeng, this monument is thought to be the first Sri Lankan-style *chedi* of the Sukhothai Kingdom. The style was later copied throughout Si Satchanalai and Sukhothai.

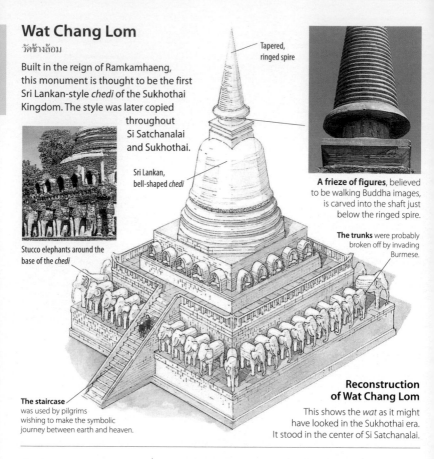

Tapered, ringed spire

Sri Lankan, bell-shaped *chedi*

A frieze of figures, believed to be walking Buddha images, is carved into the shaft just below the ringed spire.

The trunks were probably broken off by invading Burmese.

Stucco elephants around the base of the *chedi*

The staircase was used by pilgrims wishing to make the symbolic journey between earth and heaven.

Reconstruction of Wat Chang Lom
This shows the *wat* as it might have looked in the Sukhothai era. It stood in the center of Si Satchanalai.

Exploring Sawankhalok

With the introduction of new firing techniques by Chinese potters, the kilns around Si Satchanalai and Sukhothai became some of the most important producers of ceramics in Southeast Asia. At their most prolific, during the 14th–16th centuries, as the Sukhothai Kingdom came under the control of the Kingdom of Ayutthaya, it is thought that over 200 potteries lined the banks of the Yom River. They produced a variety of pottery termed Sangkhalok – a derivation of Sawankhalok, the name that was given to Si Satchanalai during the period of Ayutthaya's rule in the region. Today the name applies only to the small town of Sawankhalok,

Sangkhalok pottery

where the **Sawankha Woranayok National Museum** is located. This houses an expansive selection of Sangkhalok ceramics (*see pp164–5*), which includes plates, storage jars, bowls, temple roof tiles, figures used in religious ceremonies, and everyday statues that may have been toys. A large number of the ceramics on display were salvaged from ships wrecked in the Gulf of Thailand on their way to trade with India, China, the Philippines, and Indonesia. The museum also contains a collection of religious sculptures taken from Sawankhalok's nearby Wat Sawankharam – many were donated to the *wat* by the villagers who unearthed them.

Exploring Si Satchanalai National Park

Founded in 1981, this park covers an area of 82 sq miles (213 sq km). Dotted around the park are the Tad Dao, Tad Duen, Huai Sai, and Huai Pa Cho waterfalls. The Tara Wasan and Kang Khao caves are also worth visiting. The park is good for bird-watching, with more than 70 species recorded. Though few large mammals inhabit the park, there may be a small number of wild elephants living here.

Sawankha Woranayok National Museum
Sawankhalok, 11 miles (17 km) S of Si Satchanalai. **Tel** 0-5564-1571. **Open** Wed–Sun.

Si Satchanalai National Park
N of Si Satchanalai-Chalieng Historical Park, off Hwy 101, (0-2562-0760 or **dnp.go.th** for bungalow bookings). **Tel** 0-5591-0002. **Open** daily.

Green and ocher roof tiles at Wat Phra Si Rattana Mahathat, Phitsanulok

❽ Phitsanulok

พิษณุโลก

Phitsanulok province. ⬛ 183,000.
🚆 🚌 🚐 ℹ TAT, 209/7–8
Borommatrailokanat Rd, Phitsanulok
(0-5525-2742/3). 🛒 Wed, Sat. 🎉
Phra Buddha Chinarat (Jan/Feb),
Phitsanulok Boat Races (Oct).

Many visitors pass through
this town since it is an
important transport hub,
connecting Bangkok
and the Central Plains
to Northern Thailand.

There has been a
settlement here from
as early as the mid-
14th century, when
Wat Phra Si Rattana Mahathat
was built on the bank of the
Nan River. Initially, this *wat*
complex, also called Wat Yai,
probably housed a Sukhothai
lotus-bud *chedi*, which was later
replaced by the tall Ayutthayan
prang that can be seen today.
It was built by the Ayutthayan
king Borommatrailokanat
(1448–88), who ruled from
Phitsanulok after 1463 in order
to wage a military campaign
against the Kingdom of Lanna
(*see pp66–7*). The golden tiles
on the antefixes of the *wat*
were added during a later
renovation by King
Chulalongkorn (1868–1910).

Inside the west *wihan* is the
revered Buddha image Phra
Phuttha Chinarat (*see pp164–5*),
made of gilded bronze and
dating from the 14th century.
It attracts pilgrims from all over
Thailand, and, consequently,
a small industry of religious

The Phra Buddha
Chinarat image

paraphernalia has grown up
around it. In the gallery outside
the *prang* are dozens of Buddha
images. Across the road, in the
bot of **Wat Ratchaburana**, are
some faded 19th-century
murals, depicting scenes from
the Ramakien (*see pp44–5*).
**Sergeant Major Thawee's
Folk Museum** houses a
collection of rural folk
crafts – wood and
bamboo animal traps,
farm tools, and
basketry. Across the
street is the affiliated
Buddha Foundry,
where visitors can
watch bronze Buddha
images being forged.

Environs
Three miles (5 km) south of
Phitsanulok is the Ayutthayan,
laterite *prang* of **Wat
Chulamani**. It was built by King
Borommatrailokanat in 1464, a
year after he moved his capital
from Ayutthaya to Phitsanulok.
He was ordained as a monk here
in 1465 after abdicating in favor

of his son. Eight months later he
returned to the throne; until his
death In 1488, he ruled
Ayutthaya from Phitsanulok.

🏛 **Sergeant Major Thawee's
Folk Museum**
26/43 Wisuth Kasat Rd. **Tel** 0-5521-
2749. **Open** 8:30am–4:30pm Tue–Sun.
🖼 Buddha Foundry: **Open** Mon–Sat.

❾ Thung Salaeng Luang National Park

อุทยานแห่งชาติทุ่งแสลงหลวง

Phitsanulok province, Park HQ off Hwy
12, 50 miles (80 km) E of Phitsanulok.
Tel 0-5526-8019. ℹ TAT, Phitsanulok
(0-5525-2742/3); Forestry Dept (0-
2562-0760 or 🅦 **dnp.go.th** for
bungalow bookings). 🚌 from
Phitsanulok to Nakhon Thai, then
songthaew. 🖼

With its open fields interspersed
with forest, this 487-sq mile
(1,262-sq km) park offers good
hiking and bird-watching.
Barking deer can also be seen,
and elephants are sometimes
found at the salt licks. The
cascades of Kaeng Sopha lie
6 miles (9 km) from the park
headquarters. Farther west are
the Poi falls and smaller Kaeng
Song rapids.

Environs
At **Khao Kho**, to the east, is a
rehabilitation project for the
Hmong, displaced through
involvement in anti-Communist
fighting in the 1970s–80s. The
King takes great interest in the
program and has a palace nearby.

The thinly forested Thung Salaeng Luang National Park

NORTHERN THAILAND

Introducing Northern Thailand

Northern Thailand, home of the ancient Lanna kingdom *(see pp66–7)*, offers a great diversity of activities. The old Lanna capitals of Chiang Mai and Chiang Rai are filled with ancient monuments and museums, and markets selling the distinctive local textiles and handicrafts. Smaller towns, such as Nan and Lamphun, offer a more low-key charm. Away from the main settlements, the scenery of Northern Thailand is stupendous: mountains, forests (some of them teak), rice fields set in verdant valleys, and several spectacular national parks. The more adventurous visitor can join a trek to remote villages inhabited by hill tribes where elements of lifestyle have changed little in hundreds of years.

Mae Hong Son *(see pp220–21)*, a rapidly developing tourist center, is particularly popular with budget travelers. The town's main attraction is its beautiful mountain setting.

Chiang Mai *(see pp228–31)* is justly famed for its 300 temples, fine shopping, distinctive Northern cuisine, and (despite its size) relaxed pace of life.

Doi Inthanon National Park *(see pp234–5)* incorporates the highest mountain in Thailand. Visitors come for the stunning scenery, including several waterfalls, and rich wildlife.

Fang

Mae S

Chiang
Dao

Pai

Phrao

Mae
Hong Son

Khun
Yuam

Chiang Mai

Sop Wak

Lamphun

NORTHWEST HEARTLAND
(see pp216–241)

Lampan

Mae
Sariang

Hot

Mae Tun

Mae Tom Nua

Lampang *(see pp240–41)* is a thriving town which hosts colorful festivals. It contains a number of important *wats* and a museum of Lanna artifacts.

◀ Rice paddies against a sunset backdrop, Chiang Mai area

Doi Tung *(see p247)*, a mountain set in beautiful forested country, is crowned by an important pilgrimage site.

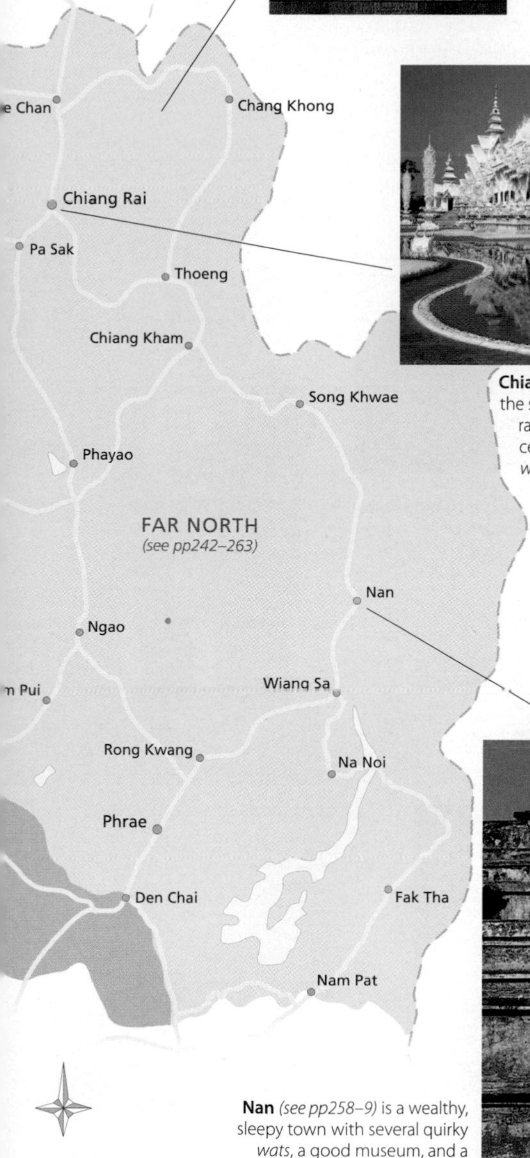

e Chan

Chang Khong

Chiang Rai

Pa Sak

Thoeng

Chiang Kham

Song Khwae

Phayao

FAR NORTH
(see pp242–263)

Nan

Ngao

m Pui

Wiang Sa

Rong Kwang

Na Noi

Phrae

Den Chai

Fak Tha

Nam Pat

Chiang Rai *(see pp254–5)* has long dwelled in the shadow of nearby Chiang Mai, but is now rapidly developing into a significant tourist center in its own right. Its monuments and *wats* may not be as numerous, but the city is an excellent source of hill-tribe handicrafts and a starting point for trekkers.

| 0 kilometers | 50 |
| 0 miles | 25 |

Nan *(see pp258–9)* is a wealthy, sleepy town with several quirky *wats*, a good museum, and a spectacular mountain setting. Every October the Nan River is filled with colorful canoes taking part in the Lanna boat races.

The Hill Tribes of Thailand

There are six main groups of hill dwellers living in Northern Thailand: the Akha, Hmong, Lisu, Karen, Lahu, and Mien. These seminomadic peoples, some 500,000 in total, began to arrive here at the end of the 19th century, pushed out of their native Tibet, Myanmar, and China by civil war and political pressures. Though widely referred to as hill tribes, this label is rather general as each group has its own heritage, language, religion, and culture. The future of the hill tribes is uncertain. Traditionally, most use the slash-and-burn method (swiddening) to grow crops, abandoning land once it is exhausted. But competing pressures on land are drawing them into the Thai market economy. Many hill-tribe teenagers have moved to Chiang Mai to work in or set up craft workshops.

This 1890s portrait is of Lahu women. Most hill tribes still wear traditional dress, though Western clothing is widely available.

Bamboo sections are pounded rhythmically to honor leaders during the Swing Ceremony.

Young Lisu women and girls wear black turbans adorned with multicolored threads, mainly for important celebrations such as New Year. Silver jewelry, sewn onto their clothes, is a display of the family's wealth.

This Hmong house has been accidentally destroyed by fire. To improve living conditions and economic opportunities, and to stop swiddening, the government aims to integrate hill tribes into the Thai way of life.

Festivals and Gatherings

Colorful ceremonies mark rites of passage such as birth, death, and marriage. Here, the Akha gather for a festival.

New Year is the most important date in the Lisu calendar. A tree is planted in front of each house in the village. A shaman and a priest then perform a ritual to cleanse the village of the past year's bad elements, while young people dance around the trees.

In the past, some hill tribes earned extra income from opium production. They are now encouraged to grow "new" crops such as cabbage.

Akha houses are characterized by a large porch connected to a square living area with a stove. They are usually constructed on high ground near the tribe's rice fields.

Akha people strive to maintain a traditional way of life, the "Akha Way." This is proving more difficult as fertile land disappears and animal numbers are depleted. Here, a villager carries out the vital chore of collecting wood.

An ornate headdress, decorated with silver or, increasingly, aluminum, is worn by Akha women.

A sash, weighed down with coins and beads, distinguishes women from girls.

While many Lahu women no longer wear traditional dress on a daily basis, they still weave distinctive shoulder bags (*yam*) from brightly colored fabrics.

Mien clothing is particularly distinctive. Women embroider colorful patterns onto black or indigo cloth and stitch red pompons onto caps worn by children.

Karen typically build houses in lowland valleys, cultivating by crop rotation rather than slash-and-burn. They are the largest and least nomadic tribe.

Spiritual Beliefs

Many hill-tribe beliefs and practices are based on animism. Villages often have two religious leaders: a priest, who performs rituals and communes with the local guardian spirit, and a shaman, who has the power to consult directly with the spirit world. Rituals influence most decisions in a village, including where it is sited. But as tribes are drawn into modern life, traditional practices and medicine are coming under threat.

Mien tools used during shamanistic ceremonies

Northern Arts and Crafts

Northern Thailand is famous for its handicrafts. The high quality of crafts produced today, such as wooden carvings, silverware, fabrics, ceramics, silk, and lacquerware, reflects centuries of Northern Thai, or Lanna, expertise. The region's ethnic minorities and hill tribes *(see pp210–11)* also produce distinctive embroidery, paintings, and silverware. Chiang Mai *(see pp228–31)* is the main crafts center, while villages such as Bo Sang and San Kamphaeng *(see pp232–3)* specialize in particular crafts. In factory-shops, visitors can watch crafts being made. Antiques and excellent copies are sold in outlets in Chiang Mai. Though teak logging has been strictly controlled in Thailand since 1989, wooden crafts produced from imported teak are still widely sold.

Ornate Akha headdresses feature silver coins and hollow baubles that are expertly crafted by the men of the hill tribe.

Animal figures, intricately carved from wood (in many cases teak), often feature in Northern *wats*. Such wooden crafts are still produced throughout the North, despite the ban on unregulated teak logging.

Northern lacquerwork typically consists of a red lacquer-coated wood or bamboo base decorated with a yellow pattern. This is a 19th- or 20th-century box.

Curved legs were designed to fit over the back of the elephant, near its head.

Royal Howdah

Before the advent of the car, elephants were used for transportation in Thailand. People sat in howdahs, or elephant chairs, on the elephants' backs. Howdahs stood some 5 ft (1.5 m) high, and their decoration revealed their passengers' status. The most basic form consisted of a seat with raised sides. Howdahs used for transporting royalty and aristocrats, such as this one from Northern Thailand, featured ornate wood carving and usually had a roof.

Umbrellas are the main craft items produced in Bo Sang. They are made of lacquered paper, stretched over a bamboo frame, then painted with traditional motifs such as elephants.

Betel sets consist of several containers used to hold the ingredients for betel-chewing (a popular activity in Southeast Asia) – betel leaf, limestone ash, and the narcotic areca palm fruit. A gold set was a sign of status.

Wooden roof brackets, seen on religious buildings, are for decoration rather than support. They often depict *nagas* (serpents) and other animals.

A roof made from lacquered woven bamboo offered shelter from the heat.

Silver ceremonial jewelry is worn for village festivals and other important occasions. While hill tribes still use old silver, melted down from Indian and Burmese coins, many Thai silversmiths in Chiang Mai nowadays rely on imported silver of a lower quality.

Handles were used for support during bumpy rides. Royal elephant seats were more comfortable than ordinary ones.

In Thailand even everyday items are decorated, such as this wooden clapper, which is painted with a flower motif. A clapper is traditionally worn by water buffalo so they can be located if they stray.

Delicately fashioned wood carving featured only on elephant chairs used by affluent members of society.

Textiles of Northern Thailand

Embroidering a striped Lahu bag

Textile production in Northern Thailand dates from the early Lanna period, and the region is known for its silk and cotton. Chiang Mai and San Kamphaeng are centers for silk clothing – also made in the Northeast *(see pp270–71)* – including the traditional *pha sin* (woman's sarong). Outlets also sell furnishings and cottonware produced in Pasang *(see p233)* such as the *pha koma* (man's sarong). Chiang Khong factory-shops produce Thai Lue cotton fabrics in stunning colors *(see p253)*, while hill tribes make and sell brightly patterned fabrics. Most textiles can be bought as lengths or as ready-made items.

A traditional cotton design

A 19th-century *pha sin*

Birds of Northern Thailand

Northern Thailand lies on the Eastern Asia Flyway, a major flight path for migrating birds. Thailand boasts some 10 percent of the world's bird species, 380 of which have been recorded in the hills around Chiang Mai. Most of these are migratory birds that have flown south in winter to the warmer climes of Thailand's forested hills. Steps have been introduced to protect bird habitats under threat from deforestation. But many sites in the north, especially Doi Suthep *(see pp226–7)* and Doi Inthanon *(see pp234–5)* national parks, still provide a habitat for numerous bird species.

Selected Migration Routes
- ▬ Arctic warblers
- ▬ Siberian rubythroats
- ▬ Herons

Black-crowned night-herons are nocturnal birds. They have a black crest, nape, and back, whitish underparts, and gray wings. Resident in various countries, they migrate to low altitudes in Northern Thailand.

Changeable hawk-eagle

The red-breasted parakeet, of deciduous woodlands, is threatened by the illegal trade in birds.

Red-wattled lapwings, named for the red patch of skin in front of the eye, reside near streams and in open forest. When alarmed they emit a loud, shrill call.

Teak tree

Silver pheasants live at various altitudes, typically over 2,300 ft (700 m). Their red feet and long tail distinguish them from other types of pheasants. They are also bred in captivity to be sold for food – because of their depleted numbers, pheasants are protected.

Pheasant-tailed jacanas have long legs, toes, and claws that enable them to walk on leaves in lowland rivers, foraging for food.

Purple herons are wetland birds that can be seen near forest streams. They have a slender, rufous (red-brown) neck.

0–1,640 ft (0–500 m)
Above sea level

Coral-billed ground-cuckoos are difficult to observe because they are rare, shy birds.

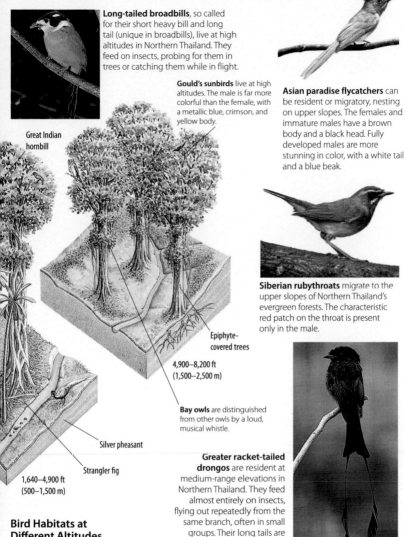

Long-tailed broadbills, so called for their short heavy bill and long tail (unique in broadbills), live at high altitudes in Northern Thailand. They feed on insects, probing for them in trees or catching them while in flight.

Gould's sunbirds live at high altitudes. The male is far more colorful than the female, with a metallic blue, crimson, and yellow body.

Asian paradise flycatchers can be resident or migratory, nesting on upper slopes. The females and immature males have a brown body and a black head. Fully developed males are more stunning in color, with a white tail and a blue beak.

Great Indian hornbill

Siberian rubythroats migrate to the upper slopes of Northern Thailand's evergreen forests. The characteristic red patch on the throat is present only in the male.

Epiphyte-covered trees

4,900–8,200 ft (1,500–2,500 m)

Bay owls are distinguished from other owls by a loud, musical whistle.

Greater racket-tailed drongos are resident at medium-range elevations in Northern Thailand. They feed almost entirely on insects, flying out repeatedly from the same branch, often in small groups. Their long tails are tipped with a vane or "racket" that ripples as the bird flies.

Silver pheasant

Strangler fig

1,640–4,900 ft (500–1,500 m)

Bird Habitats at Different Altitudes

Deciduous dipterocarp trees clothe the foothills of Northern Thailand. Here, teak forests provide a habitat for kalij pheasants, wagtails, and parakeets, and migratory wetland birds such as herons. Higher up the slopes, bazas, hornbills, hill mynas, and shikes are drawn to mixed evergreen and deciduous forests. Oaks and epiphytic plants, such as ferns, thrive on the hilltops, where arctic warblers, owls, and other small birds live.

Tips for Bird-watching

- The best time to see birds is during the "winter" months, from January to April, when resident birds are mating and most migratory species arrive. Avoid the wet season (June–October), when heavy rain and leeches can be a problem.
- National park headquarters provide leaflets detailing bird-watching trails. Guided trips can often be arranged.
- Take binoculars, plenty of water, insect repellent, and a compass. Try to wear dark green or inconspicuous clothing.
- Many birds are shy, so be patient. Walk quietly to avoid rustling leaves, and do not walk straight toward the bird.

NORTHWEST HEARTLAND

Northwest Thailand is the heartland of Lanna Thai. The ancient city of Chiang Mai, famed for its many fine temples and handicrafts, is the focal point for visitors. This and smaller towns are set in verdant valleys among thickly forested mountains. The Northwest is also home to a number of ethnic minorities, and the rich mix of diverse cultures and scenery is most enticing.

Chiang Mai, superbly sited in the Ping River Valley, was once the capital of the Lanna Kingdom. In the 12th–18th centuries this kingdom, strongly influenced by Burma (now Myanmar), ruled over what is now northern Thailand, and local Thais remain proud of their Lanna heritage. Indeed, the silverwork, woodcarving, pottery, and other crafts of the North are regarded by many as the most exquisite in Thailand. Nowhere in the country are crafts more readily available than in Chiang Mai and its environs.

Chiang Mai is also a useful base from which to explore the mountains and villages. Trekking to hill-tribe villages is a popular, though controversial, activity. Although most trekkers are genuinely interested in hill-tribe culture, there is a danger that villages will become dependent on tourism and that traditional ways of life will be lost forever.

In the west, close to the Myanmar border, the remote towns of Mae Hong Son and Mae Sariang are in some ways more Myanmar than Thai. The *wats*, for instance, have multiroofed *chedis* reminiscent of Myanmar temples. North of Chiang Mai, the streets of Chiang Dao are lined with two-story teak buildings, a reminder that the surrounding countryside was once rich in teak forests. To the south of Chiang Mai, Lanna influence can again be seen in temples and museum artifacts within the cities of Lampang and Lamphun. The latter also has surviving traces of the older Kingdom of Haripunchai.

Thailand's highest mountain, Doi Inthanon, lies west of Chiang Mai, within a national park with good facilities. Here can be seen dramatic waterfalls and a wide range of wildlife, including hundreds of migratory birds.

Boy lighting a candle at Wat Phra That Lampang Luang, one of several major *wats* in the Northwest

◀ Twin *chedis*, erected in honour of the king and queen, in Doi Inthanon National Park

Exploring the Northwest Heartland

The Northwest Heartland is a geographically spectacular region. Towering mountains, many with densely forested slopes, stretch to the Myanmar (Burma) border and contrast with the gentler scenery of the Ping and Taeng River valleys. Trekking in this beautiful landscape, with its wealth of wildlife and fascinating hill-tribe villages, is a major activity in the Northwest Heartland. Cultural attractions are also plentiful, including the ancient temples of Chiang Mai, Lamphun, and Lampang, and the unmissable Wat Phra That Lampang Luang.

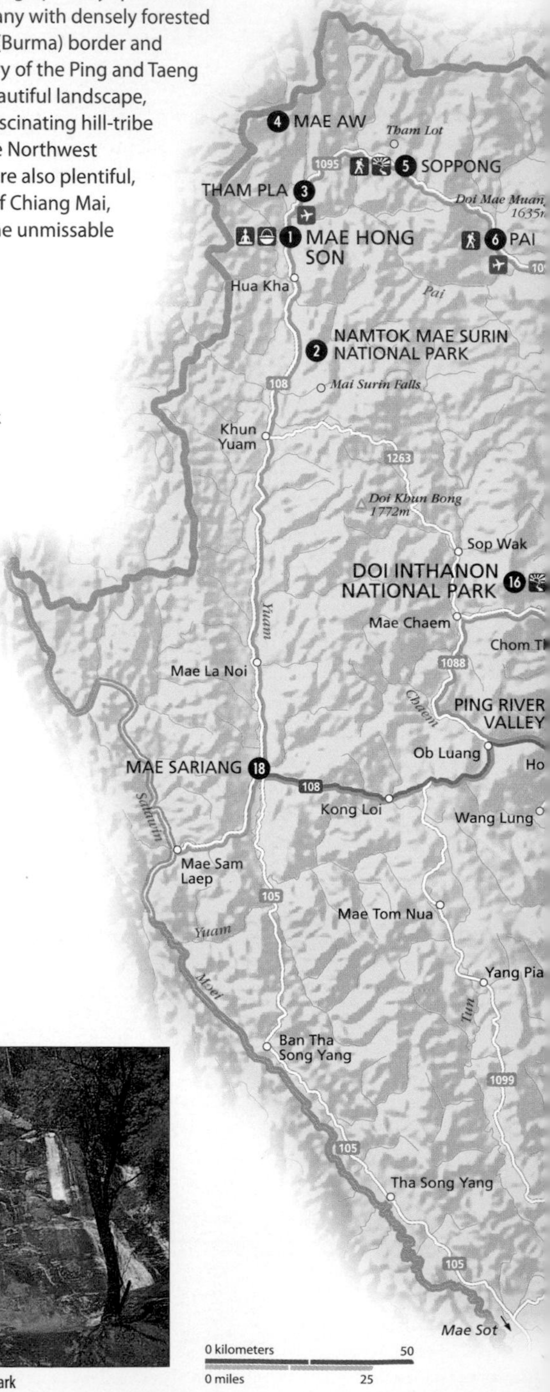

Sights at a Glance

1. *Mae Hong Son pp220–21*
2. Namtok Mae Surin National Park
3. Tham Pla
4. Mae Aw
5. Soppong
6. Pai
7. Doi Chiang Dao
8. Phrao
9. Mae Taeng Valley
10. *Doi Suthep pp226–7*
11. *Chiang Mai pp228–31*
12. Doi Saket
13. Bo Sang
14. San Kamphaeng
15. Lamphun
16. *Doi Inthanon National Park pp234–5*
17. Ping River Valley
18. Mae Sariang
19. *Wat Phra That Lampang Luang pp238–9*
20. Lampang
21. Thai Elephant Conservation Center
22. Uttaradit

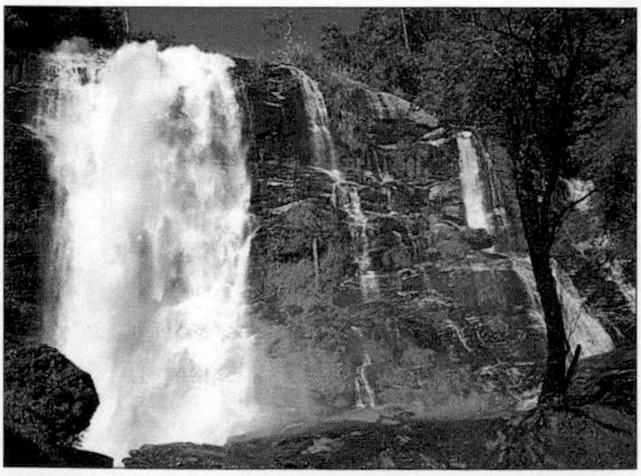

Vachirathan Waterfall, Doi Inthanon National Park

For hotels and restaurants see pp402–11 and pp418–33

Elaborately decorated pillars inside the *bot* of Chiang Mai's Wat Chiang Man

Getting Around

The highways around Chiang Mai are well maintained, and most other roads in this area are reasonable. Lampang and Mae Hong Son have domestic airports, and there is an international airport at Chiang Mai, the main transportation hub. Many trains and buses run each day between Chiang Mai and Bangkok (11–13 hours by train, via Uttaradit and Lampang; about 10 hours by bus). Frequent local bus services link most towns and villages in the region. Isolated sights are best reached by *songthaew*, and guided treks and organized tours are a good way of seeing larger areas.

Elephants at the Thai Elephant Conservation Center

For keys to symbols *see back flap*

Map labels

Fang

Pang Makham Pom

Na Wai

109

107

Wiang Pa Pao

1150

7 DOI CHIANG DAO

8 PHRAO

Chiang Dao

1001

9 MAE TAENG VALLEY

Mae Taeng

Sop eng

Luang

Chiang Rai

118

DOI THEP

10

12 DOI SAKET

San Kamphaeng Hot Springs

11

13 BO SANG

ANG MAI

14 SAN KAMPHAENG

1147

108

15 LAMPHUN

Pasang

11

Chiang Rai

Ban Hong

THAI ELEPHANT CONSERVATION CENTER

21

Hang Chat

20 LAMPANG

WAT PHRA THAT LAMPANG LUANG

19

Kor Kha

Som Ngam

11

Mae Tun

Phrae

Thung Hua Chiang

Den Chai

Li

Sop Prap

Dong Ya Thao

101

106

Thoen

11

Ping onal rk

UTTARADIT **22**

Sukhothai

Bhumibol Reservoir

1

Sam Ngao

Wang

Ping

175

Tak

Key

— Major road

===== Minor road

— Scenic route

〜〜 Railway

▬ International border

△ Summit

❶ Street-by-Street: Mae Hong Son
แม่ฮ่องสอน

Beautifully located in a valley ringed by forested mountains, Mae Hong Son sprang up in 1831 from a small camp where elephants were tethered. The town was largely isolated until it was linked by a paved highway to Chiang Mai in 1965. The province has traditionally been dominated by nearby Myanmar (Burma), as shown by its architecture. Shan and Karen people, who make up most of the population, continue to move across the border to live in Mae Hong Son and its environs. Today, the tranquil town is growing as a resort and trekking center. In the cool season, you may need to wear a sweater or jacket here.

To Airport

★ **Wat Hua Wiang**
This teak temple has a Myanmar-style, multi-roofed design. The bot – in an advanced state of decay – houses an important brass image of Buddha, Phrachao Para La'Khaeng, that was transported here from Myanmar.

UDOM CHAONITHEN

The Night Bazaar sells crafts and Thai Lue fabrics.

PRADIT CHONG K

Daily Market
This lively, pungent market, which almost spills onto the airport runway, sells a range of fresh produce, Myanmar textiles, and trekking supplies. Local hill tribes are often seen here.

The Padaung Women

Many tours from Mae Hong Son visit the "long-neck women" of the area. These women, of the Padaung, or Kayan, tribe, are distinguished by their long necks, lengthened from childhood by brass rings. Among the explanations for this old practice are that it protects the women from tiger attacks and that it enhances their looks. The practice began to die out until the Padaung realized tourists would pay to see the women. Some organizations condemn such visits.

"Long-neck women" of the Padaung tribe

Traditional Shan teak houses can be seen along this street.

Chong Kham Lake
This lake, which was originally a bathing pool for elephants, can be especially stunning in the early-morning mists that enshroud the town.

★ Wat Chong Kham
Wat Chong Kham (c.1827), which was built by the Shan, features a multi-roofed chedi. The wat houses a revered 16-ft (5-m) seated Buddha image.

Post office

Fitness park

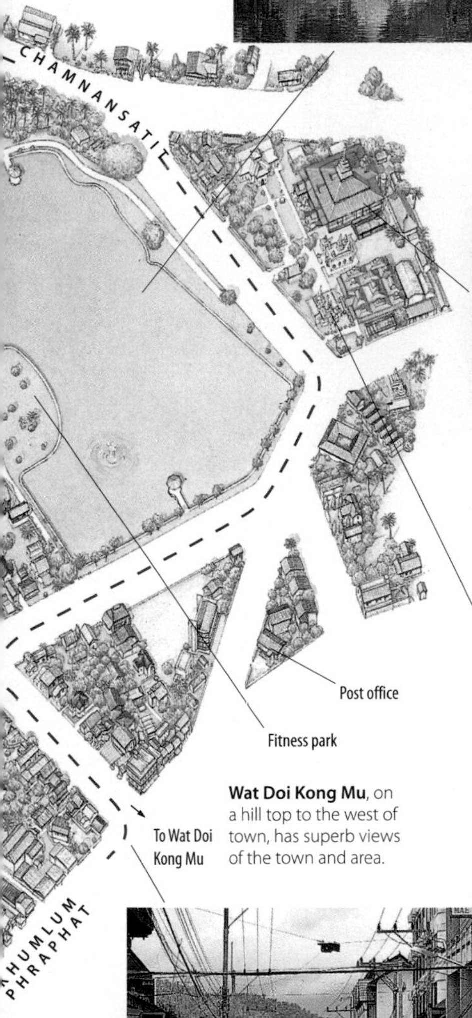

Wat Doi Kong Mu, on a hill top to the west of town, has superb views of the town and area.

To Wat Doi Kong Mu

★ Wat Chong Klang
Built in the late 19th century, this temple has distinctive white and gold *chedis*. Painted glass panels depicting the jataka tales *(see p34)* can be seen on request.

| 0 meters | 25 |
| 0 yards | 25 |

KEY

— Suggested route

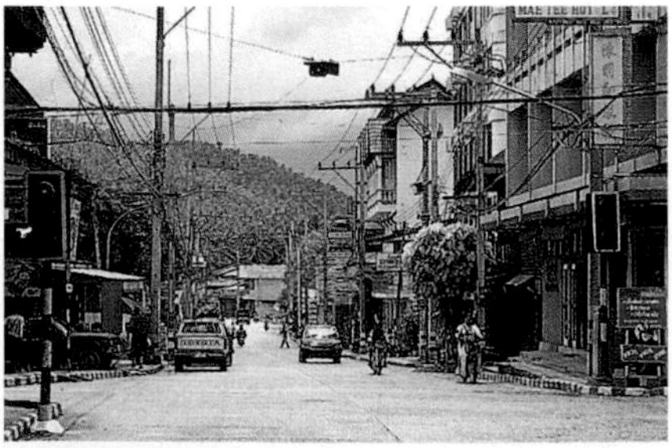

Khumlum Phraphat Road
Craft shops, restaurants, and tour companies line Mae Hong Son's main street. Hill-tribe textiles and antiques are among the items for sale.

The spectacular Mae Surin waterfall in Namtok Mae Surin National Park

❷ Namtok Mae Surin National Park

อุทยานแห่งชาติน้ำตกแม่สุรินทร์

Mae Hong Son province. Park HQ 2 miles (2.5 km) off Hwy 108, 5 miles (8 km) N of Mae Hong Son. **Tel** 0-5306-1073. _i_ TAT, Mae Hong Son (0-5361-2982-3); Forestry Dept (0-2562-0760 or 🔲 dnp.go.th for bungalow bookings). 🚌 from Khun Yuam then _songthaew_. **Open** daily. 🏕

This small park is the highlight of the area south of Mae Hong Son. Much of its lowland forest provides a habitat for the Malaysian sun bear, Asiatic black bear, and barking deer. Bird species include drongos and hornbills.

Mae Surin waterfall, which at 330 ft (100 m) is one of the highest in Thailand, is reached from the Khun Yuam district. on a dirt road. Also accessible from this road is Thung Bua Thong ("wild sunflower meadow"), which blooms in November and December.

Raft trips along the Pai River, which flows through the park, can be arranged at guesthouses in Mae Hong Son and Pai.

❸ Tham Pla

ถ้ำปลา

Mae Hong Son province. Off Hwy 1095, 11 miles (17 km) N of Mae Hong Son. _i_ TAT, Chiang Mai (0-5324-8604). 🚌 Mae Hong Son, then _songthaew_, or join tour. 🏕

Located north of Mae Hong Son, this scenic spot can be visited on a day trip from the town. Tham Pla ("fish cave") is actually a pool and stream at the base of a limestone outcrop, so named because of the huge carp that live in it. Visitors make

merit by buying papaya to feed to the fish. The peaceful surrounding gardens are perhaps the site's most attractive feature.

❹ Mae Aw

แม่ออ

Mae Hong Son province. 🔼 7,000. 🚌 Mae Hong Son, then _songthaew_, or join tour. _i_ TAT, Mae Hong Son (0-5361-2982-3). 🗓 daily.

Situated in the mountains near the Myanmar border, Mae Aw is a remote settlement built by members of the Kuomintang, or KMT _(see p246)_. Apart from superb views, the village offers an intriguing insight into life in an isolated border village. But fighting still sometimes breaks out between rival factions over control of the local opium trade, following the overthrow of Khun Sa _(see p237)_ in 1996.

The best way to get to Mae Aw is with a tour from Mae Hong Son or by jeep. Before you come, check with the local tourist information office that there is no fighting in the area.

❺ Soppong

สบปอง

Mae Hong Son province. 🔼 15,000. 🚌 from Mae Hong Son. _i_ TAT, Mae Hong Son (0-5361-2982-3). 🗓 daily.

The village of Soppong (sometimes called Pang Mapha on local maps) is perched 2,200 ft (700 m) up in the mountains. With its

Highway 1095 as it passes through Soppong

Muslim children in Pai, part of the town's mixed community

❻ Pai
ปาย

Mae Hong Son province. 🏔 27,000. 🚌 from Mae Hong Son. 🛈 TAT, Mae Hong Son (0-5361-2982-3). 🛍 daily.

Set in a beautiful valley, the town of Pai has become one of the region's most popular destinations. Although still very much a haven for backpackers, Pai is increasingly attracting larger resorts. Halfway between Chiang Mai and Mae Hong Son, the old Shan settlement is home to several hill tribes and is renowned for trekking and rafting.

The yellow and white tiles and multilayered roofs of **Wat Klang**, between the bus station and the Pai River, are typical of Shan temples. The hilltop **Wat Phra That Mae Yen**, just east of Pai, was also built by the Shan. The carved wooden doors of the main *wihan* depict scenes from nature and human life. The temple has sweeping views of the valley.

Guided treks of the area (see p225) can be arranged at many guesthouses in town.

fine views, surrounding teak forests, and air of tranquility, Soppong is becoming an increasingly popular resort. Many trekkers pass through here on the way to visit local hill-tribe villages populated by Lisu and Shan (a minority originally from Myanmar). The village itself has a thriving market where local tribespeople congregate daily.

Environs
Tham Lot, north of Soppong, is one of the largest cave systems in Southeast Asia.

The three adjoining caverns form a vast subterranean canyon, which is cut through by a large stream. The distinctive stalactites and stalagmites are especially impressive. The discovery of artifacts and huge carved teak coffins indicates that the caves were inhabited thousands of years ago. Visitors may cross the stream by raft or by elephant. Guided visits can be arranged at local guesthouses.

Thailand's Endangered Wildlife

With its diversity of landscapes, Thailand is an ideal habitat for a vast range of flora and fauna. In the 20th century, however, poaching and deforestation led to the extinction of many species, including the kouprey (a type of wild cattle) and Schomburgk's deer. Some animals are caught for food; some, including gibbons, are sold as pets, while others, like snakes, are killed through fear. Of Thailand's 282 mammal species, about 40 are endangered, and while laws exist to protect these animals, they are not always enforced. Almost all of Thailand's large mammals are in danger of extinction, and many others, including the white-handed gibbon, are, at best, rare. This alarming state of affairs is not confined to mammals: ten percent of the country's 405 reptiles and amphibians are also endangered.

Rock python – its favored forest habitat is rapidly disappearing

A rare white-handed gibbon

Tigers in Thailand

The increasing demand for dried tiger parts in traditional Chinese medicines has led to the worldwide demise of this great creature. Of the few thousand tigers that remain in Asia, about 500 are estimated to be living in Thailand, particularly in the Khao Yai National Park (see pp188–9). In 1995 the Royal Forest Department established a conservation project to try to prevent the tiger from dying out altogether in Thailand.

Pavilions and carp-filled pool in front of Tham Chiang Dao

⑦ Doi Chiang Dao
ดอยเชียงดาว

7.5 miles (12 km) W of Chiang Dao, Chiang Mai province. ℹ️ TAT, Chiang Mai (0-5324-8604). 🚌 from Chiang Mai to Chiang Dao, then *songthaew*. 🌐 **chiangmai-thai.com**

At 7,200 ft (2,195 m), this is the third-largest mountain in Thailand. Home to several Lisu and Karen villages, Doi Chiang Dao features both tropical and pine forests. Today, this peak and the surrounding area, characterized by rugged limestone scenery and dense teak forest, are more of an attraction than the nearby town, Chiang Dao.

Running for some 8.5 miles (14 km) under the mountain is a network of caves, **Tham Chiang Dao**, best reached from Chiang Dao town. Most of the caves house statues of the Buddha that, over the years, have been left by Shan pilgrims from Myanmar. The highlight of the bat-inhabited caves, however,

is their huge stalactites and stalagmites. Lanterns and guides can be hired in order to make the most of these impressive features. The tours take visitors along an illuminated walkway through the caves.

Near the caves is a temple, **Wat Tham Chiang Dao**, with a Buddhist meditation center and a small room displaying gongs and other instruments. Beyond a huge tamarind tree, by a pond, is an old Myanmar-style *chedi*. Nearby, a small market offers a wide selection of locally gathered forest

Façade of Wat Tham Chiang Dao, near Doi Chiang Dao

roots, herbs, and spices.

East of Doi Chiang Dao, and dominated by the peak, is **Chiang Dao town,** with its traditional teak buildings along the main street. It was founded in the 18th century as a place of exile for *phi pop*, ("spirit people"), who were suspected of being possessed by evil spirits. In fact, the symptoms of their true illnesses, such as malaria, had been mistaken as signs of madness.

Tham Tup Tao, 30 miles (48 km) north of Chiang Dao, are two large caverns. Tham Pha Kao ("light cave") houses two large Buddha images and a stalagmite carved in the shape of a group of elephants. Inside Tham Pha Chak ("dark cave"), which can be explored only by lantern, is a bat colony.

🏯 Tham Chiang Dao
Off Hwy 107, 3 miles (5 km) NW of Chiang Dao. **Open** daily. 🖼️ 📷

🏯 Tham Tup Tao
W of Hwy 107, Chiang Mai province. **Open** daily. 🖼️ 📷

⑧ Phrao
พร้าว

Chiang Mai province. 🏔️ 46,000. 🚌 from Chiang Mai. ℹ️ TAT, Chiang Mai (0-5324-8604). 🛍️ daily.

This small market town is a meeting place for Thai traders and hill-tribe people. Phrao was previously relatively isolated, but today Highway 1150 connects it with Wiang Pa Pao (*see p256*), making it more accessible. Phrao is still off the main tourist track. The town's principal sight is its covered market, which sells traditional textiles and locally grown fruit and vegetables.

Environs
Heading east toward Wiang Pa Pao, Highway 1150 runs through spectacular forest scenery. Several Lisu and Hmong hill-tribe villages can be seen.

Orchids in Thailand

Seen on logos throughout Thailand, the orchid is the country's most famous flower. There are over 1,300 varieties of wild orchid in Thailand, most of which are dependent on forests. But while their natural habitat is threatened by deforestation, millions are being cultivated for export to overseas markets. Export began in the 1950s, and burgeoned in the 1980s when the first orchid farms were established. In 1991 the value of exports peaked at about $80 million. Since then, as consumer trends have changed in important markets such as Japan, this figure has started to decline.

A pink orchid, one of the most popular colors for the overseas markets

A leisurely rafting trip along the Taeng River

❾ Mae Taeng Valley

แม่แตง

Chiang Mai province. 🚗
🚌 Chiang Mai, then *songthaew*.
ℹ️ TAT, Chiang Mai (0-5324-8604).

The area around Mae Taeng, especially the vicinity of the Taeng River to the northwest of the town, is very popular with trekkers. The land has been terraced and irrigated to improve agricultural production, and the variety of crops grown has created an attractive contrast of landscapes. However, most trekkers come here not only for the peaceful surroundings but also to witness everyday scenes in the region's many Lisu, Karen, and Hmong villages. Other activities, including river rafting, can be combined with treks in the area. Established in 1995, the **Elephant Nature Park**, in the beautiful Mae Taeng Valley, is home to dozens of rescued elephants. Founder Lek Chailert's efforts to save the endangered Asian elephant have received praise and awards from around the world. The center welcomes volunteer workers.

🐘 **Elephant Nature Park**
6 miles (10 km) W of Hwy 107.
Tel 0-5327-2855. **Open** daily. 🎟️
🌐 **elephantnaturefoundation.org**

Rescued elephants bathing at the Elephant Nature Park

Trekking Around Chiang Dao

Northern Thailand is renowned for its trekking *(see p448)*. Treks in the area around Chiang Dao and Mae Taeng often combine visits to hill-tribe villages with a raft trip through the stunning scenery. Most three-day treks from Chiang Mai, which can be arranged by guesthouses or trekking companies in the city, incorporate this area. Among the region's interesting towns are Mae Taeng, Phrao, and Chiang Dao, all of which have long been at the interface between the Thai-dominated lowlands and the uplands, where the hill tribes live. It is vital to trek with a guide who is familiar with the area and hill-tribe etiquette. Typical routes, lasting two to three days, are marked below.

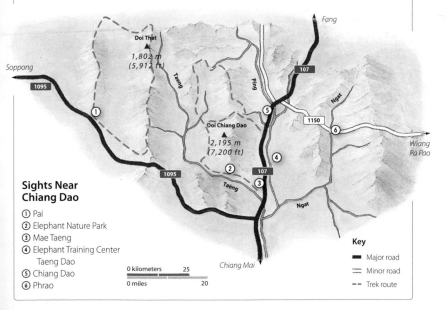

Sights Near Chiang Dao

① Pai
② Elephant Nature Park
③ Mae Taeng
④ Elephant Training Center Taeng Dao
⑤ Chiang Dao
⑥ Phrao

Key
━━ Major road
═══ Minor road
-- Trek route

Fang
Doi That
1,802 m
(5,912 ft)
Soppong
1095
Taeng
Ping
107
Ngat
Doi Chiang Dao
2,195 m
(7,200 ft)
1150
Wiang Pa Pao
1095
Taeng
107
Ngat
0 kilometers 25
0 miles 20
Chiang Mai

⑩ Doi Suthep

ดอยสุเทพ

Doi Suthep is a much-visited, thickly forested mountain in the twin-peaked Doi Suthep-Doi Pui National Park. Near its 5,250-ft (1,601-m) summit is Wat Phra That Doi Suthep, one of the most revered Buddhist shrines in Northern Thailand. The mountain is also popular with birdwatchers and trekkers. From Chiang Mai, a paved road snakes up the hillside to a village with restaurants and souvenir shops. From here, there is a choice of a steep climb or the funicular to the *wat*. Minor attractions on Doi Suthep include waterfalls, a Hmong village, and, farther along the road, the English-style gardens of Phuping Palace.

Murals in Cloister
The murals depict scenes from the Buddha's life.

★ Central Chedi
This striking gold-plated Lanna structure is a 16th-century extension of the original. The four multi-tiered gold umbrellas around it, onto which pilgrims apply gold leaf (*see p34*), are adorned with intricate filigree.

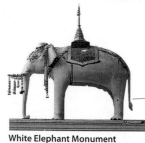

White Elephant Monument
According to legend, in the 1390s King Ku Na's elephant selected the site of the *chedi* by marching up the mountain, trumpeting and turning three times.

Wat Doi Suthep
Enshrining sacred relics, the wat *at the top of Doi Suthep, founded in the 14th century, is regarded by many as the symbol of Lanna Thailand (see pp66–7).*

Naga Staircase
Flanked by *nagas*, this sweeping staircase has 304 steps. The less energetic can take the funicular up to the temple.

Buddha Images in the Main Wihan
The gold Buddha images in the 16th-century *wihan* are the most important within the temple complex. The huge image in the back is surrounded by several smaller ones.

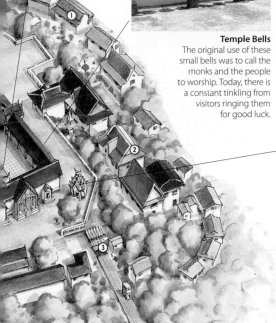

Temple Bells
The original use of these small bells was to call the monks and the people to worship. Today, there is a constant tinkling from visitors ringing them for good luck.

Bell Tower
This decorative bell tower, near the steps up to the main *wihan*, is distinctive for its multi-colored, layered roof.

★ Panoramic Views
From the edge of the temple complex there are breathtaking views of the forests of Doi Suthep-Doi Pui National Park and of Chiang Mai city, situated to the southeast.

Wildlife Around Wat Doi Suthep

With its rich and varied wildlife, Doi Suthep-Doi Pui National Park is a great attraction for nature lovers. Despite the deforestation of the western side of the park due to agriculture and the building of tourist accommodations, the park is rich in plants, butterflies, and birds such as the green cochoa. Though people have killed or driven out many indigenous mammals, 60 species still live here, including the Burmese ferret badger.

Black-collared starling, a resident of the park

KEY

① Library

② **This is one** of several buildings in the complex used as accommodation by monks.

③ Funicular

⓫ Street-by-Street: Chiang Mai

เชียงใหม่

Thailand's second most important city, Chiang Mai (literally, "new city"), was chosen in 1292 by King Mengrai to replace Chiang Rai *(see pp254–5)* as the capital of his Lanna Kingdom *(see pp66–7)*. Under Mengrai, Chiang Mai became a major base for Theravada Buddhism. It was during this period and the subsequent reign of King Tilok that many fine *wats* were built within the walled city, which is still the most atmospheric area. Today, visitors are increasingly drawn to Chiang Mai not only for its beautiful temples, but also for its excellent shopping and trekking facilities and upscale hotels and restaurants.

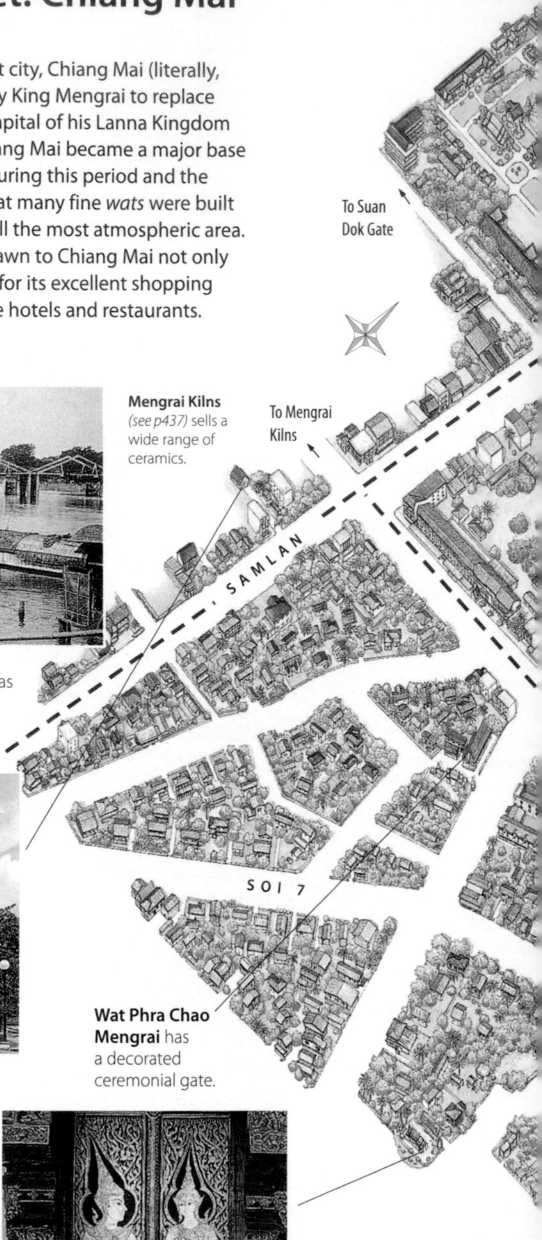

To Suan Dok Gate

Mengrai Kilns
(see p437) sells a wide range of ceramics.

To Mengrai Kilns

SAMLAN

SOI 7

Old Chiang Mai
The first bridge across the Ping River was built in 1950. Others were later added to cope with the city's growth.

Wat Muen Ngon Kong
This *wat* has exquisite lattice-work and a Lanna *chedi* topped by a Burmese finial.

Wat Phra Chao Mengrai has a decorated ceremonial gate.

| 0 meters | 100 |
| 0 yards | 100 |

Wat Phan Waen
A typical Northern Thai temple, Wat Pan Waen is set within peaceful compounds, which provide relief from the city heat. The doors of the *wihan* are decorated with religious images.

★ Wat Phra Sing
This *wat* was built in 1345 to house King Kham Fu's ashes. The Wihan Lai Kham is a superb Lanna structure with carved and gilded pediments. Murals inside depict everyday life in 19th-century Chiang Mai.

VISITORS' CHECKLIST

Practical Information
Chiang Mai province. 84,000.
TAT, 105/1 Chiang Mai–Lamphun Rd (0-5324-8604).
main office: same address as TAT (0-5324-8974). daily.
Bo Sang Festival (Jan), Flower Festival (Feb), Songkran (mid-Apr), Intakin Festival (May), Yi Peng Festival (Nov).

Transport
2 miles (3 km) SW of Chiang Mai. Charoen Muang Rd. Chiang Mai Arcade.

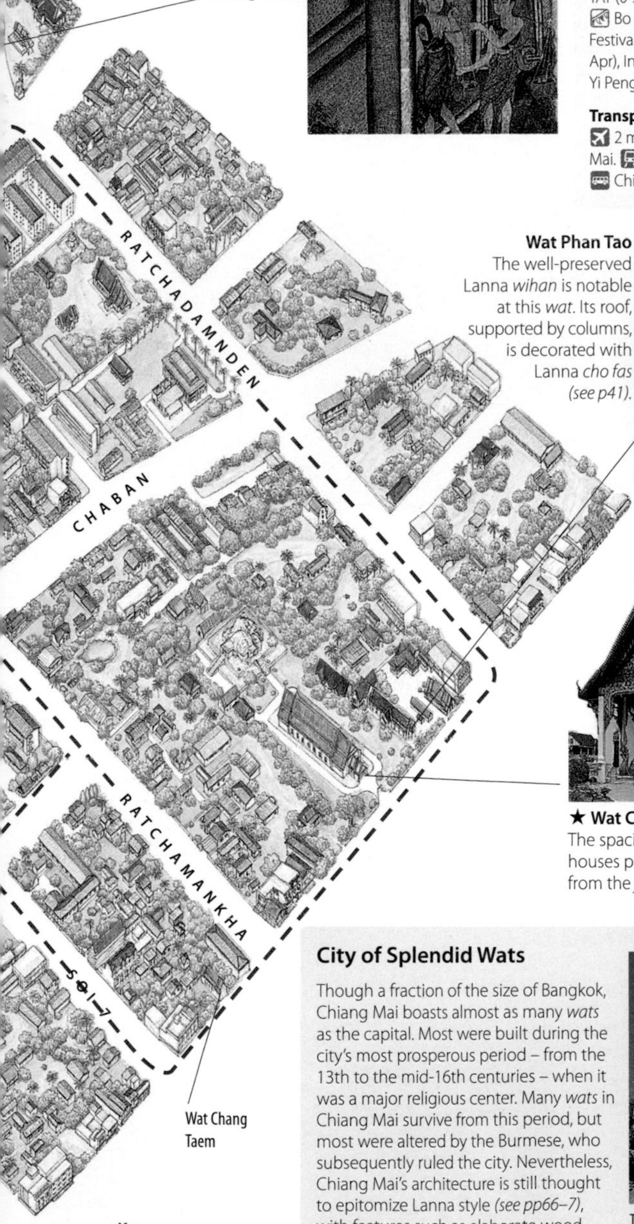

Wat Phan Tao
The well-preserved Lanna *wihan* is notable at this *wat*. Its roof, supported by columns, is decorated with Lanna *cho fas* (see p41).

★ Wat Chedi Luang
The spacious, triple-roofed *wihan* houses panels depicting scenes from the *jataka* tales (see p34).

City of Splendid Wats

Though a fraction of the size of Bangkok, Chiang Mai boasts almost as many *wats* as the capital. Most were built during the city's most prosperous period – from the 13th to the mid-16th centuries – when it was a major religious center. Many *wats* in Chiang Mai survive from this period, but most were altered by the Burmese, who subsequently ruled the city. Nevertheless, Chiang Mai's architecture is still thought to epitomize Lanna style (see pp66–7), with features such as elaborate wood-carvings on temple pillars and doors.

The 19th-century Wihan Lai Kham, Wat Phra Sing

RATCHADAMNDEN

CHABAN

RATCHAMANKHA

Wat Chang Taem

Key
— Suggested route

Exploring Chiang Mai

Often called the "rose of the North," Chiang Mai is shedding its sleepy backpacker-haven reputation and carving out a new identity for itself. The town has expanded rapidly and boutique hotels and trendy restaurants are springing up everywhere, bringing new style and sophistication. Chiang Mai boasts an exquisite location, circled by mountains. Its stunning *wats*, notably Wat Chedi Luang and Wat Phra Sing; historic sites; bustling markets; and lively nightlife make it an exciting destination. The town thrives on its crafts trade *(see pp212–13)*, as seen in the wide range sold at Warorot Market and the Night Bazaar, and along Tha Phae Road.

One of the murals inside Wat Phra Sing's Wihan Lai Kham

🏛 Wat Phra Sing
วัดพระสิงห์

Samlan Rd, near Suan Dok Gate.
Open daily.
Construction of this temple, the largest in Chiang Mai, began in 1345, though the *bot* dates from 1600. The Wihan Lai Kham ("gilded hall"), decorated with murals of everyday life, houses the revered golden Phra Buddha Sing. Like its namesakes in Bangkok *(see p92)* and Nakhon Si Thammarat *(see p383)*, the image is said to have originated in Sri Lanka.

🏛 Wat Chedi Luang
วัดเจดีย์หลวง

Phra Pok Klao Rd. **Open** daily.
Within the compound of this temple is the spot where King Mengrai was killed by lightning in 1317. The revered Emerald Buddha image was briefly housed in the *wat* in the 15th century – a previous attempt to bring it to Chiang Mai failed *(see p87)*. The *chedi*, once 295 ft (90 m) high, was damaged by an earthquake in 1465.

🏛 Wat Chiang Man
วัดเชียงมั่น

Off Ratcha Phakhinai Rd.
Open daily.
King Mengrai dedicated this residence as a *wat*, the city's oldest, while his new capital was being built. It features Lanna teak pillars and a *chedi* surrounded by stone elephant heads. The *wihan* houses the Phra Kaeo Kao, thought to have been carved in Northern India in the 6th century BC.

🛕 Tha Phae Gate
ประตูท่าแพ

Tha Phae Gate marks the beginning of Tha Phae Road, the commercial hub of Chiang Mai. Located here are bookstores, department stores, and handicraft shops. Farther east, the road becomes Highway 106, along which are shops and factories selling silk, celadon, lacquerware, and other crafts.

🛕 Suan Dok Gate
ประตูสวนดอก

This is the city's western gate, marking the start of Suthep Road, along which three important temples are situated.

🏯 Night Bazaar
ไนท์บาซาร์

Chang Khlan Rd.
Open 6–11pm daily.

With its wide range of goods at competitive prices, this easily rivals Bangkok's Chatuchak Market *(see p139)*. Inside are endless stalls selling hill-tribe crafts, leather goods, and clothing. The top floor specializes in antiques. Beware of fakes *(see p435)*, especially at the stalls outside the market. This is also a good place to try Chiang Mai's Myanmar-influenced cuisine. Shops on Wualai Road, south of Chiang Mai Gate, sell the best silverware and textiles.

🏯 Warorot Market
ตลาดวโรรส

N of Tha Phae Rd. **Open** daily.
During the day, this covered market sells local food, clothing and hill-tribe crafts, often at lower prices than the Night Bazaar. Fruits, spices, and tasty dishes are all available. By night, it is the site of a colorful flower market.

Shoppers browsing around Chiang Mai's lively Warorot Market

Environs

There are many sights outside the city center that are worth a visit. Most can be reached by local transport. For longer excursions, most hotels and guesthouses offer treks to hilltribe villages *(see pp210–11)*. There are also many tour operators on Tha Phae Road. Two-hour river cruises on the Ping River leave from **Wat Chaimongkol** on Charoen Prathet Road, taking in a variety of opulent homes and humble riverside villages.

To the north of the city is the **Chiang Mai National Museum**. Its collection ranges from Haripunchai terracottas to Lanna heads of the Buddha.

On the grounds of Chiang Mai University is the **Tribal Research Institute**. Its small museum details the history of the area's ethnic minorities. Treks to hill-tribe villages can be arranged here.

On Kaew Narawat Road, to the northeast of the city, is

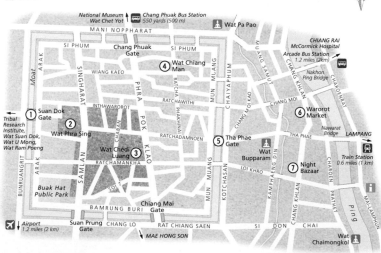

Buddha image,
National Museum

McCormick Hospital. This working hospital is typical of Chiang Mai's 19th- and 20th-century architecture, much of which was built by missionaries and officials of the British teak logging companies who came here from Myanmar (Burma).

Just west of Suan Dok Gate, on Suthep Road, is **Wat Suan Dok**. The temple was built in 1383 to house relics of the Buddha, while the open-sided *wihan* was restored in the 1930s. The small *chedis* contain ashes of members of Chiang Mai's former royal family. Farther along Suthep Road is the 14th-century **Wat U Mong**. Some of the original tunnels leading to the monks' cells can still be explored. Also of note is a disturbing image of a fasting Buddha. This temple and nearby **Wat Ram Poeng** offer meditation courses. The latter's library keeps versions of the Theravada Buddhist canon in various languages.

Wat Chet Yot, distinctive for its seven-spired *chedi*, is set in

Facade of the 14th-century Wat Suan Dok

spacious grounds. Its stuccoed design is based on the Mahabodhi Temple of Bodhgaya in India, where the Buddha is said to have achieved Enlightenment.

🏛 **Chiang Mai National Museum**
Off Superhighway **Tel** 0-5322 1308.
Open 9am–4pm Wed–Sun.
Closed public hols.

🏛 **Tribal Research Institute**
Chiang Mai University, off Huai Kaew Rd. **Tel** 0-5321-0872.
Open 8:30am–noon & 1–4:30pm Mon–Fri. **Closed** public hols.

Chiang Mai City Center

① Suan Dok Gate
② Wat Phra Sing
③ Wat Chedi Luang
④ Wat Chiang Man
⑤ Tha Phae Gate
⑥ Warorot Market
⑦ Night Bazaar

Key

▪ Street-by-Street map
see pp228–9

0 meters   500
0 yards   500

⑫ Doi Saket
ดอยสะเก็ด

Off Hwy 118, 10 miles (16 km) NE of Chiang Mai, Chiang Mai province. *i* TAT, Chiang Mai (0-5324-8604). 🚌 💺 Chiang Mai, then *songthaew*. **Open** daily. 🅿

Forming a triangle with Bo Sang and San Kamphaeng, the mountain of Doi Saket is an ideal sight to combine with these two towns on a day trip from Chiang Mai.

The main reason for visiting Doi Saket is its hilltop temple, Wat Doi Saket, which offers stunning views of the Chiang Mai valley. The *wat* is reached by a steep staircase of 300 steps, flanked on either side by a *naga*. The temple complex includes a modern *wihan*, painted in red and gold, and a white *chedi*. There is a huge, seated Buddha on the hill top and seven smaller Buddhas, one for each day of the week.

Red and gold modern *wihan* of the hill top Wat Doi Saket

Women constructing ornamental umbrellas in the village of Bo Sang

⑬ Bo Sang
บ่อสร้าง

6 miles (9 km) E of Chiang Mai, Chiang Mai province. 🔼 2,600. 🚌 from Chiang Mai. *i* TAT, Chiang Mai (0-5324-8604). 🛍 daily. 🎪 Umbrella Fair (Jan).

Bo Sang is known throughout Thailand as the "umbrella village" on account of the decorative umbrellas produced here. The village is made up almost entirely of shops and factories involved in this craft.

Each umbrella has a wooden handle, bamboo ribs, and a covering of oiled rice paper, silk, or cotton. Craftsmen will usually add names or a personalized design in bold colors if requested. The annual fair includes competitions, exhibitions, and a beauty contest.

Other handicrafts, including silverware, celadon (a grayish-green porcelain), and lacquerware, are also sold here. Aside from its umbrella making, Bo Sang is also the heart of a farming community. In the wet season (June to October), the rice fields are a deep green color. From November to January, the fields dry out and turn golden. Farmers then thresh the rice by hand.

Many houses in and around Bo Sang are traditional, wooden Northern Thai structures *(see p40)* with spacious rooms. They are typically built on stilts and set in small gardens.

⑭ San Kamphaeng
สันกำแพง

9 miles (13 km) E of Chiang Mai, Chiang Mai province. 🔼 44,000. 🚌 from Chiang Mai. *i* TAT, Chiang Mai (0-5324-8604). 🛍 daily.

This village, with its old, wooden buildings and narrow streets, is renowned for its silk and

---

Nagas: Mythical Serpents

Naga figures, seen throughout Thailand, are protective serpents. Acting as guardians against bad spirits, they often flank the walls of temples or the staircases up to them, and may also be carved on roofs, doors, gables, and windows. The significance of *nagas* is deep-rooted throughout Buddhist Asia, though their meaning may vary slightly according to the country, with overlaps between Buddhism and Hinduism. In Buddhism, their origins can be traced back to an episode in the *jataka* tales *(see p34)* in which a *garuda*, or mythical bird, attacks and subdues a *naga* that is trying to harm the Buddha. The *naga* subsequently becomes the Buddha's guardian. Its protective powers are shown when Mucilinda, a king of the *nagas*, grows several heads to shelter the Buddha from a thunderstorm. *Nagas* are also believed to control rainfall and are worshiped as givers of water during Songkran *(see p240)*.

Two-headed *naga* of Wat Chedi Luang, Chiang Saen *(see p252)*

Geyser bursting through the ground at the San Kamphaeng Hot Springs

handicraft products. There are many factories here selling good-quality silk, teak furniture, silverware, lacquerware, jade, or celadon. Prices can be high, though bargaining *(see p434)* often reduces the cost significantly. An interesting feature of most of the silk factories are their exhibits of the silk-making process. The whole procedure is shown *(see pp270–71)*, from silk moths, through the unraveling of the cocoons, to the weaving of dyed silk thread on traditional wooden looms.

Environs

To the east of San Kamphaeng, just past the village of Mu Song, are the caves of **Tam Muang On**, with impressive stalactites and stalagmites. Farther east are the **San Kamphaeng Hot Springs**, offering therapeutic baths in hot mineral water. Here, geysers spurt to incredible heights.

Tam Muang On
8.5 miles (14 km) E of San Kamphaeng. **Open** daily.

San Kamphaeng Hot Springs
12.5 miles (20 km) E of San Kamphaeng. **Open** daily.

⑮ Lamphun

ลำพูน

Lamphun province. 🕍 97,000. 🚉 🚌 *i* TAT, Chiang Mai (0-5324-8604). 🛍 daily. 🎎 Lamyai Festival (Aug).

This ancient town was the capital of the Haripunchai Kingdom from AD 750–1281. Today, Lamphun is made up of large wooden houses beside the Kuang River and is characterized by its peaceful atmosphere, ancient temples, and surrounding countryside of rice fields.

Lamphun's most important temple is **Wat Phra That Haripunchai**. The present compound was probably founded in AD 1044 by King Athitayarai of Haripunchai, though the 150-ft (46-m) high central *chedi*, topped by a nine-tier umbrella of pure gold, is thought to date from 897. In the 1930s, the temple was renovated by Khrubaa Siwichai, one of the most revered monks in Northern Thailand. One unusual structure is the rare, pyramid-shaped

Buddha head, Lamphun National Museum

chedi in the northwest of the compound. The large *bot* houses a reclining Buddha image, while a 15th-century Lanna Buddha is kept in the main *wihan*. Adjoining it is a 19th-century library, with a staircase flanked by *nagas*. To the right of the library is an open pavilion displaying a huge gong cast in 1860, alleged to be the largest in the world. Outside the main compound is a smaller *bot*, inside of which is a so-called "happy Buddha," a fat, smiling Chinese-style image.

The nearby **Lamphun National Museum** is small but excellent. It has carvings and artifacts from many periods, especially the Dvaravati, Haripunchai, and Lanna kingdoms. Modern artifacts include an ornate black and gold howdah *(see p212)* and *naga* decorations. The collection of Buddha images covers many schools of sculpture.

Wat Chama Thewi (or Wat Kukut), just west of Lamphun on Highway 1015, is noted for its two *chedis*, thought to be among the oldest in Thailand. Both built in 1218, they are the last surviving examples of Dvaravati architecture. The larger, tiered structure is adorned with Buddha images, and the smaller one is decorated with Hindu gods.

🏛 **Lamphun National Museum**
Inthayongyot Rd. **Tel** 0-5351-1186. **Open** 8:30am–4pm Wed–Sun. 🖼

Environs

Pasang, a small town 19 miles (30 km) south of Lamphun, produces excellent cottonwear of unique designs, especially sarongs and shirts. They are sold through many outlets in the town. Lamphun province, in particular the town of Nong Chang Kheun, to the north, is renowned for its *lamyai*, or longan *(see p137)* fruit. It is celebrated in a festival that features competitions and a Miss Lamyai beauty contest.

⑯ Doi Inthanon National Park

อุทยานแห่งชาติดอยอินทนนท์

Doi Inthanon, at 8,400 ft (2,565 m), is the highest mountain in Thailand. It is located in the 105-sq mile (272-sq km) Doi Inthanon National Park, and, only 36 miles (58 km) from Chiang Mai, is a popular destination for one-day excursions. The park has many types of habitat and a wide range of mammals, such as leopard cats, pangolins, and flying squirrels. The area is also popular for bird-watching, being home to nearly 400 bird species, many from North Asia (including mountain hawk eagles and Eurasian woodcocks). Karen and Hmong peoples *(see pp210–11)* also live here. In contrast to the rest of Thailand, the climate on Doi Inthanon can be chilly, so visitors to the park are advised to take warm clothing.

Twin Chedis
This shrine is inside one of the twin *chedis* of Phra That Naphamataneedon, built for King Bhumibol's 60th birthday.

Spectacular View
Walkers on Doi Inthanon are treated to impressive views. On a clear day it is possible to see for many miles over the forested landscape.

Doi Inthanon ▲
8,400 ft
(2,565 m)

① Siriphum waterfa

Mae Pan waterfall

Mae Chaem

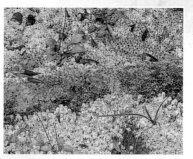

Sphagnum Moss
Doi Inthanon's cool climate allows plants such as mosses, ferns, and lichens to thrive. At the mountain's summit, sphagnum mosses form a kind of bog, the only habitat of this kind in Thailand.

Timber Beetle
For protection, this beetle's markings ape the warning coloration of wasps. Its larvae are hatched in the trunks or branches of trees.

KEY

① **Montane evergreen forests** are found on the upper levels of Doi Inthanon.

② **Deciduous and sub-montane forests** are found in low-lying areas of the national park.

Orchids

Wild orchids are in abundance on Doi Inthanon. On the higher slopes of the mountain, 8,200 ft (2,500 m) above sea level, pink and white orchids *(see p224)* can be seen draped over the branches of evergreen trees.

White-Crested Laughing Thrush

This bird takes its name from its distinctive white crest. Its common habitat is the forest crowning the upper slopes of Doi Inthanon.

Hmong Tribespeople

The Hmong *(see p210)* have been here since the 1890s. Their slash-and-burn agriculture has led to deforestation, but government programs to reduce this are now underway.

Mae Ya Waterfall

This is estimated to be the highest waterfall in the whole of Thailand. Falling over 820 ft (250 m), Mae Ya waterfall is also one of the most beautiful sights at Doi Inthanon.

Key

═══ Road

– – Trail

—·– Park border

0 kilometers   2

0 miles   2

For keys to symbols *see back flap*

Rural landscape around Hot, a town in the Ping River Valley

⓱ Ping River Valley

หุบเขาแม่น้ำปิง

Chiang Mai province. *i* TAT, Chiang Mai (0-5324-8604). Chiang Mai, then *songthaew*.

Nearly 600 km (370 miles) long, the Ping River is one of the major waterways in Northern Thailand. It rises on the Myanmar border and flows on to the Bhumibol Reservoir before merging with the Wang, Yom, and Nan rivers. This becomes the Chao Phraya River at Nakhon Sawan, in the Central Plains. The valley is a rural area where traditional life can still be observed.

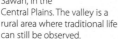

Wooden carving on the *bot* of Wat Phra That Si Chom Thong

Chom Thong, just south of Chiang Mai, at the junction of Highway 108 and the road to Doi Inthanon National Park *(see pp234–5)*, is a small but busy town. It boasts one major sight, **Wat Phra That Si Chom Thong**. The *wat* was built to enshrine a relic of the Buddha and is still an important pilgrimage site for Buddhists. Many will try to make the journey at least once a year. This *wat* is also widely considered to be one of the most beautiful in Northern Thailand. The gilded *chedi*, built in 1451, is of Myanmar design, as is the mid-16th-century *bot*, which features intricate woodcarvings depicting flowers, birds, and *nagas (see p232)*. A meditation center and a room displaying thrones, religious antiques, and weapons are also located within the temple complex.

The deep Chaem River Valley, west of Chom Thong, is known locally for its many varieties of butterfly and moth. Several villages, spread along the twisting road within the valley, are known collectively as the town of **Mae Chaem**. The town, once famous for weaving, is now modernizing rapidly. Its main temple, **Wat Pa Daet**, is worth visiting for its well-preserved Lanna buildings and extensive murals.

At the southern end of the valley is the small town of **Hot**. Originally located 10 miles (5 km) farther downstream, the town was relocated to its present site in 1964, when the land was flooded to form the Bhumibol Reservoir. Today, this reservoir is a major source of Thailand's electricity. Ruins of the original town can still be seen beside the reservoir, though they are limited to only a few *chedis*. Excavation of the site has turned up amulets, stucco carvings and gold jewelry. These artifacts are now on display in Chiang Mai's National Museum *(see p231)*. Modern-day Hot, meanwhile, is an important market town and a useful staging post for journeys westward to the town of Mae Sariang.

⓲ Mae Sariang

แม่สะเรียง

Mae Hong Son province. 48,000. *i* TAT, Chiang Mai (0-5324-8604). daily.

Mae Sariang is a pleasant town on the Yuam River. The area has historical links with nearby Myanmar, a fact that is reflected in Mae Sariang's architecture and by its large community of Myanmar Muslims. People of the Karen hill tribe – the area's main ethnic group – can be seen in the central market.

Two temples near the bus station have Myanmar features: multilayered roofs and vivid orange and yellow exterior ornamentation. **Wat Chong Sung** (also called Wat Uthayarom) was built in 1896, while **Wat Si Bunruang** dates from 1939.

Environs

The area around Mae Sariang is mountainous and forested, with many winding roads. Organized trips by boat or *songthaew* (which can be arranged in town) make the 30 mile (45-km) journey from Mae Sariang to **Mae Sam Laep**, a Karen settlement on the Myanmar border next to the Salawin River. This river was once infamous for drug running and gem smuggling. Today, Mae Sam Laep is a staging post for the (mostly illegal) teak log trade. Political troubles in Myanmar have made this area a zone for refugees, though some Myanmar minorities, such as the Lawa, have lived here longer than Thais.

Chedi of the 19th-century Wat Chong Sung in Mae Sariang

The History of Opium in Thailand

Opium was first grown in Northern Thailand in the late 19th century, when hill tribes *(see pp210–11)* arrived from Southern China, where the drug was a major commodity. Grown on poor soil at high altitudes and easily transported, it was in fact their most profitable cash crop. Opium production was outlawed in Thailand in 1959, but flourished nonetheless during the Vietnam War. It was during this lucrative period that power struggles erupted for control of the Golden Triangle's *(see pp250–51)* poppy fields. The KMT *(see p246)*, allowed by the Thai government to control the illicit drugs trade, and the Shan United Army, based in Burma (now Myanmar), were the largest of the many contenders, including the Thai, Burmese, and Lao armies. Opium production has been cut by more than 80 percent since the 1960s, and most hill tribes now grow other crops, but Thailand is still used as a channel for opium produced in nearby countries.

Smoking opium in custom-built dens became popular in parts of Asia – especially China – in the 19th century.

Britain and China fought the Opium Wars of 1839–42 and 1856–60 over British rights to import opium from India. After the wars the drug was legalized in China and freely traded.

Short sickles, used to score poppy heads, are just some of a number of poppy-cultivating implements exhibited in the House of Opium.

The thin hillside soil easily supports poppies, which favor the low nutrient, high-alkaline conditions at altitudes of over 3,300 ft (1000 m).

Opium Production

This mural in the House of Opium Museum, Sop Ruak *(see p252)*, is one of a series showing traditional poppy harvesting for opium production, a process normally carried out in December and January. The museum also houses artifacts depicting the war between the KMT and the Shan United Army.

Since the 1980s, cash crops, including cabbage, tea, and coffee, have begun to replace poppies grown for opium production. Today, fields of these new crops are a common sight in Northern Thailand.

King Bhumibol, concerned about opiate addiction and the illegal drug trade in his country, has been particularly active in encouraging replacement crops.

ⓙ Wat Phra That Lampang Luang

วัดพระธาตุลำปางหลวง

One of the most famous temples in Northern Thailand, Wat Phra That Lampang Luang is also one of the most attractive. The main buildings were constructed in the late 15th century on the site of an 8th-century fortress. This had been built on a mound to protect it from attack and was further fortified by three parallel earthen ramparts separated by moats. The ramparts are still visible in the village around the present *wat*. In 1736 a local hero, Tip Chang, successfully defended the temple from the Burmese. The buildings are distinctive for their graceful architecture and richly colored interiors, while the revered Phra Kaeo Don Tao image, allegedly carved from the same jadeite block as the Emerald Buddha *(see p87)*, is kept in the museum behind the main complex.

Buddha in Wihan Phra Phut
A huge Buddha image sits inside the 13th-century *wihan*, the oldest building on the site.

Wihan Phra Phut
With its beautifully carved façade and two-tiered roof, this *wihan*, from 1802, is a masterpiece of Lanna architecture.

Five Buddhas in Wihan Luang
The huge, open-sided main *wihan*, which dates from 1496, has an elegant, three-tiered roof. Inside are five seated Buddha images.

Main entrance

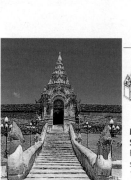

Main Staircase
Flanked by *nagas*, this stairway leads up to a 15th-century ceremonial gatehouse.

KEY

① Bodhi tree
② Bot
③ Wihan Phra Chao Sila
④ Wihan Ton Kaew

Ho Phra Phuttabat
This small, elevated *mondop* houses a sculpture of the Buddha's Footprint, which is worshipped by pilgrims during important festivals. Women may not enter the building.

★ Main Chedi
The subtle green and blue hues of the 15th-century *chedi* are due to centuries of rainfall, which have oxidized the copper. Inside is a hair, said to be from the Buddha.

★ Murals in Wihan Nam Tam
These faded murals, which depict 16th-century life and scenes from the *jataka* tales (*see p34*), adorn the walls of what may be Thailand's oldest surviving wooden structure.

Pillar Detail
This black lacquered pillar, inlaid with gold, is typical of the intricate decoration of the whole temple complex.

Ku in Wihan Luang
The Buddha image, Phra Chao Lang Thong, which dates from 1563, sits in this gilded brick *ku* (Lao-style *prang*).

Horse-drawn carriages, a popular tourist attraction in Lampang

⑳ Lampang
ลำปาง

Lampang province. 🏔 94,000. ✈ 🚌 🚆 *i* TAT, Lampang (0-5421-8823 or 0-5422-6812). 🏪 daily. 🎎 Luang Wiang Lakon (Feb).

The second-largest town in Northern Thailand, Lampang is still growing rapidly as a trading center. It offers much of the historic interest of Chiang Mai, but without the overt commercialization. Lampang is also a good base for excursions and travel within Northern Thailand.

The town was originally inhabited in the 7th century. The following century, when it was still called Kelang Nakorn, it became part of the Haripunchai Empire, which centered on Lamphun (see p233). In the 19th century, British traders came here from Myanmar and turned the town into a teak production center, bringing Myanmar workers with them. The result was the many teak houses and Myanmar-style temples seen throughout the town today. Teak furniture is just one of the traditional crafts still produced in Lampang; others are cottonware and ceramics.

Modern Lampang is distinctive for its brightly colored horse-drawn carriages, another surviving tradition. This mode of transportation was introduced to Lampang in the 19th century, and it is the only town in Thailand that uses it.

One of the most important temples in Northern Thailand is **Wat Phra That Lampang**

Luang (see pp238–9), to the southwest of the town, which is famous for its impressive 19th-century murals.

Lampang town focuses on the south side of the Wang River, although the main sights are found to the north of it. Of its temples, the most interesting is **Wat Phra Kaeo Don Tao**. The *wat* is thought to have been built about the same time the town was founded, but only the 165-ft (50-m) *chedi* survives from the original buildings. The distinctive *mondop* is notable for its nine-tier teak roof with intricate carvings and a bronze Buddha in the Mandalay style.

Between 1436 and 1468 the temple housed the revered Emerald Buddha, or Phra Kaeo

(see p87), which was later moved to Bangkok's Wat Phra Kaeo. During the same period, a similar jasper Buddha image, now in Wat Phra That Lampang Luang, was kept here. Within the compound is the **Lanna Museum**, displaying religious Lanna artifacts.

Ban Sao Nak ("many pillars house"), southeast of Wat Phra Kaeo Don Tao, is a Lanna structure built in 1896. It takes its name from the 116 square teak pillars supporting the building. Now a museum, it is furnished with Myanmar and Thai antiques. The sumptuous decoration includes lacquerware, ceramics, and silverware. **Wat Pongsanuk Tai**,

Interior of Ban Sao Nak, Lampang, decorated with antique crafts

Songkran Festivities in the North

Celebrated nationwide, but most exuberantly in and around Chiang Mai, Songkran (see p50) is one of Thailand's major festivals. Held over three days from April 12th–14th (though celebrations carry on until the 15th in towns such as Chiang Mai), Songkran marks the start of the Buddhist New Year. This public holiday has, over the centuries, evolved from a purely religious event, in which Buddha images are bathed with water to purify them, into a much greater celebration of water in the hot season. Nowadays, buckets of water are thrown over everyone in the streets (unsuspecting tourists make the best targets). Some of Songkran's original customs, such as younger Thais paying respect to their elders and monks by sprinkling their hands with perfumed water, are also maintained.

River procession in Lampang, part of the Songkran festivities

Exterior of the charming Wat Si Chum

to the west of Ban Sao Nak, is a distinctive late 18th-century Lanna temple with a copper *chedi*. An enclosure in the *mondop* contains a Bodhi tree that is surrounded by four Buddha images.

The 19th-century Myanmar-style **Wat Si Chum**, located in the south of the city, is constructed mostly from beautifully carved teak. The exquisite lacquerwork inside the main chamber shows life in Lampang during the 19th century.

🏛 **Lanna Museum**
Phra Kaeo Rd. **Tel** 0-5321-1364.
Open daily. 🈲

🏛 **Ban Sao Nak**
Ratwana Rd. **Open** daily. 🈲

❷ Thai Elephant Conservation Center

ศูนย์ฝึกลูกช้าง

Off Hwy 11, 24 miles (38 km) NW of Lampang, Lampang province.
🛈 TAT, Lampang (0-5421-8823).
Tel 0-5424-7875. 🚉 Lampang, then *songthaew*. **Open** daily; shows 9:30–11am (2pm Sat & Sun). 🈲

This is one of the best elephant training camps in Northern Thailand. About 12 animals, three to five years old, arrive here each year to be trained, and there are about 100 in total. Although their ability peaks between the ages of 40 and 50, the elephants may remain at the camp until the official retirement age of 60. During the five-year training

period the elephants learn a variety of tasks, including stacking, carrying, and pushing logs. Nowadays, such chores are part of the performances put on for tourists, and there is contro-versy surrounding this form of entertainment and its impact on the elephants' well-being (see p448). There is also a small museum focusing on the culture and the history of elephants in Thailand (see p257).

Environs
On the opposite side of the highway, the **Thung Kwian Forest Market** sells a wide range of plants and medicinal and culinary herbs, as well as lizards, beetles, and snakes. Government campaigns have attempted to end the sale of endangered species (see p223), but some, such as pangolins (scaly anteaters), are still sold here.

🏠 **Thung Kwian Forest Market**
Off Hwy 11, 22 miles (35 km) NW of Lampang. **Open** daily.

❷ Uttaradit

อุตรดิตถ์

Uttaradit province. 🖼 102,000. 🚉
🚌 🛈 TAT, Uttaradit (0-5525-2743).
🗓 daily. 🎪 Langsat Fair (Oct).

This provincial capital, relatively free of modern development and tourist paraphernalia, features on few visitors' itineraries. Nevertheless, the town's location makes it a convenient staging post between the North Central Plains and Northern Thailand.

Uttaradit rose to prominence during the Sukhothai era, and just prior to the collapse of the kingdom at the end of the 13th century the town marked its northern border. Uttaradit's most famous citizen was King Taksin, who was born here in the mid-18th century. He reunited Thailand after Myanmar sacked Ayutthaya in 1767. The town is made up of old teak buildings and narrow streets. The main temple of interest is **Wat Tha Thanon**, behind the train station. Inside is the Luang Pho Phet, a revered bronze Lanna Buddha.

To the west of Uttaradit is **Wat Phra Boromathat**, which is also known as Wat That Thung Yang. Its *wihan* is an example of the Lao Luang Prabang architectural style.

Uttaradit province is famous for the quality of its agricultural produce, particularly the *langsat* fruit.

Busy main street of Uttaradit, the birthplace of King Taksin

FAR NORTH

The Far North of Thailand is known as the Golden Triangle – the meeting point of Thailand, Myanmar, and Laos and an area historically associated with opium production. Nowadays, this picturesque region with numerous hill-tribe villages attracts large numbers of trekkers. Less well known delights in the Far North include, southeast of the Golden Triangle, quiet towns such as Phrae and Nan.

The fertile flood plains of the Mekong, which touch the tip of the Far North before running east into Laos, contrast with the breathtaking beauty of the mountains in the west and east of the area. Here can be found remote villages inhabited by hill tribes such as the Mien and Akha, who still preserve their traditional way of life. There are also settlements populated by ex-Chinese Nationalist soldiers and their descendants, who migrated here after Mao Tse-tung's Communist army won the Chinese civil war in 1949.

Chiang Rai is the main town in the Far North. Though not picturesque, it has a few sights and is used as a trekking base. Of greater interest are the towns strung out by the Mekong along the Myanmar and Lao borders, including the ancient city of Chiang Saen and Chiang Khong, a Thai Lue settlement.

Most visitors to northern Thailand travel from Chiang Mai to Chiang Rai, and then north to the Golden Triangle; thus some sights to the east are relatively unknown. The old, walled settlement of Phrae, for instance, with some of Thailand's largest teak buildings, is visited by few tourists, despite being easily accessible from the Central Plains and Chiang Mai. The town of Nan is more remote, set in a valley far from the main highway to the Golden Triangle. The diversion is worthwhile, if only to see the murals at Wat Phumin. Northeast of here, Doi Phu Kha National Park offers superb bird-watching. To the south of Nan, and far from the beaten track, is extraordinarily diverse scenery ranging from the earth pillars of Sao Din and Phea Muang Phi to the vast Sirikit Reservoir.

Thai Lue farmer plowing the fields in the time-honored way

◀ Golden Buddha statues grace the shrine inside Wat Phumin, Nan

Exploring the Far North

Thailand's northernmost region is, for many people, synonymous with the Golden Triangle. This area around the meeting point of three national borders still conjures up images of untamed wilderness, remote hill-tribe villages, and opium barons. There remains more than a grain of truth in this reputation, but the Far North is also developing rapidly as a tourist destination, centered around the one-time capital of the Lanna Kingdom, Chiang Rai. The major attraction for visitors is the spectacular geography of the region, best explored on foot or motorbike. Touring through the mighty forested mountains along the Myanmar (Burma) and Lao borders, and beside the winding Mekong, as it skirts the tip of the region, is a richly rewarding experience.

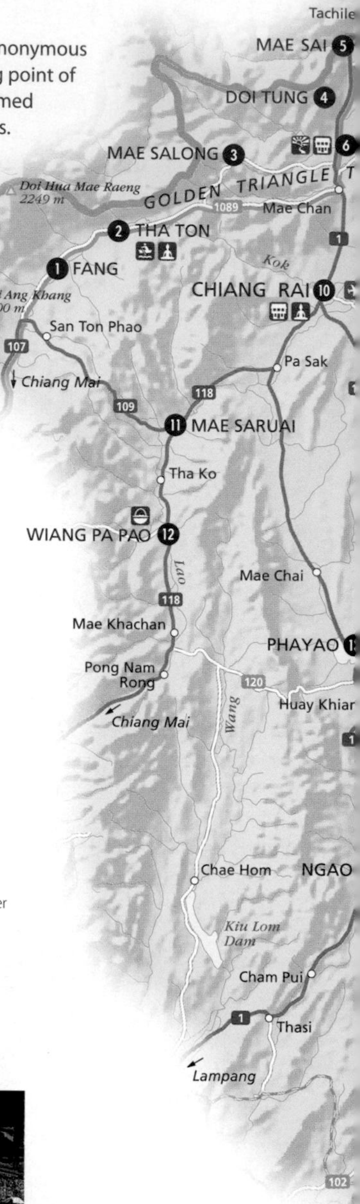

Sights at a Glance

1. Fang
2. Tha Ton
3. Mae Salong
4. Doi Tung
5. Mae Sai
7. The Golden Triangle Apex (Sop Ruak)
8. Chiang Saen
9. Chiang Khong
10. *Chiang Rai pp254–5*
11. Mae Saruai
12. Wiang Pa Pao
13. Phayao
14. Ngao
15. Nong Bua
16. Doi Phu Kha National Park
17. *Nan pp258–61*
18. *Phrae pp262–3*
19. Sirikit Reservoir

Tours
6. Golden Triangle

Key
— Major road
--- Minor road
— Scenic route
--- Railway
■ International border
△ Summit

0 kilometers 25
0 miles 15

A gathering of Lisu tribeswomen in traditional costume

For hotels and restaurants see pp402–11 and pp418–33

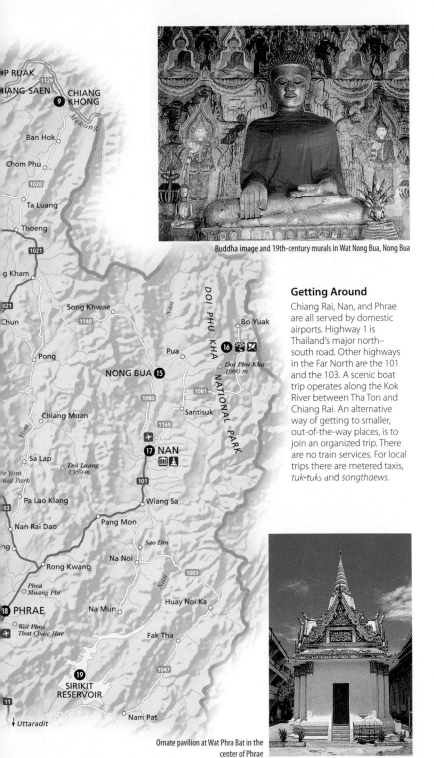

Buddha image and 19th-century murals in Wat Nong Bua, Nong Bua

P RUAK
IANG SAEN

CHIANG
KHONG **9**

Mekong

Ban Hok

Chom Phu

1020

Ta Luang

Thoeng

1021

g Kham

021

Chun

Song Khwae

1148

Pong

NONG BUA **15**

Pua

Chiang Muan

1080

1081

Santisuk

1169

NAN **17**

Sa Lap

Doi Luang
1369 m

e Yom
nal Park

101

Pa Lao Klang

Wiang Sa

03

Nan Rai Dao

Pang Mon

Sao Din

ng

Rong Kwang

Na Noi

DOI PHU KHA

Bo Yuak

16

Doi Phu Kha
1980 m

NATIONAL PARK

1083

Phea
Muang Phi

18 PHRAE

Na Mun

Huay Noi Ka

Wat Phra
That Chaw Hae

Fak Tha

19
SIRIKIT
RESERVOIR

1047

11

↓ *Uttaradit*

Nam Pat

Getting Around

Chiang Rai, Nan, and Phrae are all served by domestic airports. Highway 1 is Thailand's major north–south road. Other highways in the Far North are the 101 and the 103. A scenic boat trip operates along the Kok River between Tha Ton and Chiang Rai. An alternative way of getting to smaller, out-of-the-way places, is to join an organized trip. There are no train services. For local trips there are metered taxis, *tuk-tuks* and *songthaews*.

Ornate pavilion at Wat Phra Bat in the center of Phrae

For keys to symbols *see back flap*

Karen tribespeople trading their wares at Fang's daily market

❶ Fang
ฝาง

Chiang Mai province. 🏔 111,000.
🚌 from Chiang Mai. ℹ️ TAT, Chiang
Mai (0-5324-8604). 🛍 daily.

This town was founded as a
trading center in 1268 by King
Mengrai, who took advantage
of the site's location at the head
of a valley. At the beginning of
the 19th century the town was
destroyed by Burmese raiders,
and it lay deserted until 1880.
Today Fang is effectively a
border town between the areas
inhabited by Thais and hill tribes
(see pp210–11). The local Mien,
Karen, and Lahu tribes sell their
goods at Fang's market, and this
has made it an important
trading center.

Fang is characterized by teak
houses. The influence of
nearby Myanmar is seen in
many structures, such as
Wat Jong Paen, located
in the north of town.
The most impressive
temple in Fang,
it features a
Myanmar-style,
multiroofed *wihan*.

Environs
Drug trading in the
Fang area has been significant in
the past, and fighting between
rival drug factions in Myanmar
still occasionally spills across the
border. It is wise to check the
situation with the local tourist
office before venturing on a
guided trek. Sights in the region
include, some 6 miles (10 km)
west of Fang, sulfur springs,
whose natural energy is used
to power a nearby geothermal
plant. To the southwest of Fang,
Highway 1249 leads to the
peak of **Doi Ang Khang**, via
several Lisu, Lahu, and Hmong
hill-tribe villages.

❷ Tha Ton
ท่าตอน

Chiang Mai province. 🏔 21,000.
🚌 from Chiang Mai to Fang, then
songthaew. ℹ️ TAT, Chiang Mai
(0-5324-8604).

Located on a bend in the Kok
River, picturesque Tha Ton is
essentially a staging post for
riverboats that make regular
trips from here to Chiang Rai.
Excursions can be arranged
at guesthouses in town, and
may often be combined
with visits to nearby tribal
villages or hot springs.
Tha Ton's chief tourist
attraction is **Wat Tha
Ton**, which is notable
for a huge white
Buddha with a
striking golden
topknot. The
temple dominates
the town from its
hillside location to
the west, offering splendid
panoramic views.

Imposing white Buddha
overlooking Tha Ton

Environs
The road leading from Tha Ton
to Doi Mae Salong, 26 miles
(43 km) to the northeast, takes
in impressive mountain
scenery and villages along the
Myanmar border.

❸ Mae Salong (Santikhiree)
ดอยแม่สะลอง (ดอยสันติคีรี)

Chiang Rai province. 🏔 15,000.
🚌 Chiang Rai, then *songthaew*.
ℹ️ 0-5371-7433. 🛍 daily.

One of the main settlements in
Northern Thailand, the hillside
town of Mae Salong is also one
of the most scenic. Mae Salong
was founded in 1962 by the
Kuomintang (KMT), or Chinese
Nationalist Army, following their
defeat in China by Mao Zedong
in 1949. It became a center for
exiled Chinese soldiers, who
used it as a base for incursions
into China. The Thai military
agreed to let the KMT stay if
they helped to suppress
Communism, which they
believed would become rife
among the hill tribes at the time
of the Vietnam War. In return for
their help, the KMT were
allowed to control and tax the
local opium trade. As a result,
the area around Mae Salong
was relatively lawless and
dangerous until the 1980s.

When Khun Sa, the opium
warlord (see p237), retreated to
Myanmar in the early 1990s,
the Thai government began to
have some success in pacifying
the area. This was helped
when, soon after the end of
this turbulent period, Mae
Salong was officially renamed
Santikhiree ("hill of peace"), in
an attempt to rid the town of
its former image. The new term
is used for both the town and
the 3,950-ft (1,200-m) peak that

Chinese medicinal herbs and spices for sale
at Mae Salong market

Modern temple on the hill top of Doi Mae Salong

rises above it, Doi Mae Salong. A temple has been built at the summit, giving spectacular views of the surrounding rolling hills, which are dotted with hill-tribe villages. Akha and Mien villagers can be seen at the market in Mae Salong, but the town's main population is made up of old KMT soldiers and their descendants. The sight of low, Chinese-style houses made of bamboo and the sound of Yunnanese (a Chinese dialect) give the overall impression that Mae Salong is more of a Chinese than Thai town.

A road built to Mae Salong in the early 1980s made the settlement less isolated. Opium production is now suppressed, having been replaced by cash crops such as cabbage, tea, and Chinese herbs and medicines. This produce is sold in the town's market.

❹ Doi Tung
ดอยตุง

Chiang Rai province. *i* TAT, Chiang Rai (0-5371-7433). 🚌 from Mae Chan or Mae Sai to turn-off for Doi Tung, then *songthaew* to summit.

The mountain of Doi Tung is an impressive limestone outcrop dominating the Mekong flood plain near Mae Sai. The narrow road snakes through monsoon forest, winding its way up to the 5,900-ft (1,800-m) peak. On a clear day the views of Myanmar and lowland Thailand from the summit are stunning.

The name of the mountain means "flag peak," so called because in AD 911 King Achutarat of Chiang Saen ordered a giant flag to be flown from the summit to mark the site where two *chedis* were to be built, allegedly to house a piece of the Buddha's collarbone. Still a major pilgrimage site, the *chedis* are at the heart of **Wat Phra That Doi Tung**, which was renovated in the early 1900s. Also here is a large, rotund Chinese-style Buddha image. Pilgrims throw coins into its navel to make merit. The area around Doi

Tung has historically been the site of opium production, the poppy fields guarded by hill tribespeople and the KMT. The area has become the focus for a rural development project aimed at increasing central government control over the area. In 1988 **Doi Tung Royal Villa** was built on the mountain as part of a plan to increase tourism in the area and to discourage nearby hill tribes from producing opium. Originally a summer residence for the late mother of King Bhumibol, the villa has an attractive flower garden and a restaurant. While the plan has largely succeeded, local villagers have become dependent on hand-outs from the development project and from tourists.

Doi Tung is now connected to the other main settlements of the area by good roads. These make fascinating driving into regions that were once the preserve of drug barons. Mae Salong and Mae Sai may be reached by these routes, via Lahu and Akha hill-tribe villages. Although a strong Thai army presence has reduced drug trading in the area substantially, visitors are advised not to leave main roads.

🏛 **Doi Tung Royal Villa**
Hwy 1149. **Open** 7am–5:30pm daily.
🌿 Gardens: **Open** 6am–6pm. 🌿

A terraced hillside near Mae Salong, cultivated with new crops aimed at replacing opium as the main source of income

Big golden Buddha image overlooking the Mekong River at Sop Ruak, the apex of the Golden Triangle ▶

❺ Mae Sai
แม่สาย

Chiang Rai province. 🏠 58,000. 🚌 ℹ️
TAT, Chiang Rai (0-5371-7433). 🛍️ daily.

The northernmost town in
Thailand, Mae Sai is separated
from Myanmar (Burma) only by
a bridge. The town bustles with
traders from the neighboring
country who come here to sell
their wares. Among the handicrafts are lacquerware, gems,
and jade items, mostly made in
Myanmar. Though the town
itself is nondescript, there are
good views over the Sai River to
Myanmar. **Wat Phra That Doi
Wao** also has a good vista.

Environs
To visit the town of **Tachilek**, in
Myanmar, visitors have to exit
Thailand at the border bridge in
Mae Sai. Mynamar Immigration
charges a 500-*baht* fee for a
temporary visa that allows a
24-hour stay. Most people
simply look around the market
and return to Mae Sai. Beware
of buying counterfeit goods
such as DVDs, CDs, and mobile
phones in Tachilek, since Thai
customs may confiscate them.
   South of Mae Sai is **Tham
Luang**, a large cave complex
with crystals that change color
in the light. Farther south are
more caves, **Tham Pum** and
Tham Pla, with lakes inside.

🦇 Tham Luang
Off Hwy 110, 3.5 miles (6 km) S of Mae
Sai. **Open** daily. 🎫 ⬛

🦇 Tham Pum and Tham Pla
Off Hwy 110, 8 miles (13 km) S of Mae
Sai. **Open** daily. 🎫 ⬛

Tobacco-curing houses near the Myanmar
border, outside Mae Sai

For hotels and restaurants see pp402–11 and pp418–33

❻ Golden Triangle Driving Tour

The Golden Triangle is a 75,000 sq-mile (195,000 sq-km)
area spanning parts of Thailand, Laos, and Myanmar
(Burma). The area is historically connected to the opium
and heroin trades (thus "golden"), but it has much more to
interest visitors. This tour takes in its best features: superb
views of the "apex" of the Golden Triangle, where the three
countries meet; hill-tribe villages nestling amid stunning
mountain scenery; and the historical towns of Chiang
Saen and Chiang Khong. Illicit opium trading is thought
to continue in the region, however, and visitors should
use a qualified guide and take extra care near the
Myanmar border, which can be dangerous.

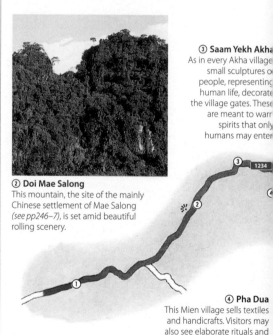

③ **Saam Yekh Akha**
As in every Akha village,
small sculptures of
people, representing
human life, decorate
the village gates. These
are meant to warn
spirits that only
humans may enter

② **Doi Mae Salong**
This mountain, the site of the mainly
Chinese settlement of Mae Salong
(see pp246–7), is set amid beautiful
rolling scenery.

④ **Pha Dua**
This Mien village sells textiles
and handicrafts. Visitors may
also see elaborate rituals and
ceremonies based on the local
hill tribe's religion, a mixture of
animism and Chinese Taoism.

① **Tha Ton**
Located near the Myanmar
border, Tha Thon *(see p246)*
is a staging post between the
lowlands and the mountains.
A huge white Buddha image,
visible from miles around,
faces eastward over the town
and surrounding countryside.

0 kilometers	15
0 miles	10

Tips for Drivers

Tour length: 125 miles (200 km).
Stopping-off points: Mae Sai,
Chiang Saen, and Chiang Khong
all have restaurants, guesthouses,
and gas stations. Smaller roads
may be difficult for travel,
especially in the wet season, so it
is best to use the numbered
roads above.

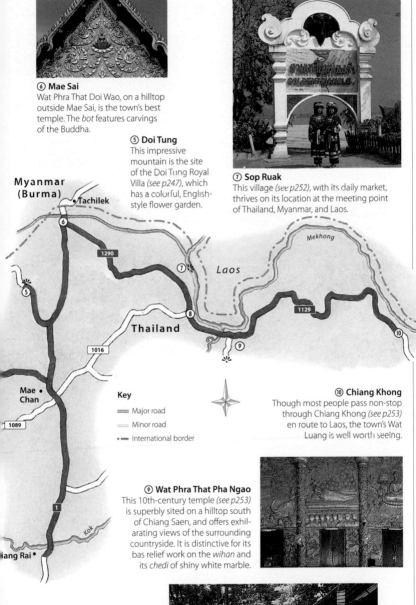

⑥ Mae Sai
Wat Phra That Doi Wao, on a hilltop outside Mae Sai, is the town's best temple. The *bot* features carvings of the Buddha.

⑤ Doi Tung
This impressive mountain is the site of the Doi Tung Royal Villa *(see p247)*, which has a colorful, English-style flower garden.

⑦ Sop Ruak
This village *(see p252)*, with its daily market, thrives on its location at the meeting point of Thailand, Myanmar, and Laos.

Myanmar (Burma)

•Tachilek

Mekhong

Laos

Thailand

Key

━━ Major road
═══ Minor road
▪━ International border

Mae • Chan

ang Rai •

Kok

⑩ Chiang Khong
Though most people pass non-stop through Chiang Khong *(see p253)* en route to Laos, the town's Wat Luang is well worth seeing.

⑨ Wat Phra That Pha Ngao
This 10th-century temple *(see p253)* is superbly sited on a hilltop south of Chiang Saen, and offers exhilarating views of the surrounding countryside. It is distinctive for its bas relief work on the *wihan* and its *chedi* of shiny white marble.

⑧ Chiang Saen
Visitors should not miss this town *(see pp252–3)* of ruined temples and teak trees, once the capital of a small kingdom. Today it boasts an excellent branch of the National Museum and a daily market specializing in Thai Lue fabrics and souvenirs.

Farmers using traditional methods to cultivate rice in paddies near Chiang Saen

❼ The Golden Triangle Apex (Sop Ruak)

สามเหลี่ยมทองคำ (สบรวก)

42 miles (68 km) NE of Chiang Rai, Chiang Rai province. ➡ from Chiang Saen. ➡ from Chiang Saen. 🚹 TAT, Chiang Rai (0-5371-7433).

The apex of the Golden Triangle is the point at which the borders of Thailand, Myanmar (Burma), and Laos meet. The junction, at a bend in the Mekong River, is near the village of **Sop Ruak**. Historically, the "Golden Triangle" referred to a much wider region – the area of Northern Thailand, Myanmar, and Laos in which opium was produced (see p237). Nowadays, though, the term refers to a much smaller area and is associated with Sop Ruak village.

Sop Ruak, eager to take advantage of its location, is growing rapidly as a tourist spot, as evidenced by its many shops, restaurants, and hotels. A museum, the **House of Opium**, displays artifacts relating to opium production. It details a battle between the KMT army (see p246) and the now-deposed opium lord, Khun Sa (see p237), over control of the local opium trade. The battle, which established the notoriety of the Golden Triangle, took place in 1967.

But the area's main attraction is the Mekong. Boat trips give views of Laos and of the Golden Triangle Paradise Resort. The resort and casino were built in Myanmar, as gambling is illegal in Thailand.

Lanna carving, National Museum

🏛 **House of Opium**
212 House of Opium, SE of Sop Ruak village center. **Tel** 0-5378-4060. **Open** 7am–7pm daily. 🚫
🌐 **houseofopium.com**

Mural in the House of Opium showing tools used to harvest poppies

❽ Chiang Saen

เชียงแสน

Chiang Rai province. 🚹 47,000. ➡
➡ 🚹 TAT, Chiang Rai (0-5374-4674). ➡ daily.

One of the oldest towns in Thailand, Chiang Saen is set beautifully on the bank of the Mekong River. The town was founded in 1328 by Saenphu, the grandson of King Mengrai, as a powerful fortification with many temples. There is evidence, however, from some of Chiang Saen's monuments, that suggests the town may be much older. In 1558, Chiang Saen was captured by the Burmese. It was liberated by King Rama I in 1804, who burned it to the ground to prevent its recapture. The present town was established in the early 1880s. Today, Chiang Saen is a quiet and peaceful settlement boasting an impressive number of monuments that survived the razing. The Fine Arts Department in Bangkok lists 66 ruins inside the walled town and 75 beyond.

The largest temple in Chiang Saen is **Wat Phra That Chedi Luang**. Its 190-ft (58-m) octagonal *chedi*, built between the 12th and the 14th centuries, is a classic Chiang Saen (more commonly known as Lanna) structure.

Beside the temple is a small market selling textiles and souvenirs made by the Thai Lue, an ethnic minority from China who came to the area in the 18th century. Also nearby is the **Chiang Saen National Museum**, with a collection of stone carvings from the Lanna period, Buddha images, and artifacts relating to hill-tribe culture *(see pp210–11)*.

The town's most attractive temple is **Wat Pa Sak** ("teak forest temple"), located outside the old walls to the west. The monument consists of seven separate ruined structures set among teak trees, which give the *wat* its name. The *chedi*, built in 1295, is the oldest in town. It is carved with flowers and mythological beasts.

On a hill to the northwest of Chiang Saen is **Wat Phra That Chom Kitti**, which may date from 10th century. The temple has little of architectural interest, it gives fine views of the town and the Mekong.

Just south of Chiang Saen is the hilltop **Wat Phra That Pha Ngao**. This temple, with a white pagoda, offers stunning views of the river and the Golden Triangle region.

Typical Thai Lue fabrics for sale in Chiang Khong

❾ Chiang Khong

เชียงของ

Chiang Rai province. ⚐ 52,000. 🚌 🚐 ℹ TAT, Chiang Rai (0-5374-4674). 🛒 daily.

On the banks of the Mekong River, Chiang Khong town is all that remains of the much larger territory of Chiang Khong, most of which was lost to the French in 1893, when they claimed it as part of French Indochina (the rest of this land now forms part of Laos). A growing border town, Chiang Khong is largely dominated by events in Laos. The town was one of the key points of arrival for refugees after the Communist victory in Laos in 1975 *(see p299)*. There is

a large Thai Lue community here too, and shops sell their distinctive, multicolored textiles. Chiang Khong's main temple is the 13th-century **Wat Luang**, in the town center. On a hillside just northwest of town is a cemetery where some 200 Chinese KMT soldiers, killed in battles against Communists in the area since the 1960s, are buried.

Environs
Visitors can take a ferry to **Huay Xai**, just inside the Lao border. Visas can be obtained on arrival at Huay Xai immigration at a cost of $35. You will need two passport-size photos. An important trading center, Huay Xai boasts the 19th-century **Wat Chan Khao Manirat**.

Thailand's Teak Industry

The use of teak (*Tectona grandis*) in Thailand dates back many centuries. Its favorable properties, including strength and resistance to pests and disease, made it a natural choice for use in buildings and furniture, while its fine grain traditionally lent itself to intricate carving. However, reckless overlogging has led to disastrous deforestation, and, as a result, most commercial teak logging and export was banned in 1989. Pockets of teak may

Transporting teak logs on the Chao Phraya River

still be seen in its natural habitat – low-lying deciduous forests of up to 1,950 ft (600 m) in elevation, with rich, moist soil (such forest is characteristic of Northern Thailand) – or in large new plantations. The trees are easily recognizable by their huge size – they can grow up to 131 ft (40 m) when mature – and by their large, floppy leaves, which fall off during the dry period of November to May. Thailand's historic use of teak is evident in rural parts of the country, as in the old wooden houses of provincial towns, including Phrae *(see pp262–3)* and Ngao *(see p256)*, both located in the North.

Lowland teak forest in Northern Thailand

⑩ Chiang Rai
เชียงราย

This ancient town was founded in 1262 by King Mengrai. He decided that the site, in a basin between mountains, would be ideal for the new capital of the Lanna Kingdom (see pp66–7). However, the capital was transferred to Chiang Mai only 34 years later, and Chiang Rai declined in importance. Today it is known as the "gateway to the Golden Triangle." While the modern town may lack the charm and architectural interest of Chiang Mai, it has a number of sights worthy of attention.

Exploring Chiang Rai

Evidence of the town's historic importance can be seen in monuments such as Wat Phra Kaeo. However, modern development is becoming increasingly prominent. The construction of hotels for tourists, who use Chiang Rai as a trekking base, and of second homes for the wealthy people of Bangkok, has made the town one of the fastest growing in Thailand. Economic activity in the area is expected to grow even further as trade increases with China, just 120 miles (200 km) to the north. Development focuses mainly on the area between the old market off Suk Sathit Road and Phahon Yothin Road, with the newest hotels on the outskirts of town and by the airport. Resorts have been built on many of the islands in the Kok River. A popular night bazaar is held in the center of town. Visitors can buy a range of crafts, enjoy a meal, and watch cultural performances. The nearby fresh fruit market is also open at night.

🔰 Wat Phra Kaeo
วัดพระแก้ว

Trirat Rd. **Open** daily.

This is the city's most revered temple. According to legend, lightning struck and cracked the *chedi* in 1354, revealing a plaster cast statue encasing the Emerald Buddha (actually made of jadeite). Today Thailand's most holy Buddha image is housed in Bangkok (see p87). A replica, presented in 1991, is now kept here. The *wat* dates from the 13th century and is also notable for its fine *bot*, decorated with elaborate woodcarving, and the Phra Chao Lang Thong, one of the largest surviving bronze statues from the early Lanna period (see pp66–7).

🔰 Wat Chet Yot
วัดเจ็ดยอด

Chet Yot Rd. **Open** daily.

This small temple, named for its unusual, seven-spired *chedi*, is similar in appearance to its namesake in Chiang Mai (see p231). The front veranda of the main *wihan* has a mural depicting astrological scenes.

🔰 Wat Phra Sing
วัดพระสิงห์

Singhakhlai Rd. **Open** daily.

Built in the late 14th century, Wat Phra Sing is a typical Northern wooden structure, with low, curved roofs. The main *wihan* houses a replica of the Phra Sing Buddha in Chiang Mai's Wat Phra Sing (see p230). Also of interest are the carved medallions below the windows of the *bot*, which depict birds and animals. Around the Bodhi tree are images of the Buddha.

Staircase leading up to a seated Buddha image at Wat Mungmuang

🔰 Wat Mungmuang
วัดมุงเมือง

Uttarakit Rd. **Open** daily.

A rotund Buddha image with one hand raised in the *vitarkha mudra* position (see p177) dominates this *wat*. The murals in the main *wihan*, depicting local mountain scenery and scenes of flooding and pollution, reflect the concern of Thais at the rapid growth of their cities, an issue of particular relevance in Chiang Rai.

🔰 Wat Phra That Doi Thong
วัดพระธาตุดอยทอง

At-am Nuai Rd, Doi Chom Thong Hill. **Open** daily.

This temple, built in the 1940s, is located on a hill top outside the town. It is on this spot that King Mengrai is said to have decided upon the location of his new capital. In the *wihan* is Chiang Rai's original *lak muang*, or "city pillar," traditionally erected in Thailand to mark the founding of a new city.

Wihan of Wat Phra Sing, housing a replica of Chiang Mai's Phra Sing Buddha

Overbrook Hospital, an example of Chiang Rai's colonial architecture

Overbrook Hospital
โรงพยาบาลโอเวอร์บรู๊ค
Singhakhlai Rd. **Tel** 0-5371-1366.

This working hospital is typical of the colonial architecture created by Westerners in the 19th and 20th centuries, when the city was a base for missionaries and traders. Such buildings are slowly being swamped in Chiang Rai as modern development proceeds apace. This trend is likely to continue as ever more trekkers and package tourists, demanding ever more comprehensive facilities, are attracted to the wild beauty of the mountainous Golden Triangle region (see pp250–52).

🏛 Hill Tribe Museum
พิพิธภัณฑ์ชาวเขา
620–625 Thanalai Rd. **Tel** 0-5374-0088.
Open 8:30am–6pm Mon–Fri, 10am–6pm Sat & Sun. 🏛 🔲 **pdacr.org**

This museum and crafts center was established in 1990 by the non-profit Population and Community Development Association (PDA), also known for raising awareness of Thailand's AIDS problem (see p120). In addition to informing tourists of the plight of hill tribes (see pp210–11), volunteers at the center work with the tribespeople, educating them on how to cope with threats to their traditional lifestyle from a rapidly modernizing society. The center displays and sells hill-tribe crafts (see pp212–13). These can also be bought at the

Hill Tribe Museum, surrounded by lush greenery, Chiang Rai

VISITORS' CHECKLIST

Practical Information
Tel 0-5371-7779. 🔲 **chiangrai province.org** Chiang Rai province.
🚹 140,000. 🎦 TAT, Singhklai Rd, Chiang Rai 0-5371-7433; 🏠 on the floor below TAT office, 🔲 daily. 🔲 Pho Khun Mengrai (Jan); Songkran and Boat Racing Festival (Apr); Lychee and Nang Lae Pineapple Fair (May); Chiang Rai Flower Festival (Dec/Jan). 🔲

Transport
✈ 5 miles (8 km) N of Chiang Rai.
🚌 off Prasopsuk Rd; 4 miles (6 km) S of Chiang Rai. 🚤 Kok River pier.

market and in shops around the center of town.

Environs
Chiang Rai is growing as a base for visiting the rest of the Far North. Vehicle rental, guided treks, and excursions can be arranged through tour companies and guesthouses. Boat trips on the Kok River include excursions to the village of **Tha Ton** (see p246). **Ruamit**, some 12 miles (20 km) west of Chiang Rai was originally inhabited solely by the Karen tribe, though many different hill tribes now live here. Guided treks can be taken from here to other villages.

Eight miles (13 km) south of Chiang Rai is the photogenic **Wat Rang Khun**. Known as the "White Temple," this unfinished wat was designed in 1997 by artist-turned-architect Chalermchai Kositpipat.

Chiang Rai Town Center
① Wat Phra That Doi Thong
② Wat Phra Kaeo
③ Overbrook Hospital
④ Wat Phra Sing
⑤ Wat Mungmuang
⑥ Wat Chet Yot
⑦ Hill Tribe Museum

0 meters 250
0 yards 250

For keys to symbols see back flap

⓫ Mae Saruai

แม่สรวย

Chiang Rai province. 🚌 84,000. 🚐 Chiang Rai, then *songthaew*. 🛈 TAT, Chiang Rai (0-5371-7433). 🕭 daily.

Situated on a plain between mountains and jagged limestone outcrops, this small market town is a popular meeting place for hill tribes, particularly Akha (*see pp210–11*). Mae Saruai is modernizing rapidly, and new agriculture, including flower production, is replacing traditional crops such as rice.

Environs
Cars can be rented in Chiang Rai to visit the Akha hill-tribe villages. The remote ones are accessible on motorcycles or by trekking. Ban Saen Chareon, 6 miles (10 km) west of Mae Saruai, was the subject of a major study of the Akha.

⓬ Wiang Pa Pao

เวียงป่าเป้า

Chiang Rai province. 🚌 61,000. 🚃 🚐 Chiang Mai, then *songthaew*; or 🚐 Chiang Rai, then *songthaew*. 🛈 TAT, Chiang Rai (0-5374-4674). 🕭 daily.

This important market town is picturesquely located in a long, thin valley surrounded by mountains. The town is composed mainly of two-story teak buildings, typical of Northern Thailand, and has quiet back streets shaded by teak trees. Many hill-tribe villagers who live in the area,

Chedi and *wihan* of Wat Si Suthawat, Wiang Pa Pao's main temple

The main street in Mae Saruai, with its two-story buildings

especially Lisu and Akha, come to trade at its market. Wiang Pa Pao's main tourist attraction is **Wat Si Suthawat**, to the east of the main road through town. This spacious old temple, with distinctive, curled *nagas* flanking the sweeping staircase that leads up to the main *wihan*, is surrounded by teak trees.

⓭ Phayao

พะเยา

Phayao province. 🚌 21,000. 🚐 🛈 TAT, Chiang Rai (0-5374-4674). 🕭 daily.

This quiet provincial capital, spectacularly sited beside a large lake, was possibly first settled in the Bronze Age. Later abandoned, it was resettled in the 12th century, when it became an independent city state. Today, Phayao is divided into two parts. The older district is confined to the promontory jutting into the lake. With its narrow streets and teak houses, it is more pleasant than the newer part.

Wat Si Komkam, situated just north of town by the lake, dates from the 12th century. Its modern *wihan* houses a 16th-century, 52-ft (16-m) Buddha image, which is thought to be the largest in the whole of Northern Thailand. The *wihan* is surrounded by 38 heads of the Buddha in the Phayao style – distinguished by their rounded heads and pointed noses – dating from the 14th century.

Angel at Wat Dok Ban, Ngao

⓮ Ngao

งาว

Lampang province. 🚌 53,000. 🚐 from Lampang or Chiang Rai. 🛈 TAT, Lampang (0-5422-1813). 🕭 daily.

Like many towns in Northern Thailand, Ngao's historical association with the teak trade is evident in its buildings. The suspension bridge over the Yom River offers wonderful views of the town, with its teak houses on stilts backing onto the fertile river valley.

Ngao's principal temple is **Wat Dok Ban**, on the east side of town. It is distinctive for its wall surrounded by about 100 kneeling angel figures of different colors.

Environs
Mae Yom National Park, northeast of Ngao, is centered on the Yom River, one of Northern Thailand's main waterways. More than 50 species of birds have been observed in the park, as well as many mammals, including the serow (a type of antelope), pangolin (scaly anteater), wild pigs, and barking deer. Within the park is the **Dong Sak Ngan Forest**, notable for its tall teak trees. The forest can be reached only on foot.

🏞 **Mae Yom National Park**
11 miles (18 km) NE of Ngao. **Tel** 0-5462-6770. 🛈 Forestry Dept (0-2579-0529). **Open** daily. 🏕

Elephants in Thailand

As well as playing a very important practical role in Thai history, elephants have traditionally been of great spiritual significance. They were first mentioned centuries ago in Hindu and Buddhist texts and since then have enjoyed a higher status in Thailand than any other animal. However, although wild elephants have been protected by law since 1921, deforestation and, to a lesser extent, poaching have reduced their numbers to just a few thousand. The introduction of machines for logging, followed by a ban on most commercial logging in 1989, has led to a sharp fall in the number of captive elephants. Tourists may still come across these being ridden by *mahouts*, and at elephant welfare camps, though some "shows" have been criticised by animal welfare groups.

Elephants were used in war, as depicted in this old manuscript

Working Elephants

Although most logging is officially banned in Thailand, elephants are still used for transporting logs in some areas. They are often looked after by one handler for all their life, and cause less damage than modern machinery.

Able to run up to 12 miles (20 km) an hour, elephants were frequently used by hunters.

This 19th-century training manual shows how to tame wild elephants.

Sacred Elephants

The spiritual significance of elephants derives from Ganesh, the Hindu god of knowledge and the remover and creator of obstacles, who is a young boy with an elephant's head. The significance of white elephants *(see p110)*, the most revered of all, has its roots in Buddhism. Only the king may own them.

Mural of elephants in one of the Buddhist heavens, Wat Suthat, Bangkok *(see pp94–5)*.

Royal white elephants, said to represent the monarch's power, are the most sacred elephants.

⓯ Nong Bua
หนองบัว

Nan province. 🗻 5,100. 🚌 Nan, then *songthaew*. 🛈 TAT, Chiang Rai (0-5374-4674). 🛒 daily.

This picturesque town, situated on a flat, fertile plain beside the Nan River, is characterized by traditional teak houses on stilts and neat vegetable gardens. It is one of a number of towns in Nan province inhabited by the Thai Lue, an ethnic minority related to the Tai people of Southern China, who began to settle in the region in 1836.

Wat Nong Bua, which was built in 1862, has features typical of a Thai Lue temple, including a two-tiered roof and a carved wooden portico. Its murals are thought to be the work of the same artists who painted those at Wat Phumin *(see pp260–61)*. Though the murals at Wat Nong Bua are more faded than Wat Phumin's, their depictions of 19th-century life are just as fascinating. As at Wat Phumin, scenes from the *jataka* tales *(see p34)* are also featured here.

To the west of town is a textile factory, where traditional Thai Lue fabrics are made using hand-operated looms. The distinctive, multicolored fabrics are for sale in the adjacent store.

Nong Bua is the site of a two-day festival held every three years in December (2014, 2017, and so on), during which the villagers pay homage to their ancestors.

A 19th-century mural depicting a hunting party, Wat Nong Bua

⓰ Doi Phu Kha National Park
อุทยานแห่งชาติดอยภูคา

Visitors' Center off Hwy 1080, 42 miles (85 km) NE of Nan. **Tel** 0-5473-1623. 🛈 TAT, Chiang Rai (0-5374-4674); Forestry Dept (0-2562-0760 or 🖵 dnp.go.th). 🚌 Nan, then *songthaew*.

Ranged around the 6,550-ft (2,000-m) peak of Doi Phu Kha, this is one of the youngest national parks in Thailand. For years, the area was widely considered a hotbed of Communist infiltration. Some of the hill-tribe villagers here were suspected of sympathizing with the Communists and were kept isolated from visitors. Tourism in the park is therefore still in its infancy. Doi Phu Kha has two main attractions, the most obvious being its beautiful scenery, such as caves and waterfalls.

Short-tailed magpie, Doi Phu Kha National Park

The visitors' center provides information on forest walks and opportunities for bird-watching.

The other points of interest in the park are the tribal villages, particularly Mien and Hmong *(see pp210–11)*, and lowland ethnic minorities such as the Htin and Thai Lue.

There are few good roads or tourist facilities in the park. The more adventurous will be rewarded by an area relatively free of development.

⓱ Nan
น่าน

Nan province. 🗻 60,000. ✈️ 🚌 🛈 TAT, Chiang Rai (0-5374-4674). 🛒 daily. 🎏 Nan Provincial Fair (Oct/Nov), Nan Boat Racing (late Oct or early Dec); Golden Orange Festival (Dec/Jan).

Nan developed as an isolated kingdom in the 13th and 14th centuries. It fell under the influence of the Sukothai and Lanna kingdoms *(see pp62–3)*, then surrendered to Burmese control in 1558. In 1788 the town became a vassal state of Bangkok, though it kept its autonomy and independent rulers until it officially became part of Thailand in 1931. Today, Nan is a prosperous town on the Nan River.

Wat Phumin *(see pp260–61)*, in the south of town, is without doubt the most important sight in Nan. Just north of it (on Highway 101) is the **Nan National Museum**, which is housed in an impressive former

Thai Lue farmers working in the rice fields around Nong Bua

royal palace dating from 1903. The ground floor is dedicated to the ethnic groups of Nan province, including the Hmong and Mien hill tribes. The second floor has a comprehensive selection of artifacts relating to the history of the region, including weapons. Notable items include a "black" elephant tusk weighing 40 lb (18 kg), supported by a sculpted *khut* (mythological eagle). Thought to date from the 17th century, the tusk is actually dark brown.

The collection of Buddhas includes some rare Lanna and Lao images. Also exhibited are skyrockets made by local farmers for the Bun Bang Fai (Rocket Festival) *(see p51)* held each May in Northeast and parts of Northern Thailand.

Façade of the *bot* of the 14th-century Wat Suan Tan in Nan

Unusually for Thai museums, many of the exhibits are labeled in English. Nearby is **Wat Chang Kham Wora Wihan**, with a magnificent 14th-century *chedi* resting on sculpted elephant heads. The *bot* and the *wihan* are guarded by *singhas* (mythological lions). Among Nan's other temples is **Wat Suan Tan**, in the northwest of town, with a 130-ft (40-m) *chedi*, crowned by a white *prang* – a rounded, Khmer-style tower that is very rarely seen in Northern Thailand. Housed in the *wihan* is a bronze Buddha image, Phra Chao Thong Thip. The image was made to the order of the king of Chiang Mai in 1449 after he conquered Nan. According to legend, the monarch gave the city's craftsmen just one week to make it.

Just southeast of Nan is the revered **Wat Phra That Chae Haeng**. Dating from 1355, the temple is set in a square compound on a hill top overlooking the Nan valley. Its gilded Lanna *chedi* is just over 180 ft (55 m) high. This, and the huge *nagas* (serpents) flanking the staircase, can be seen from several miles around. The multilayered roof of the *wihan* is Lao In style.

🏛 Nan National Museum
Hwy 101. **Open** 9am–4pm Wed–Sun. 🖼

"Black" elephant tusk in Nan National Museum

Environs

Despite its many attractions, the mountainous province of Nan was once one of the most remote and inaccessible areas in Thailand. Better roads have now greatly improved connections to the province, making it one of the country's fastest-growing tourist destinations.

To the north of Nan is **Tham Pha Tup Forest Reserve**, a limestone cave complex set in a forested area. There are some 17 caves here, which are impressive for their stalactites and stalagmites. About half of them can be reached by marked trails.

Another natural feature of the region is **Sao Din**, literally "earth pillars," which are located off Highway 1026, about 19 miles (30 km) to the south of Nan. These sculpted clay columns, created by erosion, stick out of depressions in the ground. The pillars have the same eerie appearance as those at Phea Muang Phi in Phrae province *(see p263)* and have been used as a backdrop for many Thai films.

Traditional Boat Races in Nan

Each year, at the end of October, boat races take place on the river at Nan. The races are the highlight of the two-week Nan Provincial Fair, which attracts visitors from all over Thailand. The tradition of the boat races is thought to have begun toward the end of the 19th century and marks the start of the Krathin season *(see p54)*, when the city's menfolk present new robes to the local monks. The boats, some 98 ft (30 m) in length, can hold up to 50 rowers. Each one is carved from a single log and decorated to look like a dragon-serpent or *naga (see p232)*. The sides are brightly painted with traditional motifs.

Boats competing during annual races on the Nan River

Wat Phumin
วัดภูมินทร์

One of the most beautiful temples in northern Thailand, Wat Phumin was founded in 1596 by the ruler of Nan. The *wat* was renovated in the mid-19th century and again in 1991 and is notable for its cross-shaped design, elaborate coffered ceiling, and carved doors and pillars. The highlight, however, is undoubtedly its murals. These were originally thought to have been painted by Thai Lue *(see p258)* artists during the 19th-century renovation. But the apparent depiction of French troops, unknown in the area before the French annexation of part of Nan province in 1893, suggests a date in the mid-1890s. Three main themes can be picked out from the murals: the life of the Buddha, the *jataka (see p34)* tale of his incarnation as Khatta Kumara, and scenes depicting everyday life in Nan.

Rich Official
This lavishly dressed man, smoking a pipe, may depict the ruler of Nan who commissioned the murals.

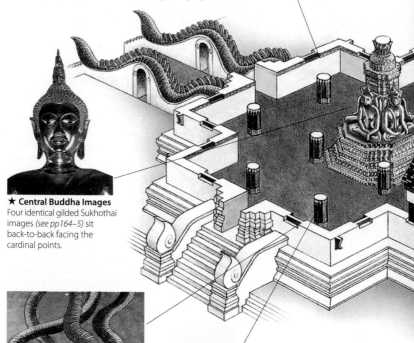

★ **Central Buddha Images**
Four identical gilded Sukhothai images *(see pp164–5)* sit back-to-back facing the cardinal points.

Decorative Pillars
These red, black, and gold pillars are all carved with the same floral pattern. The bases of some pillars feature elephant motifs while others depict *devas* (Hindu gods).

Descending Serpents
This mural shows poisonous snakes sent by angry gods to punish an unruly king in the story of Khatta Kumara.

KEY

① *Nagas* (serpents) flank the steps at the front and back of the building.

Courting Couple
This mural gives an insight into clothing worn in 19th-century Nan. The tattooed man with a Thai Lue hairstyle may be one of the artists.

VISITORS' CHECKLIST

Practical Information
Phumin village, south bank of Nan River, Phakong Rd, center of Nan town. **Open** 8:30am–4:30pm daily.

★ Story of the Buddha Mural
The mural on the northern wall above the main door is particularly outstanding. Located at the very top of the image is the Buddha, and on a lower plane are his disciples. In the bottom half, Khatta Kumara and his friends are depicted on their way to a city with a palace, which Khatta later rebuilds after its destruction by snakes and birds.

①

Main entrance

Boy, Mother, and Elephant's Footprint
In this scene, Khatta Kumara is with his mother. She bore him after drinking the god Indra's urine from an elephant's footprint. Indra had descended to earth in the form of an elephant.

The Arrival of Europeans in Nan
This scene shows characters wearing European clothes. The figures in berets may be French, and the mural could be a direct reference to the takeover of part of Nan province by the French in 1893.

⑱ Street-by-Street: Phrae

แพร่

With its distinctive charm and identity, Phrae is appealing yet surprisingly seldom visited. The town was built beside the Yom River in the 12th century and remained an independent city state until it came under Ayutthayan control. In the 18th century, the town was taken by Myanmar (Burma) and later became a base for Myanmar and Lao teak loggers. Myanmar influence is obvious in Phrae's temples, which also have Lanna features. The town prospers on agricultural produce from the surrounding fertile valley, as shown by the growing commercial district outside the walled town. Remains of the old city walls and moat can be seen in the northeast of town.

Buddhist shrine inside the museum at Wat Luang

★ Wat Luang
Phrae's oldest temple (12th century) is entered through a section of old city wall. The octagonal Lanna *chedi* is notable for its elephant caryatids. Swords, jewelry, and photographs are displayed in the museum.

Wat Phra Non, a 17th-century Lao temple, houses a reclining Buddha image.

To Wat Phra Non

To Ban Prathup Chai

KHAMLUE

KHAMLUE

Wat Phra Ruang
Several architectural styles are blended at this temple. The cruciform *bot* is more characteristic of temples in nearby Nan. The Lao *wihan* has delicately carved doors, shown here. The *chedi* is Lanna.

LUKMUANG

KHUMDERM

PHRA RUANG

NARIRUT

Wat Phra Bat
The Lao *bot* of Wat Phra Bat dates from the 18th century, while the *wihan*, housing a revered Buddha image, is modern. Part of a Buddhist university, the temple is often bustling with monks.

VISITORS' CHECKLIST

Practical Information
Phrae province. 🗺 85,000.
ℹ TAT, Chiang Rai (0-5371-7433).
📅 daily. 🎎 Phra That Chaw Hae
(Mar); Songkran (Apr).

Transport
✈ 1 mile (2 km) SE of Phrae.
🚌 off Yantarakitkosok Rd.

Wat Si Chum

The plain interiors of the *bot*
and *wihan* contrast with the
ornate Buddha images inside.
Unfortunately, the *chedi* is in a
state of ruin.

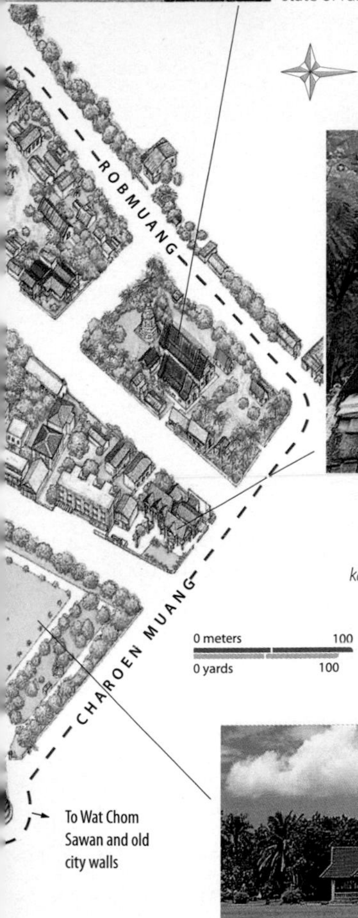

★ **Teak Houses**
These teak houses
are typical of Phrae. Their
roofs are decorated with
kalae, a feature of Northern
Thai houses (see p40).

To Wat Chom
Sawan and old
city walls

Key
— Suggested route

| 0 meters | 100 |
| 0 yards | 100 |

Public Park
This park is ideal for relaxing after
visiting Phrae's sights. Unusually for
Thai towns, it is located in the center.

Environs

Wat Chom Sawan, in the
northeast of Phrae, is an early
20th-century Shan temple with
a distinctive, copper-crowned
Myanmar *chedi*.

To the west of Phrae is **Ban
Prathup Chai**, one of Thailand's
largest teak houses, with its
ornate pillars. The structure was
assembled in the mid-1980s;
even though teak logging was
not banned then (see p253),
spare logs from nine other
houses were used to build it.

To the southeast is **Wat Phra
That Chaw Hae**, thought to date
from the 12th–13th centuries.
Staircases flanked by *nagas* and
stone lions lead through a teak
forest up to the hilltop *wat*.
The temple is named after the
satinlike cloth (*chaw hae*) that
worshipers wrap around the
110-ft (33-m) gilded *chedi*. Inside
is the revered Phra Chao Than
Chai, believed to grant wishes.

Phea Muang Phi is a popular
excursion from Phrae. This surreal
landscape (*muang phi* means
"ghost city") consists of pillars of
soil and rock that rise from the
ground like mushrooms. Like Sao
Din in Nan province (see p259),
they are the result of the erosion
of clay beneath a hard crust.

🏛 **Ban Prathup Chai**
1,100 yards (1,000 m) W of Phrae.
Open daily. 📷

🛕 **Wat Phra That Chaw Hae**
5 miles (8 km) SE of Phrae, Phrae
province. 🚌 Phrae, then *songthaew*.
Open daily. 📷

🏞 **Phae Muang Phi**
Off Hwy 101, 11 miles (18 km) NE of
Phrae, Phrae province. 🚌 Phrae, then
songthaew.

⓭ Sirikit Reservoir
เขื่อนสิริกิติ์

28 miles (45 km) SE of Phrae, Uttaradit
province. 🚌 Nan or Uttaradit, then
songthaew.

Named after Queen Sirikit and
set amid splendid scenery, this
reservoir and dam were created
in the mid-1970s on the Nan
River, a tributary of the Chao
Phraya. Built to control flooding,
the dam also provides electricity
and water to farmers in the area.

NORTHEAST
THAILAND

Introducing Northeast Thailand

The Khorat Plateau, which takes up most of the Northeast, is mostly barren scrubland; its main focus is the city of Khorat (Nakhon Ratchasima). To the north and east of this region and separating it from neighboring Laos is the Mekong River Valley. Along the Thai side of the river lie small villages, some with small docks and beaches. Known locally as Isan, the Northeast has an extremely rich history. One of the first areas in the world where rice was cultivated, silk woven, and bronze produced, it fell under Khmer rule in the 9th–13th centuries. Isan's proximity to Laos and Cambodia and its largely infertile land mean that it is seen by many Thais as a poor relation. Most of its people are ethnically Lao and are known for their friendly openness.

Nong Khai

Sangkhom

Chiang Khan

Nong
Kha

Loei

Phu Rua

Udon Thani

Nong Hin

Nong
Bualamphu

Si Buan
Ruang

Lom Sak

Khon San

Khon
Kaen

Phetchabun

KHORAT PLATEAU
(see pp272–285)

Na Chan

Ban

Chaiyaphum

Bua Yai

Nong Bua
Khok

Dan Khun
Thot

Khorat

Pak Thong Chai

Ta Phraya

Phu Kradung National Park *(see pp290–91),* with a steep-sided plateau at its center, is home to fabulous animal and plant life.

Prasat Hin Phimai *(see pp280–81),* dating from the 11th–12th centuries, is one of the most extensively restored Khmer temple complexes in Thailand.

Prasat Hin Khao Phnom Rung
(see pp284–5), covering a huge area, is one of Thailand's finest examples of Khmer architecture.

◄ Prasat Hin Phimai, Khorat

Nong Khai *(see pp296–7)* is a developed commercial town that has retained a peaceful riverside atmosphere.

ung Kan

Ban Mai

Phon Charoen

MEKONG RIVER VALLEY
(see pp286–307)

Nakhon Phanom

Wang Ta Mua

Sakhon Nakhon

That Phanom

Som Det

Mukdahan

Loeng Nok Tha

Khemmarat

Roi Et

Selaphum

Amnat Charoen

Yasothon

Suwannaphum

Meuang Chamrap

Ubon Ratchathani

Satuk

Na Phiman

Si Sa Ket

Ram

Sikhoraphum

Surin

Kantharalak

rasat

Sangkha

Wat Phra That Phanom *(see p301)* was, according to legend, built shortly after the death of the Buddha. It is the Northeast's most sacred shrine.

0 kilometers   50
0 miles   25

Prasat Khao Phra Wihan *(see p306)* enjoys a stunning location on a mountain spur on the border between Thailand and Cambodia.

The Lost Khmer Temples

When Europeans first saw mysterious ruins in the forests far east of Ayutthaya, they thought they had found an ancient Chinese, or even Greek, civilization. It was not until the 19th century that the history of the Khmers, who ruled an area covering much of modern Cambodia and Northeast Thailand from the 9th to 14th centuries, began to be uncovered. The Khmers are now acknowledged to have been among the world's greatest architects. Many sites can be visited in Thailand today; in Cambodia, restoration of Angkor, the old capital, is ongoing.

The Khmer Empire
• Major Khmer sites

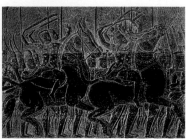

Bas-reliefs of battles adorning the walls of many Khmer sites not only display the creative and technical abilities of the Khmer craftsmen, but have also helped scholars to write Khmer history. The Khmers' main adversaries were the Thais: in 1444 Ayutthaya finally took Angkor, and the Khmer Empire was vanquished.

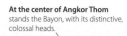

At the center of Angkor Thom stands the Bayon, with its distinctive, colossal heads.

Restoration of the most important of Thailand's 300-odd Khmer monuments was begun in 1925. The Thai Fine Arts Department has overseen work at temple complexes such as Phimai *(see pp280–81)* in the late 20th century.

Romance of the Great Temples

Khmer temple complexes were built to symbolize kingship and the universe and are awesome in their scale and beauty. The Thais borrowed elements of Khmer temple design (see p38), and a scale model, made in 1922, of Angkor Wat, the largest complex, stands at Bangkok's Wat Phra Kaeo (see pp84–7). European views of romantic ruins abound, as exemplified by engravings such as this, made in 1866–8. A reconstruction of Angkor Wat was also the centerpiece of the 1931 Colonial Exposition in Paris.

A *shivalinga* was the main object of worship at the center of many Khmer temples. It is a phallus representing the creative force of the Hindu god Shiva.

The Rediscovery of Angkor

In about 1550 a Cambodian king is said to have come upon the ruins of Angkor while hunting for elephants. He cleared part of the site where his ancestors had once held court. Before long, news filtered to Europe from Portuguese and Spanish missionaries of a vast hidden city. But few ventured into the jungle, and the artistic feats of the Khmers were to remain largely unknown for another 300 years. Interest in the ruins increased when France colonized Indochina. Henri Mouhot (1826–61) earned the dubious posthumous status of "discoverer" of Angkor on publication of his engravings and drawings of the site that he made in 1860. From his work France decided to finance proper exploration. Louis Delaporte, George Cœdès, Jean Boisselier, and Henri Parmentier were among others who spent much of their lives piecing together Khmer history.

The French scholar Parmentier in 1923

Scenes from the Ramayana, an ancient Indian epic, are found at many Khmer temples, and probably directly inspired the Thai version, the Ramakien *(see pp44–5)*.

The 19th-century artists were particularly inspired by imagery of the jungle encroaching upon the ruins.

The scale of the humans shown in the engraving is fairly accurate. The larger statues in the foreground are imaginary.

Marc Riboud, a photographer for the renowned Magnum agency, visited Angkor in the 1960s and 1980s. He took some of the most evocative and widely published pictures of Angkor before and after the war in Cambodia.

The gently smiling faces of the Buddha at the Bayon of Angkor Thom have found their way onto posters, book covers, and, here, the score of a 1921 foxtrot.

Silk Production

Finds at the prehistoric site of Ban Chiang *(see pp58–9)* indicate that silk production in Northeast Thailand may predate even that of China, where sericulture probably originated in about 2700 BC. In Thailand, silk production was beginning to die out until an American, Jim Thompson *(see pp124–5)*, revived it in the 1940s. Today, all manner of silk products are available, with silk shirts and sarongs popular with visitors. The silk industry is centered mostly in the Northeast, due to the suitability of soil in these areas for growing mulberry bushes, the main diet of the silkworm. Silk production in these areas is still based on traditional methods and comprises the stages outlined here.

2 In three to four weeks the eggs grow into silkworms. These are placed on large, woven bamboo trays and, protected from mice, ants, flies, and bright light, feed on mulberry leaves. In the larval stage, while they are still growing, each silkworm sheds its skin four times and increases its weight 10,000-fold.

Silkworm moth
(Bombyx mori)

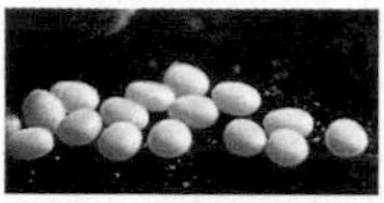

1 Female silkworm moths spend their short life of about four days mating and laying eggs.

SILKWORMS

Reeling

5 The individual silk threads are lifted out of the pot using a special forked bamboo pole. They are twisted together to form a single, larger thread, which is then reeled onto a spool.

6 Silk skeins are inspected and graded. The outer layer of cocoon gives the coarsest yarn and is used for furnishings. The best silk, from the middle and inner layers, is used for weaving.

Dyeing

7 The raw silk is soaked in soapy water to remove the sericin, a gumlike coating, leaving it softer and lighter.

8 The yarn is then dyed. The strength of the dye depends on the number of times the yarn is dipped in the solution. Tie-dyed yarn *(ikat)* is achieved by wrapping segments of yarn with dye-resistant strings, according to the design required. The thread is then dried and the strings removed, revealing the pattern.

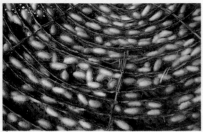

3 At the end of the 30-day growth cycle, the fully developed silkworms are ready to spin a cocoon. They are moved to a large, circular, bamboo tray with a frame that leaves them just enough space to attach their cocoons. Silkworms build their cocoons from a single white or yellow fiber secreted from the mouth at a rate of 4.5 in (12 cm) per minute.

Cocoons, which are spun in about 36 hours

4 Cocoons have to be reeled within ten days or the moths will begin to hatch and damage the silk. The cocoons are placed in a pot of water just below boiling point. This kills them and releases the silk threads.

COCOONS

Plying	Weaving

9 Up to six threads can be plied together to form a single thread, the weft.

10 The silk is woven on upright looms with foot treadles. The coarse weft is woven into fine, even warps, which even in traditional workshops are often prefabricated and imported from Japan, Korea, and Europe – the production of the warp is a time consuming business by any method. The combination of fine and coarse threads gives the fabric its unique luster.

Tools for Silk Weaving

During the silk-weaving process, the fibers must be kept clean and free from obstructions that could tangle and damage them. Each implement has a unique and vital function: delicate brushes with ornamental wooden handles help to keep the silk free from particles of dust. Carved wooden pulleys, which are attached to traditional looms, insure that the fibers run smoothly while they are being woven.

Decorative silk brushes

Traditional pulley

11 The distinctive, brightly colored silk is then made into umbrellas, scarves, ties, shirts, and sarongs, and sold around Thailand (see p441).

KHORAT PLATEAU

Though one of the most infertile areas of Thailand, and home to the nation's poorest people, the Khorat Plateau is rich in culture and historic sites from the days when the Khmer Empire held sway over the region. The people are welcoming, the cuisine fiery hot, often served with glutinous rice and raw vegetables, and the silk and cotton handicrafts are exquisite.

The vast, sandstone Khorat Plateau dominates the Northeast, a region that the Thais call Isan. The plateau, which is about 660 ft (200 m) above sea level, takes up almost a third of Thailand's land mass and is home to about a third of the population. The uneven rainfall of the region causes both floods and droughts and permits the cultivation of only one rice crop per year. As a result there is much rural poverty.

Although few tourists visit the region, there is much of historical interest to be discovered. To the north, at Ban Chiang, lies a site that has revolutionized archaeologists' views of prehistoric Southeast Asia. The Northeast is now thought to be one of the first areas in the world where rice growing, bronze making, and silk weaving were pioneered. Silk production has flourished again since the mid-20th century, and visitors are drawn to modern-day weaving villages where a wide range of silk and cotton goods are sold.

In the 9th century AD, the Khorat Plateau came under Cambodian control, which was to endure until the end of the 13th century. It was during this period that the region's splendid Khmer temples were built. The magnificent stone temples at Phnom Rung and Phimai, which once stood on a road linking the plateau with the Khmer capital of Angkor, have now been evocatively restored.

Bung Phlan Chai, a scenic lake in the center of Roi Et town

◄ Statue in the central sanctuary at Prasat Hin Khao Phnom Rung

Exploring the Khorat Plateau

The Khorat Plateau occupies most of Northeast Thailand. It is a broad stretch of barren, arid hills some 985 ft (300 m) above sea level, separated from the Central Plains to the west by the Phetchabun mountain range. Much of the region is characterized by red earth and scrub forest. Khorat city, regarded as the gateway to the Northeast, is the center of the region's transportation network. Other towns and sights of interest in the region can be reached by road from here, though distances are considerable. North of Khorat lie the towns of Khon Kaen and Roi Et; farther north still, the prehistoric site of Ban Chiang. East of Khorat the main attractions are the Khmer temples of Phimai and Phnom Rung. Nearby are Ta Klang and Surin, which are linked to the elephant trade.

Sights at a Glance

1. Udon Thani
2. Ban Chiang
3. Khon Kaen
4. Roi Et
5. Yasothon
6. *Prasat Hin Phimai (see pp280–81)*
7. Khorat
8. Dan Kwian
9. Prasat Ta Muen and Prasat Ta Muen Tot
10. Prasat Hin Muang Tam
11. *Prasat Hin Khao Phnom Rung (see pp284–5)*
12. Surin
13. Ban Ta Klang

The exquisitely restored Prasat Hin Phimai

For hotels and restaurants see pp402–11 and pp418–33

Bun Bang Fai (Rocket Festival), celebrated each year at Yasothon

Getting Around

The Khorat Plateau is well served by air-conditioned buses, which operate between Bangkok's Northern Bus Terminal (Morchit) and most towns and cities in the region. Local bus services connect small towns and villages. Journey times tend to be long because of distances and poor quality of roads. The rail route from Bangkok divides into two main sections at Khorat: it runs east toward Ubon Ratchathani in the Mekong River Valley *(see pp306–7)* and northeast to Udon Thani and Nong Khai close to the border with Laos. Khorat, Khon Kaen, Buriram and Roi Et all have domestic airports. There are relatively few organized tours available to the region from Bangkok.

Key

━━━ Expressway

━━━ Major road

┉┉┉ Minor road

━━━ Scenic route

┄┄┄ Railway

▅▅▅ International border

Elephants at Surin, part of the mass roundup *(see p282)* that takes place annually

For keys to symbols *see back flap*

Nong Prachak Park, one of the more peaceful parts of Udon Thani

❶ Udon Thani
อุดรธานี

Udon Thani province. 🗺 170,000. ✈ 🚌 🚍 𝒊 TAT, Mukmontri Rd, Udon Thani (0-4232-5406). 🗓 daily.

During the Vietnam War Udon Thani changed from a sleepy provincial capital into a booming support center for a nearby American airbase. Since the withdrawal of the GIs in 1976, Udon has retained a little of that past vibrancy, together with some rather nondescript streets, lined with Western-style coffee shops, nightclubs, and massage parlors. It has continued to grow as an industrial and commercial center within the region. The most attractive part of town is **Nong Prachak Park**, where there are some open-air restaurants. The town makes a good base for travelers wanting to visit nearby Ban Chiang.

❷ Ban Chiang
บ้านเชียง

Udon Thani province. 🗺 4,680. 🚍 from Udon Thani. 𝒊 TAT, Udon Thani (0-4232-5406). 🗓 daily.

The principal attraction for visitors to Ban Chiang is its archaeological site (see pp58–9). It was discovered by accident in 1966 by an American

sociologist who tripped over some remains. The finds provided archaeological evidence that northeast Thailand may have been one of the world's earliest centers of bronze production. Spearheads from the site are thought to date from around 3600 BC, while ceramics, dating from between 3000 BC and AD 500, testify to a high degree of technical and artistic skill.

Today, a collection of these artifacts is on display, together with ornaments such as bangles and rings, at the **Ban Chiang National Museum**.

Ban Chiang pot, c.2000 BC

A short walk from the museum, 1 mile (2 km) through dusty streets lined with quaint wooden shop-houses, two covered excavation sites lie in the grounds of **Wat Pho Si Nai**.

Here the main exhibits are graves containing skeletal remains and ceramics used for symbolic purposes in burial. Bodies were wrapped in perishable material and laid on their backs. Pots were then arranged along the edge of the grave and over the bodies themselves. Other grave goods found at the burial site include pig skulls and mandibles, jewelry, tools, weapons, and river pebbles.

Research associated with the discoveries at Wat Pho Si Nai indicates that the inhabitants of Ban Chiang were a strong, long-legged people with wide foreheads and prominent cheekbones with an average life expectancy of 31 years. The main causes of death were diseases such as malaria. As with other early peoples of Southeast Asia, the exact ethnic origins of the population of Ban Chiang remain a mystery.

🏛 **Ban Chiang National Museum**
On edge of Ban Chiang. **Tel** 0-4220-8340. **Open** 9am–4pm Wed–Sun. 🎫

❸ Khon Kaen
ขอนแก่น

Khon Kaen province. 🗺 240,000. ✈ 🚌 🚍 𝒊 TAT, 15/5 Prachasamoson Rd, Khon Kaen (0-4322-7714/5). 🗓 daily. 🎊 Silk Festival (10 days Nov/Dec). 🌐 **khonkaen.com**

Once the quiet capital of one of the poorest provinces in the northeast of Thailand, this place

Khon Kaen National Museum, home to Ban Chiang and Dvaravati relics

For hotels and restaurants see pp402–11 and pp418–33

has changed into a bustling town. Located at the heart of the region, it has consequently been a focus of regional development projects – the town now boasts the largest university in the northeast, in addition to its own television studios. There are a number of modern hotels and shopping complexes, all of which nestle rather incongruously among the town's more traditional streets and market places.

Places of interest to tourists include **Khaen Nakhon Lake**, an artifical lake beside which are some restaurants. **Khon Kaen National Museum** has a collection of Ban Chiang artifacts and a number of Dvaravati *(see pp60–61)* stelae carved with excerpts from the life of the Buddha, as well as examples of local folk art.

❹ Roi Et
ร้อยเอ็ด

Roi Et province. ⛰ 119,000. ✈ 🚌
ℹ TAT, Khon Kaen (0-4322-7714/5).
🏠 daily.

Founded in 1782, Roi Et literally means "one hundred and one," a name that is thought to be an exaggeration of 11, the number of vassal states over which the town once ruled. Today it is a steadily growing provincial capital. The modern skyline is dominated by an immense brown and ocher image of the Lord Buddha, the Phraphuttha-rattana-mongkol-maha-mani, which is situated within the grounds of **Wat Buraphaphi-ram**. Measuring 225 ft (68 m) from its base to the tip of its flame finial, this giant standing Buddha is reputed to be one of

The Phraphuttha-rattana-mongkol-maha-mani image at Roi Et

the tallest in the world. The climb up the statue offers an impressive view of the town and surrounding area. Silk and cotton are both good buys in Roi Et and can be found along Phadung Phanit Road.

The Khaen

Originating in Laos, and played widely in Northeast Thailand, the *khaen* is a large, free-reed panpipe and is constructed primarily of bamboo. Although the length and pitch of the *khaen* are not standardized, the number of pipes and the tuning are. Each *khaen* is pitched according either to the personal preference of the player, or to the range of the singer it accompanies, and has a range of two octaves – this gives a total of 15 pitches. Whereas most arts in Thailand are formally taught, *khaen* players tend to learn their skills by listening to relatives and neighbors in the village. There is no written music for the *khaen*, its repertoire having been passed down through oral transmission. It was traditionally played by young men on their way to woo their sweethearts or by blind beggars in the hope of receiving a few coins for their performances. Women never play the *khaen*.

Craftsmen assemble the *khaen* from bamboo reeds dried in the sun. Wax from the *khisut*, an insect, is used to glue the reeds together and attach them to the carved windchest.

The *khaen* consists varying lengths of bamboo, each producing a different pitch.

Holes in the reeds are fingered to create different levels of pitch.

Phin (a type of guitar)

Ponglang (a type of xylophone)

Khaen

Notes are made by blowing into this carved windchest.

Orchestra with *khaen*, *phin*, and *ponglang* players

Bun Bang Fai or "Rocket" Festival held each year at Yasothon

❺ Yasothon
ยโสธร

Yasothon province. 🏔 108,000. 🚌 ℹ️ TAT, Ubon Ratchathani (0-4524-3770). 🛗 daily. 🎊 Bun Bang Fai (Rocket) Festival (May).

Like many provincial towns across Thailand, Yasothon has only a few tourist sights. There are one or two temples that are worth visiting, in particular **Wat Thung Sawang** and **Wat Mahathat Yasothon**. Situated in the center of the town, the latter is home to the Phra That Phra Anon *chedi*, thought to have been built in the 7th century to house the relics of Phra Anon, the closest disciple of the Buddha.

Yasothon is best known, however, as the principal venue for the Bun Bang Fai or "Rocket" Festival *(see pp50–51)*. As a result of harsh weather in Northeast Thailand, this festival, the principal function of which is to appease a Hindu rain god, is one of great symbolic importance. Local people invest enormous sums of money in the construction of huge bamboo rockets. The gunpowder that goes into the rockets is pounded by young girls in the temple grounds, and, perhaps surprisingly, it is Buddhist monks who possess the expertise of building and firing the rockets. The rockets are paraded on floats through

the streets, surrounded by revelers, then shot into the clouds to "fertilize" them. The festival's sexual overtones come out in bawdy humor and flirtation, not encouraged at other times. The owners of those rockets that fail to go off are ritually coated in mud.

❻ Prasat Hin Phimai
ปราสาทหินพิมาย

See pp280–81.

❼ Khorat
โคราช

Khorat province. 🏔 207,000. ✈️ 🚆 🚌 ℹ️ TAT, 2102–4 Mittraphap Rd, Khorat (0-4421-3666). 🛗 daily. 🎊 Thao Suranari Festival (late Mar/early Apr); Phimai Boat Racing (Oct/Nov).

In former times, Khorat, or Nakhon Ratchasima, was two separate towns, Khorakhapura and Sema; they were joined during the reign of King Narai (1656–88). Today Khorat is a rapidly expanding business center. Its development stems from playing host to a nearby US airbase during the Vietnam War. At first sight Khorat

Khorat City Center

① Wat Suthachinda
② National Museum
③ Thao Suranari Monument
④ Night Market
⑤ Wat Phra Narai Maharat
⑥ Wat Sala Loi

For keys to symbols *see back flap*

Ornate pediment and façade of the *bot* at Wat Phra Narai Maharat

appears to the visitor as a sprawl of confusing roads and heavy traffic. The city center has little of interest save for the **Night Market** that sells good-value street foods and local handicrafts.

At the city's western gate, Pratu Chumphon, is the **Thao Suranari Monument**, built in memory of Khunying Mo, a woman who successfully defended Khorat against an attack by an invading Lao army in 1826. While her husband, the deputy governor of Khorat, was away on business in Bangkok, Prince Anuwong of Vientiane (*see pp298–9*) seized the city. Khunying Mo and her fellow captives allegedly served the Lao army with liquor and were then able to kill them in their drunken stupor with whatever weapons were at hand. The Lao invasion was therefore held at bay until help arrived. Khunying Mo was given the title of Thao Suranari or "brave lady" from which the monument, built in 1934, derives its name. It shows Khunying Mo standing, hand on hip, on a tall pedestal. The base of the statue is adorned with garlands and ornamental offerings made by local people in their respect for her; a week-long festival, including folk

Thao Suranari
Monument

performances of dancing, theater, and song is also held in her honor each year.

Located in the grounds of **Wat Suthachinda** is Khorat's **Maha Weerawong National Museum**. The artifacts on display here range from skeletal remains of human corpses, Dvaravati and Ayutthaya Buddha images, ceramics, and wood carvings, and were donated to Prince Maha Weerawong, from whom the museum derives its name.

Though quite a modern city, Khorat has a number of other Buddhist temples. In the *wihan* of **Wat Phra Narai Maharat** is a sandstone image of the Hindu god Vishnu, originally found at Khmer ruins near to the city.

One of the most strikingly innovative, modern Buddhist temples in northeast Thailand is **Wat Sala Loi**, or the "temple of the floating pavilion," on the banks of the Lam Takhong River. Designed in the form of a Chinese junk, the main *wihan* of this *wat* has won architectural awards. It was constructed entirely from local materials, including distinctive earthenware tiles made only at the nearby village of Dan Kwian. The original site on which Wat Sala Loi now stands dates back to the time of Khunying Mo, and her ashes are still buried here,

a fitting resting place for the heroine without whom present-day Khorat would possibly not exist.

Just outside Khorat, **Wat Khao Chan Ngam**, is the site of prehistoric finds, while at **Wat Thep Phitak Punnaram**, a large white Buddha overlooks the road.

🏛 **Maha Weerawong National Museum**
Ratchadamnoen Rd. **Open** 9am–4pm Wed–Sun. **Closed** public hols.

❽ Dan Kwian
ด่านเกวียน

Khorat province. 🚗 2,300.
ℹ TAT, Khorat (0-4421-3666).

Southeast of Khorat is Dan Kwian, first inhabited in the mid 18th century by the Mon people traveling east from the Burmese border. Since then it has become famous for its rust-colored pottery, derived from the high iron content of the local clay.

Today Dan Kwian is essentially a collection of ceramics factories, many of which can export large items for tourists. Shops selling the local pottery line the highway at the entrance point to the village. Items for sale include jewelry, elaborately decorated vases, often in the form of upstanding fish, chicken-shaped plant pots, leaf-shaped wind chimes, and traditional water jars.

Lucky Khorat Cats

Silver-colored Khorat cats are named after the Khorat Plateau. They are one of the most prized breeds in Thailand. A pair of Khorat cats is sometimes given as a wedding present in the Northeast, as they are believed to bring good fortune to their owners. They are mentioned in a book of cat poems written during the Ayutthaya period. Khorat cats were first introduced to the West in 1896, but did not gain the same popularity as their cream-colored relatives, who are still known as the original Siamese cats.

Thai stamp bearing a picture of a Khorat cat

❻ Prasat Hin Phimai

ปราสาทหินพิมาย

In the small town of Phimai, on the banks of the Mun River, lies one of Thailand's most extensively restored Khmer temple complexes. There is no definitive date for the construction of this temple, but the central sanctuary is likely to have been completed during the reign of Suryavarman I (1001–49). Prasat Hin Phimai lies on what was once a direct route to the Khmer capital at Angkor and, unusually, is oriented in a southeasterly direction to face that city. Originally a Brahmanic shrine dedicated to Shiva, Prasat Hin Phimai was rededicated as a Mahayana Buddhist temple at the end of the 12th century. Its famous lintels and pediments depict scenes from the Ramayana *(see pp44–5)* and, unique among Khmer temples, Buddhist themes. Restoration of the site was carried out by the Fine Arts Department in 1964–9.

Front View of Central Sanctuary
The white sandstone edifice is topped with a rounded *prang*, the style of which may have influenced the builders of Angkor Wat *(see pp268–9)*.

Naga Bridge
This symbolic bridge leads to the main entrance of the temple complex. The line of *nagas* that flank either side of the bridge are mythical guardian spirits.

Central Sanctuary

The word prasat, *which is used to refer to the central sanctuary, also describes the temple complex as a whole.*

KEY

① *Mandapa* (hallway of main entrance)

② **Rama and Lakshman** appear on the lintel over the western entrance to the *mandapa*. They have been tied up with a *naga*. The monkeys below despair, while above them a *garuda* (a mythical creature, half-bird, half-human) and more monkeys come to the rescue.

③ **Rama and his monkeys**, building the causeway to Lanka – a scene from the Ramayana *(see pp44–5)* – can be seen on the western pediment of the *prang*.

④ *Prang* (tower)

⑤ **The God of Justice**, on the pediment of the eastern porch, judges a feud between Rama and Tosakan *(see p45)*, good and evil.

⑥ **Trilokayavijaya**, the most important Mahayana Bodhisattva (Enlightened being), can be seen on the interior lintel of the eastern porch.

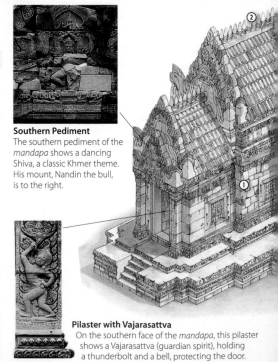

Southern Pediment
The southern pediment of the *mandapa* shows a dancing Shiva, a classic Khmer theme. His mount, Nandin the bull, is to the right.

Pilaster with Vajarasattva
On the southern face of the *mandapa*, this pilaster shows a Vajarasattva (guardian spirit), holding a thunderbolt and a bell, protecting the door.

★ Northern Porch
The centerpiece of the northern porch is this lintel depicting a three-headed, six-armed Vajarasattva. Below him crouch a group of dancing girls.

VISITORS' CHECKLIST

Practical Information
Centre of Phimai town, Khorat province. **Tel** 0-4447-1568.
i TAT, Khorat (0-4421-3666).
Open 7am–6pm daily.
Phimai Temple Festival (Nov).

Transport
Khorat, then *songthaew*.

★ Northern Pediment
This scene from the Ramayana includes Vishnu holding a conch, a lotus, a discus, and a staff.

★ Buddha under *Naga*
Seated atop a coiled *naga* and protected by an umbrella formed by the beast's head, this reproduction of a 13th-century Buddha is in the Bayon (*see p268*) style.

Plan of Complex

1 Central sanctuary
2 Inner compound
3 Outer compound
4 Royal pavilions
5 *Gopuras* (entrance pavilions)
6 *Naga* (serpent) bridge

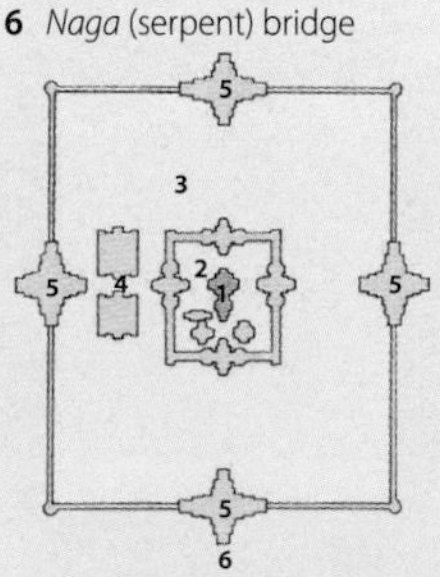

Novice Monks
Though Prasat Hin Phimai does not function as a working *wat*, it is sometimes the setting for Buddhist gatherings and celebrations.

❾ Prasat Ta Muen and Prasat Ta Muen Tot

ปราสาทตาเมือนและตาเมือนโต๊ด

Off Hwy 214, Surin province. **i** TAT, Khorat (0-4421-3666). 🚌 🚍 Surin, then preferably by organized tour. **Open** daily. ♿

In the district of Ta Muen, in Surin province, the remains of two Khmer *prasats* stand 330 ft (100 m) apart. One, Prasat Ta Muen, is a laterite chapel marking what would once have been a resting place on the long, arduous road between Angkor *(see pp268–9)* and Prasat Hin Phimai *(see pp280–81)*. The other, Prasat Ta Muen Tot, is more decayed and was originally a hospital to care for travelers along this route. Both were built by King Jayavarman VII (1181–1220).

Although both *prasats* are today largely in ruins, with their brickwork gripped and overrun by the roots of towering fig trees, they are potent reminders of the powerful Khmer Empire that once held sway over the

Border police who act as armed escorts for visitors, Prasat Ta Muen

Khorat Plateau. Because of their location along the rather dangerous Cambodian border, Ta Muen and Ta Muen Tot are best seen as part of a tour organized by one of the guesthouses in Surin, and may require a military escort. They are not easily accessible to lone tourists and cannot be visited at times of disputes and skirmishes between the various rival factions in the area.

❿ Prasat Hin Muang Tam

ปราสาทหินเมืองตำ

Off Hwy 214, Buri Ram province. **i** TAT, Khorat (0-4421-3666). 🚌 from Surin to Prakhon Chai, then *songthaew*. **Open** daily. ♿

Muang Tam, or "the lower city," stands at the foot of Khao Phnom Rung, an extinct volcano on top of which lies the Khmer site of Prasat Hin Khao Phnom Rung *(see pp284–5)*. Muang Tam postdates the earliest stages of construction of the more elaborate and well-preserved temple above and was built in brick, sandstone, and laterite between the 10th and 12th centuries as a residence for the local governor. Today little remains, and at first sight Muang Tam appears to be nothing more than an exotic heap of decaying brickwork.

The remains of four brick sanctuaries surround what would once have been a central temple containing religious icons. The reliefs on the Muang Tam lintels indicate that these icons are most likely to have been Hindu. The lintel over the northern sanctuary shows Shiva and his consort Parvati riding on Nandin the bull, another lintel depicts the four-headed Hindu god of creation, Brahma.

All the sanctuaries in the complex face east and are encircled by galleries (now collapsed). On each side there

The Surin Elephant Roundup

In the third weekend of November, Surin is transformed by the annual Elephant Roundup. The first roundup was held here in 1960, though nowadays the elephants are used less as working animals than as performers. Some 150 to 200 elephants from local farms are led into Surin by their riders. Shows include demonstrations of how elephants are captured and raised. There are war parades celebrating King Naresuan of Ayutthaya (1590–1605), who fought the Burmese on elephant back. Soldiers, dressed in Ayutthayan costume, march toward an imagined enemy with spears and shields poised. There are also demonstrations of the elephants' strength and intelligence, as well as a chance for spectators to take rides.

Elephants and riders in traditional costume, Surin

are also four *gopuras* or entrance pavilions. Beyond these lie four L-shaped ponds, decorated at each corner with majestic, multiheaded *nagas*. The ponds themselves are filled with colorful lotus blossoms.

An immense reservoir or *baray*, 3,950 ft (1,200 m) wide and 1,650 ft (500 m) long, is situated to the north of Muang Tam, pointing to the fact that this site probably once supported a sizeable population.

⓫ Prasat Hin Khao Phnom Rung

ปราสาทหินเขาพนมรุ้ง

See pp284–5.

Boiling silkworm cocoons to release the silk threads, Surin

⓬ Surin

สุรินทร์

Surin province. 🚹 214,000. 🚌 🚐 🚹 TAT, Khorat (0-4421-3666). 🏠 daily. 🐘 Elephant Roundup (Nov).

Surin is famous for its silk, its elephants, and its first ruler, Phraya Surin Phakdi Si Narong Wang, from whom it derives its name. A modern statue in the town depicts the leader dressed to go into battle. A member of the Suay tribe, Phraya Surin became ruler of Surin in 1760 when, according to legend, he was instrumental in recapturing an escaped royal white elephant (*see p110*).

The process of silk production (*see pp270–71*) can be seen in the surrounding villages. There

are over 700 patterns used by silk weavers in Surin province. Rhomboid designs are especially popular.

During the 1970s, when the Khmer Rouge seized control of, and terrorized, neighboring Cambodia, thousands of Cambodian refugees crossed the Banthat mountains into Surin province and took up residence there, alongside already established Lao refugees, Thais, and Suay tribespeople. Although most immigrants have been repatriated, some remain.

Surin's main attraction is the annual Elephant Roundup, at the **Surin Sports Park**. At other times of the year, artifacts associated with elephant capture and training can be seen at the **Surin Museum**, including buffalo-hide ropes used by Suay tribesmen to catch wild elephants. There are also exhibits of the protective clothing and amulets, inscribed with magical incantations, worn during elephant hunts. The capture and training of elephants in Surin is traditionally a male preserve. In fact, women are strictly forbidden to touch the paraphernalia of the hunt, in case they destroy the magic needed to catch the elephants.

Statue of Phraya Surin

🏛 Surin Museum

Chitramboong Rd. **Tel** 0-4451-3358. **Open** 9am–4pm Wed–Sun.

Road sign advertising Ban Ta Klang, the Elephant Village

⓭ Ban Ta Klang

บ้านตากลาง

Surin province. 🚹 15,000. 🚹 TAT, Khorat (0-4421-3666). 🏠 daily. 🐘 Elephant Roundup (Nov).

The Suay tribes people make up the population of Ban Ta Klang, which is also known as the Elephant Village, a name that reflects the Suay people's skill in capturing and training wild elephants. The Suay are thought to have migrated to Thailand from Central Asia in the early 9th century and to have been the first people to make use of elephants for building, in particular for the construction of Khmer temples. Nowadays, Ban Ta Klang is the primary training ground for the Surin Elephant Roundup. Every October, approximately one month before the roundup in Surin itself, Suay tribesmen begin to practise their skills. In the days leading up to the roundup, the training becomes intense. To participate in the roundup, the riders must walk their elephants the 32 miles (50 km) or so south to the outskirts of Surin.

An elephant feeding while the trainer takes a break, Surin

⓫ Prasat Hin Khao Phnom Rung

ปราสาทหินเขาพนมรุ้ง

Crowning the extinct volcano of Khao Phnom Rung is the splendid Khmer temple complex Prasat Hin Khao Phnom Rung. A Hindu temple, it was built here to symbolize Shiva's abode on Mount Krailasa – hence the processional way leading to the central sanctuary, its stairways, and *naga* bridges extending in total for 655 ft (200 m). The temple's construction began early in the 10th century, and, like other Khmer sites, it lies on a route to Angkor Wat in Cambodia *(see pp268–9)*. Its buildings are aligned so that at Songkran *(see p52)*, the rising sun can be seen through all 15 doors of the western *gopura*.

Western Porch Pediment
This carving shows monkeys rescuing Sita in a chariot that is itself a model of the temple.

★ Central Sanctuary
The corncob-shaped *prang* of the central sanctuary is the cosmological summit of the processional way.

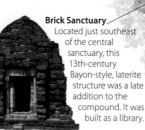

Brick Sanctuary
Located just southeast of the central sanctuary, this 13th-century Bayon-style, laterite structure was a late addition to the compound. It was built as a library.

KEY

① **Main temple compound**

② *Gopura*

③ *Naga* bridge

④ **The stairway** forms part of the processional way to the principal temple compound.

★ *Naga* Bridge
This *naga* bridge, which is located inside the main temple compound, links the east-facing entrance *gopura* to the central sanctuary. The body of the *naga* forms the bridge's balustrade.

**Pediment over Porch
of *Mandapa***
The carving on this
pediment represents
Shiva Nataraja, the dancing
Shiva, his 10 arms splayed
out in a dance of death
and destruction.

VISITORS' CHECKLIST

Practical Information
31 miles (50 km) S of Buriram,
off Hwy 24, Buriram province.
i TAT, Khorat (0-4421-3666).
Open 6am–6pm daily. 🚫 📷
📅 Phnom Rung Festival (Apr).

Transport
🚌 from Khorat or Surin to Ban
Ta Ko, then songthaew.

Nandin the Bull
This image of Nandin the bull,
the mythical mount of the
Hindu deity Shiva, is located
in the first, eastern chamber
of the central sanctuary.

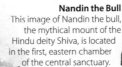

★ Ornamental Ponds
Located at the front of the entrance to the
main temple compound are four ponds. They
supposedly represent the four sacred rivers of
the Indian subcontinent. In the background,
a *naga* bridge leads into the complex.

Main entrance

★ Processional Way
This processional walkway was built to
symbolize the spiritual journey from
earth to Hindu heaven.

MEKONG RIVER VALLEY

Some 1,250 miles (2,000 km) from its source in the Tibetan Himalayas, having passed through China, Myanmar (Burma), northern Thailand, then Laos, the Mekong River reaches Chiang Khan in Northeast Thailand. From here the river forms the border with Laos until it flows into Cambodia. Although relatively few tourists visit this border country, it has many natural and cultural attractions.

The agricultural basin of the Mekong River Valley stands in contrast to the dusty, parched Khorat Plateau to the south and west and the rugged mountains on the Lao side of the river. The Mekong River Valley's relatively fertile land means fruit and vegetables can be produced on a marketable scale. Furthermore, due to its distance from Bangkok, the area has escaped widespread development and remains one of the most beautiful, unspoiled regions in the country.

Lively Nong Khai is the most important border town in the region and the access point to the Lao capital, Vientiane. The stretch of river to the west of here is dotted with numerous picturesque towns and villages with traditional teak houses. At Phu Phrabat Historical Park (near Ban Phu), a variety of mesmerizing sandstone rock formations can be seen.

Nearby are the extraordinary huge Buddhist and Hindu statues of Wat Khaek.

As the river winds its way east and then south, past Nakhon Phanom, it passes one of the most important Buddhist pilgrimage sites in Thailand, Wat Phra That Phanom. The temple supposedly dates from the death of the Lord Buddha in 543 BC.

Farther downriver is Pha Taem, a cliff face painted with huge prehistoric figures and unusual geometrical patterns. Not far away, at Khong Chiam, the Mun River flows into the Mekong, creating the phenomenon of the "two-colored river." From here the Mekong flows into Laos and then Cambodia. The Cambodian border with Thailand has been the scene of skirmishes between rival factions and, as a result, it is not always possible to reach one of the most magnificent of all Khmer monuments, Prasat Khao Phra Wihan.

View from Nakhon Phanom, looking over the Mekong River and into Laos

◄ Waterfall in Phu Kradung National Park

Exploring the Mekong River Valley

The mighty Mekong River forms a 465-mile (750-km) border between Northeast Thailand and Laos. The valley along which it flows is a relatively fertile area in an otherwise arid region of Thailand. It is possible to follow the length of the Mekong from Chiang Khan to Pha Taem by road. Some of the most attractive areas are west of Nong Khai, where visitors pass through sleepy towns and villages of pretty wooden houses. South of the northern stretch of the Mekong lie the Phu Rua, Phu Kradung, and Phu Hin Rong Kla national parks. Farther south is Ubon Rachathani, by far the largest city in the region.

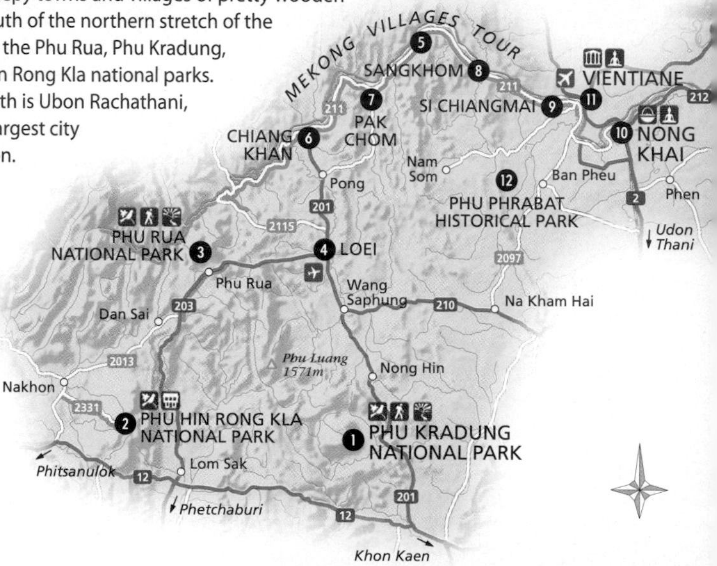

MEKONG VILLAGES TOUR

SANGKHOM ⑧
⑤
⑦ SI CHIANGMAI ⑨
VIENTIANE
⑪
PAK CHOM
CHIANG ⑥ KHAN
Nam Som
Ban Pheu
⑩ NONG KHAI
Pong
⑫
Phen
201
PHU PHRABAT HISTORICAL PARK
Udon Thani
2115
④ LOEI
2097
PHU RUA NATIONAL PARK ③
Phu Rua
Wang Saphung 210
Na Kham Hai
Dan Sai
203
Phu Luang 1571m
Nong Hin
2013
Nakhon
2331
② PHU HIN RONG KLA NATIONAL PARK
① PHU KRADUNG NATIONAL PARK
Phitsanulok 12
Lom Sak
Phetchaburi 12
201
Khon Kaen

Key

— Major road
---- Minor road
— Scenic route
~~~ Railway
■ International border
△ Summit

The colorful Phi Ta Khon Festival, held in Loei

Sights at a Glance

① Phu Kradung National Park pp290–91
② Phu Hin Rong Kla National Park
③ Phu Rua National Park
④ Loei
⑤ Mekong Villages Tour
⑥ Chiang Khan
⑦ Pak Chom
⑧ Sangkhom

⑨ Si Chiangmai
⑩ Nong Khai pp296–7
⑪ Vientiane pp298–9
⑬ Sakhon Nakhon
⑭ Nakhon Phanom
⑮ Renu Nakhon
⑱ Pha Taem
⑲ Khong Chiam
⑳ Chong Mek

㉑ Sirindhorn Dam
㉒ Prasat Khao Phra Wihan
㉓ Prasat Prang Ku
㉔ Ubon Ratchathani

Tour

⑫ Phu Phrabat Historical Park
⑯ Wat Phra That Phanom
⑰ Mukdahan

Getting Around

Nong Khai, Loei, Nakhon Phanom, and Ubon Ratchathani are the best bases from which to tour the area. Two train lines run through the region: a direct line, which divides at Khorat, connects Bangkok to Ubon Ratchathani and to Udon Thani. Travelers can pick up a connection from Udon Thani to Nong Khai. The best way to get around is by bus, rented car, or *songthaew*. Long-tail boats run on some sections of the Mekong River.

Lao-style *chedi*, Sakhon Nakhon

0 kilometers 50
0 miles 25

❶ Phu Kradung National Park

อุทยานแห่งชาติภูกระดึง

There are two legends connected to Phu Kradung, or "bell mountain": the first is that the sound of a bell, said to be that of the god Indra, once rang out from its peak; the second is that the mountain rings like a bell when struck with a staff. This steep-sided, flat-topped mountain is now a national park covering 135 sq miles (348 sq km), its 37-mile (60-km) plateau 4,450 ft (1,350 m) above sea level. This plateau has a climate cool enough for plants that cannot survive in other parts of Thailand; many animals also live in its thin pine forests and grasslands.

Asiatic Black Bear
This bear lives in forests all over Southeast Asia; it feeds on ants, insect larvae, nuts, and fruit.

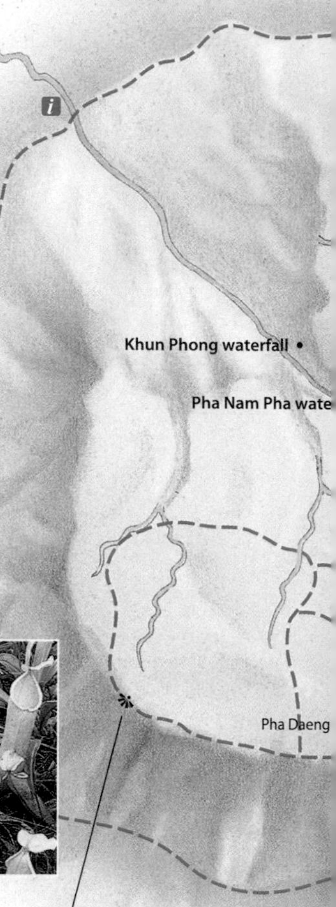

Khun Phong waterfall •

Pha Nam Pha wate

Waterfalls
Waterfalls are dotted all over Phu Kradung. They are most impressive in October (the end of the rainy season).

Pha Daeng

Pitcher Plants
Common in Phu Kradung, carnivorous pitcher plants gather nutrients lacking in the local acidic soil by "eating" insects.

Pha Lom Sak
This unusually shaped sandstone ledge is situated on the southern edge of the plateau. It provides beautiful vistas over the rolling hills and valleys. In summer, lines of people gather to photograph this popular and scenic attraction.

For hotels and restaurants see pp402–11 and pp418–33

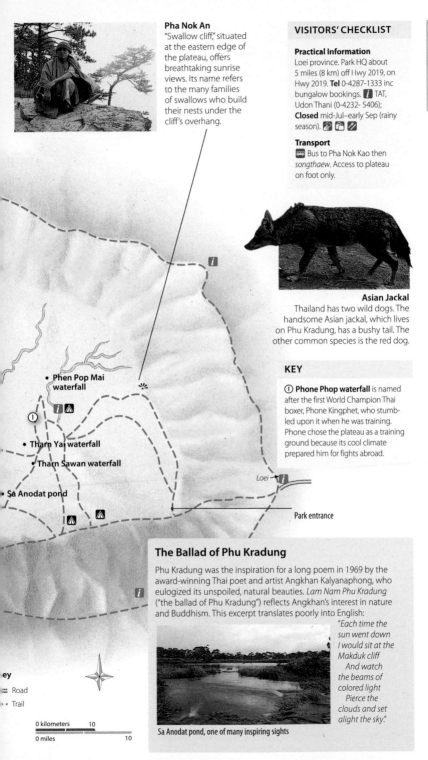

Pha Nok An

"Swallow cliff," situated at the eastern edge of the plateau, offers breathtaking sunrise views. Its name refers to the many families of swallows who build their nests under the cliff's overhang.

VISITORS' CHECKLIST

Practical Information
Loei province. Park HQ about 5 miles (8 km) off I Hwy 2019, on Hwy 2019. **Tel** 0-4287-1333 inc bungalow bookings. 🛈 TAT, Udon Thani (0-4232- 5406); **Closed** mid-Jul–early Sep (rainy season). 🌂 🏠 ✏

Transport
🚌 Bus to Pha Nok Kao then *songthaew*. Access to plateau on foot only.

Asian Jackal
Thailand has two wild dogs. The handsome Asian jackal, which lives on Phu Kradung, has a bushy tail. The other common species is the red dog.

KEY

① **Phone Phop waterfall** is named after the first World Champion Thai boxer, Phone Kingphet, who stumbled upon it when he was training. Phone chose the plateau as a training ground because its cool climate prepared him for fights abroad.

• **Phen Pop Mai waterfall**

• **Tharn Yai waterfall**

• **Tharn Sawan waterfall**

• **Sa Anodat pond**

Loei

Park entrance

The Ballad of Phu Kradung

Phu Kradung was the inspiration for a long poem in 1969 by the award-winning Thai poet and artist Angkhan Kalyanaphong, who eulogized its unspoiled, natural beauties. *Lam Nam Phu Kradung* ("the ballad of Phu Kradung") reflects Angkhan's interest in nature and Buddhism. This excerpt translates poorly into English:

"*Each time the sun went down I would sit at the Makduk cliff And watch the beams of colored light Pierce the clouds and set alight the sky.*"

Sa Anodat pond, one of many inspiring sights

Key
⎯ Road
• Trail

0 kilometers   10
0 miles   10

For keys to symbols *see back flap*

Rapids in Phu Hin Rong Kla National Park

❷ Phu Hin Rong Kla National Park

อุทยานแห่งชาติภูหินร่องกล้า

Phitsanulok province. Park HQ off Hwy 2331, 19 miles (31 km) SE of Nakhon Thai. **Tel** 0-5535-6607. 🛈 TAT, Phitsanulok (0-5525-2743); Forestry Dept (0-2562-0760 or 🅦 **dnp.go.th** for bungalow bookings). 🚌 from Loei or Phitsanulok to Nakhon Thai, then *songthaew*. 🏍

Covering an area of 120 sq miles (307 sq km), Phu Hin Rong Kla National Park has a wide variety of flora and fauna and an unusual open-air museum with exhibits of the Communist camp based here in the 1960s and '70s. The spread of Communism in Southeast Asia from the 1950s alarmed the Thai goverment, and hostilities between the Communist Party of Thailand (CPT) and the military commenced in 1964. Soon after, the open forests of the Phu Hin Rong Kla mountain range became a CPT stronghold. An average elevation of 3,300 ft (1,000 m), proximity to Laos – run by the Communist Pathet Lao from 1975 *(see p299)* – and the access this facilitated to headquarters, at Kunming in China, all made it an ideal site. The CPT was active after 1976, when thousands of students fled here after a coup in Bangkok. By 1979, disillusioned with Communism, many began to take advantage of an amnesty from the Thai government. Dwindling support and government attacks on Phu Hin Rong Kla in the early 1980s led the site to fall to the authorities in 1982.

Two years later it opened as a national park. Its highest peak, Phu Man Khao, rises to a height of 5,300 ft (1,620 m).

❸ Phu Rua National Park

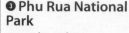

อุทยานแห่งชาติภูเรือ

Loei province. Park HQ off Hwy 203, 30 miles (60 km) W of Loei. **Tel** 0-8509-5299. 🛈 TAT, Udon Thani (0-4232-5406); Forestry Dept (0-2562-0760 or 🅦 **dnp.go.th** for bungalow bookings). 🚌 from Loei to Phu Rua village, then *songthaew*. 🏍

Phu Rua or "boat mountain" gets its name from its peak, which is shaped like a junk. It stands some 4,500 ft (1,365 m) above sea level and offers spectacular views of the town of Loei to the south and toward Laos. A modern Buddha image sits looking out over the plains in contemplation of their beauty.

It is possible to drive to the summit of Phu Rua, passing several bizarre rock formations on the way. The most remarkable is Hin Ta or "tortoise rock," with two huge sandstone boulders stacked one on top of the other, surmounted by a third, giving the structure the appearance of a giant mushroom.

For the traveler with time to explore the 47 sq miles (121 sq km) of this national park, a number of marked trails lead through a beautiful landscape of meadows, rock gardens, and pine and evergreen forests. Views across the surrounding lowlands can be seen from Phu Kut and the cliffs of Pha Lon Noi, Pha Dong Tham San, Pha Yat, and Pha Sap Thong. There are also several waterfalls located around the park, namely Huai Phai, Huai Ta Wat, and Lan Hin Taek.

Animals at Phu Rua National Park include barking deer, wild pigs, a wide variety of birds, including pheasant, and the rare *tao puru*, or Siamese big-headed turtle. Phu Rua is also famed for being one of the coolest areas of Thailand, with a record low temperature of 25° F (-4° C) having been recorded here in 1981.

Unusual rock formation at Phu Rua National Park

Relics of the war between the military and the CPT, Phu Hin Rong Kla

Rolling hills near Loei, typical of this part of the Northeast

❹ Loei

เลย

Loei province. 🗺 86,000. ✈ 🚌
ℹ TAT, Udon Thani (0-4232-5406).
🗓 daily. 🎪 Cotton Blossom Festival
(Feb), Phi Ta Khon Festival, Rocket
Festival (May/Jun).

In Thai, the word *loei* means "beyond" or "to the farthest extreme," a fitting name for a town and province that lie in the northernmost part of Northeast Thailand, straddling the edge of the Khorat Plateau. Though the province is administrated as part of Isan (the Northeast), its climate and landscape are more similar to those of Northern Thailand. In winter it is cold and foggy, in summer searingly hot. In the past, bureaucrats who had fallen out of favor with the Siamese government, based in Bangkok, were posted to the remote town of Loei as punishment for their inefficiency. One fortunate aspect of Loei's isolation is that it firmly retains its traditional flavor.

Lying along the west bank of the Loei River, Loei has a few sights of interest to visitors. There is a lively market by the bridge across the river, and next to the bridge is the **Lak Muang** or "city pillar." The town also has an old Chinese shrine, **Chao Pho Kut Pong**, a popular place of worship for the local people. The surrounding valley is rich in minerals and also produces some of the finest cotton in Thailand. Examples of this can be bought in Loei, in shops along Charoenraj Road and Ruamchai Road.

Loei also has a reasonable amount of cheap accommodations, making it a good base from which to visit Phu Rua and Phu Kradung *(see pp290–92)* national parks.

Phi Ta Khon Festival

Young men, dressed as spirits, preparing to parade a sacred Buddha around Loei town

Although a less lively version of this festival is held in the provincial capital of Loei in July, its real home is in the town of Dan Sai, 50 miles (80 km) to the west. Here Phi Ta Khon takes place in June at the beginning of the rainy season *(see pp51–3)*. Its purpose is to make Buddhist merit and call for rain. The festival's origins are in the Buddhist tale of Prince Vessandorn, the Lord Buddha's final incarnation before he attained *nirvana*. Apparently, when Vessandorn returned to his city, the welcoming procession was so enchanting that the spirits emerged to celebrate. Today, the young men of Dan Sai dress up as spirits *(phi ta khon)*, draped in robes of patchwork rags and sporting painted masks made out of coconut tree trunks with huge, gaping mouths, beaklike noses, and wicker-basket crowns. During the three-day festival, they make playful jibes at onlookers as they parade a sacred Buddha image around the town. Monks also recite the story of Vessandorn to the crowd. On the third day, the "spirits" bring the festival to a close by circumambulating the main building of the local *wat* three times, before finally casting their colorful masks into a nearby river.

Phi Ta Khon costume

Phi Ta Khon "spirits" making fun of onlookers

Ornate, Lao-style façade of Wat Tha Kok, Chiang Khan

❻ Chiang Khan

เชียงคาน

Loei province. 52,000. from Loei or Nong Khai. TAT, Udon Thani (0-4232-5406).

Chiang Khan consists of two 1-mile (2-km) long parallel streets running along the south bank of the Mekong River and lined with run-down teakwood shop-houses, restaurants, and temples. Those temples most worth a visit are Wat Santi, Wat Pa Klang, built over 100 years ago by Lao immigrants, Wat Si Khun Muang, Wat Tha Kok, and Wat Mahathat. The latter is the oldest temple in Chiang Khan, its *bot* having been built in 1654. Like Wat Tha Kok, it shows French colonial influence in its colonnades and shutters.

Wat Tha Khok has a beautiful, painted ceiling. Its exterior walls are stained red, like the river, from dust. This possibly stems from deforestation in nearby Laos, which exposes the local red topsoil.

Environs
Located 1 mile (2 km) farther east from Wat Tha Kok along the Mekong River is Wat Tha Khaek. Neglected for years, this temple is now undergoing major reconstruction in a mixture of traditional and modern styles. A further 1 mile (2 km) down river are the scenic Kaeng Kut Khu rapids.

❼ Pak Chom

ปากชม

Loei province. 29,000. from Loei or Nong Khai. TAT, Udon Thani (0-4232-5406). daily.

Pak Chom is little more than a picturesque settlement of ramshackle wooden buildings clustered by the bank of the Mekong River, 25 miles (40 km) northeast of Chiang Khan. It's a good place to stop for refreshments and to enjoy the scenery. In the 1970s and 1980s the town had a somewhat higher profile thanks to Ban Winai, a Lao-Hmong (*see p210*) refugee camp of some 15,000 inhabitants. It was established when these tribespeople fled Laos in the wake of the Pathet Lao (*see p299*), who overthrew the Lao monarchy and took control of the country in 1975. In 1992 the camp was disbanded and the Hmong moved to Chiang Kham in the Chiang Rai province of Northern Thailand.

❺ Mekong Villages Tour

As well as villages, this tour takes in temples, lush forest, and great river views. No river in the world is quite like the 2,500-mile (4,025-km) Mekong, with its distinctive red waters. Its source is in the Himalayas, and it separates Laos and Thailand for 470 miles (750 km) before flowing through Cambodia and Vietnam out into the South China Sea. Rich in agriculture, its floodplain has been a source of wealth in an otherwise infertile region.

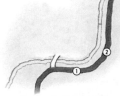

④ **Ban Muang**
Fishermen casting their nets are a common sight at this point in the Mekong River.

Tips for Travelers

Length: 75 miles (120 km).
Stopping-off points: Chiang Khan has a couple of restaurants, and four or five good guest-houses serving food. Pak Chom, Sangkhom, and Si Chiangmai all have good guesthouses offering food. Some guesthouses rent out bicycles. Food vendors can be found in most villages and towns.
Public transport: Local buses run between the main towns along the route. It is also possible to travel from Chiang Khan to Pak Chom by long-tail boat.

② **Pha Baen**
This small village is one of many with picturesque wooden buildings and river views.

③ **Pak Chom**
The journey along the stretch of river between Chiang Khan and Pak Chom can be made by road or by long-tail boat.

① **Chiang Khan**
Many of the temples and shop-houses in Chiang Khan show Lao influences.

Key
▬ Tour route
〓 Other roads
〓 Rivers

❽ Sangkhom
สังคม

Nong Khai province. 🏠 19,000.
🚌 from Loei or Nong Khai. 🛈 TAT,
Udon Thani (0-4232-5406).

The main attractions of this town are its peace and quiet and its location in a particularly lush part of the Mekong River Valley. Ranged along the bank of the river are some quaint wooden buildings. Sangkhom also makes a good base for excursions into the surrounding countryside.

Environs
The **Than Thip falls** are a major highlight of this area. Just outside Sangkhom, 2 miles (3 km) off the main highway, they are hidden in the middle of jungle and banana groves. The two main, and most accessible, levels of this waterfall have pools at their bases, making them ideal for a refreshing swim. More intre-pid travelers can explore a further three levels higher up the falls.

Topiary in the gardens of the Fisheries Department, near Si Chiangmai

❾ Si Chiangmai
ศรีเชียงใหม่

Nong Khai province. 🏠 23,000.
🚌 from Loei or Nong Khai. 🛈 TAT,
Udon Thani (0-4232-5406). 🛒 daily.

This town overlooks the Lao capital of Vientiane (see pp298–9) on the other side of the Mekong River and has a large population of Lao and Vietnamese refugees. Its main claim to fame is as the world's largest producer of spring roll wrappers. When the weather is good, they can be seen along the roadsides, spread out on bamboo racks to dry in the sun.

Environs
Located 3 miles (5 km) outside Si Chiangmai are the gardens of the **Fisheries Department**, featuring unusual elephant-shaped topiary.

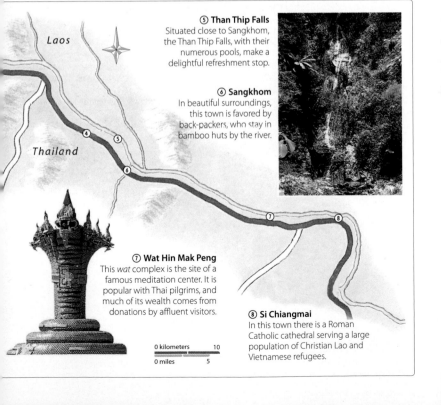

⑤ **Than Thip Falls**
Situated close to Sangkhom, the Than Thip Falls, with their numerous pools, make a delightful refreshment stop.

⑥ **Sangkhom**
In beautiful surroundings, this town is favored by back-packers, who stay in bamboo huts by the river.

Laos

Thailand

⑦ **Wat Hin Mak Peng**
This *wat* complex is the site of a famous meditation center. It is popular with Thai pilgrims, and much of its wealth comes from donations by affluent visitors.

⑧ **Si Chiangmai**
In this town there is a Roman Catholic cathedral serving a large population of Christian Lao and Vietnamese refugees.

0 kilometers   10
0 miles   5

⑩ Nong Khai

หนองคาย

Now one of the busiest commercial centers in the Northeast, this once sleepy border town continues to grow, benefitting from lively border trade with Laos. The construction, in 1994, of the Friendship Bridge, the first bridge to span the Mekong River between Thailand and Laos, was a factor in an increase in trade between the two countries. Nevertheless, the town center retains much of its original charm, and Nong Khai's main attraction for travelers is still its peaceful riverside character.

Boats moored on the River Mekong in Nong Khai

Exploring Nong Khai

Nong Khai's streets and *sois* are lined with traditional wooden shop-houses. Its most vibrant neighborhood is around the Sadet riverboat pier, with its market and adjacent restaurants overlooking the Mekong River. An influx of prosperity in the town is made obvious by the burgeoning number of restaurants as well as modern shopping centers and banking facilities.

Intricate carving on the rear of the Lao-style Wat Si Muang

🍴 Indochina Market

ตลาดอินโดจีน

Off Rimkhong Rd, Tha Sadet. **Open** daily.

This market remains the focus of lively, local trade carried out between Thailand and Laos. Reciprocal visa arrangements allow merchants from either country to visit Vientiane *(see pp298–9)* or Nong Khai for up to three days. Merchandise that can be bought at the market includes clothing, pots and pans, foodstuffs, pestles and mortars, fishing nets, and tables woven from bamboo.

Prap Ho Monument

อนุสาวรีย์ปราบฮ่อ

Janjopthit Rd.

The Prap Ho Monument, a symbol of municipal pride, was built to honor those who held off Ho Chinese invasions in 1855 and 1877. Built in 1886, and bearing Thai, Lao, Chinese, and English inscriptions, it is the site of annual celebrations on March 5.

📷 Prajak Road

ถนนประจักษ์

Along Prajak Road, visitors can pay a call at the Village Weaver shop, where traditional silk weaving is carried out. The factory/shop specializes in *mut mee*, the name given to a method of tie-dying used in the Northeast. It was established as part of a program to encourage local girls to stay and work in Nong Khai, rather than moving to larger urban centers such as Bangkok. There is also a market on Prajak Road, to the rear of the bus station.

🛕 Wat Si Muang

วัดศรีเมือง

Off Meechai Rd. **Open** daily.

The temple buildings and *chedi* of Wat Si Muang are Lao in style. The *wat* has an ornate shrine at the main entrance, cluttered with Buddhist merit offerings. Wat Si Muang is one of many such temples that line the main Meechai Road leading west toward Wat Pho Chai.

🛕 Wat Pho Chai

วัดโพธิ์ชัย

Pho Chai Rd. **Open** daily.

The somewhat gaudy Wat Pho Chai lies in the southwest of the city, adjacent to a street market of the same name. Its main chapel sports imposing *naga* balustrades and a pair of roaring lions at the top of the entrance stairs, protecting the highly revered Luang Pho Phra Sai Buddha image housed inside.

Guardian lion, Wat Pho Chai

This solid gold Buddha with a ruby-studded, flame finial was originally molded in the ancient Lao kingdom of Lan Xang. It later resided in Vientiane *(see pp298–9)*. In 1778 it was taken by Prince Chakri, later Rama I (1782–1809), following the first Thai invasion of Laos. As he attempted to ferry it across the Mekong, it fell into the river and, according to legend, miraculously resurfaced. After it had been rescued it was placed in Wat Pho Chai. Murals in the temple give a pictorial account of this story.

Luang Pho Phra Sai Buddha image, housed in Wat Pho Chai

🔟 Other Wats

Apart from its major sights, Nong Khai has a number of minor *wats* worth a visit. All of them have Lao-influenced architecture and include **Wat Haisoke, Wat Lamduan** and **Wat Si Sumang**, which all offer views of the Mekong River, and **Wat Si Khun Muang**.

Environs

Though always a major crossing point for tourists and traders bound for the Lao capital of Vientiane, Nong Khai gained significance as a commercial border post with the opening of the **Friendship Bridge** in 1994. Built with Thai, Lao, and Australian cooperation, it links

Ban Chommani on the western outskirts of Nong Khai to Tha Na Laeng on the opposite bank, some 12 miles (20 km) from Vientiane. By the foot of the bridge, on the Thai side, is a stretch of sand known as Chommani beach, a popular spot for picnicking Thais during the dry season, when the waters of the Mekong River are low.

Closer to the town center is the Lao *chedi* of **Phra That Nong Khai**, which collapsed into the Mekong River in 1847. Over the years it has slowly drifted farther and farther into the middle of the river to the point where it can now be seen only when the water is low.

By far the most unusual site of interest at Nong Khai lies some 3 miles (5 km) to the east of the town. **Wat Khaek**, also known as Sala Kaew Ku, was founded in 1978 by the charismatic Luang Pu Bunleua Surirat. This Thai-Brahmin shaman allegedly trained under a Hindu guru in Vietnam, moved on to Laos, and was then forced to Thailand by the hostile attentions of the Pathet Lao *(see p299)*. Wat Khaek is essentially an open-air theme park of enormous, concrete Hindu and Buddhist sculptures.

Seven-headed *naga*, Wat Khaek

VISITORS' CHECKLIST

Practical Information
Nong Khai province. 🅰 83,000. 🛈 TAT, Udon Thani (0-4232-5406). 🍽 daily. 🎉 Nong Khai Festival (Mar), Bun Bang Fai (Rocket) Festival (May); Naga Fireballs (Oct).

Transport
🚆 2 miles (3 km) W on Kaeo Worawut Rd. 🚌 Praserm Rd.

Among the giant gods, saints, and demons that are depicted here are Rahu, the god of eclipses and, tallest of all, a 82-ft (25-m) high seven-headed *naga* with a tiny Buddha seated on its coils.

The atmosphere of a walk through this eccentric collection of images is intensified by incense and piped music. The shrine building is an exhibition hall on two floors that contains, among other things, numerous photographs of the Luang Pu or "Venerable Grandfather." He is said to have such charisma that anyone drinking holy water offered by him will immediately donate all their belongings to the temple.

Nong Khai Town Center

① Prap Ho Monument
② Wat Haisoke
③ Indochina Market
④ Wat Si Muang
⑤ Wat Si Khun Muang
⑥ Wat Lamduan
⑦ Wat Si Sumang
⑧ Prajak Road
⑨ Wat Pho Chai

❶ Vientiane
เวียงจันทน์

In its 1,000-year history, Vientiane has come under Khmer, Vietnamese, Thai, and French colonial influence. It was capital of the Lan Xang Kingdom in the 16th century and later a vassal of Ayutthaya. The Thais sacked Vientiane in 1828. In 1893 the French annexed Laos and made Vientiane its capital. Laos gained independence in 1953; in 1975 it became a Socialist Republic. A day trip from Nong Khai *(see pp296–7)*, today Vientiane shows a side of Southeast Asia that is fast disappearing.

Exploring Vientiane

Vientiane has been isolated from change for generations. However, it has now seen some radical changes thanks to cross-border trade with Thailand, encouraged by the Friendship Bridge *(see p297)*, and investment from China and Japan. Vientiane is shaking off its sleepy image, but so far it has also remained blissfully free from mass commercialism and uncontrolled development.

Vientiane was one of three important French Indochinese cities; the others were Ho Chi Minh City (or Saigon) and Phnom Penh. French colonial influence can still be felt in the city, with its broad, tree-lined boulevards and shuttered villas.

Shop-house in Vientiane

🔯 Haw Pha Kaew
Setthathirat Rd. **Open** daily. **Closed** public hols. 🔯

This temple was once home to the Phra Kaeo or Emerald Buddha *(see p87)*, which was taken by the Thais in 1778 and placed in Wat Phra Kaeo in Bangkok. (Phra Kaeo is the preferred transliteration in Thai; Pha Kaew in Lao.) A replica, a symbol of renewed friendship, was given to Laos by Thailand in 1994. The sack of 1828 left the temple in ruins. Restored in the 20th century, it is now a museum. The beautifully carved main door is all that remains of the original *wat*.

🔯 Wat Sisaket
Lane Xang Rd. **Open** daily. **Closed** public hols. 🔯

This *wat*, built in 1818, was one of the few buildings to survive the sack of 1828. It is now the oldest *wat* in Vientiane and one of the most interesting to visit. Its most memorable feature is the 2,052 tiny Buddha images made of terra-cotta, bronze, and wood that fill niches in the walls of the cloister. Over 300 Buddha images also rest on a long shelf below the niches.

🏛 Lao Revolutionary Museum
Samsenthai Rd. **Open** 8am–noon, 1–4pm daily. **Closed** public hols. 🔯

Artifacts and photographs here detail the period of French colonialism, independence in the 1940s and 1950s, and the rise of the Pathet Lao.

🔯 Wat Mixai
Setthathirat Rd. **Open** daily. Its gates flanked by two *nyaks* or guardian giants, parts of this *wat* complex were built in 19th-century Rattanakosin style.

Vientiane City Center

① Wat Hai Sok
② Wat Ong Theu
③ Wat Mixai
④ Lao Revolutionary Museum
⑤ Wat Sisaket
⑥ Haw Pha Kaew

For keys to symbols *see back flap*

🏛 Wat Ong Theu

Setthathirat Rd. **Open** daily.

One of the most important *wat* complexes in all Laos, Wat Ong Theu was originally founded in the early 16th century. Destroyed in 1828, it was rebuilt in the 19th and 20th centuries. The *wat* houses a large, 16th-century bronze Buddha image, with two standing Buddhas either side of it. The *wat* also houses a school for monks.

🏛 Wat Hai Sok

Setthathirat Rd. **Open** daily.

Like other *wats* in Vientiane, Wat Hai Sok has undergone restoration. Its most distinctive feature is an impressive five-tiered roof.

Environs

The **Pha That Luang**, which perches, somewhat out of the way, halfway up a hill on the northeastern outskirts of the city, is the most important national and Buddhist monument in Laos. According to legend a *chedi* was built here in the 3rd century BC to house a breastbone of the Lord Buddha. More tangible evidence suggests this was the site of a Khmer *prasat*. The present structure was built in 1566, when Vientiane became the capital of the Lan Xang Kingdom. It was

damaged in the 18th and 19th centuries and restored, albeit badly, by the French in 1900. A better restoration of the site was undertaken in the 1930s.

Wat Si Muang, to the southeast of the city center, is the most popular place of worship in Vientiane. According to legend, the site was chosen by Lao sages in 1563.

Wat Sok Pa Luang is known for its instruction in *vipassana*, a type of Buddhist meditation.

Ho Nang Ussa, a rock formation in Phu Phrabat Historical Park

⑫ Phu Phrabat Historical Park

อุทยานประวัติศาสตร์ภูพระบาท

Off Hwy 2021, 6 miles (10 km) W of Ban Pheu, Udon Thani province. 🛈 TAT, Udon Thani (0-4232-5406). 🚌 from Nong Khai or Udon Thani to Ban Phu, then *songthaew*. **Open** daily. 🏛

The distinctive sandstone formations that are the central attraction of this historical park cannot fail to leave their imprint on the imagination. The local population has shrouded the site in many fantastic myths and legends. According to one of these, Princess Ussa was sent to Phu Phrabat by her father to study. However, she fell in love with Prince Barot. Outraged, her father challenged the prince to a temple-building duel, but lost. A huge sandstone slab in the park, known as Kok Ma Thao Barot, is supposedly Prince Barot's stable. The mushroom-shaped Ho Nang Ussa apparently represents Princess Ussa's residence, where she pined away many long years in exile.

The 6,000-year-old human history of this site is testified to by cave paintings found on the underside of two natural rock shelters, known locally as Tham Wua and Tham Khon or "ox cave" and "people cave."

At the entrance to the historical park stands a crude replica of Wat Phra That Phanom (*see p301*); the **Wat Phraphutthabat Bua Bok** houses the Bua Bok Buddha Footprint and is an important pilgrimage site for local Thais.

The Pathet Lao

The Lao Patriotic Front was formed after World War II and, with ties to Ho Chi Minh's Communist Party in Vietnam, opposed French rule. In 1953 Laos was declared a constitutional monarchy, backed by France and the US. The LPF's armed wing, the Pathet Lao, mounted an armed struggle against the government in the 1960s. During the Vietnam War the US repeatedly bombed Laos in order to stamp out Pathet Lao support for the North Vietnamese. With the withdrawal of American forces from the region in 1975, the Pathet Lao staged a bloodless coup and declared Laos the Lao People's Democratic Republic.

Poster supporting the Lao People's Democratic Republic

Wat Phra That Choeng Chum, the main *wat* in the old, once Khmer, town of Sakhon Nakhon

⑬ Sakhon Nakhon

สกลนคร

Sakhon Nakhon province. 🏛 120,000. ✈ 🚌 ℹ TAT, Nakhon Phanom (0-4251-3490). 🔄 daily. 🎎 Wax Castle Ceremony (Oct).

There are two sights of interest in the friendly town of Sakhon Nakhon. **Wat Phra That Choeng Chum** is a beautiful temple complex with a large *bot* and *wihan*, a 10th-century Khmer *prang*, and a whitewashed, 80-ft (24-m) Lao-style *chedi* built during the Ayutthaya period.

The old *prang* is reached through a door in the *wihan*. Etched into the *prang's* base is an ancient Khmer inscription, and around it are Lao and Khmer images of the Buddha. Also in the compound is an interesting display of *luk nimit*, which are Brahmin foundation markers that somewhat resemble giant cannon balls.

The five-layered, 11th-century Khmer *prang* of **Wat Phra That Narai Cheng Weng** was built as a Hindu monument. The name Cheng Weng is taken from the princess responsible for its construction; Narai is a Thai and Khmer name for Vishnu. The most important lintel – over the only entrance, to the east – shows Shiva dancing on the destruction of the universe, as

he tramples the head of a lion. On the northern portico is a splendid depiction of Vishnu, with a lotus and baton in two of his four hands.

⑭ Nakhon Phanom

นครพนม

Nakhon Phanom province. 🏛 114,000. ✈ 🚌 ℹ TAT, Soontornvijit Rd, Nakhon Phanom (0-4251-3490). 🔄 daily. 🎎 Illuminated Boats Procession (Oct).

Nakhon Phanom – "city of hills" – is a good town in which to spend a few relaxing days by the Mekong. In the dry season a beach by the river, **Hat Sai Tai Muang**, becomes exposed, and it is possible to walk out almost as far as Laos. However, this town cannot be used as a place to procure a visa for, or as an entry point into, Laos.

To celebrate the end of the rains, during the night of the full moon in the 11th lunar month, there is a resplendent procession of illuminated boats on the river here. Measuring some 33 ft (10 m) in length, the boats are traditionally crafted from bamboo or banana trees. They are filled with lighted candles, incense, kerosene lamps, and offerings of fragrant flowers and candies.

⑮ Renu Nakhon

เรณูนคร

Nakhon Phanom province. 🏛 39,000. 🚌 from Nakhon Phanom. ℹ TAT, Nakhon Phanom (0-4251-3490). 🔄 Wed.

Renu Nakhon is a village known primarily for its weaving and fine embroidery. At the popular Wednesday market, colorful cottons and silks are sold by the *phun*, a measure 2 ft (75 cm) long. Ready-made garments and furnishings from all over the Northeast and Laos are also sold. There is a more permanent gathering of textile stalls around **Phra That Renu**. This was built in 1918 and modeled loosely on the nearby *chedi* at That Phanom.

Shop selling a range of locally made textiles, Renu Nakhon

⑯ Wat Phra That Phanom

วัดพระธาตุพนม

This *wat*, in the remote town of That Phanom, is the most revered shrine in Northeast Thailand, famous for its central, Lao-style brick and plaster *chedi*. The *chedi* was constructed some 1,500 years ago, but according to legend it was built eight years after the death of the Buddha in 535 BC, when local dignitaries erected it as a burial place for his breastbone. The monument has been restored many times, most recently after devastating rains in 1975. Each year at the full moon of the third lunar month, during a farming holiday, a week-long temple festival attracts thousands of pilgrims from Thailand and Laos.

VISITORS' CHECKLIST

Practical Information
Center of That Phanom, Nakhon Phanom province. 🛈 TAT, Nakhon Phanom (0-4251-3490). **Open** 6am–7pm daily. 📷 Phra That Phanom Festival (Feb/Mar).

Transport
🚌 from Nakhon Phanom, Sakhon Nakhon, or Mukdahan.

Stone Lion One of two on either side of the outer compound's central path, this fierce mythical beast is a temple guardian who wards off evil forces.

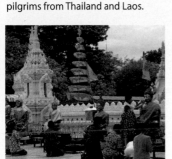

Pilgrims at Wat Phra That Phanom
Thousands come to pay homage at festival time and throughout the year. Many devotees are from Laos – the monument is the second most sacred site to them, the first being That Luang in Vientiane.

Gold decoration in the shape of a multi-leaved lotus flower represents the path to Enlightenment.

The *chedi* is studded with gemstones and gold rings.

Central Chedi

The famous 185-ft (57-m) high chedi at the center of the temple is in the shape of a stylized, elongated lotus bud. The present structure, rebuilt in 1977, is modeled on That Luang in Vientiane, Laos.

Golden Buddha Image
In *abhaya mudra* posture *(see p177)* and shaded by an umbrella, this image sits near the entrance to the inner compound.

A *chat*, or ceremonial umbrella

Numerous Buddha images
line the inner compound wall of the *chedi*. Pilgrims paste squares of gold leaf onto them as a way of making merit.

Stone panels carved in the 10th century tell the legends of the five men who supposedly built the *chedi* in the 6th century BC.

The market along the river at Mukdahan, where Lao and Vietnamese merchandise is sold

⑰ Mukdahan

มุกดาหาร

Mukdahan province. 🏔 83,000. 🚌 ℹ TAT, Nakhon Phanom (0-4251-3490). 🛒 daily. 🎊 Ruam Pao Thai Ma Kham Wan Chai Khong Fair (Jan).

Mukdahan is the capital of one of Thailand's newest provinces, created in 1980 from areas that were formerly part of Nakhon Phanom and Ubon Ratchathani provinces.

The most interesting street is Samran Chai Khong Road, along the Mekong River front. It faces the second-largest city in Laos, Suwannakhet, on the opposite bank. In 2007, a second Thai–Lao Friendship Bridge opened

Seated Buddha at Wat Yot Kaew Siwichai, Mukdahan

across the river, linking Mukdahan with Suwannakhet. Visitors can obtain a visa on arrival to enter Laos. Mukdahan is a busy trading center, and both Lao and Thai boats can be seen at the pier, loading and unloading their goods.

A market also runs most of the length of the riverside, between **Wat Si Mongkol Tai** and **Wat Yot Kaew Siwichai**. Goods for sale may be disappointing because there are few examples of traditional Lao and Vietnamese merchandise. Expect an excess of plastic ephemera, though the market is worth a visit for the local sweetmeats and its colorful atmosphere.

Wat Si Mongkhol Thai was built in 1956 by Vietnamese immigrants in the town and is distinguished by statues of mythical creatures at the entrance to its main chapel.

The gaudier Wat Yot Kaew Siwichai houses an enormous, seated, golden Buddha image. The figure sits in an open-fronted *wihan* with paneled glass on two of its sides. Near Wat Yot Kaew Siwichai, on Song Nang Sathit Road, is the Chinese **Chao Fa Mung Muang shrine**, home to Mukdahan's guardian spirit. Also here is the **Lak Muang**, or City Pillar, which is usually draped in colorful plastic garlands.

Environs
Excellent views of the entire provincial capital can be captured from the 1,650-ft (500-m) peak of **Phu Manorom**. A pavilion at the top of the hill shelters a replica of the Buddha's Footprint.

🏛 **Phu Manorom**
Off Hwy 2034, 3 miles (5 km) S of Mukdahan. **Open** daily. 🏞

⑱ Pha Taem

ผาแต้ม

11 miles (18 km) N of Khong Chiam, Ubon Ratchathani province. ℹ TAT, Ubon Ratchathani (0-4524-3770). 🚌 from Ubon Ratchathani to Khong Chiam, then tuk-tuk. **Open** daily. 🏞

The route, 11 miles (18 km) from Khong Chiam up to Pha Taem or "painted cliff," is a circuitous one, really accessible only by rental car or *tuk-tuk*. Along the way, a few kilometers before you arrive at the cliff top, an unusual, sandstone rock formation can be seen at the side of the road. Known as Sao Chaliang, it is reminiscent of the Ho Nang Ussa at Phu Phrabat Historical Park (*see p299*).

At the end of the journey, an unmarked trail leads from the parking lot to the cliff face. This is decorated with huge figures and geometrical designs. Painted in an indelible red pigment derived from soil, tree gum, and fat, the paintings are thought to date back some 4,000 years. Covering 560 ft (170 m) along the cliff face, they include depictions of fish traps, wild animals, giant cockroachlike fish, angular human beings, and a 98-ft (30-m) stretch of handprints. The artists who created these decorations are thought to be related to the early inhabitants of Ban Chiang (see p276) and were rice cultivators rather than cave dwellers.

Prehistoric cliff-painting, Pha Taem

Pha Taem is particularly beautiful at sunset, when it has tremendous views across the Mekong and of the wild Lao jungle beyond.

⓭ Khong Chiam

โขงเจียม

Ubon Ratchathani province. 🚗 30,000. 🚌 ℹ️ TAT, Ubon Ratchathani (0-4524-3770). 🛒 daily.

Khong Chiam is near the confluence of the muddy red Mekong and the indigo-blue Mun rivers, which creates the phenomenon of the *maenam song si* or "two-colored river."

Making wicker fish traps, Khong Chiam

The differing colors of the rivers derive from the amounts of sand and clay suspended in their waters. Scenic views are offered from the bank at **Wat Khong Chiam**, and boat trips out to the confluence point itself allow a full appreciation of the blend of colored waters, clearest in April. It is also possible to cross from Khong Chiam to the Lao town on the opposite side of the river, but this cannot be used by travelers as an official crossing point into Laos.

Visitors to Khong Chiam can also watch traditional conical fish traps being made out of wicker.

⓴ Chong Mek

ช่องเม็ก

Ubon Ratchathani province. 🚗 4,900. 🚌 from Ubon Ratchathani. ℹ️ TAT, Ubon Ratchathani (0-4524-3770). 🛒 daily.

Situated on the border between Thailand and Laos, Chong Mek is one of the few places at which tourists can cross into Laos. Other Lao entry points include Nong Khai (see pp296–7), Chiang Khong (see p253), and Mukdahan (see p302). Visitors can obtain a visa on arrival, valid for one month, for a fee of US$35 and two recent passport photographs.

Since the border crossing opened at Chong Mek, a vibrant market and shopping area has sprung up, attracting busloads of Thai tourists who also cross into Laos to visit the nearby town of Pakse.

For those who do not have a visa, it is possible, even without a passport, to walk some 660 ft (200 m) over the border to browse around the open-air market and duty-free shops that are set up there.

In the market, there may be groups of old women selling rare plants and flowers. However, many of the plants are, sadly, taken from the Lao jungle. Visitors to the market are advised not to buy these.

Boat on the Sirindhorn Dam

㉑ Sirindhorn Dam

เขื่อนสิรินธร

Ubon Ratchathani province. ℹ️ TAT, Ubon Ratchathani (0-4524-3770). For information about tourist accommodation call 0-4536-6085. 🚌 from Ubon Ratchathani to Chong Mek, then *songthaew*.

Named after the second daughter of King Bhumibol, the Sirindhorn Dam was built in 1971. The reservoir it created is 27 miles (43 km) from north to south; the turbines produce 24,000 kilowatts of electricity.

There is a park at the dam HQ, and a restaurant and bungalows. It is possible to walk out over the dam and to take a boat on the reservoir.

Dams in Thailand have been funded by the World Bank since the 1950s to meet Thailand's ever-increasing need for electricity. They are given support mainly by politicians and the business community. Residents and environmental groups have begun to campaign against the construction of new dams.

Golden reclining Buddha image at Wat Phra That Phanom ▶

㉒ Prasat Khao Phra Wihan
ปราสาทเขาพระวิหาร

Off Hwy 221, S of Ubon and Si Sa Ket, just inside Cambodia. *i* TAT, Ubon Ratchathani (0-4524-3770). 🚌 from Ubon or Sisaket to Kantharalak, then *songthaew*. **Open** daily. 🏛

The extraordinary site of this early Khmer temple, laid out along a spur of the Dongrek Mountains, makes it one of the most distinctive Khmer structures outside of Angkor (*see pp268–9*). Possibly older than Angkor, sadly, it was long the victim of disputes between Thailand and Cambodia. After much disagreement between the two countries, in 1962 a decision was taken by the World Court: while the easiest access to the temple is through Thailand, the temple stands firmly in Cambodia.

During the mid-1970s, the years of the Khmer Rouge regime in Cambodia, the temple became a strictly no-go area. After the

Three ruined *prangs*, all on a single base, at Prasat Prang Ku

Vietnamese invaded Cambodia in 1978, conflicts continued between rival factions in the area until the late 1980s. The site was finally cleared of land mines and opened to the public in the early 1990s, but as civil unrest

Stone relief on the Cambodian sight of Prasat Khao Phra Wihan

continues in Cambodia, this magnificent temple is forced to close down periodically.

When Khao Phra Wihan is open, tourists can walk through army checkpoints to ascend a series of grand staircases, pass through stone *gopuras*, and then walk along an 2,800-ft (850-m) *naga*-lined causeway to arrive at the central sanctuary, or *prasat*. Dedicated to the Hindu god Shiva, it is now largely in ruins. The *prang* in particular is in need of restoration. Views from the sheer cliffs here, over the Cambodian plateau, are exhilarating. If the temple is closed, elegant Khmer reliefs carved in the cliff can be viewed from the Thai side of the border.

㉓ Prasat Prang Ku
ปราสาทปรางค์กู่

Off Hwy 2234, 43 miles (70 km) SW of Si Sa Ket, Si Sa Ket province. *i* TAT, Ubon Ratchathani (0-4524-3770). 🚌 from Ubon or Sisaket to Kantharalak, then *songthaew*. **Open** daily. 🏛

Located in the district of Prang Ku in Si Sa Ket province, this 11th-century Khmer monument comprises three brick *prangs* on a single platform. The most remarkable feature is a well-preserved lintel, divided horizontally into two sections

A beautifully preserved stone *gopura*, Prasat Khao Phra Wihan

by the tails of two long *nagas*. In the center stands Vishnu on his mount, a *garuda*. On either side of the *garuda* are two lions with garlands of flowers in their open mouths. The top half of the lintel is decorated with dancing deities. In front of Prasat Prang Ku is a 1,100-yard (1,000-m) long Khmer *baray* (reservoir), a welcome feeding ground for birds.

㉔ Ubon Ratchathani
อุบลราชธานี

Ubon Ratchathani province. 🏛 118,000. ✈ 🚉 🚌 *i* TAT, 264/1 Khuan Thani Rd, Ubon Ratchathani (0-4524-3770). 🛒 daily. 🎎 Ubon Candle Festival (late Jul). 🌐 tatubon.org

From the 10th century, Ubon Ratchathani province, often simply known as Ubon, was part of the Khmer Empire. It later fell under the control of the Ayutthaya Kingdom (*see pp64–5*). The provincial capital, the city of Ubon Ratch-athani was founded by Lao immigrants on the northern bank of the Mun River at the end of the 18th century, and Lao influence can still be seen in the architectural features of some of the city's religious buildings. Following the rapid growth of Ubon during the Vietnam War, when it played host to a nearby American air base, the city is, today, one of the largest in Thailand.

At first sight, Ubon appears to be a great concrete sprawl, but the **Ubon National Museum** is one of the best in the Northeast, and some fascinating temples are dotted around the city. The museum is housed in the former country residence of King Vajiravudh (1910–25) and contains displays of Khmer, Hindu, and Lao Buddhist iconography, as well as traditional tools, utensils, and handicrafts. One of the rarest and most impressive exhibits is a giant bronze drum, dating back as far as the 4th century AD, that was used originally for ceremonial purposes.

The most interesting of Ubon's temples is **Wat Thung Si Muang** on account of its teakwood library. Founded by King Rama III (1824–51) the *wat* houses 150-year-old murals showing some of the *jatakas* (see pp34–5). The complex also includes a *mondop* with a Buddha Footprint.

Figure atop Wat Supattanaram

In 1853 King Mongkut (1851–68) gave his support to the construction of **Wat Supattanaram Worawihan** as the first temple in the Northeast dedicated to the Thammayut sect – a strict branch of Theravada Buddhism – of which the king was also a member. It consists of a highly eclectic blend of architectural styles, having been built by Vietnamese craftsmen who were under instruction to incorporate an unusual mixture of Khmer, Thai, and European architectural influences.

The more modern **Wat Phra That Nong Bua** was built in 1957 to commemorate the 2,500th anniversary of the death of the Lord Buddha. Its two four-sided, white-washed towers are decorated with standing Buddha images in niches and reliefs of tales of the Buddha in his previous lives. Ubon also has several other interesting temples: **Wat Cheng**, with its elegant Lao-style wooden carvings; **Wat Si Ubon Rattanaram**, built in 1855 and housing a topaz Buddha image, originating from Chiang Saen;

Carved Buddha images in niches at Wat Phra That Nong Bua

and the main temple, **Wat Maha Wanaram**, in which local people worship.

Ubon becomes a place of pilgrimage at the beginning of Buddhist Lent, when, during the Ubon Candle Festival *(see p53)*, large, sculpted candles are carried through the streets.

🏛 **Ubon National Museum**
Khuan Thani Rd. **Tel** 0-4525-5071.
Open 9am–4pm Wed–Sun.
Closed public hols. 🅰
ⓦ thailandmuseum.com

Ubon Ratchathani City Center

① Wat Supattanaram Worawihan
② Ubon National Museum
③ Wat Si Ubon Rattanaram
④ Wat Cheng
⑤ Wat Maha Wanaram
⑥ Wat Thung Si Muang

For keys to symbols *see back flap*

THE GULF OF THAILAND

Introducing the Gulf of Thailand

Thais and foreigners flock to the Gulf's resorts to relax on the many superb beaches and eat delicious seafood. Bangkok weekenders have long favored Cha-am and Hua Hin, while Pattaya draws lovers of sports and hectic nightlife. The towns of Chaiya and Phetchaburi contain architectural and artistic treasures and have the lively ethnic and cultural mix typical of the Western Seaboard and farther south. Inland, breathtaking flora and fauna abound in beautiful, crowd-free national parks. Thailand's once-idyllic islands have been experiencing a huge surge in popularity. Ko Samui has suffered badly from uncontrolled development and mass tourism, and Ko Samet and Ko Chang have also witnessed dramatic changes.

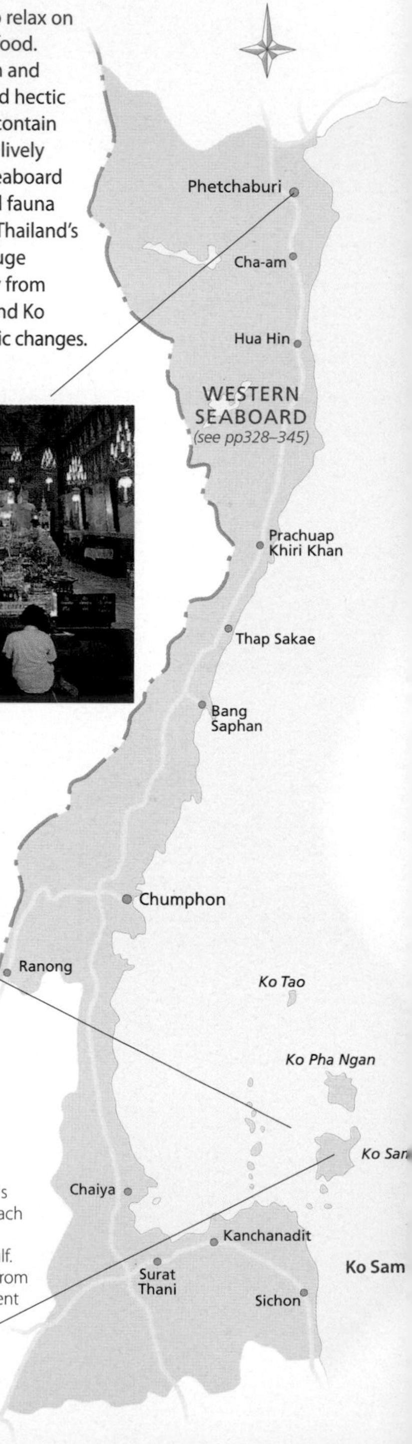

Phetchaburi

Cha-am

Hua Hin

WESTERN SEABOARD
(see pp328–345)

Prachuap Khiri Khan

Thap Sakae

Bang Saphan

Chumphon

Ranong

Ko Tao

Ko Pha Ngan

Ko Sar

Chaiya

Kanchanadit

Ko Sam

Surat Thani

Sichon

Phetchaburi *(see pp332–4)* is an important cultural center with more than 30 *wats*, including the splendid Wat Mahathat, founded in the 14th century. Despite a history dating back to the 11th century and an attractive old quarter, the town receives few visitors.

Angthong National Marine Park *(see pp344–5)*, easily accessible from Ko Samui, is a stunning group of tiny islands teeming with wildlife.

Ko Samui *(see pp340–42)* is the premier beach destination of the Western Gulf. It has suffered from overdevelopment over the years.

◀ The beautiful crescent-shaped bay at Pattaya

Ko Samet *(see pp322–3)* is a popular island destination, particularly with Thais, since it is within comfortable driving distance from Bangkok.

Pattaya *(see p321)* attracts an unlikely mix of families eager to take advantage of the beaches and excellent sports facilities, and hedonists equally eager to enjoy the renowned nightlife of the discos, go-go, and beer bars.

Ko Chang *(see pp326–7)* is the largest of an archipelago of 52 islands. It has experienced considerable development and is now a popular mainstream destination.

0 kilometers 50

0 miles 25

Beach Life and Leisure in the Gulf

Thai beach culture dates from the 1920s with the opening of both the railroad from Bangkok to Hua Hin and the first golf club, the Royal Hua Hin, designed by Scottish railroad engineer A.O. Robins. Hua Hin and its modern neighbor, Cha-am, continue to attract Thai weekenders from Bangkok, whose leisure pursuits center more around seafood dining than swimming and sunbathing. Foreigners, meanwhile, are attracted to the Gulf's clear waters and fine sands, and exceptionally good water sports. The development of resort hotels and golf courses in the Gulf continues to boom, to the alarm of many environmentalists. However, it is still possible to find seclusion and simplicity, such as on Ko Chang.

Bangpra Golf Course, Pattaya, is one of many courses within the forested hills of Chon Buri province (see p448).

Cha-am (see p334) has become increasingly developed but is still overshadowed by nearby Hua Hin.

The Sofitel Centara Grand Resort & Villas (see p335), formerly famed as the Railway Hotel, has been restored to its original 1920s colonial-style elegance.

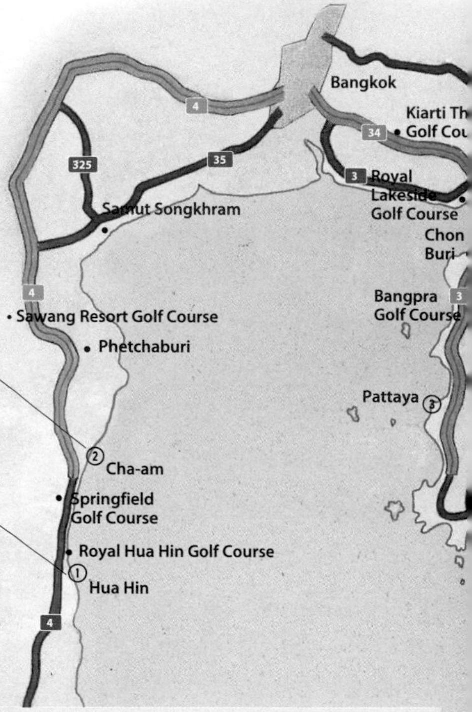

Map labels:

Bangkok

Kiarti Th Golf Cou

Royal Lakeside Golf Course

Chon Buri

Samut Songkhram

Sawang Resort Golf Course

Phetchaburi

Bangpra Golf Course

Pattaya

② Cha-am

Springfield Golf Course

Royal Hua Hin Golf Course

① Hua Hin

Best Beaches of the Northern Gulf

① Hua Hin Beach
Thailand's first beach resort. Good for the charm of the town and its seafood restaurants.

② Cha-am Beach
Popular with Thai weekenders but quiet during the week. Outstanding seafood restaurants.

③ Jomtien Beach, Pattaya
A 9-mile (14-km) long beach. Suitable for families and has excellent water sports facilities.

④ Glass Sand Beach (Hat Sai Kaeo), Ko Samet
Longest and liveliest beach on the island with sand so clean it

squeaks when walked on. Beautifully clear water, and good for water sports.

⑤ White Sand Beach (Hat Sai Khao), Ko Chang
The best and busiest beach on an unspoiled island. Fishing, snorkeling, and boat trips.

Pattaya

Thailand's biggest, brashest resort attracts single males and family package tourists in equal numbers. The former are drawn by the neon-lit go-go bars and a reputation acquired when Pattaya was used for R&R by US servicemen during the Vietnam War. Families, meanwhile, are attracted by the restaurants, golf courses, and beaches, particularly Jomtien beach (south of Pattaya beach), which has the best water sports facilities in the country.

Water sports – a major attraction of Pattaya

Si Racha
Ko Sichang
Laem Chabang Golf Course
Pattaya
Phoenix Golf Course
Eastern Star Golf Course
Sattahip
Rayong

0 kilometers 20
0 miles 10

Ko Chang

(see pp326–7) is Thailand's second-largest island after Phuket. This former backpacker haven has become increasingly developed and now receives more than 700,000 visitors a year.

Diving is possible all year round in the Gulf of Thailand along the east coast, unlike Ko Samui and the Andaman coast, which are more affected by monsoons *(see pp30–31)*.

Rayong
Ko Samet
Chanthaburi
Trat
Ko Chang
344
331
317
3
4
5
318

0 kilometers 25
0 miles 25

Thai Gemstones

Since the 15th century, Chanthaburi ("city of the moon") has been known to Western travelers for its abundance of gemstones. As a trading city its history dates back to the Khmer Empire in the 9th century *(see pp60–61)*. Along with Bangkok, Chanthaburi is world-renowned as a gem center, and for its skilled gem cutters. The gemstones – mainly rubies and sapphires, with associated deposits of zircon, spinel, and garnet – are found in alluvial deposits either on the surface or up to 20 ft (6 m) underground. Although rubies and sapphires are now overmined around Chanthaburi, farmers have previously found gemstones while plowing. Over 70 percent of the world's rubies have come from Thailand.

Gem-Mining Areas
Ruby and sapphire mines

Examining gemstones in the host rock helps formulate the correct cutting plan. This ensures that the best yield and shapes are obtained.

This machine is pumping gravel and water that may contain gemstones such as rubies.

Simple grinding wheels are often used in small businesses, which are commonly run from the owner's home. More sophisticated operations use modern equipment such as diamond saws.

Mining for Gemstones

In Chanthaburi, gem stores can arrange visits to mines. Due to over-mining locally, many of the stones cut in Chanthaburi come from mines in Cambodia or Vietnam.

Faceting Gemstones

Thai workers have a worldwide reputation for their skill and dexterity in faceting (precisely cutting) gemstones, often using simple equipment and judging angles by eye. A modern faceting machine may use a diamond blade or laser to improve speed and accuracy. After cutting, the stones are sorted and graded by size and quality, with quality being determined by sparkle, color, brilliance, and the presence or absence of imperfections.

Modern faceting equipment used to cut gemstones

Most gem buyers prefer to buy gems "in the rough," using their expertise to judge the potential of the uncut material. Later the buyers arrange the cutting of the stones, often in their own workshops. Untrained buyers should beware of potential scams (see p464).

Bargaining in gem-mining towns such as Bo Rai (see p325) is common practice. Since opinions differ as to the potential of rough material and the quality of cut stones, bargaining is hard but good natured.

Designing and making jewelry from gems demands a delicate touch and a keen eye, qualities renowned in Thai craftsmen and women. Most jewelry is made to highlight the beauty of the gems.

Whole families can often be seen searching for gemstones. Children may begin helping at a very young age.

Pans are often used to scoop up gravel that may contain gemstones. The gemstones sink to the bottom of the pan.

Of all the Thai gemstones, deep blue sapphires and blood-red rubies are highly prized, as are unusually colored (such as yellow) sapphires. Sometimes the color is enhanced permanently by heating the stones to almost 3,650° F (2,000° C).

Star sapphire

Star ruby

Green sapphire

Zircon

Ruby

Peridot

Yellow sapphire

EASTERN SEABOARD

The Eastern Seaboard of the Gulf of Thailand, stretching from Bangkok to the Cambodian border, is a region of contrasts. Remarkably picturesque and unspoiled islands lie within easy reach of brash, over developed resorts; oil refineries and industrial complexes are scattered along much of the coast, but not far inland are little-visited and spectacular national parks.

The Eastern Seaboard was a frontier between the Khmer and Sukhothai empires in the early 15th century. As Khmer power waned, large numbers of ethnic Tais settled here and discovered gem-rich deposits in the lush countryside. Chanthaburi became a centre for gem trading and in the 18th and 19th centuries had to expel first Burmese then French occupying forces. Numerous Vietnamese refugees have since settled in the town.

Though still a forested region with orchards, gem-mining, and fishing communities, the Eastern Seaboard has seen dramatic changes in the late 20th century as the oil and tourist industries have grown dramatically. However, some seaside towns have retained their charm, and in Si Racha excellent seafood can be sampled in open-air restaurants overlooking the bay. In contrast to this are the neon lights of Pattaya, an infamous destination for US marines on R&R during the Vietnam War. Despite a seedy image, it is an excellent center for water sports. South and east of Rayong there are beautiful mountainous islands and dense rainforest sheltering a wealth of fauna and flora. Trails, waterfalls, and eerie limestone caves characterize Khao Chamao, Khao Kitchakut, and Namtok Phlio national parks.

The relaxed island of Ko Samet is a popular vacation destination, with its white-sand beaches. Farther south, Ko Chang has many beautiful beaches and has become increasingly popular, attracting hundreds of thousands of visitors each year.

Temple boys in a shrine cave within the Khao Chamao-Khao Wong National Park

◄ Aerial view of the long, bungalow-lined Hat Sai Khao ("white sand beach") on Ko Chang

Exploring the Eastern Seaboard

Blessed with miles of idyllic beaches and soaring temperatures, the Eastern Seaboard is a sun-lover's paradise. Whether you want to unwind and sample the local seafood or try out water sports, there is much to choose from. Beach resorts range from the chaotic Pattaya, with its lively nightlife, to lesser-known islands such as Ko Chang, which is part of a stunning national marine park. The three other national parks in this region, characterized by tropical forests, mountains, and waterfalls, are home to a wealth of wildlife. The main town in the area is Chanthaburi, center of the thriving gem-mining industry.

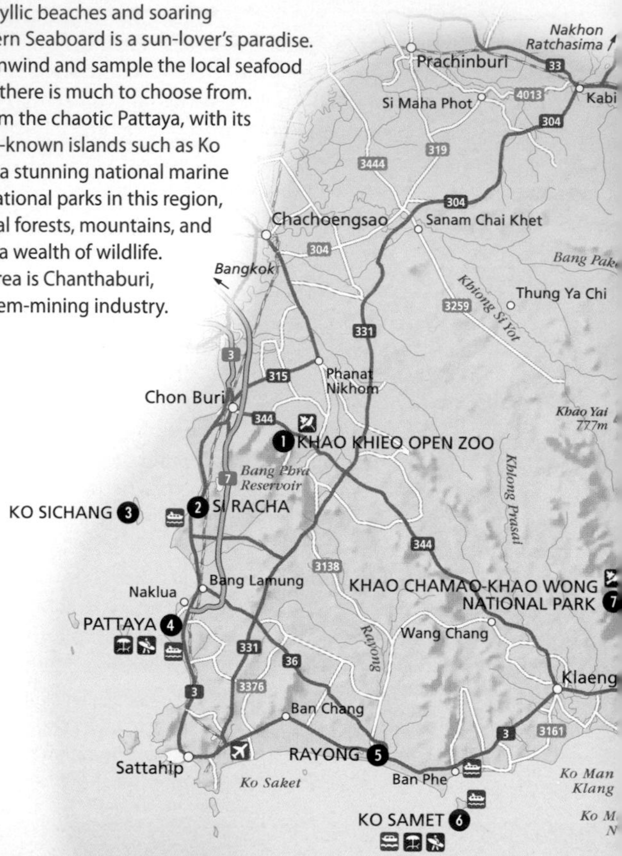

Key

- ▬▬ Motorway
- ▬ Major road
- ▭▭▭ Minor road
- ▬ Scenic route
- ▬▬ Main railway
- ▬▬ International border
- △ Summit

Relaxing on Ko Samet's beautiful white beaches

Sights at a Glance

1. Khao Khieo Open Zoo
2. Si Racha
3. Ko Sichang
4. Pattaya
5. Rayong
6. Ko Samet
7. Khao Chamao-Khao Wong National Park
8. Wat Khao Sukim
9. Khao Kitchakut National Park
10. Chanthaburi
11. Namtok Phlio National Park
12. Bo Rai
13. Ko Chang
14. Trat
15. Khlong Yai

Getting Around

The Eastern Seaboard's transport system is comprehensive on the mainland and connects to the main islands. A twice daily train service runs from Hua Lamphong Station in Bangkok to Si Racha and Pattaya. Chon Buri and Sattahip are served by domestic airports. Buses are the easiest way to get around the Eastern Seaboard: there is a regular service from Bangkok's Eastern Bus Terminal to the main towns. To visit places not on bus routes, charter a *songthaew* from a local bus station. Transportation in the mainland towns is provided by *songthaews*, *samlors* (three-wheeled bicycles), and *tuk-tuks*. Several ferries leave Ban Phe each day for Ko Samet. On the island, *songthaews* service the main beaches, and fishing boats can be hired to surrounding islands. Ko Chang and Ko Mak are reached by ferry from Laem Ngop. Infrastructure on these islands is poor, though motorcycles and *songthaews* can be hired to get around the rough roads.

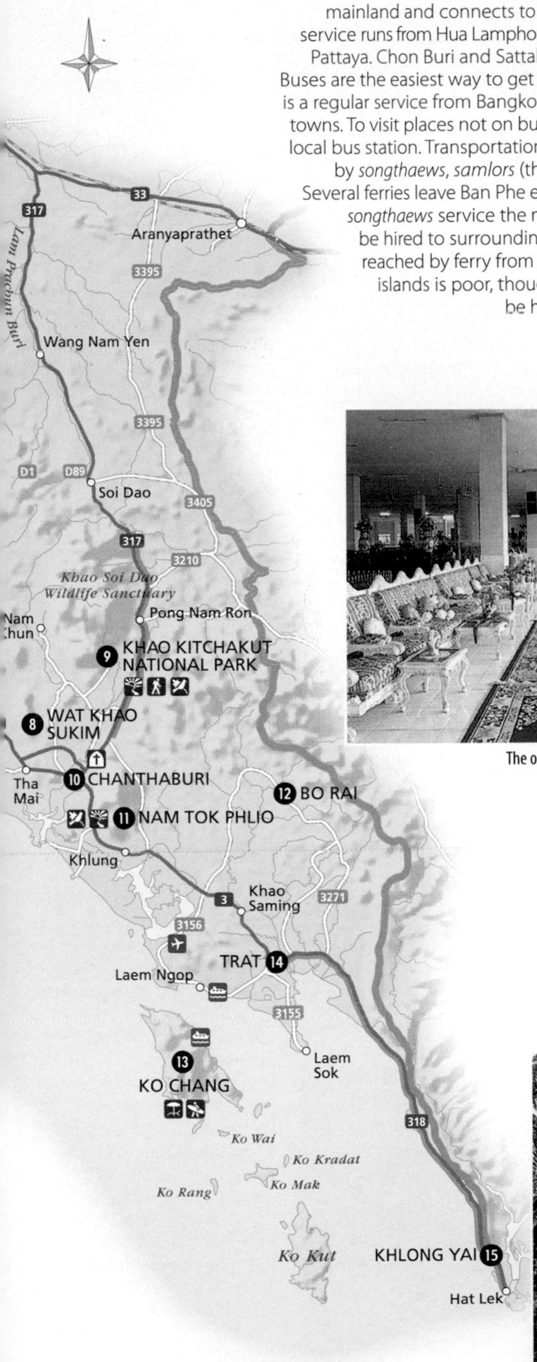

Aranyaprathet

Wang Nam Yen

Soi Dao

Khao Soi Dao Wildlife Sanctuary

Nam Chun

Pong Nam Ron

9 KHAO KITCHAKUT NATIONAL PARK

8 WAT KHAO SUKIM

Tha Mai

10 CHANTHABURI

12 BO RAI

11 NAM TOK PHLIO

Khlung

Khao Saming

3 TRAT **14**

Laem Ngop

Laem Sok

13 KO CHANG

Ko Wai

Ko Kradat

Ko Mak

Ko Rang

Ko Kut

KHLONG YAI **15**

Hat Lek

The opulent interior of the main hall of Wat Khao Sukim

0 kilometers 25

0 miles 15

Bungalows on palm-fringed Ko Chang

For keys to symbols *see back flap*

❶ Khao Khieo Open Zoo
สวนสัตว์เขาเขียว

Off Route 344, 6 miles (10 km) SE of Chon Buri, Chon Buri province. **Tel** 0-3831-8444. **W** kkopenzoo.com 🚉 🚌 Chon Buri, then *samlor*. **Open** 8am–6pm daily. 🎫

This open zoo has over 50 species of birds and animals, including deer, zebras, and tigers. The animals inhabit spacious, semifree enclosures, and the birds are kept in a large aviary. The zoo is in a peaceful, hilly setting amid woodland scenery and is best reached by car.

For bird enthusiasts, 12 miles (20 km) south of Khao Khieo is the beautiful wild marshland of **Bang Phra Reservoir**, where the brown-spotted whimbrel can be seen in winter.

❷ Si Racha
ศรีราชา

Chon Buri province. 🏠 20,000. 🚉 🚌 🚢 ℹ TAT, Pattaya (0-3842-7667). 🚢 daily.

Famed for its seafood and its spicy Si Racha sauce *(sauce phrik si racha)* – Thailand's answer to Tabasco – this small seaside town is the launching point for trips to Ko Sichang. Running off busy Jermjompol Road, Si Racha's main waterfront street, are several tentacle-like piers. At the end of the piers are breezy, open-air restaurants ideal for sampling the local delicacies: oysters *(hoi nang rom)* or mussels *(hoi thot)* dipped in Si Racha sauce. On a rocky promontory, which is also an occasional ferry pier, is **Ko Loi**, a Thai-Chinese Buddhist temple.

Just 6 miles (10 km) south of town is the **Si Racha Tiger Zoo**, with probably the world's largest collection of these big cats.

The streets of Si Racha (and Ko Sichang) resonate to the sound of spluttering motorcycle taxis. They are unique to the area – their sidecars are positioned at the rear.

Wat Atsadang, Rama V's meditation chamber on Ko Sichang

❸ Ko Sichang
เกาะสีชัง

Chon Buri province. 🏠 4,600. 🚢 from Si Racha. ℹ TAT, Pattaya (0-3842-7667 or 0-3842-8750).

A former haunt of King Chulalongkorn (Rama V), this small island, with a rugged coastline, once functioned as the customs checkpoint for Bangkok-bound ships. Now it is a relatively quiet place with some architectural ruins and a handful of guesthouses catering to visitors who want to avoid the bustle and commercialism of the resorts.

There is only one ramshackle fishing village, **Tha Bon**, on the eastern side of the island. Just north of it is the **Chinese Temple**, with colorfully decorated shrine caves.

On the west coast of the island are the beaches of **Hat Tham Pang** and **Hat Tham**. On the southern side, sprawling over a hillside, are the overgrown ruins of **Rama V's Summer Palace**. The palace was built in the 1890s but abandoned after a fleeting

Motorcycle taxis provide the transport on Si Racha and Ko Sichang

occupation by the French in 1893. In 1901 it was moved and reconstructed as Vimanmek Mansion at Dusit Park in Bangkok *(see pp106–9)*. One part of the palace complex that remains intact is the circular **Wat Atsadang** at the top of the hill. Crowned by a crumbling *chedi*, this was once a meditation chamber used by King Chulalongkorn.

The island also has a well-known temple, **Wat Tham Yai Prik**. Its gardens provide crops for the locals, and it has large underground rainwater tanks to meet the islanders' needs, since there is no other water source.

The deserted rocky hilltop offers pleasant walks and fine views. It is home to nesting seabirds and the yellow squirrel, which is endemic here.

Boats to Ko Sichang take 40 minutes from Si Racha's pier.

❹ Pattaya

พัทยา

Chon Buri province. 🗺 150,000. 🚉 🚌 ⛴ 🛈 TAT, 609 Mu 10 Phra Tamnak Rd, Pattaya (0-3842-7667). 🛥 daily. 🎉 Pattaya Festival (Apr).

Pattaya's faded beauty is now difficult to discern. The once-idyllic beaches attracted visitors as early as the 1950s and later became a destination for US troops on R&R during the Vietnam War. Now dubbed "Patpong by the Sea" *(see p120)*, the town has become one of Thailand's infamous red-light districts, with a menagerie of

A jet ski sitting ready for use on one of Pattaya's beaches

go-go bars and glitzy transvestite shows.

Despite its seedy image, Pattaya still attracts many families, who come for the good, cheap accommodations, extensive beaches (though the sea is often polluted), excellent restaurants, and the best water sports facilities in Thailand.

Pattaya consists of three bays. At its center is the 2-mile (3-km) long **Pattaya beach**. Pattaya Beach Road is packed with fast-food restaurants and souvenir shops. Walking Street, or "the strip," is where the sex industry plies its trade. North Pattaya Road, on the other hand, is more sedate, with open-air drinking spots called bar beers.

Many tourists prefer the more family-oriented 9-mile (14-km) long **Jomtien beach**, around the southern headland of Pattaya. This is also the best place for water sports, as the sea here is cleaner. Scores of companies offer water- and jet-skiing, windsurfing, sailing, parasailing, game-fishing, and scuba diving. Other activities include golf, target shooting, horseback riding, and tennis.

Quieter **Naklua bay**, to the north of Pattaya beach, has a fishing village that, despite tourism, has kept its charm.

The 2006 opening of Suvarnabhumi Airport, between Bangkok and Pattaya, sparked a building boom that led to the construction of several of Thailand's tallest skyscrapers.

Parrot fish, a common sight for divers in Pattaya's waters

❺ Rayong

ระยอง

Rayong province. 🗺 95,000. 🚌 ⛴ 🛈 TAT, 153/4 Sukhumvit Rd, Mu 12, Rayong (0-3865-5420). 🛥 daily. 🎉 Fruit Fair (May).

Rayong is a busy and prosperous fishing town best known as a starting point for trips to the nearby island of Ko Samet.

The main attractions lie outside the town. For good beaches, head 16 miles (25 km) southeast to **Ban Phe**. A 12-mile (20-km) coast road winds along from here to Laem Mae Phim.

From Ban Phe there are boats to Ko Samet *(see pp322–3)*. Ferries also run to nearby **Ko Saket, Ko Man Nok** and **Ko Man Klang** – the latter two islands are part of the Laem Ya-Mu Ko Samet National Park. The park authorities have managed to limit excessive development here, although jet-skiing is gradually eroding the coral reef.

Three miles (5 km) past Ban Phe is the beach park of **Suan Son** ("pine park"). This has crystal-white sand beaches and is a popular picnic area for Thais. It offers seafood snacks and homegrown water sports such as wave riding on inner tubes.

Rayong province is known for its succulent fruit, particularly the pineapple and durian *(see p137)*, and its *nam pla* (fish sauce) and *nam phrik kapi* (shrimp paste).

Picnicking Thais relaxing at Suan Son, a beach park near Rayong

⑥ Ko Samet

เกาะเสม็ด

Rayong province. 🗻 1,464. 🚤 from Ban Phe (Rayong) to Ao Wong Duan and Ao Phrao. 🛈 TAT, Rayong (0-3865-5420). 🚤 daily.

Ko Samet, blessed as it is with clear blue waters and crystalline sand, is popular with foreigners and Thai weekenders. Because it is only 4 miles (6 km) long and 2 miles (3 km) wide, most of the island is accessible on foot. The interior's dense jungle, home to the usual geckos and hornbills, is riddled with trails.

Despite attaining national park status in 1981, in common with all Thai resorts and islands, Ko Samet has suffered from development and has experienced a huge increase in high-quality accommodation.

The small fishing town of **Na Dan**, which links Ko Samet to Ban Phe on the mainland, was an ancient checkpoint for Chinese junks. Legend has it that its calm, sheltered waters were once the hunting ground of pirates. Several beaches on Ko Samet offer one-way boat trips back to Ban Phe.

The kite-shaped island's finest beaches are on the east coast. With its clear shallow waters, **Hat Sai Kaeo** ("glass sand beach") is the longest and liveliest beach. Water sports on the beach include windsurfing. Boat trips around Ko Samet and snorkeling day trips to nearby islands leave from here.

Ban Phe

Ban Phe

Na Dan

KO SAMET

Ao Phrao

Mermaid Statue

Hat Sai Kaeo

Ao Phai

Ban Phe

Ao Nuan

Ao Cho

Ao Wong Duan

Ao Thian

Ao Wai

Ao Kui Na Nok

Ao Kui Na Nai

Cape Khut

Ao Karang

Ao Toei

Ko Chan

Key

═══ Minor road

▪ ▪ Trail

0 kilometers ———— 1

0 miles ———— 1

Sunset walk along the coast of picturesque Ko Samet

For keys to symbols see back flap

Heading southward along the east coast are the equally popular **Ao Phai** and **Ao Nuan**. Near the first is a wind-battered statue of the prince and the mermaid in *Phra Aphaimani*, a poem by Sunthorn Phu, Thailand's most famous poet.

Farther south, the bays are less crowded, with the exception of the wide beach at **Ao Wong Duan** ("moon bay"), which can get quite busy. At the narrow isthmus of **Ao Kui**, solitude and beauty are guaranteed. It is merely a short stroll between sunrise and sunset vistas of Ao Kui Na Nok and Ao Kui Na Nai. The island's best coral is found just off the southern tip.

The only area to have undergone development on the largely inaccessible west coast is **Ao Phrao** ("coconut bay"). Due to its isolation, the beach here doesn't receive as many overnight visitors as those on the east coast.

In July 2013 the island was hit by a devastating oil spill caused by a broken pipeline. A clean-up operation has now restored the beaches to their former glory.

Upscale bungalows on peaceful Ao Phrao, Ko Samet

❼ Khao Chamao–Khao Wong National Park

อุทยานแห่งชาติเขาชะเมา–เขาวง

Rayong province. Park HQ 11 miles (17 km) N of Hwy 3 at Klaeng. 🅸 TAT, Rayong (0-3865-5420). Forestry Dept, Bangkok (0-2562-0760 or Park HQ 0-3889-4378). Bungalow bookings: 🆆 dnp.go.th 🚌 Rayong or Chanthaburi, then songthaew. 🚲 🆆 tat-rayong.com

The two mountains in this national park, Khao Wong and Khao Chamao, loom above the farming lowlands of the Eastern Seaboard.

Elephants and Asiatic black bears find refuge in the park's tropical, broadleaved, evergreen forests, away from farmers and hunters. Also resident is the *tor soro* carp. Folklore claims that the name of Chamao mountain, which means "to get drunk,"

derives from the giddy feeling induced by eating the carp.

Park highlights include the pools of the **Khao Chamao waterfall** and the 80 or so **Khao Wong caves**. Tham Pet ("diamond cave") and Tham Lakhon ("theater cave"), situated 2 miles (4 km) southeast of the park headquarters, are the most spectacular of these limestone caverns. The park's most impressive waterfall is **Klong Pla-Gang**, a 3 mile (5 km) trek from park headquarters

There are few developed trails in the park. The best route climbs alongside the cascading Khao Chamao waterfall and ends near the top of the falls at Chong Kaep.

From the park's northwest station former elephant trails lead through the fertile and wildlife-rich forest of the stunning Khlong Phlu valley.

Wat Khao Sukim's cable car, which transports visitors up to the temple

❽ Wat Khao Sukim

วัดเขาสุกิม

Khao Bai Si, Tha-Mai district, 13 miles (20 km) N of Chanthaburi, off route 3322. 🅸 TAT, Rayong (0-3865-5420). 🚌 Chanthaburi, then *songthaew*.

This huge, pale orange *wat* is perched on the side of Sukim mountain. The temple, the home of Luang Pho Somchai, one of Thailand's most popular meditation masters, is reached via a cable car or the *naga*-lined staircase. Inside are a number of tables inlaid with mother-of-pearl, while exhibits housed in a museum include an ostentatious display of jewelry and a collection of Bencharong, Khmer, and Ban Chiang pottery. They show the surprising wealth that a revered monk can accumulate from donations by merit-makers.

The Poetry of Sunthorn Phu

Sunthorn Phu (1786–1855) is Thailand's most respected poet. His long, lyrical travel verses, often with a moral lesson, made him the favorite poet of kings Rama II and Rama III. The epic *Phra Aphaimani*, Sunthorn Phu's first poem, was inspired by the surroundings of Ko Samet (then called Ko Kaew Pisadan), where he settled. The poem tells the story of a prince, Phra Aphaimani, exiled to an underwater kingdom ruled by a giantess, who is in love with him. Helped by a mermaid, the prince escapes by fleeing to Ko Samet. The giantess follows, but is defeated when the prince plays his magic flute, sending her to sleep. The prince is subsequently betrothed to a beautiful princess.

Statue on Ko Samet depicting characters in *Phra Aphaimani*

For hotels and restaurants see pp402–11 and pp418–33

❾ Khao Kitchakut National Park

อุทยานแห่งชาติเขาคิชฌกูฏ

Chanthaburi province. Park HQ off Hwy 3249, 15 miles (24 km) NE of Chanthaburi. *ℹ* Park HQ (0-3945-2074). 🚌 Chanthaburi, then *songthaew.* 🐾

Covering an area of just 23 sq miles (59 sq km), this is one of Thailand's smallest national parks. It encompasses Khao Kitchakut, a granite mountain just over 3,300 ft (1,000 m) high. The park's best known site, the 13-tier **Krathin waterfall**, is located near park headquarters. From here a relatively easy trail can be taken to the top.

Logo of the Thai national parks

More ambitious hikers and large numbers of pilgrims make the arduous four-hour climb to the summit of the impressive Phrabat mountain. They come to see two sights: an image of the Buddha's Footprint, which is etched here in granite, and a strange collection of natural rock formations shaped like an elephant, a large turtle, a pagoda, and a monk's bowl.

Khao Kitchakut is near the much larger, but less visited, **Khao Soi Dao Wildlife Sanctuary** (290 sq miles, 745 sq km). Both protected areas enclose some of the last surviving tracts of a once-great lowland forest. They are vital to the economy of the region as their slopes collect water for orchards. They also provide protection for many endangered species, including sun bears, spot-bellied eagle owls, silver pheasants, spiny-breasted giant frogs, binturongs (bear cats), and elephants. The upland forests of Khao Soi Dao provide a habitat for the tree-dwelling pileated gibbon.

☒ Khao Soi Dao Wildlife Sanctuary

Off Hwy 317, 16 miles (25 km) NW of Chanthaburi. *ℹ* TAT, Rayong (0-3865-5420). 🚌 Chanthaburi, then *songthaew.* 🐾

Shrine inside the Church of the Immaculate Conception, Chanthaburi

❿ Chanthaburi

จันทบุรี

Chanthaburi province. 🏠 50,000. 🚌 *ℹ* TAT, Rayong (0-3865-5420). 🛍 daily. 🎏 Fruit Festival (May/Jun).

Surrounded by verdant chili and rubber plantations, this prosperous and friendly town is arguably Thailand's most charming settlement. Known as a center for gem trading *(see pp314–15)* since the 15th century, Chanthaburi has attracted a wide ethnic mix. Vietnamese refugees form the largest group. They came in three waves: in the 19th century, fleeing the anti-Catholic persecutions of Cochin China; in the early 20th century, escaping French colonial rule; and after the 1975 victory in South Vietnam by North Vietnamese Communists. The Vietnamese quarter, running parallel to the river on Rim Nam Road, is lined with lattice-work wooden shop-houses.

The monarch most revered in the town today is King Taksin. In the 18th century he expelled the Burmese from the town, their last Thai stronghold, thus reuniting Thailand. Two monuments celebrate Taksin and his famous victory: **San Somdej Prachao Taksin** on Tha Luang Road is a huge statue in the shape of Taksin's hat. **Taksin Park** sports a dynamic bronze statue of the king in battle as seen on the 20-*baht* note.

On the bank of the Chanthaburi River is the **Church of the Immaculate Conception**, a French-style Catholic cathedral built on the site of an 18th-century missionary chapel.

A refreshing shower at the base of Krathin waterfall, Khao Kitchakut

Maytime Fruit Festivals

Held in three neighboring provinces – Rayong, Chanthaburi and Trat – this annual fruit festival, lasting for a few days in either May or June (whenever the harvest is ripe), is a colorful, celebratory affair. These provinces are known for their flavorsome rambutan, durian, and mangosteen, which all come into season during May. Stalls selling the produce of local orchards are set up on the main streets of each town. Parades of floral-and-fruit floats are held along with gaudy beauty pageants, which are a ubiquitous element of every provincial Thai festival. Contests for the ripest durian or most beautifully shaped fruit, among other titles, are a highlight of the year for local farmers and a great spectacle for tourists. Visitors can also see cultural shows and excellent displays of local handicrafts. In Chanthaburi there are many stalls selling one of the specialties of the province: intricately woven straw mats.

Fruit festival float, Chanthaburi

It is the largest cathedral in the country and a legacy of French occupation. The French held Chanthaburi hostage from 1893 to 1904 as a guarantee that Thailand would relinquish her hold on Lao and Cambodian land. To keep the country intact, King Chulalongkorn reluctantly agreed to surrender the territories.

The **Gem Quarter** (talat phloi), at the intersection of Si Chan and Thetsaban 4 roads, attracts gem traders from all over the world.

Statue of King Taksin, Chanthaburi

On weekends a rainbow array of gemstones from Burma, Cambodia, and the rich mines of Chanthaburi province are traded at street stalls. However, most of the best quality stones are dispatched directly to Bangkok.

⓫ Namtok Phlio National Park

อุทยานแห่งชาติน้ำตกพลิ้ว

Chanthaburi province. Park HQ off Hwy 3, 9 miles (14 km) SE of Chanthaburi. ✦ TAT, Rayong (0-3865-5420); Forestry Dept (0-2562-0760 or ⓦ dnp.go.th for bungalow bookings). ▨ Chanthaburi, then *songthaew*. ▨

Immensely popular with Thais, this 52-sq mile (135-sq km) park contains some of Thailand's richest rainforest. It is also a haven for wildlife, with over 156 species of birds and 32 of mammals, including the Asiatic black bear, tiger, leopard, barking deer, and macaque. The park's other attractions are its spectacular waterfalls – the most impressive being **Phlio waterfall**. Facing this are two *chedis*: the Alongkon *chedi* and a 10-ft (3-m) high pyramid-shaped *chedi*, built by King Chulalongkorn in honor of one of his queens, Sunantha, who drowned at Bang Pa-in (*see p185*) in 1876. The region was much loved by Chulalongkorn.

A harder hike is required to reach the 66-ft (20-m) roaring Trok Nong falls and the forest-encircled Klang waterfall. The entrance road to the park is lined with souvenir shops.

⓬ Bo Rai

บ่อไร่

Trat province. ▨ 25,000. ▨ ✦ TAT, Trat (0-3959-7259-60). ▨ daily.

This small town used to be the thriving center of the Eastern Seaboard's gem trade. The surrounding mines, once renowned for the quality of their rubies (*tab tim*), have almost dried up, so today the Bo Rai gem trade is small. Only one morning market of any significance, the **Khlong Yaw market**, remains. The market has a reverse system of buying and selling – buyers sit at makeshift tables and vendors stroll around displaying their wares.

Sadly, gem mining has destroyed large areas of Trat province, exposing the topsoil and leaving acres of despoiled land in rusty-orange mud.

Customer carefully inspecting a vendor's gems in Bo Rai market

Bungalows amid coconut trees along Khlong Phrao, Ko Chang

⑬ Ko Chang

เกาะช้าง

Trat province. 👥 5,800. 🚢 from Laem Ngop. 🛈 TAT, Trat (0-3959-7259-60).

Mountainous Ko Chang is the largest of the 50 or so islands that form the Ko Chang National Marine Park, which covers an area of 250 sq miles (650 sq km), two-thirds of which is ocean. Mangroves, cliffs, and clear waters make this one of Thailand's most scenic islands and the ideal place for a varied holiday. Increased development means that Ko Chang now has no shortage of quality hotels, resorts, and spas.

Since Thai-Chinese agricultural families first settled on Ko Chang in the mid-19th century, most of the island's wildlife has been destroyed, although some small mammals, including the barking deer,

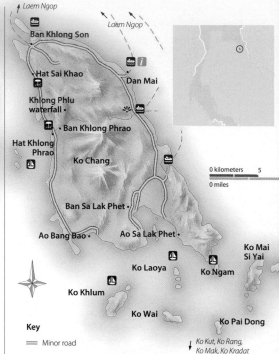

Key

═══ Minor road

stump-tailed macaque, and small Indian civet, remain. Also resident are some 75 bird species, and reptiles and amphibians such as monitor lizards, pythons, king cobras, and the endemic Ko Chang frog.

Inland exploration is difficult because of the rugged terrain. The coast road, which was begun in the early 1990s, is the first construction to improve accessibility on the island. Ko Chang's best beaches are on the west coast, especially along Ao Sai Khao, where the shell-

sprinkled, bungalow-lined **Hat Sai Khao** ("white sand beach"), the island's longest and busiest beach, is located. An information center on the beach arranges boat trips, fishing, and snorkeling. Most guesthouses also offer fishing, snorkeling, and motorcycle rental. **Hat Khlong Phrao**, south of here, is more attractive and quieter. Nearby is a fishing village, Ban Khlong Phrao. Apart from tourism, which is growing rapidly, fishing is also important.

The beaches in the south are still relatively isolated. Of these, the beach at the sheltered bay of **Ao Bang Bao**, in the southwest corner, is particularly beautiful. East of here is a long beach encircling a bay, Ao Sa Lak Phet, where there are a few fishing villages and bungalows. The wrecks of two Thai Navy ships can be visited off the coast here.

Of the island's many waterfalls, two are worth the hike. On the east coast, near the park headquarters, is the three-tiered **Than Mayom waterfall**, which has good views of the

View of Hat Khlong Phrao, one of the best beaches on Ko Chang

For keys to symbols *see back flap*

island. The other is **Khlong Phlu waterfall**, along Khlong Phrao on the west coast. The uppermost level, accessible by a gentle 2-mile (3-km) hike, has a freshwater pool.

For snorkelers, divers, and day-trippers there are stunning smaller islands off the coast of Ko Chang, with a good variety of hard and soft corals and a proliferation of giant clams.

Ko Kut, the second largest island within the group, falls outside the park boundaries. It has excellent beaches and breathtaking waterfalls.

The rocky, coral-lined coast of **Ko Wai**, south of Ko Chang, is popular for fishing. Around **Ko Rang**, farther south, is a cluster of rocky coral islets.

Ko Mak, a predominantly flat island, is covered mainly in coconut plantations. It has a secluded beach on the northwest bay, a fishing village, and good coral reefs.

Northeast of Ko Mak is the coconut-fringed **Ko Kradat**, a tiny island with some of the prettiest beaches in the island cluster. The island's name comes from the kradat tree, which is used to make paper.

Sandflies and mosquitoes are a problem on the islands, so be sure to take precautions and invest in insect repellent.

Barrel sponge, seen off Ko Chang

⑭ Trat

ตราด

Trat province. 📷 72,000. 🚌 🛥 *i* TAT, Trat (0-3959-7259 60). 🛥 daily. 🎏 Rakham Fruit Fair (May–Jun).

This provincial capital is a small but busy commercial town. Most tourists pass through Trat only en route to Ko Chang. However, the town's popularity is likely to increase in line with that of the archipelago. Trat has several attractions, including its markets, most of which are centered around Tait Mai and Sukhumvit roads. The covered market on Sukhumvit Road has a good selection of food and drink stalls. Also of interest are the gem-mining villages around Trat, such as Bo Rai, where rubies are mined *(see pp314–15)*. Local guesthouses can arrange trips. Located about 1 mile (2 km) southwest of Trat is **Wat Bupharam** ("flower temple"), set in pleasant grounds with large, shady trees. Some of the original buildings within the temple complex, including the *wihan*, the bell tower, and the monks' residences, or *kutis*, date from the late Ayutthaya period *(see pp64–5)*.

Durian vendor at one of Trat's bustling markets

⑮ Khlong Yai

คลองใหญ่

Trat province. 📷 15,000. *i* TAT, Trat (0-3959-7259-60). 🛥 daily.

This picturesque seaside town near the Cambodian border sports a handful of bustling markets and stalls selling delicious noodles with seafood.

The road from Khlong Yai to the border checkpoint of **Hat Lek** passes through spectacular scenery, with mountains on one side and the sea on the other. Tourists can now enter Cambodia at Hat Lek. A visa on arrival is available with a valid passport, recent photo, and US$30. However, border guards often demand higher fees, so it is wise to apply for a visa in advance at Bangkok's Cambodian Embassy.

Fishing trawlers, harbored on Ko Chang, which provide a significant source of income on the island

For hotels and restaurants see pp402–11 and pp418–33

WESTERN SEABOARD

The rolling landscape of the Western Seaboard extends some 370 miles (600 km) from Bangkok to Surat Thani. Its major attraction is the islands that make up the beautiful Ko Samui archipelago, such as Ko Pha Ngan, Ko Tao, and the Angthong National Marine Park. Yet visitors should not ignore the many charms of the mainland – lively towns, fine beaches, and national parks.

Miles of remote sandy beaches dominate long stretches of the Western Seaboard, which unites the Buddhist heartland of the nation with the maritime, Muslim-influenced South. Temples reflecting pre-Thai influences, simple fishing villages, verdant fruit orchards, and sand-rimmed resorts characterize this region.

The Tenasserim Mountains, rising to 4,350 ft (1,329 m), form a spine down the peninsula. They absorb much of the rain that falls during the southwest monsoon, keeping the coastal strip relatively dry. However, this coastal region is still a fertile growing area, famed for its pineapples, corn, sugar cane, "lady-finger" bananas, asparagus, and mangosteens.

Beaches easily reached from the capital cater primarily to weekenders from Bangkok. Particularly popular are the casuarina-lined waterfronts of Cha-am and Hua Hin. The latter was Thailand's first beach resort. The many golf courses within easy reach of these two tourist centers make this area arguably the country's premier golf destination. Farther south, the stunning islands of the Ko Samui archipelago offer excellent diving and sunbathing, and a well-developed tourist infrastructure.

Trekkers and bird-watchers will be drawn to Khao Sam Roi Yot and Kaeng Krachan national parks, where migratory birds rest and feed in the salt marshes from August to April.

Among the most interesting of the towns along the Western Seaboard is Phetchaburi, with its crumbling architectural remnants of the Khmer, Mon, Ayutthaya, and Rattanakosin epochs. Farther to the south, Chaiya still contains archaeological remains that reveal its important role in the Srivijaya Empire (*see pp350–51*).

Fishing boats in the bay of the peaceful town of Prachuap Khiri Khan

◄ Tham Khao Luang cave temple, Phetchaburi

Exploring the Western Seaboard

This long, narrow coastal strip, backed by mountains along the Burmese border, stretches from the cultural center of Phetchaburi to the commercial town of Surat Thani. In the north is one of Thailand's oldest beach resorts, Hua Hin, while farther north still is the modern resort of Cha-am. The area also offers natural beauty inland in the huge, hilly Kaeng Krachan National Park and the limestone outcrops of the coastal Khao Sam Roi Yot National Park. The islands of the stunning Ko Samui archipelago are the major attractions farther south. Ko Samui itself is the main resort island, while Ko Tao and Ko Pha Ngan are popular with backpackers. For spectacular, unspoiled island scenery, it is hard to beat the beautiful Angthong National Marine Park.

Sights at a Glance

1. *Phetchaburi pp332–4*
2. Kaeng Krachan National Park
3. Cha-am
4. Mareukathayawan Palace
5. Hua Hin
6. Khao Sam Roi Yot National Park
7. Prachuap Khiri Khan
8. Chumphon
9. Chaiya
10. Surat Thani
11. *Ko Samui pp340–42*
12. Ko Pha Ngan
13. Angthong National Marine Park
14. Ko Tao

Towering stacks of TV antennas on the houses along the Phet River in the center of Phetchaburi

Lapping up the sun on Ko Samui's Chaweng beach

Getting There

Most of the attractions in the region are easily accessible from the main highways 4 and 41. The major towns are linked to each other and Bangkok by bus services and trains (Bangkok to Hua Hin is 3–4 hours by bus or train; Bangkok to Surat Thani is 11 hours by bus, 11–13 hours by train). Ko Samui, Surat Thani, Prachuap Khiri Khan, and Hua Hin have domestic airports. There are several flights a day between Bangkok and Hua Hin and Ko Samui. *Songthaews* and bicycle rickshaws can be hired for trips to local sights. Cha-am, Hua Hin, and Ko Samui have car rental facilities. Surat Thani and Don Sak are the main gateways to the Ko Samui archipelago. Ko Tao is also accessible via Chumphon. The train/bus/ferry journey from Bangkok to Ko Samui takes 16 hours.

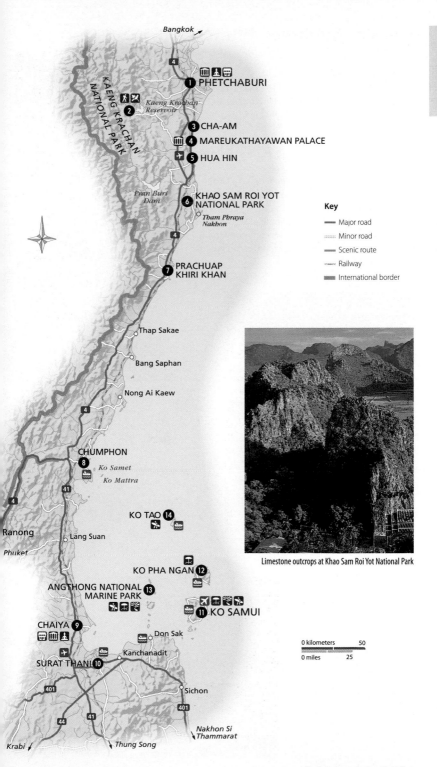

Bangkok

KAENG KRACHAN NATIONAL PARK

Kaeng Krachan Reservoir

① PHETCHABURI

②

③ CHA-AM

④ MAREUKATHAYAWAN PALACE

⑤ HUA HIN

Pran Buri Dam

⑥ KHAO SAM ROI YOT NATIONAL PARK

Tham Phraya Nakhon

⑦ PRACHUAP KHIRI KHAN

Thap Sakae

Bang Saphan

Nong Ai Kaew

CHUMPHON
⑧
Ko Samet
Ko Mattra

Ranong

Phuket

Lang Suan

KO TAO **⑭**

KO PHA NGAN **⑫**

ANGTHONG NATIONAL MARINE PARK **⑬**

⑪ KO SAMUI

CHAIYA **⑨**

Don Sak

Kanchanadit

SURAT THANI **⑩**

Sichon

Krabi

Thung Song

Nakhon Si Thammarat

Key

— Major road

···· Minor road

— Scenic route

⌐⌐ Railway

▬ International border

Limestone outcrops at Khao Sam Roi Yot National Park

0 kilometers	50
0 miles	25

For keys to symbols *see back flap*

❶ Street-by-Street: Phetchaburi

เพชรบุรี

Settled since at least the 11th century, Phetchaburi
(often spelled Phetburi) is one of Thailand's oldest
towns. It has long been an important trading and
cultural center, and Mon, Khmer, and Ayutthayan
influences can be seen in its 30 temples. During the
19th century it became a favorite royal retreat, and
King Mongkut built a summer house here on a hill,
Khao Wang, west of the center. This is now part of the
Phra Nakhon Khiri Historical Park *(see p334)*. Other
major sights are the 17th-century Wat Yai Suwannaram,
the five Khmer *prangs* of Wat Kamphaeng Laeng, and
an old quarter that has retained much of its original
charm. Despite such attractions, accommodation is
scant. Most visitors come on day trips from Bangkok,
76 miles (123 km) away.

To Phra
Nakhon Khiri
Historical Park

Phra Song Road
Several *wats* are located
on this busy road.

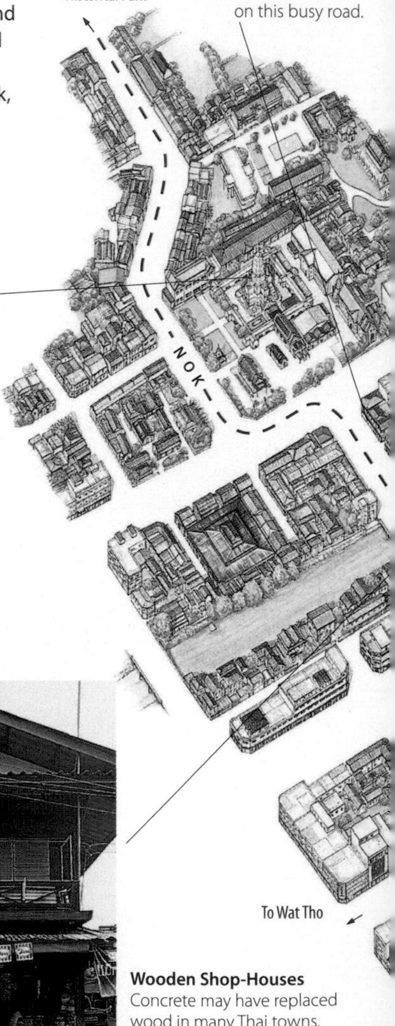

Wat Mahathat
The five white Khmer-style
prangs of this much-restored
14th-century temple dominate
the town's central skyline.
The figures of angels and gods
decorate the roofs of the main
wihan and *bot*.

0 meters 75

0 yards 75

To Wat Tho

Wooden Shop-Houses
Concrete may have replaced
wood in many Thai towns,
but attractive wooden
buildings, many lining the
riverbank, are still a feature
of Phetchaburi.

★ **Phra Nakhon Khiri Historical Park**
As an avid astronomer, King Mongkut had this observatory conveniently built next to his hilltop summer palace; this is now a museum *(see p334)*. The magnificently landscaped and forested surrounding park offers extensive views of Phetchaburi.

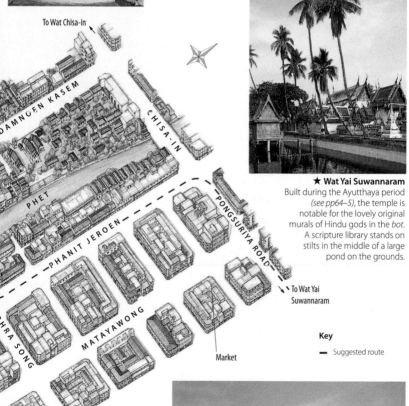

★ **Wat Yai Suwannaram**
Built during the Ayutthaya period *(see pp64–5)*, the temple is notable for the lovely original murals of Hindu gods in the *bot*. A scripture library stands on stilts in the middle of a large pond on the grounds.

To Wat Chisa-in

DAMNUEN KASEM

CHISA-IN

PHET

PHANIT JEROEN

PONGSURIYA ROAD

To Wat Yai Suwannaram

PHRA SONG

MATAYAWONG

Market

Key
— Suggested route

To Wat Kamphaeng Laeng

★ **Wat Kamphaeng Laeng**
This is one of the few surviving Khmer shrines in Thailand outside the Northeast. The five laterite *prangs* of the temple, in varying states of disrepair, are typically Khmer in design and may date from the 12th century. Originally a Hindu temple, it was later adapted for Buddhist use.

Phra Nakhon Khiri, Rama IV's ambitious 19th-century palace complex

Exploring Phetchaburi's Outer Sights

Phetchaburi is divided by the Phet River, which weaves its way past this provincial capital's 30 historic temples. Many, especially the Ayutthayan *wats*, are excellently preserved, their pinnacles dominating the skyline. In the distance, to the west, three large hills loom imperiously over the city.

Phra Nakhon Khiri, locally referred to as Khao Wang, translates as the "celestial city of the mountain." This palace complex, perched on top of 302-ft (92-m) Maha Samana hill, was commissioned by King Mongkut (Rama IV) as a summer house in the 1850s. Extravagant use of European, Chinese, and Japanese architectural styles make this a bold study in Thai and foreign architecture. Set among natural woods, rocks, and caverns, it also offers fine vistas of Phetchaburi town and panoramic views of the province.

The complex extends over three peaks. The Royal Palace and the Ho Chatchawan Wiangchai, an observatory tower (Rama IV was an accomplished amateur astronomer), are both perched on the west rise; the Phra That Chomphet, a white *chedi* erected by Rama V, stands on the central rise; and Wat Maha Samanaram, containing some fine murals, takes up the east rise. In 1988 the complex was made a Historical Park. A cable car takes visitors up the steep ascent to the palace buildings.

A short distance north of town is **Tham Khao Luang**, a cave containing stalactites, *chedis*, and Buddha images. To the right of the cave's mouth lies **Wat Bun Thawi**, notable for its intricately carved wooden door panels.

🏛 **Phra Nakhon Khiri**
Khao Wang, Phetchaburi.
Tel 0-3242-5600. **Open** daily. 🐾

🕳 **Tham Khao Luang**
Hwy 3173, 2 miles (3 km) N of Phetchaburi. **Open** daily.
🐾 donation.

❷ Kaeng Krachan National Park

อุทยานแห่งชาติแก่งกระจาน

Phetchaburi province. Park HQ off Hwy 3175, 37 miles (60 km) S of Phetchaburi. 🛈 TAT (0-3247-1005/6); Forestry Dept (0-2562-0760 or 🌐 **dnp.go.th** for bungalow bookings). 🚌 🚐 Phetchaburi then *songthaew.* 🐾

Thailand's largest national park is home to at least 40 species of large mammal, such as tiger, leopard, elephant, gibbon, two types of Asiatic bear, and two types of leaf-monkey (langur). Established in 1981,

Tiger, one of many species at Kaeng Krachan National Park

this 1,150-sq mile (2,920-sq km) preserve covers nearly half of Phetchaburi province and contains some of the most pristine tracts of tropical evergreen forest in the country.

The park is relatively unknown to tourists but offers some excellent hiking.

Its western flank is marked out by the dramatic Tenasserim mountain range and the Thai-Burmese border. Streams and rivers are the water source for the 17-sq mile (45-sq km) **Kaeng Krachan reservoir**, which can be explored by boat. Thousands of migratory birds coming from as far afield as China and Siberia rest, feed, and breed in the salt marshes.

Horse for hire at Cha-am beach

❸ Cha-am

ชะอำ

Phetchaburi province. 🏔 20,000. 🚉 🚌 🛈 TAT, 500/51 Phetkasem Rd, Cha-am (0-3247-1005/6). 🏖 daily.

Since the mid-1980s Cha-am has experienced a dramatic surge in popularity. It has been developed from a quiet fishing and market village into a lively playground for Bangkok weekenders. Tall condominiums and huge resort hotels have sprung up alongside the long, sandy beach. During the week, however, it can be remarkably quiet.

The resort caters primarily to Thais, who focus their attentions on eating and drinking rather than swimming. At umbrella-shaded tables strung along the beach like a high tide mark, visitors feast on delicious grilled fish, squid, shrimp, and mussels. Spicy dips and cold beer complete the culinary adventure. Those who prefer more formal eating will find restaurants serving the same range of succulent fare at the northern end of the beach.

❹ Mareukatha-yawan Palace

พระราชนิเวศน์มฤคทายวัน

Off Hwy 4, 5 miles (9 km) S of Cha-am. 🛈 *TAT, Cha-am (0-3247-1005/6).* 🚌 *from Cha-am.* **Open** *8:30am–4:30pm daily.* 🎫 *donation.* 🚫 *in bedroom.*

Mareukathayawan Palace ("the palace of love and hope") was the summer residence of Rama VI. Built midway between Cha-am and Hua Hin, this grand golden teak building was designed by an Italian architect and constructed in just 16 days in 1923. However, it was abandoned when Rama VI died two years later and stood neglected for decades. The palace has undergone restoration since the 1970s and is now close to its original appearance.

The building is cool and airy; its wooden halls, verandas, and royal chambers are decorated simply and painted in pastel shades. Although the palace is easily accessible, it is rarely visited by tourists.

❺ Hua Hin

หัวหิน

Prachuap Khiri Khan province. 🚉 *33,000.* ✈ 🚐 🚌 🛈 *Municipality Tourist Office, 114 Phetkasem Rd, Hua Hin (0-3247-1005).* 🛥 *daily.*

Hua Hin was Thailand's first beach resort. Its rail connection to Bangkok, completed in 1911, was key to its success, making the 118-mile (190-km) journey from Bangkok a manageable seaside excursion. A nine-hole golf course and the splendid colonial-style Railway Hotel were built in 1922 and 1923.

Hua Hin Station, vital to the resort's early success

Following the international trend for recuperative spa resorts at the time, Hua Hin became a popular retreat for minor Thai royalty, Bangkok's high society, and affluent foreigners. Prince Chulachakra-bongse built a summer palace in the town which he called **Klai Klangwon** (meaning "far from worries") in 1926. It is still used by the royal family and is not open to the public. Hua Hin's fortunes declined after World War II, but its historical connections have helped it become popular again with a new generation of Bangkokians. Hua Hin is also a hit with international retirees, who are catered for by new holiday homes and condominiums. There has also been a marked rise in boutique resorts, spas, and restaurants.

For an insight into the Hua Hin of the 1920s, visit the Railway Hotel, now called the **Sofitel Centara Grand Resort & Villas**. By the 1960s it had fallen into disrepair, but a sensitive restoration of the elegant 1920s decor, museum tearoom, and topiaries won it an Outstanding Conservation Award from the Architects' Association of Thailand in 1993. Before its refurbishment the hotel and its environs were used in the making of the film *The Killing Fields*, where it stood in for the Phnom Penh Hotel.

South of Hua Hin's main beach lies Khao Takiap (or "chopstick hill"), which is covered with miniature *chedis* and shrines. Nearby stands **Wat Khao Lad**, fronted by an impressive 66-ft (20-m) standing Buddha, which faces the sea.

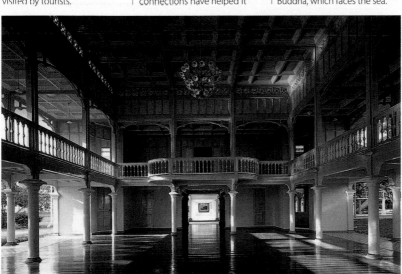

The majestic open hall and first-floor gallery in the north wing of Mareukathayawan Palace

❻ Khao Sam Roi Yot National Park

อุทยานแห่งชาติเขาสามร้อยยอด

Prachuap Khiri Khan province. Visitors' Centre off Hwy 4, 23 miles (37 km) S of Pranburi. 🛈 TAT, Cha-am (0-3247-1005/6); Forestry Dept (0-2562-0760 or 🌐 **dnp.go.th** for bungalow bookings). 🚌 Pranburi, then *songthaew*. 🐾 📷

This small coastal park sits in the narrowest part of the Thai peninsula, overlooking the Gulf of Thailand. Covering 38 sq miles (98 sq km), it is a region of contrasts: sea, sand, and marsh backed by mountains and caves. The park is best known for its distinctive limestone pinnacles (*Khao Sam Roi Yot* means "mountain of 300 peaks") that rise vertically from the marshland to a height of 2,150 ft (650 m).

The park's wetlands provide a sanctuary for water birds. Millions of migratory birds flying from Siberia to Sumatra and Australia rest, feed, and breed here between August and April. It is home to many other animals such as the rare dusky langur, the nocturnal slow loris, and the crab-eating macaque.

Beware monkeys sign, Khao Sam Roi Yot

Tham Phraya Nakon houses a grand pavilion, built for King Rama V in 1896, and **Tham Sai** contains fossilized falls.

Wat Chong Kra Chok, overlooking sedate Prachuap Khiri Khan

❼ Prachuap Khiri Khan

ประจวบคีรีขันธ์

Prachuap Khiri Khan province. 🗺 60,000. 🚉 🚌 🚢 🛈 TAT, Cha-am (0-3247-1005/6). 🚢 daily.

Prachuap Khiri Khan means "town among the mountain chain." And it is certainly true that its coastal sugar-loaf limestone outcrops at either end of a sandy bay give it a "little Rio" appearance. The local economy relies primarily on fishing; freshly caught seafood can be purchased from a number of good restaurants and stalls along the promenade. This peaceful administrative town has pleasant swimming beaches to the north and south of its main bay. The top of the delightful **Wat Chong**

Kra Chok – perched on one of the surrounding hills – offers the best view of the area. About 200 macaques live on the hill, and every evening they climb to the top to feed from the lovely frangipani trees.

❽ Chumphon

ชุมพร

Chumphon province. 🗺 84,000. 🚉 🚌 🚢 🛈 TAT, Chumphon (0-7750-1831). 🚢 daily. 🎉 Luang Suan Buddha Image Parade and Boat Race (5 days in Oct).

Chumphon is regarded by some as the point of cultural transition between the heartland of the Buddhist Tai peoples, and the peninsular south of the country, where Muslim culture is strong. The town was the home of Prince Chumphon, the Father of the Royal Thai Navy, who died in 1923. Nearby, the 225-ft (68-m) long **HMS Chumphon** torpedo boat, decommissioned in 1975, has been preserved. It forms a distinctive landmark.

The reefs around the 47 tiny islands off Chumphon's 140-mile (222-km) long coast are becoming increasingly popular with divers. Tour companies in town will arrange diving day trips to such islands as **Samet, Mattra, Ngam Yai**, and **Ngam Noi**. Chumphon is also the most convenient place from which to get a ferry to Ko Tao *(see p345)*.

Chaiya's Role in the Srivijaya Empire

Srivijayan votive tablet

The Mahayana Buddhist Empire of Srivijaya *(see pp60–61)* dominated the whole Malaysian peninsula and parts of Indonesia between the 7th and 13th centuries AD. Although the majority of scholars now believe that Palembang in Sumatra was the Srivijayan capital, discoveries of temple remains and some exquisite stone and bronze statues (many now in the National Museum in Bangkok) in Chaiya provide evidence of Chaiya's importance. Its strategic geographical position, as a then coastal port, meant the town played an important role in the east-west trade between India, the peninsula, and China. In fact, Chaiya was mentioned in the writings of the Chinese monk I Chinga, who, while visiting the area in the late 7th century, testified to its religious and cultural sophistication. It is known that some of Chaiya's rulers were connected by marriage to those of central Java. Furthermore, it is possible that the name "Chaiya" originated as a contraction of "Siwichaiya" (a different transliteration of *Srivijaya*), which follows the local tendency to emphasize the final syllable of a word.

8th-century bronze found at Chaiya

A line of Buddha images at Phra Boromathat Chaiya, one of the few remaining temples from the Srivijaya period

9 Chaiya

ไชยา

Surat Thani province. 🏔 34,000.
🚉 🚌 ℹ️ TAT, Surat Thani
(0-7728-8818). 📅 daily. 🎉 Chak
Phra Festival (Oct–Nov).

Despite the somewhat dreary look of the small railroad town of Chaiya, the settlement is actually one of the oldest and most historically significant in Southern Thailand. A number of superb examples of sculpture dating from the Srivijaya period (7th–13th centuries) have been found here.

Many of the sculptures show clear Mon and Indian influences, depicting figures such as Bengali-style Buddha images and multiarmed Hindu deities. These, and a variety of votive tablets, can be seen at the **Chaiya National Museum**. It also holds examples of Ayutthayan art. The museum is 1 mile (2 km) west of Chaiya and a 10-minute walk from the train station.

Right beside the museum is **Phra Boromathat Chaiya** (see pp350–51), an important Srivijayan temple. Within the main compound is the central *chedi*, which has been painstakingly restored. Square in plan, it has four porches that ascend in tiers and are topped with small towers. The 8th-century *chedi* is built of brick and vegetable mortar. Although the site is old, it is the memory of Phra Chaiya Wiwat, a locally venerated monk who died in 1949, that attracts the majority of worshipers today.

🏛 **Chaiya National Museum**
Phra Boromathat Chaiya.
Tel 0-7743-1066. **Open** Wed–Sun.
Closed public hols. 🎟

Environs
The International Dhamma Hermitage (see p451) at **Wat Suan Mok**, southwest of Chaiya, is a popular retreat for Buddhists from all over the world. Its attraction is its back-to-basics religious philosophy established by the *wat's* founder, Buddhadhasa Bhikkhu, who died in 1993. Within the temple a regimen of physical

Murals relating the story of the Buddha at Wat Suan Mok

labor underpins a simple monastic life devoid of elaborate religious ceremony. Ten-day residential meditation retreats are held here, starting on the first day of each month.

🧘 **Wat Suan Mok**
4 miles (7 km) S of Chaiya off Hwy 41.
Tel 0-7743-1552. **Open** daily.

10 Surat Thani

สุราษฎร์ธานี

Surat Thani province. 🏔 31,000.
✈️ 🚉 Phun Phin, 9 miles (14 km) W of Surat Thani, then bus. 🚌
🚢 Ban Don (in town); Thong, 4 miles (6 km) E of town. ℹ️ TAT, 5 Talat Mai Rd, Surat Thani (0-7728-8818).
🎉 Rambutan Fair (Aug); Chak Phra Festival (Oct–Nov).

Surat Thani, a business center and port dealing in rubber and coconuts, first grew to prominence in the Srivijaya period, since it was strategically located at the mouth of the Tapi and Phum Duang rivers. The riverside is still intriguing today with its numerous small boats ferrying people to the city's busy waterfront markets, which sell fresh products and flowers. But Surat Thani is best known as a transportation gateway to the beaches of Ko Samui and Ko Pha Ngan.

Dramatic limestone cliffs at Rachabrapha Dam, Surat Thani ▶

⑪ Ko Samui

เกาะสมุย

Ko Samui is situated 400 miles (700 km) south of Bangkok, in the Gulf of Thailand. It is the country's third-largest island, after Phuket and Ko Chang. A backpackers' haven in the 1970s, Samui has now seen tourism become its main income earner. With rapid development, the arrival of major hotel chains, and persistent promotion by the TAT, Samui has become one of the most popular islands in Southeast Asia. It also attracts foreign investors building luxury homes for wealthy business people from Hong Kong, Singapore, and Taiwan, and has a thriving luxury villa rental market serving European holiday makers.

Nathon

Nathon is Samui's capital and main ferry port. The island was first settled in the 1850s by Chinese merchants who had come in search of trade in cotton and coconuts. Nathon was founded around 1905, when the site was chosen as the island's administrative center.

Few visitors stay here, except in order to take an early morning boat to Surat Thani on the mainland. The town has a supermarket, post office, and money changing facilities.

The main transport route on the island is the 31-mile (50-km) circular road, which passes through Nathon. *Songthaews* departing from Nathon ferry port travel either northward (clockwise) toward Chaweng beach and the airport, or southward (counterclockwise) toward Lamai.

The 38-ft (12-m) "Big Buddha" on Ko Faan, just off the Samui coast

Maenam

This 2-mile (4-km) long beach is the most westerly stretch of sand on the north coast. It has extensive views of Ko Pha Ngan *(see p343)*. Visitors flock here for the excellent windsurfing opportunities, which are aided by the strong directional breezes that blow on-shore during the northeasterly

Maenam, on the north coast, one of the quieter beaches on Ko Samui

For hotels and restaurants see pp402–11 and pp418–33

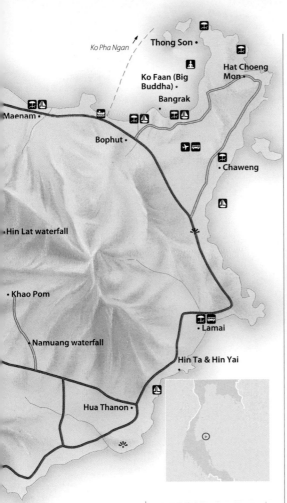

VISITORS' CHECKLIST

Practical Information
Surat Thani province. 🕰 42,000.
ℹ️ TAT, Nathon (0-7742-0504) or
TAT, Surat Thani (0-7728-8818);
Songserm (0-2808- 0734), Nathon
(0-7742-0157, for ferry bookings).
🚌 2 miles (3 km) S of Nathon
(0-7742-1281). 🚢 daily.

Transport
✈️ 14 miles (23 km) from
Nathon. 🚢 from Surat Thani,
Tha Thong and Don Sak.

Paragliding over Chaweng beach, one of
many activities

sprung up at the foot of the
naga staircase leading to the
Buddha image. From the pier at
Bangrak there is a ferry service
to Hat Rin, a beach on Ko Pha
Ngan and home of the full
moon parties.

Thong Son and Choeng Mon
On Samui's northeastern cape
there are a series of secluded
rocky coves. Hat Thong Son is a
peaceful inlet with marvelous
views across to Ko Pha Ngan.
Most of the accommodation on
the headland is concentrated at
Ao Choeng Mon, an attractive
bay with a pleasant beach and
good swimming.

monsoon from December to
February. However, the beach is
narrow and not as attractive as
others on the island.

Bophut
Bophut has better facilities
than Maenam. Its bustling
village, at the eastern end of the
next bay to the east, includes
bungalows, hotels, banks, bars,
restaurants, and a range of
water sports. The 1-mile (2-km)
long beach is popular with
families and backpackers.

Bangrak
Adjacent to Bophut is Bangrak,
also known as "Big Buddha"
beach. The sea is not as clear
here as it is off Chaweng and
Lamai beaches (see p342), but

it does offer plenty of budget
accommodations. A causeway
links the eastern end of Bangrak
beach to the tiny island of Ko
Faan, home to the large, gold-
covered Big Buddha. The
imposing statue is popular with
islanders and Asian tourists,
who come here to make merit
(see p133). A gaudy bazaar of
souvenir stalls and cafés has

Palm trees shading typical beachside huts on Ko Samui

Exploring Ko Samui: the East Coast and Minor Sights

The beautiful beaches and buzzing nightlife of Chaweng and Lamai on Samui's east coast draw tourists from all over the world. Many visitors never stray from these resorts, leaving the quieter beaches on the south and west coasts, the island's *wats*, and Samui's spectacular mountainous and forested interior relatively untouched.

Muslim fishermen landing their boats on Samui's east coast

Chaweng
Chaweng is the longest, busiest, and most beautiful beach on the island, stretching 3 miles (5 km) down the east coast. Its warm waters and white sands have attracted budget travelers for many years. Today, though, Chaweng is a mecca for package tourists and is lined with hotels and bars. The budget bungalows of yesteryear are long gone.

At the northern end of Chaweng is a tranquil 3-ft (1-m) deep lagoon, ideal for children and novice windsurfers. The long, inviting sweep of the middle and southern end of the beach is bordered by coconut palms. Chaweng is at its most scenic along its southern section where large boulders alternate with discreet sandy coves. The beach has a wide range of sports including windsurfing, canoeing, paragliding, scuba diving, tennis, and volleyball.

Chaweng has the most developed tourist infrastructure on Samui with travel agencies, banks, supermarkets, and car and bike rental among the facilities available. The main street in Chaweng is a hub for nightlife and shopping in Ko Samui. Bars, clubs, and restaurants rub shoulders with souvenir shops and upscale boutiques.

Lamai
Samui's second largest beach is also very developed, with big chain and luxury hotels along the waterfront. The main focus is at the center of the 2-mile (4-km) long beach. Behind the beach are riotous bars, nightclubs, and restaurants serving Western food.

Lamai village is at the quieter, northern end of the beach, away from the crowds. It still has many old teak houses with thatched roofs. The village's main sight is Wat Lamai Cultural Hall, built in 1826, which has a small folk museum dedicated to arts and crafts found on Samui.

On the southern promontory of Lamai beach are the Hin Ta and Hin Yai rock formations that are famous for their similarity in shape to male and female sexual organs.

South and West Coasts
There are many quiet beaches with simple huts along the south and west coasts, such as around Thong Krut. Another is Thong Yang which – although only 1 mile (1.5 km) south of the pier where the vehicle ferries from Don Sak dock – which is perfect for those seeking peaceful seclusion.

Swimming in Namuang waterfall, in the center of Samui

The Interior
For visitors tiring of the beach, the interior of Samui offers an adventurous alternative. The mix of dense tropical forest and large coconut plantations seems impenetrable, but there are rough trails – which can be negotiated by four-wheel-drive vehicle or by motorcycle – and two roads leading to Samui's picturesque waterfalls.

Namuang, an impressive 98-ft (30-m) high waterfall, is a popular destination for picnics and swimming. It is situated 6 miles (10 km) from Nathon and 3 miles (5 km) from the circular coast road. Hin Lat, 2 miles (3 km) from Nathon, is smaller than Namuang and less interesting. Both falls are at their most spectacular in December or January at the end of the rainy season, when they swell with rainwater.

Chaweng, the longest and most attractive beach on Ko Samui

For hotels and restaurants see pp402–11 and pp418–33

⑫ Ko Pha Ngan

เกาะพะงัน

Surat Thani province. 🏔 8,400.
🚢 from Nathon on Ko Samui to
Tong Sala. 🛈 TAT, Surat Thani
(0 7728-8818). 🚢 daily.

Ko Pha Ngan is 9 miles (15 km)
north of Ko Samui, and is two-
thirds its size. The island has the
same tropical combination of
powdery beaches, accessible
coral reefs, and rugged, forested
interior. Budget travelers come
to enjoy a bohemian life, staying
in rattan huts beside idyllic
bays. The island is much less
developed for tourism than
Samui, due mainly to its bad
road system. Much of it is
accessible only by sea or along
rutted tracks by pickup truck.

Tong Sala

This town is the entrance port
to Ko Pha Ngan, and, like
Nathon on Ko Samui, acts as a
service town with many banks,
a post restante, supermarkets,
travel agents, restaurants, a food
market, and weekly tourist
market. Next to the pier, an
armada of *songthaews* waits to
take visitors around the island.

Hat Rin

Hat Rin is the most commercial
town on the island, located at the
southeastern tip, 6 miles (10 km)
from Tong Sala. It is a popular
destination with backpackers and
party animals. Hat Rin has two
wide beaches flanking the headland. Its accommodations are
often fully booked for a week
either side of the monthly full
moon party, which starts after
dark and goes on beyond sunrise.

The white sands of Hat Rin beach on Ko
Pha Ngan

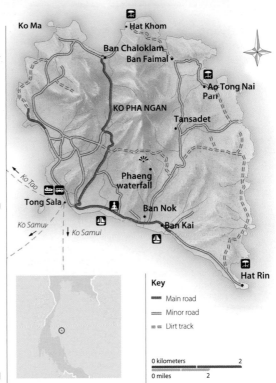

Key

━━ Main road
═══ Minor road
═ ═ Dirt track

0 kilometers ⸺⸺⸺ 2
0 miles ⸺⸺⸺ 2

Chaloklam

A strong smell of dried, salted
fish emanates from Chaloklam's
storefronts. Asian visitors often
stop here to buy fish after
visiting the revered Chao
Mae Koan Im shrine in
the center of the
island. In Chaloklam,
fishing-related
activities such as
mending nets and
gutting fish coexist
with shop-houses
selling pizza and
other tourist snacks.
The beaches near
the town tend to be
rather dirty but
improve farther to
the east, especially
as far out of town as
Khom beach.

Dried fish at Chaloklam
village

Tong Nai Pan

Although the majority of the
beaches are on the east side of
the island, the roads accessing
the beaches are fairly rugged
and some can only be reached
via rough track. The twin bays of
Tong Nai Pan Noi and Tong Nai
Pan Yai in the northeast offer
arguably the most attractive
scenery. They can be reached
by pickup truck or taxi from
Tong Sala or, between January
and September, or by small
ferry from Maenam
on Ko Samui.

Tansadet, 2 miles
(3 km) to the south, is
the island's biggest
stream and waterfall.
It owes its name,
"royal stream," to
the 10 visits King
Chulalongkorn
made between
1888 and 1909.
Since then most
Thai monarchs have
left large stone inscriptions on
rocks alongside the stream –
finding the signatures requires
scrambling among the rocks.
The stream has two falls,
Sampan and Daeng. Both are
suitable for swimming, but
heavy rainfall from September
to December makes the
stream bed too dangerous to
walk along.

For keys to symbols *see back flap*

⓭ Angthong National Marine Park

อุทยานแห่งชาติทางทะเลอ่างทอง

Surat Thani province. Park HQ on Ko Wua Talab. 🚢 from Ko Samui. ℹ TAT, Surat Thani (0-7728-8818); Park HQ (0-7728-0222); Forestry Dept (0-2562-0760). Bungalow bookings: 🅦 dnp.go.th Closed Nov–Dec.

The 40 virtually uninhabited islands of the Angthong National Marine Park display a rugged beauty distinct from palm-fringed Ko Samui 19 miles (31 km) away to the southeast. The Angthong ("golden basin") islands, covering an area of 39 sq miles (102 sq km), are the submerged peaks of a flooded range of limestone mountains that, farther south in Nakhon Si Thammarat province, rise to 6,000 ft (1,835 m).

Angthong's pristine beauty owes much to being the preserve of the Royal Thai Navy, and therefore off-limits until 1980 when it was declared a National Marine Park. Now naval boats have been replaced by tourist ferries. Most visitors come on daytrips from Ko Samui to relax on the mica-white sands, explore the lush forests and limestone caves, sea canoe around the islands' jagged coastlines, and snorkel among the colorful fan corals.

Another attraction is the abundant wildlife, both on land and in the sea. Leopard cats, squirrels, long-tailed macaques, sea otters, and pythons may be glimpsed, and a lack of natural predators has made the endearingly friendly dusky langur easy to spot. Among the 40 bird species found in the archipelago are the black baza, the edible-nest swiftlet, the brahminy kite, and the Eurasian woodcock.

Divers taking advantage of the excellent coral off **Ko Sam Sao** will probably see short- bodied mackerel (pla thu), a staple of the Thai diet. The sea around the islands is favored by the fish as a breeding ground. It is also possible to spot dolphins, although they are wary of humans because fisherman catch them for their meat. The park headquarters, and the islands' only tourist accommodations and

Key

‑ ‑ Trail

Ko Naayphud

Ko Hindab

Ko Wuakantang

Ko Sam Sao

Ko Mae Ko

Ko Phi
National Park Headquarters

Ko Wua Talab

Ko Samui

*Angthong
National Marine
Park*

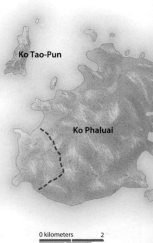

Ko Tao-Pun

Ko Phaluai

0 kilometers   2
0 miles   1

View from a trail on Ko Wua Talab, Angthong National Marine Park

For keys to symbols *see back flap*

Boat for carrying visitors from the ferry to the beach on Ko Mae Ko

facilities, are located on the largest island, **Ko Wua Talab** ("sleeping cow island"). A steep 1300-ft (400-m) climb from here leads to a vista offering wonderful panoramas of the whole archipelago and beyond to Ko Pha Ngan, Ko Samui, and the mainland. The view is at its best at sunrise and sunset. Another fairly tough climb leads to Tham Buabok ("waving lotus cave"), so named because of the shape of some of its stalactites and stalagmites.

On **Ko Mae Ko** there is a swimming beach as well as the stunning Thale Noi, a wide turquoise lake bordered by sheer cliffs. This is the "golden basin" that gives the islands their name.

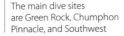
Cowrie shell, Ko Tao

⑭ Ko Tao
เกาะเต่า

Surat Thani province. 1,300. from Chumphon or Ko Samui. TAT, Surat (0-7728-8818).

Located 25 miles (40 km) north of Ko Pha Ngan, "turtle island" is the smallest and prettiest of the islands in the Samui archipelago that offer visitors accommodations. Ko Tao's major attraction is its superb offshore diving. Excellent visibility, a wide range of diving sites, and a rich variety of coral and marine life make for some of the most rewarding diving in the country. The main dive sites are Green Rock, Chumphon Pinnacle, and Southwest Pinnacle. Many sites are suitable for beginners thanks to the shallow inshore bays and clear waters. In May water visibility can approach 130 ft (40 m), which is often claimed to be the maximum possible. The island has about 10 dive companies that operate all year round, although the main season is from December to April.

The island itself is rugged, with dense forest inland, quiet coves along the east coast, and a fine sweep of sandy beach on the west side. Simple bungalow and plusher resort accommodation is available, although it can be difficult to find a room in tourist season.

A good way to get to know the island is to charter a small boat for a day trip, sailing around it and stopping at different beaches. The boatmen supply snorkeling equipment and know all the best spots.

Diving among the rich marine life and fine coral off Ko Tao

Bird's-Nest Soup

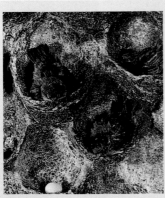
Birds' nests: a regional delicacy

Unlike such misleadingly named delicacies as Bombay duck, the main ingredient of bird's-nest soup is, indeed, birds' nests. Not just any nest will do, however. Only the homes of birds such as the brown-rumped swift, the edible-nest swiftlet, and the sea swallow are acceptable. When these delicate, saliva-thread constructions are cooked they are transformed into smooth, noodlelike strands that are considered to have aphrodisiac properties by peoples throughout Southeast and East Asia. Such is the perceived potency of the soup that the nests change hands for huge sums of money. A government license is required to collect the nests, and many of the most important sites, such as those in caves on Ko Phi Phi Ley (see p377) are protected by armed guards. The dangerous job of nest harvesting is allowed only between February and April and in September, when agile collectors must scale the cave walls on flimsy bamboo scaffolds.

SOUTHERN
THAILAND

Introducing Southern Thailand

The narrow peninsula of Southern Thailand, stretching from Ranong, on the Myanmar border, to Malaysia, is a unique region with a rich, multicultural heritage. Forested mountains run along much of the interior, and the hinterland and islands of Phangnga Bay in the Andaman Sea form Thailand's most spectacular natural landscape. Here the shallow waters are dotted with limestone stacks and craggy islands 985 ft (300 m) high. Some of the country's best sandy beaches and diving sites are also found along the southern coasts and around the Andaman islands. Though the beach resorts of Phuket and Krabi draw the most visitors to the area, the South also offers historic cultural sites, such as the towns of Songkhla and Nakhon Si Thammarat. Sadly, many parts of the region's coast were hit by the tsunami in 2004 and some 5,300 people were killed. The Thais responded rapidly, though, and most of the reconstruction was completed by 2006.

Ranong

UPPER ANDAMAN COAST
(see pp356–377)

Ko Surin

Ban Hin Lat

Takua Pa

Phanom

Khao Lak

Ko Similan

Phangnga

Ao Lu

Phangnga Bay

Thalang

Krab

Phuket Town

Ko Phi Phi

Phangnga Bay
(see pp368–71), with its weird and wonderful towering limestone stacks, is one of Southern Thailand's most famous natural beauty spots. Due to massive erosion, big tourist boats are currently banned from large areas of the bay.

Phuket *(see pp362–7)* is Thailand's largest island and richest province. Prosperous even during the 19th century, when Chinese merchants used the island as a base for sea trade, today it is one of the most popular tourist resorts in Thailand. Phuket is now a largely upscale destination with luxury hotels, restaurants, and shops lining many of the island's stunning beaches. A wide range of water sports is available, including superb diving facilities.

 Ko Phi Phi Don as seen from a viewpoint in Krabi town

Nakhon Si Thammarat
(see pp382–3), once the regional capital of the Srivijaya Empire *(see pp350–51)*, is today the South's cultural center. Despite some fine sights, including Southern Thailand's holiest shrine, Wat Mahathat, and one of the few remaining *nang talung* shadow puppet theaters, the city is not visited by many tourists.

Songkhla National Museum *(see p390)*, contains an eclectic collection of ceramics, art, and furniture. It occupies the one-time deputy governor's residence, a splendid 19th-century Chinese-style mansion.

Nakhon Si Thammarat

ıra
ng

Pak Phanang

Thung Song

Ron Phibun

ılong Thom

Huai Yot

Pak
eng

Trang

Phatthalung

Sathing Phra

Palian

Rattaphum

Songkhla

Thung Wa

Hat Yai

Na Thawi

Tarutao

Satun

Sadao

Yala

Pattani

Salburi

Ba Cho

Na

DEEP SOUTH
(see pp378–395)

Betong

Korlae **fishing boats** *(see p394)*, with painted hulls, are a colorful feature of the Muslim South. Some of the best ones can be seen at Pattani, once an independent Muslim state.

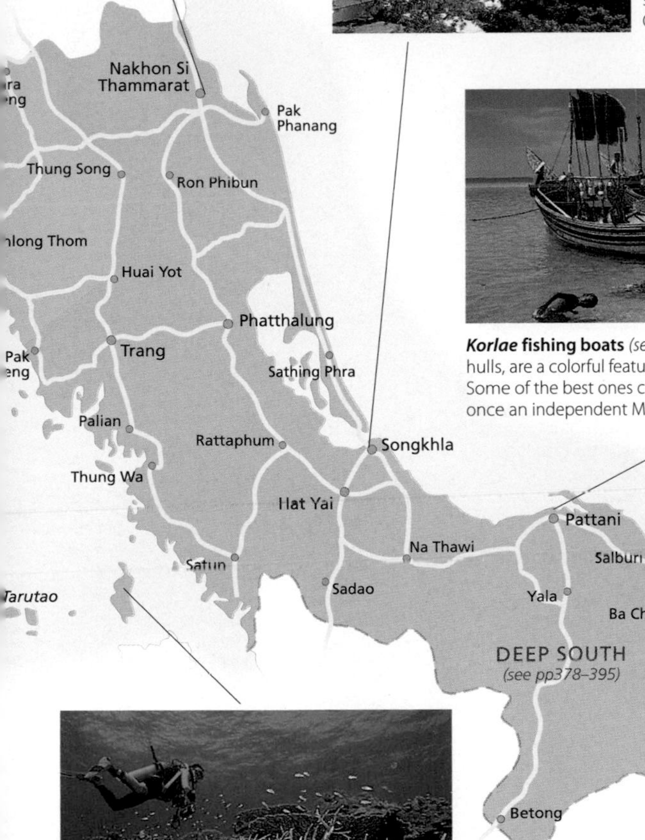

| 0 kilometers | 50 |
| 0 miles | 25 |

Tarutao National Marine Park *(see p392)* has a wide diversity of wildlife and offers some of the most stunning, unspoiled beaches and island scenery in Thailand.

The Peninsula as a Cultural Crossroads

For over 2,000 years, the peninsula that is now divided between Malaysia, Thailand, and Myanmar has been a major cultural crossroads. Finds from the Isthmus of Kra (especially the historic trading centers of Nakhon Si Thammarat, Chaiya, Sathing Phra, and Takua Pa) testify to strong links with China, India, the Middle East, and even the Roman Empire before the first millennium AD. In the 7th–13th centuries the Hindu-Buddhist Srivijaya Empire held sway over much of the region. After Srivijaya's decline, Burma and Siam, both Buddhist, pushed south, while Islam, brought by Arab traders, made a lasting impact in the southernmost part of the peninsula.

Islam, the main religion in Malaysia, is widely practiced in Southern Thailand today – minarets compete with Buddhist shrines in many towns.

There was even greater cultural diversity from the 16th century, when the British, Dutch, Portuguese, and other colonial powers developed trade routes through the Straits of Malacca.

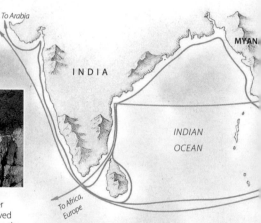

Prehistoric paintings can be found in Phangnga Bay *(see pp368–71)* and other parts of the peninsula. Humans have lived here at least since the last Ice Age, when the peninsula did not exist as such – the area from Borneo to Sumatra was then dry land.

Ceremonial drums found at the ancient cities of Chaiya and Nakhon Si Thammarat and in Sumatra, were made in Dong Son in North Vietnam c.500 BC, testifying to early trade.

The Srivijaya Empire ruled the peninsula as far north as Chaiya in the 7th–13th centuries. As first a Hindu and then a Mahayana Buddhist state, it produced many statues of Bodhisattvas – enlightened beings who delay *nirvana* in order to save mankind.

Trade Routes

The Straits of Malacca have always been a natural channel for sea routes. Chinese, Indian, and Arab vessels were trading, gathering provisions, and "wintering" at posts along the peninsula at least 2,000 years ago. European ships joined them from the 16th century. As seafaring technology developed, ships became less dependent on some ports, which subsequently declined.

| 0 kilometers | | 1,000 |
| 0 miles | | 500 |

Key

— Local routes (c. 5th century BC onward)

— Major routes during the Srivijaya period (7th–13th centuries AD)

— Major European routes (16th century onward)

This Dutch East India Company cannon is in Nakhon Si Thammarat, an ancient town in Southern Thailand (see pp382–3). The company traded all over Southeast Asia and was drawn to the peninsula by access to Chinese and Japanese goods.

Srivijayan Architecture

The Srivijaya Empire controlled trade at ports such as Chaiya (see pp336–7) and Takua Pa, on the Isthmus of Kra. Numerous Srivijayan artifacts have been found in the Gulf and South of Thailand, but most chedis, which were built of stucco and brick, have been built over. The main example to survive is an outstanding, complete chedi at Wat Phra Boromathat in Chaiya. Cruciform in shape, it has four tiers, decreasing in size as they ascend. On each corner is a smaller chedi. Built in the 8th century, it has been restored many times, most recently in 1930.

Chedi of the Javan-influenced Wat Phra Boromathat, Chaiya

This European engraving shows a march in Pattani (see p394), one of several Muslim states in the peninsula that lost autonomy to Bangkok in the early part of the 20th century.

The Thais and Burmese battled over the northern peninsula after Srivijaya waned. A fight for Phuket, or Junkceylon (see pp362–7), took place in 1785.

European trade led to extensive mapping of Southeast Asia. This 17th-century French map shows the local trade route up the east coast of the peninsula, from Batavia (Jakarta) in Java to the city of Ayutthaya in Siam.

Coral Reefs

Thailand's best coral reefs are found in the Andaman Sea. These reefs, which are composed of countless tiny marine animals, grow extremely slowly: 3 ft (1 m) of coral reef can take 1,000 years to form. As a coral reef is an excellent source of food and shelter, it provides the base for a unique and diverse marine ecosystem. The reef consists of reef builders (mainly hard corals, whose limestone skeletons form the basis of the reef) and reef dwellers, such as sea urchins, whose remains may also help build the reef when they die. Although the 2004 tsunami did damage many reefs, especially those of the Surin, Similan, and Phi Phi islands, initial reports of great devastation were inaccurate.

Snorkeling is a low-cost and easy way to explore a coral reef. Many reefs can be found in relatively shallow, clear water, which is excellent for snorkeling.

Gobies – small, spiny-finned fish with large heads – live mainly in tropical waters. They often share sand burrows with shrimp.

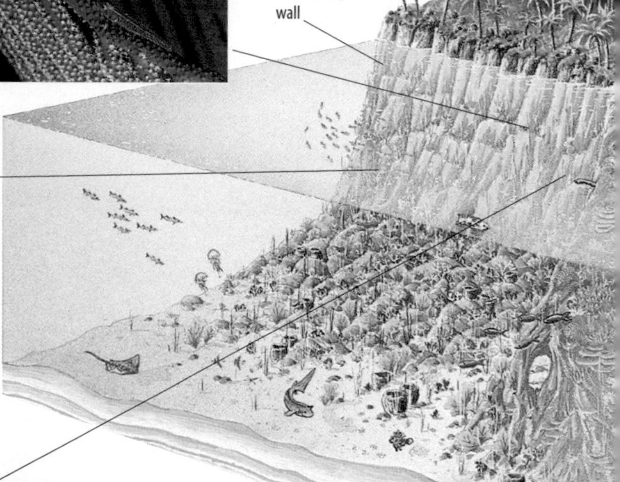

Coconut grove

West-facing wall

The clown triggerfish has an upright spine in its dorsal fin. The spine is raised to wedge the fish under rocks and ledges; this stops predators from pulling the fish out.

A Typical Reef

On the island's east side, the reef flat slopes away from the beach, rises to a crest, then slopes steeply to the sea bed. Mostly hard corals are found on the east side. The reef's west walls tend to be much steeper and rockier than the east side. Its boulders provide protection for soft corals and nooks in which creatures such as eels live.

Moray eels are voracious predators, hiding in crevices and lunging out at unsuspecting prey swimming by. Food left between a moray's teeth may be picked clean by hungry cleaner shrimp.

Leopard sharks, also known as zebra sharks, pose no threat to people. At Shark Point, near Ko Phi Phi, divers often see these timid creatures resting or cruising along the outskirts of the coral reef.

Many species of sea bird gather around islands with coral reefs to feed on the abundant fish life. This is a great egret, a large wading bird that feeds by stabbing small fish with its razor-sharp bill.

Scuba diving is an excellent way to experience diverse reef ecosystems (see pp446–7). In the South, Phuket has the most diving operators offering instruction, equipment rental, and trips to offshore islands such as Ko Phi Phi. When exploring a coral reef, you should not touch the delicate corals, as this causes permanent damage to the reef.

Rays are often seen around coral reefs. Manta rays have impressive wingspans of up to 20 ft (6 m), while blue-spotted rays have a poisonous spine in their tail.

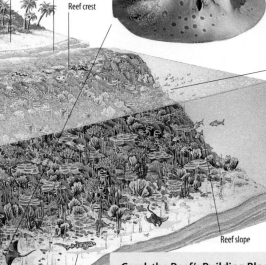

Sandy beach

Reef flat

Reef crest

Reef slope

Snapper often follow schools of feeding goatfish, devouring any small fish that escape the latter.

Coral: the Reef's Building Block

Coral is made of the skeletons of polyps, small animals related to sea anemones and jellyfish. Polyps are unusual in that they build their skeletons outside their bodies. As the polyps divide, the coral colony slowly builds up. There may be as many as 200 different species of coral in a reef, divided into hard corals such as brain coral, and colorful soft corals, which have no stony outer skeleton.

Giant hermit crabs are soft-bodied crustaceans. They protect their bodies by living and moving around the sea bed in the empty shells of mollusks such as whelks.

Hard, rocklike coral

Soft, plantlike coral

Mangrove Forests

Mangrove forests develop only in the tropics, in brackish and saltwater areas of estuaries. In Thailand they are found in pockets of the South, particularly at Phangnga Bay *(see pp368–71)*. Mangrove species are the only trees to have adapted to the inhospitable conditions of these muddy, intertidal zones. The forests typically cover networks of channels and levees created from the buildup of silt that becomes trapped in the cagelike root systems of the trees. Though often dismissed as wasteland, in its natural state a mangrove forest is a vital ecosystem – a fertile spawning, nursing, feeding, and sheltering ground for crustaceans, fish, birds, snakes, and even mammals. "Primary" mangrove grows to over 80 ft (25 m) high. Most mangrove in Thailand is "secondary," meaning it has been cut by humans and reaches only 16–33 ft (5–10 m).

The characteristic stiltlike roots of most mangrove trees support the tree against the constant movement of tidal waters. As well as holding the trunk of the tree above the high tide level, the roots trap nutrient-rich sediments.

The upward-growing roots (pneumatophores) of some trees have special "breathing" pores used during low tide.

Sonneratia are sturdy trees, tolerant of high salinity.

Breathing roots, or pneumatophores, can excrete excess salt.

Avicennia are sustained by large cable root systems below the mud.

Rhizophora *species* are associated with soft mud under strong tidal influence.

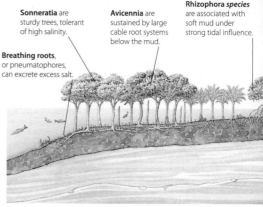

Cross Section of a Mangrove Levee

This cross section shows a typical gradation of trees in a Thai mangrove forest. The waters are at high tide, a time when small fish and invertebrates feed in the sheltered, nutrient-rich waters around the roots of the trees. At low tide, when the roots of the trees are exposed, crabs and wading birds scour the mud flats for trapped fish and decaying matter.

The mud skipper, so called for its skipping gait across mud flats at low tide, is the ubiquitous mangrove dweller. It can survive for short periods out of water.

The estuarine crocodile was once king of the mangroves. Nowadays it is bred in farms and is very rarely seen in the wild.

Small-clawed otters are often spotted in mangrove regions. They eat the smaller inhabitants such as mollusks and crabs.

Male fiddler crabs sift the silt with their one enlarged claw, selecting tiny organic particles to eat. As with most other types of crab, their colorful claws are also used in courtship displays.

***Rhizophora* trees**, such as these at Phangnga Bay, are common in Thai mangrove forests. Their colonizing ability is largely due to the unusual shape of their seed pods. With dagger-shaped stalks, these penetrate the ooze rather than floating away with the tide.

Yellow-ringed cat snakes, like other mangrove snakes, are adept swimmers and tree climbers. They rest by day and hunt fish and frogs by night.

***Bruguiera* trees** grow in compacted mud that is inundated with water only during high spring tides.

Nipa palms thrive in soft mud away from wave action. Nipa is used by Thais to wrap tobacco and as an ingredient in candies and alcohol.

Crab-eating macaques inhabit Thai mangrove forests; they are capable swimmers and forage for crabs at low tide. Seeds also form part of the macaques' diet.

The Destruction of Thailand's Mangrove Forests

Despite the provision of a national mangrove management program (set up in 1946), some 60 percent of Thailand's mangrove has been cleared since the 1960s – just 300,000 acres were

Shrimp farm in a former area of mangrove forest

thought to remain by 1996. Not only has this loss of habitat decimated marine life, but coastal erosion has also started to become a problem in parts of the South. Without the roots of mangrove trees to trap it, estuarine silt is deposited over a progressively larger area, and seawater seeps over more and more of the land. The rate of loss peaked in the late 1980s with the boom in tiger shrimp farming in former mangrove areas. After clearing mangrove trees to make way for shrimp farms, farmers use the tide-flushed mangrove channels to discharge nutrient-rich excreta from the prawn pools. This reduces oxygen levels in the adjacent natural breeding grounds of shrimp, fish, and crabs. Charcoal production is also to blame: tall mangrove species have been select-cut for decades in order to be incinerated and turned into charcoal. The fuel is sold cheaply in Thailand or shipped to Singapore for distribution within Asia. Road and harbor construction are other factors responsible for the loss of mangrove forests in Thailand.

UPPER ANDAMAN COAST

The abiding image of Thailand's Andaman Coast is of long sandy beaches backed by swaying palms and a verdant hinterland of rainforest. Centered on Ko Phuket, the upper half of this coast has many attractions. This region suffered the most from the 2004 tsunami, in particular Ranong, the Surin, Similan, and Phi Phi islands, but rebuilding and environmental restoration work has been swift.

The Andaman Coast around Phuket has long been a magnet for Thais and foreigners. Merchants were drawn by its strategic position on the spice routes between East and West (see pp350–51); prospectors came for the rich tin deposits. This is a lush, fertile region. Much of the interior is cloaked in rainforest, and rubber, coffee, cashew, banana, and durian plantations are common.

The outstanding natural beauty of the Andaman Coast is known the world over. The biggest draw in the region is Phuket, now a resort island, which has superb beaches, excellent diving facilities, and the most developed tourist infrastructure in Southern Thailand. Over the last 20 years, many traditional sea gypsy and Muslim fishing villages on Phuket and around Krabi have been transformed into vacation resorts. Long-tail boats take visitors to sights like the extraordinary limestone stacks of Phangnga Bay. In remote mangrove channels – accessible only by canoe – otters, monkeys, and sea eagles still live undisturbed.

There is outstanding scenery and diving around Ko Phi Phi, though it is now firmly on the tourist trail. Visitors wanting sand and sun without the crowds head for relatively undeveloped islands such as Ko Lanta. Unspoiled beach resorts can be found along the stretch of coast from Ranong to Phuket, and the virgin rainforest of Khao Sok National Park is located inland. West of here, the Ko Surin and Ko Similan archipelagos offer some of the world's best dive sites.

The southwest monsoon, which lasts from about June to October, makes some of the outer islands inaccessible.

Lush green environs of Andaman Sea Resort, Krabi

◀ Long-tail boats moored at Paradise Beach, Phuket

Exploring the Upper Andaman Coast

This part of Thailand's Andaman Sea coast contains some of the most inviting beach scenery in Southeast Asia. Using the international resort of Phuket as a base, visitors have 12 long sandy beaches on their doorstep and a full range of shopping, dining, entertainment, land and water sport services. The towering limestone stacks of Phangnga Bay can readily be explored in a day. An alternative base is quieter Krabi, which combines fine beaches with spectacular cliff landscapes. The idyllic island scenery of Ko Phi Phi is accessible from Krabi and Phuket. The monsoon forests of the Tenasserim mountain range provide a backdrop to the little frequented beaches of Khao Lak. Avid divers and snorkelers can visit the remote Similan and Surin archipelagos acclaimed for their superlative corals and aquatic life.

Yachting off the coast of the unspoiled Similan archipelago

0 kilometers   25
0 miles   15

4 KO SURIN

Ko Chang

Ko Phayam

K

Khao Lang Kha
13

4

Khura E

KH

NATION

Takua Pa

40

KHAO LAK COAST

3 Khao Lak

Tap Lamu

4 KO SIMILAN

A N D A M A N   S E A

Phangnga

Thai Muang

4

Ko Khao
Phing Khan

BA

402

Thalang

Ko Ya
Y

PHUKET 5

Patong   Phuket T

A deserted beach on Ko Phi Phi – still possible to find despite its ever-increasing popularity

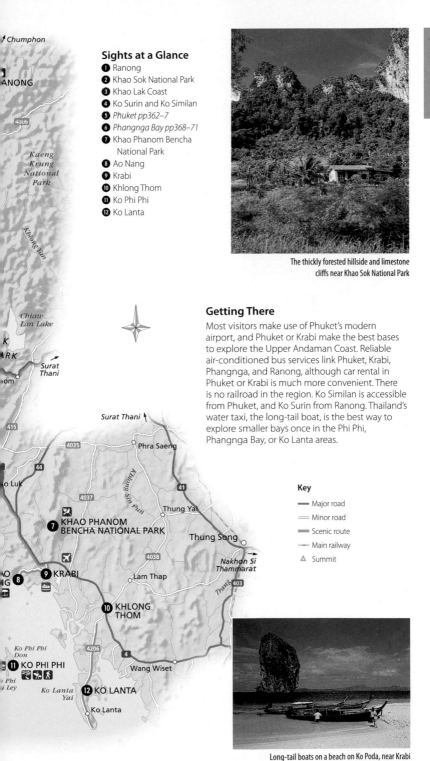

Chumphon

ANONG

400b

*Kaeng
Krung
National
Park*

Khlong Yan

*Chiaw
Lan Lake*

K
RK

*Surat
Thani*
om

415

4035

o Luk

44

4037

Phra Saeng

Khlong Sin Pun

41

Thung Yai

KHAO PHANOM
BENCHA NATIONAL PARK

Thung Song

4038

Nakhon Si
Thammarat

Trang
403

Lam Thap

KHLONG
THOM

Ko Phi Phi
Don

KO PHI PHI

Phi
Ley

*Ko Lanta
Yai*

KO LANTA

Ko Lanta

4206

4

Wang Wiset

O
G

KRABI

Surat Thani

Sights at a Glance

1. Ranong
2. Khao Sok National Park
3. Khao Lak Coast
4. Ko Surin and Ko Similan
5. *Phuket pp362–7*
6. *Phangnga Bay pp368–71*
7. Khao Phanom Bencha
   National Park
8. Ao Nang
9. Krabi
10. Khlong Thom
11. Ko Phi Phi
12. Ko Lanta

The thickly forested hillside and limestone
cliffs near Khao Sok National Park

Getting There

Most visitors make use of Phuket's modern
airport, and Phuket or Krabi make the best bases
to explore the Upper Andaman Coast. Reliable
air-conditioned bus services link Phuket, Krabi,
Phangnga, and Ranong, although car rental in
Phuket or Krabi is much more convenient. There
is no railroad in the region. Ko Similan is accessible
from Phuket, and Ko Surin from Ranong. Thailand's
water taxi, the long-tail boat, is the best way to
explore smaller bays once in the Phi Phi,
Phangnga Bay, or Ko Lanta areas.

Key

—— Major road
=== Minor road
▬▬ Scenic route
▬▬ Main railway
△ Summit

Long-tail boats on a beach on Ko Poda, near Krabi

For keys to symbols *see back flap*

Collecting water from one of Ranong's geothermal springs

❶ Ranong

ระนอง

Ranong province. ⛰ 69,000. 🚌
🚌 🚆 daily. 🛈 TAT, Chumphon
(0-7750-1831).

Ranong was originally settled in the late 18th century by Hokkien Chinese who were hired to work as laborers in the region's tin mines. The area grew rich, and Ranong is now a major border town. From here Thai nationals may travel to **Victoria Point** in Myanmar (Burma) on a half- or full-day boat trip. Referred to as Kaw Thaung by the Burmese, the town is well known for bargain duty-free goods and handicrafts. Officially, foreigners may not go to Victoria Point without a visa, but this is not always enforced.

In Ranong, the natural hot springs are the main attraction. They rise beside the Khlong Hat Sompen River at **Wat Tapotaram**, 1,100 yds (1 km) east of the town center, and are channeled into three concrete tubs called Mother, Father, and Child. At an average temperature of 150° F (65° C), the water is too hot for bathing. A short walk down the river, the Jansom Thara Spa Resort Hotel has tapped and cooled the water to 110° F (42° C). Those not staying at the hotel can use the spa for a nominal fee.

❷ Khao Sok National Park

อุทยานแห่งชาติเขาสก

Surat Thani province. Park HQ off Hwy 401, 25 miles (40 km) E of Takua Pa. 🛈 TAT, Surat Thani (0-7728-8818) or Forestry Dept (0-2562-0760 or 🌐 **dnp.go.th** for bungalow bookings). 🚌 from Surat Thani or Takua Pa. 🚣

Together with nearby preserves, Khao Sok National Park forms the largest and most dramatic tract of virgin forest in South Thailand. The 285-sq mile (738-sq km) park rises to a height of 3,150 ft (960 m) and includes 100 spectacular islands, formed when the Rachabrapha Dam was built in 1982.

Elephants, tigers, bears, boars, and monkeys live in the park, along with at least 188 species of birds, including hornbills and the argus pheasant. Sightings of the larger mammals are usually at night and animal tracks, are regularly seen along the park's many marked trails. Sadly, poaching of tigers and elephants persists despite the efforts of national park officers.

The area is popular with tourists eager to trek, canoe, watch birds, and spot animals. The park also contains interesting flora, such as the rare giant Rafflesia flower. Many of the hiking trails are suitable for all levels, with more demanding hikes for the experienced. Khao Sok receives the brunt of both summer and winter monsoons, causing a long wet season from May to November. The best time to visit is between January and April.

❸ Khao Lak Coast

เขาหลัก

Phangnga province. 🛈 TAT, Phuket (0-7621-1036). 🚌 from Takua Pa or Phuket.

The coastline south of Takua Pa consists of long stretches of rocky and sandy beaches. Commercial development is on the rise and a variety of accommodation can now be found here. Khao Lak, halfway between Takua Pa and Thai Muang, has a fine beach and is a good base from which to explore the area.

The nearby **Khao Lak (Lam Ru) National Park** is famous for its scenery: steep ridges of monsoon forest extend to the winding coast. Barking deer and small bears are among the wildlife living in the forest but, sadly, the park is plagued by encroachment and poaching.

Barking deer at Khao Lak

The Similan Islands are only 4 hours away by boat, and many visitors come here to book their dive trips. Between November and April, Tap Lamu fishing port and Hat Khao Lak operate as ferry points for Ko Similan.

Badly hit by the 2004 tsunami, this coast has now made a full recovery.

🏞 **Khao Lak (Lam Ru) National Park**
HQ 16 miles (25 km) S of Takua Pa.
🛈 Forestry Dept (0-2562-0760). 🚣

Khao Sok, a wilderness of virgin forest, limestone cliffs, and waterfalls

Similan's boulders, under which are massive underwater grottoes

❶ Ko Surin and Ko Similan

เกาะสุรินทร์และสิมิลัน

Phangnga province. ℹ TAT, Phuket (0-7621-1036) or Forestry Dept (0-2562-0760 or 🌐 **dnp.go.th**) for bungalow bookings. Surin: 🚤 from Khuraburi Pier, 1 mile (2 km) off Hwy 4. 🚤 Similan: 🚤 from Tap Lamu, off Hwy 4, 24 miles (39 km) S of Takua Pa; or by diving trips from Khao Lak Coast or Ko Phuket. **Open** Best time for diving is Dec–early May. **Closed** mid-May–mid-Nov. 🚤

Ko Surin and Ko Similan, 37 miles (60 km) off the west coast and 62 miles (100 km) apart, are the most remote islands in Thailand. Because of the southwesterly monsoon, from May to October they are virtually inaccessible. In season, however, the two archipelagos offer some of the best diving sites in the world and some of the most spectacular wildlife and scenery in Thailand.

The five **Surin** islands are virtually uninhabited, home only to a few sea gypsies and national park officials. There is a park dormitory on Ko Surin Nua, but most people camp on the islands.

The two largest islands, Ko Surin Nua and Ko Surin Tai, are heavily forested with tall hardwood trees. Sea eagles, monitor lizards, and crab-eating macaques are common sights. The surrounding sea offers an outstanding array of soft corals and frequent sightings of

shovel-nose rays, bow-mouthed guitar fish, and whale sharks. However, overfishing has led to the depletion of the marine life of Ko Surin, and many divers maintain that the best sightings of sealife are around the Similans instead.

Of the nine **Similan** islands 4, 7, 8, and 9 were damaged by the 2004 tsunami but are still open to tourists and divers. The name Similan is thought to derive from the Malaysian word *sembilan*, meaning nine, and the islands are numbered Ko 1 through to Ko 9. Ko 4 (Ko Miang) has the park HQ, a restaurant, bungalows, and campsite (with a supply of two-person tents). Also important is Ko 9, where the ranger

sub-station can be found. The interiors of these islands consist of crystal-white sand and lush rainforest, while the headlands are made up of distinctive, giant granite boulders the size of houses. Beneath these rocks are underwater grottoes and swim-through tunnels, which appeal to divers and snorkelers.

The sea bed is decorated with staghorn, star, and branching corals, and a range of fish, including manta rays, and giant sea turtles. Other, more threatening, fish include giant groupers, and poisonous stonefish, and lionfish. Sharks around the islands include black and white tips, leopard sharks, hammerheads, bull sharks, and whale sharks.

Diver exploring the colorful coral around Ko Similan

The World's Largest Flower

Khao Sok is one of the few places in the world where the giant *Rafflesia kerri* grows. This foul-smelling tropical plant has no roots or leaves and is wholly parasitic. For most of the year it lies dormant in the form of microscopic threads inside the roots of a host tree. Once a year, however, a small flower breaks the surface of the host's bark. Over a period of months the bud swells to the size of a

Rafflesia flower in full bloom, Khao Sok National Park

watermelon and eventually opens to become the world's largest flower, with a diameter up to 31 inches (80 cm). The flower's fetid smell attracts insects that assist in the pollination process. After a few days the orange-red flower shrivels to a vile, unsightly, putrescent mass. Occasionally a Rafflesia in flower may be found at the end of a marked path at Khao Sok.

❺ Phuket

ภูเก็ต

Thailand's largest island, Phuket first became prosperous thanks to tin production, but tourism is now the major earner. Southeast Asia's most popular vacation destination attracts visitors from across the globe with its stunning beaches, crystal-clear waters, and vibrant nightlife. Phuket has also seen a huge growth in chic boutique resorts and spas. The northern tip of the island is separated from the mainland by only a narrow channel of sea, over which runs the 765-yard (700-m) long Sarasin Bridge.

Game fishing
Tuna, barracuda, and other fish are hunted from boats.

Half-Buried Buddha
Wat Phra Tong is built around an unusual, gold-leafed Buddha image, half buried in the ground. Legend says that whoever tries to remove it will die.

Key

━━ Main road

═══ Minor road

KEY

① **Cape Promthep** is the southernmost point on Ko Phuket. The views from this rugged headland are some of the most stunning on the island, particularly at sunset.

② **The Gibbon Rehabilitation Project** in the Khao Phra Taew Forest Park encourages once-domesticated gibbons to fend for themselves in the wild.

③ **Phuket town** is notable for its 19th-century Sino-Portuguese-style residences. It acts as a transit and service center.

★ **West Coast Beaches**
The clearest waters, best sand, and most luxurious hotels are on the west coast. Patong is the most densely developed resort; Karon and Kata are quieter.

0 kilometers 5

0 miles 5

Sarasin Bridge •

Hat Sai Kaeo •

Hat Mai Khao •

Hat Nai Yang •

Hat Nai Thon •

Wat Phra To

Thalang

Ao Bang Tao

Hat Pansea •

Hat Surin •

Hat Kamala

Phuket FantaSea •

Kathu waterfall •

Hat Patong •

• Hat Karon Noi

Wat Chalong

Hat Karon •

Hat Kata Yai •

Hat Kata Noi •

Hat Nai Harn •

Hat Raw

Ko Bon

Ko Ngam
Cape Khut •

Ko Raet

Ko Naga Yai
Ao Po

(2)
• Bang Pae waterfall
• Khao Phra
Taew Forest
Park
on Sai
aterfall

Ko Naga Noi

Naga Pearl
Farm

halang Museum

Ao Sapam
Ko Rang Yai

Ko Maphrao Yai

(3)

Ko Sire Gypsy Village

halong

• Phuket Deep Sea Port

→ Ko Phi Phi

Cape Phanwa
Marine Research
Center

Lone

VISITORS' CHECKLIST

Practical Information
Phuket province. 102,000.
TAT, 191 Thalang Rd (0-7621-
1036). Tourist Police, Yawarat
Rd (1155). Vegetarian Festival
(late Sep/early Oct, for nine days);
King's Cup Regatta (Dec).
W phuket.com

Transport
18 miles (29 km) N of Phuket
town. Phangnga Rd, Phuket
town. from Ko Phi Phi to
Phuket Deep Sea Port.

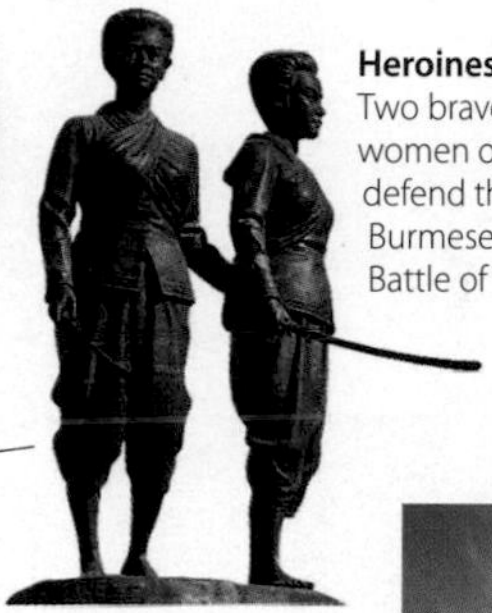

Heroines' Monument
Two brave sisters rallied the
women of Phuket to successfully
defend the island against
Burmese invaders during the
Battle of Thalang in 1785.

Ko Sirey
This small, hilly island is
home to rubber and
coconut plantations and
quiet beaches. The temple
of Wat Ko Sirey can also
be found here, on the top
of a hill that offers
wonderful views.

Monkey Hill
In addition to the resident
macaques, for which this
place is named, Monkey
Hill is a good spot to visit
for views and a popular
Taoist shrine.

★ Marine Research Center
A well-designed aquarium at the
center includes salt- and freshwater
fish, lobsters, turtles, and mollusks.

For keys to symbols *see back flap*

Phuket Town

Phuket Town grew to prominence around the beginning of the 19th century, when the island's tin resources attracted thousands of Chinese migrants. Many merchants made fortunes from tin, built splendid residences, and sent their children to British Penang to be educated. Hokkien-speaking tin-mining families soon intermarried with the indigenous Thai population. Today, the bustling downtown area retains some of its earlier charm, though, unlike most of the island, it is geared toward residents rather than tourists. The Chinese heritage is preserved in the Sino-Portuguese shop-houses, temples, the local cuisine, and the Vegetarian Festival.

One of the grand old Sino-Portuguese mansions in Phuket town

🏛 Chinese Mansions

Thalang, Yaowarat, Dibuk, Krabi, Ranong, and Phangnga roads.
The heart of Phuket town is the old Sino-Portuguese quarter with its spacious, if now rather run-down, colonial-style residences set in large grounds. Most date from the reigns of Rama IV and Rama V (1851–1910). Among the best examples are those used today as offices by the Standard Chartered Bank and Thai Airways on Ranong Road. Unfortunately, no one has yet seen fit to convert any of the old mansions into a museum, and none can be visited. Many of the commercial Chinese shop-houses are also dilapidated.

🏛 Thavorn Hotel Lobby Exhibition

ห้องแสดงของเก่าโรงแรมถาวร
74 Rasada Rd. **Tel** 0-7621-1334.
Open daily. 🖼
The owner of this hotel in the center of town has assembled a collection of Phuket artifacts and pictures that he now displays in the lobby and adjacent function rooms. Among the exhibits are models of tin mines, pictures of the town center in the 19th century, Chinese treasure chests, and weavers' tables, all of which are imaginatively displayed.

🛒 Fresh Produce Market

ตลาดสด
Ranong Rd. **Open** daily.
The 24-hour wet market is a treat that assaults the senses. The market and adjacent lanes are full of colorful characters hawking condiments, dried herbs and spices, pungent pickled *kapi* fish, squirming eels, and succulent durians.

🏯 Rang Hill

เขารัง
On the top of this hill overlooking the town stands a statue of Khaw Sim Bee Na-Ranong (1857–1913), governor of Phuket for 12 years from 1901. He enjoyed considerable autonomy from Bangkok but is credited with bringing the island firmly under central rule, and also with importing the first rubber tree into Thailand.

🏯 Bang Niew Temple

ศาลเจ้าบางเหนียว
Phuket Rd. **Open** daily.
This temple is where *naga* devotees climb knife ladders during the Vegetarian Festival. The inner compound is devoted to a number of Chinese mythological gods, the most prominent being Siew, Hok, and Lok, who represent longevity, power, and happiness.

Phuket Town's Vegetarian Festival

At the start of the ninth Chinese lunar month, Phuket town hosts a nine-day Vegetarian Festival accompanied by gruesome rites. The tradition began over 150 years ago when a troupe of Chinese entertainers in Phuket recovered from the plague by adhering to austere rituals practiced in China. Today, believers use the festival to purge the body and soul of impure thoughts and deeds. Devotees dress in white, follow a vegetarian diet, and refrain from alcohol and sex. The highlight is the parade of *nagas* (spirit mediums) with their flesh pierced by metal rods. Other *nagas* climb ladders of knives, plunge their hands into hot oil, or walk on burning coals. The worse the suffering, the greater reward for the *naga* and his temple.

Nagas parading through the town

Wat Mongkol Nimit, a typical example of Rattanakosin architecture

🏯 Wat Mongkol Nimit
วัดมงคลนิมิต

Yaowarat Rd. **Open** daily.

This large, Rattanakosin-style temple has finely carved doors. Its compound acts as a community center where monks play *takraw* with the laity.

🏯 Chui Tui Temple
ศาลเจ้าจุ๊ยตุ่ย

Ranong Rd. **Open** daily.

A steady flow of people visit this Chinese temple to shake numbered sticks from a canister dedicated to vegetarian god Kiu Wong In. Each number corresponds to a preprinted fate that, according to belief, the person will inherit.

Environs

The island of **Ko Sirey** is linked to Phuket by a short bridge just beyond the commercial fishing port area. On this small but hilly island, rubber and coconut plantations vie with the natural fauna, and quiet beaches offer excellent seafood at low prices. Atop a hill in the center of the island, the temple of Wat Ko Sirey has great views and a massive image of a reclining Buddha. The island is also home to "sea gypsies," who arrived here long before the current inhabitants, and do not speak Thai. Ko Sirey is developing though – the Westin Sirey Bay Resort, on the south of the island, offers every luxury.

Just east of the town, **Monkey Hill**, or Khao To Sae, offers scenic views, some culture in the form of a Taoist shrine, and a population of macaques quite accustomed to being offered food. They are great fun to watch, but afford them the respect you would any wild animal – don't get too close or try to touch them. The Taoist shrine near the base of the hill reveres three resident spirits and attracts many locals wishing to win the lottery. The hill is also popular with fitness enthusiasts – the road is closed to vehicular traffic after 5pm, making it ideal for a sunset run, and there is a small fitness park as well. Don't bother trying to reach the summit – the views and the ambience are marred somewhat by television and cell phone towers.

Phuket Town Center

① Rang Hill
② Chinese Mansions
③ Wat Mongkol Nimit
④ Chui Tui Temple
⑤ Fresh Produce Market
⑥ Thavorn Hotel Lobby Exhibition
⑦ Bang Niew Temple

0 meters 600
0 yards 600

For keys to symbols *see back flap*

Exploring Phuket

Phuket was called Junkceylon by early European traders, but its modern name may derive from the Malay word *bukit*, meaning hill. On arrival, many visitors head straight for a beach resort and do not leave it for the duration of their vacation – the best of the island's beaches are strung out along the west coast. However, there are several historical and cultural sights to complement the beachside attractions, and the lush, hilly interior is also worth exploring.

High-rise hotel overlooking the popular, tree-lined beach at Patong

Hat Patong

Phuket's most developed beach is the 2-mile (3-km) long Hat Patong. Once a quiet banana plantation, it is now almost a city by the sea. The area has a lively nightlife, with a vibrant mix of hotels, restaurants, discos, and bars. During the day there are many water activities, such as parasailing, waterskiing, diving, and deep-sea fishing.

Although Patong continues to expand, the beaches along the southern headland of Patong bay are far quieter, such as Freedom Beach, which is only accessible by boat from Patong.

Hat Karon and Hat Kata

South of Patong, and almost as popular, are the beaches of Karon and Kata. Karon has one long stretch of sand lined with accommodations, and a second beach at tiny Karon Noi. Kata's beaches, along the bays of Kata Yai and Kata Noi, are smaller and prettier, sheltered by rocky promontories. There are a number of good restaurants on the headland between Karon and Kata.

Other Western Beaches

North of Patong, fringed by palm-covered headlands, lie the smaller beaches of Kamala, Surin, and Pansea. Hat Kamala is relatively undeveloped, with some Muslim fishermen's houses and a few restaurants. Just to the south, however, is **Phuket FantaSea**, a huge Las Vegas-style cultural theme complex that hosts a spectacular live night-time stage show with music, dance, special effects, and elephants.

Farther north from Hat Kamala, Ao Bang Tao offers a quiet, enchanting retreat, popular with families. Fronted by a few exclusive hotels, the beach is good for water sports.

Round the next few headlands are three beaches: Hat Nai Thon, a gorgeous, un-developed stretch; Hat Nai Yang, which is visited by Thais on weekends; and Hat Mai Khao, a deserted 7.5-mile (12-km) stretch of sand.

🏠 **Phuket FantaSea**
99 Kamala Beach. **Tel** 0-7638-5000.
Open 5:30–11:30pm Fri–Wed.

Cape Promthep, one of the best vistas on Phuket – a good place for spectacular sunsets

Sea Gypsies of the Andaman Sea

Sea gypsies, known as *chao ley* in Thai, may originate from the Andaman or Nicobar islands, across the Andaman Sea from Thailand. Phuket's sea gypsy population settled the area around 200 years ago, following routes from the Mergui archipelago, west of the Burmese mainland. Today, they can be found in Phuket at Rawai, Ko Sire, near Sapam village, and in northern Phuket's villages of Laem La and Nua. Ethnically, they comprise three groups: Moklen, Moken, and Urak

Lawoi. Sea gypsies live throughout the Andaman Sea at Ko Surin, Ko Phra Tong in Phangnga, and farther south at the islands of Phi Phi, Lanta, Talibong, Tarutao, and Langkawi. They speak their own language and have animistic beliefs. Once a year they hold a spiritual cleansing ceremony, placing human mementos on a small boat before pushing it out to sea to get rid of bad spirits.

Cleaning fish, an everyday part of life for Andaman sea gypsies

Southeastern Capes and Bays

Hat Nai Harn, a bay near the southern tip of Phuket, is the home of the exclusive Phuket Yacht Club. The beach (open to all) is one of the most beautiful on the island. Cape Promthep, 1 mile (2 km) away on the southern tip of Phuket, offers wonderful views, especially at sunset.

North of Promthep, on the east side of the island, are Hat Rawai, and farther along, Ao Chalong. The sands around this bay are not as white as those on the west coast, but there are many excellent seafood shacks here. Ao Chalong acts as an anchorage for international yachts exploiting its sheltered location, and is also a departure point for boat excursions to the charming islands of Lone, Hai, and Bon, where there is good snorkeling.

Farther up the coast at Cape Phanwa is the interesting and much-visited Phuket Aquarium, which forms part of the **Marine Research Center**.

Ghost crab at Marine Center

Marine Research Center
Tip of Cape Phanwa. **Tel** 0-7639-1126. **Open** 9am–4pm daily.

Northeast Coast
Ko Naga Noi, an island off Phuket's northeast coast, has a tranquil, sandy beach that makes a fine halt for swimming and relaxing. The island is home to the **Naga Pearl Farm**, whose owners give demonstrations of the process of culturing South Sea pearls.

At Phuket's northeasternmost point, on the Cape Khut headland, there are sweeping views of the monoliths of Phangnga Bay *(see pp368–71)*. The placid waters of the narrow channel between Phuket and Phangnga province are exploited by Muslim fishermen who farm sea bass here.

Naga Pearl Farm
Ko Naga Noi. **Open** daily.

Thalang
This town in central Phuket was the site of a famous battle in 1785 against the Burmese, which is commemorated by the Heroines' Monument 5 miles (8 km) to the south. A short walk east of the monument is the Thalang Museum, which outlines the rich heritage of Phuket. Among the exhibits are

5th-century religious icons, Chinese porcelain, life-size figures recreated from the Burmese battle, and information on the sea gypsies.

In Thalang itself there is a good market and, nearby, Wat Phra Thong. In the center of the *wat* lies a gold-covered Buddha image, half buried in the ground. Legend has it that disaster will come to anyone who tries to move the image.

Thalang National Museum
Off Hwy 402, opposite Heroines' Monument. **Tel** 0-7631-1025, 0-7631-1426. **Open** daily. **Closed** public hols.

Khao Phra Taew Forest Park
Some 2.5 miles (4 km) east of Thalang is the spectacular Khao Phra Taew Forest Park. The preserve is important, as it preserves the last of Phuket's primary rainforest.

Within the park are two fine waterfalls. Ton Sai waterfall is the prettiest and is at its best from June to December. On the eastern fringe of the preserve is the Bang Pae waterfall.

Near the latter is the **Gibbon Rehabilitation Project**. This volunteer-run program aims to reintroduce domesticated gibbons into the forest by encouraging them to fend for themselves. Visitors' donations buy food for the gibbons.

Khao Phra Taew Forest Park
Thalang district. **Open** daily.

Gibbon Rehabilitation Project
Near Bang Pae falls. **Tel** 0-7626-0491. **Open** daily.

A barrel of limes for sale at Thalang market in central Phuket

❻ Phangnga Bay
อ่าวพังงา

No one area epitomizes the splendor of the South's landscape as succinctly as 155-sq mile (400-sq km) Phangnga Bay. Its scenic grandeur derives from towering limestone stacks rising sheer from calm, shallow waters up to 1,150 ft (350 m) high. Inside many of the 40-odd stacks are narrow tunnels and sea caves. Inland, too, this coastal area boasts majestic, scrub-clad pinnacles. Phangnga is, in fact, the most spectacular remnant of the once mighty Tenasserim Mountains, which still form a spine through Thailand to China.

Protected Mangroves
The heavily silted northern end of Phangnga Bay, where several rivers meet the sea, is Thailand's largest and best preserved area of mangrove *(see pp354–5)*.

Undercut Cliffs
The action of waves erodes the base of the stacks at a rate of about 3 ft (1 m) every 5,000 years.

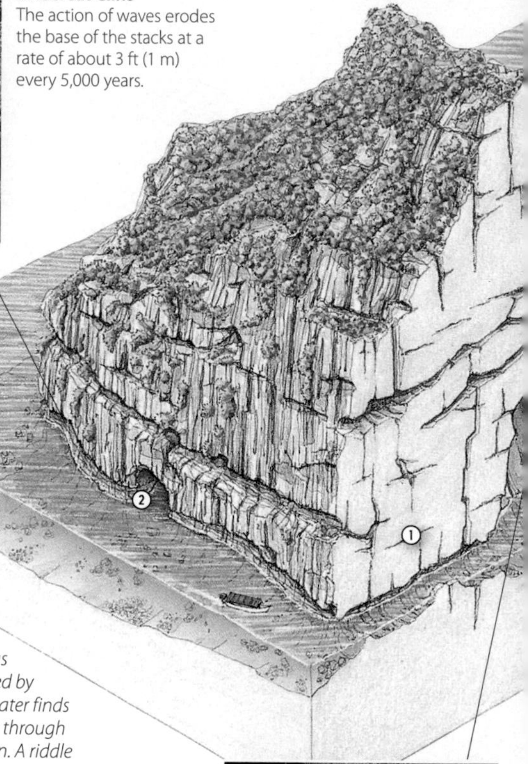

Cross Section of Typical Stacks in Phangnga Bay

The limestone landscape at Phangnga Bay is known by geologists as drowned karstland. Karst is characterized by its internal drainage system, whereby water finds its way into the interior of the limestone through fissures, then erodes the rock from within. A riddle of tunnels is typical; chasms and vast sea chambers (hongs) are also common at Phangnga.

KEY

① **Fissures** allow water to penetrate and erode the limestone.

② **Caves** form quickly at sea level. Some are exposed only at low tide.

③ **The weakened roof** of the cave will eventually collapse.

④ **Forest scrub** clings to cracks in the limestone.

Calcite Deposits in Caves
Within most caves are stalagmites, stalactites, and other structures formed from dripping calcite.

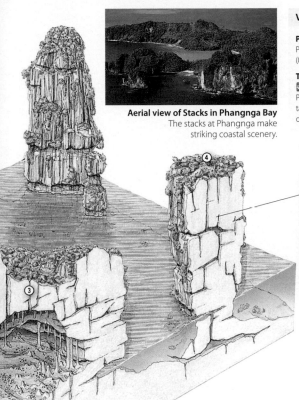

Aerial view of Stacks in Phangnga Bay
The stacks at Phangnga make striking coastal scenery.

Isolated Stacks
There are a number of sheer, thin stacks in the bay. These columns of rock are splinters of limestone that have been heavily eroded by the sea.

How Phangnga Bay was Formed

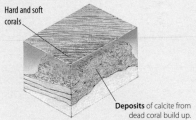

Hard and soft corals

Deposits of calcite from dead coral build up.

130 million years ago the area was under water and part of a vast coral reef. Calcite deposits from dead coral built up in thick layers.

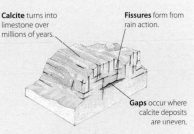

Calcite turns into limestone over millions of years.

Fissures form from rain action.

Gaps occur where calcite deposits are uneven.

75 million years ago plate movements pushed these deposits, which had turned to limestone, out of the ocean. The rigid rock ruptured.

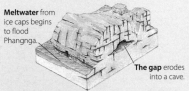

Meltwater from ice caps begins to flood Phangnga.

The gap erodes into a cave.

20,000 years ago, at the end of the last Ice Age, the sea level rose, flooding Phangnga. Wave and tide action accelerated the process of erosion.

Wave action sculpts the stacks.

The cave is much larger.

8,000 years ago the sea reached its highest level, about 13 ft (4 m) above its present height, sculpting a shelf, visible on most of the stacks.

Exploring Phangnga Bay

Boat tours of the bay once took in the best-known sights, such as the fishing village built over water in the shadow of Ko Panyi, and "James Bond Island," as well as a number of fascinating caves. Some of the eerie caverns contain prehistoric paintings and Buddhist shrines. Due to massive erosion however, big tourist boats are currently banned from large areas of Phangnga Bay. The karst scenery continues inland to the east, where cliffs soar above hidden valleys with cascading rivers.

Phangnga town

★ **Panyi Fishing Village**
About 120 Muslim families live in this village, which is built on stilts above the water. Islanders sell fish sauce, dried shrimp, and shrimp paste.

Suwan Kuha Cave (Wat Tham)
A reclining Buddha, tiny shrines, and *chedis* are found among stalactites and stalagmites in this cave temple.

★ **James Bond Island**
This island (Ko Khao Phing Kan) and nearby Ko Tapu ("nail island") both appeared memorably in the 1974 James Bond classic, *The Man With the Golden Gun*.

Ko Hong
A vast network of lagoons, chasms, and tunnels runs underneath this island. As a conservation measure access to the area is forbidden at present.

Areas of Mangrove
It is possible to explore many mangrove channels in a small boat at high tide, though skillful piloting is required.

Rubber Plantations
Rubber is a major industry around Phangnga. Latex, tapped from rubber trees, is left to harden in shallow trays.

• **Ao Luk**

②

Tanboke Koranee National Park
In Ao Luk district, this national park is known for its series of miniature waterfalls amid beautiful limestone scenery.

0 kilometers   10

0 miles   5

KEY

① **Tham Lot** is a 165-ft (50-m) long sea tunnel through limestone with stalactites hanging from its roof.

② **Tham Hua Gralok** ("skull cave") contains prehistoric paintings, in black and red pigment, of humans and strange animals.

③ **Ko Phanak** contains a number of sea *hongs* with vegetation-clad walls and marooned snakes and monkeys.

James Bond and the Island Hideout

In the film *The Man With the Golden Gun* (1974), James Bond (Roger Moore) comes to the Orient in search of the villain Scaramanga (Christopher Lee). Bond is eventually taken to Scaramanga's hideout, an island just off China. In fact, the island seen is Ko Khao Phing Kan in Phangnga Bay; the sheer rock nearby, containing the secret weapon, is Ko Tapu.

Scaramanga and Bond

Aerial view of Ko Hong, Phangnga Bay ▶

❼ Khao Phanom Bencha National Park
อุทยานแห่งชาติเขาพนมเบญจา

Krabi province. Park HQ off Hwy 4, 12.5 miles (20 km) N of Krabi. TAT, Krabi (0-7562-2163); Forestry Dept (0-2562-0760); Park HQ (0-7566-0716). Krabi, then local bus.

This 193-sq mile (500-sq km) national park of mostly tropical monsoon forest is named for the five-shouldered peak of Khao Phanom Bencha, which rises to a height of 4,580 ft (1,397 m).

Despite illegal logging and poaching, the park's rainforest still holds at least 156 species of bird, including the white-crowned hornbill and the striped wren-babbler. Among the 32 mammal species catalogued are the Asiatic black bear, Malaysian sun bear, clouded leopard, wild boar, binturong, and serow.

Clouded leopard in Khao Phanom Bencha

The thundering **Huay To waterfall** and **Huay Sadeh waterfall** are located less than 2 miles (3 km) from the park headquarters. Park attendants can arrange treks to the summit. The climb is difficult but rewarding – from the top there are spectacular views of the surrounding forest.

❽ Ao Nang
อ่าวนาง

11 miles (18 km) W of Krabi town, Krabi province. TAT, Krabi (0-7562-2163). Krabi, then songthaew.

From November to April, Ao Nang sees the arrival of thousands of tourists attracted by the spectacular scenery, pristine beaches, and laid-back atmosphere.

Until the early 1980s, fishing and coconut and rubber plantations were the mainstay for the Muslim villagers at Ao Nang. Today the 1-mile (2-km) sandy beach sports a growing number of hotels, seafood restaurants, scuba diving outlets, and canoe tour companies.

Visitors can rent a sea canoe to paddle in the turquoise waters in the shadow of the 330-ft (100-m) rocky eastern end of the bay. Nearby is uncrowded Pai Plong beach. In season, Ao Nang is a pleasant base for day trips by long-tail boat to the striking **Railay-Phra Nang headland**, 2 miles (3 km) to the southeast. Its sheer limestone cliffs, pure white sand, and emerald sea attract many visitors.

Hat Phra Nang, west of the Phra Nang headland, is the most attractive beach in the area. Rising above it is a high

Strolling along a beach on Ko Poda, a small island near Ao Nang

limestone cliff into which **Tham Phra Nang Nok** ("outer princess cave") is carved. Inside is a shrine to the lost spirit of a princess, Phra Nang, whose ship allegedly sank near the beach in the 4th century BC. Today, local fishermen place offerings of incense, fruit, and water at the shrine to bring them a plentiful catch. Inside the cliff is **Sa Phra Nang**, a lagoon reached by a steep path.

Flanking Phra Nang are the white sand beaches of East and West Railay, the latter being much finer. There are boats from West Railay and Phra Nang beaches to **Ko Poda**, southwest of Phra Nang, where striped tiger fish can be fed by hand from the shallow shore, and **Ko Hua Khwan**, or Chicken Island, located farther south. Both islands offer excellent diving and snorkeling.

On **Ko Hong**, 16 miles (25 km) northwest of Ao Nang, the prized nests of the edible-nest swiftlet (see p345) are collected from the island's intricate network of caves.

The headquarters of the **Phi Phi-Hat Nopparat Thara National Marine Park**, to the west of Ao Nang, overlook stunning beaches. The park covers an area of 150 sq miles (390 sq km), which includes Ko Phi Phi (see pp376–7), Ko Mai Phai, and Ko Yung (also known as Ko Mosquito).

Phi Phi-Hat Nopparat Thara National Marine Park
Park HQ 2 miles (3 km) W of Ao Nang. TAT, Krabi office (0-7562-2163). Krabi, then songthaew.

Idyllic bay within the Phi Phi-Hat Nopparat Thara National Marine Park

❾ Krabi
กระบี่

Krabi province. 🏯 68,000. 🚌
🚢 ✈ 🛈 TAT, Maharat Rd,
Krabi (0-7562-2163). 🛒 daily.
🌐 **tourismthailand.org/krabi**

This small fishing town, the capital of beautiful Krabi province, has an important role as the ferry embarkation point for islands such as Ko Lanta to the south, Ko Phi Phi to the southwest, and the beaches around Ao Nang to the west. Set on the banks of the Krabi Estuary, the town takes its name from a sword, or *krabi*, allegedly discovered nearby. It is surrounded by towering limestone outcrops, similar to those in Phangnga Bay *(see pp368–71)*, which have become the symbol of Krabi province. Among the most notable are **Kanap Nam twin limestone peaks**, which stand like sentinels at each side of the river. To the east, the town is flanked by mangrove-lined shorelines. These outcrops and mangroves can be toured by renting a long-tail boat from the Chao Fa pier in the center of town.

Environs
Located 5 miles (8 km) north of town is **Wat Tham Sua** ("tiger cave temple"), named after a rock formation that resembles a tiger paw. It is one of the most renowned forest *wats* in Southern Thailand, with the

Swimmers enjoying a hot spring spa in the forest near Khlong Thom

main hall, where meditation is practiced, built inside a cave. A circular path in the nearby forest hollow offers a pleasant walk among towering, buttressed trees and *kutis*, simple huts inhabited by monks and nuns. A 985-ft-high staircase (300-m) leads to a large Buddha image and Buddha Footprint on top of the cliff. From here there are panoramic views of the province.

Buddha image on the cliff top by Wat Tham Sua, Krabi province

❿ Khlong Thom
คลองท่อม

Krabi province. 🏯 60,000. 🚌 🛈 TAT, Krabi (0-7562-2163). 🛒 daily.

Some 25 miles (40 km) south of Krabi town, Khlong Thom is known locally for the small museum within **Wat Khlong Thom**. The temple's abbot has assembled an array of archaeological icons and weapons from the area. One of the most interesting exhibits is a collection of distinctive beads called *lukbat*.

A maritime port, Kuan Lukbat, was once located on the site of Khlong Thom. From the 5th century AD onward, the port was used by foreign merchants and emissaries crossing the peninsula to Nakhon Si Thammarat and Surat Thani *(see pp350–51)*. Few traders wanted to sail through the treacherous, pirate-infested Straits of Malacca, so they traveled overland instead.

Environs
A bumpy 7.5-mile (12-km) ride inland from Khlong Thom leads to a natural hot spring in the forest – ideal for swimming.

About 5 miles (8 km) farther on is the rewarding **Tung Tieo forest trail** in Khao No Chuchi lowland forest. The well-marked paths lead through this protected area, skirting emerald pools along the way. The surrounding woodland is the only known area in the world where the colorful ground-dwelling Gurney's pitta survives. Previously, this bird was thought to be extinct.

Climbing Krabi's Stacks
Krabi and Ko Phi Phi are the only places in Thailand where organized rock-climbing takes place. The honeycombed limestone stacks around the Phra Nang headland, near Krabi, and Ko Phi Phi offer challenging conditions and attract rock climbers from around

the world. Only the south of France is said to offer such arduous climbs. They vary in difficulty from an easy "4" according to the French system, to a very difficult "8b." Climbers can cool off with a swim between climbs.

Climber on Thaiwand Wall, Tham Phra Nang near Ao Nang

⓫ Ko Phi Phi

เกาะพีพี

Krabi province. ⌂ 7,700. ⛴ from Phuket or Krabi. 🛈 TAT, Phuket (0-7621-2213). ⛩ Chinese New Year (Feb), Songkran (Apr), Loy Krathong (Nov). Ⓦ **phi-phi.com**

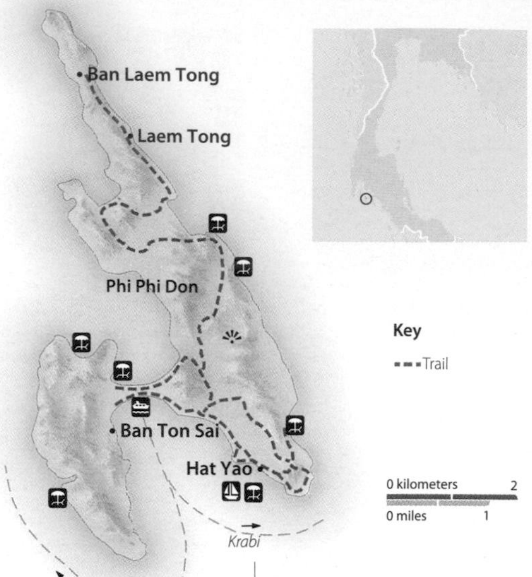

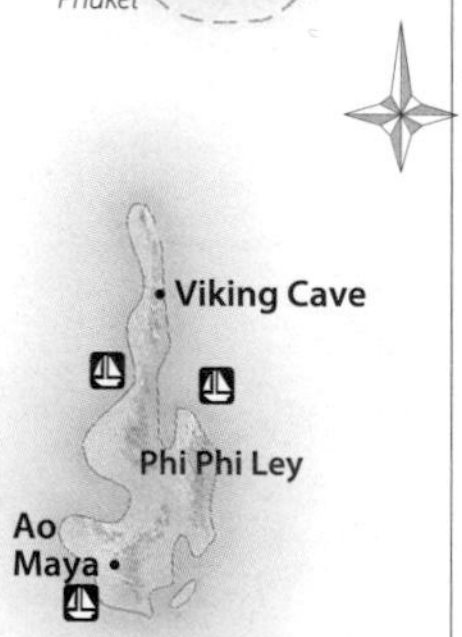

Spectacular Ko Phi Phi, pronounced "PP," 25 miles (40 km) south of Krabi town, is in fact two separate islands: Phi Phi Don and Phi Phi Ley. Both islands belong to the **Phi Phi-Hat Nopparat Thara National Park**, which also takes in part of the mainland near Ao Nang (see p374).

The islands are famed for their spectacular landscapes. Rock climbers are attracted by the breathtaking cliffs (see p375), with tall sheer walls of limestone rising to 1,030 ft (314 m) on Phi Phi Don, and 1,230 ft (374 m) on Phi Phi Ley. Nature lovers will find a haven in the islands' coral beds, teeming with sea life.

Phi Phi Don

The two sections of Phi Phi Don, the larger of the two islands, are linked by a 1,100-yard (1,000 m) isthmus of sand. Here stands the island's original Muslim fishing village, Ban Ton Sai. This area was badly damaged by the 2004 tsunami but the reconstruction work was completed quickly. Since development began on Phi Phi Don following the arrival of the

• Ban Laem Tong

• Laem Tong

Phi Phi Don

• Ban Ton Sai

Hat Yao

Krabi

Phuket

Key
- - - Trail

0 kilometers ——— 2
0 miles ——— 1

• Viking Cave

Phi Phi Ley

Ao Maya •

first visitors in the 1970s, the island has given itself up to tourism. However, there is still plenty of natural beauty to enjoy here. A pleasant one-hour coastal walk from Ban Ton Sai leads to Hat Yao ("long beach"), with tantalizing white sands, vibrant offshore marine life, and unhindered views of the soaring flanks of Phi Phi Ley, 2.5 miles (4 km) away.

It is also worth climbing the steep trails on Phi Phi Don's two massifs, which afford wonderful vistas of the island. The eastern route is well marked and the least strenuous.

Superb coral beds at Hin Pae off Hat Yao, and at Ko Phai ("bamboo island"), to the northeast of Phi Phi Don, provide some of the best diving and snorkeling in Thailand.

To the north is Ban Laem Tong. This village's sea gypsy

A typical view of Ko Phi Phi's stunning scenery, now enjoyed by large numbers of vacationers

For keys to symbols see back flap

One of Ko Phi Phi's enticing, dazzling, white-sand beaches

population still survives on fish caught in the isolated coves of nearby Laem Tong.

Phi Phi Ley

Unlike Phi Phi Don, Phi Phi Ley remains uninhabited and unspoiled. Boats from Phi Phi Don bring visitors on day trips to see the paintings in Viking Cave. Another feature of the cave are the nests of the edible-nest swiftlet (see p345), which are used in bird's-nest soup. Agile collectors climb rickety bamboo scaffolding to reach the nests, which are so valuable that the caves are protected by armed guards and staying overnight on the island is prohibited. There is excellent snorkeling at the coral reefs of Ao Maya.

Environs

Many of the islands in the area shelter endangered bird species such as the white-bellied sea eagle and the *mukimaki* flycatcher.

⓬ Ko Lanta

เกาะลันตา

Krabi province. ⛰ 26,000. 🚌 from Krabi or Bo Muang. 🛈 TAT, Krabi (0-7562-2163).

Close to the mainland in the southeast corner of Krabi province, Ko Lanta is a group of 52 islands, 15 of which belong to the Ko Lanta National Marine Park. Most of the wildlife can

Cave Paintings of the Andaman Islands

There are many prehistoric paintings in Phangnga (see pp368–71) and Krabi (see p375) provinces, especially in caves on the Andaman Islands. Most are stylized red and black outlines depicting human forms, hands, fish, and, in some cases, broken line patterns that are thought to have had symbolic value. Some of the unidentifiable images are of monstrous beings – half-human, half sea-creatures – that still mystify archaeologists. Such paintings may have been drawn as part of magical-religious rituals to bring good fortune for hunting, fishing, food gathering, and tribal battles. Many paintings can be reliably dated to Neolithic times, but the drawings of junklike boats at Phangnga Bay and in the misleadingly named Viking Cave on Phi Phi Ley may be only a few hundred years old.

Paintings of boats in a cave at Phangnga Bay

be found on the smaller, remoter islands. The ramshackle wooden port of Ban Sala Dan is the gateway to **Ko Lanta Yai**, a predominantly Muslim fishing island. Some 15 miles (25 km) long, this is the main island in the archipelago, and it is covered with undulating forested hills sweeping down to numerous west-facing sandy bays. The natural beauty of the island has attracted many resorts, and Ko Lanta Yai is now popular with tourists, although there are still some lovely unspoiled beaches to explore.

The Laem Kaw Kwang headland in the northwest of the island has views across to Ko Phi Phi. At the southern tip, a 2-mile (3-km) coastal trail leads to a solar-powered lighthouse on a steep promontory beside the park headquarters.

Sea gypsies inhabit the nearby village, Ban Sangka-u. They are renowned for their colorful rituals, such as the *loi rua* ceremony. As part of the festivities, a 6-ft (2-m) replica boat is sent out to sea to banish the ill fate built up throughout the past year.

Bungalow accommodations on the island of Ko Lanta

For hotels and restaurants see pp402–11 and pp418–33

DEEP SOUTH

The Deep South of Thailand has more in common with Malaysia than with the distant Thai heartland to the north. Many visitors come here to experience the region's distinct culture, dialect, and food, and to learn about the local history and religion. The scenery, with spectacular mountains in the interior of the peninsula and unspoiled beaches and islands on the west coast, is equally alluring.

In many ways Thailand's Deep South doesn't feel like Thailand at all. The influence of Indian, Chinese, and Malaysian culture can be seen in the region's architecture and ethnic makeup. Skin tones are noticeably darker than the rest of the country. The population speaks an unusually intonated dialect of Thai, and Yawi, a language related to Malay and Indonesian. Also, the food is spicier, characterized by often bitter curries laced with turmeric.

South of Songkhla, especially near the coasts, most people are Muslim, and the minarets of mosques replace the gilded peaks of Buddhist temples. Indeed, Pattani, an important Malay kingdom in the 17th century, is still a center of Islamic scholarship. Even so, Wat Phra Mahathat in Nakhon Si Thammarat, the South's cultural capital, is one of the most revered Buddhist temples in Thailand. Also, numerous Hindu shrines and customs, not least the Hindu-inspired *manohra* dance, are evidence of Nakhon's role as a major religious center on the ocean trade routes between India and China.

Modern Songkhla has become the educational capital of the South. Nearby Hat Yai has grown from an agricultural service and railroad town into an important shopping and entertainment center. However, tourism in the area remains low-key due to spiraling separatist violence perpetrated by Muslim extremists seeking local autonomy. In the troubled southern provinces of Songkhla, Pattani, Yala, and Narathiwat, hostilities are ongoing, and tourists are advised against all but essential travel in these areas.

Pattani Grand Mosque, one of many mosques in the Deep South

◀ Some of the 173 smaller *chedis* surrounding the monumental Chedi Phra Baromathat at Wat Phra Mahathat, Nakhon Si Thammarat

Exploring the Deep South

The eastern lowlands of the Deep South are among the most fertile in the country. Year-round heat and high humidity are ideal conditions for fast-growing coffee beans, pineapples, cashews, rambutans, and oil and rubber palms. The South's commercial capital, Hat Yai, is in this region, but Nakhon Si Thammarat and Songkhla are the cultural centers. In the west, the Trang coast and Tarutao archipelago both have fine sand beaches, spectacular corals, and few visitors by virtue of undeveloped tourist facilities. The east coast offers fewer natural attractions, but charming towns such as Songkhla are well worth visiting. The three provinces south of Hat Yai – Yala, Pattani, and Narathiwat – are strongly influenced by Muslim Malaysia. The differences in language, cuisine, and religion are obvious even to casual visitors. Densely forested mountains near the Malaysian border shelter tigers, elephants, and other wildlife.

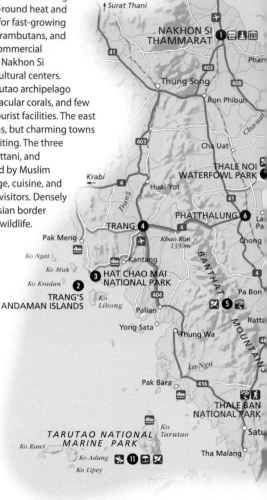

Minaret of Friday Mosque, Nakhon Si Thammarat

Sights at a Glance

1. *Nakhon Si Thammarat pp382–3*
2. Trang's Andaman Islands
3. Hat Chao Mai National Park
4. Trang
5. Banthat Mountains
6. Phatthalung
7. Thale Noi Waterfowl Park
8. Songkhla
9. Hat Yai
10. Thale Ban National Park
11. Tarutao National Marine Park
12. Pattani
13. Yala
14. Betong
15. Narathiwat

Typically deserted beach in the Tarutao archipelago

For hotels and restaurants see pp402–11 and pp418–33

Getting Around

Hat Yai is the main transportation hub of the Deep South. The 580-mile (930-km) trip to Hat Yai from Bangkok takes about 14 hours by bus and 17 by train. Most of the other big towns have bus and rail connections. Highways 4 and 41 are the major north-south roads. Most roads are paved, and local buses run to many sights. There are six small regional airports. Many Singaporeans and Malaysians visit the area on tours; most other visitors are independent travelers. A rental car is the easiest way to get around. The west coast islands can be reached from Pak Meng, Pak Bara, and Kantang.

Fishing village in Narathiwat province

Key

━━━ Major road

⋯⋯ Minor road

━━━ Scenic route

╌╌╌ Main railway

▬▬ International border

△ Summit

GULF OF THAILAND

Sathing Phra

408

Thale Sap Songkhla

Ko Yo

8 SONGKHLA

43

9 HAT YAI

Chana

43

Thepha

Nong Chik

Na Thawi

42

42

Thepha

Sadao

409

410

Wat Khuha Phimuk

13 YALA

Kabang

Bannang Sata

Pattani

Saiburi

PATTANI

12

42

Panare

Mayo

Saiburi

Ba Cho

Yi-Ngo

42

15 NARATHIWAT

Tak Bai

Bang Lang Dam

Sungai Kolok

410

To Mo

0 kilometers 50

0 miles 25

14 BETONG

❶ Nakhon Si Thammarat

นครศรีธรรมราช

Although Nakhon Si Thammarat is featured on few tourist itineraries, the most historic town in the South is a lively center with several attractions. Under the name of Ligor, it is thought to have been the capital of Tambralinga, a peninsular kingdom prior to the 7th century. From the 7th–13th centuries it was an important city of the Srivijaya Empire *(see pp350–51)*, when it became a religious center with the Sanskrit name Nagara Sri Dhammaraja, meaning "city of the sacred dharma king." Many Indian traders settled in Nakhon – as the town is popularly known – and Hindu shrines are a feature here, together with *nang talung* shadow puppet plays *(see p389)* and intricately etched nielloware *(see p437)*.

The relaxing way to take in Nakhon's sights

🏛 Nakhon Si Thammarat National Museum

พิพิธภัณฑสถานแห่งชาตินครศรีธรรมราช
Rachadamnoen Rd, 1.5 miles (2.5 km) S of train station. **Tel** 0-7534-1075. **Open** Wed–Sun. **Closed** public hols. 🖼 📷

The centerpiece of this branch of the National Museum is the 9th-century statue of Vishnu in the Pala style of South India. It was found in the base of a tree in Kapong district near Takua Pha in Phangnga, then a major transit point for Indians colonizing the south.

Two rare bronze drums made by the Dong Son people of northern Vietnam are another highlight. The Thai gallery displays religious art from Dvaravati and Srivijayan periods to the Rattanakosin era. Look out for Buddha images in the distinctive local Sing style, characterized by stumpy features and animated faces.

🏯 Shadow Puppet Theater (Suchart House)

บ้านหนังตะลุงสุชาติ
10/18 Si Thammasok Soi 3. **Tel** 0-7534-6394. **Open** daily. 🖼

The *nang talung* workshop of Suchart Subsin keeps alive a uniquely Southeast Asian form of entertainment in danger of dying out. Visitors can watch the puppets being cut from leather and buy the finished product. Sometimes impromptu shows are staged.

🏛 Wat Phra Mahathat

วัดพระมหาธาตุ
Rachadamnoen Rd, 1 mile (2 km) S of train station. **Open** daily.

Wat Phra Mahathat is one of Thailand's most sacred temples. Although its age is disputed, the *wat* is thought to be at least 1,500 years old. The present *chedi* dates from the 13th century and was supposedly built to house relics of the Buddha that were brought here from Sri Lanka. It is 255 ft (77 m) high and topped with gold variously estimated to weigh between 1,350 and 2,200 lbs (600 and 1,000 kg).

The Wihan Luang chapel has an intricately painted 18th-century ceiling, although the Wihan Phra Ma hall is perhaps more impressive. It features an elaborate, emerald-inlay door from the Sukhothai period, carved with the figures of Phrom and Vishnu. A small museum displays an evocative but unlabeled selection of archaeological finds, jewelry, and religious sculptures including Dvaravati pieces from the 6th to 13th centuries.

🏛 Ho Phra I-suan (Shiva)

หอพระอิศวร
Rachadamnoen Rd. **Open** daily.
In the hall of this shrine is a 3-ft (1-m) *shivalinga*, a phallic image

The gold-topped *chedi* of Nakhon's splendid Wat Phra Mahathat

of the Hindu god Shiva, that may date back to the 6th century AD. The worship of Shiva was a potent force in the early peninsular city-states of the first millennium AD.

Ho Phra Buddha Sihing
หอพระพุทธสิหิงค์

Rachadamnoen Rd. **Open** Wed–Sun.

The Phra Buddha Sing is one of Thailand's most revered images. The replica kept in this shrine is of an original cast in Sri Lanka in AD 157 and brought to Nakhon at the end of the 13th century. Local artisans put their characteristic stamp on the Buddha by giving it a half smile, a rounder face, and a full chest. It is similar to Buddha images in Wat Phra Sing in Chiang Mai.

Ho Phra Buddha Sing, home of the sacred Phra Buddha Sing image

Ho Phra Narai
หอพระนารายณ์

Rachadamnoen Rd. **Open** daily.

Five *lingas* (phallic sculptures) discovered on the site of this shrine may date from before AD 1000. They are now in the Wat Mahathat Museum.

Tha Chang Road
ถนนท่าช้าง

The tradition of gold and silver shops along this road dates from 1804, when migrants from Saiburi district moved to Nakhon. Only skilled gold- and silversmiths were allowed to settle here, to the west of Sanam Na Muang parade ground.

Ancient City Wall & North Gate
กำแพงเมืองเก่า

Just E of Rachadamnoen Rd.

The ancient city wall originally contained an area 440 yds by 2,450 yds (400 m by 2,230 m). The red brick North Gate is a reconstruction.

Wat Sao Thong Tong
วัดเสาธงทอง

Rachadamnoen Rd. **Open** daily.

Adjoining the compound of Wang Tawan Tok temple,

Typical nielloware pot

this *wat's* main attraction is the Southern Thai wooden house, started in 1888 and finished in 1901. It is actually three houses joined together and features delicately carved wooden door panels, gables, and window surrounds. The Architects' Association of Thailand gave a conservation award to the building in 1993.

Bovorn Bazaar
บวรบาซาร์

Rachadamnoen Rd. **Open** daily.

The city center bazaar is a peaceful courtyard and popular meeting place with cafés, bars, and two good restaurants.

Nakhon Si Thammarat Town Center

① Bovorn Bazaar
② Wat Sao Thong Tong
③ Tha Chang Road
④ Ancient City Wall & North Gate
⑤ Ho Phra I-suan (Shiva)
⑥ Ho Phra Narai
⑦ Ho Phra Buddha Sing
⑧ Shadow Puppet Theater
⑨ Wat Phra Mahathat

Airport
9 miles (15 km)

PHATHANAKAN KHU KWANG
WATYO
PAK NAKHON
BOHANG
PHANIAT
SI PRAT
RACHADAMNOEN
YOMMARAT
KAROM
THA CHANG
Khlong Ta Wang
SI THAMMARAT
NANG NGAM
PHATHANAKAN KHU KWANG
SI THAMMASOK
RACHADAMNOEN

Wat Sao Thong Tong ②
① Bovorn Bazaar
Train Station
Bus Terminal ③ THA CHANG
Ancient City Wall & North Gate ④
Ho Phra Narai ⑥
Ho Phra I-suan (Shiva) ⑤
Ho Phra Buddha Sing ⑦
Shadow Puppet Theater ⑧
Wat Phra Mahathat ⑨

National Museum, PHATTHALUNG

0 meters 500
0 yards 500

For keys to symbols *see back flap*

Lush lowland scenery at Hat Chao Mai National Park

❷ Trang's Andaman Islands

หมู่เกาะอันดามันจังหวัดตรัง

Trang province. 🚤 long-tail from Kantang to Ko Muk, Ko Kradan and Ko Libong, and from Pak Meng to Ko Hai and Ko Muk. ℹ️ TAT, Trang (0-7521-5867); Forestry Dept (0-2562-0760).

Tourist development has barely touched the 50 or so small islands off the coast of Trang province. Their stunning sands, pristine corals, and rich bird and marine life remain the preserve of a handful of solitude seekers.

Forested **Ko Hai**, or **Ko Ngai**, is the island most easily reached from Pak Meng on the mainland and offers the widest choice of accommodation. There are wonderful beaches, particularly on the east coast, and magnificent coral offshore.

Ko Muk, 5 miles (8 km) southeast of Ko Hai, is best known for Tham Morakhot ("emerald cave") on its west coast. A long limestone tunnel leads from the sea to an inl and beach surrounded by vegetation-clad cliffs. It can be entered only by boat at low tide.

Arguably the most beautiful and remotest of Trang's Andaman islands, **Ko Kradan** offers white sand beaches and good snorkeling.

Farther south and close to the mainland, **Ko Libong** is the largest of the islands. It is famed for its spectacular birdlife, which is at its best during March and April.

❸ Hat Chao Mai National Park

อุทยานแห่งชาติหาดเจ้าไหม

Trang province. ℹ️ TAT, Trang (0-7521-5867); Forestry Dept (0-2562-0760 inc bungalow bookings). 🚌 from Trang to Kantang, then *songthaew*.

Around 31 miles (50 km) west of Trang town, the varied coastal landscape of Hat Chao Mai National Park includes mangrove creeks, coastal karsts, and hidden beaches, accessed through caves around Yao and Yongling beaches. The casuarina trees lining Pak Meng beach in the north of the park is popular. This is also the main departure point for boat tours around Trang's islands, nine of which

Tuk-tuk in Trang town

are also under park control. Dugongs can sometimes be spotted between the mainland and the islands.

❹ Trang

ตรัง

Trang province. 👥 83,000. ✈️ 🚉 🚌 ℹ️ TAT, Trang (0-7521-5867). 🍴 daily. 🎉 Vegetarian Festival (Oct).

Trang has been a trading center since at least the 1st century AD. It grew to prosperity between the 7th and 13th centuries during the Srivijaya period and remains an important commercial town today. Rubber, palm oil, and fishing are the mainstays of its economy. Tourism has not yet made much impact, although this may change if Trang's Andaman islands start to be more intensively developed.

The town has a strong Chinese character (and good Chinese restaurants) as a result of an influx of immigrant labor in the latter half of the 19th century. Trang's Vegetarian Festival, mirroring its better-known counterpart on the island of Phuket (*see p364*), is renowned for the intensity of its ascetic rites, which include body piercing.

A monument to Khaw Sim Bee Na-Ranong, the first governor of Trang from 1890 to 1901, stands in the Fitness Park at the eastern end

Tranquil landing pier on the estuary of the Trang River

For hotels and restaurants see pp402–11 and pp418–33

of Phatthalung Road. The statue attracts many merit-makers, especially on April 10, the day dedicated to the former governor. The Clarion MP Hotel is notable for being partially built in the shape of an ocean liner.

Environs

Trang province was dependent on tin mining until the first rubber tree seedlings were brought into Thailand around 1901. The first rubber tree can still be seen in Kantang, 14 miles (22 km) southwest of Trang, near a small museum dedicated to Khaw Sim Bee Na-Ranong. Boats run from Kantang to many of the nearby islands.

Dense rainforest on the steep slopes of the Banthat Mountains

Slender rubber trees in one of Trang province's many plantations

❺ Banthat Mountains

เขาบรรทัด

Trang province. 🛈 TAT, Trang (0-7521-5867); Forestry Dept (0-2562-0760).

The verdant Banthat Mountains, which run down the peninsula as far as the Malaysian border, mark the eastern boundary of Trang province.

The forested higher elevations of the mountains, which rise to 4,430 ft (1,350 m) at Khao Ron, are one of the few places in South Thailand where the Sakai tribe still maintain their hunter-gatherer existence.

These ethnically unique Negrito people speak a language related to Mon-Khmer. Traditionally they live in groups of 10 to 30 in simple lean-to leaf and grass shelters near running water, and hunt with poison blow darts. Forest clearance and exposure to lowland culture has led to some Sakai becoming agricultural laborers.

The mountains are also home to many amphibian and reptile species, including dwarf geckos and wrinkled frogs. Rare birds include hornbills, spiderhunters, hawk cuckoos, and the narcissus flycatcher. A worthwhile excursion is to the **Khao Chong Nature and Wildlife Study Center**, 12 miles (20 km) east of Trang off Highway 4. It contains an

impressive open zoo and two waterfalls. Just to the south, a bird sanctuary at **Khlong Lamchan** has a reservoir that attracts many species of duck.

The minor road heading south along the western flanks of the Banthat Mountains gives access to a series of spectacular waterfalls, caves, and shady picnic places. Highlights include the huge **Ton Tay falls**, the spray rainbow that often forms by mid-afternoon over the **Sairung falls**, and the stalactites and stalagmites of **Tham Chang Hai** ("lost elephant cave") near Muansari village in Nayong district.

Much farther south, and easily accessible from Satun, is the spectacular Thale Ban National Park (see p392).

Dugongs

The once common dugong, or sea cow, was brought to the brink of extinction in Thai waters by hunting and by accidental drowning in commercial fishing nets. Today numbers are slowly increasing. The area around the Trang islands of the Andaman Sea is one of the few places they can be spotted. These herbivores feed on the seagrass beds around Ko Libong and the Trang Estuary. They grow up to 10 ft (3 m) long and can weigh 880 lbs (400 kg). In local folklore, the tears of a dugong act as a love potion.

The dugong – a rare, gentle giant now protected by law

Palm huts on the beach at Ko Hai, a small island off the coast of Trang province ▶

❻ Phatthalung

พัทลุง

Phatthalung province. ⚊ 81,000.
🚌 🚐 🚤 *i* TAT, Hat Yai (0-7423-
1055). 🛍 daily. 🎭 Phon Lak Phra
Competition (3 days in Oct or Nov).

One of the few rice-growing
areas in Southern Thailand,
Phatthalung province has
earned a steady income from
the crop throughout its history.
It is better known, though, as
the place where *nang talung*
(shadow puppetry) was first
performed in Thailand – the
name *nang talung* may even
derive from Phatthalung.
This popular form of theater,
related to Indonesian shadow
puppetry, is performed mainly
in Phatthalung and Nakhon Si
Thammarat provinces.

Phatthalung town was
established in the 19th century
during the reign of Rama III
(see pp68–9). Today's modern
town is set out in a grid and is
surrounded by limestone hills
to the north and the fertile
Thale Luang lake to the east.

Phatthalung lies between
two attractive peaks: **Khao Ok
Talu** ("punctured chest
mountain") to the northeast,
and **Khao Hua Taek** ("broken
head mountain") to the
northwest. According to local
legend, these two mountains,
"the mistress" and "the wife,"
fought over Khao Muang (the
male mountain), located to the
north. It is said that they still
nurse their battle scars from
this confrontation. In fact, Khao
Ok Talu has a naturally

Khao Ok Talu ("punctured chest mountain") overlooking Phatthalung

occurring tunnel in its peak
(the punctured chest), while
Khao Hua Taek has a dent in
its peak (the broken head).
In the latter are the Buddhist
grottoes of **Wat Tham Kuha
Sawan**. Inside the lower cave
are statues of monks and the
Buddha, while the upper cave
has views of Khao Ok Talu and
most of Phatthalung and the
surrounding area.

Environs
Lush rice fields surround
Phatthalung. At **Lam Pam**, a
small fishing village 4 miles

(6 km) east of Phatthalung,
slow-flowing canals empty
into the large Thale Luang
inland sea. The breezy but
peaceful area at Sansuk beach
has a few restaurants serving
good seafood. Boats can be
hired to the nearby islands,
Ko Si and Ko Ha.

One mile (2 km) before Lam
Pam is **Wat Wang**, Phatthalung's
oldest temple, thought to
have been founded at the same
time as the town. Next to the
chedi is a *bot* with faded murals
depicting Buddhist and
Ramakien *(see pp44–5)* themes.

The restored **Governor's
Palace** occupies a peaceful
site nearby. Built in 1889, the
palace comprises two
individual buildings. The
outer teak structure, nearer
the road, functioned as living
quarters for the governor's
family. The main building,
beside the river, is built
around a courtyard with a
large tree.

🏛 **Governor's Palace**
Hwy 4047, 2 miles (4 km) E of
Phatthalung. **Open** 8:30am–
4pm daily.

The elevated structures of the Governor's Palace in Lam Pam

For hotels and restaurants see pp402–11 and pp418–33

❼ Thale Noi Waterfowl Park

ทะเลน้อย

20 miles (32 km) NE of Phatthalung, Phatthalung province. 🛈 TAT, Hat Yai (0-7423-1055); Forestry Dept, Bangkok (0-2562-0760) 🌐 dnp.go.th 🚌 from Phatthalung, then hire a long-tail. **Open** 8:30am–4pm daily. 📷

Long-tail boat at Thale Noi Waterfowl Park

The largest wetland bird sanctuary in Thailand, this park serves as a resting and feeding ground for thousands of exotic migratory birds flying to Sumatra and Australia to escape winter in Siberia and China. The best way to explore the watery preserve, covering 12 sq miles (30 sq km), is by long-tail boat, which can be hired from Phatthalung for a two-hour round trip.

Thale Noi has the appearance of a swamp, but it is predominantly a freshwater lake, with a depth of up to 5 ft (1.5 m). Only in periods of high southerly winds does the lake become brackish, when saltier water from

White-throated kingfisher

Thale Luang and Songkhla Lake to the south is pushed northward. Dawn is the best time for bird-watching, especially between the months of January and April. Many of the 150 or so species of birds who visit the park arrive during this time, swelling its population to as much as 100,000. In May the population begins to shrink, and from October to December there are only small numbers of native species left. A viewing platform in the lake is the ideal place for

bird-watching. Among the birds here are the purple swamp hen, bronze-winged jacana, whistling teal, white-throated kingfisher, the long-legged *nok i-kong*, and the white ibis and gray heron.

One of the major forms of vegetation in the park is *don kok*, a reed which the *nok i-kong* use to build "platforms".

Around 100 families live along the shores of Thale Noi, mostly in raised wooden houses. They make a living from fishing and by weaving bulrush reeds into mats.

Shadow Puppets – Nang Talung

Nang talung is the popular Thai version of shadow puppetry, an art form that originated as early as 400 BC in Asia. *Nang talung* performances, which begin late at night and last several hours, are still an essential part of village life in the Deep South. It is the task of a single person, the *nai nag* (puppet master), to create the whole show. Sitting behind an illuminated screen, he maneuvers up to six puppets per scene. The puppets, about 20 in (50 cm) high, are made from leather, or *nang*, which is carved, colored, and rendered movable by joints. The changing tone of the puppeteer's voice differentiates between the characters, while a band of musicians adds tension to the plot. While the more formal *nang yai* is based on the Ramakien *(see pp44–5)*, *nang talung* takes its inspiration from everyday life, with themes such as family problems. Each story is created by the *nai nag* and includes easily recognizable characters, such as comic figures with exaggerated features. Once a year the apprentices commemorate the puppet master in a *wai kru* ("paying respect to the teacher") ceremony.

Shadow puppet of a Ramakien character

A puppeteer, sitting behind a screen, using his skills to perform *nang talung*

The audience's view of *nang talung*

❽ Songkhla

สงขลา

Songkhla province. 🚹 86,000. ✈
🚉 at Hat Yai, 22 miles (36 km) SW of
Songkhla. 🚌 🚢 ℹ TAT, Hat Yai
(0-7424-3747). 🏪 daily. 🎎 Chinese
Lunar Festival (Sep/Oct).

Once known as Singora ("lion
city"), Songkhla grew
to prominence during
the Srivijaya period
(see pp350–51).
It once had a
reputation as a pirate
base but gradually
attracted Arab,
Indian, Khmer, and
Chinese traders.
The cuisine and
language of
Songkhla reflect its
multicultural heritage, and a
subtle Portuguese influence is
evident in the architecture of
the houses along Nakhon Nok
and Nakhon Nai roads.

Today the city, built on
the headland between the
Gulf of Thailand and Thale
Sap – the country's largest
lake – is a fishing port and
an administrative and
educational center.

Songkhla's main beach, **Hat
Samila**, which is presided over
by the bronze **Mermaid Statue**,
is pleasant to walk along and
it has several good seafood
restaurants. Farther south, at
Khao Seng, is a Muslim fishing

*Wat Chai Mongkhon,
Songkhla*

village where colorful *korlae*
fishing boats (see p394) can
be seen. A local myth says
that if you can move the Nai
Bang's Head boulder on the
headland beside the village,
you will inherit the gold
buried underneath.

The beautiful, evocative
building housing the **Songkhla
National Museum** is
an attraction in itself.
It was built in 1878 in
the Southern Thai-
Chinese style as
the residence of
deputy Songkhla
governor Phraya
Suntharanuraksa.
A hidden grass
courtyard flanks two
spiraling staircases
leading to the
wooden paneled second story,
where most exhibits are kept.
Highlights include Bencharong
pottery, earthenware jars
recovered from the sea around
Songkhla, 7th- to 9th-century
Dvaravati plinths and Buddha
images, and Ban Chiang pottery
said to date from 3000 BC.

The **Patrsee Museum** in Wat
Matchimawat (sometimes
called Wat Klang), south of the
National Museum, is no less
important. Its 14-in (35-cm)
stone image of Ganesh, the elephant god, is thought to date
from the late 6th century,
making it the earliest such
image found in the peninsula.

Chinese painted enamelware
from the Qwing Ching dynasty,
15th-century U Thong wares,
and 18th-century European
plates all indicate the
importance of Songkhla's
former maritime trade links.

The city's other main temple,
Wat Chai Mongkhon, has a
Buddha relic from Sri Lanka
buried beneath it.

Songkhla is an attractive city
to walk around, taking in the
topiary garden at **Khao Noi** and
the view of Thale Sap from the
peak of **Khao Tung Kuan**.
Restaurants and live music
bars can be found around
Chaiya Road.

🏛 **Songkhla National Museum**
Wichianchom Rd. **Tel** 0-7431-1728.
Open Wed–Sun. **Closed** public
hols. 🎫

Elaborately decorated door at the Songkhla
National Museum

Songkhla Town Center

① Mermaid Statue
② Khao Noi
③ Khao Tung Kuan
④ Songkhla National Museum
⑤ Wat Chai Mongkhon
⑥ Patrsee Museum
⑦ Old Portuguese Houses

0 meters 500
0 yards 500

KHAO SENG

Mermaid ① Statue
LEAP RIM THALE LUANG
RATCHADAMNOEN
② Khao Noi
Wat Chai Mongkhon ⑤
Songkhla National ④ Museum
Bus Station
③ Khao Tung Kuan
Patrsee Museum ⑥
⑦ Old Portuguese Houses

Hat Samila
RATCHADAMNOEN NAI
SADAO CHAIYA
SUKHUM
CHAIMON GKHON
THALE LUANG
KO YO
HAT YAI
RAMWITHI
CHONCHAROEN
SAIBURI
LEAM SAI
NAKHON NAI
NAKHON NOK
LANG PHRARAM
Ferry pier
Thale Sap

Patrsee Museum
Wat Matchimawat, Saiburi Rd.
Open Wed–Sun. **Closed** public
hols.

Environs
The Prem Tinsulanonda bridge connects Songkhla with the narrow coastal strip to the north. Once the longest bridge in Thailand, it traverses Thale Sap via the island of **Ko Yo** on the western side of the lake. The link has boosted the island's active cotton-weaving industry and fish farms.

Ko Yo is home to the excellent **Folklore Museum**, on a hilltop overlooking the lake. The museum, which aims to preserve the rich folk traditions of the South, houses displays on history, ethnology, and religion. Exhibits include fabrics, pottery, and metalware, and traditional arts from the South, such as rattan and brassware from Ranong, Muslim *kris* knives from Pattani, *krajude* grass mats from Chumphon, and dove cages from Songkhla.

Wat Pha Kho, in **Sathing Phra** district, to the north of Songkhla, is believed to be the oldest temple in Songkhla province. Archaeological finds around the *wat* suggest Sathing Phra was once an important port selling ceramics, produced at nearby Pa-o, to Khmer, Cham, and Chinese traders.

Folklore Museum
Institute of Southern Thai Studies,
Ko Yo, 8 miles (14 km) SW of Songkhla.
Open daily.

Three young devotees venerating a Buddhist shrine in Hat Yai

❾ Hat Yai
หาดใหญ่

Songkhla province. 70,000.
7 miles (12 km) W of Hat Yai.
TAT, 1/1 Soi 2, Niphat U-thit Rd,
Hat Yai (0-7424-3747). next to TAT
(0-7424-6733). daily. Chinese
Lunar Festival (Sep/Oct).

The commercial and transport capital of Southern Thailand, Hat Yai wins no prizes for beauty. It has grown affluent due to its strategic railroad junction, its cut-price products, and a constant flow of Malaysian tourists who converge on the city on weekends to enjoy its dining, shopping, and nightlife. Malay, English, Yawi, Hokkien, Mandarin, and the clipped syllables of Southern Thai dialect can be heard around the cosmopolitan downtown area.

Seller displaying produce at Hat Yai market

Be aware that some parlors here advertising "ancient massage" will probably offer more than a quick rubdown.

Hat Yai's cultural attractions are few, so most visitors spend daylight hours shopping in Thailand's third-largest city. Electrical goods at the Kim Yong market, durians and apples from street vendors, and Bangkok-made leather goods and fashions in the department stores are a few of Hat Yai's popular buys. Bullfighting takes place in the city on the first Saturday of every month at different locations. Bulls are pitted against each other, and the winner is the animal that forces its opponent to retreat. The furious betting is often as much of a spectacle as the fight itself.

Wat Hat Yai Nai, 1 mile (2 km) west of the city center, has the third-largest reclining Buddha image in the world, measuring 115 ft (35 m) long and 49 ft (15 m) high. You can walk inside the image, entering via a small shrine room. Herbal saunas and massages are offered in the temple grounds.

Environs
Ton Nga Chang ("elephant tusk") waterfall, 15 miles (24 km) west of Hat Yai, takes its name from the two streams of water that tumble over the seven tiers of falls. They are best seen in the cool season, starting in November.

Extensive fish farms beside Ko Yo on Thale Sap lake, near Songkhla

For hotels and restaurants see pp402–11 and pp418–33

Taking the ferry from Pak Bara to Tarutao National Marine Park

⑩ Thale Ban National Park
อุทยานแห่งชาติทะเลบัน

Satun province. Off Hwy 4184, 23 miles (37 km) from Satun. 🛈 TAT, Hat Yai (0-7423-1055); Forestry Dept (0-2562-0760)or 🌐 **dnp.go.th** for bungalow bookings. 🚌 Satun, then *songthaew*. 🚗

Thale Ban is a lush expanse of dense tropical rainforest scattered with waterfalls that extends over the Banthat Mountains *(see p385)* close to the Malaysian border. It covers only 40 sq miles (102 sq km) but contains a staggering variety of wildlife including sun bears, tigers, and rare birds such as bat hawks. The park has some marked trails, the Yaroy waterfall, 3 miles (5 km) north of the park headquarters, and several swimming pools.

Satun is the nearest town and gateway to the park. It is within easy reach of Pak Bara, from which ferries depart for Tarutao, and the west coast.

⑪ Tarutao National Marine Park
อุทยานแห่งชาติตะรุเตา

Satun province. 14 miles (22 km) from Pak Bara. 🛈 TAT, Hat Yai (0-7423-1055) or Park HQ (0-7478-3485). 🚤 from Pak Bara; regular crossings mid-Nov to mid-Apr only. 🚗

The 51 islands of the Tarutao National Marine Park are the most southwesterly in Thailand, located only 5 miles (8 km) from the Malaysian island of Langkawi. Tarutao is famous for its superb diving sites, said to be among the world's best.

Offshore sightings of sperm and minke whales, dugongs, and dolphins are common. There is also a rich concentration of fish life with 92 species of coral fish and around 25 percent of all the world's fish species in the surrounding seas.

For centuries the islands had a more sinister reputation as a lair for pirates. It wasn't until the 1960s that the British Royal Navy finally curtailed the pirate raids. The archipelago, extending over 580 sq miles (1,490 sq km), became Thailand's first national marine park in 1974.

The park includes spectacular, unspoiled scenery, a wide variety of wildlife, and good coral. However, these attractions are accessible to visitors only from mid-November to mid-May as monsoon storms make the ferry trip from Pak Bara too risky at other times.

The largest island in the group, 16-mile (26-km) long

Hawksbill turtle, a resident of Tarutao

Ko Tarutao, offers the greatest scenic variety. Tropical rainforest covers most of its surface, which reaches a height of 2,300 ft (708 m). Most accommodations and the best facilities for visitors are found near the wonderful, pristine beaches of the west coast.

Ferries from Pak Bara dock at Ao Phante Malaka, which is where the park headquarters, bungalows, two restaurants, and the island's only store are located. Worthwhile excursions from here include the half-hour climb to To-bo cliff with its fine views, particularly at sunset, and the 1-mile (2-km) boat trip to stalagmite-filled Crocodile cave. No crocodiles have been seen for many years, but the island does support a wide variety of fauna including deer, wild pigs, macaques, otters, and soft-shelled turtles. **Ko Adang** and **Ko Lipey** are the only other islands in the park to offer (rudimentary) accommodations and food for visitors. Rugged Ko Adang, 39 miles (62 km) west of the mainland, rises to 2,300 ft (703 m). It is thickly forested and has many year-round waterfalls, such as the Rattana falls on the southwest coast. Here, you can take a freshwater rock pool swim while overlooking the sea.

The smaller island of Ko Lipey, 1 mile (2 km) south of Ko Adang, has pleasant footpaths through coconut plantations and the immaculate sands of Pattaya beach. It is also home to a community of sea gypsies, displaced from Ko Rawi and Ko Adang when the park was created. Relations between the gypsies and the park authorities are strained.

Ko Kra, off Lipey's east coast, has excellent corals, as does Ko Yang, midway between Rawi and Adang islands.

Tiny Ko Khai ("egg island"), west of Tarutao, has a dramatic rock arch and is surrounded by fine sands. These are a major breeding ground for sea turtles, hence the island's name.

Colorful corals, part of a reef in the Tarutao National Marine Park

Seafood of the South

One of the greatest culinary treats Thailand provides is the abundant fresh seafood of the South. Throughout the year, a wide range of fish, crabs, lobsters, mussels, shrimp, mollusks, and squid are available along both the Gulf of Thailand and Andaman Sea coasts. Although flash-frozen and container-freighted seafood is available all over the country today, it is hard to beat the flavor of a freshly caught fish, simply cooked and served up whole on a plate by the shore. Nor does it have to be expensive: for every five-star restaurant offering lobster bisque there are half a dozen street cafés serving an enormous range of seafood cooked in an amazing variety of styles.

Hoi nang rom sot, a simple Thai hors d'oeuvre of fresh oysters, is served out of the shell with slices of zesty lime.

Green mussels from the Gulf of Thailand

Whelks from the Andaman Sea

Andaman Sea cockles

Fresh crab from Phuket

Saltwater tiger shrimp

Charamet fish, prized for its succulent, soft flesh, is cooked here in sweet plum sauce (*neung buay*), accompanied by ginger, lemon grass, and chili peppers.

Barbecued Seafood

Barbecued seafood, known as thale phao, *is popular with both Thais and foreign visitors. Diners make their selection of freshly caught fish and shellfish displayed on banks of crushed ice. Pricing is usually by weight.*

Thot man kung (deep fried shrimp cakes) are served with a sweet sauce dip. This is a favorite dish with those who don't like very spicy food.

Meuk op sos noei (squid baked in butter sauce) is decorated with exquisitely carved vegetable "flowers" and "leaves." Garnishes of this type accompany many Thai dishes and are generally not eaten.

Kung mangkon phat phrik phao (barbecued lobster with chili sauce) is particularly popular around Phuket, where lobsters abound.

Phanaeng kung makheuathet is a creamy, fragrant dish of tomatoes stuffed with a shrimp and coconut milk curry. It is a specialty of Hat Yai and Phuket.

⑫ Pattani
ปัตตานี

Pattani province. ⛰ 74,000. 🚌 🚌
ℹ TAT, Narathiwat (0-7352-2411). 🛒
daily. 🎉 Lim Ko Niaw Festival (Mar).

Founded in the early 1400s,
Pattani was once a semiauto-
nomous Malay-speaking
sultanate. Today, it is the heart
of Muslim South Thailand
(75 percent of the province's
population are followers of
Islam). Pattani is one of four
southern provinces that have
seen rising violence by Islamic
extremists against the minority
Buddhist population.

Apart from the **Matsayit
Klang** mosque, there are
few notable sights, but
the town is lively,
particularly around the
harbor with its brightly
colored boats.

Environs
The mosque of **Kru Se**,
4 miles (7 km) east of
town, is unremarkable in
design but has an
interesting story behind
it. In the 1570s, Lim To Khieng,
a Chinese merchant, married a

Wat Khuha Phimuk, with its adjacent cave containing a reclining Buddha

Muslim women in
Pattani

local woman and converted to
Islam. To show his devotion to
his new faith he started
building a mosque. His sister,
Lim Ko Niaw, sailed from
China to protest about his
conversion, and he swore
he would return to
China as soon as the
mosque was finished.
However, he made
sure that it never was,
and his sister, on her
deathbed, cursed the
building and
anyone who attempted
to complete it. Her
shrine and the still
unfinished mosque attract huge
numbers of devotees.

Korlae Fishing Boats
Along mainly the east coast of the peninsula, from Ko Samui
southward, colorful, painted fishing boats called *korlae* have been
built and decorated by Muslim fishermen for hundreds of years.
The finest examples of this now declining industry originate in the
boatyards of Saiburi district, Pattani. Originally sailboats, they are now
run with engines by fishermen. Among the characters commonly
depicted on the superbly detailed hull designs are the *singha* lion,
the *gagasura* horned bird, *payanak* sea serpent, and the *garuda* bird
from Asian mythologies. Artists, however, don't feel anything is amiss
if they add a Swiss Alpine background.

Battling mythical beasts, intricately painted on a *korlae* boat

⑬ Yala
ยะลา

Yala province. ⛰ 93,000. 🚌 🚌
ℹ TAT, Narathiwat (0-7352-2411).
🎉 ASEAN Barred Ground Dove
Festival (1st weekend Mar); Yala City
Pillar Celebrations (end of May).

Yala, often heralded as the
cleanest town in Thailand, is laid
out in an orderly fashion with a
grid pattern of streets and tree-
lined boulevards. It's a prosperous
and rather staid place, at its most
lively during the annual cooing
competition of the ASEAN
Barred Ground Dove Festival,
which attracts entrants from all
over Southeast Asia. Yala's
mosque is the largest in Thailand.

Environs
For many people, the main
reason to visit Yala is **Wat Khuha
Phimuk**, called Wat Na Tham
locally, located 5 miles (8 km)
outside the town. It is one of the
most sacred and important
archaeological sites in South
Thailand. A cave next to the
temple contains an 82-ft-long
(25-m) reclining Buddha. The
statue, which allegedly once
had the head of the Hindu god
Vishnu, dates from the 8th
century, the beginning of the
Srivijaya period.

Among the priceless icons
from that era found here are
votive *stupas* from Northeast
India and 9th-century bronze
standing Buddha images in the
style of South India.

The small museum hall, at the
foot of the *naga* staircase
leading up to the temple cave,
displays a range of Srivijayan
artifacts found in the area.

⑭ Betong

เบตง

Yala province. 🚹 29,000. 🚌 *i* TAT, Narathiwat (0-7352-2411). 🏠 daily.

Betong is the southernmost town in Thailand. It sits high in the hills, 3 miles (5 km) from the Malaysian border and 87 miles (140 km) from Yala.

The surrounding countryside is of more interest than the town itself, which has few sights other than the 130-ft-high (40-m) *stupa* in **Wat Phuttha Tiwat**. This was built in the late 1980s in a modified Srivijayan style.

Environs

The winding road from Yala to Betong climbs through remote mountain forests where bands of the Sakai tribe still hunt.

From the 1940s until the 1980s this dense forest was home to an active unit of the Communist Party of Malaya, taking refuge in Thailand. A paved road leads to their former underground guerrilla camp, **Piya Mit**, which has now been converted into a museum. Around 180 Communists lived here undetected in 1,100 yds (1 km) of tunnels, 33 ft (10 m) below the surface.

The end came peacefully in 1989 when "an honorable settlement" was reached with the Malaysian and Thai governments. Most of the former revolutionaries settled in the area, and some now guide visitors through the network of dank tunnels and explain the camp's facilities. The cleverly constructed kitchen area has a flue that would disperse smoke on the other side of the hill, thus concealing the camp's location. It was so successful that the stronghold remained undetected until the end. Other items on display include old shoes, uniforms, knives, and torches used by the fugitive comrades. Simple modern bungalows are available.

🏛 Piya Mit

Betong province. Off Hwy 410, 12 miles (19 km) N of Betong. **Open** daily.

⑮ Narathiwat

นราธิวาส

Narathiwat province. 🚹 68,000. ✈ 🚉 🚌 *i* TAT, Narathiwat (0-7352-2411). 🎭 Chao Mae Toe Moe Festival (late Apr or early May), Narathiwat Fair (3rd week Sep).

The town of Narathiwat is visited by few tourists, but it makes a useful base for exploring the surrounding region. However, caution is advised as the province experiences frequent acts of violence carried out by Islamic extremists. The Muslim fishing village is a good place to see the traditional painted *korlae* boats. There are a number of good beaches near the town – the best is Ao Manao, 4 miles (6 km) to the south.

Environs

Taksin Palace, south of town, is the summer residence of the King and Queen. It is open to

Immense golden-tiled Buddha on Khao Kong, Narathiwat

the public when the royal family is not in residence. The gardens have views of the adjacent beach and an aviary with peacocks and cockatoos.

On the road to Rangae is the hill **Khao Kong**, perched upon which is the tallest seated Buddha image in Thailand. The 79-ft (24-m) statue is covered in golden tiles.

Close to the Malaysian border, 21 miles (34 km) south of Narathiwat, is the lovely village of **Tak Bai**. Its main attraction is Wat Chonthara Sing He: an outpost of Thai Buddhism in an almost exclusively Malay-speaking, Muslim area. The *wat* was erected in 1873 by King Chulalongkorn to stake his claim to a region that the British wanted to incorporate into Malaya (Malaysia).

The architecture of the temple mixes Southern Thai with Chinese influences, the latter being particularly evident in the tiered roof. One of the buildings in the large grounds contains a reclining Buddha decorated with Chinese ceramics from the Song dynasty. Another temple building is adorned with a number of fine murals depicting many aspects of local life painted during the reign of King Mongkut.

🏛 Taksin Palace

Off Hwy 4084, 5 miles (8 km) S of Narathiwat. **Open** daily. **Closed** usually Aug & Sep.

A lively scene of daily life from a mural at Wat Chonthara Sing He

TRAVELERS' NEEDS

WHERE TO STAY

Places to stay in Thailand come in all price ranges, and the distribution of hotels is surprisingly good in all but the remotest parts of the country. All major cities have several international-class hotels, while Bangkok boasts of some of the best hotels in the world. These are equipped with spas, swimming pools, fitness clubs, restaurants, business services, and other luxury facilities. Mid-range accommodation is available in most towns and, although it may be lacking in character, it is uniformly clean, efficient, and friendly. The current trend in Thailand is for luxurious spas, resorts, and pool villas featuring contemporary Thai design and decor. These fabulously chic properties can now be found across the country. Guesthouses provide remarkably cheap accommodations for budget travelers. Other alternatives include camping or staying in bungalows in the national parks.

Shangri-La's sumptuous lounge *(see p403)*

Hotel Grading and Facilities

Hotels are not officially graded, although some are registered with the **Thai Hotels Association**. Price is therefore the only indication of what to expect *(see p400)*. Accommodations range from basic to luxury. Even at the low end of the market rooms are usually spotlessly clean.

Often the best value is to be found in the once-luxury establishments that have been downgraded since the arrival of international luxury chains. These hotels offer the facilities available in first-class hotels at a fraction of the cost.

Luxury Hotels

Thailand's luxury hotels are probably the equal of any in the world – and their number and standards are rising year after year. Expect to be treated like a visiting dignitary in the air-conditioned retreats of Bangkok and the other major cities. Rooms are sure to have every conceivable luxury, from a king-size bed and massive television to a well-stocked minibar and perhaps even a marble Jacuzzi or private pool. In such world-famous hotels as the Mandarin Oriental and the Shangri-La Bangkok, the magnificent views of the Chao Phraya River are an added privilege.

These first-class hotels offer their guests a huge range of facilities, including spas, business centers, conference rooms, designer-brand shops, coffee shops, fitness centers, and swimming pools, as well as numerous food outlets.

Resort Hotels

Like the urban luxury hotels, the resort hotels of Thailand are unsurpassed in style, comfort, and elegance. They also usually offer stunning views. Such resorts as the Four Seasons in Chiang Mai, Honeymoon Private Island Resort in Phuket, and the Chiva Som Resort in Cha-am are luxury designer-built oases of tranquility and opulence. Expect the best of everything, with charming service provided by traditionally dressed waiting staff. The cuisine served is varied and of excellent standards.

Modern Hotels

A modern, mid-range hotel in Thailand might be anything between a former top-line hotel that has been downgraded as newer places open with better facilities, and a new boutique hotel that offers personalized service at competitive prices. Mid-range accommodation can be found in just about every town in Thailand, and in remote areas, they might sometimes be the only available options. Some of these places offer all

The luxurious Conrad Room at the Mandarin Oriental Hotel, Bangkok *(see p403)*

◄ Painted parasols on display in Bo Sang, Chiang Mai

The beautiful swimming pool at Kanchanaburi's Felix River Kwai Resort *(see p404)*

the same in-room facilities as a top-end hotel, such as air-conditioning, satellite TV, and even little extras like hair dryer or tea- and coffee-making facilities. For visitors who do not need extravagant amenities such as a private plunge pool or in-room spa facilities, these modern hotels provide the best-value accommodation.

Guesthouses

Guesthouses in Thailand date from the backpacker explosion of the 1970s. Still frequented primarily by Western travelers, they offer a superb value for money and often a lot of charm.

In Bangkok, Khao San Road is the primary haunt of budget travelers. Offering low-cost accommodation in an otherwise expensive capital city seems to have taken priority over comfort, and, with a few exceptions, Bangkok guesthouses are, at best, unremarkable.

Outside the capital, however, and especially in Chiang Mai, guesthouses are usually clean, friendly, and astoundingly cheap. Most have rooms with air-conditioning or fans, as well as en-suite bathrooms. Some establishments offer swimming pools, restaurants, and good service for around 500 *baht* a night, just a fraction of the cost of a top resort hotel. Cheap guesthouses may cost as little as 150 *baht*, but for this expect basic facilities, with communal Asian toilets and showers, although the quality of service should still be good.

Budget Hotels and Backpacker Hostels

Budget hotels can be found just about everywhere in Thailand. They generally offer basic facilities, often without Western-style toilets (these are clean, but require squatting rather than sitting), and are cheap and functional, but unexceptional.

Budget hotels are architecturally unexciting, generally being multi-story concrete blocks containing numerous identical rooms. As ever in Thailand, however, they are usually clean and the service is friendly. Most will offer guests a choice between air-conditioned rooms *(hong air)* and fan-cooled rooms *(hong patlom)*.

Only a few budget hotels are equipped with restaurants. However, in some remote areas, particularly little-visited areas of the Central Plains and Northeast Thailand,

these hotels may well provide the only option for travelers.

Backpacker hostels are a more recent trend in Thai accommodation and as yet are only available in Bangkok and the bigger cities. These comprise segregated dorms, shared bathrooms, and communal facilities such as a café and movie room. They offer less personal service than guesthouses but are very convenient for large groups traveling together.

Serviced Apartments

Serviced apartments are an increasingly popular choice for visitors intending to stay in Thailand for a month or longer. Properties usually occupy prime locations and offer guests the service and convenience of a five-star hotel at significantly lower prices. For more information, visit www.sabaai.com.

A charming guesthouse in rural surroundings, in the north of the country

Staying in National Parks

The majority of national parks allow camping for a minimal fee, although the facilities provided are extremely basic when compared to those available in Europe and North America. Camping has limited appeal in Thailand, as most Thais prefer to sleep in a hotel if one is available. Campers will have to face the perils of the outdoors; mosquito nets and copious amounts of insect repellent are essential.

A traditional-style bedroom with mattresses on the floor

In many national parks visitors can also stay in log-cabin-style bungalows; these have few facilities. Advance booking is necessary, either through the **Department of National Parks** website or by phoning the **Forestry Department** in Bangkok.

Prices

Thailand's extraordinary range of accommodations includes something to suit every visitor's budget. At the top end of the market, which includes such hotels as Bangkok's Mandarin Oriental *(see p403)* and Chiang

Mai's Four Seasons *(see p405)*, the sky is the limit. Celebrities and heads of state may take suites at 40,000 *baht* a night, although for more everyday luxury expect to pay between 5,000 and 15,000 *baht* a night.

Mid-range accommodations cost from 1,000 to 5,000 *baht* a night in Bangkok, Chiang Mai, Pattaya, Phuket, or Ko Samui. A comfortable air-conditioned room in a standard provincial hotel goes for between 700 and 2,000 *baht*, depending on the season. Prices everywhere are at their highest in the cool season (November to February).

In the hot season (March to May) and the rainy season (May to October), rates often fall, except in the capital, which remains busy all year round. A clean but spartan room in a budget hotel in Bangkok will cost around 500 *baht*, falling to 200 to 400 *baht* in the provinces.

Local factors should also be taken into consideration. For example, in Surin hotel prices soar during the Elephant Roundup in November, when rooms in this otherwise moderately priced city are booked up months in advance.

The best deals available are probably the guesthouses of Chiang Mai and other tourism-oriented towns. It is possible to stay in traditional Thai houses, with teak walls and stilts, for between 200 and 500 *baht* a night. This is difficult to beat, and visitors often stay for weeks longer than planned. Beach bungalows are similarly priced, but less comfortable, and more prone to invasion by insects.

Booking

Advance booking is advisable for luxury hotels and mid-range establishments, especially during national and local festivals. Budget hotels and guesthouses are unlikely to take bookings. In popular tourist areas, and at luxury hotels, staff speak English. Elsewhere, making a booking may be difficult unless you speak some Thai. However, **Tourism Authority of Thailand** offices are able to make bookings on behalf of tourists.

An idyllic setting: tent and bungalows at Ao Phrao on Ko Samet

Taxes

The tax situation in Thailand is rather confusing and apparently irregular. All hotels should charge seven percent VAT (value added tax), and some luxury hotels will also add a 10 percent service charge on top of their basic rates. Most cheap hotels include this tax in their rates, but many of the more expensive places do not. Thus, it is important to ask whether this is included in the price when booking or before checking in.

At small hotels outside the main resorts, tax is rarely (if ever) charged, and service is paid for (if at all) by tipping.

Bargaining

It is always a good idea to ask about the possibility of a reduction in price. The worst that can happen is a polite refusal, and very often, especially outside Bangkok and out of season, such an inquiry can lead to substantial savings, particularly if booking for several nights. It is not considered impolite to ask, but it is bad manners to press the point. Many hotels give discounts if bookings are low, and if special rates are available, most Thai proprietors will certainly let you know.

Tipping

Outside the capital and the major destinations of Ko Samui, Phuket, Pattaya, and Chiang Mai, tipping is unusual. Porters will expect a tip, and staff are rewarded for good service. Use your discretion: if you have received particularly good service, then leave a tip if you wish. Thanks, and a smile, are also much appreciated.

Khon Kaen Hotel, Khorat Plateau (see p407)

There are no hard and fast rules, and the standard British 10 percent – let alone the American 15 percent – would be far too much on a large bill. Between 10 and 50 *baht* is adequate in almost every circumstance. Expensive hotels will automatically include a service charge on the bill.

Facilities for Children

Thais love children and are incredibly tolerant of them, especially if they are blond-haired and blue-eyed. Such kids seem as exotic and doll-like to Thais as their own offspring do to the average Westerner. However, very few mid-range hotels have facilities for children or nursing mothers, and supervised play areas are rare.

By contrast, the majority of seaside resorts and luxury hotels offer some kind of babysitting services, and children can often stay in their parents' room for free. Wading pools may be provided, but guests must supervise their own children.

Disabled Travelers

Even luxury hotels in Thailand have only a few facilities for disabled visitors. Wheelchair ramps are beginning to make an appearance in newly commissioned luxury hotels, and nearly every luxury or tourist-class establishment has an elevator. However, that is the limit of facilities in most hotels.

Thailand has a fast-developing economy and a booming tourist trade, but it is likely to be many years before a serious awareness of the needs of the disabled develops. Hotels should be carefully chosen, with the help of the Thai Hotels Association, and bookings made well in advance.

Recommended Hotels

The lodging recommendations in the pages that follow have been selected for their ambience, room and food quality, and/or good value. They span the spectrum across all price levels and types, from rustic, family-owned inns and simple budget hotels to deluxe beachfront resorts and chic contemporary boutique hotels. Hotels are listed by area, and within these areas by price. Map references for hotels in Bangkok refer to pp152–9.

For the best of the best, look out for hotels featuring the DK Choice symbol. These establishments have been highlighted in recognition of an exceptional feature – a stunning location, notable architecture, ambience, or outstanding facilities, etc. The majority of these are extremely popular among local residents and visitors, so be sure to reserve well ahead of time.

Where to Stay

Bangkok

Old City

Lamphu Tree House ⓑ
Boutique **Map** 2 E4
*Soi Baan Pan Thom, 155 Wanchat
Bridge, Prachatipatai Rd, Phra
Nakorn, 10200*
Tel *0-2282-0991-2*
ⓦ lamphutreehotel.com
Tranquil spot in a residential area
close to the Grand Palace. Classic
decor with teakwood furniture.

Arun Residence ⓑⓑ
Boutique **Map** 5 C1
*36–38 Soi Pratu Nok Yung, Tha
Maharat, Maharat Rd, Ratanakosin
Island, 10200*
Tel *0-2221-9158*
ⓦ arunresidence.com
Sino-Portuguese mansion on
the river, in the heart of historic
Bangkok. Good split-level rooms
with balconies.

Navalai River Resort ⓑⓑ
Modern **Map** 2 D3
45 Phra Athit Rd, Banglampoo, 10200
Tel *0-2280-9955*
ⓦ navalai.com
Pleasant hotel on the riverside
with Colonial- and Thai-themed
rooms. Close to Khao San Road.

DK Choice

Chakrabongse Villas ⓑⓑⓑ
Boutique **Map** 5 B1
*396 Maharat Rd, Phra Nakorn,
Tha Tien, 10200*
Tel *0-2222-1290*
ⓦ thaivillas.com
Located on the banks of the
Chao Praya River, within walking
distance of the Grand Palace,
this unique boutique hotel was
once the residence of a Thai
prince. It is surrounded by lush
gardens with fantastic views
of the temples. The four free-
standing suites and three
rooms are furnished in Thai,
Chinese, and Moroccan motifs.
The service is first-rate.

Chinatown

Chinatown Hotel ⓑ
Modern **Map** 6 E2
*526 Yaowarat Rd,
Sampphantawong, 10100*
Tel *0-2225-0204*
ⓦ chinatownhotel.co.th
Clean hotel with modern, if
somewhat spartan, decor.
Great location in the middle
of Chinatown.

Riverview Guesthouse ⓑ
Guesthouse **Map** 6 F3
*768 Soi Panurangsi, Songwat Rd,
San Jao Tosuekong, 10100*
Tel *0-2234-5429*
ⓦ riverviewbkk.com
Basic rooms in a hard-to-find
location, but with superb views
of Chinatown and the river.
Dorms available, too.

Grand China Princess Hotel ⓑⓑ
Modern **Map** 6 E1
*215 Yaowarat Rd, Samphantawong,
10100*
Tel *0-2224-9977*
ⓦ grandchina.com
A 21-story hotel with a rotating
restaurant. Some rooms are a bit
dated, but the views are superb.

Shanghai Mansion ⓑⓑ
Boutique **Map** 6 F2
*479–481 Yaowarat Rd,
Samphantawong, 10100*
Tel *0-2221-2121*
ⓦ shanghaimansion.com
Lavish rooms with traditional
Chinese decor. Exceptional
service and delicious breakfasts.

Dusit

Hotel de Moc ⓑⓑ
Boutique **Map** 2 E3
78 Prajatipatai Rd, Phra Nakorn, 10200
Tel *0-2629-2100–4*
ⓦ hoteldemoc.com
Large rooms with retro 1960s
decor. Pool and spa facilities.

DK Choice

The Siam ⓑⓑⓑ
Boutique **Map** 2 E1
*3/2 Thanon Khao, Vacirapayabal,
10300*
Tel *0-2206-6999*
ⓦ thesiamhotel.com
Located upstream from the
Grand Palace/Khao San Road
area on the Chao Phraya River,
this hotel provides a tranquility
unlike anywhere else in Bangkok.
Sumptuously decorated suites
have antique furniture and river
views. Fantastic service.

Downtown

A One Inn ⓑ
Guesthouse **Map** 8 E1
*25/13–15 Soi Kasamsunt 1, Rama I Rd,
10330*
Tel *0-2215-3029*
ⓦ aoneinn.com
Basic rooms, but in a great location
close to the best shopping areas
and the Skytrain.

Price Guide

Prices are based on one night's stay in
high season for a standard double room,
inclusive of service charges and taxes.

ⓑ	up to 1,500 *baht*
ⓑⓑ	1,500 to 4,000 *baht*
ⓑⓑⓑ	over 4,000 *baht*

City Lodge ⓑ
Budget
137/1–3 Sukumvit Soi 9, 10110
Tel *0-2253-7705*
ⓦ mosaic-collection.com
Good value choice in a part
of town known for its nightlife.
Opt for a quiet room at the back.

Lub-d Silom ⓑ
Hostel **Map** 7 B4
4 Decho Rd, Bangrak, 10500
Tel *0-2634-7999.*
ⓦ lubd.com
Slick and trendy backpackers' place.
Private ensuite rooms plus dorms.
Free Wi-Fi and a friendly bar.

Red Planet Asoke ⓑ
Modern
7 Sukumvit Soi 14, 10110
Tel *0-2613-5888*
ⓦ redplanethotels.com
In a prime location, this quiet
hotel is great value for money.

Baan K Residence ⓑⓑ
Modern **Map** 8 D4
12/1 Sathorn Soi 2 Sathorn Rd, 10120
Tel *0-2633-9911*
ⓦ baankresidence.com
These large suites and studio
apartments are ideal for families.

Silom Convent Garden ⓑⓑ
Apartments **Map** 7 C4
35/1 Sio Phiphat 2, Soi Convent Rd, 10500
Tel *0-2667-0130*
ⓦ silomconventgarden.com
These serviced apartments,
near Silom Road, have cooking
facilities. Great for longer stays.

River views from the Chakrabongse Villas

Triple Two Silom ⓦⓑ
Boutique
222 Silom Rd, 10500
Tel *0-2627-2222*
ⓦ tripletwosilom.com
This stylish low-rise is popular
with business travelers.

**Anantara Baan Rajprasong
Suites** ⓑⓑⓑ
Luxury **Map** 8 D2
*3 Soi Mahardlekluang 3,
Ratchadamri Rd, 10330*
Tel *0-2264-6464*
ⓦ rajprasong-bangkok.
anantara.com
Luxurious one-bedroom suites.
Fantastic fitness center and sauna.

**AriyasomVilla
Boutique Hotel** ⓑⓑⓑ
Boutique **Map** 8 F1
65 Soi 1 Sukhumvit Rd, 10110
Tel *0-2254-8880*
ⓦ ariyasom.com
This 1940s mansion is a serene
urban oasis. Lovely garden and
pool, and great vegetarian food.

The Banyan Tree ⓑⓑⓑ
Luxury **Map** 8 D4
*5 South Sathorn Tai, Sathorn,
Pathumwan, 10120*
Tel *0-2679-1200*
ⓦ banyantree.com
Sleek modern decor. Great spa
and outdoor rooftop restaurant.

The Mandarin Oriental ⓑⓑⓑ
Luxury **Map** 6 F4
*Charoen Krung Soi 41, 48 Oriental
Ave, 10500*
Tel *0-2659-9000*
ⓦ mandarinoriental.com
Established in the 19th century,
this hotel offers a great riverside
location and impeccable service.

Plaza Athenee ⓑⓑⓑ
Luxury **Map** 8 E2
61 Wireless Rd, 10330
Tel *0-2650-8800*
ⓦ plazaatheneebangkok.com
Ultra-modern hotel with superb
rooms and decadent dining.

Shangri-La Hotel ⓑⓑⓑ
Luxury **Map** 6 F5
*89 Soi Watr Suan Plu, Charoen Krung
Rd, 10500*
Tel *0-2236-7777*
ⓦ shangri-la.com
Located close to the river boats
and Skytrain. With a famous spa,
private butlers, and great views.

Siam Kempinski ⓑⓑⓑ
Luxury **Map** 4 D5
991/9 Rama 1 Rd, 10330
Tel *0-2162-9000*
ⓦ kempinski.com
Stylish hotel close to the best shopping areas. Several dining choices.

Elegant decor and great views at Shangri-La

The St. Regis ⓑⓑⓑ
Luxury **Map** 8 D2
159 Ratchadamri Rd, 10330
Tel *0-2207-7777*
ⓦ stregisbangkok.com
Contemporary high-rise hotel
with elegant decor. Friendly staff.

The Sukhothai ⓑⓑⓑ
Luxury **Map** 8 D4
13/3 South Sathorn Rd, 10120
Tel *0-2344-8888*
ⓦ sukhothai.com
Sumptuous rooms with a
modern take on traditional
Thai furnishings. Magnificent
pool and gardens.

Swisshôtel Nai Lert Park ⓑⓑⓑ
Luxury **Map** 8 E1
2 Wireless Rd, Pathumwan, 10330
Tel *0-2253-0123*
ⓦ swissotel.com
Central, plush low-rise resort set
in expansive tropical gardens.

Thon Buri

Ibrik Resort on the River ⓑⓑ
Boutique **Map** 1 B5
*256 Soi Wat Rakhang, Arunamarin
Rd, 10700*
Tel *0-2848-9220*
ⓦ ibrikresort.com
Comfortable rooms in a quiet
but convenient location by
the river.

**Anantara Bangkok Riverside
Resort & Spa** ⓑⓑⓑ
Luxury
257/1–3 Charoennakorn Rd, 10600
Tel *0-2476-0022*
ⓦ bangkok-riverside.anantara.com
Expansive riverside gardens, a
lovely spa, and several restaurants.
Great for families.

The Peninsula ⓑⓑⓑ
Luxury **Map** 6 E5
*333 Charoen Nakorn Rd, Klong San,
10600*
Tel *0-2861-2888*
ⓦ peninsula.com
Rooms on the waterfront with
excellent views and elegant decor.

Farther Afield

Amari Don Muang Hotel ⓑⓑ
Modern
333 Chertwudthakas Rd, 10210
Tel *0-2566-1020*
ⓦ amari.com
Good location close to Don
Muang airport. Clean, affordable,
and well-thought-out rooms.

Bangkok Tree House ⓑⓑⓑ
Luxury
*60 Moo 1, Petch Cha Heung Rd, Bang
Namphueng, Phra Padaeng, 10130*
Tel *08-2995-1150*
ⓦ bangkoktreehouse.com
Popular eco-resort accessible
only by boat or on foot. Delicious
organic food on offer.

**Novotel Suvarnabhumi
Airport Hotel** ⓑⓑⓑ
Luxury
*Moo 1, Nongprue, Bang Phli, Samut
Prakarn, 10540*
Tel *0-2131-1111*
ⓦ novotel.com
Very high standards for an airport
hotel. Elegant rooms, excellent
spa, and good food.

South Central Plains

AYUTTHAYA: Bann Kun Pra ⓑ
Hostel
48 U Thong Rd, 13000
Tel *0-3524-1978*
ⓦ bannkunpra.com
Double and dorm rooms with
delightfully quirky decor.
Romantic restaurant serving
fusion cuisine.

**AYUTTHAYA: Prom Tong
Mansion** ⓑ
Budget
*23 Pathon Soi 19, Pathon Rd,
T Pratuchai, 13000*
Tel *08-9165-6297*
ⓦ promtong.com
Centrally located hotel with
simply furnished family rooms.
Free Wi-Fi and use of nearby
swimming pool.

For more information on types of hotels *see pp398–401*

One of many dining options at Krungsri River Hotel

DK Choice

**AYUTTHAYA:
Kantary Hotel** ⓑⓑ
Modern
168 Moo 1, Rojana Rd, 13000
Tel *0-3533-7177*
Ⓦ kantarycollection.com
One of the most stylish hotels
in Ayutthaya. Expect excellent
comfort, impeccable service, and
great value for money. Choose
between studios with separate
living areas, and one- or two-
room apartments with kitchens
and washing machines.

**AYUTTHAYA:
Krungsri River** ⓑⓑ
Modern
27/2 Moo, 11 Rojana Rd, 13000
Tel *0-3524-4333*
Ⓦ krungsririver.com
Lacking in character, but in a great
location just across the river from
many of the sights. A lovely pool.

**KANCHANABURI: Apple's
Retreat** ⓑ
Guesthouse
153/4 Moo 4, Thamakham, 71000
Tel *0-3451-2017*
Ⓦ applesguesthouse.com
Located across the river from town.
Restful place with clean, simple
rooms. Offers cookery classes.

**KANCHANABURI:
Ploy Guest House** ⓑ
Guesthouse
79/2 Mae Nam Kwae Rd, 71000
Tel *0-3451-4437*
Ⓦ ploygh.com
Stylish riverside place with a
small pool, terrace dining, and
kitchen facilities.

**KANCHANABURI: Felix River
Kwai Resort** ⓑⓑ
Modern
9/1 Moo 3, Thamakham, 71000
Tel *0-3455-1000-23*
Ⓦ felixriverkwai.co.th
Large, centrally located resort with
lush grounds, extensive facilities,
and a business center.

**KANCHANABURI: Royal River
Kwai Resort** ⓑⓑ
Boutique
88 Kanchanaburi–Saiyok Rd, 71000
Tel *0-3467-0621*
Ⓦ royalriverkwairesort.com
Beautifully designed resort with a
spa, a pool, and riverside restaurant.

**KANCHANABURI:
U Inchantree** ⓑⓑ
Boutique
443 Mae Nam Kwae Rd, 71000
Tel *0-3452-1584*
Ⓦ uhotelsresorts.com
Close to the famous bridge on the
Khwae Yai River, with delightful
gardens. Part of a hotel chain.

LOP BURI: Lopburi Inn ⓑ
Budget
28/9 Narai Maharat Rd, 15000
Tel *0-3641-2609*
Spacious rooms in a very central
location. Dated decor.

LOP BURI: Nett Hotel ⓑ
Budget
*17/1–2 Soi 2, Ratchadamnoen Rd,
15000*
Tel *0-3641-1738*
Basic rooms at rock-bottom rates.
Convenient for the ruins.

**SANGKHLA BURI:
Samprasob Resort** ⓑⓑ
Modern
122 Moo 3, Nonglu, 71240
Tel *0-3459-5050*
Ⓦ samprasob.com
On a hill overlooking the river and
the Mon bridge, the Samprasob
offers a range of rooms, including
free-standing cabins.

North Central Plains

**KAMPHAENG PHET:
Phet Hotel B** ⓑ
Modern
189 Bumrungrat Rd, 62000
Tel *0-5571-2810*
Ⓦ phethotel.com
Large, clean rooms with private
bathrooms. Friendly staff.

KAMPHAENG PHET: Three J ⓑ
Guesthouse
79 Rajwithee Rd, 62000
Tel *0-5572-0384, 0-8188-7419*
Ⓦ threejguesthouse.com
Welcoming place with creative
decor and great communal areas.
A relaxed backpacker haven.

MAE SOT: Ban Thai ⓑ
Guesthouse
740/1 Inthakhiri Rd, 63110
Tel *0-5553-1590*
Good range of rooms, from small
basic rooms with fans to big, air-
conditioned bungalows.

**MAE SOT: Centara Mae
Sot Hill Resort** ⓑ
Modern
100 Asia Highway, 63110
Tel *0-5553-2601-8*
Ⓦ centarahotelsresorts.com
Located 2km outside the center,
this is one of Mae Sot's top hotels.
Spacious rooms and a huge pool.

PHITSANULOK: Pailyn Hotel ⓑ
Budget
38 Baroma Trailokanart Rd, 65000
Tel *0-5525-2411*
Busy high-rise hotel in a central
location. Good views from the
top floors.

**PHITSANULOK:
Yodia Heritage** ⓑⓑ
Boutique
89/1 Puttabucha Rd, 65000
Tel *0-5521-4677*
Ⓦ yodiaheritage.com
Gorgeous, riverside boutique
hotel with stylish decor and top-
notch service.

**SUKHOTHAI:
At Home Sukhothai** ⓑ
Guesthouse
184 Wichienchamnong Rd, 64000
Tel *0-5561-0172*
Ⓦ athomesukhothai.com
Cozy rooms in a beautifully
restored traditional teak house.
Free bicycle use.

SUKHOTHAI: Lotus Village ⓑ
Budget
170 Ratchathani Rd, 65000
Tel *0-5562-1484*
Ⓦ lotus-village.com
Teak rooms on stilts set in a lush,
tropical garden. Run by a friendly
Thai/French couple.

SUKHOTHAI: Ruean Thai ⓑⓑ
Modern
*181/20 Soi Pracharuammit, Jarod
Withithong Rd, 65000*
Tel *0-5561-2444*
Ⓦ rueanthaihotel.com
A beautifully decorated traditional
teak house with lovely rooms set
around a pool. Wi-Fi available.

DK Choice

SUKHOTHAI:
Tharaburi Resort ฿฿
Luxury
113 Srisomboon Rd, 65000
Tel *0-5569-7132*
[W] tharaburiresort.com
Located right beside the historical park, this resort oozes style with canopied beds, private balconies, and tasteful artwork on the walls. The lavish suites make guests feel like Siamese royalty. Offers cookery classes for guests. Bicycles are also available for hire.

TAK: Viang Tak Riverside ฿
Budget
236 Chompol Rd, 63000
Tel *0-5551-2507*
[W] viangtakriverside.com
Slightly faded decor, but in a great location. Free Wi-Fi, friendly staff and a very good restaurant.

UMPHANG: Tu Ka Su Cottage ฿
Budget
40 Moo 6, 63170
Tel *0-5556-1295*
[W] tukasu.webs.com
Offers a range of cozy cottages set in shady gardens. The very helpful owners also run trips to Thi Lo Su falls.

Northwest Heartland

CHIANG DAO:
Chiang Dao Nest ฿
B&B
144/4 Moo 5, 50170
Tel *0-5345-6242*
[W] chiangdaonest.com
Well-appointed bungalows with a rustic feel. This place also offers organized treks up the mountain.

Pavilion at the Four Seasons Resort

CHIANG MAI: Baan Kaew ฿
Guesthouse
142 Charoenprathet Rd, 50100
Tel *0-5327-1606*
[W] baankaew-guesthouse.com
Comfortable hotel near the Night Bazaar, with simple but spotless rooms. Very friendly staff.

CHIANG MAI: Hollanda Montri ฿
Guesthouse
365 Charoenrat Rd, 50000
Tel *0-5324-2450*
[W] hollandamontri.com
Long-standing riverside option with basic rooms. A bit outside the town center.

CHIANG MAI: Micasa ฿
Modern
2/2 Soi 4, Tha Pae Rd, 50100
Tel *0-5320-9127*
[W] thaimicasa.com
Centrally located hotel with attractive, well-equipped rooms and helpful staff.

CHIANG MAI: Roong Ruang ฿
Budget
398 Tha Pae Rd, 50300
Tel *0-5323-4746*
[W] roongruang.com
Spacious rooms set around a courtyard a few steps from Tha Phae Gate. Great value for money.

DK Choice

CHIANG MAI: Baan Orapin ฿฿
Historic
150 Charoenrat Rd, 50000
Tel *0-5324-3677*
[W] baanorapin.com
Traditonally decorated teak rooms in a century-old, Colonial-style house. Set in a relaxing, tropical garden, the hotel is a short distance from some of the town's best restaurants and shops on the east bank of the Ping River.

CHIANG MAI: Chiang Mai Gate Hotel ฿฿
Modern
11/10 Suriyawong Rd, 50100
Tel *0-5320-3895*
[W] chiangmaigatehotel.com
Smart rooms with Lanna decor, just south of the old city and near the Saturday Walking Street.

CHIANG MAI:
De Naga Chiang Mai ฿฿
Boutique
21 Soi 2, Ratchamanka, Moon Muang Rd, 50100
Tel *0-5320-9030*
[W] denagahotel.com
Stay in beautiful Thai-style rooms in a great location in the old city, near the temples.

CHIANG MAI: Kanatary Hills ฿฿
Modern
44/1–2, Soi 12, Nimmanheimin Rd, 50200
Tel *0-5322-2111*
[W] kantarycollection.com
Spacious rooms and efficient service at this smart hotel.

CHIANG MAI: U Chiang Mai ฿฿
Boutique
70 Ratchadamnoen Rd, 50200
Tel *0-5332-7000*
[W] uhotelsresorts.com
Beautiful rooms in a resort ideally situated in the old city.

CHIANG MAI: Anantara Chiang Mai ฿฿฿
Luxury
123 Charoen Prathet Rd, 50100
Tel *0-5325-3333*
[W] chiang-mai.anantara.com
Sleek contemporary rooms and stunning grounds. Great location.

CHIANG MAI:
Dhara Dhevi ฿฿฿
Luxury
51/4 Chiang Mai–Sankampaeng Rd, Moo 1, 50000
Tel *0-5388-8888*
[W] dharadhevi.com
Dreamlike Lanna-style village with a renowned spa and a choice of villas, suites, or stately "residences".

CHIANG MAI:
Four Seasons Resort ฿฿฿
Luxury
Mae Rim–Old Samoeng Rd, 50180
Tel *0-5329-8181*
[W] fourseasons.com/chiangmai
Opulent Lanna-style pavilions overlooking rice fields.

CHIANG MAI: Ping Nakara ฿฿฿
Luxury
135/9 Charoen Prathet Rd, 50100
Tel *0 5325-2999*
[W] pingnakara.com
Colonial-style rooms in a stunning building. Superb spa facilities and service.

CHIANG MAI:
Rachamankha ฿฿฿
Luxury
6 Rachamankha 9, 50200
Tel *0-5390-4111*
[W] rachamankha.com
Reminiscent of a temple complex, this hotel offers stylish rooms with plenty of privacy.

CHIANG MAI:
Tamarind Village ฿฿฿
Luxury
50/1 Ratchadamnoen Rd, 50200
Tel *0-5341-8896-9*
[W] tamarindvillage.com
Peaceful compound in the old city. Well-equipped rooms.

For more information on types of hotels *see pp398–401*

LAMPANG: The Riverside Guest House ⓑ
Guesthouse
286 Talad Kao Rd, 52000
Tel *0-5422-7005*
Ⓦ theriverside-lampang.com
One of the best places to stay in Lampang. Choose between simple rooms and large suites.

LAMPANG: Lampang River Lodge ⓑⓑ
Boutique
330 Moo 11, Tambol Chompoo, 52100
Tel *0-5433-6640-1*
Ⓦ lampangriverlodge.com
Restful retreat on the banks of the Wang River, with two restaurants.

DK Choice

**MAE HONG SON:
Fern Resort** ⓑⓑ
Boutique
64 Moo 10, Ban Hua Nam Mae Sakut, Tambol Pha Bong, 58000
Tel *0-5368-6110*
Ⓦ fernresort.info
This wonderful eco-lodge has gorgeous, Shan-style wooden bungalows set among rice paddy fields. Tastefully furnished rooms with private balconies. Complete seclusion, with no TVs or phones in the rooms.

MAE HONG SON: Golden Pai & Suites Resort ⓑⓑ
Modern
285/1 Ban Pangmoo, 58000
Tel *0-5362-0653-5*
Ⓦ goldenpairesort.com
Large, comfortably furnished bungalows scattered around an expansive tropical garden.

MAE HONG SON: Imperial Mae Hong Son ⓑⓑ
Modern
149 Moo 8, Tambol Pang Moo, 58000
Tel *0-5368-4444*
Ⓦ imperialhotels.com
Spacious rooms with fantastic views of lush hillsides.

PAI: Baan Tawan ⓑ
Guesthouse
117 Moo 4, 58130
Tel *0-5369-8116*
Ⓦ baantawan-pai.com
Teak wood houses on stilts in lush gardens by the riverside. Huge bungalows available for families.

PAI: Pai Island ⓑⓑ
Boutique
333 Moo 1, Tambon Vieng-Tai, 58130
Tel *0-5369-9999*
Ⓦ paiislandresort.com
A luxurious resort in a truly spectacular setting. It offers total privacy.

Far North

CHIANG KHONG: Mekong Riverside Hotel ⓑ
Budget
174–176 Moo 8, Chiang Khong, 57140
Tel *0-5379-1796*
Ⓦ namkhongriverside.net
Right on the Mekong, with stunning views over to Laos. Simple rooms at excellent rates.

CHIANG RAI: Chat House ⓑ
B&B
3/2 Sangkaew Trirat Rd, 57000
Tel *0-5371-1481*
Ⓦ chatguesthouse.com
A classic travelers' hang-out. Run for over 30 years by the same friendly and helpful family. Good food in the restaurant.

CHIANG RAI: Imperial River House Resort ⓑⓑ
Boutique
482 Moo 4, Mae Kok Rd, 57000
Tel *0-5375-0830-4*
Ⓦ imperialriverhouse.com
Imperial River House is the best of several sumptuous resorts beside the Kok River. Lavish rooms and first-rate service.

CHIANG RAI: Le Meridien ⓑⓑⓑ
Luxury
221/2 Moo 20, Kwaewai Rd, 57000
Tel *0-5360-3333*
Ⓦ lemeridienchiangrai.com
Slick modern rooms on the banks of the Mae Kok. Close to the city center, with a good sized pool.

CHIANG SAEN: Gin's Mekhong View Resort ⓑ
Budget
225 Moo 8, T. Wiang, 57150
Close to town, these pleasant rooms and bungalows offer great views of the Mekong. Good spa services.

DK Choice

CHIANG SAEN: Anantara Golden Triangle Resort & Spa ⓑⓑⓑ
Luxury
229 Moo 1, Golden Triangle, Sop Ruak 57150
Tel *0-5378-4084*
Ⓦ goldentriangle.anantara.com
A splendid resort with well-appointed rooms that overlook the borders of three countries. A particularly good place to get up close with elephants on their mahout training course. Facilities include a cooking school and a luxurious spa. First-rate staff.

CHIANG SAEN: Four Seasons Tented Camp ⓑⓑⓑ
Luxury
Golden Triangle, Sop Ruak, 57150
Tel *0-5391-0200*
Ⓦ fourseasons.com/goldentriangle
Enjoy river cruises along the Mekong, and stay in some truly luxurious tents.

**MAE CHAN:
Chang Garden Resort** ⓑⓑ
Modern
69 Moo 6, 57110
Tel *0-80-1270-526*
Ⓦ chang-garden.com
A family resort of villas, with a pool, playground, restaurant, bar, and even a fish pond.

MAE SAI: Mae Sai ⓑ
Guesthouse
Riverside Rd, 57130
Tel *0-5373-2021*
No-frills family-run place by the riverbank. Friendly staff.

NAN: Sukkasem Hotel ⓑ
Budget
119–121 Anantaworarichidet Rd, 55000
Tel *0-5477-2555*
Centrally-located hotel in the offering compact doubles and family rooms.

NAN: Phuka Nanfa ⓑⓑ
Boutique
369 Sumonthevaraj Rd, 55000
Tel *0-5477-1111*
Ⓦ pukhananfahotel.co.th
An 80-year-old hotel, beautifully decorated in a mixture of antique and modern styles. Wi-Fi available.

PHRAE: Mae Yom Palace Hotel ⓑⓑ
Modern
181/6 Yantrakitkosan Rd, 54000
Tel *0-5452-1029*
With helpful staff and the town's only swimming pool, this is one of the best places to stay in Phrae.

Camping at the Four Seasons

THA TON: Old Tree's House ⓑⓑ
Modern
323 Ban Rumthai, 50280
Tel *08-5722-9002*
ⓦ oldtreeshouse.net
Six luxurious bungalows with
great views, and two large pools.

Khorat Plateau

**BAN CHIANG: Lakeside
Sunrise** ⓑ
Guesthouse
West side of lake, 36260
Tel *08-0193-4300*
Friendly guesthouse close to the
archaeological site. Large rooms.

**CHAIYAPHUM:
Lert Namit Hotel** ⓑ
Budget
447/1 Nivesrat Rd, 36000
Tel *0-4481-1522*
ⓦ lertnimit.com
Great for visiting nearby villages.
Book a suite for air-conditioning.

KHON KAEN: Khon Kaen Hotel ⓑ
Budget
43/2 Pimpasute Rd, 40000
Tel *0-4333-3222*
ⓦ khonkaen-hotel.com
Popular business hotel with
large, well-equipped rooms
and great entertainment.

**KHON KAEN: Charoen Thani
Princess** ⓑⓑ
Modern
260 Si Chan Rd, 40000
Tel *0-4322-0400*
ⓦ charoenthani.com
A centrally located hotel with
cozy rooms and good facilities.

**KHON KAEN: Pullman Khon
Kaen Raja Orchid** ⓑⓑ
Modern
9/9 Prachasamran Rd, 40000
Tel *0-4332-2155*
ⓦ pullmanhotels.com
Plush carpeted rooms, a large pool,
and a magnificent central atrium.

KHORAT: Lamai Homestay ⓑ
Guesthouse
23/1 Moo 3, Ban Khopet, 30000
Tel *08-6258-5894*
ⓦ thailandhomestay.com
The owners at this simple guesthouse treat you like old friends and
act as your personal tour guides.

KHORAT: Siri Hotel ⓑ
Budget
688–690 Pho Klang Rd, 30000
Tel *0-4434-1822*
ⓦ sirihotelkorat.com
Charming rooms in a convenient
location, with a restaurant,
karaoke room, and family room.

The striking façade of the Pullman Khon Kaen

**KHORAT:
Dusit Princess Khorat** ⓑⓑ
Modern
1137 Suranarai Rd, 30000
Tel *0-4425-6629*
ⓦ dusit.com
An excellent standard of
accommodation, with spacious
rooms, extensive facilities, and
efficient service.

DK Choice

KHORAT: Sima Thani ⓑⓑ
Modern
2112/2 Mittraphap Rd, 30000
Tel *0-4421-3100*
ⓦ simathani.com
The Sima Thani features a
stunning five-story atrium and
offers spacious, comfortable,
carpeted rooms. The extensive
facilities include a swimming
pool, sauna, fitness center,
and a choice of restaurants.
There are also many business
and conference facilities
on site.

PHIMAI: Phimai Inn Hotel ⓑ
Budget
33/1 Bypass Rd, 30110
Tel *0-4428-7228*
ⓦ phimaiinn.com
Well-maintained hotel with a
huge pool, a decent restaurant,
and free Wi-Fi. Located near the
ruins at Phimai.

ROI ET: Phrae Thong Hotel ⓑ
B&B
45–47 Th Ploenchit, 45000
Tel *0-4351-1127*
Simple, low-cost rooms with a
light and airy feel in the center
of Roi Et.

SURIN: Pirom's House ⓑ
Guesthouse
55/326 Soi Arunee, Thungpo Rd, 32000
Tel *0-4451-5140*
This place is particularly popular
for the local knowledge of the
owners, who also help organize
tours. Basic but well-kept rooms.

SURIN: Surin Majestic ⓑⓑ
Modern
99 Jitbumrung Rd, 32000
Tel *0-4471-3980-3*
ⓦ surinmajestic.com
Situated right in the town
center. A comfortable hotel
with a large pool and well-
appointed rooms.

**UDON THANI: Centara Hotel
& Convention Centre** ⓑⓑ
Modern
277/1 Prajaksillapakhom Rd, 41000
Tel *0-4234-3555*
ⓦ centarahotelsresorts.com
The Centara is a business and
leisure hotel boasting many
facilities, including a spa.
Conveniently located near
shops in the center of town.
Very friendly staff.

Mekong River Valley

**CHIANG KHAN: Husband &
Wife** ⓑ
Guesthouse
241 Chaikhong Rd, 42110
Tel *08-5464-8008*
Attached to a craft shop, this rustic
riverside retreat is like an extension
of the imaginative goods on sale.
Every detail is beautifully crafted.

**CHIANG KHAN:
Chiang Khan Hill Resort** ⓑⓑ
Boutique
*28/2 Ruam Chai Narumit Rd, Kaeng
Khut Khu, 42110*
Tel *0-4282-1285*
ⓦ chiangkhanhill.com
In an idyllic spot by the Mekong
River, a little downstream from
Chiang Khan, this well-equipped
resort is calm and restful.

LOEI: Sugar Guesthouse ⓑ
Guesthouse
4/1 Soi 2, Wisuttitep Rd, 42000
Tel *0-4281-2982*
This friendly place has fan rooms
with shared bathrooms and air-
conditioned rooms with en-suites.

DK Choice

LOEI: Loei Palace Hotel ⓑⓑ
Modern
167/4 Charoenrat Rd, 42000
Tel *0-4281-5668-73*
Ⓦ oamhotels.com/loeipalace
This is an excellent base for
visiting the nearby national
parks. Rooms are decorated in
warm colors and are equipped
with every amenity. Opt for a
room on the upper floors to
enjoy the panoramic views.

MUKDAHAN: Ploy Palace ⓑⓑ
Modern
40 Phitak Phanom Khet Rd, 49000
Tel *0-4263-1111*
Ⓦ ploypalace.com
Pleasant rooms and some great
views from the upper floors.
Friendly staff.

**NAKHON PHANOM:
Viewkong Hotel** ⓑ
Budget
527 Sunthorn Wichit Rd, 48000
Tel *0-4251-3564*
Ⓦ viewkonghotel.com
Lovely views of the Mekong, as
the name suggests. Spacious
well-appointed rooms.

NONG KHAI: Mut Mee ⓑ
Guesthouse
1111/4 Kaew Worawut Rd, 43000
Tel *0-4246-0717*
Ⓦ mutmee.com
This first-rate guesthouse has a
choice of basic and more well-
equipped rooms. Friendly staff.

NONG KHAI: Pantawee Hotel ⓑ
Budget
1049 Haisoke Rd, 43000
Tel *0-4241-1568-9*
Ⓦ pantawee.com
Excellent hotel with a range of
facilities, including computers
in rooms and a small pool.

**NONG KHAI: Grand Paradise
Hotel** ⓑⓑ
Modern
*589 Moo 5, Nong Khai–Poanpisai Rd,
43000*
Tel *0-4242-0033, 090-5806499*
Ⓦ grandparadisenongkhai.com
A great base to explore the area,
with large, clean and comfortable
rooms. A lovely rooftop restaurant.

**PHU KRADUNG: Phu Kradung
National Park Bungalows** ⓑ
Guesthouse
Phu Kradung National Park, 42180
Tel *0-2562-0760*
Ⓦ dnp.go.th
These basic bungalows are good
for big groups. Available for hikers
every year from October to May.

Luxury private villas at Soneva Kiri

**THAT PHANOM:
Kritsadarimkhong Hotel** ⓑ
Budget
90–93 Rimkhong Rd, 48110
Tel *0-4254-0088*
Ⓦ ksdresort.com
Basic accommodation by the
river in this tiny but charming
town. A pleasant restaurant.

**UBON RATCHATHANI:
Ratchathani Hotel** ⓑ
Budget
297 Khuenthani Rd, 34000
Tel *0-4524-4388*
Smart decor and a central
location. Ask for a quiet room
at the back.

UBON RATCHATHANI: Sri Isan ⓑ
Budget
62 Phadaeng Rd, 34000
Tel *0-4526-1011*
Ⓦ sriisanhotel.com
Well-equipped but compact
rooms. Great location in the
town center.

**UBON RATCHATHANI: Tohsang
City Hotel** ⓑⓑ
Modern
251 Phalochai Rd, 34000
Tel *0-4524-5531*
Ⓦ tohsang.com
This sophisticated hotel offers
lots of amenities, superb service,
and fine dining.

Eastern Seaboard

**CHANTHABURI: Baan Luang
Rajamaitri Historic Inn** ⓑⓑ
Boutique
252 Sukhaphiban Rd, Watmai, 22000
Tel *0-66-81-915-8815*
Ⓦ baanluangrajamaitri.com
As much a museum as a hotel,
this former residence of a local
governor was built in the 1800s
right on the river. Incomparable.

KO CHANG: Kaibae Hut Resort ⓑ
Budget
Kai Bae Beach, 23170
Tel *0-3955-7142*
Ⓦ kaibaehutresort.com
Well-run place with a variety of
simple rooms and bungalows.
Good food.

KO CHANG: Nirvana ⓑⓑ
Modern
Ao Bang Bao, 23170
Tel *0-3955-8061*
Ⓦ nirvanakohchang.com
Splendidly isolated hotel on the
island's southern tip. Two pools.

**KO CHANG:
Sea View Resort and Spa** ⓑⓑ
Boutique
Hat Kaibae, 23170
Tel *0-3955-2888*
Ⓦ seaviewkohchang.com
Beautiful garden and a fantastic
spa. Variety of accommodation
types and prices. Great value.

**KO CHANG:
Siam Beach Resort** ⓑⓑ
Modern
Hat Tha Nam, 23170
Tel *08-4524-4321*
Ⓦ siambeachresort.in.th
Fantastic location away from the
busy beach area, with bungalows
built on a hillside. Delicious food.

**KO CHANG:
Aiyapura Resort** ⓑⓑⓑ
Luxury
Baan Khlong Son, 23170
Tel *0-3955-5111*
Ⓦ aiyapura.com
Expansive beachfront location,
with organic gardens and a
lovely pool. Good for families.

**KO CHANG:
Emerald Cove Resort** ⓑⓑⓑ
Luxury
Hat Khlong Phrao, 23170
Tel *0-3955-2000*
Ⓦ emeraldcovekohchang.com
Well-managed hotel with large
rooms, a huge pool, an Italian
restaurant and kids' activities.

DK Choice

KO KUT: Soneva Kiri ⓑⓑⓑ
Luxury
110 Moo 4, 23000
Tel *0-3961-9800*
Ⓦ soneva.com
This spectacular villa resort is
original in both design and
service. The owners operate on
an ethos of sustainability and the
"Slow Life". There are many family-
oriented activities. A private
plane brings guests from
Bangkok airport to the island.

KO MAK: Lazy Day the Resort ⓑⓑ
Boutique
Ko Mak, 23120
Tel *08-1882-4002*
Aptly named beachside resort with clean rooms and a serene, restful ambience.

KO SAMET: Tub Tim Resort ⓑ
Budget
Ao Tub Tim, 21160
Tel *0-3864-4025*
Ⓦ tubtimresort.com
Set at the southern end of a pretty bay. Comfortable and quiet rooms in a great location near the beach.

KO SAMET: Samed Villa ⓑⓑ
Modern
Ao Phai, 21160
Tel *08-1761-5578*
Ⓦ samedvilla.com
Lovely collection of bungalows run by a Swiss/Thai family. Ask for rooms with a sea view.

**KO SAMET: Sang Thian
Beach Resort** ⓑⓑ
Modern
Ao Thian, 21160
Tel *0-3864-4255*
Ⓦ sangthianbeachresort.com
Clean well-kept rooms on one of the quieter beaches on the island. The staff speak limited English.

KO SAMET: Le Vimarn ⓑⓑⓑ
Luxury
Ao Phrao, 21160
Tel *0-3864-4104*
Ⓦ levimarncottage.com
Opulent resort on Ko Samet's quiet west coast. The teak villas are furnished in bamboo and woven fabrics. Private Jacuzzis.

PATTAYA: Ice Inn ⓑ
Budget
528/2–3 Second Rd, Soi 12, 20260
Tel *0 3872-0671*
Ⓦ iceinnpattaya.com
Clean, functional, and very close to the beach. The quietest rooms are at the back.

PATTAYA: Hard Rock Hotel ⓑⓑ
Modern
429 Moo 9, Beach Rd, 20260
Tel *0-3842-8755-9*
Ⓦ hardrockhotels.net
A lively hotel with a dedicated entertainment team. Huge pool, excellent spa, and Western food.

PATTAYA: Woodlands Resort ⓑⓑ
Modern
164/1 Moo 5, Pattaya–Naklua Rd, 20150
Tel *0-3842-1707*
Ⓦ woodland-resort.com
Attractive Colonial-style resort in a quiet area. Ideal for families. Cooking classes offered.

**PATTAYA: Royal Cliff
Hotels Group** ⓑⓑⓑ
Luxury
353 Moo 12, Pratumnak Rd, 20150
Tel *0-3825-0421*
Ⓦ royalcliff.com
One of Pattaya's largest resorts, with a private beach and a wide range of facilities.

**PATTAYA:
Sheraton Pattaya Resort** ⓑⓑⓑ
Luxury
437 Pratumnak Rd, 20150
Tel *0-3825-9888*
Ⓦ sheratonpattayaresort.com
On a picturesque headland, with a small private beach. Superb spa and gourmet dining.

PATTAYA: Sugar Hut ⓑⓑⓑ
Luxury
391/18 Moo 10, Thabpraya Rd, 20260
Tel *0-3825-1686*
Ⓦ sugar-hut.com
Thai-style villas set back from the beach with superb gardens. Very good restaurant.

RAYONG: Wang Gaew ⓑⓑ
Modern
214 Pae-Klaeng Rd, Charkpong, 21110
Tel *0-3863-8067*
Ⓦ wangkaew.co.th
An eclectic collection of beach houses with kitchens on a private bay. Good for longer stays.

TRAT: Ban Jaidee ⓑ
Guesthouse
67 Chaimongkhon Rd, 23000
Tel *0-3952-0678*
Simple clean rooms and a warm friendly atmosphere.

Western Seaboard

CHA AM: Beach Terrace ⓑⓑ
Modern
854/4 Suksamer Rd, Bang Saiyoy, 76120
Tel *0-3250-8502*
Peaceful beachfront hotel away from the center. Friendly and efficient management. Great value for the region.

CHA-AM: Sofitel So ⓑⓑⓑ
Luxury
115 Moo 7, Tambol Bangkao, 76120
Tel *0-3270-9555*
Ⓦ sofitel.com
Sophisticated, contemporary decor. Rooms surround a huge reflecting pool.

HUA HIN: Amara Resort ⓑ
Budget
16/55 Hua Hin Soi 94, 77110
Tel *0-3251-6315*
Ⓦ amarahuahin.com
This quiet, clean place located away from the beach offers gardens and a pool.

HUA HIN: K Place Guest House ⓑ
Budget
116 Naresdamri Rd, 77110
Tel *0-3251-1396*
Close to the beach and the Night Market, this place has spacious, spotless rooms.

HUA HIN: Anantasila Villas ⓑⓑ
Boutique
35/15 Phethkasem Rd, Nongkae, 77110
Tel *0-3253-6364*
Ⓦ anantasila.com
Beachfront resort south of town, next to a fishing village. With sleek rooms, a lovely a big pool, and lots of activities for kids.

**HUA HIN: Evergreen
Boutique Hotel** ⓑⓑ
Boutique
Phetkasem Rd, Soi 45, 77110
Tel *0-3251-3318*
Near the beach, this hotel is popular with golfers. Nice decor and a great breakfast buffet.

**HUA HIN:
Anantara Resort & Spa** ⓑⓑⓑ
Luxury
45/1 Phetkusem Rd, 77110
Tel *0-3252-0250*
Ⓦ anantara.com
Choose from lagoon- or sea-facing rooms with private pools. Guests can relax in the expansive gardens or in the spa. Great dining choices.

Stunning views from Royal Cliff Hotels Group

For more information on types of hotels *see pp398–401*

DK Choice

HUA HIN: Chiva Som ⑧⑧⑧
Luxury
73/4 Phetkasem Rd, 77110
Tel *0-3253-6536*
W chivasom.com
Long before spas became a
trendy amenity, Chiva Som was
offering serious wellness
programs focusing on
wholesome diets and holistic
practices such as massage and
yoga. Expect attentive service
and a luxurious experience.

**KO PHA NGAN: Blue Lotus
Resort** ⑧
B&B
Ban Kai, 84280
Tel *0-7723-8489*
W bluelotusresort.com
Quiet beachside resort with a
relaxing atmosphere. Thai and
Mexican cuisine on offer.

**KO PHA NGAN: Blue Ocean
Garden Resort** ⑧⑧
Boutique
Chao Pao Beach, 84280
Tel *08-7086-2697*
W blueoceangarden.com
Well-managed resort in a stunning
beachside setting. Italian food.

**KO PHA NGAN:
Cocohut Village** ⑧⑧⑧
Resort
Sekantang Beach, 84280
Tel *0-7737-5368*
W cocohut.com
Located on Sunset Beach,
Cocohut offers a variety of
luxurious accommodations.

KO SAMUI: Free House ⑧
Budget
175/7 Moo 1, Bophut, 84140
Tel *0-7742-7516*
W freehousesamui.com
Great beachfront huts in
relatively quiet Bophut. Non-
guests come just for the food.

KO SAMUI: Code ⑧⑧
Boutique
*55/13 Moo 6, Bang Por Soi 4, Mae
Nam, 84140*
Tel *0-7760-2122*
W samuicode.com
Hillside suites and villas with
minimalist contemporary decor.
Superb views. Great for couples.

KO SAMUI: Coral Cove Chalet ⑧⑧
Modern
210 Moo 4, Tong Takian Beach, 84140
Tel *0-7742-2260*
W coralcovechalet.com
Attractive chalets on a palm-
covered hill, with a private white-
sand beach and good snorkeling.

KO SAMUI: Four Seasons ⑧⑧⑧
Luxury
*219 Moo 5, Ang Thong, Laem Yai,
84140*
Tel *0-7724-3000*
W fourseasons.com/kohsamui
Luxurious villas with spectacular
sea views and private infinity
pools. World-class spa and cuisine.

KO SAMUI: The Library ⑧⑧⑧
Boutique
14/1 Moo 2, Chaweng Beach, 84140
Tel *0-7742-2767*
W thelibrary.co.th
Free-standing villas with
contemporary decor and original
artwork. Huge library.

KO SAMUI: The Saboey ⑧⑧
Boutique
51/4 Moo 4, Big Buddha Beach, 84140
Tel *0-7743-0456*
W saboey.com
Beautifully designed suites and
villas. Superb seafood restaurant.

DK Choice

**KO SAMUI: Six Senses
Hideaway** ⑧⑧⑧
Luxury
*9/10 Moo 5, Baan Plai Laem,
Bophut, 84320*
Tel *0-7724-5678*
W sixsenses.com
Set on a hillside overlooking the
Gulf of Thailand on Ko Samui's
quiet north coast, this collection
of 66 villas offers truly opulent
accommodation in an unrivaled
setting. Each villa has either a
Jacuzzi or a private infinity pool.
Excellent service and food.

KO TAO: JP Resort ⑧
Budget
18/4 Moo 3, ChalokBanKao Bay, 84000
Tel *0-7745-6099*
W jpresort.asia
Good value hotel close to the
beach. Quiet location and
great restaurant.

**KO TAO: Jamahkiri
Resort & Spa** ⑧⑧⑧
Boutique
Thian Ok Bay, 84000
Tel *0-7745-6400*
W jamahkiri.com
Stay in one of 12 pavilions set
amid boulders in an isolated bay.
Superb spa and diving school.

**PHETCHABURI: Fisherman's
Resort** ⑧⑧⑧
Luxury
170 Mu 1, Haad Chao Samrin, 76000
Tel *0-3244-1370*
W thefishermansresort.com
Lavish beachfront villas set in a
traditional fishing village. Superb

spa plus fishing, water sports,
hiking, and biking.

**PRACHUAP KHIRI KHAN:
Coral Hotel** ⑧⑧
Resort
Bang Saphan, Ban Suan Luan, 77140
Tel *0-3281-7121*
W coral-hotel.com
This lovely Thai-style resort offers
large quarters for families. Fishing
and diving trips can be arranged.

**PRACHUAP KHIRI KHAN:
Sailom Resort BB** ⑧⑧
Modern
*299 Moo 5, Mae Rumpeung, Bang
Saphan, 85000*
Tel *0-3269-1003*
W sailombangsaphan.com
Spacious rooms and a fantastic
pool. Great for families.

**SURAT THANI: 100 Islands
Resort & Spa** ⑧
Boutique
*19/6 Mu 3 Bypass Rd, Makhamtia,
84000*
Tel *0-7720-1150*
W roikoh.com
On the outskirts of town, this
excellent value teak palace has
lovely gardens, a spa, and a pool.

Upper Andaman
Coast

**PHANGNGA BAY: Six Senses
Yao Noi** ⑧⑧⑧
Luxury
56 Mu 5, Koh Yao Noi, 82160
Tel *0-7641-8500*
W sixsenses.com
Luxury beyond comparison.
Villas with private pools and
personal service. Excellent spa
and great chefs at the restaurant.

Stunning villa with private pool at Six Senses

PHANGNGA COAST: Golden Buddha Beach Resort ฿฿
Modern
Ko Phra Thong, 82210
Tel *08-1892-2208*
W goldenbuddharesort.com
Individually designed teak cottages on a peaceful, undeveloped island, with yoga and vegetarian food.

PHANGNGA COAST: Aleenta ฿฿฿
Luxury
33 Moo 2, Khok Kloy, 82210
Tel *0-7658-0333*
W aleenta.com
Secluded hotel with trendy minimalist decor. Good spa.

PHUKET: Casa Brazil ฿
B&B
9 Moo 3 Soi Luang Por Chuan 1, Karon Beach, 83000
Tel *0-7639-6317*
W phukethomestay.com
Quirky decor and friendly staff at this homestay and gallery. Nice central courtyard with garden.

PHUKET: Fantasy Hill Bungalow ฿
Guesthouse
8/1 Patak Rd, Karon Beach, 83100
Tel *0-7633-0106*
Spacious rooms with large balconies. Quiet hilltop location, but convenient for the beaches.

PHUKET: Shanti Lodge ฿
Guesthouse
1/2 Soi Bangrae, Choafa Nok Rd, Ao Chalong, 83000
Tel *0-7628-0233*
W shantilodge.com
Bungalows in a quiet village away from the coast. A calm and relaxing place. Yoga offered.

PHUKET: Baipho ฿฿
Boutique
205/12–13 Rat-U-Tit Rd, Patong Beach, 83150
Tel *0-7629-2074*
W baipho.com
Chic centrally located place with friendly staff. Modern decor and tasty European food.

PHUKET: Sino House ฿฿
Boutique
1 Montree Rd, 83000
Tel *0-7623-2495*
W sinohousephuket.com
Well-located hotel with lovely Chinese decor. Small on-site spa.

PHUKET: Sugar Marina Resort Fashion ฿฿
Modern
20/10 Kata Rd, Kata Beach, 83160
Tel *0-7628-4404*
W sugarmarina-fashion.com
This stylish, lively resort close to the beach has spacious rooms.

Sleek contemporary decor at the secluded resort Indigo Pearl

PHUKET: Amanpuri ฿฿฿
Luxury
118 Moo 3, Sri Santhorn Rd, Pansea Beach, 83110
Tel *0-7632-4333*
W amanresorts.com
Phuket's original six-star resort and spa, still considered the best by many. Impeccable service.

PHUKET: Banyan Tree Resort ฿฿฿
Luxury
33/37 Moo 4, Sri Soonthorn Rd, Cherng Thalae, 83110
Tel *0-7637-2400*
W banyantree.com
Lavish pool villas on a tranquil lagoon. Superb food and spa.

PHUKET: Indigo Pearl ฿฿฿
Luxury
Nai Yang Beach, adjoining Nai Yang National Park, 83110
Tel *0-7632-7006*
W indigo-pearl.com
Chic luxurious rooms designed using industrial materials. Unique hotel in an isolated location.

PHUKET: The Royal Phuket Yacht Club ฿฿฿
Luxury
23/3 Moo 1, Viset Rd Rawai, 83100
Tel *0-7638-0200-19*
W puravarna.com
Phuket's original luxury hotel, the Royal Phuket Yacht Club is built on a hillside on the southern tip of the island. Understated elegance.

DK Choice

PHUKET: Villa Royale ฿฿฿
Boutique
12 Kata Noi Rd, Kata Noi Beach, 83100
Tel *0-7633-3569*
W villaroyalephuket.com
This hotel is a long-established oasis of good taste, luxury, and high standards. Choose from gorgeous suites or free-standing villas. The food is famous, and there is an on-site gourmet Thai cooking school. Charming, friendly staff.

RANONG: Sabai-Sabai Beach Bungalows ฿
Budget
Near Mook Bay, Ko Phayam, 85000
Tel *08-7895-4653*
W sabai-bungalows.com
Enjoy yoga and cooking classes at this affordable but clean place. It also offers a wide variety of room types. You can even camp on the beach if you wish.

Deep South

HAT YAI: Centara ฿฿
Modern
3 Sanehanusorn Rd, 90110
Tel *0-7435-2222*
W centarahotelsresorts.com
This modern high-rise hotel is part of a Thai chain and popular with business clientele. A delightful rooftop pool.

HAT YAI: Regency ฿฿
Modern
23 Prachatipat Rd, 90110
Tel *0-7435-3333-47*
W theregencyhatyai.com
Spread over 28 floors in two wings, the Regent and the fancier Royal offer over 400 rooms. Plush lobby area and a great location.

SONGKHLA: BP Samila Beach Hotel ฿
Budget
8 Rachadamnoen Nok Rd, 90000
Tel *0-7444-0222*
Great beachside setting, yet close to center of town. Glory somewhat faded, but fantastic views and friendly staff.

SONGKHLA: Rajamangala Pavilion Beach Resort ฿฿
Modern
1 Rachadamnoen Nok Rd, 90000
Tel *0-7448-7222*
W pavilionhotels.com
Located a short drive away from downtown Songkhla. All rooms have views of the Gulf of Thailand from their private balconies.

For more information on types of hotels *see pp398–401*

WHERE TO EAT

Thailand is fortunate in being a land of plenty. Because much of the land is fertile and the population has always been small relative to the size of the country, famine is all but unknown. In the 13th century King Ramkamhaeng of Sukhothai, the first Thai kingdom, recorded: "This land is thriving … in the water are fish, in the fields there is rice." He might also have mentioned the wide range of tropical fruits, vegetables, and spices – to which have been added, since his day, a wealth of imports from tropical America, thriving in their new Old World setting. The range of dishes, as well as the variety and freshness of the ingredients, make for one of the world's great cuisines. Thais love to eat: six or seven meals a day is not uncommon. Wherever there are people there are restaurants and food stands. As well being famed for its flavor and freshness, Thai cuisine is beautifully presented, and dishes are often be garnished with flowers and rosettes carved out of colorful vegetables and fruit.

Sino-Portuguese style decor at Fujian, Chiang Mai (see p423)

Restaurants

Bangkok's dining scene is one of the most cosmopolitan in Southeast Asia. Italian and French cuisine have long been part of the culinary landscape, but now diners can also enjoy trendy Mexican bars and grills, sophisticated Japanese restaurants, five-star hotel Sunday brunches, and traditional Thai food served up with contemporary flair. Most urban restaurants, especially those serving Western food, open at about 11am and close between 10pm and midnight. This can mean that finding an early Western-style breakfast is difficult away from the tourist scene, in which case a Thai omelet may have to serve as a substitute.

Restaurants are almost always listed in free tourist magazines – virtually every major city and resort in Thailand will issue these. They can be picked up in hotel reception lobbies, at banks and money changers, as well as in many restaurants. These magazines usually list places by cuisine and specialty, often giving details of how to get there, along with telephone numbers for booking tables. Away from the major tourist destinations, the main hotels in every town will usually have air-conditioned restaurants offering a mixture of Thai and Chinese cuisine.

Thais have taken to Western cuisine, and especially to the Western fast-food culture, with

Restaurant in the Sadet Market at Nong Khai, by the Mekong River

enthusiasm. McDonald's and Kentucky Fried Chicken are increasingly visible, but the most popular imports appear to be pizza and pasta, which can be found in just about any provincial capital. However, quality does vary from place to place.

Coffee Shops

Over the last decade, franchised Western coffee shops and their local equivalents have become extremely popular, particularly in the big cities and resort towns. The clean, air-conditioned shops have been a hit with the younger generation, who often gather there after school or college. Local coffee shops are still favored by older citizens, who prefer strong, sweet coffee, filtered through a cotton bag. Served with condensed milk, the coffee is excellent with youtiao, a traditional deep-fried Chinese breakfast doughnut.

Roadside and Market Food Stands

Some of the best and most reasonably priced food in Thailand can be found at any of the numerous roadside food stalls. Generally speaking, such establishments are clean and unpretentious. These stands are often mobile, allowing the proprietors to push them home and clean them every night. The ingredients are openly displayed behind glass panels. Fast cooking processes, such as flash-frying, grilling over charcoal, or boiling are often used. This means that the fare, invariably fresh, should also be well-cooked and safe to eat.

A sure way of measuring a stall's popularity, as anywhere in the world, is by its patrons. If there are plenty of locals sitting at the simple tables most stalls provide, then the chances are the food is good. It is not surprising to find a businessman with a Mercedes parked nearby sitting at the same stall as a *tuk-tuk* driver. Thais from all sectors of society know how to appreciate good, cheap food.

Menus are rarely in English, so it is a good idea to memorize the names of your favorite dishes from the food glossary *(see pp414–15)*. Alternatively, point at a dish and ask to taste – few Thais expect foreign visitors to speak their language, and they are always willing to help.

Street vendor cooking satay for passers-by in a Bangkok park

Khantoke Dining

A traditional style of dining in Northern Thailand, *khantoke* dinners are often arranged for guests by hotels in Chiang Mai and other Northern cities. Diners sit on mats around a low, circular table. The meal includes a variety of Northern dishes such as *nam phrik num* (a very spicy dip), *kap mu* (pork skin) and *kaeng kai* (a chicken and vegetable curry), all of which are served with *khao niaw* (sticky rice) and washed down with local beer. A *khantoke* dinner is often accompanied by displays of traditional Thai dancing.

Prices

Buying meals is one of the cheapest aspects of a visit to Thailand. The cost of alcohol, however, can often be more than the meal itself. It is common practice for prices to be displayed. Menus invariably list them next to each dish. The prices for shellfish are often given by weight. In larger establishments and international-class hotels a service charge and tax will usually be levied. These extra costs will be clearly detailed on the check.

Even at very small establishments prices are nearly always fixed and marked (in Arabic numerals) on a board. Bargaining for foodstuffs is surprisingly rare.

Tipping

Tipping was once unknown, but its popularity is increasing as Thais grow accustomed to tips from tourists. Do not apply a percentage: 10 percent of 50 *baht* may well be appropriate, but 10 percent of an expensive meal would be far too much.

Eating Habits in Thailand

The Thai philosophy of nutrition is simple – if you are hungry, eat. Nothing should stand in the way. Most Thais, moreover, eat little but often, sometimes snacking six or seven times a day. The concept of three meals simply does not apply in Thailand. Even though people do indeed eat breakfast, lunch, and dinner, they may also stop for a bowl of noodles, a fried snack, or a sweet at any time of day.

Eating is a simple pleasure and does not involve complex rituals of etiquette, although visitors should note a few rules. Thais eat with a fork held in the left hand and a spoon held in the right hand. The fork is used solely to push food onto the spoon; eating straight from a fork is considered crude. Since food – especially meat – is cut into pieces before it is cooked, knives are not needed.

Thai noodle dishes are often strongly influenced by Chinese culinary traditions, and they are eaten using chopsticks and a spoon. Another exception to the general rule is sticky rice *(khao niaw)*, which is eaten – delicately – using fingers.

Food in Thailand is generally served communally in a series of bowls. Only small rice bowls are reserved for individual use. Rice is traditionally served first, and then a spoon is used to ladle a spoonful from the communal bowls on top of the rice. Feel free to come back for more as necessary. Overloading your plate is regarded as uncouth – there is no hurry, and there is always plenty more in the kitchen.

Recommended Restaurants

The restaurants on the following pages have been carefully selected to give a cross-section of options from across the country. Included are not only those places that excel in producing tasty Thai cuisine, but also those that serve other Asian cuisines, such as Japanese and Vietnamese, as well as restaurants serving international favorites like steaks, salads, and burgers. Besides the quality of food, these recommendations take into account the ambience and level of service. However, since taste is much more important than presentation for most Thai diners, many of the places listed here lack the kind of sophisticated ambience so sought after by restaurants in the West. For the best of the best, look out for the restaurants featuring the DK Choice label.

The Flavors of Thailand

Thai food is popular worldwide for its aromatic and spicy qualities. Chili peppers were first imported to Thailand from the New World in the 16th century by European traders. They were adopted into Thai cuisine (especially the small, fiery ones) with great enthusiasm, but mildly spiced dishes are also widely available. Although influences from China and India can be detected in stir-fries and curries, Thai inventiveness has resulted in a dizzying range of dishes unique to the country. The cuisine is full of distinctive flavors and complementary textures, nutritionally balanced and delightfully presented.

Nam pla phrik

Fish for sale on a local market stall in Chiang Rai

Rice and Noodles

In common with those of all its Southeast Asian neighbours, the Thai diet is based on the staples of rice and noodles. The most popular type of rice is the long-grained *khao hom mali*, or fragrant jasmine rice, which is usually steamed. However, in the north and northeast, locals prefer *khao niaw*, or sticky rice, which is eaten with the fingers,

rolled into little balls, and dipped in sauces. Rice porridge (*jok*) is a typical breakfast dish, often with egg, chilies, and rice vinegar stirred in.

Noodles, made of rice (*kuaytiaw*), wheat and egg (*bami*), or mung beans (*wun sen*), are usually served fried or in a soup. The most well-known Thai noodle dish among foreigners is *phad thai* (literally "Thai fry"). An irresistible mix of noodles fried with fresh or dried shrimp, egg, beancurd (tofu), and beansprouts, it vies with *tom yam kung* for the title of Thai national dish.

The Four Flavors

All Thai dishes strike a balance between the "four flavors" – sweet, sour, salty, and hot –

Kaffir lime leaves — Lemongrass — Ginger — Turmeric — Shallots — Thai basil — Galangal — Chilies

Selection of typical Thai herbs, spices and flavorings

Regional Dishes and Specialities

Central Thai food is strongly influenced by Chinese cuisine and accounts for most dishes on menus nationwide, including the country's signature dish *tom yam kung*. Northern Thai cuisine takes much of its inspiration from Burma and Yunnan province in China. Examples include *khao soi*, a delicious dish of boiled and crispy noodles in a mild curry broth, and *kaeng hang le*. Northeastern Thais like their food with a kick, and one of their best-known imports from nearby Laos is tangy, crunchy *som tam* salad. Southern food is the fieriest of the lot, with creamy coconut, vibrant turmeric, and sharp ng in such typical dishes as sour and spicy *kaeng luang pla*.

Pea eggplants (aubergines)

Tom Yam Kung uses lemon grass, galangal, kaffir lime, and chili to flavor the hot and sour shrimp broth.

Traders selling fruit and vegetables at Damnoen Saduak Floating Market

although the balance varies from dish to dish. While Thai cuisine has a reputation for being liberal with its use of chilies, it also features a wide range of subtly flavoured dishes that make use of aromatic herbs and spices such as galangal, lemon grass, kaffir lime leaves, basil, and coriander (cilantro) to enhance aroma and taste. Pastes using these ingredients are pounded by hand in a mortar to ensure the freshest flavor. However, the real key to Thai cuisine is fish sauce *(nam pla)*, which adds its piquancy to the vast majority of dishes. Mixed with chilies, garlic, and lemon, it becomes the popular condiment *nam pla phrik*.

The Thai Meal

A typical Thai meal consists of a soup, a curry, a stir-fry, and a spicy Thai salad, as well as side dishes of raw or steamed vegetables, served with a big bowl of rice. The meal is rarely divided into formal courses. Westerners who do not realize this often order a soup or a salad as a starter whereas, in fact, the spiciness of these dishes is intended to be toned down by eating them with rice. However, Thai

Melon, expertly carved in the Thai style, as a table decoration

restaurant staff are very likely to serve all dishes ordered at the same time anyway. The only concession that Thais make to courses is with dessert, which is usually a plate of mixed fruit intended to clear the palate after the savory dishes. Many foreign visitors also like to indulge in a national favorite – *khao niaw mamuang*, or mango with sticky coconut rice.

WHAT TO DRINK

Fruit juices Thailand's wealth of luscious fruits, such as watermelon, mango, lychee, and papaya, are blended into juices, shakes and smoothies. Chilled coconut juice, drunk through a straw straight from the nut, is perfect for slaking a thirst on the beach.

Beers There is a good range of beers available. Popular choices are the full-bodied local Singha and Chang.

Wines and spirits As well as locally made rice wine, wines from Europe and the New World are widely available, and Thai vineyards are also starting to produce acceptable varieties. The local spirits, Sang Som and Hong Thong, are very palatable when mixed with ice and soda.

Coffee and tea While not traditional Thai drinks, excellent varieties of both are now grown in the northern hills.

Kaeng Hang Le, a dry, mild curry of pork with ginger, peanuts, and garlic, is served with rice and Chinese greens.

Som Tam is shredded unripe papaya and other vegetables, with lime juice, chili, fish sauce, and dried shrimps.

Kaeng Lueng Pla is a spicy fish soup with bamboo shoots, flavored with tamarind, chili, garlic, and palm sugar.

A Glossary of Typical Thai Dishes

Thai cuisine is famously creative and varied *(see pp42–3)*. Even street vendors delight in their culinary skills, and it is not uncommon to see food being encased in a banana leaf as delicately as if it were being gift wrapped. Such artful presentations and the sheer range of dishes can be bewildering to newcomers: it may not even be obvious what is savory or sweet. This glossary covers typical dishes; phonetic guidance for food words is on pages 510–11.

A street vendor cooking over charcoal on a roadside stall

Choosing Dishes

Restaurant menus in tourist areas may include descriptions in English, and sometimes other languages. The Thai names of dishes often derive simply from the main elements – for instance, the dish *khao mu daeng* translates literally as "rice, pork, red." Thus, the basic components of any dish can often be worked out with only a little knowledge of Thai. If there is no menu, the dishes of the day will be on display. If you don't recognize the dish, pointing and saying *"nee arai na?"* ("what's this?") should elicit a list of ingredients.

Vegetarians should find it easy to order food without meat *(mai ao nua)*, but ought to be aware that fish sauce is used in many dishes. Dairy products feature only rarely in Thai cuisine, so vegans should not fare worse than vegetarians. Thais are accustomed to foreigners asking if a dish is spicy *(phed mai?)*, or requesting a non-spicy meal *(mai ao phet na)*. To enliven any dish, diners can use the ubiquitous condiments of chilies in vinegar, chili flakes, sugar (for savory dishes), and fish sauce usually found on tables.

Snacks

Thais love to snack. Almost every street corner has a selection of food stalls selling raw and freshly cooked snacks.

Bami mu daeng
บะหมี่หมูแดง
Egg noodles with red pork.

Khai ping
ไข่ปิ้ง
Charcoal-roasted eggs.

Kai yang
ไก่ย่าง
Charcoal-grilled chicken.

Khanom beuang
ขนมเบื้อง
Filled, sweet, crisp pancakes.

Khanom khrok
ขนมครก
Coconut puddings.

Khao tom mud
ข้าวต้มมัด
Sticky rice served in banana leaves.

Kluay ping
กล้วยปิ้ง
Charcoal-grilled bananas.

Look chin ping
ลูกชิ้นปิ้ง
Meatballs with a chili sauce.

Po pia tod
ปอเปี๊ยะ
Deep-fried spring rolls.

Sai krok
ไส้กรอก
Thai beef or pork sausages.

Satay
สะเต๊ะ
Slivers of beef, pork, or chicken grilled on a stick, served with peanut sauce and cucumber.

Tua thod
ถั่วทอด
Roasted cashews or peanuts.

Noodles

Rice noodles come as *sen yai* (broad), *sen lek* (medium), and *sen mi* (thin). *Bami* are egg noodles. *Woon sen* are thin, transparent soy noodles.

Bami nam
บะหมี่น้ำ
Egg noodles in a broth with vegetables and meat or fish.

Kuaytiaw haeng
ก๋วยเตี๋ยวแห้ง
Rice noodles served "dry" with vegetables and meat or fish.

Kuaytiaw look chin pla
ลูกชิ้นปลา
Fishballs with noodles.

Kuaytiaw nam
ก๋วยเตี๋ยวน้ำ
Rice noodles in a broth with vegetables and meat or fish.

Phad thai
ผัดไทย
Rice noodles fried with beancurd, egg, dried shrimp, peanuts, bean sprouts, and chili.

Street sellers and their customers in a Bangkok market

Rice Dishes

Rice is the staple food. A familiar Thai greeting, equivalent to "how are you?" is *kin khao ru yang?*, literally "have you eaten rice?"

Khao man kai
ข้าวมันไก่
Chinese-style chicken with rice cooked in chicken stock.

Khao mok kai
ข้าวหมกไก่
Thai-style chicken biriyani.

Khao mu daeng
ข้าวหมูแดง
Chinese-style red pork served on a bed of fragrant rice.

Khao na ped
ข้าวหน้าเป็ด
Roast duck served on a bed of fragrant rice.

Khao phad mu/kung
ข้าวผัดหมูหรือกุ้ง
Fried rice with pork or shrimp.

Soups

Soups are diverse and inventive. Some, such as *jok*, are eaten for breakfast. The word *"sup"* is widely recognized.

Jok
โจ๊ก
Ground rice porridge with minced pork and ginger.

Khao tom
ข้าวต้ม
Rice soup with a selection of meat and vegetable side dishes.

Tom jeud tao hu
ต้มจืดเต้าหู้
Mild broth with beancurd and minced pork.

Tom kha kai
ต้มข่าไก่
Chicken soup with galingale, coconut milk, and lemon grass.

Tom yam kung
ต้มยำกุ้ง
Shrimp, mushrooms, lemon grass, galingale, and coriander.

Curries

Curries are served either *rat khao* (on a plate of rice) or in a bowl as an accompaniment to a central bowl of rice.

Kaeng kari kai
แกงกะหรี่ไก่
Indian-style chicken and potato.

Kaeng khiaw wan
แกงเขียวหวาน
Slightly sweet green curry.

Fragrant green leaves make a perfect wrapping for sticky rice

Kaeng matsaman
แกงมัสมั่น
A mild curry from the Muslim South with chicken, peanuts, potatoes, and coconut milk.

Kaeng phanaeng
แกงแพนง
Southern-style "dry" curry with coconut and basil.

Kaeng phed
แกงเผ็ด
A hot curry with red chilies, lemon grass, and coriander.

Kaeng som
แกงส้ม
Hot and sour curry, often with fish.

Seafood

An amazing variety of seafood is available at reasonable prices, particularly in the South.

Hoi malaeng pu op
หอยแมลงภู่อบ
Steamed green mussels.

Hoi thod
หอยทอด
Oysters fried in batter with egg on a bed of beansprouts.

Hu chalam
หูฉลาม
Shark's fin soup.

Kung mangkon phao
กุ้งมังกรเผา
Grilled lobster.

Pla meuk yang
ปลาหมึกย่าง
Roasted sliced squid.

Pla nung khing
ปลานึ่งขิง
Steamed fish with ginger, chili, and mushrooms.

Pla thod
ปลาทอด
Deep-fried fish.

Pu neung
ปูนึ่ง
Steamed crab.

Regional Dishes

Kaeng hang le
แกงฮังเล
Pork, peanut, and ginger curry from Chiang Mai.

Khao soi
ข้าวซอย
Chicken or beef curry served with wheat noodles, fresh lime, and pickled cabbage. A Northern specialty.

Larb ped
ลาบเป็ด
Northern spicy minced duck.

Som tam
ส้มตำ
Green papaya salad with peanuts, from the Northeast.

Yam thalay
ยำทะเล
Southern spicy seafood salad.

Desserts

Known as *khong wan* or "sweet things," these are mostly coconut- or fruit-based.

Foy thong
ฝอยทอง
Sweet, shredded egg yolk.

Khao niaw mamuang
ข้าวเหนียวมะม่วง
Fresh mango served with sticky rice and coconut milk.

Kluay buat chi
กล้วยบวชชี
Bananas in coconut milk.

Mo kaeng
หม้อแกง
Thai-style egg custard.

Drinks

Bia
เบียร์
Beer. Usually served in bottles.

Cha (nom) ron
ชาร้อน
Hot tea with condensed milk.

Kafae
กาแฟ
Coffee, often instant.

Nam cha
น้ำชา
Chinese-style tea without milk.

Nam kuad
น้ำขวด
Bottled water.

Coconut seller on the Floating Market

Where to Eat and Drink

Bangkok

Old City

Roti Mataba ⓑ
Indian/Malay **Map** 2 D3
136 Phra Athit Rd, Chanasongkram, 10200
Tel *0-2282-2119* **Closed** *Mon*
Roti Mataba is an inexpensive no-frills place where you can enjoy a classic Indian/Malay *roti*, a delicious fried flatbread, stuffed with various fillings and served with a small bowl of *dhal* or curry sauce for dipping. They serve good curries too. Very busy at lunchtimes.

Aquatini ⓑⓑ
Thai **Map** 1 C3
45/1 Phra Athit Rd, Chanasongkram, 10200
Tel *0-2280-9955*
With a large, breezy riverside terrace beside the Phra Athit Pier, Aquatini is a convenient spot to enjoy a seafood dish or Thai curry washed down with a cold beverage.

Deck by the River ⓑⓑ
Thai **Map** 5 C1
Arun Residence, 36–38 Soi Pratu Nok Yoong, Maharaj Rd, 10200
Tel *0-2221-9158*
The food at Deck by the River is prepared with great skill and only the highest-quality ingredients. Traditional Thai fare, with a few Western dishes. Enjoy great views of the famous Wat Arun across the river, especially at sunset.

Jay Fai ⓑⓑ
Thai **Map** 3 E4
327 Mahachai Rd, 10200
Tel *0-2223-9384*
Jay Fai is an unpretentious local favorite renowned for its *phad khii mao*, literally drunkard's noodles, a spicy fried noodle dish with chicken and basil. This place can get very busy, but it's worth the wait.

Kai Yang Boran ⓑⓑ
Issan **Map** 2 D5
474–476 Tanao Rd, Banglamphu, 10200
Tel *0-2622-2349*
This is an excellent choice for those wishing to sample the food from Thailand's northeastern Issan region. The place takes its name from the region's signature dish, *kai yang*, or roasted marinated chicken. Pleasant air-conditioned interior.

Sala Rattanakosin Eatery & Bar ⓑⓑⓑ
Thai/Western **Map** 5 B1
39 Maharat Rd, Tha Thien (behind Wat Pho), 10200
Tel *0-2622-1388*
With views of the river and Wat Arun, the scenery here rivals the excellent food as an attraction. Thai and imaginative Western dishes are offered. Don't miss the rooftop bar.

Chinatown

Nai Sow ⓑ
Chinese/Thai **Map** 6 F1
3/1 Maitrichit Rd, Pom Prap Sattru Phai, 10220
Tel *0-2222-1539*
Don't be fooled by the humble surroundings and simple decor; this place dishes up truly excellent Chinese and Thai food. Try favorites such as *tom yam kung* or *hoi thod*. Popular with office workers at lunchtime.

Thip Samai ⓑ
Thai **Map** 2 E5
313 Maha Chai Rd, Samramrat, Pra Nakorn, 10220
Tel *0-2221-6280*
Established in 1966, this place has a solid reputation for serving the best *phad thai* in Bangkok. Delicious fresh shrimp also on offer, wrapped in an omelet, or with added shrimp fat.

Harmonique ⓑⓑ
Thai **Map** 6 F3
Soi Wat Muang Khae, Charoen Krung Rd, 10100
Tel *0-2237-8175*
Great atmosphere with a quiet off-street garden and ramshackle decor inside. Good Thai food prepared to Western tastes. Nice pastries as well.

Hua Seng Hong ⓑⓑ
Chinese **Map** 6 E2
371–373 Yaowarat Rd, 10100
Tel *0-2222-0635*
Classic Hong Kong-style Chinese restaurant with an extensive menu. Try the duck, clay pot prawns, or choose from a wide selection of dim sum. Efficient service.

Seven Spoons ⓑⓑ
Mediterranean **Map** 2 F4
22–24 Chakkrapatiphong Rd, 10100
Tel *0-2629-9214* **Closed** *Mon*
A unique spot in Bangkok, serving up good cocktails and inventive Mediterranean cuisine. Lots of vegetarian specialties –

try the quinoa salad with mango, avocado, and mushroom. Book ahead.

T & K Seafood ⓑⓑ
Seafood **Map** 6 F2
49–51 Soi Phadung Dao, 10100
Tel *0-2223-4519*
Choose from the wide selection of fresh seafood displayed on ice in front of this raucously busy place. Gets particularly crowded in the late evening. The whole-steamed fish is great, as is the crab curry. All items sold by weight.

Dusit

Krua Apsorn ⓑ
Thai **Map** 2 E1
503–505 Samsen Rd Soi 9, 10200
Tel *02-241-8528* **Closed** *Sun*
Authentic and tasty Thai dishes served in a basic but clean setting. This is the first and the best of three branches in the city. Try the mussels fried *phad cha*-style, with basil, yellow chili, wild ginger, and green peppercorn, or one of the Southern Thai curries.

May Kaidee ⓑ
Vegetarian **Map** 2 D3
33 Samsen Rd opposite Soi 2, 10200
Tel *0-2281-7699*
An institution for Bangkok's vegetarians, May Kaidee serves mostly Thai dishes with some Western choices thrown in. Delicious spring rolls, green curry

The off-street garden at Harmonique

European à la carte dining at Biscotti

with tofu, and *phad thai*. Good buffet. The chef offers cooking classes, and has published a cookbook of Thai vegetarian food.

Downtown

Hai Somtam
Issan   ⓦ
Map 7 C4
2/4–5 Convent Rd, Silom, 10120
Tel 0-2631-0216
Great place for Northeastern Thai food, known as *aharn issan*. An unassuming, open-fronted restaurant, packed at lunchtimes and early evenings with locals eating spicy *som tam* (green papaya salad), grilled chicken, sun-dried pork, sticky rice, and other Issan favorites.

Lamyai
Thai   ⓦ
Map 8 D2
Lang Suan Rd Soi 6, 10330
    Closed *evenings, Sat & Sun*
Try *khao soi*, the famous Northern Thai curried noodles at this foodie's favorite in Bangkok. The wheat noodles with chicken or pork and fragrant spices is a must-try. Great for lunch.

Mrs. Balbir's
Indian   ⓦ
155/1–2 Sukumvit Soi 11/1, 10110
Tel 0-2651-0498   **Closed** *Tue*
Unpretentious restaurant serving good Northern Indian favorites. The owner is a local TV personality who gives Indian cooking classes. Of the several branches in the city, this is the original restaurant and it is still the best.

Suda
Thai   ⓦ
6-6/1 Sukumvit Soi 14, 10110
Tel 0-2229-4664
Suda is a favorite evening haunt of expatriates in the Sukhumvit area, thanks to its inexpensive and delicious cuisine. Thai office workers flock here for lunch too.

Popular choices include tuna with chilies and cashews, and green curry with rice.

Biscotti
Italian   ⓦⓦ
Map 8 E1
Ratchadamri Rd, 10330
Tel 0 2126 8866
Located in the swish Four Seasons Hotel, Biscotti is a stylish but warm and friendly Italian restaurant with an open kitchen. The menu is not limited to haute cuisine, and features pasta and other comfort foods as well. Top-quality service and great value.

Bua
Thai   ⓦⓦ
Map 7 C4
Siboonrueng Building, 1/4 Convent Rd, Silom, 10120
Tel 0-2237-6640
For over 20 years, Bua has served both locals and tourists an extensive menu of delicious dishes from four of Thailand's main culinary regions. Try the *pla neung mannao* (steamed sea bass in lime juice).

Coyote Bar & Grill
Mexican   ⓦⓦ
Map 7 C4
Sukhumvit Soi 11, 10110
Tel 0-2651-3313
Coyote Bar & Grill is Bangkok's most popular Mexican eatery. Tuck into quesadillas, burritos, enchiladas, and racks of pork ribs, and choose from more than 75 different types of margaritas. Bright, lively ambience.

Le Dalat Indochine
French/Vietnamese   ⓦⓦ
14 Soi 23, Sukhumvit Rd, 10110
Tel 0-2259-9593
Run by a French-Vietnamese family, this restaurant is renowned for the culinary blend of these two different cultures, also reflected in the decor. Try the angel hair

sautéed with crab meat and shiitake mushrooms.

Eat Me
International   ⓦⓦ
Map 7 C4
1/6 Soi Phipat 2, off Convent Rd, Silom, 10120
Tel 0-2238-0931
The exposed beams give a loft-style look to this place, which is fitting as it is both a restaurant and an art gallery. The excellent fusion food nevertheless remains the main attraction. Try the pan-seared Alaskan sea scallops, or the *nduja* (spicy sausage) tartine with goat's cheese and pine nuts.

Indus
Indian   ⓦⓦ
71 Soi 26, Sukumvit Rd, 10110
Tel 0-2258-4900
The light, simple dishes at Indus place an emphasis on health without sacrificing flavor. The dining room decor draws on northern India's cultural heritage, with stunning results. A lovely bar and café add to the ambience.

Thanying
Thai   ⓦⓦ
Map 7 A5
10 Pramuan Rd, Silom, 10500
Tel 0-2236-4361
A Thai title for ladies of nobility, the name of this restaurant reflects the type of aristocratic but traditional fare on offer. In a lovely old house off Silom, the ambience is good, but the food is even better. Fantastic attention to detail.

Uncle John
French/Thai   ⓦⓦ
Map 8 D5
279/2 Suan Phlu Soi 8, 10120
Tel 08-1373-3865
Soi Suan Phlu, near Sathorn Rd, is full of excellent street food and bars. Uncle John serves quality home-style French dishes at prices far below those paid in fancier places.

For more information on types of restaurants *see pp412–13*

Le Beaulieu
French   ⓦⓦⓦ
Map 8 F2
Athenee Office Tower, 63 Wireless Rd,
10330
Tel *0-2168-8220*
This long-standing local favorite
serves authentic French cuisine
in an elegant setting. Try the
premium Fines de Claire oysters,
simple bouillabaisse, roasted
Bresse chicken, home-made
pâtés, or côte de boeuf
(rib-eye steak).

Bo.lan
Thai   ⓦⓦⓦ
24 Sukhumvit Soi 53, 10110
Tel *0-2260-2962*   **Closed** *Wed*
A true taste of Thailand, this place
refuses to soften traditional Thai
flavors to Western tastes. All the
food here is made with fresh,
locally sourced ingredients. Opt
for the tasting menu, which
changes every two months.
Sleek, wood-themed decor.

The China House
Chinese   ⓦⓦⓦ
Map 6 F4
Mandarin Oriental Hotel,
48 Oriental Ave, 10500
Tel *0-2659-9000*
In a beautifully restored house
in the Art Deco style of 1930s
Shanghai, this restaurant dishes
up classic Cantonese cuisine with
a contemporary twist. Try the
delicious home-made tofu and
oven-roasted Peking duck.

Issaya Siamese Club
Thai   ⓦⓦⓦ
Map 8 F5
4 Soi Sri Aksorn, Chua Ploeng Rd,
Sathorn, 10120
Tel *0-2672-9040-1*
On offer here is delicious Thai
food with a contemporary twist.
Try the *moo manao* (thinly sliced
pork topped with lime and
edible flowers), glazed pork ribs,
and *pla ob prik* (baked fish with a
chili glaze). The setting is a 1920s
mansion complete with bright,
quirky furnishings.

Koi
Japanese   ⓦⓦⓦ
26 Sukhumvit Soi 20, 10110
Tel *0-2258-1590*
This trendy Japanese restaurant
is a stunning addition to the
city's increasingly eclectic dining
scene. One of the most talked
about restaurants in Bangkok, it
has attracted a host of famous
celebrities and models. All come
for delicious sushi and sashimi
presented with flair.

Naj
Thai   ⓦⓦⓦ
Map 7 C4
42 Convent Rd, Silom 10120
Tel *0-2632-2811*
First-rate Thai food served in an
elegant three-story Colonial-style
house. Try the coconut-milk soup
with chicken and *galangal*, wing-
bean salad with minced pork and
shrimps, or a sizzling seafood hot
plate. Exceptional service.

Le Normandie
French   ⓦⓦⓦ
Map 6 F4
Mandarin Oriental Hotel, 48 Oriental
Ave, 10500
Tel *0-2659-9000*
Said to be Asia's finest French
restaurant, Le Normandie offers
a charming river-view setting,
impeccable service, and an
exceptional wine list. Choose
from a wide selection of superb
dishes on the à la carte menu.
Highlights include breast of
Bresse pigeon with *foie gras*.

Vertigo Grill and Moon Bar ⓦⓦⓦ
International   Map 8 D4
21/100 South Sathorn Rd, 10120
Tel *0-2679-1200*
A fabulous open-air restaurant
on the 61st floor of the Banyan
Tree Hotel. Breathtaking views,
fantastic cocktails, and great
barbecue food. Specialties
include red mullet *en papillote*
with thyme, and grilled scallops
with coriander butter. Go at
sunset for the very best views.

Thon Buri

DK Choice

Supatra River House   ⓦⓦ
Thai   Map 1 B4
266 Soi Wat Rakhang, Arun
Amarin Rd, 10700
Tel *0-2411-0305*
ⓦ supatrariverhouse.com
With superb views of the
Grand Palace and Wat Arun,
this riverside venue offers an
evening to remember. Excellent
Thai food and wonderful dance
performances. Guests are picked
up by boat from Maharaj Pier in
the Old City.

Prime
Steak house   ⓦⓦⓦ
Map 6 F3
Millenium Hilton, 123
Charoennakorn Rd, 10600
Tel *0-2442-2000*
Considered one of the city's
best steak houses, Prime offers
top-quality imported beef, as
well as seafood and side dishes.
Relaxing contemporary
atmosphere, with great views
of the river.

Trader Vic's
Asian   ⓦⓦⓦ
Anantara Riverside Resort & Spa,
257 Charoennakorn Rd, 10700
Tel *0-2476-0022*   **Closed** *Mon*
Promises a unique experience,
with Polynesian decor, fine food
from across Asia, and delicious
cocktails on the riverside deck.
Try the spectacular Sunday
Mai Tai jazz brunch, a fabulous
spread of international
gourmet cuisine.

Farther Afield

Cedar
Lebanese   ⓦⓦ
Sukumvit Rd, Soi 49/9,10110
Tel *0-2119-7206*
Popular with Bangkok's expat
community, Cedar is known for
its delicious Middle Eastern fare.
Choose from over 30 types of the
famous meze appetizers, as well
as hearty main courses and great
desserts. Knowledgeable and
friendly service.

Taling Pling
Thai   ⓦⓦ
25 Sukhumvit Soi 34, 10110
Tel *0-2258-5308-9*
In a converted family home
with a bright contemporary
design. Serves tasty Thai food at
reasonable prices. Since many
of the dishes are unusual, the
picture menu, with clear
descriptions, is useful.

The elegant dining room at Le Normandie

Tasty morsels on offer at Tony's Place

South Central Plains

AYUTTHAYA: Bann Kun Pra Ⓑ
Thai
48 U Thong Rd, 13000
Tel *0-3524-1978*
One of Ayutthaya's most popular guesthouses also has a riverside restaurant that serves good Thai food, the specialty being seafood.

AYUTTHAYA: Chainam Ⓑ
Thai/Western
36/2 U Thong Rd, 13000
Tel *0-3525-2013*
Occupying an attractive spot on the west bank of the Pasak River, this family-run restaurant serves both Thai and Western dishes, including a wide range of breakfast options.

AYUTTHAYA: Malakor Ⓑ
Thai/Western
Chikun Rd, 13000
Tel *0-8171-2577-9*
Simple restaurant right next to Wat Ratchaburana, serving tasty Thai food and a few Western dishes like burgers. Good choice for an evening meal, with great views of the illuminated ruins.

AYUTTHAYA: Pae Krung Kao Ⓑ
Thai/Chinese
4 Moo 2, U Thong Rd, 13000
Tel *0-3524-1555*
This floating restaurant is popular with tourists for its authentic Thai and Chinese dishes. Try catfish salad and the specialty – river prawns. Lovely terrace with views of the Pa Sak river.

AYUTTHAYA: Street Lamp Ⓑ
Thai/Western
Naresuan Rd Soi 2, 13000
Tel *09-2902-9100*
With live music most evenings, this place is better known as a popular nightlife venue, but it does serve delicious Thai and international dishes. Pleasant outdoor seating.

AYUTTHAYA: Tony's Place Ⓑ
Thai/Western
Naresuan Soi 2, 13000
Tel *0-3525-2578*
Part of a popular guesthouse, this place serves a basic but reliable range of Thai and Western classic dishes. The bar becomes very busy later in the evening, with live music most nights.

AYUTTHAYA: California Steak House ⒷⒷ
Western
Kantary Hotel, 168 Moo 1, Rojana Rd, 13000
Tel *0-3533-7177*
Great choice for those longing to enjoy a good steak in a relaxing environment. Only imported meats are used. Several seafood options are also available.

DK Choice

KANCHANABURI: Blue Rice Restaurant by Apple & Noi Ⓑ
Thai
153/4 Moo 4, Thamakham, 71000
Tel *0-3451-2017*
This is a very popular restaurant with an attached guesthouse. The signature dish is *massaman* curry, made with coconut milk and cashews. Extensive menu with excellent set dinner options. The chefs also offer cookery classes for around 1500 *baht* a day. Be prepared to wait a while as all dishes are made to order.

KANCHANABURI: Nita's Raft House Ⓑ
Thai
271/1 Pak Praek Rd, 71000
Tel *0-3451-4521*
Relax on the bamboo deck and enjoy outstanding home-style cooking. Try the fiery *tom yam kung* or Japanese *okonomiyaki* (rich savoury pancakes). Friendly, English-speaking staff.

KANCHANABURI: Schluck Ⓑ
Thai/Western
20/1 Mae Nam Kwae Rd, 71000
Tel *0-3462-4599*
A fantastic place for those craving Western comfort foods such as pasta or steak, though they also have an extensive menu of Thai dishes and delicious desserts.

KANCHANABURI: Peppers ⒷⒷ
Thai/Western
443 Mae Nam Kwae Rd, 71000
Tel *0-3452-1584*
Located in the luxury U Inchantree Resort, this restaurant offers a modern take on traditional Thai cuisine. Dine on the stunning riverside terrace or in the cool, air-conditioned interior.

LOP BURI: Maad Mee Ⓑ
Thai
8/18 Phra Sri Mahosote Rd, Talay Chup Sorn, 15000
Tel *0-3641-2883*
Offering great food, this simple place is popular with locals and visitors. Try the *gaeng khua* with pandan-leaf-wrapped meatballs.

North Central Plains

MAE SOT: Bai Fern Ⓑ
Thai/Western
660/2 Intharakiri Rd, 63110
Tel *0-5553-3343*
Double-fronted restaurant with a fantastic selection of Thai, Burmese, Mexican, and Italian dishes. Uses local ingredients like mushrooms and ferns.

MAE SOT: Krua Canadian Ⓑ
Thai/Western
3 Sri Phanit Rd, 63110
Tel *0-5553-4659*
Simple but well-run café, popular among local workers for its generous breakfasts and good coffee.

DK Choice

MAE SOT: Khaomao-Khaofang Restaurant ⒷⒷ
Thai
382 Moo 9, Mae Sot–Mae Ramat Rd, 63110
Tel *0-5553-2483*
Ⓦ khaomaokhaofang.com
Delightful restaurant designed and owned by a botanist. Waterfalls, palms, and ferns combine to create a magical, romantic atmosphere. The food is also top-notch, with authentic Thai dishes and delicious desserts. Super-attentive staff.

An array of options at Kalare Night Bazaar

PHITSANULOK: Ban Mai ฿
Thai
93/30 U Thong Rd, 65000
Tel *0-5525-8548*
Tucked away in Phitsanulok's backstreets, this place offers a short menu of very good Thai dishes. Do not miss the *yam takrai* (lemongrass salad). A pleasant setting with smartly laid tables.

PHITSANULOK: Amore ฿฿
Italian/Thai
Yodia Heritage Hotel, 89/1 Puttabucha Rd, 65000
Tel *0-5521-4677*
Romantic setting for a tasty Italian meal, though there are also a few token Thai dishes on offer. Sleek decor inside, and a nice outdoor seating area.

SUKHOTHAI: Dharma Cafe ฿
Thai/French
83 Jarodvithi Thong Rd, 64000
Tel *09-5686-4354*
This pleasant bistro is great for an evening out. The European owner and his Thai family offer home-cooked Thai food and a variety of Western dishes, mainly French but often other specials.

SUKHOTHAI: May Klang Kroong ฿
Thai
139 Charodvithitong Rd, 64000
Tel *0-5562-1882*
Possibly the best place to sample Sukhothai noodles, a dish made of sweet rice noodles, pork rind, peanuts, and chicken. There is no English signage, so look out for the old bicycle parked in front.

SUKHOTHAI: Pai Sukhothai Cafe ฿
Thai/Western
3 Prawet Nakhon, 64000
Tel *0-0898-8848*
A stylish spot that serves much more than coffee. Choose from Thai mains, pasta dishes, salads, and sandwiches. Comfortable seating and a relaxed atmosphere.

SUKHOTHAI: Poo ฿
Thai/Western
24/3 Charodvithitong Rd, 64000
Tel *09-3197-4070*
This classic travelers' café, on the main road in the new town, is well-regarded for its range of delicious Thai and international food, along with expensive Belgian beer.

SUKHOTHAI: Dream Café ฿฿
Thai
88/1 Singhawat Rd, 64000
Tel *0-5561-2081*
The clutter of period furniture and old-world ornaments may make Dream Café look more like an antique shop than a restaurant, but the food and service are excellent.

SUKHOTHAI: Ruean Thai Restaurant & Bar ฿฿
Thai
181/20 Soi Pracharummit, 64000
Tel *0-5561-2444*
In the hotel of the same name, near the town center, this place offers excellent Thai standards, as well as imaginative Thai/Western fusion dishes. Indoor and outdoor dining. Nice Thai-style desserts.

TAK: Rimping Terrace ฿
Thai/Western
Viang Tak Riverside Hotel, 236 Chompol Rd, 63000
Tel *0-5551-2507*
Tuck into spicy Thai dishes or Western food while being serenaded by singers and enjoying good riverside views. Friendly and efficient service.

UMPHANG: Phu Doi ฿
Thai
294 Moo 1 Prawet Wan Rd, 63170
Tel *0-5556-1049*
There are limited dining options in tiny Umphang, but this place turns out decent Thai food such as the spicy *tom yam kung* and delicious curries. There are also a good range of refreshing beers.

Northwest Heartland

CHIANG MAI: Art Café ฿
Thai/Western
291 Tha Pae Rd, 50100
Tel *0-5320-6365*
Occupying a prime spot opposite Tha Phae Gate, this is a good place for people-watching through the large plate-glass windows. The wide-ranging and eclectic menu offers Thai, Italian, and Mexican dishes.

CHIANG MAI: Dada Kafe ฿
Thai/Western
20/1 Ratchamanka Rd, 50200
Tel *0-5344-9718*
Dada Kafe is a great option for health-conscious diners, with a range of nutritious salads. Great central spot for breakfast, with a wide selection of international newspapers and magazines.

CHIANG MAI: Hin Lay ฿
Indian
8/1 Nawatket Rd, 50000
Tel *0-5324-2621*
Serves superb and flavorful Indian curries, ranging from explosive *vindaloo* to mild *korma*. Pleasant garden setting. It is a bit tricky to find, but worth the effort.

CHIANG MAI: Huen Phen ฿
Thai
112 Ratchamanka Rd, 50200
Tel *0-5327-7103*
Huen Phen is known for its excellent lunchtime *khao soi* (noodles in curry broth) and other tasty Northern Thai dishes. Lunch is served in a simple dining space out front, while dinner is in the antique-laden house next door.

CHIANG MAI: Kalare Night Bazaar Food Court ฿
Thai
Chang Klan Rd, 50100
Opposite the main Night Bazaar building behind the streetside shops, this bustling food court is a great pit stop for refreshments after shopping. Diners can enjoy the nightly traditional dance performance as they eat.

CHIANG MAI: New Lamduan Faham Khao Soi ฿
Regional
352/22 Charoenrat Rd, 50000
Tel *0-5324-3519*
One of the best places to sample Chiang Mai's famous lunchtime dish, *khao soi*. They also have a wide variety of Northern Thai curries and excellent satay. Closes promptly at 4pm.

Key to Price Guide *see page 418*

CHIANG MAI: Ratana's Kitchen ®
Thai/Western
320-322 Tha Pae Rd, 50300
Tel *0-5387-4173*
This cozy café offers a huge menu of Thai and Western favorites at cheap prices. Located on the city's main street, it is perfect for people-watching, especially from the outdoor terrace upstairs.

CHIANG MAI: Chez Marco ®®
Mediterranean
15/7 Loy Kroh Rd, 50100
Tel *0-5320-7032*   **Closed** *Sun*
A warm, friendly place serving excellent Italian and French food. Try rainbow trout with almond butter sauce and duck steak with apple sauce. There is also a kids' menu. Open evenings only.

CHIANG MAI: Dash Teak House ®®
Thai/Western
38/2 Moonmuang Rd, 50200
Tel *0-5327-9230*
Delicious Thai and Western dishes served in an attractive two-story teakwood house. Ask for a table outdoors, either on the terrace or in the garden. Try the sea bass steamed with lime or stir-fried eggplant in chili sauce.

CHIANG MAI: Ginger & Kafe ®®
Thai/Western
199 Moonmuang Rd, 50200
Tel *0-5341-9011*
A stylish restaurant adjoining a quirky gift shop. Choose from a short but excellent menu of Thai and Western dishes, such as soft-shell crab with black pepper and lamb kebabs with roasted pepper.

CHIANG MAI: Pulcinella da Stefano ®®
Italian
2/1–2 Chang Moi Kao Rd, 50300
Tel *0-5387-4189*
This is a popular place right near Tha Phae Gate offering

northern Italian dishes in a relaxed environment. Generous portions, daily specials, great service, and an extensive wine list. Book ahead.

CHIANG MAI: Rachamankha ®®
Thai/Fusion
6 Rachamankha Soi 9, 50200
Tel *0-5390-4111*
This is one of the city's classiest restaurants, located in the elegant Rachamankha Hotel. Dine in the lovely courtyard and choose from a range of superb Thai, Shan, and Burmese dishes.

CHIANG MAI: Riverside ®®
Thai/Western
9–11 Charoenrat Rd, 50000
Tel *0-5324-3239*
Something of a Chiang Mai institution, Riverside is a one-stop eating, drinking, and entertainment venue. For those willing to splurge, reserve a spot on the dinner cruise.

DK Choice

CHIANG MAI: Ruen Tamarind ®®
Thai/Western
Tamarind Village, 50/1 Ratchadamnoen Rd, 50200
Tel *0-5341-8896*
This elegant restaurant is part of the Tamarind Village hotel and looks out onto the swimming pool. Though there are a few Western dishes on the menu, it is the exquisitely prepared Thai options that are the draw here: try the tamarind-glazed pork spare ribs or the spiced mushroom tempura.

CHIANG MAI: Whole Earth ®®
Thai/Indian
88 Sridonchai Rd, 50100
Tel *0-5328-2463*
With tables inside an elegant dining room and on the terrace

of an attractive traditional house, this is a good choice for a dinner after shopping in the nearby Night Bazaar. The menu also has several vegetarian options.

CHIANG MAI: Fujian ®®®
Chinese
Mandarin Oriental Dhara Dhevi Resort, 51/4 Moo 1, Chiang Mai–Sankamphaeng Rd, 50000
Tel *0-5388-8888*
Atmospheric 1930s-style Chinese restaurant famed for its dim sum lunches. The evening menu is classic Chinese with a degustation option, complemented by an excellent wine list.

CHIANG MAI: Latest Recipe ®®®
International
108 Chang Klan Rd, 50100
Tel *0-5325-3666*
Part of Le Meridien hotel, this buffet serves everything from green curry to steaks. Food is beautifully presented and chefs are always on hand to advise. Chic modern decor.

CHIANG MAI: Le Coq d'Or ®®®
French
11 Koh Klang Rd, Nong Hoi, 50000
Tel *0-5314-1555*
Formal French restaurant housed in a Colonial-style building. The menu includes *foie gras*, caviar, and lobster, and a comprehensive wine list. Live classical music some evenings.

CHIANG MAI: Moxie ®®®
Thai/Western
Dusit D2 Hotel, 100 Changklan Rd, 50100
Tel *0-5399-9999*
This chic hotel restaurant offers a range of Thai and Western dishes. Try the spaghetti with Chiang Mai sausage, followed by *crème brûlée*.

The 1930s-inspired decor at Chinese restaurant Fujian, renowned for its dim sum

For more information on types of restaurants *see pp412–13*

CHIANG MAI: Ping Nakara ⓑⓑⓑ
Thai/International
135/9 Charoenprathet Rd, 50100
Tel *0-5325-2999*
A hotel restaurant serving Thai
cuisine as well as a delightful
afternoon tea of sandwiches
and Thai desserts. Guests at the
hotel can book a special chef's
tasting menu.

DK Choice

**CHIANG MAI:
Sala Mae Rim** ⓑⓑⓑ
Thai
*Four Seasons Resort, Mae Rim–
Samoeng Old Rd, 50180*
Tel *0-5329-8181*
Although on the outskirts of
town, Sala Mae Rim is worth
traveling to for sublime Thai
cuisine in an idyllic setting, with
spectacular views of rice paddy
fields. Try the *gaeng pah* (Thai
jungle curry) and *poo nim
kapraow grob* (crispy soft-shell
crab with holy basil). Very good
service and wine list.

**CHIANG MAI: Tengoku De
Cuisine** ⓑⓑⓑ
Japanese
Tambon Tha Sala, 50000
Tel *0-5385-1133*
Across the street from the Dhara
Dhevi Hotel, Tengoku serves the
best Japanese in Chiang Mai,
including sashimi and sushi.
Choose from the à la carte or great-
value buffet menu.

LAMPANG: Aroy One Baht ⓑ
Thai
Tipchang Rd, 52000
Tel *08-7900-9444*
This bustling place is always
packed with locals and serves
authentic Thai cuisine. The food
is delicious and excellent value.

LAMPANG: Riverside ⓑ
Thai/International
328 Tipchang Rd, 52000
Tel *0-5422-1861*
Long-standing eatery on the
banks of the Wang River, with
live bands entertaining in the
evening. Excellent *tom yam
khung* and wood-fired pizzas.

LAMPANG: Wienglakor Hotel ⓑ
Thai/International
138/35 Phaholyothin Rd, 52000
Tel *0-5431-6430-5*
The restaurant at Wienglakor
Hotel is one of the best in
Lampang. The relaxing
ambience, serene decor,
reliable food quality, and polite
service make for a delightful
dining experience.

LAMPHUN: Lamphun Ice ⓑ
Thai/Western
6 Chaimongkol Rd, 51000
Tel *0-5351-1452*
Decked out like a 1950s American
diner, this is a great place to relax
after visiting Wat Haripunchai,
Lamphun's main attraction.
The varied menu includes curries,
ice creams, and hot dogs.

MAE HONG SON: Kai Mook ⓑ
Thai/Chinese
23 Udom Chao Nithet Rd, 58000
Tel *0-5361-2092*
Centrally located restaurant
serving a huge range of dishes,
including local specialties like
wild boar with red curry. There
are also daily specials.

**MAE HONG SON:
Salween River** ⓑ
Thai/Western/Burmese
23 Pradit Jongkham, 58000
Tel *0-5361-3421*
This welcoming spot beside
Jongkham Lake serves excellent
Western breakfasts along with
Thai and Shan dishes. Some great
healthy options too; try the
delicious green-tea salad.

**MAE HONG SON:
Golden Teak** ⓑⓑ
Thai/Western/Chinese
*Imperial Hotel, 149 Moo 8,
Pang Moo, 58000*
Tel *0-5368-4444-9*
A short ride away from the
town center, Golden Teak is
worth the trip for its delectable
Thai, Chinese, and Western
dishes. Lovely views from the
outside terrace.

MAE SARIANG: Inthira ⓑ
Thai
Wiang Mai Rd, 58110
Tel *0-5368-1529*
This no-frills place, very popular
with locals on Mae Sariang's main
road, serves authentic Thai soups,
stir-fries, and curries. Try the
Salween river fish.

PAI: Baan Benjarong ⓑ
Thai
Rangsiyanon Rd, 58130
Tel *0-5369-8010*
There may nothing fancy about
the decor here, but the big
attraction is the well-prepared
Thai food. Go for the fiery *tom
yam kung* or banana flower salad.

PAI: Boomelicious ⓑ
Western
Soi 1 Corner Plaza, 58130
Tel *08-6329-3014*
This hip café is typical of
eateries in trendy Pai, and is a
great place to linger over a lazy

brunch. Choose from all-day
breakfasts, burgers, soups,
and salads.

PAI: Burger House ⓑ
American
Rangsiyanon Rd, 58130
Tel *0-5369-9093* **Closed** *Mon*
A wide range of juicy burgers
made using prime imported
meats. Try the Mexican burger
with chili and salsa, or the bacon
cheeseburger. There are also
baguettes and other main dishes
on the menu.

PAI: Na's Kitchen ⓑ
Thai
Ratchadamrong Rd, 58130
Tel *08-1387-0234*
The owner Na does everything
here – takes orders, cooks, clears
tables, and washes dishes. Things
might take a while, but the
delicious food is worth the wait.

Far North

CHIANG KHONG: Fai Nguen ⓑ
Thai/Western
*Nam Khong Riverside Hotel,
Sai Klang Rd, 57140*
Tel *0-5379-1796*
Perhaps the best of the many
resort restaurants in Chiang
Khong. The extensive menu
covers Thai and international
favourites. Karaoke starts every
night at 8pm.

**CHIANG RAI: Baan Chivit Mai
Bakery** ⓑ
Thai/Western
172 Thanon Prasop Sook, 57000
Tel *0-5371-2357*
This Scandinavian-run bakery is
located right by the bus station
and sells a delicious range of
cakes and pastries. All profits go
to support local disadvantaged
young people and social projects.

Alfresco dining at Sala Mae Rim

CHIANG RAI:
Cabbages & Condoms   Ⓑ
Thai
620/25 Thanalai Rd, 57000
Tel *0-5371-9167*
Run by the Population &
Community Development
Association (PDA), this place serves
yummy Thai food, including
some local specialties. Profits go
to promote safe sex and other
social development programs.

CHIANG RAI: Night Market   Ⓑ
Thai/International
Phaholyothin Rd, 57000
The Night Market is Chiang Rai's
biggest after-dark attraction, and
there are plenty of alfresco eating
options here. Shop for souvenirs,
then sit down for spicy soups,
noodles, sushi, or pizza.

CHIANG RAI: Phu Lae   Ⓑ
Thai
673/1 Thanalai Rd, 57000
Very popular among locals for its
Northern Thai dishes such as
gaeng haeng lae (pork curry with
ginger) and *sai oua* (spicy sausage).
Packed on Saturdays when the
Walking Street Market is outside.

DK Choice

CHIANG RAI: Salungkham   Ⓑ
Thai
834/3 Phaholyothin Rd, 57000
Tel *0-5371-7192*
This excellent place may be a
bit tricky to spot on the busy
main road as there is no English
signage. Located opposite the
PT petrol station, it boasts
wonderful Thai cuisine, including
heart of palm curry with spare
ribs and banana flower salad
with prawns. Dine in the
restaurant's relaxing interior or
in the pretty garden.

CHIANG RAI: Aye's   ⒷⒷ
Thai/Western
869/170 Phaholyothin Rd, 57000
Tel *0-5375-2534*
Stylish place with bamboo decor,
and generous portions of Thai
and international food. On the
downside, prices are steep and
service can be slow.

CHIANG RAI: Chinatown   ⒷⒷ
Chinese
*Dusit Island Resort, 1129 Kraisorasit Rd,
57000*
Tel *0-5360-7999*
Indulge in some lunchtime dim
sum or an evening feast of
Cantonese dishes at this elegant
restaurant in Dusit Island
Resort. The perfect place for a
special occasion.

Riverside seating area at Nan Steak House

CHIANG RAI: Yunnan   ⒷⒷ
Yunnanese
211/5 Khwae Wai Rd, 57000
Tel *0-5371-3263*
This place serves Thai staples
such as *tom yam kung*, but also
many Yunnanese specialities
such as stewed pork leg with
preserved vegetables, and
Kunming-style fried milk.

CHIANG SAEN: Sriwan   Ⓑ
Thai
150 Moo 1, Tambon Wiang, 57150
Tel *0-5378-4025*
One of the best restaurants in
Sop Ruak, a village just outside
Chiang Saen. Several set menus
to choose from and superb views
over three countries – Thailand,
Myanmar and Laos – from an
open-sided pavilion.

CHIANG SAEN: Baan Dahlia   ⒷⒷⒷ
Italian/Mediterranean
*Anantara Golden Triangle Resort,
229 Moo 1, 57150*
Tel *0-5378-4084*
Head here for a special treat at
the Golden Triangle. Enjoy the
view over the Mekong River
while sampling dishes such
as tiger prawns with pesto and
pine nuts, and sipping a glass
of wine.

MAE SAI: Kik Kok   Ⓑ
Thai
Phaholyothin Rd, 57130
No-frills eatery south of the
bridge serving a huge range of
traditional Thai dishes. There is a
helpful English picture menu to
choose from, and the dishes are
reliably tasty.

MAE SAI: Rabiang Kaew   Ⓑ
Thai
356/1 Phaholyothin Rd, 57130
Tel *0-5373-1172*
On an atmospheric terrace just
near the bridge to Myanmar, this
restaurant serves Thai dishes and a
few international ones. Antiques
in the dining room create a sense
of rustic charm. Closes early.

MAE SALONG: Khum Nai
Phol Resort   Ⓑ
Thai/Chinese
58 Moo 1, Doi Mae Salong, 57110
Tel *0-5376-5000-4*
Located in a large, open-sided,
wooden building by the evening
market, this place serves an
extensive range of Thai and
Chinese dishes along with a
few local specialties.

MAE SALONG:
Mae Salong Villa   Ⓑ
Yunnanese
5 Moo 1, Maesalongnok, 57110
Tel *0-5376-5114-5*
Specializes in dishes such as roast
pork with a spicy gravy and black
chicken with herb soup. As a
bonus, there are superb views
across the hilly landscape from
the terrace.

NAN: Poom Sam   Ⓑ
Thai/Chinese
Anantaworarichides Rd, 55000
Tel *0-5477-2100*
This no-frills place may look like
nothing special, but it rustles
up some delicious, good value
dishes. Try the *massaman*
curry or the eggplant with
minced pork.

NAN: Tanaya Kitchen   Ⓑ
Thai/Vegetarian
Anantaworarichides Rd, 55000
Tel *0-5471-0930*   **Closed** *Sun*
Right next to Poom Sam, this
small restaurant is easy to miss,
but is worth hunting down for
its varied vegetarian menu. It's a
popular place, so arrive early to
avoid a wait.

NAN: Nan Steak House   ⒷⒷ
Western
15/7 Sumonthevaraj Rd, 55000
Tel *08-1982-8500*
With a fantastic view of the
river, this is a great spot to
grab some Western food.
Steaks of all kinds, including
ostrich, as well as pizza
and sandwiches.

For more information on types of restaurants *see pp412–13*

The elegant dining room at Pavilion Café

PHRAE: Gingerbread House Gallery and Café ⓑ
Thai
94/1 Chareon Muang Rd, 54000
Tel *0-5452-3671*
A restaurant that is both homely and welcoming. Tuck into tasty noodles in broth, before browsing the gift shop and gallery upstairs.

PHRAE: Night Market ⓑ
Thai
Charoen Muang Rd, 54000
There are not many tourist-friendly eateries in Phrae, so the best bet for a meal is at the Night Market, where you can find simple but good noodles or rice dishes.

PHRAE: Pan Jai ⓑ
Thai
2 Weera Rd, 54000
Tel *0-5462-0727*
On a quiet backstreet in the old town, this is a pleasant restaurant surrounded by a lush garden. The specialty is *khanom jeen* – spicy rice noodles.

Khorat Plateau

BURIRAM: Bamboo Bar & Restaurant ⓑ
Thai/Western
14/13 Romburi Rd, 31000
Tel *0-4462-5577*
A favorite among Buriram's expat community, this place serves steaks, schnitzels, and pasta, as well as Thai staples. As the name suggests, the decor is predominantly bamboo-themed.

KHON KAEN: Didine ⓑ
Thai/International
19/21 Prachasamran Rd, 40000
Tel *08-0011-0180*
Welcoming place serving some excellent European food and a good range of Thai dishes. Try the chicken fillet with tarragon

sauce or the mixed grill. A great selection of Belgian and American craft beers. Opens at 5pm.

KHON KAEN: Mama Big ⓑ
Thai/Western/Fusion
140/456 Kanlapaphruek Rd, 40000
Tel *0-4324-5789*
Smart place near the university serving a wide choice of Thai and international cuisine, including several fusion dishes. Save room for the mouthwatering desserts.

DK Choice

KHON KAEN: Bua Luang ⓑⓑ
Thai/Chinese
Rop Bueng Kaen Nakhon Rd, 40000
Tel *0-4322-2504*
Perched on the north shore of a scenic lake with a terrace jutting out over the water, this fancy restaurant is where locals usually take guests for a first-class meal. Seafood is the specialty here, so go for a fish dish with the one of the many sauces on offer.

KHON KAEN: Pavilion Café ⓑⓑ
Thai/International
Pullman Khon Kaen Raja Orchid Hotel, 9/9 Prachasamran Rd, 40000
Tel *0-4332-2155*
Located in the lobby of the Pullman Raja Orchid Hotel, the Pavilion Café serves up a scrumptious, if expensive, buffet of Thai and Western dishes for lunch and dinner.

KHON KAEN: Pomodoro ⓑⓑ
Italian
348/16 Prachasamran Rd, 40000
Tel *0-4327-0464*
Centrally located Italian eatery serving pizzas, ravioli, and meatballs from 4pm. Fantastic desserts include a top-notch tiramisu. Helpful staff and great service.

KHORAT: Amphawa ⓑ
Thai/Western
264 Yommarat Rd, Nakhon Ratchasima, 30000
Tel *0-4400-7488*
This lively, casual place opens at 4pm. It has a nice garden area, and bands play in the evening, mainly Thai rock. Thai food is well prepared and tasty, and there are also standard Western favorites.

KHORAT: Seaw Seaw Restaurant ⓑ
Chinese
77 Bua Rong Rd, Nakhon Ratchasima, 30000
Tel *0-4424-3180*
Family-run restaurant serving up traditional Chinese food, including Peking duck and fish and crab dishes.

KHORAT: Veterans of Foreign Wars Café ⓑ
American
Pho Klang Rd, 30000
Tel *0-4425-3432* **Closed** Mon
This centrally located café next to the Siri Hotel is a remnant of the US air base that was here during the Vietnam War. Western breakfasts and burgers feature on the menu.

KHORAT: Chez Andy ⓑⓑ
European
5–7 Manat Rd, 30000
Tel *0-4428-9556*
Probably Khorat's classiest restaurant, Chez Andy is run by a Swiss chef, and offers imported steaks and oysters along with a handful of Thai dishes.

PHIMAI: Phimai Inn Hotel ⓑ
Thai/Western
33/1 Bypass Rd, 30110
Tel *0-4428-7228*
Though a little away from the town center, this is one of the best place for refreshments before or after a visit to the Khmer ruins at Phimai.

ROI ET: White Elephant ⓑ
German/Thai
59/2 Robmuang Rd, 45000
Tel *0-4351-4778*
Located beside the old moat around Roi Et, this German-run restaurant offers schnitzels, sauerkraut, and sausages, plus well-prepared Thai food. Imported beers and a pool table.

SURIN: Mae Phim Pla Phao ⓑ
Thai
555 Tessaban Rd 1, 32000
Tel *08-1977-0096*
Customers come to this renowned, simple eatery for its excellent barbecued fish, served

with dipping sauces and other Central Thai favorites. Issan dishes such as *laab* and *somtam* also feature on the menu.

SURIN: Starbeam Restaurant ⓑ
Western
32/6 Soi Saboran 2, 32000
Tel 08-6877-4447
This clean place with its simple decor offers a very wide variety of Western cuisine, such as burgers, Mexican food, and pizzas. Good salads and vegetarian dishes, too.

UDON THANI: Rabiang Patchanee ⓑ
Thai/Issan
53 Suphakit Janya Rd, 41000
Tel 0-4224-4015
A serene oasis in a busy city, this restaurant occupies an excellent spot overlooking the Nong Prajak Lake. Enjoy classic cuisine and some less commonly found Issan dishes.

Mekong River Valley

CHIANG KHAN: Rabiang Kong ⓑ
Thai
Chai Khong Rd, 42110
Located directly on the river, Rabiang Kong offers a good variety of affordable Thai dishes, including fresh Mekong fish. The venue is popular with locals and visitors alike.

LOEI: Loei Danang ⓑ
Thai/Vietnamese
22/60 Chumsai Rd, 42000
Tel 0-4283-0413
This lively place serves both Thai and Vietnamese dishes in a clean, cool environment. There is a helpful picture menu to choose from and musicians sometimes perform in the evenings.

LOEI: Night Market ⓑ
Thai
Chumsai Rd, 42000
As in many rural, non-tourist Thai towns where restaurants don't have English menus, the best bet for dinner is to stroll through Loei's Night Market and point at something that appeals.

MUKDAHAN: Night Market ⓑ
Issan/Vietnamese
Song Nang Sathit Rd, 49000
This bustling evening market offers classic Issan dishes such as *kai yang* (grilled chicken) and *som tam*, as well as crunchy bugs and tasty spring rolls.

MUKDAHAN: The Waterfront ⓑ
Thai/Western
103/4 Samran Chai Khong Rd, 49000
Tel 0-4263-2577
Located about 1 km (0.5 mile) south of the town center, Riverside serves up well-prepared river fish and other regional and Western dishes. Breezy terrace with views across to Laos.

MUKDAHAN: Wine Wild Why? ⓑ
Thai
11 Samran Chai Khong Rd, 49000
Tel 0-4263-3122
The unusual name of this riverside restaurant reflects its distinctive character, though unfortunately the choice of wines is limited. Excellent Thai dishes served in an atmospheric teakwood house.

NAKHON PHANOM: Satang ⓑ
Thai
766 Sunthorn Wichit Rd, 48000
Perhaps the best of the several riverside restaurants in Nakhon Phanom, despite there being no English menu. Go for the *hor mok talay*, a spicy seafood soufflé steamed in a banana leaf.

NAKHON PHANOM: Chomkong ⓑⓑ
Thai/Western/Chinese
527 Sunthorn Wichit Rd, 48000
Tel 0-4251-3564
Located at the Viewkong Hotel, Chomkong serves Thai, Chinese, and Western cuisine. Try a classic Thai dish such as *gaeng kiaw waan*, a sweet green curry.

NONG KHAI: Daeng Namnuang ⓑ
Vietnamese
526 Rimkhong Rd, 43000
Tel 0-4246-0647
The big Vietnamese community in Northeast Thailand is reflected in the restaurants in the region. This riverside spot is especially popular among locals for its fresh spring rolls.

NONG KHAI: DD Phochana ⓑ
Thai/Chinese
1155/9 Prajak Silipakorn Rd, 43000
Tel 0-4241-1548
The drab decor of this restaurant belies the outstanding food on offer. The extensive menu includes excellent *tort man pla* (fish cakes).

NONG KHAI: Mut Mee Guest House ⓑ
Thai/International
1111/4 Kaew Worawut Rd, 43000
Tel 0-4246-0717
Mut Mee Guest House serves up a range of delicious Western and Thai dishes, including fresh apple pie. Dine in the shady riverside garden or on their boat, *Nagarina*.

THAT PHANOM: That Phanom Phochana ⓑ
Thai/Issan
31 Phanom Phanarak Rd, 48110
Tel 0-4254-1189
This no-frills place turns out consistently good Thai dishes such as *phad thai* with beansprouts and egg, as well as some fiery Issan dishes.

UBON RATCHATHANI: Krua Suanpla ⓑ
Thai/Fusion
50 Soi Chayangkul 12, Chayangkul Rd, 34000
Tel 0-4531-5432
Good Thai, Chinese, and other Asian flavors are to be had here, delivered in attractive surroundings. The restaurant is frequented by locals, which is always a good sign.

UBON RATCHATHANI: Jumpa-Hom ⓑⓑ
Thai
49/3 Phichitrungsan Rd, 34000
Tel 0-4526-0398
This sophisticated place would not look out of place in Bangkok, so is quite a surprise to find it in

The riverside garden at Mut Mee Guest House

For more information on types of restaurants *see pp412–13*

such a remote town. Choose from a great menu that includes both common and not-so-common Thai dishes.

DK Choice

UBON RATCHATHANI:
Pratheung Thong   ⓑⓑ
Thai/International
Tohsang City Hotel, 251
Phalochai Rd, 34000
Tel *0-4524-5531*
Pratheung Thong might be pricier than other restaurants in the area, but is well worth it. With subdued lighting, smartly dressed and attentive wait staff, a menu of tempting Thai and international dishes, and songstresses serenading you long into the evening, this place guarantees a meal to remember.

The terrace at Naga restaurant

Eastern Seaboard

CHANTHABURI:
Chanthorn Pochana   ⓑⓑ
Thai
102/5–8 Benchamarachathutit Rd,
22000
Tel *0-3931-2339*
Centrally located restaurant with a tempting variety of curries, spicy salads, and delicious stir-fries on the extensive menu. Try the local specialty *sen mi phad pu* – a bowl of egg noodles topped with crab meat.

CHANTHABURI: Tamajun   ⓑⓑ
Thai
Sukhaphiban Rd, Chantaboon
District, 22000
Acoustic guitar music enhances the atmosphere while looking over the river in old Chanthaburi. Thai favorites feature on the menu; try the *pla krapong phat prik thai dam* (sea bass) with peppercorns and vegetables.

KO CHANG: Chow Lay   ⓑ
Seafood
Pier, Baan Bang Bao, 23170
Chow Lay is one of several seafood restaurants located on the pier in this picturesque fishing village. Good food served in a rustic yet sophisticated atmosphere. Good range of cocktails.

KO CHANG: Oodie's Place   ⓑ
Thai/French
Hat Sai Khao, 23170
Tel *0-3955-1193*
A lively place where the owner and his band play classic rock covers after 10pm most evenings.

Good choice of food and drinks, both Thai and Western. Great spot to relax and sing along.

KO CHANG: Invito Al Cibo   ⓑⓑ
Italian
Hat Sai Khao, 23170
Tel *08-5275-7915*
Enjoy great views from this restaurant's hilltop perch above Hat Sai Khao. The food is excellent – from simple pizzas to fine dining choices that cover all the regional cuisines of Italy. Nice breezy outdoor terrace.

KO CHANG: Paddy's Palms   ⓑⓑ
Irish
Hat Sai Khao, 23170
Tel *0-3961-9085*
Ko Chang's original Irish pub, Paddy's pours out draught Guinness and Kilkenny to go with authentic Irish food such as beer-marinated beef and shepherd's pie. They also do an excellent Sunday roast. Lively atmosphere.

KO CHANG: Tonsai   ⓑⓑ
Thai/Western
Hat Klong Prao, 23170
Tel *08-9895-7229*
Excellent Thai and Western food, with many vegetarian choices. Try the stir-fried fish with ginger. Especially good for large groups.

KO SAMET: Naga   ⓑ
Thai/Western
Ao Hin Khok, 21160
Tel *0-3864-4035*
This restaurant is part of a bungalow complex and serves up simple but hearty fare using baked goods from the in-house bakery. Good choice of vegetarian curries and Thai stir-fries.

KO SAMET: Ao Prao Resort   ⓑⓑ
International
Ao Prao, 21160
Tel *0-3864-4100*
Chic and fancy by local standards, Ao Prao's restaurant serves beautifully prepared

seafood and other Thai dishes cooked to Western tastes. Located on the west side of island.

KO SAMET: Ploy Talay   ⓑⓑ
Seafood
Hat Sai Kaew, 21160
Tel *0-3864-4212*
Perhaps the best of the many restaurants that set up in the evening along Hat Sai Kaew. Sit comfortably on cushions surrounding a low, candle-lit table and enjoy fresh seafood. Prices fluctuate according to supply, so check beforehand.

KO SAMET: Red Ginger   ⓑⓑ
Thai/Western
Samet Village, 21160
Tel *08-4383-4917*
A great alternative to the standard Thai curries and seafood you find on all the beaches. Imaginative international cuisine in an intimate and quiet spot close to the ferry landing.

KO SAMET: Tub Tim Resort   ⓑⓑ
Seafood
Ao Tub Tim, 21160
Tel *0-3864-4025*
Tub Tim Resort's restaurant promises excellent seafood and nice views of the beach. Try the *hor mok talae*, a spicy soufflé with seafood steamed in a banana leaf.

PATTAYA: Food Wave   ⓑ
Thai
Royal Garden Plaza, Beach Rd, 20260
This food court offers a wide range of cuisines, including Thai, Vietnamese, Indian, Japanese, Turkish, and Western. Good views of the bay.

PATTAYA: Ali Baba   ⓑⓑ
Indian
1/13–14 Central Pattaya Rd, 20260
Tel *0-3836-1620*
Good range of high-quality North Indian cuisine, including *tandoori* and curry dishes, with several vegetarian options.

PATTAYA: Blue Olive ⓑⓑ
Mediterranean
62/147 Moo 12 Theprasit Soi 8, 20150
Tel *0-3841-6285*
Although located a little out of town, it is worth making the trip to Blue Olive for the excellent Italian, Spanish, and Greek cuisine, and for the restaurant's famous steaks. A relaxed atmosphere, away from the buzz of the city.

PATTAYA: Lobster Pot ⓑⓑ
Seafood
228 Beach Rd, 20150
Tel *0-3842-6083*
Perched on the fishing pier in South Pattaya, Lobster Pot is just a few steps from raucous Walking Street, but the serene setting makes it seem a world away. Try the lobster or grilled tiger prawns.

DK Choice

PATTAYA: Mantra ⓑⓑⓑ
International
Amari Orchid Resort, Beach Rd, 20150
Tel *0-3842-9591*
This restaurant embodies Pattaya: excessive, outrageous, and lots of fun. Seven open kitchens prepare scrumptious Japanese, Chinese, Indian, and Western dishes. With two levels of seating, including private alcoves with names like The Sultan's Table or Opium Den, this place is an event as much as a restaurant. Entertainment every night.

PATTAYA: The Grill House ⓑⓑⓑ
International
Rabbit Resort, Dongtan Beach, Jomtien, 20150
Tel *0-3825-1730*
A romantic restaurant in Jomtien, the Grill House serves a wide range of Thai and Western dishes,

The setting at Mantra, fitting in perfectly with Pattaya's outrageous spirit

from a massive buffet breakfast, to steaks and seafood skewers from the charcoal beach grill.

TRAT: Uncle Jong ⓑ
Thai
140 Soi Rak Muang, Wang Krajae District, 23000
Tel *08-6317-7975*
Great family-style Thai cooking is served here in a laid-back and comfortable atmosphere. Food is cooked to order – tell them if you don't like it too spicy.

TRAT: Sang Fah Restaurant ⓑⓑ
Thai/Chinese
157 Sukhumvit Rd, 23000
Tel *0-3951-1222*
Locals flock here for the best Thai and Chinese food in town. House specialty is *nam phik puu khai*, a dip made from crabs' eggs, but less obscure dishes are available.

Western Seaboard

CHA-AM: Harry's Pizzeria & Bar ⓑ
Thai/Western
933/32 Buriram Rd, Ban Kwai, 76120
Tel *08-4318-6413*
Run by an amiable Australian/Thai couple, Harry's specializes in pizza and pasta dishes but also offers excellent Thai food, using herbs fresh from their garden.

CHA-AM: Raya Restaurant ⓑⓑ
Thai/Western
264 Ruamjit Rd, 76120
Tel *0-3247-2641*
This swanky place near the beach has a wide variety on the menu. The Thai food is good, albeit somewhat Westernized. Excellent desserts, which you can eat at the tables on the beach.

CHA-AM: Siam Jasmine ⓑⓑ
Thai
Gaolai Rd, 76120
Tel *0-3247-0609*
Located in the hotel of the same name, right on the beach in Cha-am, the Siam Jasmine has developed a following for its excellent Thai offerings, especially seafood. Very clean place, with good service.

CHUMPHON: Papa Seafood ⓑⓑ
Seafood
Rot Fai Rd, Tha Tapao, 86160
Tel *0-7750-4504*
This indoor/outdoor seafood emporium lets diners choose from the tank and serves up delectable, fresh meals. Good service, attention to detail, and a vibrant atmosphere.

HUA HIN: Chao Lay Seafood ⓑ
Seafood
15 Naresdamri Rd, 77110
Tel *0-3251-3436*
This mainly outdoor restaurant on a wooden pier is a favorite with tourists and local families. Thai seafood specialties made using the freshest produce available. Very busy on weekends; go early to secure a table.

HUA HIN: Chatchai Market ⓑ
Seafood
Soi 72, b/w Phetkasem and Sa Song Rds, 77110
Tel
Definitely "street food", but of a much higher standard than some. Try the classic *phad thai* with fresh shrimps, *hoi thot* (fried oyster omelet), one of the many noodle soups, or hearty portions of fresh fish.

HUA HIN: I Rice ⓑ
Thai/International
Rod Fai Rd, Soi 68–70, 77110
Tel *0-89137-6009*
No-frills homely restaurant serving good-value Thai food prepared to Western tastes, although it can be made more authentic by asking. Good European mains and cheap beer.

HUA HIN: Baan Itsara ⓑⓑ
Thai
7 Napkehad Rd, 77110
Tel *0-3251-1673*
A seaside spot north of Hua Hin, this casual restaurant was once the home of a Thai artist. The menu consists of standard Thai seafood dishes, but the food is prepared with exceptional skill.

HUA HIN: Cool Breeze ⓑⓑ
Spanish
62 Naresdamri Rd, 77110
Tel *0-3253-1062*
Located in a Colonial-style seafront house, this is a good choice for a light meal. Excellent selection of sandwiches, tapas, dips, and salads, as well as hearty mains. Be sure to sample the paella.

HUA HIN: Let's Sea ⓑⓑ
Thai
83/155 Soi Talay 12, Khao Takiab, 77110
Tel *0-3253-6888*
In a nice resort location south of town, Let's Sea serves delicious seafood with lovely views of the bay. The cuisine is Thai with an international twist. Try the fish cakes wrapped in mini-croutons and lobster carpaccio.

For more information on types of restaurants *see pp412–13*

HUA HIN: Shiva ⓑⓑ
Indian
*Soi 88, 38/11 Khao Hin Lek Fai 2 Rd,
77110*
Tel *0-3265-2546*
A little hard to find (opposite the
Chom Dong Villa) but well worth
the effort, Shiva serves delicious
curries, from super-spicy *vindaloo*
to smooth *palak paneer*, each
with a distinctive flavor.

HUA HIN: Hagi ⓑⓑⓑ
Japanese
*Sofitel Centara Grand Resort and
Villas, 1 Damnoernkasem Rd, 77110*
Tel *0-3251-2021*
Stylish restaurant serving both
contemporary and traditional
Japanese dishes, beautifully
executed and presented. The
16-seat tepanyaki kitchen turns
cooking into theater and makes
for a dramatic dining experience.

HUA HIN: Salathai ⓑⓑⓑ
Thai
*Sofitel Centara Grand Resort and
Villas, 1 Damnoernkasem Rd, 77110*
Tel *0-3251-2021*
Located between Cha-am and
Hua Hin, Salathai has excellent
choices of Thai food prepared
with quality ingredients. Lovely
outdoor seating in a garden with
an adjacent pool. Service and
ambience worthy of the price.
Reservations recommended.

HUA HIN: White Lotus ⓑⓑⓑ
Chinese
*Hilton Hua Hin Resort & Spa, 33
Naresdamri Rd, 77110*
Tel *0-3253-8999*
On the 17th floor of the
impressive Hilton Resort, White
Lotus enjoys stunning views
of the town and coastline.
The contemporary Chinese
menu focuses on Sichuan and
Cantonese styles, with a couple
of degustation menus. Great
dim sum lunch.

KO PHA NGAN: Om Ganesh ⓑ
Indian/Thai
Had Rin, 84280
Tel *0-7737-5123*
Authentic Indian curries served
in a vibrant setting. Nice *thali*
platters and *lassis*. Meat
dishes and Thai food also
available. Favorite haunt of
tired backpackers.

KO PHA NGAN: Luna Lounge ⓑⓑ
French/Thai
Thong Nai Pan Noi Beach, 84280
Tel *0-7744-5035*
Considered by many to be the
best place to eat on the island,
Luna Lounge offers a wide choice
of Western and Thai food served

in a comfortable and sophisticated
atmosphere. Try the lamb curry
or barbecued kingfish.

KO SAMUI: Islander ⓑ
International
Chaweng Center, Bophut, 84140
Tel *0-7723-0836*
This backpacker favorite in the
heart of Chaweng offers basic
international food in a lively
setting. Thai options also
available. With a kids' menu,
pool tables, and a sports TV.

KO SAMUI: Phensiri Thai Bistro ⓑ
Thai
80/30 Chaweng Beach Rd, 84140
Tel *0-7795-2412*
The atmosphere is pleasant here,
amid the bustle of Chaweng
Beach, with a nice little garden
for outdoor dining. Serves very
tasty and healthy Thai food,
with an emphasis on cleanliness.
Great desserts.

KO SAMUI: Will Wait ⓑ
International
Main Rd, Lamai Beach, 84140
Tel *0-7742-4263*
With Thai, Chinese, Western, and
even some Japanese on the
menu, this place has something
for everyone. Nothing innovative,
but the food is decent and well-
priced. Good home-made bread
and pastries. Contrary to the
name, their service is quick.

KO SAMUI: Barracuda @ The Wharf ⓑⓑ
Mediterranean
62/9 Moo 1, Bophut, 84140
Tel *0-7743-0003*
Barracuda's German chef prepares
imaginative Mediterranean
cuisine with a nod to Thai flavors.
The understated decor belies
the excellent food and service.
Opt for the lamb or the
consistently good daily specials.

KO SAMUI: The Boudoir ⓑⓑ
French
14/21 Moo 1, Maenam, 84140
Tel *08-5783-1031*
Located between Bophut and
Maenam, The Boudoir serves
fantastic French food. But what
keeps people coming back is the
romantic atmosphere. The French
couple running it are great hosts.

KO SAMUI: The Duke Pub & Restaurant ⓑⓑ
British
*12 Moo 2 Chaweng Beach Rd,
84140*
Tel *0-7730-0348*
Comfort food and drink for home-
sick Brits. Great bangers and

mash, pies, and fish 'n' chips await,
and live music in the evenings.
Rowdy at times, but friendly.

KO SAMUI: Le Napoleon ⓑⓑ
French
Lamai 4 Rd, Lamai Beach, 84140
Tel *08-5478-4571*
Consistently well-rated for its
classic French food, Le Napoleon
features traditional decor
including white tablecloths. Of
the many French dishes on offer,
be sure to try the gratinated
mussels and *tournedos flambé*
in cognac. Excellent set menus.

KO SAMUI: Rocky's Bistro ⓑⓑ
Thai/Fusion
Rocky's Resort, Lamai Beach, 84140
Tel *0-7723-3020*
This resort's casual dining
venue gets excellent reviews
for its fusion cuisine, but its
international dishes are also
noteworthy. Modern Thai decor
with lovely poolside tables.
Good value for quality fare.

DK Choice

KO SAMUI: Dining on the Rocks ⓑⓑⓑ
Asian
*Six Senses Hideaway, Baan Plai
Laem Bophut, 84140*
Tel *0-7724-5678*
This sophisticated restaurant is
spread over 10 terraced decks –
some covered – perched on
boulders with incredible views.
Serves unique and delicious
interpretations of a range of
Asian dishes. The Thai staple
tom yam, for instance, is served
with a tangy foam, scallops, and
a crumbly cracker of parmesan
cheese. Impeccable service.
Promises a memorable meal.

The top deck at Dining on the Rocks

Cheerful outdoor dining area at Je t'aime

KO SAMUI: H Bistro ⓑⓑⓑ
French/Mediterranean
Hansar Resort, Bophut, 84140
Tel *0-7724-5511*
Amid modern, almost urban stone-and-wood decor, H Bistro offers a menu that includes traditional European, Thai, fusion, and even vegetarian specialties. Excellent service. One of the best eateries on the island.

KO SAMUI: Tree Tops ⓑⓑⓑ
Thai/Western
Anantara Lawana Resort, North Chaweng Beach, 84140
Tel *0-7796-0333*
With individual pavilions built into a rain forest, this restaurant offers a lush and shady respite from the beach. The menu includes sophisticated interpretations of Thai and Western dishes. Friendly service.

KO SAMUI: Zazen ⓑⓑⓑ
French/Thai
Zazen Resort, Bophut Beach, 84140
Tel *0-7743-0345*
Dine in a relaxed yet opulent atmosphere right on the beach. The chef prides himself on his interpretations of French and Thai classics. Try the popular lobster set menu.

KO TAO: Porto Bello Bistro ⓑ
Italian
Hat Sairee, 84000
Tel *0-7745-7029*
Well-prepared Italian food made using lots of local seafood. Friendly atmosphere and good service. Tasty home-made pastas and mouthwatering desserts.

KO TAO: Starlight ⓑⓑ
International
Charm Churee Resort, Jansom Bay, 84000
Tel *0-7745-6394*
In a lovely resort south of the busier beaches on the island. Offers not only great sunset views and a pleasant dining atmosphere, but scrumptious Thai and Western dishes, including imported steaks.

PHETCHABURI: Swiss Palazzo ⓑ
Italian
37/4 Thumbol Tongchai, Khlong Krachaeng, 77110
Tel *0-3240-0250*
Limited but delicious menu – everything is pasta-based in the best Italian style, with excellent and diverse sauces. Gnocchi is a favorite here. They also make their own superb ice cream.

PHETCHABURI: Rabiang Rim Nam ⓑⓑ
Thai
1 Shesrain Rd, 76000
Tel *0-3242-5707*
Choose from a range of tasty and good-value dishes served in this guesthouse-based restaurant. Centrally located with a nice garden setting next to the river. Popular with tourists.

PRACHUAP KHIRI KHAN: Twigg's Bakery & Cafe ⓑ
Western/Thai
201/1–2 Salacheep Rd, 85000
Tel *0-3260-1188*
A local institution, Twigg's serves up pizza, steaks, Thai food, and superb pastries. Excellent for breakfast and travel tips.

PRACHUAP KHIRI KHAN: Phloen Samut ⓑⓑ
Thai
44 Beach Rd, 85000
Tel *0-3260-1866*
Popular with both locals and visitors to Prachuap, this restaurant is a good place to try the local specialty *pla samli daet diaw* (flash-fried, sundried cotton fish, served with a green mango salad). The other Thai and seafood dishes on the menu are also excellent.

SURAT THANI: Mouth2Mouth Cafe & Restaurant ⓑⓑ
Thai/Western/Fusion
Soi Talat Mai 4, 84000
This hip but family-friendly place has a bit of everything – from ice cream to imported beers – and the interesting menu has a Western take on Thai classics.

Upper Andaman Coast

PHANGNGA BAY: Je t'aime ⓑ
International
21/1 Moo 1 Market, Koh Yao Noi, 82160
Tel *0-7659-7495* **Closed** *Fri*
Je t'aime's Danish owner-chef prepares a wide variety of tasty dishes including fresh fish, excellent lobster, and baked goods, all at reasonable prices.

PHANGNGA BAY: Duang ⓑⓑ
Thai/Chinese
122 Phetkasem Rd, 82000
Tel *0-7641-2216*
This restaurant serves both Chinese and Southern Thai cuisine, and is noted for its seafood specialties. Try the *tom yam talay* (spicy seafood soup) or *yam pla duk fu*, a twice-cooked catfish topped with freshly shredded green mango.

PHANGNGA BAY: Tasai Seafood ⓑⓑ
Thai
Bor Saen District, 82000
Tel *08-9469-3392*
A little out of town (near Bor Saen Villa Resort), this restaurant is well worth the journey to dine in a mangrove forest. Popular with locals for its tranquil ambience and excellent Thai seafood.

PHANGNGA COAST: Stempfer Café ⓑ
German
Phetkasem Rd, Baan La On, Khao Lak, 82210
This is a long-standing local favorite for its very filling breakfasts. It is also well-known for its cakes, pastries, sandwich lunches, and beer.

PHANGNGA COAST: Enzo ⓑⓑ
Japanese Fusion
62/2 Moo 5, Kukkhak, Khao Lak, 82190
Tel *0-7648-6671*
Enzo is a stylish place serving traditional and modern Japanese food. The unlimited buffet, with its varying prices, is quite popular. The restaurant has a lovely ambience.

For more information on types of restaurants *see pp412–13*

Cheerful decor at Ka Jok See

**PHANGNGA COAST:
Everyday Lasy House
Restaurant & Bar** ⓑⓑ
Thai/Western
Phetkasem Rd, Khao Lak, 82210
Tel *08-1397-2802*
An unpretentious restaurant offering well-presented Central Thai favorites and some Western choices. Vegetarian and seafood dishes are also offered.

PHUKET: Angus O'Tool's ⓑ
Irish
516/20 Patak Rd, Soi Islandia, Karon, 83100
Tel *0-7639-8262*
Known for one of the heartiest breakfasts in all of Phuket, Angus also has excellent nightly specials, and a famous Sunday roast. Guinness draught available.

PHUKET: China Inn Café ⓑ
Thai/International
20 Thalang Rd, 83000
Tel *0-7635-6239*
In a restored Sino-Portuguese building, this café resembles a tasteful but eclectic antique shop. Mainly Thai dishes but some Western choices as well. Great for breakfast.

PHUKET: Flip Side ⓑ
Western
469 Viset Rd, Rawai, 83100
Tel *09-0869-5552*
As far away from a burger chain as you can get – think sun-dried tomatoes, buffalo mozzarella, Italian basil, rocket, burger relish, and balsamic glaze. Nice ambience and good craft beers.

PHUKET: Natural Restaurant ⓑ
International
66/5 Soi Phuthon, Bangkok Rd, 83000
Tel *0-7622-4287*
This garden restaurant is full of hidden nooks and crannies and even little waterfalls. A relaxing and amusing whimsical oasis. Selection of world cuisines, from Japanese to German and Thai.

PHUKET: Pepper's Sports Bar ⓑ
Western/Thai
16–18 Lagoon Rd, Cherng Talay, 83110
Phuket's favorite sports bar shows games on six high-definition screens. Food is good, too: English breakfasts, Sunday roasts, and a few Thai dishes. Family friendly.

**PHUKET: Red Duck
Restaurant** ⓑ
Thai
6/23 Moo 2, Patak Rd, Kata Beach, 83160
Tel *08-4850-2929* **Closed** *Mon*
Standard Thai fare prepared with an attention to quality and served in a no-frills, comfortable dining space. Excellent curries that can be tuned to different tastes, from mild to super spicy.

PHUKET: Red Onion ⓑ
International
Patak Rd E, Karon, 83160
Tel *0-7639-6827*
A bit basic in appearance, but the standard Western food is substantial and tasty. Try the chicken steak with fries and the Weiner schnitzel. Popular with locals, so get there early.

PHUKET: Somjit Noodles ⓑ
Thai
214/6 Phuket Rd, 83000
Tel *0-7625-6701*
A small, clean, unassuming daytime noodle shop with an excellent range of Hokkein and Thai noodle dishes. Try the island's best-known noodle dish, *khanom chin nam ya Phuket* (Chinese noodles in a curried fish sauce).

PHUKET: Baluchi ⓑⓑ
Indian
Horizon Beach Resort, Soi Kepsap, Patong, 83100
Tel *0-7629-2526*
Considered by many to be the best Indian restaurant in Phuket, Baluchi serves top-notch North Indian specialties. The chefs are

from the subcontinent as are a big section of the loyal clientele. Good vegetarian choices.

PHUKET: Ka Jok See ⓑⓑ
Thai
26 Takua Pa Rd, 83000
Tel *0-7621-7903* **Closed** *Sun & Mon*
Hidden down a small side street in the center of town, Ka Jok See is famous throughout Thailand for its lively, sometimes raucous, atmosphere. Thai dishes prepared with flair, along with live music, dancing, and a cabaret show. Reserve ahead.

**PHUKET: Kan Eang
Seafood II** ⓑⓑ
Seafood
9/3 Chofa Rd, Chalong Bay, 83110
Tel *0-7638-1323*
A seafood institution for over 30 years, this lovely restaurant with a garden started as a streetside stand. Well-priced meals. Play for area for kids on the adjacent sandy beach.

PHUKET: Linda Seafood ⓑⓑ
Seafood
Ratutit Rd, near Soi Koknam, Patong, 83110
This humble place gets consistently good reviews for the freshness of its seafood, legitimately priced without the hidden extras that sometimes spoil local seafood emporiums. Clean and unpretentious.

**PHUKET: Paan Yah Thai
Restaurant** ⓑⓑ
Thai
249 Prabaramee Rd, Patong, 83110
Tel *0-7629-0451*
Excellent choice in Patong for its reasonably priced fare and quality views. Classic Thai seafood and noodle dishes, carefully prepared with fresh ingredients. Outdoor deck with shaded seating.

PHUKET: Salvatore's ⓑⓑ
Italian
15 Rasada Rd, Phuket Town, 83000
Tel *0-7622-5958* **Closed** *Mon; Sun lunch*
Typical *trattoria*-style place, with the food done to perfection and competently served in a tasteful and laid-back atmosphere. There is also a separate pizzeria next door.

PHUKET: Tatonka ⓑⓑ
Fusion
Srisoonthon Rd, Bang Thao, 83110
Tel *0-7632-4349* **Closed** *Wed*
Offers "globetrotter cuisine", with influences from the many countries the owner has lived in. Many tasty, unique creations, such as the sashimi spring rolls.

PHUKET: Baan Rim Pa ⑧⑧⑧
Thai
Novotel Phuket Resort, 62 Praburamee Rd, Patong, 83150
Tel *0-7634-0789*
Royal Thai cuisine served in a two-story teakwood villa on a rocky point overlooking the ocean. Lively piano bar. Classy but casual ambience. Ask for a table outside.

PHUKET: Black Ginger ⑧⑧⑧
Thai
Indigo Pearl Resort, Nai Yang Beach, 83110
Tel *0-7632-7006*
A traditional Thai pavilion built on stilts over a lake, and reached by boat. Aside from the stunning surroundings, Black Ginger also promises an elegant dining experience with superb renditions of Thai classics on offer.

DK Choice

PHUKET: The Blue Elephant ⑧⑧⑧
Thai
96 Krabi Rd, 83000
Tel *0-7635-4355*
Housed in the former Phuket governor's mansion, a gem of Sino-Portuguese architecture, The Blue Elephant serves food that is up to the setting. The traditional Thai cuisine (often spicy, but the menu gives a "chili count") is of the highest standard. The southern Thai massaman curry is unrivaled. Set menus and à la carte, as well as vegetarian choices. There is even a cooking school.

PHUKET: The Boathouse Wine & Grill ⑧⑧⑧
French/Thai
West Patak Rd, Kata, 83100
Tel *0-7633-0015-7*
Thai and Mediterranean food on the menu, with modern, innovative interpretations of classic dishes. The beachside setting is superb, the service

impeccable, and the wine list unparalleled. Many special events including cooking classes.

PHUKET: Lim's ⑧⑧⑧
Thai
28 Phra Baramee Soi 7, Kalim, 83100
Tel *0-7634-4834*
Head to this effortlessly chic restaurant located away from the beach crowds on a hill above Kalim Bay, just north of Patong. Savor authentic and modern Thai cuisine prepared with superb attention to detail. Nice adjacent lounge bar. Popular with locals.

PHUKET: La Gaetana ⑧⑧⑧
Italian
352 Phuket Rd, Phuket Town, 83000
Tel *0 7625-0523*
An intimate eatery known for its Italian haute cuisine. Go for the mixed carpaccio of salmon, tuna, beef, and smoked duck breast followed by baked portobello mushrooms in Gorgonzola sauce.

PHUKET: Siam Supper Club ⑧⑧⑧
International
Tinlay Place, Bang Tao, Cherng Talay, 83110
Tel *0-7627-0936*
This restaurant offers a mainly Western menu of seafood, steaks, and pastas. An elegant yet informal atmosphere and a good spot for families. Popular bar. Try the excellent cheesecake.

RANONG: Buono @ Ranong ⑧
Italian
1/12 Chonraru Road, Khao Niwet, 85000
Tel *08-3632-9844*
A great place for Italian comfort food such as pasta and pizzas, along with burgers and some Thai fare. Rustic, with friendly staff.

RANONG: Ranong Hideaway ⑧
Thai/Western
323/7 Ruangrat Rd, 85000
Tel *0-7783-2730*
This is one of the primary backpacker hangouts in Ranong, and a good place to gather travel

tips. The menu includes a wide choice of both Western and Thai dishes, and the restaurant is set in a pleasant garden. Swift, efficient service.

Deep South

HAT YAI: Sumatra ⑧
Indonesian
55/1 Ratthakan Rd, 90110
Tel *0-7424-6459*
This modest eatery serves good halal food. Try typical dishes such as the *mee goreng* (fried yellow noodles mixed with eggs and shrimp), or *rojak* (a filling spicy salad with a peanut sauce). No alcohol.

HAT YAI: Basil ⑧⑧
Thai/Western
9, Soi 2 Punnakun Rd, 90110
Tel *0-8191-9321* **Closed** *Mon*
Surprisingly good Western food in a place not usually associated with international cuisine. Good pizzas, grills, and salads served up in a friendly atmosphere. The tuna with sesame sauce is a must-try. Popular with students from the nearby university.

HAT YAI: Kaopan ⑧⑧
Japanese
1/51 Tanon Jiranakorn, 90110
Tel *0-7423-3156* **Closed** *Mon*
A fantastic place to go for really fresh sushi, as well as other Japanese dishes. Locals and expats prefer it to the chain Japanese places for quality and value.

SONGKHLA: The Hot Bread Shop ⑧
Western/Thai
61 Srisuda Rd, 90000
Tel *0-7432-1399*
A good bakery that serves nice pastries and coffees. The sandwiches here are considered the best in town. Cooked Western food and Thai dishes as well.

Chic dining area at Black Ginger

For more information on types of restaurants *see pp412–13*

SHOPPING IN THAILAND

Thailand is well known as a country that offers good shopping. The high quality, wide variety, and low prices of many Thai goods are a major attraction for tourists. Arts and crafts are probably the most tempting buys. These range from inexpensive wicker rice steamers to valuable antiques, and include many typically Thai items such as triangular cushions, colorful hill-tribe artifacts, and finely crafted silver jewelry. Many are available from specialty crafts centers. Thai silk has an international reputation and comes in a huge variety of designs, both traditional and modern. Tailors, particularly in Bangkok, can make clothes in silk or any other fabric to high standards for low prices. The country is also known for its rich supply of gems, and the capital is a major gem trading center. With the appearance of huge, luxurious shopping malls in Bangkok alongside vibrant, chaotic markets and street stands, Thailand offers shoppers a mix of the contemporary and the traditional.

Asia Books – one of the best book chains in Thailand

Opening Hours

Most small stores open from about 8am to 8pm or 9pm, while department stores, shopping malls, and tourist shops typically open from 10:30am until 9pm or 10pm in busy areas. Business days are normally Monday to Saturday, but most shops in Bangkok, tourist areas, and resorts also open on Sundays and public holidays. During the Chinese and Thai new years (in February and April) many shops shut for several days. Market hours are usually dawn to mid-afternoon for fresh produce, or late afternoon to midnight or even later for tourist markets.

How to Pay

The Thai *baht*, linked to the US dollar, has been a stable currency since the mid-1980s. *Baht* will always be accepted throughout the country (and in Laos). Credit cards can be used in many stores in Bangkok and resorts, and increasingly so in provincial towns. VISA and American Express are probably the most widely accepted,

followed by MasterCard. Upscale places usually take all major cards. Be warned, though, that many shops will add on a surcharge of up to five percent if you pay by credit card.

Rights and Refunds

When buying expensive items, ask for a written receipt *(bai set)* with the shop's address and tax number. For goods on which you want to reclaim the seven per-cent sales tax, shops should fill out a form for you to present to customs at the airport. However, the hassle and handling fees involved mean that this is rarely worth the trouble.

If you are arranging to have goods shipped home make sure you confirm all the costs involved with the supplier in advance, including insurance, tax, and shipping charges.

Refunds are almost unheard of, but exchange of faulty or poorly fitting non-sale goods from reputable stores should be possible, if sometimes complicated. In small shops you may succeed through charm.

Bargaining

The trend in cities, especially Bangkok, is toward chain stores with fixed prices and endless discount sales. However, the Thai love of bargaining means you can still often negotiate at small shops, specialty retailers, and, of course, market stands. There are a few tips for successful bargaining. Be aware of the going rate for items so as not to offer embarrassingly low sums. Talking in Thai numbers may restrain the vendor's initial bid. You can try faking disinterest if the seller's bids remain high. This is a better policy than enthusiastically bargaining, then deciding not to buy when the vendor agrees on your price.

Department Stores and Malls

International-style department stores are a mainstay of Bangkok shopping. However, Thai market

Jewelry stall on Khao San Road, Bangkok

The huge Siam Paragon shopping complex in downtown Bangkok

habits die hard, and many stores fill their aisles with bargain stands.

The two main Thai chains are **Robinson's**, with a branch on Sukhumvit road; and the upscale **Central** at the Silom Complex, farther down Silom Road, Chidlom, and Lad Phrao.

The scale of the change in Thai shopping habits is remarkable. Residents of Bangkok already have countless downtown malls, such as **Peninsula Plaza**, to choose from, as well as luxury shopping complexes like **Emporium**, **Central World Plaza** and **Siam Paragon**. But the trend is for vast malls out of the center of the city – such as **Fashion Island** on Ramindra Road. These are the focus for growing suburbs and resemble self-contained, air-conditioned towns, selling not only fashion and domestic items, but even houses and cars. They incorporate huge food courts, water parks, movie theaters, concert halls, skating rinks, bowling alleys and entertainment theme parks.

Two of the world's five biggest shopping malls are in outer Bangkok. **Seacon Square** on Srinakharin Road, southeast of the city, contains a fun fair and stretches for more than 1,100 yds (1 km). The rest of Thailand has yet to experience such excesses, but a few modern malls are now appearing in the larger towns and resorts. Examples include

Kad Suan Kaew in Chiang Mai and the **Mike Shopping Mall** and **Central Pattaya Festival Beach Shopping** in Pattaya.

English-language Bookstores

Thailand has three English-language book and magazine chains: **Asia Books**, **Kinokuniya**, and **Bookazine**. All have several branches in Bangkok; there are Asia Books branches in Chiang Mai malls, and smaller Bookazine shops in any area frequented by foreigners. Smaller independent bookshops specialize in good-value used books.

Markets and Street Vendors

There is a market at the heart of every Thai town. Even the smallest will offer a good range of fresh produce, and the larger markets often sell everything from arts and crafts to fruit and vegetables and household items. The most notable are Chatuchak Market (see p139), the Chiang Mai Night Bazaar (see p230), the Pattaya Floating Market, and the night market in Chiang Rai. For markets in central Bangkok, see pages 144–5.

Impromptu roadside stands are also found all over the country. Some sell devotional items such as jasmine rings (see p35), and others are good for souvenirs (though many of the goods are of dubious legality). Chiang Mai, Pattaya, and Patong in Phuket have many such stands. In Bangkok they are found on Silom and Sukhumvit roads, and in Banglampu and Patpong districts.

Factories and Craft Centers

Tours of factory outlets and craft centers are popular, particularly in the North and Northeast. No bargaining is required as prices are fixed, but be aware that guides take commissions.

Fake Goods

Thailand's trade in fakes is so notorious that many people seek out the most kitsch items as souvenirs. Most prized are goods with a deliberately fake quality, using famous logos on products they'd never normally grace, such as Louis Vuitton fanny packs or Chanel T-shirts. Conversely, identical copies with spoof labels like Live's Jeans are even becoming collectors' items. Original manufacturers are understandably outraged by the piracy. Although it could be argued that aping an original is a way for a developing country to gain skill on which to build new industries, it is still illegal. In fact, a growing copyright clampdown has shrunk the trade in fakes and even led to some forgers becoming official import agents. Be warned that customs officers may confiscate fakes.

Street stall in Pattaya selling fake versions of expensive watches

Thai Silk

The ancient art of Thai silk-weaving (see pp270–71) was revived by American Jim Thompson (see pp122–3) after World War II and is now a booming export business. Silk can be plain, patterned, or in the subtle *mut mee* style made from pre-tie-dyed *(ikat)* thread. Aside from Thai designs, this heavy, bright, and slightly rough cloth is now imaginatively used for ties, dresses, shirts, skirts, and other Western fashion items, plus cushions, hangings, and sundry ornaments. Many shops will tailor clothes to your measurements, even to your own designs.

Most silk comes from the Northeast and the North, but some is woven in and around Bangkok. For range and quality, Surawong Road in Bangkok is reliable, particularly **Jim Thompson's**, as well as **Shinawatra** on Sukhumvit Road. Chiang Mai's San Kamphaeng Road is renowned for its silk, the most famous producer being **T. Shinawatra Thai Silk**.

The Thai Silk Fair is held annually in Khon Kaen in late November or early December, when the town is packed with vendors and their bolts of cloth. If you miss the fair, **Prathamakant** sells a superb selection of silk all year round.

A dazzling selection of swatches of colorful Thai silk

Clothes

Thai tailors can make suits and dresses to order for low prices. Resist the rip-off 24-hour package deals including a "free gift." You get better service by

Made-to-measure suits are a specialty of many tailors in Thailand

seriously assessing the designs, fabric, and cut, and insisting on one or two intermediate fittings. In Bangkok, countless Chinese and Indian tailors advertise in tourist magazines and outside their shops along Sukhumvit, Charoen Krung, and Khao San Roads. Designs are usually copied, often with considerable skill, from magazines or catalogues of famous brands such as Armani and Hugo Boss. The quality of workmanship can vary considerably. Ask around for recommendations.

Other popular items of Thai clothing include baggy fishermen's pants; batik sarongs (especially in the South, such as at Ko Yo, Songkhla); vests and trousers made from hill-tribe fabrics; Thai silk and other Northeastern fabrics.

Arts and Crafts

Most Thai handicrafts are produced in the North and Northeast, and Chiang Mai is undoubtedly where visitors will find the widest choice of goods. The vibrant, diverse Night Bazaar sells everything from lacquerware to teak furniture, and you will need several hours if you want to peruse the often overpriced shops on San Kamphaeng Road (Highway 1006).

Prathamakant in Khon Kaen stocks a fine selection of Northeastern items such as the colorful triangular pillows.

Ayutthaya is a good source of crafts and antiques, particularly around Wat Phra Si Sanphet and

on Si Sanphet Road, where you can find unique stone carvings at **Kim Jeng**. Nearby **Bang Sai Folk Arts and Crafts Center** is the focus of Queen Sirikit's SUPPORT Foundation, which enables villagers to make a living from preserving their traditions (see p109). The fine pieces they produce are also sold at the dozen **Chitrlada** shops around Thailand. High-quality ethnic crafts are available from boutiques in most top hotels, **Silom Village**, **River City**, and the less expensive **Narai Phand** department store in Bangkok. The open-air **Patong OTOP Shopping Paradise** in Phuket has lots to choose from.

Hill-Tribe Artifacts

The costumes and artifacts of the hill tribes make fascinating anthropological souvenirs. Items might include Akha coin head-dresses, Lahu geometric blankets and cushion covers, Hmong red-ruffled black jackets, brightly colored Lisu tunics, wooden cattle bells, almond-shaped bamboo boxes, wooden boxes with carvings, and woven rattan.

Some of the best outlets in Chiang Mai are the **Hill Tribe Products Foundation**, **Thai Tribal Crafts**, and the **Old Chiang Mai Cultural Center**. The **Chiang Rai Handicraft Center** also has a large range. In Bangkok, the best selection is found at Chatuchak Market (see p139). Buying from the shop at **Cabbages and Condoms** will ensure that your money goes to the tribes.

Lisu tribeswoman, selling tribal goods at a Chiang Rai bazaar

Roadside basket seller in Northern Thailand

Wood, Bamboo, and Rattan

Bamboo, rattan, and wooden items are very cheap and can be shipped home. Carved wooden friezes, screens, headboards, doors, and lintels are readily available. Chiang Mai is the best source – **Pen Phong** is good for rattan/bamboo. Woodcarving is a specialty of Mae Tha and Ban Luk near Lampang, as well as the Bo Hang district of Chiang Mai. Hang Dong and Saraphi, south of Chiang Mai, are known for their intricate basketware.

Be aware that if you buy wooden items, you may be contributing to Thailand's already disastrous deforestation problem.

Attractive celadon and blue and white ceramics in Bangkok

Ceramics

Delicate Bencharong pottery was historically made in China and sent to Thailand to be decorated with intricate floral patterns using five colors. Today the entire process occurs in Thailand. You can buy complete dinner services in Bencharong, and myriad designs, including the more typical spherical pots. In Bangkok, Chatuchak Market is cheaper and offers a wider choice than the downtown shops.

The heavy celadon pottery style is distinguished by its etched designs under a thick, translucent green, blue, or brown glaze with a cracked patina. It's best bought direct from the potteries in Chiang Mai, where the top producer is **Mengrai Kilns**, but is also available in Bangkok from **Thai Celadon House** and many craft shops including those on Silom and Charoen Krung roads.

Lampang is notable for its fine blue and white ceramics, produced by companies such as **Indra Ceramics**.

Lacquerware

Lacquerware is a Northern Thai specialty. It usually has floral, flame, or portrait designs in black and gold on bamboo and wood. More common is the Burmese style of red ocher on bamboo and rattan with pictorial scenes or floral designs. Traditional items include boxes for food and jewelry. Lacquerware is plentiful in the craft shops of Chiang Mai and Bangkok.

Nielloware and Pewterware

Nielloware, the intricate process of silver (or, more rarely, gold) inlay in a black metal amalgam in floral and flame patterns, makes for beautiful items like cufflinks, pill boxes, and jewelry. Some of the finest is from Nakhon Si Thammarat.

Southern Thailand has significant tin deposits, so pewterware has become a major craft. Typical items include tankards, plates, vases, and boxes. Department stores in Bangkok and stores in Phuket town stock good selections.

Kalaga Tapestries

The weaving of *kalaga* tapestries involves metallic and multicolored threads, beads, patches, and sequins sewn onto a padded black background. It is a 200-year-old Burmese art but has only now been revived, so antique examples are rare and very expensive. The ubiquitous modern embroideries are often gaudy and sloppily made, but the more carefully constructed (and more expensive) simple traditional designs can make attractive cushions, hangings, bags, and even caps. Towns near to the Burmese border such as Mae Sot and Mae Sai are usually the best sources.

Musical Instruments, Masks and Puppets

Musical instruments including *khaens* (Northeastern "pan pipes"), *piphat* ensemble gongs, and drums make impressive souvenirs. They are available at Chiang Mai's Night Bazaar and at Silom Village, Narayanaphand, Chatuchak, and Nakorn Kasem markets in Bangkok. These places are also good sources of *khon* masks and theatrical items such as intricate *hoon krabok* puppets and *nang taloong* and *nang yai* shadow puppets.

In the South, Nakhon Si Thammarat is the place for shadow puppets. They can be bought from the **Shadow Puppet Theater**, and, if you phone in advance, the master puppet-maker will show you how the puppets are made.

Narai Phand, a government-sponsored store in Bangkok

Antiques

The delicacy and charm of Thai antiques are so appealing to shoppers that the few antiques remaining in the country are very expensive, fakes, or illegally obtained. Thailand is, in fact, one of the principal outlets for antiques from all over Southeast Asia. Some shops resemble museums, jumbled with tapestries, statues, cabinets, bells, puppets, ceramics, baskets, lacquerware, and temple artifacts. They're enchanting even if you're not buying.

Bargains are rare, although prices are lower than in Hong Kong or Singapore. Chiang Mai's Tha Phae and Loi Khro Roads are a bit cheaper than the main sources in Bangkok: Charoen Krung Road, River City, Chatuchak Market, and in Chinatown at Wang Burapha and Nakorn Kasem Market. There are antique auctions at River City on the first Saturday of each month. The excellent copies available are a cheaper, more culturally responsible alternative.

Recommended shops include **Amaravadee Antiques** and **Borisoothi Antiques** in Chiang Mai, and Bangkok's **The Fine Arts** and **NeOld**.

Export permits are required for antiques and all Buddha images from the Fine Arts Department via the **National Museum** and take at least a week to obtain *(see p459)*. Not surprisingly, given that so much of their cultural heritage has left the country, Thai customs officers are vigilant in enforcing this regulation.

Shoppers admiring gold jewelry in Bangkok's Chinatown

Jewelry

Thai jewelry tends to be large and expressive, often with superb detailing. The country has a long history of silverwork, particularly in the North and Northeast and among the hill tribes. The Wualai Road shops in Chiang Mai offer a good selection.

Necklaces, bracelets, earrings, and Lao-style belts are typical in employing silver thread and filigree detail, often incorporating silver beads and large, plate-like pendants. Contemporary and international styles are increasingly preferred in cities and resorts. More affordable modern costume jewelry sells well in Siam Square and Chatuchak Market in Bangkok, where you can buy inexpensive ethnic wares and jewelry created from such diverse materials as nuts, seeds, shells, and beans.

Intricate bejeweled silver pendant

Some of Thailand's best jewelry is found in Bangkok's **Peninsula Plaza** shopping mall as well as hotels such as the Dusit Thani. Some shops will work to your own specifications, notably **Uthai's Gems** in Bangkok and **Shiraz** in Chiang Mai. Richard Brown designs personalized Vedic astrological jewelry at **Astral Gemstone Talismans**.

Gold is a popular, age-old form of portable wealth, and the most common type is the very yellow, Chinese-style gold. There are Chinese-owned gold shops in most sizable towns. Be warned that amulets are not classed as jewelry and the trade in these sacred items is widely disapproved of, not least by the Buddhist authorities who believe it exploits and encourages superstition. You need a licence to export them.

Gems

Bangkok is possibly the world's biggest gem-trading center. The local stones are rubies, red and blue spinels, orange and white zircons, and yellow and blue sapphires *(see pp314–5)*. Markets operate around Chanthaburi, Kanchanaburi, Mae Sai, and in Mae Sot on the Burmese border, where gems are cheaper than in Bangkok. However, you'll need an expert eye to pick out the bargains and should be wary of illegally smuggled gems. Phuket is Thailand's only good source of high-quality pearls; the reputable **Pearl of Phuket** is worth a visit.

Gem scams are notorious in Bangkok and Chiang Mai, so run a mile if someone friendly says it's a public holiday so there's a government suspension of tax. Countless people have fallen for this ruse before being coaxed into parting with large sums of money by clever salesmanship and even, sometimes, drugged drinks.

It is possible to learn gemology and have stones authenticated and graded (but not valued) at the **Asian Institute of Gemological Sciences** in Bangkok.

Antiques in one of Bangkok's more exclusive shops

DIRECTORY

Department Stores and Malls

Central Department Store
Silom Complex, 191 Silom Rd, Bangkok. **Map** 7 A4.
Tel 0-2231-3333.

Central Pattaya Festival Beach Shopping
333/9 Beach Rd & 2nd Rd, Pattaya.
Tel 0-3300-3999.

Central World Plaza
Soi 4, Ratchadamri Rd, Bangkok. **Map** 8 D1.
Tel 0-2264-5555.

Emporium
622 Sukhumvit Rd, Prompong, Bangkok.
Map 8 F1.
Tel 0-2269-1000.

Fashion Island
589/719 Ramindra Rd, Bangkok.
Tel 0-2947-5000.

Kad Suan Kaew
99/4 Mu 2, Huai Kaew Rd, Chiang Mai. **Tel** 0-5322-4444, 0-8691-7372-4.

Mike Shopping Mall
262 Mu 10, 2nd Rd, Pattaya.
Tel 0-3841-2000.

Peninsula Plaza
153 Ratchadamri Rd, Bangkok. **Map** 8 D1.
Tel 0-2253-9762.

Robinson's
55 Srinakarin Rd, Nong Bon, Bangkok.
Tel 0-2651-1533.

Seacon Square
904 Srinakharin Rd, Bangkok. **Tel** 0-2721-8888.

Siam Paragon Shopping Center
Rama I Rd, Bangkok.
Map 7 C1. **Tel** 0-2690-1000, 02-610-8000.

English-Language Bookstores

Asia Books
221 Sukhumvit Rd, Bangkok. **Tel** 0-2651-0428, 0-2252-7277.

Kinokuniya
Floor 6, Isetan, Ratchadamri Rd, Bangkok.
Map 8 D1.
Tel 0-2255-9834.

Thai Silk

Jim Thompson's
9 Surawong Rd, Bangkok.
Map 7 C3.
Tel 0-2235-8931.

Prathamakant
79/2–3 Ruenrom Rd, Khon Kaen.
Tel 0-4322-4080.

Shinawatra
145/1–2 Chiang Mai-San Kamphaeng Rd, Chiang Mai.
Tel 0-5333-8053.

T. Shinawatra Thai Silk
94 Sukhumvit Rd, Soi 23, Bangkok.
Tel 0-2258-0295.

Arts and Crafts

Bang Sai Folk Arts and Crafts Center
Tambon, Bang Sai, Ayutthaya province.
Tel 0-3536-6252, 0-3536-2253.

Chitrlada Shop
Chitrlada Palace, Bangkok.
Map 3 B2.
Tel 0-2229-4611.

Kim Jeng
12 Mu 2, Kamang, Ayutthaya.

Narai Phand
President Tower, Ploenchit Rd, Bangkok. **Map** 8 E1.
Tel 0-2656-0398.

Patong OTOP Shopping Paradise
Ratutit Rd, Patong, Phuket.

River City
23 Trok Rongnamkaeng, Yotha Rd, Bangkok.
Map 6 F3. **Tel** 0-2237-0077, 0-2237-0078.

Silom Village
286 Silom Rd, Bangkok.
Map 7 A4.
Tel 0-2635-6810.

Hill-Tribe Artifacts

Cabbages and Condoms
6 Sukhumvit, Soi 12, Bangkok. **Map** 8 F1. **Tel** 0-2229-4611, 0-2229-4610.

Chiang Rai Handicrafts Center
732 Mu 5 Rimkok, Phahon Yothin Rd, Chiang Rai.
Tel 0-5371-3355.

Hill Tribe Products Foundation
21/17 Besibewat Suan Dok, Suthep Rd, Chiang Mai. **Tel** 0-5327-7743.

Old Chiang Mai Cultural Center
185 Wualai Rd, Chiang Mai. **Tel** 0-5320-2993.

Thai Tribal Crafts
208 Bamrung Rad Rd, Chiang Mai. **Tel** 0-5324-1043, 081-023-8842.

Wood, Bamboo, and Rattan

Pen Phong
189/25 Nongkaew Rd, Hangdong, Chiang Mai.
Tel 0-5343-3745.

Ceramics

Indra Ceramics
382 Mu 1, Lampang–Denchai Rd, Lampang.
Tel 0-5422-1189, 0-5431-0583.

Mengrai Kilns
79/2 Araks Rd, Samlarn Soi 6, Chiang Mai.
Tel 0-5327-2063.

Thai Celadon House
8/3–8/5 Ratchadapisek Rd, Sukhumvit, Bangkok.
Tel 0-2229-4383.

Puppets

Shadow Puppet Theater
10/18 Si Thammasok Soi 3, Nakhon Si Thammarat.
Tel 0-7534-6394.

Antiques

Amaravadee Antiques
141 Chiang Mai–Hot Rd, Chiang Mai.
Tel 0-5344-1628.

Borisoothi Antiques
15/2 Chiangmai-San Kamphaeng Rd, Chiang Mai. **Tel** 0-5333-8460.

The Fine Arts
3/F Room 354 River City, Bangkok. **Map** 6 F3.
Tel 0-2237-0077 ext.354.

National Museum
Fine Arts Department, I Na Phra That Rd, Bangkok.
Map 1 C4.
Tel 0-2224-1402.

NeOld
149/2–3 Surawong Rd, Bangkok. **Map** 7 B4.
Tel 0-2235-8352, 0-2235-8919.

Jewelry

Astral Gemstone Talismans
All Seasons Place, Conrad Hotel, 87/208 Wireless Rd, Bangkok.
Tel 0-2252-1230.

Shiraz
170 Thapae Rd, Chiang Mai. **Tel** 0-5325-2382.

Thai Lapidary
1009–1011 Silom Rd, Bangkok. **Map** 7 C4.
Tel 0-2236-2134.

Uthai's Gems
28/7 Soi Ruam Rudi, Ploenchit Rd, Bangkok
Map 8 F2.
Tel 0-2253-8582.

Gems

Asian Institute of Gemological Sciences
33rd Floor, Jewellery Trade Center, 919/1 Silom Rd, Bangkok. **Map** 7 A4.
Tel 0-2267-4315.

Pearl of Phuket
Baan Sapam, Ko Kaew Rd, Phuket town.
Tel 0-7637-7730.

What to Buy in Thailand

Thai market stalls, craft centers, and specialty shops offer a wide and tempting range of souvenirs and gifts. Handicrafts are particularly good buys, and there are few regions of the country without their own specialty. In the south you can find delicately worked nielloware, pewter, and shadow puppets; colorful hill-tribe artifacts, lacquerware, and silver jewelry are made in the North; the Northeast is famed for its silk and cushions. The widest selection is available in major cities such as Bangkok and Chiang Mai.

Nang talung puppet

Traditional Masks and Puppets

Thailand has a rich tradition of masked dance and puppetry, and although performances are becoming increasingly rare, masks and puppets make evocative souvenirs. Most depict characters from the Ramakien *(see pp44–5)* and include huge leather *nang yai* figures, smaller *nang talung* shadow puppets, *hoon krabok* marionettes, and the smaller *hoon lek (see pp46–7)*. Puppets can be bought in the South as well as at markets such as Chatuchak in Bangkok.

Figure of a Thai musician

Khon mask of a demon

Rattan and Wickerwork come in many guises, from simple rice steamers to attractive and durable sets of rattan furniture. Trays, boxes, and bags are popular and can be found for sale in many Thai markets, particularly in Bangkok and Chiang Mai. Reputable shops can arrange for large items to be shipped overseas.

Nielloware is an ancient craft that has been practiced in the South of Thailand for several centuries. Nakhon Si Thammarat province is the center of Thai nielloware production today. The process involves the decorative etching of silver and gold items that are then rubbed with a black metal alloy. Jewelry and small boxes are the most affordable items.

Wood-Carving is a highly skilled profession, and visitors can buy everything from tiny carved bowls and pill boxes to huge screens, cabinets, and beds. However, be aware that some hardwood items may be made from illegally felled trees.

Lacquerware items include jewelry boxes, bangles, bowls, and trays. The process of coating split bamboo or wood with lacquer and then adding delicate hand-paintings is a specialty of the north. The two most common styles of decoration are gold on black lacquer and the Burmese style of yellow and green on red. Chiang Mai is the best source.

Hill-Tribe Artifacts

are sold in towns and villages all over Northern Thailand, although Chiang Mai undoubtedly has the widest range of handicrafts. Among the most attractive items are patchwork bags, brightly colored blankets, delicately wrought silver jewelry, and hand-embroidered jackets and hats. If you go on a trek it is likely that you will visit at least one hill-tribe village, enabling you to buy the local handicrafts direct from the producers and, sometimes, see them being made.

Blue and white dinner service

Bencharong
pot

Celadon
vase

Ceramics have been produced in Thailand for hundreds of years. Although many styles show a pronounced Chinese influence, there are also several types of ceramics that are given a distinctive Thai stamp. One is the colorfully enameled Bencharong pottery that is most commonly found as small pots and vases. Celadon is another example. It is recognizable by its characteristic crazed surface on a typically light green glaze.

Silverware is another traditional Northern Thai craft. Beaten silver bowls, vases, and boxes, often with expertly worked relief patterns, are popular buys, particularly in Chiang Mai. Delicate silver jewelry in traditional and modern designs is also widely available throughout the North and in Bangkok.

Yellow and blue
sapphire ring

Silver bird

Orchid jewelry

A selection of sapphires

Silver bowl

Hanuman on
silver box lid

Jewelry and gems are particularly tempting purchases in Thailand. Not only is the country one of the world's major sources of rubies and sapphires, but it is also well known for skillfully crafted jewelry. Jewelers who display their work in the shops within the top hotels usually offer good quality at fair prices, but it is unwise to buy gems with the intention of reselling at a profit unless you are an expert.

Thai Fabrics

Silk is without doubt the best known Thai fabric and probably the number-one buy for visitors *(see p436)*. It comes in an enormous range of styles, weights, and designs, both ancient and modern, including tie-dyed *mud mee*. Thai cotton goods are also excellent – *pha sin* skirts and triangular *mawn sam liam* cushions often feature complex patterns. The hill tribes are known for their bold, geometric fabric designs. In the South, batik sarongs and baggy fishermen's trousers are widely available.

Hill-tribe (Hmong) tapestry

Mawn sam liam cushion

Patterned
silk tie

Scarf of raw Thai silk

Traditional cotton
fishermen's trousers

Cotton *pha sin* skirt

ENTERTAINMENT IN THAILAND

Modern Thailand may have adopted many foreign pursuits, from Hollywood movies to karaoke, but traditional entertainments still flourish. Although the graceful movements of classical *khon* dance-dramas survive mainly as tourist shows, the grassroots following of such typically Thai obsessions as muay thai boxing remains as strong as ever.

High-spirited *sanuk* (fun) is an all-embracing activity, even on the most serious of occasions such as religious festivals. Indulging in the local passions is essential to understanding life in Thailand, whether it be a song-filled night out at a bar or folk music club, a colorful temple fair, a classical concert, a *takraw* game, or watching the latest Thai movie.

The Thailand Cultural Center, the country's premier concert venue

Information Sources

Details of the major events and festivals throughout Thailand are provided in a booklet available from TAT offices. Monthly magazines *Bangkok 101* and *Big Chilli* are good sources of information on events, venues, and new restaurants in Bangkok. It is also worthwhile consulting the English-language newspapers, the *Bangkok Post* and the *Nation*, and the many free tourist magazines. Good hotels should also be able to provide information.

Bangkok's listings magazine

Booking Tickets

Major hotels and travel agencies can book tickets for cultural shows and sports events. Alternatively, you can buy tickets direct from venues or, for major events, from Thai TicketMajor counters at Central Department Store *(see p439)*. To book by phone call 0-2262-3456, or visit www.thaiticketmajor.com.

Traditional Theater and Dance

Watching the stylized royal all-male masked dance *khon* is like seeing the murals of Wat Phra Kaeo come to life. Sadly, popular interest in the mostly Ramakien-based dance-dramas is waning, and performances of *khon*, and of the equally elaborate but less formal *lakhon*, are becoming increasingly rare. In even greater danger of extinction are the *hoon lek* marionette shows *(see pp46–7)*.

The most atmospheric place to watch traditional dance is at Sanam Luang on the evening of royal ceremonies such as the king's birthday or a funeral. At such times dozens of stages provide entertainment long into the night. Complete performances can last days, so abridged scenes are chosen for shows at the **National Theater** (indoors on the last Saturday and Sunday of the month; outdoors every Saturday and Sunday from December to May) and the hi-tech **Royal Chalermkrung Theater** in Bangkok and at the **Old Chiang Mai Cultural Center**.

Countless tourist dinner shows in the major cities and resorts offer bills of dances from all over the country. Chiang Mai's famous *khantoke* dinners *(see p42)*, including dancing, can be experienced at the **Khantoke Palace** and

Khum Kaew Khantoke Palace. Reliable venues in Bangkok include the **Sampran Riverside** and **Silom Village**, while the Oriental's **Sala Rim Nam** restaurant presents authentic *khon*. *Lakhon* can also be witnessed at Bangkok's Lak Muang shrine near Sanam Luang, and the Erawan Shrine. Traditional Thai puppetry can be seen at the **Aksra Theatre**.

The most widespread dance-drama is *likay*, a regular feature of temple fairs, festivals, and TV. Its bawdy, slapstick, and satirical elements have allowed it to retain a popular contemporary following. The ancient equivalent from the South of Thailand is *manora*.

Still widespread in Malaysia and Indonesia, *nang talung* shadow puppet shows survive only in the Deep South at Phatthalung and Nakhon Si Thammarat *(see p389)*. Performances of *nang talung* at local festivals can run all night, but an hour or two is usually enough for most tourists. Even rarer are performances of *nang yai*, in which enormous, flat leather puppets are manipulated by a team of puppeteers.

A traditional khon performance

Concerts, Exhibitions, and Modern Theater

Thailand's major concert and exhibition halls are located in Bangkok. The state-of-the-art **Thailand Cultural Center** has excellent performance facilities and attracts popular international names. The German **Goethe-Institut** and the **Alliance Française** host first-rate exhibitions and concerts. Top stars frequently perform in the ballrooms of luxury hotels such as the **Dusit Thani**.

Bangkok Playhouse often stages plays in English and it also houses the **Art Corner** gallery, though **H Gallery** is the best place to go and see contemporary Thai art. The **Bangkok Art & Culture Center** also holds fascinating exhibitions, and stages concerts, performances, lectures, and film screenings.

Exhibition space at Bangkok Art and Culture Center

Movies

Thais are avid movie-goers. Bangkok now has a number of huge multiplexes, but there are still 2,000 mobile units in the country that offer impromptu open-air screenings in villages.

The film industry in Thailand has a long, erratic history. Despite socially aware classics like *Luk Isan* (1978), it has mostly produced formulaic melodramas, comedies, and violent action films. Hong Kong action movies have long been popular, but, since the early 1990s, Hollywood movies have dominated the Thai market. However, Thai cinema has been enjoying a renaissance and it is now regarded as one of the most creative in Southeast Asia. The capital also hosts the increasingly prestigious annual Bangkok International Film Festival.

Some of the theaters in Bangkok (such as **The Lido** and **Siam Cinema**), Chiang Mai, Pattaya, Phuket, and Hat Yai show movies with their original soundtracks.

Discos, Bars, Comedy, Music, and Folk Clubs

Challenged by international rock and sugary Thai pop, folk music has retained its popularity. It can be heard on the radio and TV, in bars, at festivals, and impromptu gatherings, particularly outside the capital, although concerts are rarely publicized in English. It is also played in the unsalubrious cafés staging *talok* (comedy), which do not welcome tourists.

The main styles include the exuberant, rhythmic *rum wong*, which is often accompanied by a jocular dance; *look thung* ("country music"), combining big band music, costumed dance troupes, and singing; and the schmaltzy, ballad-based *look kroong*. Favored by bus and taxi drivers, the faster Northeastern *mo'lam* sound is distinguished by *khaen* pipes and rap like vocals. The Khmer-style *kantrum* music of the southern region of the Northeast can be heard in Surin's **Petchkasem Hotel** on weekends. The plaintive, radical *phleng phua chiwit* ("songs for life") emerged during the student protests of the 1970s and has a few dedicated spots, such as **Raintree**, in Bangkok.

"Adult" entertainment from the King's Group

Emerging rock bands often play at **Flann O'Brien's Irish Pub**, while hotels host classier venues: **Spasso** (Grand Hyatt Erawan), **Angelini** (Shangri-La), and the Oriental's **Lord Jim's** and jazzy **Bamboo Bar**.

Friends sharing food and whisky while listening to live music is the nightlife formula throughout Thailand, although karaoke, discos, and themed bars are gaining ground. In Bangkok, fashionable districts come and go at great speed. A long-term live-music favorite is **Brown Sugar Jazz Boutique**, which features some of the city's top performers, mainly jazz. The gay night scene takes place on Silom Soi's 2 and 4, with Soi 2 starting later and going longer and wilder. **Saxophone Pub** is a long-standing favorite for live jazz and blues. In Chiang Mai, **The Riverside** leads a string of venues beside the Ping River.

Discos can be found throughout all of the major resorts in Thailand. The many large Bangkok nightclubs include the ever-popular **Narz Club**.

The flesh-trade districts – such as Patpong *(see p120)*, Nana Entertainment Plaza (Sukhumvit Soi 3), and Soi Cowboy (off Soi Asoke) in Bangkok, plus Pattaya and Patong in Phuket – are notorious for their bizarre gynecological "entertainments." Rip-offs are common, although the King's Group's bars are among the most "reputable." One of Thailand's most infamous and popular attractions on stage and TV is its cross-dressing *katoeys*, or "ladyboys." Tourists flock to their sanitized transvestite shows at **Calypso Cabaret** in Bangkok, **Chiang Mai Cabaret** in Chiang Mai, **Simon Cabaret** in Patong, and **Alcazar** in Pattaya, which boasts the best performers.

Temple Fairs and Festivals

The Thai calendar is packed with national holidays and local festivals *(see pp50–55).* These festivals may be religious or in honor of a local hero, to promote seasonal produce, or dedicated to other activities like boat racing and kite flying.

As well as often hosting other events, most *wats* stage temple fairs. But apart from scheduled major fairs such as the Golden Mount Temple Fair in Bangkok at Loy Krathong *(see p54),* it's usually a matter of chance whether you encounter one. The sideshows are often as entertaining as the ceremonies with vendors selling food and trinkets, colorful characters like the cross-dressing *katoeys,* folk music such as *likay* and *lam wong,* beauty contests, and who-can-eat-the-hottest-*som-tam* competitions. Other activities might include cock fighting or Siamese fighting fish contests.

Staged spectaculars aimed at tourists include the sound-and-light, fireworks, and other festivities at the Sukhothai ruins during Loy Krathong in November and during the Khwae River Bridge Week at Kanchanaburi *(see p54).*

Parade during the Loy Krathong festival in Lampang

Muay Thai and Krabi-Krabong

Thai kick boxing, *muay thai,* is a national passion *(see pp48–9).* Most provinces have a boxing arena, but the nation's top two venues are in the capital. **Ratchadamnoen Boxing Stadium** has bouts on Mondays, Wednesdays, Thursdays, and Sundays;

Muay thai boxing – passionately followed all over Thailand

and boxing can be seen at **Lumphini Stadium** on Tuesdays, Fridays, and Saturdays.

If you are interested in learning, rather than simply watching, the skills involved in *muay thai,* then contact the **International Amateur Muay Thai Federation,** who should be able to recommend suitable gyms and instructors.

Another revered, long-established Thai martial art is *krabi-krabong,* named "sword-staff" after some of the hand weaponry used. The techniques are taught to ancient standards, although skill and stamina rather than injuries inflicted are now the measures of an accomplished fighter. Demonstrations are often included in tourist cultural shows.

Takraw

The acrobatic Southeast Asian sport of *takraw* is played by young males at seemingly any clear patch of ground in Thailand. The idea is to keep a woven rattan ball in the air using any part of your body except your hands. The players' extraordinary agility, balletic leaps, and speed of reactions are a revelation to visitors reared on more ponderous sports.

There are elaborate versions emphasizing individual skill, but the classic original style has a team trying to get the ball into a basketball-like net more times in a set period than their rivals. Despite the competitive

version, *sepak takraw,* which resembles volleyball, now being incorporated into the Asian Games, professional games are played surprisingly rarely.

The remarkably acrobatic *takraw*

Soccer, Rugby, and Snooker

Thais have developed a feverish enthusiasm for soccer. Major foreign teams often visit Thailand for both official and "friendly" matches. Rugby has also sparked remarkable interest, with established clubs competing in a league and the Hong Kong Sevens. Games are mostly held in Bangkok at the **Pathumwan Stadium, Hua Mark Stadiums, Army Stadium,** and **Royal Bangkok Sports Club.**

Thailand is the most successful non-Anglophone country to adopt snooker, which has become hugely popular. Its dangerous association with underground gambling makes it hard for players to emulate champions like James Wattana, though there are some safe clubs around. Thailand hosts world ranking tournaments in March and September.

DIRECTORY

Traditional Theater and Dance

Aksra Theatre
Rangnam Rd, Bangkok.
Map 4 E4.
Tel 0-2677-8888.

Khantoke Palace
288/19 Chang Khlan Rd,
Chiang Mai.
Tel 0-5327-2757.

Khumkaew Palace Khantoke Vista Hotel
252/19–23 Phra Pok Klao
Rd, Chiang Mai.
Tel 0-5321-0663.

National Theater
Rachinee Rd (Prapinklao
Bridge), Pranakorn,
Bangkok. **Map** 1 C4.
Tel 0-2224-1342.

Old Chiang Mai Cultural Center
185/3 Wualai Rd,
Chiang Mai.
Tel 0-5327-5097.

Royal Chalermkrung Theater
66 Charoen Krung Rd,
Bangkok.
Map 6 D1.
Tel 0-2222-0434.

Sala Rim Nam
Oriental Hotel,
48 Oriental Ave, Bangkok.
Map 6 F4.
Tel 0-2236-0400.

Sampran Riverside
Off Hwy 4, 32 km
(20 miles) W of Bangkok.
Tel 0-3432-2588.

Silom Village
286 Silom Rd, Bangkok.
Map 7 A4.
Tel 0-2635-6810.

Concerts, Exhibitions, and Modern Theater

Alliance Française
29 Sathorn Tai Rd,
Yannawa, Bangkok.
Map 8 D4.
Tel 0-2670-4200.
W **alliancefr.org**

Bangkok Art and Culture Center
939 Rama I Road,
Bangkok
Map 7 C1.
Tel 0-2214-6630

Bangkok Playhouse/ Art Corner
2884/2 New Phetchaburi
Rd, Bangkok.
Tel 0-2718-0600.

Goethe-Institut
18/1 Soi Atthakan Prasit,
Sathorn Tai Rd, Bangkok.
Map 8 E4.
Tel 0-2287 0942.
W **goethe.de/bangkok**

H Gallery
201 Sathorn Soi 12,
Bangkok. **Map** 7 A5.
Tel 08-5021-5508.
W **hgallerybkk.com**

Thailand Cultural Center
Ratchadaphisek Rd,
Bangkok.
Tel 0-2247-0028.

Movies

The Lido
256 Rama I Rd, Siam
Square, Bangkok.
Map 7 C1.
Tel 0-2252-6498.

Siam Cinema
216 Siam Square Soi 1,
Rama I Rd, Pathumwan,
Bangkok. **Map** 7 C1.
Tel 0 2252-9976.

Discos, Bars, Comedy, Music, and Folk Clubs

Alcazar
Pattaya Second Rd,
Pattaya.
Tel 0-3841-0224-5.
W **alcazarpattaya.com**

Angelini
Shangri-La Hotel, 89 Soi
Wat Suan Phu, Bangkok.
Map 6 F5.
Tel 0-2236-7777.

Bamboo Bar
Oriental Hotel,
48 Oriental Ave, Bangkok.
Map 6 F4.
Tel 0-2236-0400.

Brown Sugar Jazz Boutique
Phrasumen Rd, Bangkok.
Map 2 D3.
Tel 0-2282-0396.
W **brownsugar-bangkok.com**

Calypso Cabaret
Asia Hotel, 296 Phayathai
Rd, Bangkok.
Tel 0-2653-3960.

Chiang Mai Cabaret
Anusarn Night Bazaar,
Chang Klan Rd,
Chiang Mai.

Flann O'Brien's Irish Pub
62 Silom Rd, Bangkok.
Map 8 C4.
Tel 0-2632-7515.

Lord Jim's
Oriental Hotel,
48 Oriental Ave, Bangkok.
Map 6 F4.
Tel 0-2236-0400.

Narz Club
112 Sukhumvit Soi 23,
Bangkok.
Tel 0-2258-4805.
W **narzclubbangkok.net**

Petchkasem Hotel
104 Chitbumrung Rd,
Surin.
Tel 0-4451-1274.

Raintree
116/64 Soi Rang Nam, off
Phaya Thai Rd, Bangkok.
Tel 0-2245-7230.

The Riverside
9–11 Charoenraj Rd,
Chiang Mai.
Tel 0-5324-3239.

Saxophone Pub
Victory Monument,
Bangkok. **Map** 4 E3.
Tel 0-2246-5472.

Simon Cabaret
100/6–8 Mu 4, Karon Rd,
Patong, Phuket.
Tel 0-7634-2011.

Spasso
Grand Hyatt Erawan
Hotel, 494 Ratchadamri
Rd, Bangkok.
Map 8 D1.
Tel 0-2254-1234.

Muay Thai and Krabi-Krabong

International Amateur Muay Thai Federation
Pathumwan Stadium, 154
Rama I Rd, Bangkok.
Map 7 B1.
Tel 0-2215-6212-4.

Lumphini Stadium
6 Ram Indra Rd, Bangkok.
Tel 0-2284-3141.
W **muaythailumpinee.net**

Ratchadamnoen Boxing Stadium
1 Ratchadamnoen Nok
Rd, Bangkok.
Map 2 F4.
Tel 0-2281-4205.

Soccer, Rugby, and Snooker

Army Stadium
Wiphawadirangsit Rd,
Bangkok.
Tel 0-2278-5000.

Hua Mark Indoor and Outdoor Stadiums
2088 Ramkhamhaeng Rd,
Bangkok. **Tel** 0-2318-0940, 0-2318-0944.

Pathumwan Stadium
154 Rama I Rd, Bangkok.
Map 7 B1.
Tel 0-2214-0120.

Royal Bangkok Sports Club
1 Henri Dunant Rd,
Pathumwan, Bangkok.
Map 8 D2.
Tel 0-2652-5000.
W **rbsc.org**

OUTDOOR ACTIVITIES & SPECIAL INTERESTS

Thailand offers an impressive range of outdoor activities and special interests. The coastline in the south is ideal for aquatic fun, from sailing, waterskiing, and windsurfing to big-game fishing and diving to see some spectacular coral reefs. Northern Thailand's mountainous forests are famous for their waterfalls, caves, and wildlife, including rare birds, gibbons, elephants, and tigers. Trekking in this beautiful region to see hill tribes is a controversial activity, and there are claims that constant visits from outsiders are eroding traditional culture,

so be sure to choose a responsible trekking company with knowledgeable guides. Thailand also has an extensive network of national parks. Exciting ways to explore the country's natural wilderness include sea canoeing, bamboo rafting, white-water rafting and rock climbing.

Some visitors take advantage of the growing number of excellent golf courses. Others come to learn cultural skills such as Buddhist meditation, traditional massage, and Thai cooking techniques, which include delicate vegetable carving.

Diving and Snorkeling

Abundant coral reefs thronging with aquatic life – serviced by countless diving operations – make Thailand one of the world's most accessible and rewarding destinations for underwater exploration. The Andaman coast and islands, in particular, have some stunning reefs, ocean drop-offs, and submerged pinnacles. The visibility in these areas often exceeds 30 m (100 ft) – a distance unheard of in most parts of the world. A rich variety of marine life can be spotted in these waters, such as whale sharks off the Burma Banks.

Much of the best diving is to be found in the national marine parks containing the Surin, Similan, and Tarutao archipelagos in the Andaman Sea; Ko Tao in the western Gulf of Thailand; and Ko Chang in the eastern Gulf. The once-

magnificent Ko Phi Phi has not been protected by this preserve status, and has been heartbreakingly damaged by careless anchoring and snorkelers breaking the coral. Reckless fishing with dragnets, harpoons, and explosives has also killed some reefs, while siltation and pollution pose growing threats. Though the devastating tsunami of 2004 caused a tragic loss of lives, its effect on the coral reefs of the Andaman Sea was fortunately minimal.

Because of rough weather brought on by monsoons *(see pp30–31)*, the Andaman sites are accessible from November to April; the shallower waters of the western Gulf are best visited between January and October. The Eastern Seaboard is accessible all year round.

Diving trips vary in length from one to several days, and many tours accommodate

Spectacular diving around the reefs off Thailand's coasts and islands

snorkelers, too. Selected dive companies are listed in the directory *(see pp452–3)*, and fuller listings and details of dive sites appear in the books *Asian Diver Scuba Guide: Thailand* (Asian Diver) and *Diving in Thailand* (Asia Books).

PADI- and NAUI-approved diving courses are widely available in Thailand. The main centers offering courses are Phuket, Pattaya, Khao Lak, Ko Tao, Ko Samui, Ko Phi Phi, and Krabi.

Basic diving rules include: inspect your equipment and get the right fit; don't dive unless you are confident in your instructor and have been well trained; make sure there's a buddy system; check that your group is small enough for the dive masters to monitor; and never touch the coral.

For people who do not want to spend the time or money on

Snorkeling with the marine life off the upper Andaman coast

the training necessary to become a certified diver, snorkeling is an excellent alternative, since all you need is the ability to swim. Most hotels and guesthouses located near reefs can rent out equipment, but to make the most of the experience, it's best to buy your own. While the beautiful patterns of the corals and brilliant colors of the fish that live among them can be mesmerizing, it's important to be constantly aware of your position and not to venture too far from the shore.

Sailing

Thailand's dramatic coastline is popular with the yachting fraternity, who come to Phuket every December for the King's Cup Regatta. Chartering a yacht – with or without a skipper – is possible, though daily rates for this very exclusive sport are not cheap.

Gulf Charters Thailand operates on the Eastern Seaboard, where sea breezes are often ideal, but the widest choice of sailing companies is found on Phuket. Some of the best are **Phuket Sailing**, **Yachtpro**, and **South East Asia Liveaboards**.

Water Sports

Water sports are hugely popular at many Thai beach resorts, but the disturbance they cause to holidaymakers is of concern, and in places such as Krabi they are banned. However, at most other seaside towns it is possible to rent windsurfing boards, and jet skis and banana-boat rides are becoming commonplace even in national marine parks such as Ko Samet.

For the best range of water sports, including paragliding, waterskiing, and motorboat rental, head for Jomtien beach at Pattaya; Hua Hin and Cha-am; and Patong and Karon beaches on Phuket.

Anglers can make use of the excellent facilities for big-game fishing at Pattaya and Phuket. This can be a thrilling way to

Jet-skiing: an ever-popular but increasingly controversial activity

pass a day, but be prepared to pay in excess of 10,000 *baht* for boat rental.

See the directory *(pp452–3)* for details of service providers.

Canoeing

Sea canoeing is not just the most peaceful way to enjoy the unusual karst islets of Phangnga Bay and the Angthong archipelago, but also the only way to explore their collapsed sea caves. Ringed by forest and often containing tiny beaches, many of these spectacular *hong* (literally "rooms") were first discovered by **Sea Canoe Thailand**, which runs the most responsible tours to these fragile "lost worlds." Another reliable outfit that operates tours around Phangnga Bay, Ko Tarutao National Marine Park, and the huge reservoir in Khao Sok National Park is **Paddle Asia**.

White-Water Rafting and Kayaking

Sedate bamboo rafting is a popular tourist pastime, particularly on the rivers in the north. More exciting, though, is white-water rafting on hardy inflatables. No experience is necessary apart from the ability to swim, since instruction is given to paddlers before setting out, and each raft has a capable crew to deal with any emergency. The upper reaches of the Pai and Moei rivers in the north are ideal for this thrilling sport, and Umphang's Mae Klong district near Mae Sot is particularly notable for world-class rafting. **Thai Adventure Rafting**, **Siam Rivers**, and **The Wild Lodge** are a few of the best trip organizers.

For athletic types looking for a challenge, white-water kayaking offers plenty of thrills and spills. Siam Rivers offers day courses for beginners on the Mae Taeng River, just north of Chiang Mai, and tougher, five-day trips on the Nam Wa River in Nan Province.

The season for white-water rafting and kayaking in Thailand lasts from July to December: this is when water levels are high enough to ensure an exciting ride.

Canoeing is a peaceful way to explore the splendid Thai coastline

Golf

With green and caddie fees cheaper than in the West, it's easy to see why so many visitors include a round of golf on their itinerary. Golf is very popular in Thailand, and the country has hosted several international competitions at its growing number of courses, many designed by the game's top names. The greens around Bangkok are mostly flat and uninteresting, but there are some beautiful backdrops at golfing resorts in Phuket, Khao Yai, and Chiang Mai.

Exclusivity is a feature of some clubs, though many are open to non-members, and golfing vacation packages are particularly popular at places such as Pattaya, Phuket, and Hua Hin. Visit www.golf thailand.net for an idea of what is on offer. The best printed guides to courses are the *Thailand Golf Map* and *Thailand Golf Guide*; TAT also publishes a free directory of the country's top 75 courses. For improving your handicap, there's a David Leadbetter Academy of Golf at the **Thana City Golf and Country Club**.

See the directory *(pp452–3)* for additional golf clubs.

Elephant Riding

After the mechanization of logging, and then its supposed ban in 1989, working elephants were no longer in great

Kayaking in the beautiful waters of Phang Nga Bay

demand, and their *mahouts* were reduced to begging on city streets for a living. Offering elephant rides was an obvious way to generate income and was perceived by many as a positive step toward securing the survival of this national symbol, since the elephants' lowland forest habitat had been largely destroyed.

However, recent research has provided us with greater knowledge of the intelligence and emotions of these animals, and animal welfare groups have expressed serious concerns about the ethics of training and riding elephants, and of forcing them to perform elaborate shows for the amusement of tourists.

There are many ways to enjoy the landscape and wildlife of Thailand without riding an elephant, such as trekking,

kayaking, white-water rafting, or taking a river cruise. If you wish to make a positive contribution to elephant conservation, consider a visit to the Elephant Nature Park in northwest Thailand *(see p225)*, where you can observe rescued elephants (and a whole menagerie of other animals), and spend a day or a week as a volunteer helper.

Trekking

Thailand has some ideal terrain for hiking, from the precipitous karst forests of Krabi and Khao Sok in the south to the undulating mountains around Mae Hong Son and Loei in the north.

Aside from the country's outstanding natural beauty, it is the opportunity to visit hill tribes that has caused the trekking business to boom. The novelty of encountering hill tribespeople in elaborate costumes undeniably adds cultural interest to a trek. However, over time, traditional tribal values cannot but be eroded by continued exposure to tourists. Many villages close to Chiang Mai, Chiang Rai, Pai, and Mae Hong Son are depressingly exploited. Additionally, there is the issue of trekkers feeling like voyeurs, especially at cynical shows such as the long-necked Padaung *(see p220)*. Try to establish a rapport with tribespeople and always ask their permission before taking photos.

Be wary of Burmese border areas, especially around Mae Sariang, where there is a chance of skirmishes between the Burmese military and ethnic armies fighting for independence. Malaria is also a risk around these parts, as it is in Kanchanaburi. In general, the health risks increase the farther you travel away from the towns. For nature-based treks, head for **Khao Yai National Park** *(see pp188–9)*. Many treks also include poling on a bamboo raft, if the rivers are high enough. Treks can last a week,

Lining up a putt at one of Thailand's growing number of golf courses. As well as the sport, visitors can enjoy the beautiful settings of the courses

Trekking through Thailand's beautiful and varied forests

but most take place over two to three nights and include visits to several villages. Be aware that scams are commonplace; to avoid being swindled, ask TAT for the list of companies recognized by the Professional Guide Association of Chiang Mai or the Jungle Tour Club of Northern Thailand, of which **Eagle House** and **Mae Ping Riverside Tours** are both members.

All treks should be led by at least two competent guides (who should speak the tribal languages and be aware of local customs). Check that the group doesn't exceed about eight trekkers, that the trek is registered with the police, and that transportation is not by public buses. Useful tips include lining backpacks with plastic bags to keep damp out; sleeping in dry clothes (even if it means wearing wet clothes by day); wearing a sun hat and cream, long trousers to protect against leeches, insect repellent, and worn-in hiking boots or at least supportive athletic shoes. Nights are cold in the mountains, so take warm layers: thermal tops and leggings, and silk sleeping bags. The best times to trek are November to February and early in the wet season, in June and July. For eco-friendly visitors, **Siam Safari**, **The Trekking Collective**, **The Wild Lodge** (see *White-water Rafting*

and Kayaking), and **Phuket Trekking Club** have a good reputation, and **Friends of Nature** organizes genuinely ecological treks.

Wildlife Watching

Unfortunately, Thailand's wildlife has been hunted almost to extinction, so there is little point in spending a few days in a hide in the hope of seeing a wild tiger or a bear. However, the country has a wide network of national parks, where some effort has been made to protect pockets of natural beauty. Here, visitors might well see rare and colorful birds, huge butterflies, and foot-long centipedes. The entrance fee to national parks for foreigners has been doubled to 400 *baht*, and while this may be justified for a stay of a few days, it is hardly worth paying for a brief visit. Some parks have camp sites, and most have log-cabin-style accommodation that can be reserved through the **National Park, Wildlife, and Plant Conservation Department**. The more popular parks, such as Khao Yai (*see pp188–9*), Khao Sok (*see p360*), Phu Kradung (*see pp290–91*), and Doi Inthanon (*see pp234–5*), have well-marked trails, but in less popular parks, visitors should ask

Wildlife encounter at Khao Yai National Park

park rangers to lead them to interesting features.

Boat Trips

Before the arrival of the motor car, boats were the only form of transportation in Thailand apart from walking. Low-lying areas of the country, such as the Central Plains, were criss-crossed by canals that enabled locals to visit friends and do their shopping. These days, floating markets are strictly for tourists, where visitors can enjoy the colorful spectacle and bustle of boats at places like Damnoen Saduak (*see p136*).

Apart from the floating markets, there are several other opportunities for sightseeing by boat. In Bangkok, **Chao Phraya Express Boats** offers short tours with commentary on the main riverside sights, such as the Grand Palace and Wat Arun. In the south, companies like **Sayan Tour** organize half-day and day trips in long-tail boats around the limestone stacks in Phangnga Bay, with the option of canoeing for an hour. In the north, long-tail boats cruise on the Ping River in Chiang Mai. Another popular trip is along the Mae Kok River from Tha Ton to Chiang Rai, either on bamboo rafts that take a couple of days or on long-tail boats that roar downriver in a few hours. Some of these tours, which can be arranged at the jetty in Tha Ton, include a stop at the Karen village of Ruammit for visitors to take a quick elephant ride.

The traditional long-tail boat, now popular for tourist excursions

Cycling

With cycling growing in popularity worldwide, it is no surprise that more and more people consider touring Thailand by bike, on a model either brought from home or rented locally. Not only is cycling healthy and environmentally sound, it also guarantees meaningful encounters with local people along the way. Though traffic on main roads can be dangerous to negotiate, it is possible to put a bike on a bus or train and head for quieter rural areas. Mostly the terrain is cyclist-friendly, and several companies organize guided rides along country lanes.

Anyone considering a cycling holiday would be advised to consult www.thaicycling.com and www.mrpumpy.net for information on possible itineraries. One of the most popular routes in the country follows the flow of the Mekong River from Chiang Khan to Nong Khai, or even right round to Mukdahan.

The best time to cycle in Thailand is from November to February, when temperatures are cooler, particularly in the north; the worst is between March and May, when pedalers are guaranteed to end each day dripping with sweat. Cycling in the rainy season (June–October) is worth considering, since there is frequently cloud cover, tropical storms tend to pass over quickly, and the landscapes are at their most lush at this time.

See the directory (pp452–3) for cycling tour operators.

Rock Climbing

Those looking for an activity that gets the adrenalin flowing will find that rock climbing is hard to beat. Providing dramatic views from limestone peaks at the end of a climb, Thailand is one of the world's most popular destinations for this sport.

The epicenter of rock climbing in Thailand is around Krabi, especially at Railay beach, where several companies offer half-day to three-day courses for beginners and rent out equipment to experienced climbers; the more reliable operators here include **Tex Rock Climbing**, **King Climbers**, and **Hot Rock**. More than 700 bolted routes in the region offer climbs ranging from 5a to 8c in terms of difficulty, graded according to the French system. For more details of rock climbing and other activities in this area, visit www.railay.com.

Ko Phi Phi has a similar limestone terrain, and a few local companies, like **Spider Monkey**, offer instruction for beginners at Ton Sai Tower or Hin Taek. Rock climbing is also getting a foothold in the north, where **Chiang Mai Rock Climbing**

Adventures runs climbs on more than 100 bolted routes at Crazy Horse Buttress, near San Kamphaeng, about 25 miles (40 km) east of Chiang Mai. These routes range in difficulty from easy to extremely challenging.

The large cave system of Tham Lot, containing artifacts dating back 1,700 years

Caving

Though Thailand's limestone landscapes are peppered with caves, few are set up for visitors to explore, so caving remains an activity largely for specialists. However, one cave that has been popularized is **Tham Lot** (see p223), near Soppong, in the northwest of the country. It contains some coffins that date back 1,700 years, and each evening there is a spectacular sight when hundreds of thousands of swifts return to nest in the cave. **Cave Lodge** is an ideal base from which to explore Tham Lot, and they can even arrange kayaking trips that pass right through the cave.

Bungee Jumping and Ziplining

Visitors who fancy having their feet bound and being thrown off a platform 165 ft (50 m) above the ground should head to **Jungle Bungy Jump**, a successful company operating in popular tourist locations such as Phuket, Pattaya, and Chiang Mai. A certificate is issued on completion of the jump.

Thailand's best rock climbing, at Railay beach, near Krabi

Ziplining is a popular activity that lets you sweep through the forest canopy on a steel cable secured to a body harness. The course's rest stations are ideal for enjoying the jungle's sounds.

Horse Racing and Riding

Plenty of people enjoy a day at the races in their homeland, so why not try your luck in tropical Thailand? It may be difficult to decipher the form card, but a keen eye on the runners in the paddock might just land a winner. As one of the few forms of gambling allowed in Thailand, horse racing attracts a strong local following, and the atmosphere is always vibrant. Races are held on weekends in Bangkok at the **Royal Bangkok Sports Club** (see p121) and the **Royal Turf Club**.

Air Sports

As if visitors to Chiang Mai didn't have enough activities to keep them busy, a couple more options, depending on weather conditions, are microlighting and hot-air ballooning. **Chiang Mai Sky Adventure** offers regular take-offs from bases just northeast of Chiang Mai during the cool season, giving the chance for a bird's-eye view of the Ping Valley and some spectacular photos.

Parasailing over the heads of sun-worshippers lining the beach

Cultural Study

Courses in meditation can give a valuable insight into Thai culture and, if followed diligently, also provide an invaluable skill to help cope with stress in the modern world. Participants are required to dress in white and adhere to the fundamental vows of Buddhism, which include refraining from killing, stealing, lying, and eating after midday. Practitioners are also expected to be up before dawn and to plan their day around sessions of walking and sitting meditation, as well as abstaining from entertainment (for example, no watching TV or listening to music) and idle chat (no mobile phones). Since the Dharma (literally, "Way of the Higher Truths," or code of conduct) is given for free, most places suggest that students make a donation to cover their lodging and food.

For meditation sessions in English and longer, disciplined retreats, contact the **World Fellowship of Buddhists** or visit www.dhammathai.org. Visitors are welcome to join the 10-day course that is run by the **International Dhamma Hermitage** at the beginning of each month at Wat Suan Mokkh, near Chaiya in the south. Other options include the **Northern Insight Meditation Center**'s month-long retreats at Wat Ram Poeng in Chiang Mai, **Wat Mahathat** in Bangkok, and **Wat Kow Tahm** on Ko Pha Ngan. Some locations have facilities where women can study, while others are only for men.

Visitors also come to Thailand to study traditional Thai massage, a vigorous combination of yoga, reflexology, and acupressure.

Learning to cook Thai food the Thai way

Courses typically tend to last between a week and two weeks and consist of theory, demonstration, and practice, leading to certification of competence.

Popular training in English is conducted at **Wat Pho** (see pp96–7) in Bangkok and in Chiang Mai's subtler style at centers including the **Old Medicine Hospital** and the **Thai Massage School of Chiang Mai**.

Delicately carved vegetables

The techniques of preparing Thai food – including fruit and vegetable carving – can be learned at various hotels and cooking schools, such as the **Blue Elephant** restaurant and cooking school with branches in Bangkok and Phuket, and **Baipai Thai Cooking School** in Bangkok. Reliable schools in the north include the **Chiang Mai Thai Cookery School** and **Baan Thai Cookery School**. Students can sign up for either a day or several days, and a typical day's "study" includes a shopping trip to the market, a demonstration of how to prepare a few dishes, followed by practice, then the best part – the eating – in which students get to taste and savor their own culinary creations.

DIRECTORY

Diving and Snorkeling

The Dive Academy
Bo Phut Beach,
Ko Samui.
Tel 09-2464-3264.

Dive Asia
24 Karon Rd, Kata Beach,
Phuket.
Tel 0-7633-0598.
w diveasia.com

Ko Tao Dive Info
Chuancheun Village,
Pattanakarn 57,
Bangkok.
Tel 0-8182-5960-7.
w diveinfo.net

New Way Diving
Sairee Rd,
Ko Tao.
Tel 0-7745-6528.

Phi Phi Scuba
Ton Sai Bay, Ko Phi Phi.
Tel 0-7560-1148.
w ppscuba.com

Santana Diving & Canoeing
273 Rat-U-Thit 200 Pi Rd,
Patong Beach,
Phuket.
Tel 0-7629-4220.
w santanaphuket.com

Sea Dragon Dive Center
5/51 Moo 7, Khao Lak.
Tel 0-7648-5420.
w seadragondive
center.com

Sailing

Gulf Charters Thailand
Ocean Marina, 167/5
Sukhumvit Rd, Sattahip.
Tel 0-3823-7752.
Island View Resort,
Ao Salak Pet, Ko Chang.
Tel 08-1813-8023.
w gulfcharters
thailand.com

Pattaya Yacht Charters
Ocean Marina, Sattahip.
Tel 08-7645-7771.
w pattayayacht
charters.com

Phuket Sailing
20/28 Soi Suksan, Moo 4,
Tambon Rawai, Phuket.
Tel 0-8990-9695-9 or
0-8189-5182-6.
w phuket-sailing.com

South East Asia Liveaboards
A10 The Royal Place,
96/68 Praphuketkhew Rd,
Kathu, Phuket.
Tel 0-7661-2655.
w seal-asia.com

Yachtpro
Adjacent to Yacht Haven
Marina, Phuket.
Tel 0-7633-1615.
w sailing-thailand.com

Water Sports

Phuket Fishing Charters
48/12 Mu 9,
Chalong, Phuket.
Tel 08-1370-8181.
w phuketfishing
charters.com

Wahoo Fishing Charters
48/20 Mu 9,
Chalong, Phuket.
Tel 0-7628-1510.

Canoeing

Paddle Asia
18/58 Thanon
Rasdanusorn, T Rasada,
Ban Kuku, Phuket.
Tel 0-7624-1519.
w paddleasia.com

Sea Canoe Thailand
125/461 Moo 5,
Baan Sapan Rd,
Muang Phuket.
Tel 0-7652-8839/40.
w seacanoe.net

White-Water Rafting and Kayaking

Siam Rivers
17 Ratchawithi Rd,
Chiang Mai.
Tel 0-8951-5191-7.
w siamrivers.com

Thai Adventure Rafting
54/5 Moo 2, Soi 14,
Tambol Tasala,
Chiang Mai.
Tel 0-5385-0160.
w activethailand.com

The Wild Lodge
666 Sukhumvit 24,
Bangkok.
Tel 0-2261-4412.
w thewildlodge.com

Golf

Laem Chabang International Country Club
106/8 Moo 4,
Beung, Siracha,
near Pattaya.
Tel 0-3837-2273.
w laemchabang
golf.com

Lanna Golf Club
Chotana Rd,
Chiang Mai.
Tel 0-5322-1911.

Red Mountain Golf Course
119 Wijittsongkram Rd,
Kathu District, Phuket.
Tel 0-7632-2000.
w redmountain
phuket.com

Thana City Golf and Country Club
100-100/1 Moo 4,
Bang Na Trat Rd,
Km 14, Bangplee,
Samutprakarn.
Tel 08-3304-4455.

Trekking

Eagle House
16 Chang Moi Kao,
Chiang Mai.
Tel 0-5323-5387.
w eaglehouse.com

Friends of Nature
133/21 Ratchaprarop Rd,
Bangkok.
Map 4 E4–5.
Tel 0-2642-4426.
w friendsofnature
93.com

Mae Ping Riverside Tours
101 Chiang Mai-
Lamphun Rd,
Chiang Mai.
Tel 0-5330-2121.
w tours-chiangmai.
com

Phuket Trekking Club
55/779–780 Villa
Daowroong Village,
East Chaofah Rd,
Tambon Vichit,
Phuket.
Tel 0-7637-7344.
w phukettrekking
club.com

Siam Safari
17/2 Soi Yodsanae,
Chao Far Rd,
Chalong,
Phuket.
Tel 0-7638-4456,
0-7638-4777.
w siamsafari.com

The Trekking Collective
3/5 Loy Kroh
Road Soi 1,
Chiang Mai.
Tel 0-5320-8340.
w trekking
collective.com

Wildlife Watching

National Park, Wildlife, and Plant Conservation Department
61 Phaholyothin Rd,
Chatuchak, Bangkok.
Tel 0-2561-0777,
0-2579-6666.
w dnp.go.th

DIRECTORY

Boat Trips

Chao Phraya Express Boats
78/24–29 Maharaj Rd,
Phra Nakhorn,
Bangkok.
Tel 0-2623-6001.
w chaophrayaexpress
boat.com

Sayan Tour
209 Phangnga Bus
Terminal,
Phangnga
Tel 0-7643-0348.
w sayantour.com

Cycling

Bike & Travel
Prathum Thani.
Tel 0-2990-0274.
w cyclingthailand.com

Click and Travel
158/42 Chiang
Mai-Hod Rd,
Chiang Mai.
Tel 0-5328-1553.
w clickandtravel
online.com

Spice Roads
14/1-B Soi Promsri 2,
Sukhumvit Soi 39,
Bangkok.
Tel 0-2381-7490.
w spiceroads.com

Rock Climbing

Chiang Mai Rock Climbing Adventures
55/3 Ratchapakinai Rd,
Chiang Mai.
Tel 0-5320-7102.
w thailandclimbing.
com

Hot Rock
245 Moo 5, Sai Tai, Krabi.
Tel 0-7566-2245,
085-641-9842.
w railayadventure.com

King Climbers
Railay Beach,
near Krabi.
Tel 0-7562-2096.

Spider Monkey
Ton Sai Village,
Ko Phi Phi Don.
Tel 0-7581-9384.

Tex Rock Climbing
East Railay Beach,
Krabi.
Tel 0-7563-1509.

Caving

Cave Lodge
15 Moo 1,
Pang Mapha,
near Mae Hong Son.
Tel 0-5361-7203.
w cavelodge.com

Bungee Jumping and Ziplining

Jungle Bungy Jump
61/3 Wichitsongkram,
Kathu, Phuket.
Tel 076-321-351.
w phuketbungy.com

Flight of the Gibbon
Mae Kampong Village,
Chiang Mai.
Tel 0-5301-0660.
Khao Khiao Safari Park,
Chonburi.
Tel 08-9833-5503.
w treetopasia.com

Flying Hanuman
Soi Nam Tok Kathu,
Wichitsongkram Rd,
Phuket.
Tel 0-7632-3264.
w flyinghanuman.com

Horse Racing and Riding

Phuket Riding Club
95 Viset Rd,
Rawai, Maung,
Phuket.
Tel 0-7628-8213.

Royal Turf Club
Phitsanulok Rd,
Dusit, Bangkok.
Tel 0-2628-1810.
w rtcot.com

Air Sports

Chiang Mai Sky Adventure
190 Mu 3,
T Nong Yhang, Sansai,
Chiang Mai.
Tel 0-5325-5588.
w skyadventures.info

Cultural Study

Baan Thai Cookery School
11 Rachadamnern Rd,
Soi 5, Chiang Mai.
Tel 0-5335-7339.
w cookinthai.com

Baipai Thai Cooking School
8/91 Ngam Wongwan Rd,
Soi 54, Ladyao,
Chatuchak,
Bangkok.
Tel 0-2561-1404.
w baipai.com

Blue Elephant
233 South Sathorn Rd,
Bangkok.
Tel 0-2673-9353.
96 Krabi Rd, Phuket.
Tel 0-7635-4355.
w blueelephant.co.th

Chiang Mai Thai Cookery School
47/2 Moon Muang Rd
Chiang Mai. Tel 0-5320-
6388. w thaicookery
school.com

International Dhamma Hermltage
Wat Suan Mokkh, Chaiya,
Surat Thani.
Tel 0-7743-1552.
w suanmokkh-idh.org

Northern Insight Meditation Center
Wat Ram Poeng, Canal Rd,
Chiang Mai.
Tel 0-5327-8620.
w palikanon.com/
vipassana/tapotaram/
tapotaram.htm

Old Medicine Hospital
238/8 Wualai Rd,
Chiang Mai.
Tel 0-5320-1663.
w thaimassageschool.
ac.th

Thai Massage School of Chiang Mai
203/6 Mae Jo Rd, Chiang
Mai. Tel 0-5385-4330.
w tmcschool.com

Wat Kow Tahm
Near Ban Tai,
Ko Pha Ngan.
Tel 08-3593-3597.
w kowtahm.com

Wat Mahathat (Section Five)
Maharat Rd, Bangkok.
Tel 0-2222-6011.

World Fellowship of Buddhists
616 Benjasiri Park, Soi
Medhinivet, off
Sukhumvit 24, Bangkok.
Tel 0-2661-1284.

Spa Breaks in Thailand

Thailand has thousands of spas offering every kind of treatment possible, and its sultry temperatures, idyllic landscapes, and sense of tranquility make it an ideal destination for a spa break. Traditional Thai architecture, serene Zen-minimalist decor, and enchanting gardens blend with the Thai people's gentle and giving nature to make a truly memorable spa experience. Massage has been practiced in Thailand for some 2,500 years, and while it's possible to have a cheap shoulder rub in simple backstreet shop fronts, nothing beats some serious pampering at a luxury resort or an indulgent afternoon at a day spa.

Relaxing in the peaceful garden environment of the Anantara Resort & Spa

Hotel & Resort Spas

Travelers tend to visit a hotel or resort spa as part of a wider holiday, with the main focus being a beach or cultural experience. However, Thailand's luxury five-star hotels and resorts are home to some of the world's very best spas, offering a wide range of professional, unique, and blissful treatments.

The greatest concentration of spas is on the islands of Phuket and Ko Samui, in the beach resort towns of Hua Hin and Cha-am, and in the northern Chiang Mai area.

The country's foremost spa resorts include the **Four Seasons Resort Koh Samui**, the **Banyan Tree Spa Phuket**, **Six Senses Yao Noi**, and the **Anantara Resort & Spa** in Hua Hin and Ko Samui.

Spa treatments are generally an added extra, but many resorts are now increasingly offering all-inclusive packages.

The Anantara resorts offer three-day and seven-day programs that include between four and ten treatments.

Spa Retreats

Thailand has a number of luxury resorts situated in truly breathtaking settings. Visitors looking for an intimate getaway on a deserted white-sand beach skirted by palm trees should head to the **Six Senses Hideaway Hua Hin**, south of Hua Hin, or the **Aleenta Resort & Spa Phang Nga**. Those who like the sound of a plush villa with a private infinity pool set among tropical jungle overlooking lush rice fields – or, more dramatically, the Mekong River across to Burma – should book at the **Four Seasons Chiang Mai** or the **Four Seasons Tented Camp at the Golden Triangle**. The aim of staying here is to experience the local culture

and lush environment as much as it is to have a spa experience. The fact that these resorts are often set in remote locations and may be accessible only by speedboat (such as the **Rayavadee Spa** near Krabi) or traditional long-tail boat (the Four Seasons Tented Camp at the Golden Triangle) adds to the allure. The spas at these resorts offer longer programs of daily treatments for those who really want to unwind.

Destination Spas

Revitalizing the mind, body, and spirit is the central purpose of destination spas, with guests rarely leaving the resort after checking in. Thailand's first and best, the **Chiva-Som International Health Resort**, offers more than 150 treatments focused on relaxation and rejuvenation, stress relief, detoxification, and weight loss. Guests undergo an extensive health consultation upon arrival, and a program is created to match their goals. There is a three-night minimum stay, though most guests stay a week or more, and nutritious spa cuisine, activities, and treatments are included in the rate. Another famous destination spa is the **Kamalaya Wellness Sanctuary & Holistic Spa** in Ko Samui.

Because spa resorts tend to provide an array of non-spa activities – from golf to white-water rafting and mountain climbing – signature

A poultice massage at Banyan Tree Spa Phuket, a popular spa resort

treatments at destination spas cater for travelers who may be suffering some after-effects. The signature treatment at the Four Seasons Tented Camp, for instance, is where poultices filled with camphor, lime, and lemongrass are used to massage the body and inner thighs – the perfect antidote for aching muscles.

Day Spas

All over Thailand, travelers can find day spas – stand-alone operations not attached to resorts or hotels – and many hotels also offer treatments to non-guests on a per-session basis. Most day spas are in Bangkok and include the stylish **Oasis Spa** and **Thann Sanctuary**, the **Harnn Heritage Spa**, and **Health Land**. Chiang Mai also has excellent day spas.

Spa Treatments

Despite Thailand's long history of therapeutic massage and natural healing – including Thai massage, medicinal herbs, and natural springs – the country

Working out stress through yoga at Chiva-Som International Health Resort

is at the cutting edge of spa offerings. Expect to see anything and everything on a spa menu, from Tropical Sprinkles and Tranquility Mists at the Banyan Tree Spa Phuket, to their famous four-hand Harmony Banyan treatment, where two therapists work on you at once. Other spas, such as the Six Senses Spa and Anantara Spas, also offer versions of this indulgent treatment. While some treatments are indigenous

to Thailand – traditional Thai massage, for example – others, such as hydrotherapy, thalassotherapy, aromatherapy, and Ayurvedic treatments, can be found all over the world. Many spas have also developed their own signature treatments. The Four Seasons Spas have an array of sensual offerings connected to the cycles of the moon, with treatments that should be experienced only during certain lunar phases.

DIRECTORY

Hotel & Resort Spas

Anantara Resort & Spa Hua Hin
43/1 Phetkasem Beach Rd, Hua Hin.
Tel 0-3252-0250.
W anantara.com

Anantara Resort & Spa Koh Samui
99/9 Moo 1, Bo Phut Bay, Ko Samui. **Tel** 0-7742-8300. W anantara.com

Banyan Tree Spa Phuket
33 Moo 4, Srisoonthorn Rd, Cherngtalay, Phuket.
Tel 0-7632-4374.
W banyantreespa.com

Four Seasons Resort Koh Samui
219 Moo 5, Angthong, Ko Samui. **Tel** 0-7724-3000.
W fourseasons.com

Six Senses Yao Noi
Yao Noi Island,
Phang Nga Bay.
Tel 0-7641-8500.
W sixsenses.com

Spa Retreats

Aleenta Resort & Spa Phang Nga
33 Moo 5, T Khokkloy, Phang Nga.
Tel 0-7658-0333.
W aleenta.com

Six Senses Hideaway Hua Hin
9/22 Moo 5, Paknampran Beach, Pranburi.
Tel 0-3263-2111.
W sixsenses.com/ hideaway-huahin

Four Seasons Chiang Mai
Mae Rim-Old Samoeng Rd, Mae Rim, Chiang Mai.
Tel 0-5329-8181.
W fourseasons.com

Four Seasons Tented Camp at the Golden Triangle
49 Moo 1, Chaeng Saen Rd, Chaeng Saen, Chiang Rai. **Tel** 0-5391-0200.
W fourseasons.com

Rayavadee Spa
214 Moo 2, Tambol Ao-Nang, Amphur Muang, Krabi.
Tel 0-7562-0740-3.
W rayavadee.com

Destination Spas

Chiva-Som International Health Resort
73/4 Petchkasem Rd, Hua Hin. **Tel** 0-3253-6536.
W chivasom.com

Kamalaya Wellness Sanctuary & Holistic Spa
102/9 Moo 3, Laem Set Rd, Na-Muang, Ko Samui.
Tel 0-7742-9800.
W kamalaya.com

Day Spas

Harnn Heritage Spa
Siam Paragon, 991 Silom Rd, 4th Floor, Bangkok.
Tel 0-2610-9715-6.

Health Land
120 Sathorn Rd, Bangkok.
Tel 0-2637-8883.

Oasis Spa
88 Soi Sukhumvit, 51 Klongton Nua, Bangkok.
Tel 0-2662-6171.

Thann Sanctuary
Gaysorn Plaza, 4th floor, Ploenchit Rd, Bangkok.
Tel 0-2658-0550.

SURVIVAL GUIDE

PRACTICAL INFORMATION

Thailand caters well to its growing number of tourists. The 12 million people who visit each year find one of the biggest and best-organized tourist industries in Asia. The headquarters of the helpful Tourism Authority of Thailand (TAT) is in Bangkok, and there are offices across the country and several overseas branches. The relevant address and telephone number is given for each town and sight throughout this guide. The tourist industry has developed so rapidly that the adventurous traveler is no longer restricted to organized tours or major tourist destinations such as Bangkok and Phuket – the whole country is accessible to independent travelers. There are many reputable travel agencies all over Thailand. They offer advice, book flights and accommodations, and organize sightseeing tours. Some pre-travel planning is necessary to avoid the worst of the rainy season and holiday periods such as the Chinese New Year *(see pp52–5)*.

When to Go

Thailand's weather can be tempestuous, with year-round humidity, rocketing temperatures, and torrential rainstorms. However, the optimum time to visit the country is during the cooler, drier months from November to February. It is no coincidence that this is the peak tourist season, when sights may get crowded. The hot season, from March to May, can be unbearable, while the rainy season, which generally lasts from June to October, is the least predictable of the three periods. Climate and rainfall charts can be found on pages 52–5.

Tourists relaxing in the sun at Patong beach, Phuket

Advance Booking

Bangkok is a popular launching point for other Southeast Asian destinations, so it is necessary to book airline tickets well in advance. This is especially true during Thailand's peak tourist season, November to February, when flights and hotels are heavily booked. If you plan to travel during this period, it is wise to make arrangements at least three to six months prior to departure.

Visas and Passports

Many nationalities, including the citizens of most European countries, Australia, and the US, can enter Thailand for up to 30 days without a pre-arranged visa. Proof of adequate funds for the duration of a visitor's stay (10,000 *baht* per person or 20,000 *baht* per family) can be requested upon arrival – a credit card is sufficient proof of this. Also be aware that certain visas have minimum fund requirements – check with your local Thai embassy before traveling for current information. Proof of a confirmed return flight or other on-going travel arrangements might also be required, although this is rare. The 30-day period is extendible for a maximum of 10 days. Nationals of several smaller European countries must obtain a visa before traveling. For those wishing to stay longer, a 60-day tourist visa (extendable by 30 days at an immigration office) can be arranged from a Thai embassy or consulate prior to arrival in Thailand. This usually takes two to three working days to process, but may take longer during busy periods.

A 90-day nonimmigrant visa must be applied for in your home country and requires a letter of verification from a Thai source giving a valid reason, such as business or study, for spending three months in Thailand. This visa is slightly more expensive than the 60-day tourist visa.

With all visas, entry into Thailand must occur within 90 days of issue. Visa extensions are at the discretion of the **Immigration Department** in Bangkok or any other immigration office in Thailand. Overstaying a visa carries a fine of 500 *baht* per day and can result in serious penalties. Single and multiple re-entry visas can be obtained relatively easily, allowing the visitor to leave the country and return within 60 days. These can be applied for at the Immigration Department in Bangkok. Strictly speaking, travelers entering Thailand should have at least six months left on their passport. It is best to confirm all such details with a Thai embassy or consulate before traveling. Crossing the border into neighboring countries generally depends on the current political situation, *(see p464)* so it is wise to check prior to travel. A 24-hour visa for Myanmar, for a stay in

◄ The railway market stalls at Maeklong in Samut Songkhram, a short distance from Bangkok

the town over the border, costs 500 *baht* to the Myanmar immigration. The quickest way to obtain a 30-day tourist visa for Laos is to apply for it at a travel agency in major cities such as Bangkok or Chiang Mai. Visitors to Cambodia can obtain a 30-day tourist visa free of charge upon arrival at Phnom Penh airport.

Travel Safety Advice

Visitors can get up-to-date travel safety information from the **Foreign and Commonwealth Office** in the UK, the **State Department** in the US, and the **Department of Foreign Affairs and Trade** in Australia.

Customs Information

Customs regulations in Thailand are standard. During an inbound flight you will be given a customs form that must be filled in and handed over at the customs desk after claiming your baggage. Thai customs restrictions for goods carried into the country are 200 cigarettes and/or one liter of wine or spirits. For complete details about export declarations, duty payments, and VAT refunds visit www.customs.go.th.

A car or motorbike can be brought into the country for touring purposes for up to six months, but this requires prior arrange-ment through the Thai embassy in your home country. The carrying of drugs *(see p464)*, fire-arms, or pornography is strictly prohibited.

There are no restric-tions on the maximum amount of money an individual may bring into the country, however there are sometimes minimum require-ments *(see Visas and Passports)*. It is illegal to leave Thailand with more than 50,000 *baht* without the correct authorization. Antiques and Buddha images are not allowed out of Thailand with-out authorization. If you wish to export such

items you must first contact the **Fine Arts Department** of the National Museum in Bangkok at least five days before the date of shipment and fill in a form accom-panied by two frontal photographs of the object being purchased (no more than five pieces to be shown in any one photograph). Contemporary "works of art," such as paintings bought in markets, can be taken out of the country without permission.

Tourist Information

The many branches of the **Tourism Authority of Thailand (TAT)** are very helpful, offering plenty of practical and back-ground information on sights and festivals, as well as maps, brochures, mini-guides, and posters. They also have a useful list of reputable travel agents and hotels. There is a small informa-tion booth in Suvarnabhumi airport. Many of the provincial capitals in Thailand have a TAT office (listed throughout this guide), as do some overseas countries. The TAT website is also a useful source of information.

Admission Prices

Admission charges to sights in Thailand are usually nominal, ranging between 10 and 50 *baht* for government-run establish-ments. National parks, however, charge either 200 or 400 *baht* per person (children are usually admitted at half price). Private museums are generally either free or charge up to 200 *baht*. Occasionally, foreigners may be

Local travel agency offering tourist information

DIRECTORY

Immigration Department
507 Soi Suanphlu, Sathorn Tai Rd, Bangkok. **Tel** 0-2287-3101.
W immigration.go.th

Fine Arts Department
National Museum, 1 Na Phra That Rd, Phra Nakhon, Bangkok.
Tel 0-2628-5033. W national museumfineart.go.th

TAT Headquarters
1600 New Phetburi Rd, Bangkok.
Tel 1672 or 0-2250-5500.
W tourismthailand.org

Embassies

Cambodia
518/4 Pracha Uthit Rd, Soi Ramkamhaeng 39, Bangkok.
Tel 0-2957-5851 (then dial 100).

Canada
15th Floor, Abdulrahim Place, 990 Rama 4 Rd, Bangkok.
Tel 0-2636-0540.

Malaysia
33–35 South Sathorn Rd, Bangkok. **Tel** 0-2629-6800.

Myanmar (Burma)
132 Sathorn Nua Rd, Bangkok.
Tel 0-2234-4698, 0-2233-2237.

United Kingdom
14 Witthayu (Wireless) Rd, Bangkok. **Tel** 0-2305-8333.

United States
95 Witthayu (Wireless) Rd, Bangkok. **Tel** 0-2205-4000.
W bangkok.usembassy.gov

Travel Safety Advice

Australia
Department of Foreign Affairs and Trade. W dfat.gov.au/ smartraveller.gov.au/

United Kingdom
Foreign and Commonwealth Office. W gov.uk/foreign-travel-advice

United States
US Department of State.
W travel.state.gov/

charged a higher admission price than locals on the assump-tion that they earn more than most Thais. Under Thai law this is not totally legal, but to prevent embarrassment it is usually best to pay the extra amount. A few major tourist *wats* charge a set fee; in others there is usually a box for donations.

Opening Hours

Most sights can be visited throughout the year, though access to some of the southern islands may be limited in the rainy season. In general, major tourist attractions open at 8am or 9am and close any time between 3:30pm and 6pm. A few also shut for lunch

Typical entrance tickets to major historical sites

between noon and 1pm. Most major sights are open daily, but some national museums close for public holidays and on Mondays and Tuesdays.

Department stores are usually open daily, 10am–9pm, and smaller shops are open 8am–9pm. Commercial offices open 8am–noon and 1–5pm Monday to Friday. Government offices are open 8:30am–noon and 1–4:30pm Monday to Friday. During the Chinese New Year, many businesses close, especially in the south. For banking hours, *see page 468*.

What to Take

As the climate in Thailand is generally hot and humid, it is advisable to dress in cool, nonrestricting clothes made from natural fibers. A sweater may be needed in northern and northeastern regions during the cool season. The rainy season brings sudden downpours when a light raincoat is handy. If visiting temples, appropriate dress is required *(see p463)*, as is easily removable footwear. A first-aid kit is also useful *(see p466)*.

Travelers with Special Needs

There are few facilities for disabled travelers in Thailand. Sidewalks can be uneven and pedestrian bridges are often accessed only by steep steps. Wheelchair access is limited to the top-class hotels. The easiest way to travel is to book an organized tour *(see p475)* or to contact the **Association of Physically Handicapped People** for further information.

Traveling with Children

Children are always welcome in Thailand. The larger hotels have baby-sitting services, and TAT offers advice on attractions for kids. Hats and sunblock are a must for children out in the sun. There are plenty of fast-food outlets and adaptable chefs who will gladly provide a choice of suitable alternatives to spicy meals.

Senior Travelers

Older citizens of Thailand are treated with great respect, as are senior citizens from other countries. Unfortunately, this higher status does not translate into any discounts or savings.

Gay and Lesbian Travelers

On the whole Thai society takes a fairly relaxed attitude to homosexuality. A number of bars, clubs, and other venues cater exclusively to a gay and lesbian crowd. However, at heart, Thai society is still quite conservative, and public displays of affection by both homosexuals and heterosexuals are frowned upon.

Prominent gay and lesbian scenes can be found in Bangkok, Pattaya, and Phuket, and to a lesser extent in Chiang Mai. General information for gay and lesbian visitors is available online at **Dragoncastle**, and both this website and **Utopia** are excellent for details of gay and lesbian related activities and events in Thailand.

Centers of Worship for Visitors

There are many facilities for visitors to undertake Buddhist studies *(see p451)*. The International Buddhist Meditation Center has details of English-language courses at wats in and around Bangkok. Most other religious denominations are represented in Thailand – listed below are religious centers in Bangkok offering services in English. Christ Church holds Anglican and Episcopalian services. The International Church has services on Sundays, as does the Holy Redeemer Catholic Church. The Jewish Association of Thailand has occasional services at the Jewish Community Center. The Haroon Mosque has services for Muslims.

Language

It is always useful to learn a few Thai phrases *(see pp508–11)*. Many local people in tourist towns speak some English, as do most hotel receptionists. Sight and road names in these areas are transliterated, and menus are often in English as well as in Thai. Prices and road numbers are generally in Arabic numerals. Transliterated spellings vary in different maps and guides, and on signs. Note that "j" and "ch" are interchangeable, as are "d" and "t." The letters "ph" (e.g. as in Phuket) are pronounced "p," never "f." Likewise, the "h" in "th" is always silent (e.g. Thailand).

Thai Time Systems and Calendar

Bangkok time is seven hours ahead of Greenwich Mean Time (GMT), 12 hours ahead

Transliterated road sign

of Eastern Standard Time, and 15 hours ahead of Pacific Standard Time (6, 11, and 14 hours ahead, respectively, during Daylight Saving Hours). Although the standard clock and 24-hour clock are used and widely understood, Thailand also has its own unique system. Thais divide the day into four segments of six hours each. For example, 7am for us is 1am for Thais.

Two calendars are used in Thailand: the Gregorian (Western) and the Buddhist calendars. The Buddhist Era (BE) starts 543 years before the Gregorian era. To convert from the Gregorian calendar to the Buddhist calendar, add 543 years. For example, AD 1957 is the equivalent of 2500 BE.

Conversion Chart

US Standard to Metric
1 inch = 2.54 centimeters
1 foot = 30 centimeters
1 mile = 1.6 kilometers
1 ounce = 28 grams
1 pound = 454 grams
1 US quart = 0.947 liter
1 US gallon = 3.6 liters

Metric to US Standard
1 centimeter = 0.4 inch
1 meter = 3 feet 3 inches
1 kilometer = 0.6 mile
1 gram = 0.04 ounce
1 kilogram = 2.2 pounds
1 liter = 1.1 US quarts

A range of plugs and adaptors that can be used in Thailand

Electricity

The electric current throughout Thailand is 220 volts AC, 50 cycles. Dual-prong rounded plugs as well as flat-pin plugs can be used. Major hotels also have 110-volt outlets for electric razors. Adaptors and power-surge cables (for laptops) are sold in department stores and electrical stores.

In smaller towns, especially during the rainy season, there can be power failures and flashlights can be useful.

Responsible Travel

Attitudes towards environmental issues are slowly beginning to change in Thailand. The authorities are actively promoting awareness of the need for conservation, from prohibiting locals fishing with dynamite and drag-netting coral reefs, to encouraging tourists to "leave nothing but your footprints". Ecologically aware dive companies forbid visitors to take anything away, even a seashell, and the use of plastic bags and plastic water bottles in national parks, where they might be abandoned, is increasingly discouraged.

Open World, an ecological tour operator, conducts culture, nature, and conservation tours throughout Thailand, which include a tiger conservation program, flora and fauna and birdwatching tours. The **Thailand Environment Institute** website has information about environmental projects and the conservation of natural resources in Thailand.

Set against all this good work, visitors should be aware that in some areas there are still environmentally destructive shrimp farms, the clearing of natural forest for palm oil plantations, and the farming of tigers in captivity for their body parts under the guise of "tiger zoos".

DIRECTORY

Travelers with Special Needs

Association of Physically Handicapped People
73/7-8 Tivanond Rd, Talad Kwan, Nonthaburi.
Tel 0-2951-0445.

Gay and Lesbian Travelers

Dragoncastle
w dragoncastle.net

Utopia
w utopia-asia.com

Centers of Worship

Christ Church
11 Covent Rd, Bangkok.
Tel 0-2234-3634.
w christchurch bangkok.org

Haroon Mosque
25 Charoen Krung 36 Rd, Chinatown, Bangkok.
Tel 0-2630-9435.

Holy Redeemer Catholic Church
123/19 Soi Ruam Rudi, 5 Witthayu (Wireless) Rd, Bangkok. **Tel** 0-2256-6305.
w holyredeemer bangkok.net

International Buddhist Meditation Center

Wat Mahathat, 3 Maharaj Rd, Bangkok.
Tel 0-2623-6326.

International Church
61/2 Soi Saen Sabai, Sukhumvit 36, Bangkok.
Tel 0-2258-5821.
w icbangkok.org

Jewish Community Center
121 Soi Sainamtip 2, Soi 22 Sukhumvit Rd, Bangkok.
Tel 0-2663-0244.
w jewishthailand.com

Responsible Travel

Open World International Travel Service
89/14–15 Phahonyothin 54/1, Saimai, Bangkok.
Tel 0-2974-3867.
w openworldthailand. com

Thailand Environment Institute
16/151 Muang Thong Thani, Bond Rd, Pakkred, Nonthaburi.
Tel 0-2503-3333.
w tei.or.th

Etiquette

It is not by accident that Thailand is often referred to as "the land of smiles." The Thais are exceptionally friendly and helpful people, and getting along with them is easy – simply smile wide and laugh a lot. Being Buddhists, they are an amazingly tolerant people. Avoiding offensive behavior can generally be achieved through simple courtesy and common sense. A few taboos do exist, though, mostly with regard to the monarchy and Buddhism. Visitors should be particularly careful to behave respectfully at *wats* and in front of any Buddha image. Confrontation is also considered extremely rude, and Thais will bend over backward to avoid arguments of any sort. Losing your temper or shouting, whatever the situation, is seen as an embarrassing loss of face.

King Bhumibol and Queen Sirikit

Royalty

The royal family is the most revered institution in Thailand. Criticizing or defaming it in any way can be considered *lèse-majesté*. Not only could this mean a jail sentence, but Thai people will nearly always be deeply offended. Coins, bills, and stamps bear the images of kings and therefore should not be treated lightly. Similarly, you cannot photograph certain sacred sights connected to royalty, such as the *bot* of Wat Phra Kaeo, which houses the highly revered Emerald Buddha image.

Two Thais addressing each other with a *wai*, the traditional greeting

Greeting People

The Thai greeting is known as the *wai* and consists of the palms being pressed together and lifted towards the chin. The *wai* evolved from an ancient greeting used to show that neither party was carrying weapons. The *wai* is layered with intricacies of class, gender, and age: each of these dictates a certain height at which the two hands must be held. The inferior party initiates the *wai* and holds it higher and for longer than the superior, who returns it according to his or her social standing. Non-Thais are not expected to be familiar with these complexities, and the easiest method is simply to mirror whatever greeting you receive. As a general rule of thumb, however, you should not *wai* children or workers such as waiters, waitresses, and street vendors.

Thais use first names to address people, even in formal situations. The polite form of address is the gender-neutral title Khun, followed by the first name or nickname. Every Thai person has a nickname, usually a one- or two-syllable name with a simple meaning, such as Moo (pig) or Koong (shrimp).

Body Language

The head is considered a sacred part of the body by Thais. Never touch someone's head, not even that of a child. The feet are seen as the lowliest part of the body and to point your feet toward someone or rest them on a table is considered rude. When sitting on the floor, especially inside a temple, tuck your legs away behind you or to the side and try not to step over people sitting around you; allow them time to move out of your way.

National Anthems

The royal anthem is played twice a day, at 8am and 6pm, at Skytrain stations and on the Metro. At these times it is polite to stop whatever you are doing and stand still. In theaters, the royal anthem is played before all performances. When it is playing the audience stands in silent respect to a portrait of the king on the screen. A different Thai folk tune is

Devotees kneeling before a Buddha, their feet facing away from the image

A man offering food to a line of monks on the daily alms round

played on radio and TV on behalf of the National Council for Peace and Order.

Monks

The monkhood *(sangha)* is a respected institution that comes just below royalty in the social hierarchy. Most taboos in dealing with monks concern women: it is prohibited for a monk to touch a woman or for him to receive anything directly from her. Therefore, when traveling by public transportation, women should avoid sitting near or next to a monk If she has to offer anything to a monk she should either use a middleman or place the item nearby for him to pick up. These rules are confined to monks and do not apply to nuns.

It is not forbidden for people to talk to monks – many are eager to try out their English. However, monks never return *wais*.

Etiquette at Wats

As in churches and other houses of worship, a certain decorum should be observed when entering the grounds of any *wat*. Temples are calm, quiet places, so try to avoid disturbing the peace. Dress should be clean, respectable, and unrevealing (strictly speaking, the upper arms and legs down to mid-calf should be covered). Shoes should be removed when entering any temple building. Step over, not on, the thresholds of *wat* buildings as Thais believe that one of the nine spirits that inhabit buildings lives in the threshold.

All Buddha images are sacred no matter how small, ruined, or neglected, and you must never sit with your feet pointing toward them.

Some areas of a temple may be off limits for women – there is usually a sign indicating such areas.

Suitable Dress

Because the Thais are a modest people, clothing should be kept respectable whether you are in the city or in the country. Women especially should take care not to wear revealing skirts, shorts, or skimpy tops. In formal settings and restaurants you will rarely see Thai women with bare shoulders; sleeveless dresses or tops are considered too revealing for such situations. Topless sunbathing

"No shoes" sign outside Wat Phra Kaeo, Bangkok

is frowned upon greatly – regardless of whether others are doing it – even in resorts dominated by Western tourists. Most Thais find the practice embarrassing and many of them find it offensive.

Communicating

Bargaining is common throughout Thailand *(see p434)*. Though everyone develops a personal technique – whether it involves smiling or remaining poker-faced – it is important not to get too tough or too mean. Likewise, be patient with receptionists, waitresses, and others whom you may deal with. In general, you should avoid raising your voice or becoming obviously irritable – Thais learn in childhood always to speak softly and avoid direct conflict. Foreigners who may be used to getting results if they show impatience are likely to find Thais ignoring them rather than.attempting to continue communicating with them.

Tourists bargaining with vendors on the platform of Hua Hin Station

Tipping

Traditionally, tipping is not common practice in Thailand, though in Westernized establishments it is fast becoming so. Taxi drivers expect tips – as a rule you should round up the fare to the nearest ten *baht*. Porters, hairdressers, and barbers also often expect tips. A service charge of ten percent is common on up-scale restaurant and hotel bills, even if they also charge government tax *(see p401 and p413)*.

Smoking

Smoking is prohibited in all public areas such as theaters, department stores, government buildings, and on all public transport systems. It is also banned in restaurants (except on terraces), nightclubs, and pubs. Fines for smoking in public places can be hefty, usually 2,000 *baht*.

Personal Security and Health

Thailand is a fairly safe country, and simple health and safety precautions keep the vast majority of travelers out of trouble. For instance, ignore hustlers, keep away from troubled border areas, take care of valuables, and avoid staying or eating in unsanitary conditions. The infrastructure of emergency services for both health and crime is efficient throughout Bangkok and provincial capitals. As a rule of thumb, the more remote the area, the higher the health risk and the less support available in the event of any mishap. The main hospitals in Bangkok, Chiang Mai, the main resorts, and other large cities have modern equipment and well-trained doctors, many of whom speak some English.

Tourist policeman wearing a beret, and an ordinary officer

In an Emergency

There are no national emergency telephone lines except for ambulances, and operators do not speak English. For English-speaking help, call the Tourist Assistance Center, which will contact the appropriate service for you. Lines are open from 8am to midnight, after which you will have to rely on English-speaking hotel staff. During office hours, TAT (see p459) may also be able to help. The Metropolitan Mobile Police cover general emergencies in Bangkok. All Bangkok's hospitals have 24-hour accident and emergency departments.

Fire engine

Ambulance

Police car

General Precautions

Despite its size, Bangkok is relatively safe. Crime and violence do exist, but most travelers are untouched by it. Discretion and sobriety are the best means of avoiding problems. Be alert at tourist sights and bus and train stations, where hustlers and pickpockets occasionally operate: scam artists outside the Grand Palace (see pp84–5) direct tourists to pricier, less impressive sights. Do not flash large amounts of cash or leave your luggage unattended. If you are leaving valuables in a hotel safe, make sure to get a receipt, and do not let credit cards out of your sight when paying for shopping.

The drugging, then robbing, of tourists on long-distance trains and buses has occurred, so politely decline food or drink from strangers. Thailand is an excellent place to buy gems (see p438), but do not be tempted into buying large quantities to sell back at home unless you are familiar with the market and its pitfalls. Extra care is necessary in more remote areas of the country where locals are less accustomed to tourists and you are more likely to stand out. Care should also be taken in poorer parts of cities, particularly at night, or if traveling alone.

Drugs

Thai law prohibits the sale or purchase of opium, heroin, or marijuana. Charges for possession, smuggling, or dealing drugs can lead to a 2–15-year jail sentence or, in extreme cases, the death sentence. Border areas in the north attract drug runners. Be wary of strangers in these areas, and do not leave baggage unattended, or offer to check in a stranger's suitcase at airports.

Danger Spots

Border areas are sometimes precarious places. Changing political conditions, tribal skirmishes, and the haziness of border lines have made a few areas of Thailand dangerous.

There are sporadic clashes on the Myanmar (Burmese) and Cambodian borders, so it is best to avoid traveling alone on remote roads in those areas. In the three Deep South provinces of Narathiwat, Pattani, and Yala, the militant Malay-Muslim group, PULO (Pattani United Liberation Organization) represents a real danger, and has made travel in this region extremely difficult. Again, common sense should prevail and it is wise to stay away from the most remote border areas.

Women Travelers

Female travelers are unlikely to be harassed in Thailand. Bangkok itself is not dangerous for women; hotels are safe, and taxis are readily available. If traveling alone it is a good idea to keep in touch with someone in Bangkok and let them know where you are going and for how long. Note that Thais perceive lone travelers as people to be pitied, and may offer to accompany you without any ulterior motive.

Tourist Police

There are tourist police stations in the main tourist cities. Tourist police officers all speak some English and are attached to TAT offices. Set up to deal with tourist-related crime, they help with anything from credit card scams to ludicrous bar surcharges. They are also helpful in emergencies and can act as an English-speaking liaison. Foreign residents also volunteer with the tourist police. The Bangkok branch of the tourist police is located in front of the southwest entrance to Lumphini Park. The Tourist Assistance Center is also helpful in emergencies, and is experienced in dealing with complaints such as fraudulent business charges.

Badge identifying the tourist police

Legal Assistance

Some insurance policies cover legal costs, for example, after an accident. If involved in an crash when driving a rental car, it may be wise to go to the nearest telephone and call the tourist police or the Tourist Assistance Center, then return to the scene of the accident. In Thailand there are no legal bodies specifically representing foreigners.

In an emergency, contact your embassy *(see p459).* At night there is an answering service, giving the number of the duty officer. If you are not insured for legal proceedings, then you should contact your nearest consulate for advice.

Pharmacy sign found throughout Thailand

Logo of the Thai Red Cross Society, part of Chulalongkorn University

Medical Facilities

Medical insurance is advisable when traveling in Thailand. Some policies pay bills direct, while others refund you later. Hospitals in Bangkok, both public and private, are modern, clean, and efficient, although waiting times are longer at public ones. Some doctors are Western-trained and speak good English.

Outside the capital the best facilities are in large towns: Khon Kaen in the northeast, Chiang Mai in the north, or Phuket in the south. Emergency care is available from military hospitals. For dental or eye care, it is best to seek treatment in Bangkok. The Thai Red Cross on Rama IV Road does not offer medical treatment, but is able to deal with vaccinations and snake bites.

Pharmacies

There is no shortage of well-stocked pharmacies in Bangkok – there will be several on every main street and shopping mall, and supermarkets will have drugstore kiosks. They are all supplied with up-to-date medications and can dispense antibiotics over the counter without a prescription.

Most pharmacies are open from 8am to 9pm. In the central areas of Bangkok, around Silom and Sukhumvit Roads, a few stay open until 10pm or 11pm. Pharmacy signs are the same all over the country. In small towns pharmacies are less prolific and have fewer supplies. For instance, disposable diapers and tampons can be hard to find in remote areas.

DIRECTORY

Emergency Numbers

Metropolitan Mobile Police
Tel 191.

Tourist Assistance Center
Tel 1155 (Bangkok).

Tourist Police

Bangkok
Tel 0-2356-0582/3/4 or 1155.

Chiang Mai
Tel 0-5324-7317-8 or 1155.

Ko Samui
Tel 0-774-3018 or 1155.

Pattaya
Tel 0-3842-93/1 or 1155.

Phuket
Tel 0-7622-3891/2 or 1155.

Surat Thani
Tel 0-7740-5575 or 1155.

Trat
Tel 0-3955-7382/3 or 1155.

Hospitals

Bangkok
Bangkok General Hospital,
Soi Soonvijai, New Petchaburi Rd.
Tel 0-2310-3000 or 1719.
w bangkokhospital.com

Bumrungrad Hospital,
Sukhumvit, Soi 3.
Tel 0-2667-1000.
w bumrungrad.com

Chiang Mai
McCormick Hospital, Kaew Nawarat Rd.
Tel 0-5392-1/77.
w mccormick.in.th

Phuket
Phuket International Hospital,
44 Chalermprakiat Ror 9 Rd.
Tel 0-7624-9400.
w phuketinternational
hospital.com

Ambulance

Tel 1554 (whole country).

Public Toilets

All hotels and many guest-houses have Western-style flush toilets. In some restaurants and at many major sights, you will encounter the Asian squat toilet. Nearby will be a bucket of water, used to sluice out the toilet after use. Paper is disposed of in a bin.

Immunization

There are no legal immunization requirements unless you are traveling from a country known to be infected with yellow fever. It is recommended that everyone be immunized against polio, tetanus, typhoid, and hepatitis A. In addition, for those travelers going to remote or rural areas, or who are staying more than two to three weeks, BCG (tuberculosis), hepatitis B, rabies, diphtheria, and Japanese encephalitis vaccinations are advised. For the most up-to-date advice, contact your doctor, who will also be able to advise on the current guidelines for malaria prevention, as the drug recommendations change fairly often.

Some vaccines need to be given separately or in stages. Some malaria tablets, meanwhile, are started a week before traveling and continued for several weeks after returning. Therefore, it is advisable to contact your doctor at least eight weeks before departure.

Coping with the Heat

Acclimatization to the sometimes oppressive humidity and heat of Thailand can often take longer than expected. In the first few days it is not advisable to exert yourself. Make sure you drink plenty of bottled water, take plenty of rest in the shade, and avoid being out and about in the midday sun. Once you are acclimatized, dehydration and salt deficiency can still be a problem – always keep up a high intake of bottled water. Minor fungal infections can occur due to the heat, especially if tight clothing or shoes are worn.

Perspiration trapped beneath the skin can cause the itchy rash called prickly heat. The local remedy and

A fan to beat the heat

prophylactic for this is a talcum powder that contains a tingling cooling agent. Clothing should be loose and light – 100 percent cotton is best.

The sun, especially at midday and on the islands, is very powerful; sunscreen and a wide-brimmed hat are indispensable.

First-Aid Kit

Although most first-aid items can be obtained from any pharmacy in main towns, when traveling to rural areas or quiet islands it is advisable to carry a basic first-aid kit. This should include the following: any personal medication; aspirin or paracetamol for fevers and minor aches and pains; an antiseptic for minor cuts and bites; a digestive preparation to soothe upset stomachs; insect repellent; bandages; scissors, tweezers, and a thermometer. Tiger Balm, available at any pharmacy, is Asia's miracle cure-all, relieving headaches, muscle pains, and insect bites.

Minor Stomach Upsets

If you should contract diarrhea, eat plain foods for a few days and drink plenty of fluids. Do not drink the tap water – bottled water is readily available throughout the country. Ice should be fine in main hotels and restaurants, but avoid crushed iced drinks from street vendors. Eating in hotels and restaurants is generally safe. It is when you venture into the street vendors' moveable feasts that the danger of "Bangkok belly" can arise. Choose food stalls that are popular with locals, and watch how the dishes are prepared. It can take time for visitors' stomachs to adjust to new foods. If your constitution is delicate, stick to unpeeled fruits and well-cooked foods, and make sure you eat dishes while they are still hot.

Treatment for prickly heat

Drugs such as Lomotil and Imodium can bring relief to diarrhea, but rehydrating solutions are usually the best remedy. For immediate relief, a single 500 mg dose of the prescription called Ciprofloxacin is effective and safe.

Tiger Balm – provides relief from aches, pains, bites, and strains

Cuts and Bites

Always take precautions in rural areas: wear boots and long trousers when walking through grassland or forested areas to protect against snake bites and leeches (in the rainy season). Few snake bites are dangerous. If you are bitten, apply an elastic bandage firmly to the bite, keep the limb immobile, and seek immediate medical help.

Jellyfish stings are painful – vinegar will soothe the wound. Coral cuts are slow to heal as coral contains a mild poison. Cuts should be treated with an antiseptic to prevent infection. Bandages keep wounds wet so should be used only sparingly.

Insect-Borne Diseases

Seven of Thailand's 410 mosquito species carry malaria. Symptoms of the disease include headache, fever, and violent chills. If you experience such symptoms, seek medical advice immediately. Pollution in the main towns and

Essentials for the outdoor life – mosquito coil and insect repellent

Spicy curries from food stalls – best avoided if your stomach is delicate

resorts keeps them largely free of malarial mosquitoes. The areas of greatest risk are the Myanmar (Burmese) and Cambodian border regions and some rural areas north of Chiang Mai. However, malarial zones are continually changing. For up-to-date information and advice on the most suitable prophylactic drug, visit your doctor or contact a specialist travel clinic.

Mosquitoes have become resistant to certain malaria tablets. Prevention is by far the best defense against the disease. Malarial mosquitoes are active from sundown till sunrise, during which time you should spray on plenty of repellent, wear long-sleeved clothing in light colors (dark attracts mosquitoes), and use mosquito nets and coils. Dengue fever, another mosquito-borne disease, is a risk during the daytime. However, few mosquitoes are infected with the virus, and the symptoms, though intense and unpleasant, are rarely fatal. These include fever, headache, severe joint and muscle pains, and a rash. Cases of Dengue fever have increased, so avoid stagnant bodies of water. No preventive treatment or vaccination is available.

In Northern Thailand and some rural areas there is a risk of contracting Japanese encephalitis, spread by night-biting ticks and mosquitoes. The symptoms are headache, fever, chills, and vomiting. Vaccination is advisable for travel to rural areas (particularly during the rainy season) or trekking. Should any of the above symptoms occur seek immediate medical help.

People- and Animal-Borne Diseases

Acquired immune deficiency syndrome (AIDS) is passed through bodily fluids. Blood transfusion methods in Thailand are not always reliable – it is safest to seek treatment in the main hospitals. The same goes for inoculations – make sure needles are new or bring your own supply. Be wary of all procedures involving needles, including ear-piercing, dentistry, and tattooing.

The high turnover of clients in Thailand's pervasive sex industry means that unprotected sex carries a serious risk (see p120). Not only AIDS, but other sexually transmitted diseases are commonplace.

Hepatitis B is also transmitted through bodily fluids. Symptoms include fever, nausea, fatigue, and jaundice, and it can lead to severe liver damage. A prophylactic vaccine is available.

Rabies is carried in the saliva of infected animals and can be passed on by a bite or lick to a wound or scratch. Any bite from a dog, cat, or monkey should be cleaned immediately and checked by a doctor. Treatment involves a long series of inoculations.

Tetanus is a potentially lethal disease transmitted through infected cuts and animal bites. The first symptoms are difficulty in swallowing (tetanus is also known as lockjaw) and muscle stiffness in the neck area, which can lead to convulsions. As with rabies, all wounds should be speedily cleaned and examined by a doctor. Effective vaccinations are available.

Bilharzia is contracted from tiny worms that infect some types of freshwater snail. They burrow into the skin and cause a general feeling of sickness and abdominal pain. Avoid swimming in untested rivers and lakes.

Food- and Water-Borne Diseases

Dysentery, a severe form of food or water poisoning, is rare in Thailand, but not unknown. Bacillary dysentery – characterized by stomach pains, vomiting, and fever – is highly contagious but rarely lasts longer than a week. Amebic dysentery has similar symptoms but takes longer to develop. It can recur and cause chronic health problems. Medical help should be sought without delay if you think you have either type.

Bottled water

Hepatitis A is passed on in conditions of poor sanitation (contaminated water or food) and can be prevented with a vaccine. Symptoms include fatigue, aching, fever, chills, and jaundice. Little can be done to treat it beyond rest. Typhoid is transmitted through contaminated water or food, and fluid replacement is the most important treatment. Symptoms are similar to those of flu but quickly accelerate to fever, weight loss, and severe dehydration. Medical attention is essential as complications such as pneumonia can easily occur. Although a vaccination is available, it is not always reliable.

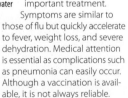

Banking and Local Currency

Throughout Bangkok and the main provincial towns, banking facilities and exchange services are plentiful, well-run, and easy to access. In the major centers, tellers often speak some English. Exchange booths are usually located in the central parts of towns, and mobile exchange units are stationed near larger tourist attractions. Automatic Teller Machines (ATMs) can be found in all cities. Smaller towns are less likely to have exchange facilities, but most have banks or ATMs. Rural villages, unless they are tourist destinations, probably will not have banking or currency exchange services.

HSBC, an international bank operating in Bangkok

Banks and Banking Hours

The four main banks are the **Bangkok Bank**, the **Kasikorn Bank**, the **Siam Commercial Bank**, and the **Krung Thai Bank**. The **Bank of Ayudhya** and **CIMB Thai** also have branches throughout the country. Foreign-owned banks offering full banking services include the **Bank of America**, **Citibank**, **Deutsche Bank**, **Hongkong and Shanghai Bank (HSBC)** and **Standard Chartered Bank**.

Banking hours are generally 8:30am–3:30pm, Monday to Friday. Some banks have branches in department stores which are open 10am–8pm. Exchange booths are open daily, until late. Major banks can arrange international money transfers.

ATM Services

Most ATMs provide instructions in both Thai and English. Any ATM displaying the VISA or MasterCard sign will accept these cards and dispense cash in *baht* using your PIN. There are

Automatic Teller Machines, found in Bangkok and many Thai towns

surcharges for such transactions. If you are planning an extended stay in Thailand, it might be worth opening an account at a Thai bank. This allows access to all ATMs, free of exchange rates or charges.

Changing Money

Banks offer the best exchange rates, and rates differ little between them. Hotels usually offer the worst rates, while those at exchange booths can vary. US dollars are widely accepted when buying *baht*, although sterling and euro are also taken. In Bangkok, hole-in-the-wall exchange booths can be found in large department stores and shopping malls and on major roads. Mobile exchange units are located near tourist attractions and market areas and are open daily between 7am and 9pm. Exchange rates are published daily in the *Bangkok Post* and the *Nation*.

DIRECTORY

Thai Banks

Bangkok Bank
333 Silom Rd, Bangkok.
Tel 0-2231-4333.
W bangkokbank.com

Bank of Ayudhya
1222 Rama 3, Bangkok.
Tel 0-2683-1000.
W krungsri.com

CIMB Thai
44 Langsuan Rd, Bangkok.
Tel 0-2626-7000.
W cimbthai.com

Kasikorn Bank
1 Kasikornthai Lane,
Ratburana Rd, Bangkok.
Tel 0-2888-8888.
W kasikornbank.com

Krung Thai Bank
35 Sukhumvit Rd,
Bangkok.
Tel 0-2208-8699.
W ktb.co.th

Siam Commercial Bank
9 Rachadaphisak Rd,
Bangkok. **Tel** 0-2544-1000. W scb.co.th

Foreign Banks

Bank of America
All Seasons Place, CRC Tower, 33rd Floor, 87/2 Wireless Rd, Bangkok.
Tel 0-2305-2900.
W bankofamerica.com/th

Citibank
399 Sukhumvit Rd,
Bangkok.
Tel 1588 or
0-2788-2000.
W citibank.co.th

Deutsche Bank
Athenee Tower,
Levels 27–29,
63 Wireless Rd, Bangkok.
Tel 0-2646-5000. W db.com/thailand

HSBC
HSBC Building,
968 Rama IV Rd,
Bangkok.
Tel 0-2614-4000.
W hsbc.co.th

Standard Chartered Bank
90 Fl. 16A Building 3,
North Sathorn Rd,
Bangkok.
Tel 0-2724-4777.
W standardchartered.co.th

Cards

American Express
Tel 0-2273-5544, 0-2273-5522.

Diners Club
Tel 0-2232-4100.
W dinersclub.com

MasterCard
Tel 0-2673-7555.

VISA
Tel 001-800-441-3485.

Credit and Debit Cards

Credit cards are accepted in department stores, major hotels, and upscale shops and restaurants. They can also be used at banks (and some exchange kiosks) for cash advances. A surcharge will be applied. **VISA** and **MasterCard** are the most widely accepted cards; the use of **Diners Club** and **American Express** is more limited.

MasterCard debit cards can be used to withdraw cash at most foreign exchange booths, and at Bangkok Bank and Siam Commercial Bank. VISA debit cards can do the same at the Kasikorn Bank. Debit cards can also be used at ATMs, but a surcharge will be levied.

As the popularity of plastic money increases, so too does the incidence of credit-card fraud. Visitors should always carefully check what they sign.

Travelers' Checks

Travelers' checks are the safest method of carrying money. Banks, main hotels, and most exchange booths cash them, with banks providing the lowest surcharge. Banks charge a fee per check cashed, so using large-denomination checks works out cheapest.

Currency

The Thai unit of currency is the *baht*, usually seen abbreviated to "B." There are 100 *satang* in a

◇ **Bangkok Bank**
The Asian International Bank

Logo for one of Thailand's long-established banks

baht, but the *satang* represents such a small sum today that it is scarcely used. You may hear 25 *satang* referred to as a *saleung*. However, inflation is rendering this colloquial term redundant.

Banknotes come in the following denominations: 20 *baht*, 50 *baht*, 100 *baht*, 500 *baht*, and 1,000 *baht*. Changing large denomination notes in rural areas may prove difficult.

The coin denominations are 25 *satang* (1 *saleung*), 50 *satang*, 1 *baht*, 2 *baht*, 5 *baht*, 10 *baht*. The gold 2 *baht* coin is slightly bigger than the silver

1 *baht* coin. The silver 5 *baht* coin has a copper rim and the 10 *baht* coin has a bronze center surrounded by a silver outer ring. Old coins feature Thai numerals only, while newer coins have both Thai and Arabic numerals.

VAT

Thailand imposes a 7 percent Value Added Tax (VAT) on goods and services, generally levied only in upscale hotels, restaurants, and shops. There is a VAT refund scheme for tourists who are in the country for less than 180 days. Look out for shops displaying a "VAT Refund For Tourists" sign.

20 *baht*

50 *baht*

100 *baht*

500 *baht*

1,000 *baht*

Coins come in the following denominations:

25 *satang*

50 *satang*

1 *baht*

2 *baht*

5 *baht*

10 *baht*

Communications and Media

Thailand's communication network is becoming increasingly sophisticated. The telephone system is run by the Telephone Organization of Thailand (TOT) under the umbrella of the Communications Authority of Thailand (CAT). It is possible to make international calls and send faxes from all business centers and main hotels. Public phones can be found on all main roads and many minor ones. The postal system, however, can be erratic; the Thai EMS service is very reliable with tracking and less expensive than international couriers. Many major international newspapers and magazines can be easily obtained. Locally published English-language newspapers and magazines can be bought in almost every hotel and bookstore, and at many curbside newsstands.

A green card-phone for local and long-distance domestic calls

International Calls

All major hotels and most guesthouses offer international dialing services. Business centers and Internet cafés in small towns will usually provide phone, fax, and printing services.

Bangkok's Central Post Office on Charoen Krung New Road and some major post offices around the country have a CAT center that can arrange collect and credit card calls. In Bangkok these are open from 7am until midnight, with reduced hours in the provinces.

To dial directly from a hotel room, either contact the reception, or dial 001 (for an international line) followed by the country code and telephone number. It is also possible to use 007, 008, or 009 to prefix your number – these offer cheaper rates. Alternatively, dial the international operator at 100.

Blue and yellow international pay phones can be found on the street, in shopping malls, and in airports. The blue phones take some credit cards. The yellow phones accept Lenso phonecards, which are sold in the post office and by agents displaying the Lenso logo.

Local Calls

Local calls can be made from any public pay phone other than the blue-and-yellow international pay phones.

Domestic calls can be made from blue-and-silver coin phones or green card-phones. Coin-operated phones accept one-, five-, and ten-*baht* coins. Calls within the same area code cost one *baht* for three minutes.

Cards for green and orange card-phones can be bought at most post offices, bookstores, and hotels and come in several denominations: 25 *baht*, 50 *baht*, 100 *baht*, and 240 *baht*.

The long-distance domestic service also covers Malaysia and Laos, as well as regional Thai calls.

Cell Phones

There are four main GSM (Global System for Mobile Communications) frequencies in use around the world, so if you want to guarantee that your phone will work, make sure you have a quad-band phone. Contact your service provider for clarification. Cell phones are extremely cheap in Thailand. There are several operating companies, including AIS, True, and DTAC. SIM cards can be bought from cell phone shops, but there is a registration process for which tourists must have their passport photographed. Customers can pay monthly or buy a scratch card with a dial-in top-up code. Cards are available from 7-Eleven stores and range from 50 to 500 *baht* in value.

Internet and Email

Internet access is available in Internet cafés, hotels, and guesthouses all over Thailand. Charges range from 20 *baht* per hour in a local Internet café to 250 *baht* per hour in a five-star hotel. In some places, Wi-Fi hotspots are available for free (ask staff for the code). However, in airports and upmarket hotels there can be a charge of as much as 600 *baht* per day.

Connections in Bangkok and some of the larger provincial centers are usually fast, but generally speaking the further you move away from urban centers, the slower the connection. Even the most remote islands now have reasonable, if slow, Internet connections.

One of Thailand's many Internet cafés

Postal Services

Thailand has a reliable postal system. Letters and postcards usually take at least one week to reach Europe and North America. Stamps are available at all post offices and at many hotels. Packages should be sent by registered mail or via International Express Mail

Service (EMS), which can be a cheaper alternative to international shipping companies.

General delivery facilities are available at all main post offices. Letters will normally be held for up to three months. To claim mail from general delivery, you must show your passport and sometimes pay a small fee. Letters should be addressed to you (last name written in capitals and underlined), poste restante, GPO, address, town, Thailand. Thus for Bangkok's main GPO, correspondents should send mail care of GPO, Charoen Krung Road, Bangkok.

Post offices are usually open 8:30am–4:30pm Monday to Friday and 9am–noon on Saturdays. The main international courier companies, such as **DHL**, **FedEx**, and **UPS**, operate in Thailand.

Television and Radio

Thailand has numerous television channels; programs are mostly in Thai, though in Bangkok some are broadcast with an English simulcast on FM radio. Most international English-language satellite and cable networks such as the BBC, CNN, Al Jazeera, and CNBC are readily available. Many hotels provide satellite and cable television as well as an in-house video channel. Check the *Bangkok Post* and *The Nation* for details.

English-language radio stations are listed in the *Outlook* section of the *Bangkok Post*. The national public radio station, Radio Thailand, broadcasts English-language programs on 107 and 105 FM 24 hours a day, and listings for short-wave frequencies are found in the *Bangkok Post* and *The Nation*.

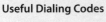
Thai mail box

Newspapers and Magazines

The main English-language newspapers are the *Bangkok Post* and *The Nation*. Both provide reliable local, regional, and international coverage. Their daily inserts include features on lifestyle and travel, as well as listings for food, films, concerts, and exhibitions in Bangkok. Both are sold in news kiosks and shops throughout Bangkok.

The *International Herald Tribune* and the *Asian Wall Street Journal* are sold in hotels and bookstores such as Asia Books and Bookazine, which also stock international magazines. News weeklies *The Economist*, *Time*, and *Newsweek* are widely available. Among the local English-language monthly publications is the useful listings guide *Big Chilli*. In addition to this, helpful free guides that are widely available, including in restaurants, bars, and bookstores, are *BK Magazine*, *Absolute Lifestyle*, and *Thaiways*.

Useful Dialing Codes

- Whether calling from within or outside the province, you need to dial a 9-digit number for Bangkok and all other provinces.
- For international calls, dial 001, 007, 008, or 009, followed by the country code.
- Country codes are: UK 44; Ireland 353; France 33; US & Canada 1; Australia 61; New Zealand 64. It may be necessary to omit the first digit of the destinat- ion area code. This will also apply when calling international mobile numbers.
- For directory assistance dial 1133 from anywhere in the country.
- To put a call through the international operator, or to report technical problems, dial 101.
- To speak to the domestic operator, dial 101.
- To make a reverse charge (collect) call dial 101 for the international operator.
- Note that the speaking clock and similar telephone services such as directory assistance are all in Thai.
- For a wake-up call, contact your hotel switchboard or front desk.

Newspaper seller on the beach

TRAVEL INFORMATION

For most visitors, flying is the most convenient way of getting to Thailand. Other routes include ferry, road, and rail via Malaysia; ferry and road via Cambodia; and limited but rapidly improving road links via Laos. Domestic flights within Thailand are easy and cut journey times considerably, with provincial airports dotted generously around the country. Flights to surrounding countries are cheaper if booked within

Thailand. Regular rail services run between Bangkok and Singapore, via Kuala Lumpur, Butterworth (for Penang), and some Southern Thai towns. Rail travel is efficient, clean, and comfortable, but there is a limited number of lines. Long-distance and provincial buses of varying quality run to all towns and to most villages. At a local level there is a variety of taxis, *songthaews*, and *tuk-tuks* with which to get around.

Green Travel

Travel around Thailand is easy, convenient, and cheap, but not really very green. Most people will travel by train, long-distance coach, or car hire – the latter being the most flexible and user-friendly, as the kingdom's roads are uniformly good and well-maintained (though driving can be hazardous at times). The only possibility for green travel in terms of fuel is the use of Liquid Petroleum Gas (LPG). This less-polluting fuel has been introduced in an attempt to combat increasing exhaust pollution in large cities and rising oil prices. However, vehicles using LPG are still relatively few, so the best that can reasonably be hoped for is the use of Gasohol, which combines ordinary benzene with fuel derived from sugar cane.

Some of Bangkok's newer local buses now use LPG and the city authorities are slowly replacing the old polluting buses, but this will take time. Both LPG and Gasohol are, to some extent, subsidized by the government in an attempt to encourage their use.

A Boeing 747 in the traditional livery of Thai Airways

Bangkok's Skytrain and MRT underground have made a huge difference to the city's once clogged arteries, providing transport for thousands of commuters who would previously have used their cars.

Arriving by Air

Thailand is served by numerous airlines from all over the world. Direct flights are available from North America, Europe, Australasia, and Asia. **Thai Airways** operates direct flights from Los Angeles to Bangkok, and **British Airways**, **United Airlines**, and **Delta** have a connecting service from New York. **Qantas** has direct flights to Bangkok from Sydney, Melbourne, and London, and **Singapore Airlines** flies from Australia to Bangkok via Singapore. International flights also land at U-Tapao Airport, located 45 minutes from Pattaya. Flights from Asian countries may land at Phuket, Chiang Mai, Hat Yai, Krabi, or Ko Samui.

Air Fares

The cost of flying to and from Thailand varies according to the destination, the airline, and the time of year. In the northern hemisphere low fares are available from September to April, and in the southern hemisphere from March to November. Bangkok is one of the cheapest cities in the world to fly out of due to loose government restrictions on air fares and fierce competition between the airlines and Bangkok's travel agencies.

International Flights

One of the busiest airports in Asia, **Suvarnabhumi** (BKK) is used for international as well as domestic flights. This huge modern airport is in Racha Thewa in Bang Phli district, Samut Prakan Province, 18 miles (30 km) east of the capital. Named by King Bhumibol, Suvarnabhumi means "Golden Land." In total, the airport stretches over 11 miles (17 km) and has the world's tallest air traffic control tower.

Arriving passengers enter the terminal on the second floor of the concourse buildings.

Gasohol service station

After passing through passport control and customs, they can proceed to the arrivals hall, where they will find transportation and accommodation counters and tourist information. A meeting point is on the third floor.

The older but refurbished **Don Muang Airport** (DMK), north of the city, is the hub for Thai Air Asia, Nok Air, and many budget airlines such as Tiger, Scoot, and Thai Smile. Many domestic flights also go from Don Muang.

If transferring between the airports, allow at least 3 hours between your first flight's arrival and your next departure. A free shuttle bus (on production of a valid air ticket) takes around 50 minutes and leaves from the bus stand outside the main exit at arrivals. Taxis also leave from here, with a surcharge of 50 *baht*. The taxi booking stands are inside the airport. The nearest rail connections are at Morchit (Skytrain) and Chatuchak Park (MRT Metro), and there is a shuttle bus A1 to both.

Airport Shopping

With more than 100 duty free shops, Suvarnabhumi Airport is a shopper's paradise.

Suvarnabhumi International Airport

Tourists should, however, refrain from touching or moving merchandise that they do not intend to buy. Such actions might give the impression of shoplifting, and this may result in detention and questioning by the police.

Getting to and from Suvarnabhumi International Airport

Metered taxis are available outside the first floor. There is a surcharge of 50 *baht* in addition to the meter fare. A trip into the city will cost roughly 400 *baht*, including expressway charges, and take around 45 minutes, depending on traffic. Passengers can also take a shuttle bus or the rail link.

People traveling to the airport by road are strongly advised to allow at least one hour for travel time and to take the expressway.

Check-ins, particularly at the Thai Airways counter, are often subject to delays. The walk from the passport checkpoint to the flight departure lounge is also a considerable distance.

A direct airport rail link runs every 40 minutes from Bangkok City Airport Terminal at Makkasan Station in the center of Bangkok to Suvarnabhumi Airport. The non-stop journey takes 15 minutes, while the stopping service takes about 30 minutes. Both services have considerably cut the journey time between the airport and the center of Bangkok.

Travelers wishing to go to Suvarnabhumi Airport from outside Bangkok should allow plenty of time – at least two hours per 60 miles (100 km) of the journey. It is advisable to shop around for taxis as fares can vary greatly. Many tourist areas now have air-conditioned regular minibus services at a fraction of the cost of private taxis (130 *baht* from Pattaya, for example).

Planes on the tarmac at Suvarnabhumi Airport

Airport	**📞 Information**	Distance to Town or Resort	Average Taxi Fare	Average Journey Time
Bangkok: Don Muang	0-2535-1111 0-2535-1253	City center 16 miles (25 km)	300 baht	Rail: 50 minutes Road: 1–2 hours
Bangkok: Suvarnabhumi	0-2132-1888	City center 18 miles (30 km)	400 baht	Rail link: 15 mins Road: 45–60 mins
Chiang Mai	0-5327-0222	City center 2.5 miles (4 km)	100 baht	Road: 20 minutes
Phuket	0-7632-7230-7	Patong 20 miles (32 km)	550 baht	Road: 45 minutes
Ko Samui	0-7742-8500	Chaweng 16 miles (26 km)	300 baht	Road: 30 minutes
Hat Yai	0-7422-7000	City center 7.5 miles (12 km)	200 baht	Road: 30 minutes

Domestic Flights

While a good number of domestic flights from Bangkok leave from Suvarnabhumi, many also fly from Don Muang Airport. Located on Bangkok's Vibhavadi Rangsit Road, Don Muang serves all the domestic flights of local budget carrier **Nok Air**.

Thai Lion Air flies to many major destinations, such as Chiang Mai, Hat Yai, Phuket, and Surat Thani. It also serves towns such as Krabi and Chiang Rai. Other airlines using Don Muang as their main hub include **Thai Air Asia** and **Orient Thai Airlines**. Tickets can be bought through travel agents and hotels, or booked directly through the airlines – in this case, passengers will need to pick up their ticket at the airport at least one hour before flying.

On public holidays (see p55) and on weekends, when there are more people traveling, it can be difficult to get a flight, so book tickets well in advance or travel during the week.

Arriving via Land or Water

Thailand shares land borders with four countries – Myanmar (Burma), Laos, Cambodia, and Malaysia. There are six border crossings with Myanmar, seven with Laos, six with Cambodia, and seven with Malaysia. Visas obtained at a land border crossing are only valid for 15 days.

Myanmar is the most difficult country to enter Thailand from, with the authorities regularly closing border points and causing many other problems for independent travelers. It is not recommended to enter Thailand from Myanmar via any of the land routes.

The crossings from Laos are Huay Xai to Chiang Khong; Nam Hong to Nakasing; Tha Na Leng to Nong Khai via the Friendship Bridge; Paksan to Beung Khan; Tha Khaek to Nakhon Phanom; Savannakhet to Mukdahan; and Vang Tao to Chong Mek. The Friendship Bridge is the most popular entry point as it is close to the capital, Vientiane.

Entry from Cambodia is relatively easy. Crossings include Poipet to Aranya Prathet; Cham Yeam to Hat Lek; O'Smach to Chong Jom; Anlong Veng to Chong Sa-Ngam; Phsa Prom Pailin to Ban Pakard; and Daun Lem to Ban Laem.

Entry from Malaysia has in the past been a formality, but with ongoing troubles in the three southernmost, mainly Muslim provinces, Narathiwat, Pattani, and Yala, many Western governments may advise against crossing the border in these areas. Currently there are two crossings in Satun Province that are safe: Wang Prajan next to the Thale Ban National Park and Kuala Perlis to Satun town. The Butterworth to Bangkok express train uses the Padang Besar to Sadao crossing and this is also a safe point for crossing.

A Nok Air Boeing 737-400 at Don Muang airport

DIRECTORY

Airlines

Bangkok Airways
Tel 1771.
W bangkokair.com

British Airways
Tel 0-2627-1701.
Tel (0844) 493 0787 (UK).
W britishairways.com

Delta
Tel 0-2660-6900.
Tel (800) 221 1212 (US).
W delta.com

Etihad Airlines
Tel 0-2787-3377.
W etihad.com

Nok Air
Tel 1318.
W nokair.com

Orient Thai Airlines
Tel 1126.
W flyorientthai.com

Qantas
Tel 0-2236-2800.
Tel (0845) 774 7767 (UK).
W qantas.com.au

Singapore Airlines
Tel 0-2353-6000.
Tel (800) 742-3333 (US).
W singaporeair.com

Thai Air Asia
Tel 0-2515-9999.
W airasia.com

Thai Airways
Tel 0-2356-1111.
Tel (800) 426-5204 (US).
W thaiair.com

Thai Lion Air
Tel 0-2529-9999.
W lionairthai.com

United Airlines
Tel 0-2353-3939.
Tel (800) 538-2929 (US).

Entrance to the Friendship Bridge, the border crossing to Thailand from Laos

Organized Tours

Hundreds of tour companies are based in Bangkok, Chiang Mai, and major resorts such as Phuket, and most hotels throughout the country offer tours of one sort or another. Typical excursions available range from one-day city tours covering the main sights to more comprehensive itineraries taking in several towns and locations over several days. Costs are naturally higher than taking public transit, but in some cases – for instance many sights in the Greater Bangkok region – much time and effort simply in getting to the destination may be saved. The drawback of most organized tours is, of course, that there is rarely time to linger.

as are jeeps for gaining access to remote areas. Most vehicles are well maintained and safe.

Boat tours are popular in many resorts, though the majority of operators follow the same routes. Day trips to islands, including opportunities for water sports, are common. Transfers to and from hotels are often part of the deal. Trips to remote islands, usually offering diving facilities on board *(see p446)*, can span several days, and accommodation may be provided on the boat itself.

Booking a Tour

It should be possible to book a tour of Thailand from your home country that will include all travel and accommodations. Such all-inclusive tours typically last between one and two weeks and include a few nights in Bangkok followed by excursions to Chiang Mai and other Northern locations, or to a beach resort. Other packages are more specialized, concentrating, say, on trekking in the North *(see p448)*, and may vary from a few days to several weeks in duration. Based in Bangkok, **Diethelm Travel** and **Exo Travel** are major operators.

Most regional hotels and many guesthouses offer tours of the surrounding area, or are in close contact with local tour companies. The local TAT office will also be able to recommend reputable tour companies. Day trips to the most popular sights can usually be booked just one day in advance. Tours to more distant sights should

include arrangements for accommodations, and usually have at least one departure day each week. In most cases, the tour company will pick you up direct from your hotel or guesthouse.

Tour Buses and Boats

Many tour companies use luxury, or "VIP," coaches, with reclining seats, on-board refreshments, air-conditioning, and a toilet. Air-conditioned minibuses are also common,

Guided Tours

Bilingual guides accompany many tours, especially to popular cultural sights such as Ayutthaya. In Northern Thailand a knowledgeable guide is essential for safety reasons when trekking through the jungle and visiting hill-tribe villages. The quality of guides varies considerably: a listing of reputable ones is published by the Professional Guide Association and available from TAT *(see p459)*.

A boat sails across the Chao Phraya River, Bangkok

Traveling around by Train, Bus, and Boat

Thailand has an efficient railroad system known as the SRT (State Railway of Thailand), with four major lines connecting Bangkok with the North, Northeast, East, and South. Though trains are comfortable and safe, trip times are similar, sometimes even longer, than by bus, and the number of towns on the network is limited. Phuket and Chiang Rai, for instance, do not have train stations. By contrast, comfortable, well maintained, long-distance buses connect all major cities to Bangkok, and provincial buses serve all smaller towns as well as many villages. The main islands are accessible via regular scheduled ferry services.

Railroad Network

The main station in Bangkok is **Hua Lampong**, which serves all four major lines. The first line runs to **Chiang Mai** via the Central Plains. A second, which later divides in two, runs to Nong Khai and Ubon Ratchathani in Northeast Thailand. A third connects Bangkok to the Eastern Seaboard and Cambodia, and a fourth runs down the peninsula to Malaysia. **Thon Buri Station** in Bangkok Noi is the principal departure point for trains to Kanchanaburi and the Khwae River Bridge.

Trains

Train services in Thailand are labeled Special Express (the fastest), Express, Rapid (slower than Express), and Ordinary. Travel times, even on Express trains, can be longer than by road. The trip from Bangkok to Chiang Mai, for instance, takes between 11 and 13 hours. First-class coaches (available on Express and Special Express trains) consist of individual cabins with air-conditioning. Second-class coaches have reclining seats and a choice of fans or air-conditioning. Sleepers in this class have individual seats that are converted into curtained-off beds at night. Toilets (there should be at least one Western toilet) and washing facilities are at the end of coaches. Most tourists find that second class is comfortable enough for long distances and far more relaxing than a bus journey.

Third-class coaches have wooden benches, each seating two or three passengers: these coaches are cheap but are not recommended for long distances. Seats cannot be booked in advance.

Most trains are clean and well maintained. Uniformed vendors stroll up and down the aisles with refreshments, and buffet cars are attached to trains on long-distance routes.

Train Tickets and Fares

A train timetable in English is available from Hua Lampong Station in Bangkok. Be aware that trains at peak periods (weekends and holidays) can be sold out days in advance. Hua Lampong has an advance booking office with English-speaking staff. Some travel agents will also book tickets.

Fares depend on the speed of the train and the class of the carriage. A second-class ticket between Bangkok and Chiang Mai is about 431 *baht*. Shorter trips, such as from Bangkok to Ayutthaya, cost anything between 15–120 *baht*. Tourists can also buy 20-day rail passes which cost 1,500–3,000 *baht*. Information about these is available from Hua Lampong Station.

Long-distance Buses

Long-distance buses run from the **Eastern (Ekamai)**, **Northern (Morchit)**, and **Southern (Pin Klao)** bus terminals in Bangkok. Most provincial capitals can be reached direct from Bangkok. Large cities such as **Chiang Mai**, Phitsanulok, Khorat, and **Surat Thani** also act as transit hubs, with both long-distance and local connections. Buses can be faster than trains: Bangkok to Chiang Mai takes about ten hours. Vehicles are air-conditioned, with a toilet, reclining seats, and plenty of leg room. "VIP" buses have the best facilities, including free refreshments served by a stewardess at a halfway rest point. Overnight services can get rather chilly – blankets should be provided.

Bus Tickets and Fares

Fares for long-distance bus trips are similar in price to second-class train tickets. "VIP" buses are at the top of the price range. Book well in advance through a travel agent or at the bus station if traveling on the weekend or during a public holiday. Other-wise, just turn up at the coach station at least half an hour before departure. Tickets are always bought as one-way.

Fountain in front of Hua Lampong Station, Bangkok

Eastern & Oriental Express

The world-renowned Eastern & Oriental Express operates between Bangkok and Singapore. The journey takes three days and two nights, including stops at Butterworth (Penang) and Kuala Lumpur in Malaysia. The 22 carriages are bedecked with fabrics and fittings evocative of 1930s rail travel. Double and single cabins come in private and presidential classes, and there are two restaurants, a saloon car, a bar, and an observation deck. Such luxuries are, of course, reflected in the price.

Dining car on the Eastern & Oriental Express

Provincial Buses

The government bus company is called *Bor Kor Sor* (BKS). Its buses are frequent, relatively reliable, and the cheapest form of transportation in Thailand. Booking is rarely necessary. On many buses simply pay the driver or conductor. Almost every town will have a terminal. The non air-conditioned *(rot thamadaa)* buses are the cheapest and slowest, and they stop almost everywhere along the way. Air-conditioned *(rot aer)* local buses do not necessarily provide blankets, so take a jacket or sweater, especially when traveling at night.

Traveling on provincial buses is a good way to meet local people and reach many villages and sights. Beware, though, that refreshment and toilet stops may be infrequent, buses may be in a poor state of repair, and the road skills of drivers will vary. Local services are nearly always slow and crowded. Back seats are reserved for monks, so be prepared to move or stand. Women should avoid sitting next to monks *(see p463)*.

Boats to the Islands

Scheduled ferries are always erratic, since their service is dependent on the weather; some do not operate at all in the rainy season (Mar–Nov). Regular services are available to Ko Samui, Ko Pha Ngan, and Ko Tao from Chumphon and Surat Thani. Ko Phi Phi is served by ferries from Phuket and Krabi. A regular daily service ferries cars and passengers between Laem Ngop and Ko Chang. Smaller islands have less regular services, sometimes just a makeshift ferry run by local fishermen. Travel agents will be able to give you rough timetables, but these will vary. Many services stop in the rainy season. Some companies offer deals on train and boat tickets combining Bangkok and the islands of Ko Samui, Ko Pha Ngan, and Ko Tao. Reliable operators include **Lomprayah**, **Seatran** and **Songserm**.

Small island ferry service

DIRECTORY

Train Information

Chiang Mai Station
Charoen Muang Rd, Chiang Mai.
Tel 0-5324-7462 or 0-5324-4795.

Eastern & Oriental Express
Tel (020) 7921 4010 (UK).
Tel (800) 524-2420 or (843) 937-9068 (US).
Tel 0-2255-9150 (Bangkok).
Tel (65) 392 3500 (Singapore).
W orient-express.com

Hua Lampong Station, Bangkok
Rama IV, Bangkok.
Tel 1690.
W railway.co.th/English

Advance booking office open 7am–4pm daily.

Seat 61
W seat61.com

Surat Thani Station
14 km (9 miles) west of Surat Thani in Kha Tham town.
Tel 0-7731-1963 or 0-7731-1213.

Thon Buri/Bangkok Noi Station
Arun Amarin Rd, Bangkok Noi.
Tel 0-2411-3102.

Bus Terminals

Chiang Mai
Chiang Mai Arcade, Kaew Nawarat Rd, Chiang Mai.
Tel 0-5324-2664.

Eastern/Ekamai Bus Terminal, Bangkok
Sukhumvit Rd, Bangkok.
Tel 0-2391-8097 (Ekamai).

Northern and Northeastern/ Morchit Bus Terminal, Bangkok
Kampheng Phet Rd, Morchit, Bangkok.
Tel 0-2936-0657.

Southern/Pin Klao Bus Terminal, Bangkok
Boromratchonnee Rd, Phra Pin Klao, Bangkok.
Tel 0-2872-1777 (dial 2 for operator).

Surat Thani
Talat Kaset Bus Terminal, Tha Thong Rd, Surat Thani.
Tel 0-7720-0032.

Ferry Information

Lomprayah
Ko Samui Office.
Tel 0-7742-7765/6.
W lomprayah.com

Seatran Discovery Ferry
Bangkok Office.
Tel 0-2240-2582.
Ko Samui Office.
Tel 0-7724-6086.
W seatrandiscovery.

Songserm Express Boat
Khao San Road Office, Bangkok.
Tel 0-2280-8076.
Chumphon Office.
Tel 0-7750-6205.
W songserm-expressboat.com

Renting a Car, Moped, or Bicycle

Driving in Thailand is not for the faint-hearted. Hazards come in the form of potholed roads, confusing intersections, and dangerous driving. However, the main expressways, prefixed "AH" (Asia Highway), are excellent, with rest areas, shops, and refreshments. For those visitors who want to explore away from the usual tour routes, the best option may be to hire a car with a driver who is used to the roads. International car rental firms operate in Bangkok and provincial capitals. The standard of local rental companies varies enormously.

Sign for a local car rental company: check if insurance is included

Renting a Car

A valid international driver's license is a necessity for most visitors, while those from ASEAN countries (Association of Southeast Asian Nations) need only have a license from their home countries. International rental agencies offer safe cars and the most extensive insurance and backup services. **Avis**, **Budget**, and **Hertz** have desks at some airports and in major cities. Charges range from about 1,800 *baht* for a day to 35,000 *baht* for a month.

With other car rental companies, you should check the small print on the contract for liabilities. Insurance may not be included. Obtain a copy of the vehicle registration and carry it around with you. You should also have with you your passport and driving license, or at the very least good copies of these.

Hiring a Chauffeur-Driven Car

Hiring an experienced driver with a car is gaining popularity in Thailand. The cost can be surprisingly low – often less than 50 percent extra on top of the normal price of car rental. Some drivers are knowledgeable about sights and will suggest interesting itineraries. Most car rental firms can arrange drivers. **Siam Express** offers packages including a chauffeur, car, and accommodation in a wide range of hotels.

Renting a Moped

Mopeds and motorcycles are widely available for rent in the resorts, provincial capitals, and other large towns. If you have never driven a motorbike before it's best to rent one of the small automatic gear 80cc bikes. Driver's licenses are rarely requested, and few firms bother with insurance. Costs are low: 200–400 *baht* is average for a day's rental. Safety precautions are essential. Check tires, oil, and brakes before you set out. Wear a helmet (compulsory in Thailand) and proper shoes. Long sleeves and trousers will minimize cuts and grazes in a minor accident. Take care on dirt roads and avoid driving alone in rural areas.

Gasoline and Servicing

Gas stations in Thailand are well manned and are located on main roads in towns and along highways. They are modern and most provide unleaded gas. Attendants will fill your tank, wash your windows, and pump up your tires. Some garages have a resident mechanic, or will at least be able to recommend one. Most of them have a small general shop, and all have Asian toilet facilities. Many garages open 24 hours, while others close at 8pm.

Logo of PTT, a gasoline company with stations throughout Thailand

Parking

Multistory parking lots in Bangkok are generally attached to major hotels and department stores. Parking is usually free for hotel guests, and for visitors for up to two or three hours. A ticket is issued on entry and should be stamped by a cashier; pay on the way out. Apart from these arrangements, parking can be difficult in Bangkok.

Throughout Thailand, pavements painted with red and white stripes indicate a no-parking zone. In provincial cities, many hotels and large guesthouses provide free parking facilities for guests. In quieter towns you can generally park anywhere that is not obstructive.

Roads

In addition to regular roads, multilane elevated highways can be found in and around Bangkok. A toll is charged to travel on these expressways, including the ones to the airports. The fees vary but are indicated above the booth – the exact change is required at manually operated booths. The expressways are less congested than other Bangkok roads, but they are still prone to traffic jams. Many roads in

Mopeds and motorcycles for rent

Traffic policeman waving vehicles through at a Bangkok intersection

Bangkok are one-way, though a lane may be reserved for buses moving in the opposite direction during peak hours. Be sure to look both ways when crossing the road at these times.

There are four major highways leading out of Bangkok. These are good dual carriageways, with AH1 and AH4 part of the Asia Highway network. In more rural and jungle areas, a concrete road may turn into a dirt track. Main roads in towns are called *thanons*; numbered lanes leading off these are called *sois* and *trawks*. In the rainy season, all roads can become flooded.

The signage on main roads is very good, in both English and Thai. Driving is on the left, but be aware of the dangers of night driving. Motorcyclists in dark clothing and with no lights may suddenly appear on the wrong side of the road.

Rules of the Road

Driving is on the left. The speed limit is 60 kph (35 mph) within city limits, unless signed otherwise, and 80 kph (50 mph) on open roads. On expressways and major highways the speed limit is 110 kph (70 mph). The standard international road rules apply, but are of little interest to Thais. The only consistent rule of thumb is that "size wins."

The eccentric use of indicators and headlights can be unnerving. A left signal can indicate to another driver that it is alright to pass, while a right signal can indicate hazardous oncoming traffic, and a flash of the headlights means: "I'm coming through."

Horns are not used enough as Thais tend to see them as impolite. When they are used it is often as a warning of presence rather than obvious danger. Drivers think nothing of straddling lanes and passing on curves and up hill. Yield to larger vehicles at unmarked intersections. It is legal to turn left at red lights if there is a blue sign with a white left arrow, or occasionally if you are in the left lane. On minor roads, beware of animals.

Traffic fines are most commonly imposed for illegal turns. If you get a ticket and your license is taken, go to the local police station, the address of which will be on the ticket, and pay the fine. Drive slowly through army checkpoints in border areas, and be prepared to stop.

Typical road scene with several lanes of one-way traffic

Road Maps

Tourist maps are widely available but cover major roads only. Some provincial, foldout maps produced by the Prannok Witthaya Map Center are useful, showing all roads and reliefs. The *Thailand Highways Map* by the Auto Guide Company and the *Thailand Highway Map* by the Roads Association are the best atlases, and are written in Thai and Roman scripts.

Renting a Bicycle

In the cool season, cycling in quiet areas is a pleasant way to get around. Guesthouses and small agencies often have

bicycles for rent for 20–100 *baht* a day, though the bikes may be rickety. New mountain bikes may be available, but, perhaps surprisingly, costs may exceed those of mopeds. Taking plenty of water is essential and, of course, great care is always necessary on the roads.

Local Transportation

Transportation in the provinces is certainly less frenetic than in Bangkok: bicycle rickshas *(samlors)* and colorful *tuk-tuks* run alongside services such as *songthaews,* and bargaining for the fare on *samlors* is part of the Thai experience. Do not climb on before agreeing a price, or you may be taken for a ride in more ways than one. The one city outside of Bangkok to run its own bus service is Chiang Mai and this has only been in operation a few years, so the most convenient form of transportation in most towns and resorts is the ubiquitous *songthaew.*

A *songthaew* – uncomfortable, but cheaper and safer than a *tuk-tuk*

Taxis

Meter taxis operate in Bangkok, Chiang Mai, Chiang Rai, Hat Yai, and Pattaya and are distinguishable by the "Taxi-Meter" sign on the roof. Drivers tend to know only the names and locations of the major hotels and sights. In nonmeter taxis, mainly found in Ko Samui and Phuket, you need to bargain for the fare before getting in.

Motorcycle taxis operate in some towns.

TAXI-METER

Roof sign of a metered taxi

Drivers tend to congregate near markets and long *sois* (streets) and can be identified by their colorful numbered vests. Prices are negotiated. Although motorcycle taxis are sometimes the quickest way to get between two points think twice about using them as they are not the safest form of transportation. They are also not practical if you are hauling a suitcase.

Shared taxis are not too common except in the Deep South where it's possible to share a taxi between Hat Yai and the Malaysian border and beyond. Drivers wait for cars to fill up, usually with a maximum of six people, before departing.

Songthaews

Songthaews (literally translated as "two rows") are vans with two rows of seats in the back. They are more common than city buses outside Bangkok and run popular routes for set fares, typically between 20 and 40 *baht*. Drivers may wait until they are at least half full before starting out. Routes are sometimes written in English on the sides of the vans. On the whole they don't usually have a terminus but cluster around large markets and shopping centers. *Songthaews* can be hailed anywhere along a route and will stop just about anywhere. To let the driver know you need to get off, press one of the buzzers located along the inner side of the roof. *Songthaews* can be rented like taxis, but are far less comfortable.

Samlors and Tuk-tuks

Samlors are three-wheeled vehicles that can transport one or two people up to a few kilometers. Motorized samlors are known as *tuk-tuks* – their two-stroke engines, introduced by the Japanese during World War II, are notoriously noisy.

In heavy traffic or during the rainy season, *tuk-tuks* can be uncomfortable and unstable, but are always popular with tourists. Nonmotorized *samlors* are often in the form of bicycle rickshas. You should negotiate a price in advance: 30–60 *baht* is reasonable for short hops.

Long-tail Boats

Thailand is a country of waterways, especially in the central region around Bangkok, and where there's a waterway there's a long-tail boat waiting to take passengers. The water-taxis in Bangkok should be used with caution; passengers are often splashed by dirty canal water. Other areas of the country, such as Krabi, also play host to a variety of long-tail boats. The greatest drawback of these elegant boats is the extremely noisy diesel engines clamped to the back. A maximum of twenty passengers is the norm and costs vary depending on whether the boat has been privately hired. Expect to pay around 200 *baht* an hour to rent a boat privately *(see p78).*

Three-wheeled bicycle ricksha, or *samlor,* in a seaside resort

Getting Around Bangkok

Following years of chronic traffic congestion, Bangkok launched the mass-transit BTS Skytrain in 1999 and the underground MRT in 2004. These fast, clean, relatively cheap services, in conjunction with the Chao Phraya Express riverboats, have revolutionized travel in the city. (For a map of the MRT and Skytrain network, see the back endpaper.) Unfortunately, these services don't cover the whole city and a huge fleet of sometimes dirty, noisy buses fill in the gaps. Older, smoke- belching buses have mostly been replaced over the last few years by new, cleaner ones, but there is a long way to go before Bangkok's streets are pollution free.

Bangkok's mass-transit BTS Skytrain

BTS Skytrain

Downtown, the efficient, fast **BTS Skytrain** has two lines: the Sukhumvit route from Morchit Station in the north to Onnut Station in the east, and the Silom route from the National Stadium to Wongwian Yai in Thonburi, with an interchange between the two at the Siam Center. The Sukhumvit line is being extended to Baering, in the Bang Na District of eastern Bangkok, and is due to open in 2017.

The airport rail link has an express service from the Phaya Thai and Makkasan stations. The City line makes eight stops along the same route, serving areas east of downtown.

Trains run daily every 3 to 6 minutes from 6:30am to midnight. Fares are calculated by distance, and magnetic fare cards are sold at all stations in values from 15 to 40 *baht*. Several passes are available, but of most interest to the visitor is the One-Day Pass costing 120 *baht* and offering limitless use of the Skytrain.

MRT

The **MRT** (Mass Rapid Transit) underground runs 12 miles (20 km) from Hua Lampong Station to Bang Sue in the north of Bangkok. There are at present 18 stations with more planned for the future. Silom and Sukhumvit stations connect with the BTS Skytrain network. Trains run daily every 4 to 10 minutes from 6am to midnight. Fares range from 16 to 41 *baht* with black tokens issued for a single journey. Unlimited 1-, 3-, and 30-day passes cost 120, 230, and 1,200 *baht* respectively.

Waterways

Chao Phraya Express boats serve popular piers on the Chao Phraya River. The company runs different routes recognizable by the color of flag each is flying. Tickets are purchased on board and range from 10 to 29 *baht* depending on the flag. The orange flag boats are the most useful as they stop at all piers

Chao Phraya Express

and are also the most frequent (they have a set fare of 14 *baht*). Ferries also link east and west banks.

Buses

The *Tourist Map Bangkok City* and *Tour 'n' Guide Map Bangkok* show bus routes. Blue air-conditioned buses ("AC" in the transport details for each Bangkok sight), and white metrobuses (indicated by "M") are comfortable and cover the popular routes. Ordinary (non air-conditioned) buses are cheap, cover all of Bangkok, and run all night.

Taxis

Metered taxis operate all over Bangkok. The minimum fare is 35 *baht* for the first kilometer and then 5 *baht* per kilometer for the second to the 12th kilometer. Some taxi drivers will attempt not to use the meter and try to charge a fixed fare, it is always best to insist on the meter.

On Foot

Bangkok is not much of a place for exploring on foot. Walking areas that might be considered include the Ratanakosin District around the Grand Palace and Wat Pho, and parts of Chinatown between Sampeng Lane and Yaowarat Road. Other than this it's best to take local transport between sights.

DIRECTORY

Transportation in Bangkok

Airport Rail Link
Tel 1690.
W bangkokairporttrain.com

BTS Skytrain
1000 Phahonyothin Rd.
Tel 0-2617-6000 (Hotline).
W bts.co.th

Chao Phraya Express
Tel 0-2445-8888.
W chaophrayaexpressboat.com

MRT
189 Rama IX Rd.
Tel 0-2354-2000.
W bangkokmetro.co.th

General Index

Acknowledgments

Dorling Kindersley would like to thank the following people whose contributions and assistance have made the preparation of this book possible.

Main Contributor
Philip Cornwel-Smith is a journalist focusing on entertainment, lifestyle and topical issues. After working on guides to London, in 1994 he moved to Thailand and was founding editor of the Bangkok listings magazine *Metro*.

Andrew Forbes has studied Thai history and culture for more than 20 years and has lived in the country on and off since 1984. He writes for the *Asian Wall Street Journal* and *Far Eastern Economic Review* among other publications.

Tim Forsyth is a writer and lecturer at the London School of Economics. He has travelled extensively throughout Northern Thailand and other parts of Southeast Asia.

Rachel Harrison has lectured at the School of Oriental and African Studies in London and contributed to Thai phrase books. She has a special interest in Northeast Thailand. David Henley is director of Crescent Press Agency's Thailand Bureau and has lived in Thailand for more than a decade. An authority on Thai cuisine, he contributes regularly to the *Bangkok Post* and *The Australian*.

John Hoskin has been based in Bangkok since 1980. He is the author of several books on travel, art and culture in Thailand and Indochina, including *The Mekong: A River and Its People*.

Gavin Pattison is a London-based writer who has contributed to the *Blue Guide to Thailand* among other titles. He has travelled extensively in Thailand, Indonesia, and other parts of Southeast Asia.

Picture Research Sumita Khatwani, Vicky Peel, Ellen Root.
Additional Illustrations Robert Ashby, Graham Bell, Peter Bull, Joanna Cameron, Chris Forsey, Paul Guest, Stephen Gyapay, Ruth Lindsay, Maltings Partnership, Mel Pickering, Robbie Polley, Sally Anne Reisen, Mike Taylor, Pat Thorne, Paul Weston.
Additional Photography Alberto Cassio, Peter Chadwick, CPA Media, Philip Dowell, Neil Fletcher, Allen Hopkins, Dave King, Brent Madison, James Marshall, Alan Newnham, Ian O'Leary, Alex Robinson, Rough Guides/Martin Richardson, Rough Guides/Karen Trist; Mick Shippen, Harry Taylor.
Additional Cartography Christine Purcell and Gary Bowes (ERA-Maptec Ltd).
Revisions Team Alexander Allan, Emma Anacootee, Gillian Allan, Douglas Amrine, Vicky Barber, Kate Berens, Tessa Bindloss, Rohan Bolton, Vivien Crump, Catherine Day, Lara Dunston, Conrad Van Dyk, Ron Emmons, Emer FitzGerald, Fay Franklin, Silvia Gaillard, Victoria Heyworth-Dunne, Paul Hines, Leanne Hogbin, Peter Holmshaw, Laura Jones, Nancy Jones, Priya Kukadia, Esther Labi, Jason Little, James Marshall, Victor Matthews, Bhavika Mathur, Sonal Modha, Catherine Palmi, Helen Partington, Sudarat Ponpangpa, Rada Radojicic, Mani Ramaswamy, Lee Redmond, Natalie Revie, Neil Ray, Natalie Revie, Erin Richards, Sands Publishing Solutions, Julian Sheather, Ellie Smith, Avantika Sukhia, Priyanka Thakur, David Tombesi-Walton, Nikky Twyman, Ajay Verma, Richa Verma, Veronica Wood, Sophie Wright.
Additional Research Parita Boonyoo, Debbie Guthrie Haer, Sathorn Leelakachornjit, Elizabeth Lu, James Mahon, Pharadee Narkkarphunchiwan, Warangkana Nibhatsukit, Larry O'Sullivan, Mick Shippen, Pimalaporn Wongchinsri, Wanee Tipchindachaikul, Somchai Worasart.
Proofreader Denise Heywood.
Index Helen Peters.
Special Assistance Dorling Kindersley would like to thank all the regional branches of the Tourism Authority of Thailand (TAT). Particular thanks also to: the Ayutthaya Historical Studies Centre (Thailand), Dr Peter Barrett (Medical Advisory Service for Travellers Abroad, London), William Booth (Jim Thompson's House, Bangkok), Alberto Cassio (Photobank, Bangkok), Crescent Press Agency (Chiang Mai), Gerald Cubitt, John Dransfield (Kew Gardens Herbarium, London), Michael Freeman, Helen Goldie (Durham University), Philip Harris (Bahn Thai Restaurant, London), Kietisak Itchayanan (National Culture Commission, Bangkok), Elizabeth Moore (London School of Oriental and African Studies), Tony Moore (British Thai Boxing Council), Phra Maha Pradit Panyatulo (Wat Buddhapadipa, London), Paisarn Piammattawat, Rattika Rhienpanish (Mai Thai Restaurant, London), Vidhisha Nayanthara Samarasekara, Philip Stott (London School of Oriental and African Studies), Dusadee Swangviboonpong (London School of Oriental and African Studies), Thai Airways (London), William Warren (Bangkok), Terri S Yamaka (TAT, London).

Photography Permissions Dorling Kindersley would like to thank the following for their assistance and kind permission to photograph at their establishments: Ancient City, Ayutthaya Historical Park, Ban Chiang National Museum, Ban Phin (House of Opium), Chakra Bongse House, Chan Kasem National Museum, Chao Sam Phraya National Museum, Chiang Mai National Museum, In Buri National Museum, Jim Thompson's Thai Silk Shop, Kamphaeng Phet Historical Park, Khon Kaen National Museum, Khorat (Nakhon Ratchasima) National Museum, Lampang National Museum, Lamphun National Museum, Lop Buri National Museum, Muang Tam Historical Park, Nakhon Pathom National Museum, Nakhon Si Thammarat National Museum, Nan National Museum, Narai Ratchaniwet Palace, National Gallery, National Museum (Bangkok), Oriental Hotel, Pha Taem, Phimai National Museum, Phnom Rung Historical Park, Prasart Museum, Ramkamhaeng National Museum, Ratchaburi National Museum, Royal Barge Museum, Sawankha Woranayok National Museum, Siriraj Hospital, Si Satchanalai-Chalieng Historical Park, Songkhla National Museum, Sukhothai Historical Park, Surin National Museum, Ubon Ratchathani National Museum, U Thong National Museum. Also all the other temples, museums, hotels, restaurants, shops, galleries and sights too numerous to thank individually.

Picture Credits
a = above; b = below/bottom; c = centre; f = far; l = left; r = right; t = top.

The publisher would like to thank the following individuals, companies and picture libraries for kind permission to reproduce their photographs.

123RF.com: Mr. Rapisan Swangphon 456-7.

Alamy Images: AA World Travel Library 146br; Peter Adams Photography Ltd 24; Piti Anchaleesahakorn 142bc; Greg Balfour Evans 422tl; Blue Eyes Photography Ltd 98; Asia 415tl; Simone van den Berg 414cla; William Casey 142cla; Danita Delimont 134; Danita Delimont/Paul Souders 83bl; Design Pics Inc. - RM Content 272; Emilio Ereza 415c; EmmePi Travel 8-9; Gary Dublanko 448tc; Greg Balfour Evans 255c; Philip Game 471br; Hemis.fr/Bertrand Gardel 443clb; Henry Westheim Photography 449tl; Julia Hiebaum 168; Zach Holmes 449br; INTERFOTO 237cr; John Kellerman 475crb; Norma Joseph 142cr; Alistair Laming 16tr; Jason Lindsey 74-5; Jon Maliones 474tr; Antony Nettle 472cr; The Photolibrary Wales 450bl; robertharding 268-269c; Fredrik Renander 470crb; Anders Ryman 450cra; Michael Snell 146cl; Rick Strange 296cla; Nat Sumanatemeya 446bl; SuperStock/RGB Ventures LLC dba 242; Aroon Thaewchatturat 269br; Daan Toner 110c; Topcris 147cra; Terry Whittaker 474bl; Andrew Woodley 447tc; **Aman Resorts:** 454cl; **Ardea London:** Francois Gohier 215tl; Wardene Weisser 215crb; **Asia Access:** Jeffrey Alford 384tl; Naomi Duguid 28bl, 384br; **Asia Images:**
© 1988 46–7c, 50br; © 1993 Matthew Burns 51cr, 271br; © 1995 Matthew Burns 42br; © 1990 Allen W Hopkins 287b, 312tr; © 1991 Allen W Hopkins 448bl; © 1995 Allen W Hopkins 91br; **Auscapes International:** Kevin Deacon 353ca; **Axiom:** © 1995 Jim Holmes 306c/bl.

Ban Phin (House of Opium): 237clb, 252bl; **Banyan Tree Spas:** 454br; **BFI Stills Posters & Designs:** © 1974 Danjaq, LLC and United Artists Corporation Inc. All Rights Reserved 371br; **Black Ginger Restaurant:** 433b; **The Bowers Museum of Cultural Art:** 58cl/clb; **Ashley J Boyd:** 321c, 327c, 345c/cr, 349bl, 352ca/clb/bl/br, 353cr/bl/bc/br, 361cr, 363bc, 392c/bl; **By Permission of the British Library:** Manuscript Or 14025: 34–5c; **Demetrio Carrasco:** 27br, 36cla, 51bl, 288cb, **Chakrabongse Villas:** 402br; **Chao Phraya Express Boat Co.:** 481bc; **Chiva-Som International Health Resorts:** 455tr; **Corbis:** Bronek Kaminski

186-7; Demotix/Steve Storey 55bl; Anders Ryman 451tr; Luca Tettoni 118br; **CPA Media:** 399tl; Joe Cummings 299bl; Ron Emmons 313c; David Henley 27c, 30tr, 34tr, 42bl, 43tr, 44bl/br, 45crb/br, 48clb, 55cra, 57b, 65br, 67ca, 68crb, 69tl/ca/bc, 70ca, 71tc, 72bl, 79bl, 85cra, 95bc, 103crb, 124clb, 125cra/br, 129tl, 137 all except cl, 138br, 167tl/br, 179tl, 210tr/clb/br, 211tl/br, 212tr, 229br, 230br, 258tr, 279br, 351tl/br/bl, 380cl, 381tr, 436br, 444cr, John Hobday 32fclb, 223crb; Daniel Kestenholz 106ca; Rainer Krack 359br, 369cra, 458cr; **Gerald Cubitt:** 28tc, 32 all except fclb, 33 all except crb/bl, 59tl, 85tl, 87tl, 109br, 137cl, 163tc/crb, 188tr/ bl, 189 all, 195tl, 209br, 211bl, 214cla/c/crb, 218bl, 223clb/bl, 225tl, 227bl, 234cb/bl, 235tl/ca, 237bl, 253bl, 258c, 259tr, 260bc, 284cla, 291cra, 293tl, 301cla, 310ca/clb, 311br, 314–15c, 319br, 327b, 330c, 331crb, 350tr, 353tl, 354cla/ clb/bl/bc, 355tl/tr/cr, 358bl, 359tr, 360c, 374c/bl, 377clb, 385tr/cl, 391c, 437tl, 438bl, 467tl; **Michael Cuthbert:** 374tr, 375c, 380br.

James Davis Travel Photography: 163br, 312cla, 348cl; **Dhara Dhevi Resort:** Arnon Tanfun 423b; **Dreamstime.com:** Anekoho 14tc; Anusorn62 17bl; Yulia Belousova 10br; Blanscape 14br; Panom Bounak 209cra; Chatchai5172 264-5; Comzeal 160-1; Rene Drouyer 316; Elvirkinsa 357b; Esusek 17tr; Finallast 208br; Hinokami 216; Xin Hua 11cr; Ihar Balaikin 348br; Jeeragone Inrut 248-9; Javarman 80; Kajornyot 215cra; Vichaya Kiatying-angsulee 26tl, 114; Kamonrutum 12tc; Patryk Kosmider 370bl; Aliaksandr Mazurkevich 13tr; Matee Nuserm 241tl, Nattyply 16bl; Khajohnsak Ngaolakon 304-305; Numskyman 206-7; Pattavikornp 378; Dmitry Pichugin 2-3; Poppap337 215tr; Pptara 286; Pattanachai Puempun 15br; Riverrail 12br; Saiko3p 224tl; Sarapon 26b; Takepicsforfun 160-1; Thaifairs 84tr; Thor Jorgen Udvang 308-9; Yongkiet 338-9; Ziggymars 4br; **Jean-Leo Dugast:** 34cl.

John Everingham: 4t, 5t, 30bl, 31tl, 34br, 42cl, 43tc, 44–45c, 45tr/cra/cr/bl, 49cra, 52bl, 136tl, 224bl, 225cra, 244bl, 271cb, 313crb 340b, 341cr/br, 342bl, 352tr, 355bl, 358cl, 362cl, 366tr, 367ca, 368cla, 370cla, 444tr.

Feature Magazine: 325tr, 385br; **Michael Freeman:** 27tl, 42tr, 46cla/ca 53cla, 60–1c, 61tl, 62c/clb, 65tl/ca/crb, 67t/clb, 68bl, 73tc, 87br, 88bl, 89br, 109tr, 111br, 124bc, 140bl, 164cla/c/crb/br, 165cb/bl, 182t, 183tr, 191b, 195bc, 204cb, 208tr, 210ca, 211tr/cra, 212bl, 213tc/bl/br, 217b, 229cra, 267br, 268cl, 269tl, 274bl, 314cla, 315cr, 334tl, 335b, 361tl, 438c, 441tc; **Tim Forsyth:** 211crb, 260bl; **Four Seasons Hotels And Resorts:** 405bl, 406br, 419t, 424br; **Fujian:** 412cl.

Getty Images: Bill Brennan 356; Mark Horn 372-373; The Image Bank/Angelo Cavalli 473tr; Chumsak Kanoknan 462tr; John S Lander 328.

Robert Harding Picture Library: 76clb, 78cl, 86cl, 240br, 248-249, 270tr, 271tl, 293crb/br, 353tr, 444clb; age fotostock/Mikel Bilbao 104, 346-7; age fotostock/P. Narayan 112-3; Eurasia 126; Alain Evrard 51tl, 53crb, 120bl; © Robert McCleod 53br; © Luca Tettoni 275tr, 282bl; © Ken Wilson 185br; **Christine Hemmet:** 35bl, 389crb; **The Hutchison Library:** 1.

The Image Bank: © Peter Hendrie 84tr; © Andrea Pistolesi 134; **Indigo Pearl:** 411tr.

Je T'aime Restaurant: 431tl; **Jewelry Realty Ltd, Bangkok:** 315tr. **Dr Oy Kanchavanit:** 361bc; **Suthep Kritsanavarin:** 133cl; **Krungsri River Hotel:** 404tl.

Frank Lane Picture Agency: © D Fleetham/Silvestris 33crb; © T & P Garner 354br; © David Hosking 172b; © E & D Hosking 188cb, 214bc, 367c; © L Lee Rue 33bl; © T Whittaker 290tr;

© De Zylva 345bl; **Leonardo MediaBank:** 312clb. **Mantra Restaurant & Bar:** 429bl. **Magnum:** © Marc Riboud 269bc; **Stuart Miller:** 375bl; **Mut Mee Garden Guest House:** 427br.

Nan Steak House: 424tr; **The National Museum (Bangkok):** 59cl/tc, 66–7c, 83cra, 92tr/cl, 93tr/cr/crb.

OnAsia: 72–3; Peter Charlesworth 421clb; Vinai Dithajohn 120tl; 472tl; Thierry Falise 123cb; **The Oriental Bangkok:** 116br.

Photobank (Bangkok): 28c, 29tl, 30–1c, 31tr/cra, 35tl/cra, 42–3c, 43bl, 44tr/cl, 45t, 46tr/clb/br, 47tl/tr/ca/bl/bc/br, 50cl, 58ca/cr, 59cra/crb, 60ca/cl, 61ca/crb, 62cla, 63crb, 64clb, 66c/clb, 68cla, 70–1c, 71crb, 73cra, 76tr, 79tc, 84clb, 92bl, 93tl, 103cl/bl/br, 133cr/cb/bl, 144cla, 145cra, 160–1, 162cl/bl, 163cra, 164–5c, 165ca, 166cl, 167cr, 169b, 174br, 188cl, 199br, 208cl, 220bc, 234cla, 237br, 253crb, 259br 267cr, 268bl, 298c, 311bl, 313cla, 314br, 321bl, 329b, 332cl, 334bc, 336bl/ br, 350bl/ br, 354tr, 363c 364bc, 369tc, 371tl/tr, 376b, 377tl/tr/br, 390cr, 413tr, 416tr/bl, 441cra, 442cla/br, 446cr, 473clb; **Photobank (Singapore):** 34clb, 43cr, 46bl, 47cra/crb, 48ca, 48–9c, 49tc, 56, 58–9c, 59c, 60cb, 63tc/cla, 64cla/cra, 67cb, 68ca/cra, 68–9c, 69crb 70clb/cb, 72cr, 77cra/bl, 89tl, 90bl, 96cla, 110bl, 124tr/cl, 125tc/cr, 128bl, 129bc, 165tl/crb, 166bl, 166–/c, 182br, 183tl, 184cl, 190, 210bl, 210–11c, 212cla, 212–13c, 213tr/cra/c/crb, 228cla, 229tc, 230cla, 245tl, 257 all, 260tr, 261 all, 266clb/bc, 269cla, 271bl/bc, 351cr, 389br, 438tr; **Photo EFEO:** 269tr; **Photolibrary:** Montgomery Jock 447br; JTB Photo 451bl; **Photoshot/NHPA:** Gerald Cubbitt 449c; **Pictures Colour Library:** 73crb, 251tr, 310bl; Picture Finders 143ca; **Popperfoto:** 119bc; **Pullman Khon Kaen Raja Orchid:** 407tr, 426tl; **PTT Public Company Limited:** 478cr.

Neil Ray: 30cb, 247b; **Reuters:** Ho New 73br; Sukree Sukplang 73cla; **River Books (Bangkok):** 35cr, 72cl, 106clb, 165tr; **Royal Cliff Hotels:** 409br; **Seaco Picture Library:** 463cr, 477tc; **Shangri-La Hotel, Bangkok:** 398cl, 403tr; **www.siamparagon. co.th:** 435tl; **Six Senses:** 410br, 430br; **Soneva Resorts:** 408tc; **Tony Stone Images:** Glen Allison 52cr; **SuperStock Ltd:** 130cl, 342cla; imagebroker.net 386-7; Steve Vidler 396-7.

Jim Thompson's Thai Silk Company: 270cl/c/bc; **Tony's Place Ayutthaya:** 421tl; **Tourism Authority of Thailand:** 29cr, 54bl, 277cr/bl; **Travel Ink:** Alan Hartley 76cla, 131tc, 311cra, 318bl, 330bl, Pauline Thornton 25ca, 130bl.

Wellcome Institute Library (London): 237cla.

Front endpaper: All special photography except **Alamy Images:** Design Pics Inc. - RM Content Rtc; Rene Drouyer Rcr; Julia Hiebaum Lcr; Alistair Laming Rbc; SuperStock/RGB Ventures LLC dba Ltr; **Dreamstime.com:** Hinokami Ltc; Pattavikornp Lbr; Pptara Rtr; **Getty Images** Bill Brennan Lbc; John S Lander Rc; **Photobank (Singapore):** Lc; Back endpapers: **Alamy Images:** Blue Eyes Photography Ltd Rbl; **Dreamstime.com:** Javarman Lbr; Vichaya Kiatyingangsulee Rcr; **Robert Harding Picture Library**: age fotostock/ Mikel Bilbao Rtc; Eurasia Ltl; Jacket – Front and spine: **Getty Images:** Genesis/Korawee Ratchapakdee.

All other pictures © Dorling Kindersley. See www.dkimages.com for more information.

Special Editions of DK Travel Guides

DK Travel Guides can be purchased in bulk quantities at discounted prices for use in promotions or as premiums. We are also able to offer special editions and personalized jackets, corporate imprints, and excerpts from all of our books, tailored specifically to meet your own needs.

To find out more, please contact:
in the United States **specialsales@dk.com**
in the UK **travelguides@uk.dk.com**
in Canada DK Special Sales at
specialmarkets@dk.com
in Australia **penguincorporatesales@ penguinrandomhouse.com.au**

Phrase Book

Thai is a tonal language and regarded by most linguists as head of a distinct language group, though it incorporates many Sanskrit words from ancient India, and some of modern English ones, too. There are five tones: mid, high, low, rising, and falling. The particular tone, or pitch, at which each syllable is pronounced determines its meaning. For instance "mâi" (falling tone) means "not," but "maˇi" (rising tone) is "silk."

The Thai script, meanwhile, is one of the most elaborate in the world, running left to right and using over 80 letters. In the third column of this phrase book is a phonetic transliteration for English speakers, including guidance for tones in the form of accents. This differs from the system used elsewhere in the guide, which follows the Thai Royal Institute's recommended romanization of common names.

Guidelines for Pronunciation

When reading the phonetics, pronounce syllables as if they form English words. For instance:

a	as in "ago"
e	as in "hen"
i	as in "thin"
o	as in "on"
u	as in "gun"
ah	as in "rather"
ai	as in "Thai"
air	as in "pair"
ao	as in "Mao Zedong"
ay	as in "day"
er	as in "enter"
ew	as in "few"
oh	as in "go"
oo	as in "boot"
OO	as in "book"
oy	as in "toy"
g	as in "give"
ng	as in "sing"

These sounds have no close equivalents in English:

eu	can be likened to a sound of disgust – the sound could be written as **"errgh"**
bp	a single sound between a "b" and a "p"
dt	a single sound between a "d" and a "t"

Note that when "p," "t," and "k" occur at the end of Thai words, the sound is "swallowed." Also note that many Thais use an "l" instead of an "r" sound.

The Five Tones

Accents indicate the tone of each syllable.

no mark	The **mid tone** is voiced at the speaker's normal, even pitch.
á é í ó ú	The **high tone** is pitched slightly higher than the mid tone.
à è ì ò ù	The **low tone** is pitched slightly lower than the mid tone.
aˇ eˇ iˇ oˇ uˇ	The **rising tone** sounds like a questioning pitch, starting low and rising.
â ê î ô û	The **falling tone** sounds similar to an English speaker stressing a one-syllable word for emphasis.

Male and Female Polite Forms

In polite speech, Thai men add the particle **"krúp"** at the end of each sentence; women add **"ká"** at the end of questions and **"kâ"** at the end of statements. These particles have been omitted from all but the most essential polite terms in this phrase book, but they should be used as much as possible. The polite forms of the word "I" are, for men, **"poˇm"** and, for women, **"dee-chún."**

In an Emergency

Help!	ช่วยด้วย	chôo-ay dôo-ay!
Fire!	ไฟไหม้	fai mâi!
Where is the nearest hospital?	แถวนี้มีโรงพยาบาล อยู่ที่ไหน	taˇir-o née mee rohng pa-yah-bahn yòo têe-nǎi?
Call an ambulance!	เรียกรถพยาบาล ให้หน่อย	rêe-uk rót pa-yah-bahn hâi nòy!
Call the police!	เรียกตำรวจให้หน่อย	rêe-uk dtum ròo-ut hâi nòy!
Call a doctor!	เรียกหมอให้หน่อย	rêe-uk mǒr hâi nòy!

Communication Essentials

Yes.	ใช่ อๆ ครับ/ค่ะ	châi or krúp/kâ
No.	ไม่ใช่ or ไม่ครับ/ไม่ค่ะ	mâi châi or mâi krúp/ mâi kâ
May I have …?	ขอ …	kǒr …
Please can you …?	ช่วย …	chôo-ay …
Thank you.	ขอบคุณ	kap-kOOn (krúp/ka)
No, thank you.	ไม่เอา ขอบคุณ	mâi ao kòrp-kOOn
Excuse me/sorry.	ขอโทษ (ครับ/ค่ะ)	kǒr-tôht (krúp/kâ)
Never mind.	ไม่เป็นไร	mâi bpen rai
Hello.	สวัสดี (ครับ/ค่ะ)	sa-wùt dee (krúp/kâ)
Goodbye.	ลาก่อนนะ	lah gòrn ná
Here.	ที่นี่	têe-nêe
There.	ที่โน่น	têe-nûn
What?	อะไร	a-rai?
Why?	ทำไม	tum-mai?
Where?	ที่ไหน	têe nǎi?
How?	ยังไง	yung ngai?

Useful Phrases

How are you?	คุณสบายดีหรือ (ครับ/คะ)	kOOn sa-bai dee reu (krúp/kâ)?
Very well, thank you – and you?	สบายดี (ครับ/ค่ะ) แล้วคุณล่ะ	sa-bai dee (krúp/kâ) – láir-o kOOn lâ?
What is your name?	คุณชื่ออะไร (ครับ/คะ)	kOOn chêu a-rai (krúp/kâ)?
My name is …	(ผม/ดิฉัน) ชื่อ …	(pǒm/dee-chún) chêu ….
Where is/are …?	… อยู่ที่ไหน	…. yòo têe-nǎi?
How do I get to …?	… ไปยังไง	…. bpai yung-ngai?
Do you speak English?	คุณพูดภาษาอังกฤษ เป็นไหม	kOOn pôot pah-sǎh ung-grìt bpen mái?
I understand.	เข้าใจ	kâo-jai
I don't understand.	ไม่เข้าใจ	mâi kâo-jai
Could you speak slowly?	ช่วยพูดช้าๆหน่อย ได้ไหม	chôo-ay pôot cháh cháh nòy dâi mái?